Star Wars Toys
A Super Collector's Wish Book

Geoffrey T. Carlton

Schiffer Publishing Ltd

4880 Lower Valley Road • Atglen, PA 19310

Other Schiffer Books By The Author:
The Star Wars Super Collector's Wish Book. ISBN: 9780764338625. $34.99

Other Schiffer Books on Related Subjects:
Action Figures of the 1980s. John Marshall. ISBN: 0764304941. $29.95
Collecting Star Wars® Toys: An Unauthorized Practical Guide, 1977-Present. Jeffrey B. Snyder. ISBN: 0764309064. $29.95

Copyright © 2012 by Geoffrey T. Carlton

Library of Congress Control Number: 2012938088

Designed by Geoffrey T. Carlton
Type set in ITC Avant Garde Gothic (T1)/Helvetica Neue

ISBN: 978-0-7643-4160-1
Printed in China

Schiffer Books are available at special discounts for bulk purchases for sales promotions or premiums. Special editions, including personalized covers, corporate imprints, and excerpts can be created in large quantities for special needs. For more information contact the publisher:

Published by Schiffer Publishing Ltd.
4880 Lower Valley Road
Atglen, PA 19310
Phone: (610) 593-1777; Fax: (610) 593-2002
E-mail: Info@schifferbooks.com

For the largest selection of fine reference books on this and related subjects, please visit our website at
www.schifferbooks.com
We are always looking for people to write books on new and related subjects. If you have an idea for a book, please contact us at
proposals@schifferbooks.com

This book may be purchased from the publisher.
Please try your bookstore first.
You may write for a free catalog.

In Europe, Schiffer books are distributed by
Bushwood Books
6 Marksbury Ave.
Kew Gardens
Surrey TW9 4JF England
Phone: 44 (0) 20 8392 8585; Fax: 44 (0) 20 8392 9876
E-mail: info@bushwoodbooks.co.uk
Website: www.bushwoodbooks.co.uk

CONTENTS

Articles and Reference

Introduction

The Star Wars collectibles covered by this book are not individually unique. They are mass-produced, with prices and availability subject to the whims and desires of investment speculators, dealers, fans, and collectors.

The selling price of any given collectible can skyrocket during the clamoring interest at the time of its initial release, only to plateau and plummet once any mania turns to focus on the next marketing spotlighted piece. Hundreds of collectibles illustrate this principle by having sold for significantly more money initially and which aren't even worth their original retail price today. Not every piece of Star Wars merchandise is a diamond to be polished for an easy profit. On the other hand, a select few turn out to be pure gold.

Purchasers need to understand whether the going price for an item is due to popularity (short term) or desirability (prolonged duration). When a wanted piece becomes available, it could mean the difference between whether the acquisition should be made decisively (long term value), or if patience would prove to be more profitable (price drops as popularity fades).

Some collectors buy extra pieces to resell, which helps to finance their own habits. This brings up the question of who is a collector and who is a dealer. A true collector buys for long-term holding, perhaps ten to thirty years. Dealers buy for the short-term, no more than ten to thirty weeks. Many dealers also collect. Few collectors routinely deal.

Calculating values is tricky, which is why a printed guide is essential. As with any other investment choices, the strategy is the classic "buy low; sell high." So, should the value of an item be calculated based upon the lowest it can obtained for by a nondescript buyer, or would it make more sense to report the value on the highest amount an established dealer could get for the piece? The debate has raged for years and often depends on whether the point of view is that of the buyer or that of the seller. Values expressed in this book are median, providing a baseline for buyers and sellers to adjust according to market, availability, and special grading considerations.

A determining factor to be made when establishing a specific price is whether or not the collectible is "investment grade." For every mass-produced item distributed, some become damaged, some acquire wear, some are opened for use or display, and a percentage remains sealed for the posterity of collecting. Of the last group of items, most are "hobby grade." Only a small percentage of those are truly investment grade. Investment grade collectibles have the ability to command a price greater than their published value. To illustrate, a vintage action figure with a value of a couple of hundred dollars could double or triple in price if it receives a top score from a professional grading house. Its increase in value has no effect on the value of equivalent condition action figures that have not been professionally graded.

Online trade and auction sites add to the mystique of the mathematics of values. It's rare to hear a person complain that they paid too much in a situation where they got to offer their own price to the seller. All too often when a bid is placed on an item, somebody else who values the item even more places a higher bid. The purpose of this type of transaction is for the buyer to obtain items at less than they are worth. Sellers may sacrifice the profit of true value for the sake of a quick turn of inventory, or to try to minimize their own losses on items. Items posted at below their value and receiving no bid whatsoever doesn't reduce the value of all like pieces, it simply indicates current lack of the auction community's interest in the movement for that piece, or a flaw in the system, such as when items are categorized or identified incorrectly.

Star Wars is a volatile market for speculation and acquisition. The property is too fast paced to capture more than a snapshot of the market. New merchandise is released every month worldwide for collectors and fans to search out. There is a huge secondary market right below the retail level which seems to specialize in obtaining the highest demand goods, marking them up and turning them around quickly to the public who become concerned when items are released and cannot be found immediately at the retail level. When the next wave of merchandise is released, the previous is all but forgotten as focus shifts the newer goods. By the time a third additional wave or series is released, the true value of the original items is revealed—a value based up desirability instead of popularity.

It is this value, the *durable value* of items once out of the population's eye for popularity, that this book reports. Less than investment grade conditioned items can be found for a lower street price. Professional graded items have the ability to go for a higher price. Ultimately though, the calculation of a selling price of an item is definitely based upon the foundation of its historically recorded value.

Evolution of Design
Separate titles for collectibles and toys.

This book is the next progression of *The Star Wars Super Collector's Wish Book*, which was published from 2001-2010 by Collector Books in Paducah, Kentucky. The fifth and final edition in that series weighed in at 464 pages and encompassed toys, collectibles, and memorabilia. This title continues that theme, varying only by splitting the collectibles and toys into separate books, giving each the needed space to continue expanding as the licensees produce record numbers of items to track, evaluate, and appraise.

Every edition incorporates and builds upon the previous editions with new layouts and different photo selections. This allows each book the ability to stand upon its own merit. Each book also contains unique focuses and features, providing owners of previous editions an expanded library of references to draw upon.

Organization of Items

Instead of pigeonholing every collectible into broad categories (ceramics, household, paper goods, etc.) where you may have to guess the location of every item, this book has all items listed alphabetically by their specific type.

If you want "Puzzles," look in "P." "Yo Yos?" Look in "Y." There are a couple of logical exceptions. Crafts, Figures, and Games each have sub-groups.

Photo References
Taking the mystery out of the bracketed numbers.

To continue showing new, improved, or alternate images of collectibles from around the world, not every item or set which has been shown in previous editions has been included in the current edition. To aid readers, any item pictured in previous editions of *The Star Wars Super Collector's Wish Book* that are not included in this edition will have a reference indicating the most recent edition and page number the photos appeared on. For example, on page 38, the 18" Episode III Mylar helium balloon by Party Express is not pictured in this edition. Its photo caption says (4:21), which indicates it can be seen in the fourth edition of *The Star Wars Super Collector's Wish Book*, page 21. Photos are referenced back to the first edition, as necessary.

Reference Photographs

Photographs in this guide are included solely for identification purposes and may not be reproduced. It is important to note that they are not in scale with one another. Completely different sized pieces may be printed next to each other and appear to be the same size. Photos should be viewed individually and not comparatively.

Designed to Survive the Internet

"Print is dead." "Information is free." These are the mantras of our time and by-and-large resound with the ring of truth. Where they tend to fall short is when expertise, detail, accuracy, completeness, coverage, and convenience are all required or desired.

The master database from which this series of books is compiled contains over 64,000 unique entries and the author has 54,000 photos of toys and collectibles, including alternate angles and conditions. 12,800 of those photos are incorporated in this edition, giving you access for education and identification immediately. As websites evolve, redesign, change hands, and expire, this book will forever be a durable and familiar reference. Among the charms of the guide are all of the obscure, limited edition, and international releases that will never be found on a website's content, much less give an accurate appraisal for when they are encountered by our readers in need of knowledge. (Who would blog about Domino games from Argentina or Touma mini-figures from Japan?)

Beyond the Book

Don't stop exploring when you reach the last of the collectible listings on page 445. Every book ends with a section referred to as "becoming one with the Force" where other collectors and clubs share their own unique experiences with the Star Wars universe, and invite you to look into their worlds and activities. It's a reminder that while the films, television, and books may give us the basic stories, where we go with them, in our imaginations and with our own hands, has always been up to us.

Contributing

Geoffrey Carlton invites you to join the collecting conversation by sending in any information or photos helpful in filling in any gaps in listings or photography. The current list of contributors appears on page 447.

Contact the Author

Mr. Carlton oversees the Star Wars collecting website at *www.StarWarsGuide.net* and may be reached via email at: *info@StarwarsGuide.net* with any questions, comments, or information contributions for the collecting community.

Action Figure 1:4 Scale Dolls

QS001   QS002   QS003   QS004   QS005   QS006   QS007   QS008

V1A001   V1A002   V1A003   V2A001

Action Figure 1:4 Scale Dolls

Diamond Select Toys
Voice and effects from the films, multi-layered cloth costumes, realistic sculpts, over twenty-five points of articulation.
__ Anakin Skywalker [QS001].............................80.00
__ Darth Maul [QS002] 80.00
__ Emperor Palpatine [QS003] 80.00
__ Han Solo, Hoth [QS004] 80.00
__ Han Solo, Mos Eisley 80.00
__ Luke Skywalker, Jedi Knight [QS005].............80.00
__ Mace Windu [QS006].....................................80.00
__ Obi-Wan Kenobi, ANH [QS007]......................80.00
__ Obi-Wan Kenobi, EPIII [QS008] 80.00

Action Figure 12" Creatures 1995-1999 (POTF2)

Hasbro
__ Captain Tarpals and Kaadu, exclusive to Target [V1A001]..65.00
__ Dewback and Sandtrooper, exclusive to Toys R Us [V1A002]..95.00

Kenner
__ Han Solo and Tauntaun, exclusive to Toys R Us [V1A003]..65.00

Toys: Action Figure 12" Creatures 2002-2004 (Saga)

Hasbro
Star Wars Saga, classic trilogy.
__ Luke Skywalker and Tauntaun, exclusive to Toys R Us [V2A001]...60.00

Action Figure 12" Dolls

Chronicle Books
Masterpiece editions. Includes collectible doll and book.
__ Anakin Skywalker [AAV001]...........................35.00
__ Aurra Sing [AAV002] 40.00
__ C-3PO [AAV003]...25.00

Hot Toys, Hong Kong
__ George Lucas, limited to 500 [AAV004]..........85.00

Medicom, Japan
Real Action Heroes.
__ 501st Clone Trooper, limited to 1,000, numbered [AAV005]..150.00
__ Anakin Skywalker, numbered [AAV006] 180.00
__ Boba Fett, limited to 1,000, numbered [AAV007]..225.00
__ Boba Fett - ROTJ Version [AAV008].............175.00
__ C-3PO [AAV009] 200.00
__ Clone Trooper (AOTC) [AAV010]..................150.00

__ Clone Trooper (ROTS 501st), limited to 1,000, numbered [AAV011]....................................225.00
__ Clone Trooper (ROTS) [AAV012]..................175.00
__ Clone Trooper Captain 175.00
__ Clone Trooper Commander, limited to 1,000, numbered [AAV013]....................................150.00
__ Darth Maul, limited to 1,000, numbered [AAV014]..150.00
__ Darth Vader [AAV015] 250.00
__ Darth Vader burned face, limited to 1,000, exclusive to Japan 275.00
__ Han Solo, numbered [AAV016]....................180.00
__ Jango Fett, numbered [AAV017]..................150.00
__ Jango Fett - 2nd Jett Pack Vers. [AAV018] ..175.00
__ Luke Skywalker, Jedi Knight [AAV019].........250.00
__ R2-D2 [AAV020]...200.00
__ Royal Guard [AAV021] 165.00
__ Sandtrooper, limited to 1,000, numbered, exclusive to Star Wars Celebration IV [AAV022]..........225.00
__ Shadow Stormtrooper [AAV023] 225.00
__ Shock Trooper, limited to 1,000, numbered [AAV024]..235.00

AAV001   AAV002   AAV003

AAV004   AAV005   AAV006   AAV007   AAV008   AAV009   AAV010   AAV011

AAV012

AAV013

AAV014

AAV015

AAV016

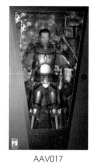
AAV017

AAV018

AAV019

AAV020

AAV021

AAV022

AAV023

AAV024

AAV025

AAV026

__ Stormtrooper [AAV025].................................225.00
__ TIE Fighter Pilot 150.00

Robert Tonner

__ Queen Amidala trunk set, limited to 200, exclusive to FAO Schwarz [AAV026] 1975.00

Action Figure 12" Dolls 1978-1986 (Vintage)

Kenner

__ Ben Kenobi, SW [A1V001] 495.00
   loose, mint, complete 200.00
__ Boba Fett, SW [A1V002] 1,100.00
__ Boba Fett, ESB [A1V003]........................... 1,100.00
   loose, mint, complete 200.00
__ C-3PO, SW [A1V004]....................................295.00
   loose, mint, complete 65.00
__ Chewbacca, SW [A1V005]............................200.00
   loose, mint, complete 95.00

__ Darth Vader [A1V006] 550.00
   loose, mint, complete 110.00
__ Han Solo [A1V007]......................................650.00
   loose, mint, complete 180.00
__ IG-88, ESB [A1V008] 1,500.00
   loose, mint, complete 300.00
__ Jawa [A1V009]..310.00
   loose, mint, complete 75.00
__ Luke Skywalker [A1V010]............................425.00
   loose, mint, complete 90.00
__ Princess Leia Organa [A1V011] 260.00
   loose, mint, complete 120.00
__ R2-D2 [A1V012] 295.00
   loose, mint, complete 60.00
__ Stormtrooper [A1V013].................................425.00
   loose, mint, complete 95.00

Kenner, Australia

ESB packaging.
__ Chewbacca [2:10] 1,750.00
__ Darth Vader.. 1,750.00

Lili Ledy, Mexico

__ Darth Vader... 2,250.00
__ Han Solo [2:10] 980.00
__ Jawa [2:10]..950.00
__ Luke Skywalker [2:10]............................... 2,200.00
__ Princess Leia [2:10]................................... 1,050.00

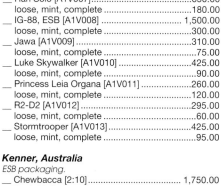
A1V001

A1V002

A1V003

A1V004

A1V005

A1V006

A1V007

A1V008

A1V009

A1V010

A1V011

A1V012

A1V013

Action Figure 12" Dolls

A2V001

A2V002

A2V003

A2V004

A2V005

A2V006

A2V007

A2V008

A2V009

A2V010

A2V011

A2V012

A2V013

A2V014 cover closed and open

A2V015

A2V016

```
__ R2-D2 [2:10].............................. 1,000.00
__ Tusken Raider [2:10]................. 2,070.00
```

Meccano, France
```
__ Chewbacca, ESB...........................415.00
__ Jawa, SW [2:10]...........................555.00
__ Princess Leia, SW.........................590.00
__ Stormtrooper, SW.........................545.00
```

Toltoys, Australia
```
__ Boba Fett......................................675.00
```

Action Figure 12" Dolls 1995-2000 (POTF2)

Hasbro
```
__ Chewbacca with sculpted fur [A2V001]..........15.00
__ Han Solo wi/magnetic detonators [A2V002]...30.00
__ Luke Skywalker with tentacle [A2V003]..........20.00
__ Obi-Wan, glow in the dark saber [A2V004].....20.00
__ Ponda Baba with removable arm [A2V005]....20.00
__ Princess Leia with chain [A2V006]..................25.00
```

A2V017

A2V018

Kenner
2-Packs.
```
__ Death Star Gunner and Grand Moff Tarkin, limited
   to 15,000, exclusive to FAO Schwarz
   [A2V007].............................................65.00
__ Emperor Palpatine and Emperor's Royal Guard,
   exclusive to Target [A2V008]..........................50.00
```

```
__ Han Solo and Luke Skywalker in Stormtrooper
   Disguises, limited to 20,000, exclusive to KB Toys
   [A2V009]...........................................60.00
__ Han Solo in Carbonite, exclusive to Target
   [A2V010].............................................35.00
__ Luke and Bib Fortuna Bib not wearing gloves,
   exclusive to FAO Schwarz [A2V011]...............85.00
```

A2V019

A2V020

A2V021

A2V022

A2V023

8

A2V024

A2V025

A2V026

A2V027

A2V028

A2V029

A2V030

A2V031

A2V032

A2V033

A2V034

A2V035

A2V036

A2V037

A2V038

A2V039

A2V040   A2V041

A2V042

A2V043

A2V044

A2V045

A2V046

A2V047

__ Luke and Bib Fortuna Bib wearing gloves, exclusive to FAO Schwarz [A2V012] 85.00
__ Luke and Wampa, exclusive to Target [A2V013]...45.00
__ Princess Leia as Jabba's Prisoner and Bartender R2-D2, exclusive to FAO Schwarz [A2V014] ..65.00

__ Wedge Antilles and Biggs Darklighter, exclusive to FAO Schwarz [A2V015]..................................75.00

3-Packs.
__ Luke Skywalker, Darth Vader, Obi-Wan Kenobi, 1997 Hong Kong commemorative [A2V016] ..85.00

__ Luke Skywalker, Princess Leia as Boushh, Han Solo in Bespin Outfit, exclusive to KB Toys [A2V017]..60.00

4-packs.
__ Luke Skywalker (Hoth), Han Solo (Hoth), Snowtrooper, AT-AT Driver, exclusive to JC Penney [A2V018]...50.00

6" Series.
__ Jawa [A2V019] 15.00
__ R2-D2 detachable utility arms [A2V020].........25.00
__ R2-D2 with retractable leg [A2V021] 25.00
__ R5-D4 [A2V022] 25.00
__ Wicket, exclusive to Walmart [A2V023] 25.00
__ Yoda [5:303]...40.00

Flap boxes.
__ Admiral Ackbar [A2V024]...............................20.00
__ AT-AT Driver, exclusive to Service Merchandise [A2V025]..30.00
__ Boba Fett [A2V026].......................................40.00
__ C-3PO [A2V027] 35.00
__ Cantina Band Member: Doikk N'ats, exclusive to Walmart [A2V028]..35.00
__ Cantina Band member: Figrin D'an, exclusive to Walmart [A2V029] 35.00
__ Cantina Band Member: Ickabel, exclusive to Walmart [A2V030]..35.00
__ Cantina Band Member: Nalan, exclusive to Walmart [A2V031]..35.00
__ Cantina Band member: Tech, exclusive to Walmart [A2V032]..35.00
__ Cantina Band Member: Tedn, exclusive to Walmart [A2V033]..35.00
__ Chewbacca [A2V034] 45.00
__ Darth Vader dark blue card, black lightsaber [A2V035]..30.00

A2V048

A2V049

A2V050

A2V051

A2V052

A2V053

A2V054

A2V055

A2V056

A2V057

A2V058

A2V059

A2V060

A2V061

A2V062

25

Action Figure 12" Dolls

A2V063   A2V064   A2V065   A2V066   A2V067   A2V068   A2V069   A2V070

__ Darth Vader light blue card, black and silver lightsaber 20.00
__ Darth Vader light blue card, black and silver lightsaber, black and gold foil logo................20.00
__ Darth Vader light blue card, black lightsaber .20.00
__ Greedo, exclusive to JC Penney [A2V036] 25.00
__ Han Solo dark blue card [A2V037]..................30.00
__ Han Solo light blue card, painted pouch 20.00
__ Han Solo light blue card, painted pouch, black and gold foil logo 20.00
__ Han Solo light blue card, unpainted pouch 20.00
__ Lando Calrissian [A2V038].............................20.00
__ Luke Skywalker dark blue card, binoculars on belt, black lightsaber [A2V039] 30.00
__ Luke Skywalker dark blue card, binoculars on card, black lightsaber 20.00
__ Luke Skywalker light blue card, black and silver lightsaber 20.00
__ Luke Skywalker light blue card, black and silver lightsaber, black and gold foil logo................20.00
__ Luke Skywalker light blue card, black lightsaber 20.00

__ Luke Skywalker Bespin Fatigues [A2V040] 20.00
__ Luke Skywalker X-Wing Pilot [A2V041] 25.00
__ Obi-Wan Kenobi dark blue card, silver belt buckle, black lightsaber [A2V042] 25.00
__ Obi-Wan Kenobi light blue card, gold belt buckle, black and silver lightsaber 20.00
__ Obi-Wan Kenobi light blue card, gold belt buckle, black and silver lightsaber, black and gold foil logo 45.00
__ Obi-Wan Kenobi light blue card, silver belt buckle, black and silver lightsaber 20.00
__ Obi-Wan Kenobi light blue card, silver belt buckle, black lightsaber 20.00
__ Princess Leia [A2V043] 25.00
__ Sandtrooper, exclusive to Diamond [A2V044]...35.00
__ Stormtrooper [A2V045]...................................30.00
__ TIE Fighter Pilot [A2V046] 35.00
__ Tusken Raider with blaster and macrobinoculars printed warning [A2V047] 25.00
__ Tusken Raider with blaster and macrobinoculars warning sticker..25.00

__ Tusken Raider with gaderffii stick printed warning 30.00
__ Tusken Raider with gaderffii stick warning sticker 30.00

Window boxes.
__ AT-AT Driver [A2V048]....................................25.00
__ Barquin D'an [A2V049]....................................15.00
__ Chewbacca Boushh's bounty [A2V050] 25.00
__ Emperor Palpatine [A2V051]...........................15.00
__ Emperor Palpatine fully posable [A2V052]......15.00
__ Grand Moff Tarkin with Interrogation Droid [A2V053]..20.00
__ Greedo [A2V054]...20.00
__ Han Solo Hoth Gear [A2V055] 20.00
__ Luke Skywalker Ceremonial [A2V056]............15.00
__ Luke Skywalker Hoth Gear [A2V057]..............20.00
__ Luke Skywalker Jedi [A2V058].......................20.00
__ Luke Skywalker Jedi with glow-in-dark lightsaber [A2V059]..20.00
__ Princess Leia in Hoth Gear, exclusive to Service Merchandise [A2V060]..................................20.00

A6V001   A6V002   A6V003   A6V004   A6V005   A7V001   A7V002

A7V003   A7V004   A3V001   A3V002   A3V003

A3V004   A3V005   A3V006   A3V007   A3V008   A3V009   A3V009 detail - correct spelling "Federation"

10

A3V010 detail - incorrect spelling "Fedration"

A3V011

A3V012

A3V013

A3V014

A3V015

A3V016

 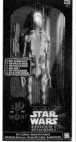 

A3V017   A3V018   A3V019

__ Sandtrooper with Imperial Droid [A2V061] 30.00
__ Snowtrooper blue highlights........................200.00
__ Snowtrooper gray highlights [A2V062] 20.00

Kenner, Italy
Deluxe figures.
__ Han Solo quick draw action [A2V063] 70.00
__ Luke Skywalker swinging lightsaber action [A2V064]..35.00

__ Boba Fett...35.00
__ Dark Vador [A2V065] 32.00
__ Han Solo [A2V066]...................................45.00
__ Luke Skywalker [A2V067] 45.00
__ Obi-Wan Kenobi [A2V068]..........................32.00
__ Princess Leia...35.00

Kenner, UK
__ Han Solo quick draw action [A2V069] 70.00
__ Luke Skywalker swinging lightsaber action [A2V070]..45.00

Action Figure 12" Dolls
1999-2000 Portrait Edition

Hasbro
__ 1999 #1 Princess Leia ceremonial gown [A6V001]..20.00
__ 1999 #2 Queen Amidala black travel gown [A6V002]..25.00
__ 1999 #3 Queen Amidala red senate gown [A6V003]..25.00
__ 2000 Queen Amidala Return to Naboo [A6V004]..25.00
__ 2000 Queen Amidala and Qui-Gon Jinn Defense of Naboo [A6V005]...80.00

Action Figure 12" Dolls
1999-2000 Queen Amidala Fashion

Hasbro
__ Beautiful Braids Padme [A7V001]..................12.00
__ Hidden Majesty [A7V002] 12.00
__ Royal Elegance [A7V003]............................12.00
__ Ultimate Hair [A7V004]...............................12.00

Action Figure 12" Dolls
1999-2001 (TPM)

Hasbro
6" Series.
__ Anakin Skywalker [A3V001] 15.00
__ Pit Droids [A3V002].....................................15.00
__ R2-A6 [A3V003] 15.00

Frame boxes.
__ Battle Droid [A3V004] 20.00
__ Chancellor Valorum and Senate Guard [A3V005]..65.00
__ Darth Maul [A3V006]....................................35.00
__ Jar Jar Binks [A3V007]..................................20.00
__ Obi-Wan Kenobi [A3V008]............................20.00
__ Qui-Gon Jinn [A3V009]................................20.00
__ Qui-Gon Jinn typographical error on back of box ("Fedration") [A3V010] 35.00
__ Watto [A3V011] 15.00

Window boxes.
__ Anakin Skywalker podracer [A3V012].............50.00
__ Battle Droid Commander [A3V013] 30.00
__ Boss Nass [A3V014] 40.00
__ Mace Windu [A3V015] 35.00
__ Qui-Gon Jinn Tatooine gray poncho 50.00

__ Qui-Gon Jinn Tatooine tan poncho [A3V016].25.00
__ Sebulba [A3V017] 30.00

Hasbro, UK
Multi-language packaging.
__ Battle Droid [A3V018] 20.00
__ Watto [A3V019]...15.00

Action Figure 12" Dolls
2001-2002 (POTJ)

Hasbro
2-Packs.
__ Luke Skywalker and Yoda [A4V001]...............45.00
__ Sith Lords Darth Vader and Darth Maul [A4V002]..60.00

Deluxe packaging.
__ Luke Skywalker 100th Figure [A4V003]..........50.00

Green packaging.
__ 4-LOM with concussion rifle [A4V004] 40.00
__ Bossk with blaster rifle [A4V005] 35.00
__ Death Star Droid [A4V006]............................25.00
__ Death Star Trooper [A4V007].........................20.00
__ Han Solo stormtrooper disguise [A4V008] 30.00
__ IG-88 [A4V009] 40.00

Action Figure 12" Dolls
2002-2004 (Saga)

Hasbro
Blue packaging, deluxe.
__ Jango Fett [A5V001] 70.00
__ Princess Leia in Boushh Disguise and Han Solo in Carbonite [A5V002].......................................30.00

A4V001   A4V002   A4V003   A4V004

A4V005   A4V006   A4V007   A4V008   A4V009   A5V001   A5V002

Action Figure 12" Dolls

| A5V003 | A5V004 | A5V005 | A5V006 | A5V007 | A5V008 | A5V009 | A5V010 | A5V011 | A5V012 |

| A5V013 | A5V014 | A5V015 | A5V016 | A5V017 | A5V018 | A5V019 | A5V020 | A5V021 | A5V022 |

| A5V023 | A5V024 | A5V025 | A5V026 | A5V027 | A5V028 | A5V029 | A5V030 | A5V031 |

Blue packaging.
__ Anakin Skywalker [A5V003] 25.00
__ Anakin Skywalker Battle [A5V004].................30.00
__ AT-ST Driver [A5V005].....................................30.00
__ Clone Commander (yellow), exclusive to KB Toys [A5V006]...30.00

__ Clone Trooper [A5V007] 30.00
__ Clone Trooper (red), exclusive to KB Toys [A5V008]...30.00
__ Count Dooku [A5V009] 30.00
__ Dengar [A5V010]...30.00
__ Gamorrean Guard [A5V011] 30.00

__ Genosian Warrior [A5V012]............................25.00
__ Han Solo [A5V013]..20.00
__ Imperial Officer [A5V014] 25.00
__ Ki-Adi Mundi [A5V015].....................................40.00
__ Lando Calrissian Skiff Guard helmet down [A5V016]..30.00
__ Lando Calrissian Skiff Guard helmet forward [A5V017]..30.00
__ Mace Windu, excl. to Toys R Us [A5V018] 30.00
__ Obi-Wan Kenobi [A5V019] 20.00
__ Padme Amidala [A5V020] 40.00
__ Plo Koon, exclusive to Fan Club [A5V021] ...165.00
__ Super Battle Droid [A5V022].........................20.00
__ Zam Wesell [A5V023]......................................15.00
__ Zuckuss [A5V024]...30.00

Gold bar packaging.
__ Biker Scout [A5V025]......................................60.00
__ Garindan [A5V026]..20.00
__ Luke Skywalker Jedi [A5V027]......................20.00
__ Obi-Wan Kenobi [A5V028] 25.00
__ Yoda [A5V029] 30.00

| A8V001 | A8V002 | A8V003 | A8V004 |

| A9V001 | A9V002 | A9V003 | A9V004 | A9V005 | A9V006 | A9V007 |

12

| B1001 | B1002 | B1003 | B1004 | B1005 | B1006 |

Gold bar packaging. 2-packs.
__ Ewoks [A5V030] 40.00
__ Jawas [A5V031] 25.00

Action Figure 12" Dolls
2004 (Original Trilogy Collection)

Hasbro
__ Boba Fett blue jumpsuit 60.00
__ Boba Fett blue jumpsuit with Star Wars sticker on box [A8V001] 70.00
__ Boba Fett gray jumpsuit 40.00
__ Boba Fett gray jumpsuit with Star Wars sticker on boc 40.00
__ Chewbacca, exclusive to KB Toys [A8V002] 35.00
__ Luke Skywalker..25.00
__ Luke Skywalker Star Wars sticker on box [A8V003] 35.00
__ Stormtrooper [A8V004] 40.00
__ Stormtrooper with Star Wars sticker on box ..50.00

Action Figure 12" Dolls
2005 (ROTS)

Hasbro
__ Anakin Skywalker Ultimate Villain [A9V001] ...60.00
__ Bariss Offee [A9V002].....................................20.00
__ Chewbacca, exclusive to KB Toys [A9V003]..39.00
__ Clone Trooper [A9V004] 30.00
__ General Grievous [A9V005]..............................30.00
__ Shaak Ti [A9V006]..25.00
__ The Emperor [A9V007]....................................20.00

Action Figure 12" Dolls 2005-2011

Gentle Giant Studios
Vintage figures scaled to 12".
__ Ben (Obi-Wan) Kenobi, limited to 2,500 ....100.00
__ Boba Fett, limited to 1,500, exclusive to Star Wars Celebration V [B1001]...................................340.00
__ Chewbacca, limited to 2,500 [B1002]...........100.00
__ Darth Vader, limited to 2,500 [B1003]...........100.00

| B1007 | B1008 |

__ Han Solo large head, ltd. to 2,000 [B1004]...100.00
__ Han Solo small head, limited to 2,500...........100.00
__ Jawa cloth cape, limited to 2,500 [B1005] 100.00
__ Luke Skywalker, limited to 2,500 [B1006] 100.00
__ Princess Leia, limited to 2,500 [B1007] 100.00
__ Sand People, limited to 2,500 ....100.00

| B1009 | B1010 | B1011 | B1012 | B1013 | B1014 | B1015 | B1016 | B1017 |

| B1018 | B1019 | B1020 | B1021 | B1022 | B1023 | B1024 | B1025 |

| B1026 | B1027 | B1028 | B1029 | B1030 | B1031 |

Action Figure 12" Dolls

| B1032 | B1033 | B1034 | B1035 | B1036 | B1037 | B1038 | B1039 | B1040 |

| B1041 | B1042 | B1043 | B1044 | B1045 | B1046 |

__ Stormtrooper, limited to 1,500, exclusive to SanDiego Comic-Con [B1008] 300.00

Sideshow Collectibles

__ 2-Pack: Han Solo and Luke Skywalker in Stormtrooper Disguise, limited to 2,000, exclusive to Comicon 295.00
__ 212th Attack Battalion: Utapau Clone Trooper [B1009]...100.00
__ 212th Attack Battalion: Utapau Clone Trooper with exclusive figure base, limited to 1,500, exclusive to Sideshow Collectibles 135.00
__ Aayla Secura, limited to 3,000, exclusive to SanDiego Comic-Con [B1010] 135.00
__ Admiral Piett, limited to 1,500, exclusive to Sideshow Collectibles [B1011] 90.00
__ Anakin Skywalker [B1012] 80.00
__ Anakin Skywalker with exclusive hologram, exclusive to Sideshow Collectibles 175.00
__ Anakin Skywalker, Clone Wars General, limited to 1,500 [B1013]..100.00

__ Anakin Skywalker, Clone Wars General with Rotta the Hutt, limited to 750 ....150.00
__ Asajj Ventress 75.00
__ Asajj Ventress with exclusive interchangeable portraits, limited to 2,000, exclusive to Sideshow Collectibles [B1014]......................................115.00
__ Bib Fortuna [B1015]......................................65.00
__ Bib Fortuna with exclusive ceremonial staff, limited to 2,500, exclusive to Sideshow Collectibles ...100.00
__ Blackhole Stormtrooper, exclusive to Sideshow Collectibles [B1016].....................................160.00
__ Captain Antilles, limited to 2,500 [B1017].......85.00
__ Clone Lieutenant, limited to 1,000, exclusive to Sideshow 120.00
__ Clone Lieutenant, limited to 300, exclusive to SanDiego Comic-Con [B1018] 175.00
__ Commander Praji, limited to 3,000, exclusive to Sideshow Collectibles [B1019] 75.00
__ Darth Maul 95.00
__ Darth Maul with damaged saber hilt, exclusive to Sideshow Collectibles [B1020] 80.00

__ Darth Sidious hologram with walking mechano-chair, exclusive to SanDiego Comic-Con [B1021] .135.00
__ Darth Vader, limited to 6,500 [B1022]..........150.00
__ Darth Vader with unique "force choke" hand, limited to 1,977, exclusive to Sideshow Collectibles ...180.00
__ Darth Vader (Anakin Skywalker) Sith Apprentice, limited to 6,000, exclusive to SanDiego Comic-Con [B1023]..325.00
__ Gamorrean Guard, limited to TBD [B1024]...150.00
__ Han Solo Bespin [B1025].............................100.00
__ Han Solo Bespin with exclusive Mynock, exclusive to Sideshow Collectibles 150.00
__ Han Solo, smuggler - Tatooine.......................75.00
__ Han Solo, smuggler - Tatooine with unique blaster pistol, exclusive to Sideshow Collectibles [B1026]..175.00
__ Imperial Stormtrooper [B1027] 75.00
__ Infantry Soldier [B1028] 95.00
__ Jabba the Hutt, limited to 4000, exclusive to Sideshow Collectibles 135.00
__ Jabba the Hutt with exclusive cup, exclusive to Sideshow Collectibles [B1029] 165.00
__ Ki-Adi-Mundi [B1030] 75.00
__ Kit Fisto [B1031] 100.00
__ Kit Fisto with exclusive battle droid head, exclusive to Sideshow Collectibles [B1032]................150.00
__ Lando Calrissian, limited to 1,500, exclusive to Sideshow Collectibles 80.00
__ Lando Calrissian with Bespin communicator, limited to 750, exclusive to Sideshow Collectibles [B1033]..95.00
__ Luke Skywalker Jedi [B1034]..........................90.00
__ Luke Skywalker Jedi with exclusive blaster, exclusive to Sideshow Collectibles 150.00
__ Luke Skywalker, Moisture Farmer [B1035].....75.00
__ Luke Skywalker, Rebel Commander - Bespin, limited to 5,000, exclusive to Sideshow Collectibles [B1036]..75.00

| B1047 | B1048 | B1049 | B1050 | B1051 | B1052 | B1053 | B1054 |

| B1055 | B1056 | B1057 front and back | B1058 | B1059 | B1060 |

A1A001 A1A002 A1A003 A1A004 A3A001 A3A002

__ Luke Skywalker, Rebel Commander - Bespin with auto-tourniquet, limited to 1,980, exclusive to Sideshow Collectibles 115.00
__ Luke Skywalker, Yavin Ceremony, exclusive to Star Wars Celebration IV [B1037]............................95.00
__ Mace Windu [B1038] 95.00
__ Mace Windu with exclusive Jango Fett helmet, exclusive to Sideshow Collectibles 150.00
__ Obi-Wan Kenobi 100.00
__ Obi-Wan Kenobi with exclusive General Grievous blaster, exclusive to Sideshow Collectibles [B1039]...175.00
__ Obi-Wan Kenobi, ANH [B1040] 75.00
__ Obi-Wan Kenobi, ANH with exclusive Leia transmission, limited to 1977, exclusive to Sideshow Collectibles 120.00
__ Obi-Wan Kenobi: General - Clone Wars.........95.00
__ Obi-Wan Kenobi: General - Clone Wars with exclusive hologram of Captain Rex, limited to 1,500, exclusive to Sideshow Collectibles [B1041].135.00
__ Obi-Wan Kenobi: Jedi Knight [B1042]...........85.00
__ Obi-Wan Kenobi: Jedi Knight with exclusive Kamino dart, limited to 1,000, exclusive to Sideshow Collectibles 125.00
__ Padme Amidala, Ilum Mission, limited to 3,500 [B1043]...65.00
__ Plo Koon, limited to 5,500 ....65.00
__ Plo Koon with twin bladed lightsaber gauntlet, limited to 1,500, exclusive to Sideshow Collectibles [B1044]...80.00
__ Princess Leia [B1045] 75.00
__ Princess Leia with exclusive wrist binders, limited to 1977, exclusive to Sideshow Collectibles 115.00
__ Princess Leia as Boushh, limited to 6,500 [B1046]...65.00
__ Princess Leia as Boushh with exclusive Ubese blaster pistol, limited to 2,500, exclusive to Sideshow Collectibles 135.00
__ Qui-Gon Jinn, limited to 7,500 [B1047] 50.00
__ Qui-Gon Jinn with moisture farmer poncho, limited to 2,000, exclusive to Sideshow Collectibles .75.00
__ Rebel Commando Infantryman [B1048] 95.00
__ Rebel Commando Pathfinder [B1049]..............95.00
__ Rebel Commando Sergeant [B1050]..............95.00
__ Rebel Fleet Trooper [B1051]............................75.00
__ Salacious B. Crumb, Creature Pack, limited to 4500, exclusive to Sideshow Collectibles [B1052] ...35.00
__ Salacious B. Crumb, Creature Pack with exclusive dwarf varactyl, exclusive to Sideshow Collectibles 45.00
__ Sandtrooper [B1053] 125.00
__ Sandtrooper with exclusive droid part, limited to 1,000, exclusive to Sideshow Collectibles [B1054]...160.00

A2A001 A2A002 A2A003 A2A004 A2A005

__ Stormtrooper with stormtrooper blaster pistol, limited to 1,500, exclusive to Sideshow Collectibles [B1055]...160.00
__ Stormtrooper Commander [B1056] 100.00
__ Stormtrooper Commander w/exclusive base, ltd. to 1,000, exclusive to Sideshow Collectibles ...135.00

2-Pack.
__ Palpatine and Darth Sidious, limited to 3,000 [B1057]...150.00

Environments.
__ Han Solo in Carbonite, limited to 2,000, exclusive to Sideshow Collectibles 250.00
__ Jabba's Throne, limited to 4,200, exclusive to Sideshow Collectibles 220.00

Expansion packs.
__ Buboicullaar Creature Pack (3 creatures) Bubo, Rock wart, Womp rat, limited to 3,000, numbered..45.00
__ Buboicullaar Creature Pack (4 creatures) Bubo, Rock wart, Womp rat, scratching womp rat, limited to 1,500, numbered, exclusive to Sideshow Collectibles [B1059]......................................75.00
__ Dejarik holochess set.......................................75.00
__ Sith Probe Droids [B1060] 45.00

Action Figure 12" Dolls: Electronic 1995-1999 (POTF2)

Kenner
__ Boba Fett, exclusive to KB Toys [A1A001].....75.00
__ Darth Vader [A1A002] 40.00

2-Packs.
__ C-3PO and R2-D2 [A1A003].........................50.00
__ Obi-Wan vs. Darth Vader, exclusive to JC Penney [A1A004] 35.00

Action Figure 12" Dolls: Electronic 1999-2000 (TPM)

Hasbro
__ C-3PO [A2A001] 40.00
__ Darth Maul [A2A002].....................................20.00
__ Jar Jar Binks [A2A003] 20.00
__ Qui-Gon Jinn [A2A004] 20.00
__ TC-14, exclusive to KB Toys [A2A005]...........30.00

Action Figure 12" Dolls: Electronic 2002 (AOTC)

Hasbro
__ Jango Fett [A3A001]......................................30.00
__ Obi-Wan Kenobi [A3A002]............................25.00

Action Figure 12" Vehicles 1995-1999 (POTF2)

Hasbro
__ Speeder Bike with Scout Trooper [A1B001].100.00

A1B001

A2B001

A3B001

A4B001

Action Figure 12" Vehicles

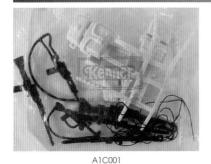
A1C001

A1C002

A1C003

A1C004

A1C005

A1C006

A1C007

A1C008

A1C009

A1C0010

Action Figure 12" Vehicles 1999-2000 (TPM)

Hasbro
__ Darth Maul with Sith Speeder [A2B001] 75.00

Action Figure 12" Vehicles 2001-2002 (POTJ)

Hasbro
__ Speeder Bike with Luke Skywalker [A3B001] .70.00

Action Figure 12" Vehicles 2002-2004 (Saga)

Hasbro
__ Princess Leia on Speeder Bike [A4B001] 50.00

Action Figure Accessories 1978-1986 (Vintage)

Kenner
__ Survival Kit mail-in promotion [A1C001] 20.00

ESB packaging.
__ Radar Laser Cannon [A1C002] 20.00
__ Tri-Pod Laser Cannon [A1C003] 20.00
__ Vehicle Maintenance Energizer [A1C004] 20.00

ROTJ packaging.
__ Ewok Assault Catapult [A1C005] 40.00
__ Ewok Combat Glider [A1C006] 40.00
__ Radar Laser Cannon [A1C007] 15.00
__ Tri-Pod Laser Cannon [A1C008] 15.00
__ Vehicle Maintenance Energizer [A1C009] 15.00

Lili Ledy, Mexico
ROTJ packaging.
__ Ewok Assault Catapult 90.00
__ Ewok Combat Glider 160.00
__ Tri-Pod Laser Cannon [A1C010] 85.00
__ Vehicle Maintenance Energizer 72.00

Action Figure Accessories 1995-1999 (POTF2)

Kenner
__ Binocular freeze-frame viewer with 2 exclusive slides [A2C001] 25.00
__ Freeze-frame storage folder [A2C002] 15.00

Kenner, Mexico
__ Binocular freeze-frame viewer, 2 excl. slides .25.00

Action Figure Accessories 1999-2001 (TPM)

Hasbro
__ Flash Cannon [A3C001] 15.00
__ Gungan Assault Cannon with Jar Jar Binks [A3C002] 15.00
__ Gungan Catapult [A3C003] 15.00

Accessory packs.
__ Hyperdrive Repair Kit 5 removable panels and 4 tools [A3C004] 30.00
__ Naboo retracting grappling hook backpack [A3C005] 6.00
__ Podracer Fuel Station fuel dispenser shoots water [A3C006] 25.00
__ Rappel Line Attack rolling rappel line [A3C007] 12.00

__ Sith firing backpack and 3 droid missiles [A3C008] 6.00
__ Tatooine pull-back droid [A3C009] 6.00
__ Tatooine Disguise Set spring-activated attack backpack [A3C010] 25.00
__ Underwater bubbling backpack [A3C011] 6.00

Battle bags.
__ Sea Creatures I Faa, Colo Claw Fish, Grouper, Sando Aqua Monster 5.00
__ Sea Creatures II Angel Fish, Trigger, Soe, Opee Sea Killer 5.00
__ Swamp Creatures III Mott, Ikopi, Kaadu, Falumpaset 5.00
__ Swamp Creatures IIII Nuna, Shaak, Pikobis, Fambaa [A3C012] 5.00

CommTech chip readers.
__ 0.00 with logo sticker 20.00
__ 0.00 without logo sticker 20.00
__ 0.01 with logo sticker 20.00
__ 0.01 without logo sticker [A3C013] 20.00

A2C001

A2C002

A3C001

A3C002

A3C003

A3C004

A3C005

A3C006   A3C007   A3C008   A3C009   A3C010   A3C011

A3C012   A3C013   A3C014 front and back   A3C015

A3C016   A3C017   A3C018   A4C001

__ CommTech Chip, model 2, any [A3C014] 35.00

Hasbro, Canada
__ Gungan Assault Cannon with Jar Jar Binks [A3C015] 15.00

Trilingual packaging.
__ CommTech chip reader [A3C016] 20.00

Hasbro, Spain
__ CommTalk chip reader [A3C017] 20.00

Hasbro, UK
__ Gungan Assault Cannon with Jar Jar Binks [A3C018] 15.00

Accessory packs. Trilingual packaging.
__ Naboo retracting grappling hook backpack 8.00
__ Sith firing backpack and 3 droid missiles 8.00
__ Tatooine pull-back droid 8.00
__ Underwater bubbling backpack 8.00

Action Figure Accessories 2002-2004 (Saga)

Hasbro
__ Attack Glider with Ewok [A4C001] 20.00

Single figure with movie accessories.
__ Arena Conflict AOTC [A4C002] 15.00
__ Death Star ANH [A4C003] 15.00
__ Endor Victory ROTJ [A4C004] 15.00
__ Hoth Survival ESB [A4C005] 15.00

Hasbro, UK
Single figure with movie accessories.
__ Arena Conflict AOTC 15.00

A4C002   A4C003   A4C004   A4C005

__ Death Star ANH 15.00
__ Endor Victory ROTJ 15.00
__ Hoth Survival ESB 15.00

Action Figure Creatures 1978-1986 (Vintage)

Kenner
Collector series.
__ Patrol Dewback [A1D001] 100.00

ESB packaging.
__ Hoth Wampa $1 rebate sticker 195.00
__ Hoth Wampa box shows Luke in Hoth gear [A1D002] 85.00
__ Tauntaun open belly [A1D003] 80.00
__ Tauntaun solid belly [A1D004] 75.00
__ Wampa box shows Rebel Commander 100.00

ROTJ packaging.
__ Rancor Monster [A1D005] 85.00

SW packaging.
__ Patrol Dewback [A1D006] 120.00

Kenner, Canada
ESB packaging.
__ Patrol Dewback 250.00
__ Patrol Dewback includes Stormtrooper figure 500.00
__ Patrol Dewback includes Stormtrooper figure orange sticker 900.00

Lili Ledy, Mexico
ROTJ packaging.
__ Rancor Monster 185.00

Meccano, France
ROTJ packaging.
__ Hoth Wampa 90.00

Palitoy, UK
ESB packaging.
__ Tauntaun open belly 135.00

A1D001

A1D002

A1D003

A1D004

ROTJ packaging.

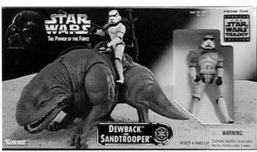

A1D005

A1D006

ROTJ packaging.
__ Hoth Wampa...75.00
__ Rancor Monster 185.00

Action Figure Creatures 1995-1999 (POTF2)

Kenner

__ Bantha and Tusken Raider .00 [A2D001]........48.00
__ Dewback and Sandtrooper .00.......................45.00
__ Dewback and Sandtrooper .01 [A2D002].......20.00
__ Jabba and Han Solo .00 ....60.00
__ Jabba and Han Solo .01 ....20.00
__ Jabba and Han Solo .02 [A2D003] 15.00
__ Rancor and Luke .00 [A2D004]......................50.00
__ Ronto and Jawa .00 [A2D005] 15.00
__ Tauntaun and Han Solo .00 [A2D006] 45.00

__ Tauntaun and Luke .00 [A2D007] 20.00
__ Wampa and Luke .00 [A2D008].....................50.00

Kenner, Italy
__ Jabba and Han Solo 40.00

Kenner, UK
__ Jabba and Han Solo 40.00
__ Ronto and Jawa [A2D009] 45.00

Action Figure Creatures 1999-2001 (TPM)

Hasbro
__ Eopie with Qui-Gon Jinn [A3D001] 130.00
__ Falumpaset with Ammo Wagon [A3D002]......50.00

__ Fambaa with Shield Generator [A3D003] 125.00
__ Jabba Glob [A3D004] 10.00
__ Jabba with 2-Headed Announcer [A3D005]...30.00
__ Kaadu with Jar Jar Binks [A3D006] 15.00
__ Opee with Qui-Gon Jinn [A3D007] 10.00

Hasbro, UK
__ Falumpaset with Ammo Wagon [A3D008]......35.00
__ Jabba the Hutt with 2-Headed Announcer.....20.00
__ Opee with Qui-Gon Jinn 20.00

Action Figure Creatures 2002-2004 (AOTC)

Hasbro
__ Acklay .00 missing claw graphic [A4D001].....35.00

A2D001

A2D002

A2D003

A2D004

A2D005

A2D006

A2D007   A2D008   A2D009

A3D001   A3D002   A3D003

A3D004   A3D005   A3D006

__ Acklay .01 claw graphic restored to packaging
[A4D002] 35.00
__ Nexu [A4D003]...15.00
__ Nexu new pose [A4D004] 12.00
__ Reek [A4D005]...15.00

Hasbro, Canada
Trilingual packaging.
__ Acklay [A4D006]...35.00
__ Nexu [A4D007]...8.00
__ Reek [A4D008]...25.00

Hasbro
__ Jabba the Hutt [A5D001] 15.00

A3D007   A3D008   A4D001   A4D001 package close-up

A4D002 package close-up   A4D003   A4D004   A4D005

Action Figure Creatures

A4D006

A4D007

A4D008

A5D001

A5D002

A5D003

A6D001

B1P001

B1P002

B1R001

B1R002

Action Figure Creatures: 2008

Hasbro
__ Battle Rancor, The Force Unleashed, exclusive to Target [B1R001]...45.00
__ Jabba's Rancor with Luke Skywalker, exclusive to Target [B1R002]...55.00

Action Figure Creatures: 2009

Hasbro
__ Dewback, exclusive to Walmart [B2R001]......45.00
__ Qui-Gin Jiin and Eopie, exclusive to mail-in [B2R002] 25.00

Action Figure Display Stands

Hasbro
__ 40-pack individual figure stands, exclusive to HasbroToyShop.com.....................................35.00

__ Jabba's Palace Court Denizens [A5D002]......20.00
__ Wampa with Hoth cave [A5D003]...................20.00

Action Figure Creatures 2007 (30th anniversary)

Hasbro
__ Arena Encounter [B1P001] 130.00
__ Bantha with Tusken Raiders brown Bantha [B1P002] 45.00
__ Bantha with Tusken Raiders red Bantha 45.00

Action Figure Creatures: 2005 (ROTS)

Hasbro
__ Boga with Obi-Wan Kenobi [A6D001] 25.00

B2R001

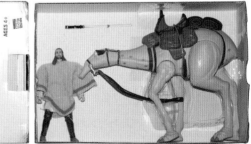

B2R002 package and contents in tray

AVA2001

AVA2002

A1F001

A1F002

A1F003

A1F004

A1F005

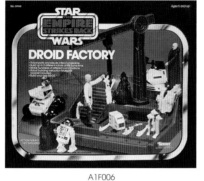

A1F006

A1F007

Kenner
Vintage.
__ Display Arena mailer packaging 245.00
__ Display Stand mailer packaging 350.00
__ Display Stand SW packaging [AVA2001] 450.00

Pride Displays, UK
__ A New Hope display dioramas, limited to 3,000 [AVA2002] 55.00

Action Figure Playsets
1978-1986 (Vintage)

Kenner
ESB packaging.
__ Cloud City, exclusive to Sears [A1F001].......420.00
__ Dagobah Jedi training sticker [A1F002]........135.00
__ Dagobah Jedi training backpack sticker, $1.00

rebate sticker 135.00
__ Dagobah package shows Luke and Yoda with training backpack [A1F003] 120.00
__ Dagobah package shows Darth Vader and Luke battling [A1F004]..150.00
__ Darth Vader's Star Destroyer [A1F005].........145.00
__ Droid Factory [A1F006]................................125.00
__ Hoth Ice Planet [A1F007]............................225.00
__ Imperial Attack Base [A1F008] 125.00
__ Rebel Command Center [A1F009]................245.00
__ Turret and Probot [A1F010]..........................145.00

ROTJ packaging.
__ Ewok Village [A1F011]..............................300.00
__ Jabba the Hutt [A1F012]................................65.00
__ Jabba the Hutt action playset, exclusive to Sears 75.00

__ Jabba the Hutt Dungeon with 8D8, exclusive to Sears [A1F013] 125.00
__ Jabba the Hutt Dungeon with Amanaman [A1F014] 300.00

SW packaging.
__ Cantina Adventure Set, exclusive to Sears [A1F015]..700.00
__ Creature Cantina [A1F016] 250.00
__ Death Star Space Station [A1F017]..............500.00
__ Droid Factory [A1F018]................................125.00
__ Land of the Jawas [A1F019] 160.00
__ Land of the Jawas with rebate sticker..........160.00

Kenner, Canada
ESB packaging.
__ Hoth Ice Planet with 3 free mini-figures offer..... 1500.00
__ Hoth Ice Planet includes Imperial Snow Stormtrooper 1500.00

A1F008

A1F009

A1F010

A1F011

A1F012

A1F013

A1F014

A1F015

A1F016

A1F017

A1F018

A1F019

A1F020

A1F021

A1F022

A1F023

A2F001

A2F002

A2F003

A2F004

A2F005

A2F006

__ Turret and Probot 195.00

ROTJ packaging.
__ Jabba the Hutt 85.00

SW packaging.
__ Death Star 230.00
__ Land of the Jawas incl. one mini-figure.... 1000.00

Lili Ledy, Mexico
ROTJ packaging.
__ Jabba the Hutt 155.00

Meccano, France
ROTJ packaging.
__ Ewok Village.................................135.00

Palitoy, UK
ESB packaging.
__ Darth Vader's Star Destroyer........................165.00
__ Turret and Probot 160.00

ROTJ tri-logo packaging.
__ Endor Chase 350.00
__ Ewok Combat 350.00
__ Ewok Village...................................220.00
__ Hoth Rescue 275.00

SW packaging.
__ Cantina [A1F021].............................450.00
__ Cantina 4 free mini-figures offer, sales samples only. 900.00
__ Death Star [A1F020]...............................1350.00
__ Droid Factory [A1F022].........................430.00
__ Land of the Jawas [A1F023] 675.00

Toltoys, Australia
SW packaging.
__ Death Star.....................................585.00

Hasbro
__ Jabba's Palace Pop-Up with Han Solo in Carbonite [A2F001]..20.00
__ Mos Eisley Pop-Up Cantina with Sandtrooper [A2F002]...20.00

Kenner
__ Cantina at Mos Eisley [A2F003].....................25.00
__ Death Star Escape [A2F004]...........................20.00

A2F007

A2F008

A2F009

A3F001

A2F010

A2F011

A3F002

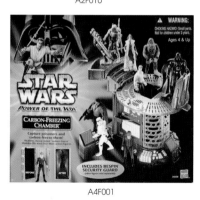
A4F001

A5F001

A6F001

A6F002

A7F001

A7F002

Action Figure Playsets

A1G001

A1G002

A1G003

__ Detention Block Rescue [A2F005] 20.00
__ Endor Attack [A2F006] 35.00
__ Hoth Battle [A2F007] 40.00

Kenner, UK
Green multi-language packaging.
__ Death Star Escape [A2F008] 35.00
__ Detention Block Rescue [A2F009] 35.00

Red multi-language packaging.
__ Death Star Escape [A2F010] 20.00
__ Detention Block Rescue [A2F011] 20.00

Action Figure Playsets 1999-2001 (TPM)

Hasbro
__ Theed Generator Complex [A3F001] 25.00
__ Theed Hangar [A3F002] 35.00

Action Figure Playsets 2001-2002 (POTJ)

Hasbro
__ Carbon Freezing Chamber [A4F001] 50.00

Action Figure Playsets 2002-2004 (Saga)

Hasbro
__ Arena Battle [A5F001] 50.00

Action Figure Playsets 2005 (ROTS)

Hasbro
__ Mustafar Final Battle [A6F001] 35.00
__ Mustafar Final Battle with four bonus clone troopers, exclusive to Sam's Club [A6F002] ..60.00

Toys: Action Figure Playsets 2010

Hasbro
__ Defense of Hoth [A7F0001] 45.00
__ Jabba's Throne [A7F0002] 45.00

Action Figure Storage Cases 1978-1986 (Vintage)

Kenner
__ C-3PO metallic finish, ROTJ [A1G001] 35.00
__ Chewbacca Bandolier ROTJ [A1G002] 20.00
__ Darth Vader ESB [A1G003] 40.00
__ Darth Vader ESB 3 free figs 600.00
__ Darth Vader ROTJ 255.00
__ Laser Rifle ROTJ [A1G004] 40.00
__ Vinyl case ESB logo [A1G005] 60.00
__ Vinyl case ESB Yoda / Wampa [A1G006] 80.00
__ Vinyl case ROTJ [A1G007] 135.00
__ Vinyl case SW [A1G008] 45.00

Kenner, UK
__ Star Wars [A1G009] 35.00

Action Figure Storage Cases 1995-1999 (POTF2)

JusToys
__ Darth Vader for Bend-ems figures [A2G001] ..20.00

Kenner
__ C-3PO talking [A2G002] 35.00
__ Collector's Case [A2G003] 65.00

Millennium Falcon with bonus figure included.
__ Imperial Scan Technician [A2G004] 30.00
__ Imperial Scan Technician made in Mexico sticker covers UPC 30.00
__ Wedge figure, 1st helmet 35.00
__ Wedge figure corrected helmet [A2G005] 25.00

Action Figure Storage Cases 1999-2001 (TPM)

Hasbro
__ R2-D2 with exclusive rolling Destroyer Droid figure [A3G001] 20.00

Action Figure Storage Cases 2004 (Original Trilogy Collection)

Hasbro
__ C-3PO with bonus Chewbacca and Han Solo figures, exclusive to Walmart [A4G001] 50.00

A1G004

A1G005

A1G006

A1G007

A1G008

A1G009

A2G001

A2G002

A2G003

A2G004

A2G005

A3G001

A4G001

A4G002

__ Darth Vader bonus Boba Fett and Stormtrooper figures, exclusive to Walmart [A4G002] 60.00

Action Figure Storage Cases 2005 (ROTS)

Hasbro
__ Darth Vader with Anakin Skywalker and Clonetrooper figures, exclusive to Walmart [A4J001]...........50.00
__ Darth Vader with bonus Darth Vader and Obi-Wan Kenobi figures, exclusive to K-Mart 25.00

Clear clamshells.
__ 5-pack, exclusive to Target [A4J002] 12.00
__ 5-pack recalled, exclusive to Target [A4J003]...15.00

A4J001

A4J002

A4J003

A1H001

A1H002

A1H003

A1H004

A1H005

A1H006

A1H007

A1H008

Action Figure Vehicles

A1H009

A1H010

A1H011

A1H012

A1H013

A1H014

A1H015

A1H016

A1H017

A1H018

A1H019

A1H020

A1H021

__ ATL Interceptor [A1H007] 175.00
__ Side Gunner [A1H008] 100.00

ESB packaging.
__ AT-AT All Terrain Attack Transport
    [A1H009] 450.00

__ AT-AT All Terrain Attack Transport $1.00 off
    sticker 495.00
__ AT-AT All Terrain Attack Transport $1.00 off sticker,
    10 accessories included sticker 560.00
__ AT-ST Scout Walker [A1H010] 85.00
__ Imperial Cruiser [A1H011]...........................125.00

__ Imperial Troop Transport 150.00
__ Millennium Falcon [A1H012] 400.00
__ Rebel Armored Snowspeeder blue background
    [A1H013] 225.00
__ Rebel Armored Snowspeeder blue background
    $1.00 rebate sticker 225.00

A1H022

A1H023

A1H024

A1H025

A1H026

A1H027

A1H028

A1H029

A1H030

A1H031

A1H032

A1H033

A1H034

A1H035

A1H036

Action Figure Vehicles

__ Rebel Armored Snowspeeder pink background [A1H014] 130.00
__ Rebel Transport blue background [A1H015] 190.00
__ Rebel Transport yellow background [A1H016] 175.00
__ Slave I [A1H017] 200.00
__ Slave I action play setting........................1220.00
__ TIE Fighter [A1H018] 195.00
__ Twin-Pod Cloud Car [A1H019] 135.00
__ X-Wing Fighter Dagobah box art (not battle damaged) [A1H020]..............................495.00
__ X-Wing Fighter red box [A1H021]................250.00
__ X-Wing Fighter with Battle Damage [A1H022] 275.00

EWOK BATTLE WAGON

A1H037

IMPERIAL SNIPER

A1H038

SAND SKIMMER

A1H039

SECURITY SCOUT

A1H040

TATOOINE SKIFF

A1H041

AT-AT

A1H042

SCOUT WALKER

A1H043

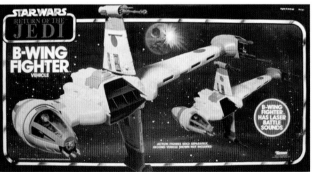

B-WING FIGHTER

A1H044

IMPERIAL SHUTTLE

A1H045

MILLENNIUM FALCON

A1H046

SPEEDER BIKE

A1H047

"BATTLE-DAMAGED" IMPERIAL TIE FIGHTER

A1H048

TIE INTERCEPTOR

A1H049

"BATTLE DAMAGED" X-WING FIGHTER

A1H050

Y-WING FIGHTER

A1H051

DARTH VADER TIE FIGHTER

A1H052

28

A1H053

A1H054

A1H055

A1H056

A1H057

A1H058

A1H059

A1H060

A1H061

Mini-rigs. ESB packaging.
__ CAP-2 Captivator [A1H023]............................35.00
__ INT-4 Interceptor [A1H024].............................30.00
__ INT-4 Interceptor $1.00 rebate sticker 30.00
__ MLC-3 Mobile Laser Cannon [A1H025]...........35.00
__ MLC-3 Mobile Laser Cannon $1.00 rebate offer sticker 235.00
__ MLC-3 Mobile Laser Cannon includes Rebel Commander 600.00
__ MTV-7 Multi-Terrain Vehicle [A1H026] 35.00
__ MTV-7 Multi-Terrain Vehicle 35.00
__ MTV-7 Multi-Terrain Vehicle $1.00 rebate offer sticker 375.00
__ MTV-7 Multi-Terrain Vehicle includes AT-AT Driver 600.00
__ PDT-8 Personnel Deployment Transport [A1H027] 30.00

Mini-rigs. ROTJ packaging.
__ AST-5 Armored Sentinel Transport [A1H028].25.00
__ CAP-2 Captivator [A1H029]............................25.00
__ Desert Sail Skiff [A1H030]...............................55.00
__ Endor Forest Ranger [A1H031].......................75.00
__ INT-4 Interceptor [A1H032].............................45.00
__ ISP-6 Imperial Shuttle Pod [A1H033] 25.00
__ MLC-3 Mobile Laser Cannon [A1H034].............35.00
__ MTV-7 Multi-Terrain Vehicle [A1H035] 25.00
__ PDT-8 Personnel Deployment Transport [A1H036] 20.00

POTF packaging
__ Ewok Battle Wagon [A1H037] 325.00
__ Imperial Sniper [A1H038]...............................125.00
__ One-Man Sand Skimmer POTF [A1H039] 85.00
__ Security Scout [A1H040]...................................95.00
__ Tatooine Skiff [A1H041] 485.00

ROTJ packaging.
__ AT-AT All Terrain Attack Transport [A1H042] 375.00
__ AT-ST Scout Walker Endor scene [A1H043] ..65.00
__ AT-ST Scout Walker Hoth scene..................225.00
__ B-Wing Fighter [A1H044]...............................250.00
__ Imperial Shuttle [A1H045]..............................450.00
__ Millennium Falcon [A1H046].........................250.00
__ Speeder Bike [A1H047]...................................35.00
__ TIE Fighter with Battle Damage [A1H048] 145.00
__ TIE Interceptor [A1H049] 195.00
__ X-Wing Fighter with Battle Damage [A1H050] 165.00
__ Y-Wing Fighter [A1H051] 175.00

SW packaging.
__ Darth Vader TIE Fighter [A1H052]..................175.00
__ Imperial Troop Transport [A1H053] 175.00
__ Landspeeder [A1H054].....................................75.00
__ Landspeeder Company store sticker 205.00
__ Landspeeder special offer 475.00
__ Landspeeder, Sonic radio controlled [A1H055] 620.00
__ Millennium Falcon [A1H056].........................450.00
__ Sandcrawler radio controlled [A1H057].......665.00
__ TIE Fighter [A1H058].....................................140.00
__ TIE Fighter free figures.................................950.00
__ X-Wing Fighter [A1H059] 175.00

Kenner, Canada
ESB packaging.
__ AT-ST Scout Walker includes mini-action figure..750.00
__ Rebel Armored Snowspeeder includes mini-action figure... 1,500.00
__ Sandcrawler radio controlled........................750.00

__ Slave I includes mini-action figure............ 1,500.00
__ Twin-Pod Cloud Car includes mini-action figure.. 1,250.00

ROTJ packaging.
__ B-Wing Fighter..185.00

SW packaging.
__ Darth Vader TIE Fighter 140.00

Lili Ledy, Mexico
Mini-rigs. ROTJ packaging.
__ CAP-2 Captivator...100.00
__ CLM-3 Cannon Laser Mobile 100.00
__ INT-4 Interceptor 100.00

ROTJ packaging.
__ AT-ST...145.00
__ B-Wing Fighter..355.00
__ Darth Vader's TIE Fighter.............................225.00
__ Imperial Shuttle..750.00
__ Millennium Falcon...575.00
__ Rebel Snowspeeder......................................185.00
__ Speederbike..135.00
__ Y-Wing Fighter..290.00

Meccano, France
__ AT-ST...550.00

SW packaging.
__ Landspeeder...350.00

Palitoy, UK
ESB packaging.
__ AT-AT All Terrain Attack Transport...............375.00
__ Millennium Falcon...260.00

A2H001

__ Rebel Armored Snowspeeder......................185.00
__ Slave I 225.00
__ X-Wing Fighter with Battle Damage 290.00

Mini-rigs. ESB packaging.
__ CAP-2 Captivator...25.00
__ MTV-7 Multi-Terrain Vehicle 25.00

Mini-rigs. ROTJ packaging.
__ AST-5 Armoured Sentinel Transport 25.00
__ CAP-2 Captivator...25.00
__ Desert Sail Skiff 75.00
__ Endor Forest Ranger......................................75.00
__ Imperial Sniper...175.00
__ INT-4 Interceptor...25.00
__ MLC-3 Mobile Laser Cannon 25.00
__ On-Man Sail Skiff 55.00
__ One-Man Sand Skimmer 75.00
__ Security Scout 200.00

ROTJ packaging.
__ AT-ST Scout Walker 95.00

A2H002

A2H003

A2H004

__ Imperial Shuttle...650.00
__ Rebel Snowspeeder 185.00
__ Slave I 265.00
__ Speeder Bike 50.00

SW packaging.
__ Darth Vader's TIE...215.00
__ Imperial Troop Transport 165.00
__ Landspeeder [A1H060] 150.00

A2H005

A2H006

A2H007

A2H008

A2H009

A2H010

A2H011

A2H012

A2H013

A2H014

A2H015

A2H016

A2H017

A2H018

A2H019

A2H020

A2H021

A2H022

A2H022 detail

A2H023

A2H023 detail

A2H024

A2H025

A2H026

A2H0228

A2H029

A2H030

A2H031

SNOWSPEEDER

A2H032

A-WING FIGHTER

A2H033

DARTH VADER'S TIE FIGHTER

A2H034

IMPERIAL AT-ST

A2H035

LANDSPEEDER

A2H036

2 in 1 LUKE'S T-16 SKYHOPPER

A2H0037

MILLENNIUM FALCON

A2H038

REBEL SNOWSPEEDER

A2H039

__ TIE Fighter...270.00
__ X-Wing Fighter [A1H061] 235.00

Action Figure Vehicles
1995-1999 (POTF2)

Hasbro

__ Tatooine Skiff with unique Jedi Knight Luke Skywalker green, exclusive to Target 80.00
__ Tatooine Skiff with unique Jedi Knight Luke Skywalker tan, exclusive to Target [A2H001] .50.00
__ Y-Wing Fighter with Y-Wing Pilot, exclusive to Target [A2H002] 95.00

Kenner

__ A-Wing Fighter .00 with A-Wing Fighter Pilot [A2H003] 35.00
__ Airspeeder .00 with Airspeeder Pilot [A2H004] 20.00

__ Boba Fett's Slave I .00 SOTE [A2H005] 50.00
__ Boba Fett's Slave I .01 [A2H006]....................60.00
__ Boba Fett's Slave I .01 with Topps widevision card inside [A2H007]...60.00

__ Cloud Car with Cloud Car Pilot [A2H008].......18.00
__ Cruisemissile Trooper .00 [A2H009] 25.00
__ Darth Vader's TIE Fighter .00 [A2H010]..........40.00
__ Dash Rendar's Outrider .00 SOTE [A2H011]..48.00

SPEEDER BIKE

A2H040

IMPERIAL / IMPERIALES SPEEDER BIKE

A2H041

IMPERIAL SPEEDER BIKE

A2H042

SPEEDER BIKE

A2H043

SPEEDER BIKE

A2H044

TIE FIGHTER

A2H045

TIE FIGHTER

A2H046

X-WING FIGHTER

A2H047

X-WING FIGHTER

A2H048

A3H001

A3H002

A3H003

A3H004

A3H005

A3H006

A3H007

A3H008

A3H009

A3H010

A3H011

A3H012

A3H013

A3H014

A3H015

A3H016

A3H017

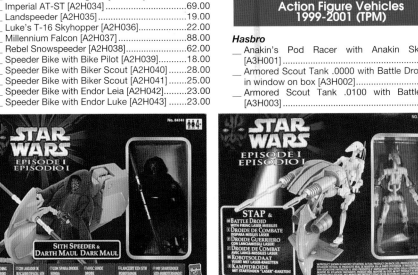

NABOO FIGHTER

A3H018

__ Speeder Bike with Bike Pilot .00 Expanded universe
[A2H020] 15.00
__ Speeder Bike with Endor Leia .00 [A2H021]...25.00
__ Speeder Bike with Endor Leia .02 [A2H022] ...15.00
__ Speeder Bike with Endor Luke .00 no glove on box
photo [A2H022]...20.00
__ Speeder Bike with Endor Luke .00 no glove on box
photo or figure 25.00
__ Speeder Bike with Endor Luke .01 [A2H023] .18.00
__ Swoop with Swoop Rider .00 [A2H024] 15.00
__ TIE Fighter .00 [A2H025]................................50.00
__ X-Wing Fighter .00 red box [A2H026].............35.00
__ X-Wing Fighter .01 green box [A2H027].........90.00
__ X-Wing Fighter, Power FX [A2H028]...............80.00

Kenner, Canada
__ Speeder Bike EU with Biker Pilot Leia without
poncho packed in [A2H029] 16.00

Kenner, Italy
__ Luke e il T-16 Skyhopper [A2H030]................40.00
__ Rebel Snowspeeder [A2H031]........................45.00

Kenner, UK
__ A-Wing Fighter with A-Wing Fighter Pilot
[A2H032] 23.00
__ Darth Vader's TIE Fighter [A2H033]................23.00
__ Imperial AT-ST [A2H034] 69.00
__ Landspeeder [A2H035] 19.00
__ Luke's T-16 Skyhopper [A2H036]....................22.00
__ Millennium Falcon [A2H037] 88.00
__ Rebel Snowspeeder [A2H038].........................62.00
__ Speeder Bike with Bike Pilot [A2H039]...........18.00
__ Speeder Bike with Biker Scout [A2H040].........28.00
__ Speeder Bike with Biker Scout [A2H041].........25.00
__ Speeder Bike with Endor Leia [A2H042]..........23.00
__ Speeder Bike with Endor Luke [A2H043] 23.00

__ TIE Fighter [A2H044]......................................36.00
__ TIE Fighter with free Stormtrooper figure
[A2H045]..85.00
__ X-Wing Fighter [A2H046] 42.00
__ X-Wing Fighter with free Luke Skywalker figure
[A2H047] 85.00

Action Figure Vehicles
1999-2001 (TPM)

Hasbro
__ Anakin's Pod Racer with Anakin Skywalker
[A3H001] 20.00
__ Armored Scout Tank .0000 with Battle Droid droid
in window on box [A3H002]............................25.00
__ Armored Scout Tank .0100 with Battle Droid
[A3H003] 15.00

A3H019

A3H020

STAP & BATTLE DROID

A3H021

A3H0022

A3H023

A4H001

B-WING FIGHTER

A4H002

A4H003

TIE BOMBER

A4H004

TIE INTERCEPTOR

A4H005

A5H001

A5H002

A5H003

A5H004

A5H005

A5H006

A5H007

A5H008

A5H009

A5H010

A5H011

A5H012

A5H013

A5H014

A5H015

A5H016

A5H017

A5H018

A5H019

A5H020

__ Flash Speeder [A3H004].................................15.00
__ Gungan Scout Sub with Obi-Wan Kenobi [A3H005]...25.00
__ Naboo Fighter .01 "Launching Proton Torpedo," old logo [A3H006]...................................48.00
__ Naboo Fighter .0200 "Launching Proton Torpedo With Real Sounds," old logo [A3H007]...........35.00

__ Naboo Fighter .0300 "With Real Movie Lights and Sounds," new logo [A3H008].........................20.00
__ Naboo Royal Starship [A3H009]...................175.00
__ Sebulba's Pod Racer with Sebulba [A3H010] 20.00
__ Sith Attack Speeder with Darth Maul [A3H011]...25.00
__ Sith Speeder with Darth Maul [A3H012].........10.00

__ Stap and Battledroid [A3H013].......................20.00
__ Trade Federation Droid Fighters [A3H014].....20.00
__ Trade Federation Tank [A3H015]....................65.00

Hasbro, Canada
__ Armored Scout Tank with Battle Droid...........10.00
__ Sith Speeder with Darth Maul........................17.00
__ STAP and Battledroid 24.00

Hasbro, Italy
__ Armored Scout Tank with Battle Droid...........16.00

Hasbro, UK
__ Anakin's Pod Racer with Anakin Skywalker [A3H016] 25.00
__ Armored Scout Tank with Battle Droid [A3H017] 16.00
__ Naboo Fighter [A3H018] 18.00
__ Sebulba's Pod Racer with Sebulba [A3H019] 25.00
__ Sith Speeder with Darth Maul [A3H020].........10.00
__ Stap and Battledroid [A3H021].......................24.00
__ Trade Federation Droid Fighters [A3H022].....16.00

A6H001

A6H002

A6H003

A6H004

A6H005

A6H006

A7H001

A7H002

A7H003

A7H004

A7H005

A7H006

A7H007

A7H008

A7H009

A7H010

Kenner

__ STAP and Battledroid Sneak Preview packaging beige support rod [A3H023] 20.00
__ STAP and Battledroid Sneak Preview packaging white support rod 20.00

Kenner, UK

__ STAP and Battledroid Sneak Preview 11.00

Action Figure Vehicles 2001-2002 (POTJ)

Hasbro

__ AT-ST and Speederbike with Paploo [A4H001] 100.00
__ B-Wing Fighter with Unique Rebel Pilot [A4H002] 100.00
__ Luke Skywalker's Snowspeeder [A4H003] 70.00
__ Tie Bomber with Unique Imperial Pilot [A4H004].....65.00
__ Tie Interceptor with Unique Imperial Pilot [A4H005] 95.00

Action Figure Vehicles 2002-2004 (Saga)

Hasbro

__ A-Wing Fighter with Pilot [A5H001] 35.00
__ Anakin Skywalker's Speeder [A5H002] 16.00
__ Anakin Skywalker's Swoop [A5H003].............25.00
__ Darth Tyrannus's Geonosian Speeder Bike [A5H004] 25.00
__ Imperial Shuttle, exclusive to FAO Schwarz

[A5H005] 225.00
__ Imperial TIE Fighter with TIE Pilot, exclusive to KB Toys [A5H006] 50.00
__ Jango Fett's Slave I [A5H007] 50.00
__ Jedi Starfighter [A5H008].............................30.00
__ Jedi Starfighter with Obi-Wan Kenobi, window box [A5H009] 40.00
__ Landspeeder with Luke Skywalker, exclusive to Toys R Us [A5H010].......................................30.00
__ Luke Skywalker's X-Wing Fighter with R2-D2 figure, exclusive to Toys R Us [A5H012] 60.00
__ Red Leader's X-Wing Fighter [A5H011]..........60.00
__ Republic Gunship [A5H013].........................85.00
__ Tie Bomber with Imperial Pilot [A5H014]........50.00
__ Zam Wesell's Speeder [A5H015]....................16.00

Hasbro, Canada

__ Jedi Starfighter [A5H016]...............................30.00
__ Republic Gunship [A5H017] 50.00
__ Zam Wesell's Speeder [A5H018] 20.00

Multi-language packaging.
__ Anakin Skywalker's Speeder [A5H019] 20.00
__ Jango Fett's Slave I [A5H020] 35.00

Action Figure Vehicles 2003-2005 (Clone Wars)

Hasbro

__ AAT Armored Assault Tank [A6H001].............75.00
__ Anakin Skywalker's Jedi Starfighter [A6H002] 90.00
__ Geonosian Starfighter [A6H003] 60.00

__ Hailfire Droid [A6H004] 90.00
__ Jedi Starfighter [A6H005]...............................70.00
__ Republic Gun Ship [A6H006]........................100.00

Action Figure Vehicles 2004-2005 (Original Trilogy Collection)

Hasbro

__ Darth Vader's Fighter with Darth Vader [A7H001] 70.00
__ Millennium Falcon [A7H002]..........................55.00
__ Millennium Falcon with 6 figures, exclusive to Sam's Club [A7H003] 75.00
__ Sandcrawler with RA-7 [A7H004] 70.00
__ Slave I with Boba Fett, exclusive to Target [A7H005] 85.00
__ TIE Fighter [A7H006].....................................60.00
__ X-Wing Fighter [A7H007] 50.00

A8H001

A8H002

A8H003

A8H004

A8H005

A8H006

A8H007

A8H008

A8H009

A8H010

A8H011

A8H012

A8H013

A8H014

A8H015

A8H016

A9H001

A9H002

A9H003

A9H004

A9H005

A9H006

A9H007

A9H008

A9H009

A9H010

A9H011

A9H012

A9H013

__ Y-Wing Fighter [A7H008] 100.00

2-Packs.
__ TIE Fighter and X-Wing Fighter [A7H009].....150.00
__ TIE Fighter and X-Wing Fighter warning sticker [A7H010] 150.00

Action Figure Vehicles 2005-2006 (ROTS)

Hasbro
__ Anakin's Jedi Starfighter [A8H001].................30.00
__ Anakin's Jedi Starfighter sneak preview [A8H002] 45.00
__ Anakin's Jedi Starfighter with Anakin Skywalker [A8H003] 85.00
__ ARC-170 Fighter [A8H004] 75.00
__ ARC-170 Fighter with bonus 3 Clone Pilots and R2 droid, exclusive to Sam's Club [A8H005] 100.00
__ AT-RT with AT-RT Driver [A8H006] 25.00

__ AT-RT with AT-RT Driver and bonus clone trooper [A8H007] 50.00
__ Barc Speeder with Barc Trooper [A8H008] 25.00
__ Barc Speeder with Barc Trooper and bonus wookiee warrior [A8H009]..............................50.00
__ Droid Tri-Fighter [A8H010]..............................30.00
__ Grievous' Wheelbike [A8H011] 30.00
__ Obi-Wan Kenobi's Jedi Starfighter [A8H012] .30.00
__ Obi-Wan Kenobi's Jedi Starfighter with Obi-Wan Kenobi [A8H013]..50.00
__ Plo Koon's Jedi Starfighter [A8H014] 60.00
__ Republic Gunship [A8H015] 85.00
__ Wookiee Flyer [A8H016] 25.00

Hasbro, Canada
Multi-language packaging.
__ Anakin's Jedi Starfighter.................................20.00
__ Anakin's Jedi Starfighter sneak preview........20.00
__ Anakin's Jedi Starfighter with Anakin Skywalker 25.00
__ AT-RT with AT-RT Driver 20.00

A9H014   A9H015

__ Barc Speeder with Barc Trooper 20.00
__ Droid Tri-Fighter..20.00
__ Grievous' Wheelbike 20.00
__ Obi-Wan Kenobi's Jedi Starfighter 20.00
__ Republic Gunship 35.00
__ Wookiee Flyer with Wookiee Warrior..............25.00

AVA001

AVA002

AVA003

AVA004

AVA005

AVA006

AVA007

AVA008

AVA009

AVA010

AVA011

AVA012

AVA013

AVA014

AVA015

AVA016

AVA017

AVA018

AVA019

AVA020

Action Figure Vehicles
2005-2006 (The Saga Collection)

Hasbro

__ Anakin's Jedi Starfighter [A9H001] 25.00
__ Darth Vader's TIE Fighter caution sticker on box [A9H002] 35.00
__ Darth Vader's TIE Fighter printed warning on box [A9H003] 25.00
__ Droid Tri-Fighter [A9H004]...........................35.00
__ Endor AT-AT [A9H005] 90.00
__ Grievous' Wheelbike [A9H006] 30.00
__ Kit Fisto's Jedi Starfigher "starfighter" misspelled, exclusive to Target [A9H007].......................35.00
__ Luke Skywalker's Dagobah X-Wing dragonsnake near shore, exclusive to Toys R Us 45.00
__ Luke Skywalker's Dagobah X-Wing dragonsnake under wing, exclusive to Toys R Us [A9H008]45.00
__ Mace Windu's Jedi Starfighter [A9H009].......30.00
__ Millennium Falcon, exclusive to Toys R Us [A9H010] 55.00
__ Obi-Wan's Jedi Starfighter [A9H011] 30.00
__ Republic Gunship Clone Wars deco [A9H012] 100.00
__ Rogue Two Snowspeeder with Zev Senesca, exclusive to Target [A9H013]......................45.00
__ TIE Fighter exclusive paint deco POTF2 pilot, exclusive to Toys R Us [A9H014] 50.00
__ TIE Fighter with pilot, exclusive to Target [A9H015] 80.00

AVA021

Action Figure Vehicles
2006-2007 (30th anniversary)

Hasbro

__ AAT [AVA001] 35.00
__ Anakin Skywalker's Jedi Starfighter [AVA002] 25.00
__ Anakin Skywalker's Starfighter [AVA003] 25.00
__ ARC-170 Clone Wars deco, exclusive to Target [AVA004] 50.00
__ AT-AP [AVA005]...35.00
__ Darth Vader's Sith Starfighter [AVA006] 35.00
__ Darth Vader's TIE Advanced x1 Starfighter [AVA007]..35.00
__ General Grievous Starfighter [AVA008]...........35.00
__ Hailfire Droid [AVA009] 35.00

__ Mace Windu's Jedi Starfighter [AVA010]........35.00
__ Obi-Wan Kenobi's Jedi Starfighter [AVA011] .35.00
__ Obi-Wan Kenobi's Jedi Starfighter with Hyperspace ring, exclusive to Toys R Us [AVA012]............40.00
__ Obi-Wan Kenobi's Starfighter [AVA013].........25.00
__ Saesee Tiin's Jedi Starfighter [AVA014] 35.00
__ Sith Infiltrator [AVA015]..................................35.00
__ TIE Bomber, exclusive to Target [AVA016].....35.00
__ TIE Fighter [AVA017].....................................35.00
__ TIE Interceptor [AVA018] 35.00
__ V-Wing Starfighter [AVA019]..........................35.00
__ V-Wing Starfighter black tape on lower right corner [AVA020] 35.00
__ Y-Wing fighter, excl. to Toys R Us [AVA021]..35.00

B2S001

B2S002

B2S003

B2S004

B2S005

B2S006

B2S007

B2S008

B2S009

B2S010

B2S011

B2S012

B2S013

B1S001

B1S002

B1S003

B1S004

B1S005

B1S006

B1S007

Action Figure Vehicles 2008 (Clone Wars)

Hasbro
__ Anakin Skywalker's Modified Jedi Starfighter [B2S001] 25.00
__ ARC-170 Fighter [B2S002] 75.00
__ AT-AP Walker [B2S003].................................25.00
__ AT-TE includes Clone Trooper [B2S004]......150.00
__ Darth Vader's TIE Advanced X1 Starfighter....25.00
__ General Grievous Starfighter [B2S005]...........25.00
__ Hailfire Droid with General Grievous, exclusive to Toys R Us [B2S006]...................................35.00
__ Homing Spider Droid [B2S007] 35.00
__ Magna Guard Fighter......................................35.00
__ Obi-Wan Kenobi's Starfighter blue [B2S008] .25.00
__ Republic Gunship [B2S009].............................65.00
__ Trade Federation AAT [B2S010]......................35.00
__ V-19 Torrent Starfighter [B2S011] 30.00
__ V-Wing Fighter with V-Wing pilot, exclusive to Toys R Us [B2S012] 35.00
__ V-Wing Starfighter [B2S013]...........................25.00

Action Figure Vehicles 2008 (The Legacy Collection)

Hasbro
__ A-Wing Fighter, Green Leader's, exclusive to Walmart [B1S001]..40.00

__ Aayla Secura's Jedi Starfighter, exclusive to Target [B1S002] 25.00
__ B-Wing Fighter Dagger squadron, exclusive to Toys R Us [B1S003] 45.00
__ Darth Vader's TIE Advanced x1 Starfighter....25.00
__ Imperial TIE Fighter [B1S004] 25.00
__ Millennium Falcon includes Han Solo and Chewbacca [B1S005] 175.00
__ TIE Fighter includes TIE Pilot, exclusive to Toys R Us [B1S006]..40.00
__ TIE Fighter (rebel decor) with Hobbie Klivian, exclusive to Previews [B1S007].....................60.00

Hasbro, Canada
__ Darth Vader's TIE Advanced x1 Starfighter....25.00
__ Millennium Falcon includes Han Solo and Chewbacca...175.00

Action Figure Vehicles 2009 (Clone Wars)

Hasbro
__ Ahsoka Tano's Jedi Starfighter [B2T001] 35.00
__ Anakin's Jedi Starfighter [B2T002] 35.00
__ ARC-170 Fighter [B2T003]...............................50.00
__ Armored Assault Tank (AAT)...........................40.00
__ Clone Turbo Tank with launching speeder bike [B2T004]...135.00
__ Corporate Alliance Tank Droid [B2T005] 35.00

__ General Grievous' Starfighter 40.00
__ Obi-Wan's Jedi Starfighter [B2T006]..............35.00
__ Octuparra Droid, exclusive to Walmart...........45.00
__ Republic Fighter Tank [B2T007].......................40.00
__ Republic Gunship [B2T008].............................65.00
__ Turbo Tank..165.00
__ V-19 Torrent Starfighter [B2T009]...................40.00
__ V-Wing Fighter with V-Wing Pilot, exclusive to Toys R Us 50.00
__ Vulture Droid [B2T010].....................................40.00
__ Y-Wing Bomber [B2T011]..............................80.00

Hasbro, UK
__ Anakin's Jedi Starfighter..................................35.00
__ ARC-170 Fighter..50.00
__ Armored Assault Tank (AAT)...........................40.00
__ Epic Encounter [B2T012]..................................75.00
__ General Grievous' Starfighter 40.00
__ Magnaguard Fighter...40.00
__ Obi-Wan's Jedi Starfighter 35.00
__ Republic Fighter Tank......................................40.00
__ V-19 Torrent Starfighter 40.00
__ Vulture Droid..40.00

Action Figure Vehicles 2009 (The Legacy Collection)

Hasbro
__ AT-ST, exclusive to Walmart [A2T001]...........40.00

B2T001

B2T002

B2T003

B2T004

B2T006

B2T005

B2T009

B2T008

B2T007

Action Figure Vehicles

B2T010

B2T011

B2T012

A2T001

A2T002

A2T003

A2T004

A2T005

B3T001

B3T002

B3T003

B3T004

B3T005

B3T006

B3T007

B3T008

B3T009

B3T010

B3T011

B3T012

B3T013

B3T014

B3T015

__ Darth Vader's TIE Advanced [A2T002] 35.00
__ Imperial TIE Fighter with Pilot [A2T003]..........45.00
__ TIE Interceptor, excl. to Toys R Us [A2T004]..45.00
__ Wedge Antille's X-Wing Fighter, exclusive to Target
   [A2T005]...45.00

Hasbro, UK

__ Darth Vader's TIE Advanced X1 Starfighter....35.00
__ Imperial TIE Fighter with Pilot.........................45.00

Action Figure Vehicles
2010 (Clone Wars)

Hasbro

__ AAT (Armored Assault Tank) [B3T001] 35.00
__ Anakin's Jedi Starfighter [B3T002] 35.00
__ AT-AP (All Terrain Attack Pod) [B3T003] 35.00

__ Droid Gunship [B3T004] 50.00
__ Droid Tri-Fighter [B3T005] 35.00
__ Hyena Bomber [B3T006] 35.00
__ Jedi Turbo Speeder [B3T007]........................35.00
__ Kit Fisto's Jedi Starfighter [B3T008] 35.00
__ Obi-Wan's Jedi Starfighter [B3T009].............35.00
__ Plo Koon's Jedi Starfighter [B3T010] 35.00
__ Republic Fighter Tank [B3T011] 35.00
__ Republic Swamp Speeder [B3T012]...............35.00
__ V-19 Torrent Starfighter [B3T013].................35.00
__ Xanadu Blood [B3T014].................................35.00

Ultimate battle packs.
__ Rise of Boba Fett [B3T015]...........................135.00

Hasbro, Canada
Ultimate battle packs.
__ Rise of Boba Fett...135.00

Action Figure Vehicles
2010 (The Legacy Collection)

Hasbro

__ Bespin Cloud Car [B4T001] 35.00
__ Imperial AT-AT [B4T002]................................95.00
__ Imperial TIE Bomber, exclusive to Walmart
   [B4T003]...35.00
__ Luke Skywalker's Snowspeeder.....................35.00

Vintage style packaging.
__ AT-AT (All Terrain Armored Transport),
   exclusive to Toys R Us [B4T004].................150.00
__ Imperial TIE Fighter, exclusive to Target
   [B4T005]...45.00
__ Rebel Armored Snowspeeder, exclusive to Target
   [B4T006]...45.00

B4T001

B4T002

B4T003

B4T004

B4T005

B4T006

Action Figures

Star Wars (Vintage)

Star Wars logo with chrome style double border.

12-back have price box on top left corner.

20-back have Boba Fett offer on front.

1978-1979

The Empire Strikes Back (Vintage)

ESB logo with chrome style single border.

Several promotional offer stickers possible on front.

1980-1983

Return of the Jedi (Vintage)

ROTJ logo with chrome style single border.

Several promotional offer stickers possible on front.

1983-1985

Power of the Force (Vintage)

POTF logo. Figure on left with collector coin mounted above.

Referred to as "Final 17" because these were the last 17 vintage movie based action figures produced.

1985-1986

Droids (Vintage)

Series logo. Figure on right with collector coin mounted above.

Figure sketch on left. Based upon cartoon spin-offs: the adventures of R2-D2 and C-3PO.

1985

Ewoks (Vintage)

Series logo. Figure on right with collector coin mounted above.

Figure sketch on left. Based upon cartoon spin-offs: the adventures of Wicket and the Ewoks.

1985

Power of the Force

Modern restart of the series which ended in 1986.

Referred to by collectors as Power of the Force 2 (POTF2)

Can be called "Red Card" or "Orange Card"

1995-1996

Power of the Force

Considered part of the POTF2 series.

Can be called "Green Card."

Character foil was present in 1996 / 97. Not applied consistently to every figure in 1997 / 98.

1996-1998

Shadows of the Empire

Abbreviated as SOTE.

Not usually considered to be part of the POTF2 series.

Six figures in this short run series.

1997

Expanded Universe

Considered part of the POTF2 series.

Thick cardback contains fold-out play scene.

Nine characters from books, comics, and games.

1998

Freeze Frame

Considered part of the POTF2 series.

Stripe at bottom can be yellow, blue, or red, depending on the character.

Freeze Frame Weequay is the most sought valuable single figure in the modern line.

1998-1999

Flashback

Considered part of the POTF2 series.

Manufacturer brand changed from Kenner to Hasbro mid way through production.

R2-D2 was packaged with lightsaber on the left and on the right.

1999

Comm-Tech

Considered part of the POTF2 series.

Comm-Tech chips may have either a foil or a white background behind character graphic.

Greedo was manufactured with either blue or yellow articulation pins.

1999-2000

Episode I

Not usually referred to as Comm-Tech.

First modern series without Darth Vader on the card.

Comm-Tech chips may have either a foil or a white background behind character graphic.

1999-2000

Power of the Jedi

Darth Vader and Obi-Wan represent first series with original and prequel characters in same line.

Green card with high star burst.

Fold out Jedi Force File with character information.

2000-2001

Saga

First retail release had background insert behind character.

Included the initial release of *Episode II: Attack of the Clones* figures.

First rectangular card since vintage figures.

2001-2002

Saga 2

Star burst background.

Gold bar boarder starts higher to logo than previous year and tapers on the left side.

2002-2003

Gold Bar Saga & Hall of Fame

2003 repackaged figures have no bases. 2004 saga figures include dark bases. All saga figures are in numbered series.

Hall of Fame figures can each have either dark or clear bases and are not numbered.

2003-2004

Clone Wars

Realistic figures of animated characters.

Based upon Cartoon Network's *Clone Wars* cartoon series, season 1.

2003-2004

Clone Wars

Animated style character action figures.

Based upon Cartoon Network's *Clone Wars* cartoon series, seasons 1-3.

2003-2005

Revenge of the Sith Sneak Preview & Revenge of the Sith

First line of figures dedicated to a specific movie without figures of any other source, since *Episode I.*

2005-2006

Saga Collection & Greatest Battles & Heroes and Villains

Saga collection was introduction of Ultimate Galactic Hunt packaging promotion.

C-3PO packaged with either lava or corridor base stand.

2006-2007

30th Anniversary Collection

Abbreviated as TAC.

Figure on left with coin mounted on right; sketch of character on card.

Ultimate Galactic Hunt figures included gold colored coins.

2007-2008

Saga Legends

Figure on left with coin mounted on right; sketch of character on card.

Saga Legends and TAC have first pack-in coins since 1998 Millennium Minted Coin (MMC) boxed action figures.

2007-2008

30th Anniversary Transition & The Force Unleashed

Interconnecting base, stamped with movie or era for included figure.

Approximately 30% of transition figures are TAC re-released with stands instead of coins.

2008

Legacy Collection & Greatest Hits

Card shaped like a stormtrooper helmet.

Helmet eyes can be printed black or blue.

Droid part pack-ins.

Greatest Hits only has four figures in the series.

2008-2009

The Clone Wars

Card shaped like a clone trooper helmet.

Helmet visor can be printed black or blue.

First day of release stickers on some figures.

2008-2009

Legacy Collection & Saga Legends

Legacy Collection also called "Droid Factory" set. Each figure includes a piece to collect to build a unique droid figure.

Saga Legends each includes extra "Clone gear."

2009-2010

Legacy Collection

Orange background with character sketch.

Includes game stats card and dice as pack-ins.

Figures are based upon repackaged or repainted updates of previously released figures.

2010-2011

The Clone Wars

Blue background with character sketch.

Include game stats card and dice as pack-ins.

All figures are animated style, based upon 3D *Clone Wars* cartoon.

2010-2011

P3U001

P3U002

Hasbro
__ Naboo Fighter with 8 mini-figures [P3U001]...75.00
__ Naboo Fighter with Anakin figure [P3U002]....25.00

Action Figures 1978-1986 (Vintage)

Clipper, Netherlands
ESB packaging, double-stem bubbles.
__ 4-LOM..400.00
__ AT-AT Commander...90.00

__ Ben Kenobi 125.00
__ Bespin Security Guard................................135.00
__ Dengar 95.00
__ Hammerhead 120.00
__ Rebel Commander.......................................140.00
__ Rebel Soldier 75.00
__ Walrus Man...160.00
__ Zuckuss 125.00

Return of the Jedi.
__ Biker Scout 85.00
__ Chief Chirpa..65.00
__ Darth Vader...85.00
__ Luke Skywalker (Jedi Knight).........................95.00
__ Lumat...95.00

ROTJ packaging.
__ Ree Yees..65.00

Star Wars 12-back cards. Produced in the Netherlands.
__ Artoo-Detoo..425.00
__ Darth Vader..850.00
__ Jawa 290.00
__ Sand People 390.00
__ See-Threepio 350.00

SW 12-back cards.
__ Ben Kenobi [AV001].....................................360.00
__ Chewbacca [AV002] 340.00
__ Death Squad Commander............................320.00
__ Han Solo [AV003]...590.00
__ Luke Skywalker [AV004] 540.00
__ Princess Leia Organa [AV005] 480.00
__ Stormtrooper [AV006] 360.00

Csillagok Haboruja, Hungary
__ Biker Scout 325.00
__ Boba Fett 1500.00
__ C-3PO..325.00
__ Chewbacca...325.00
__ Darth Vader..450.00
__ Han Solo 325.00
__ Luke Skywalker..350.00
__ Princess Leia 325.00
__ Snowtrooper 325.00
__ Wicket...235.00

Glasslite
__ C-3PO [AV007] 300.00

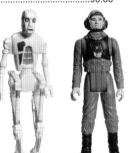

LMC001   LMC002   LMC003   LMC004   LMC005   LMC006   LMC007   LMC008

LMC009   LMC010   LMC011   LMC012   LMC013   LMC014   LMC015   LMC016   LMC017

LMC018   LMC019   LMC020   LMC021   LMC022   LMC023   LMC024   LMC025

LMC026

LMC027

LMC028

LMC029

LMC030

LMC031

LMC032

LMC033

LMC034

LMC035

LMC036

LMC037

LMC038

LMC039

LMC040

LMC041

LMC042

LMC043

LMC044

LMC045

LMC046

LMC047

LMC48

LMC049

LMC050

LMC051

LMC052

LMC053

LMC054

LMC055

LMC056

LMC057

LMC058

LMC059

LMC060

LMC061

LMC062

LMC063

LMC064

LMC065

LMC066

LMC067

LMC068

LMC069

LMC070

LMC071

LMC072

LMC073

LMC074

LMC075

LMC076

LMC077

LMC078

LMC079

LMC080

LMC081

LMC082

LMC083

LMC084

LMC085

LMC086

LMC087

LMC088

LMC089

LMC090

LMC091

LMC092

LMC093

LMC094

LMC095

LMC096

LMC097

LMC098

LMC099

LMC100

LMC101

LMC102

LMC103

LMC104

LMC105

LMC106

LMC107

__ Chewbacca [AV008] 300.00
__ Darth Vader [AV009] 400.00
__ Guerreiro Imperial 600.00
__ Han Solo [AV010] 275.00
__ Luke Skywalker [AV011] 300.00
__ Princess Leia 350.00
__ R2-D2 [AV012] 155.00

Harbert, Italy
Empire Strikes Back.
__ Bespin Security Guard (White)......................60.00
__ Boba Fett 400.00
__ Lando Calrissian 80.00
__ Luke Skywalker 95.00
__ Princess Leia 295.00
__ Rebel Soldier 75.00
__ Yoda 270.00

Star Wars.
__ Ben (Obi-Wan) Kenobi [AV013]....................450.00
__ C1P8 (R2-D2) [AV014] 325.00
__ Capo Jawa (Jawa) [AV015]..........................250.00
__ Chewbacca [AV016] 395.00
__ Comandante Squadra [AV017] 250.00
__ D3B0 (C-3PO) [AV018] 525.00
__ Death Star Droid 230.00
__ Greedo 295.00
__ Hammerhead 270.00
__ Lord Darth Fener (Darth Vader) [AV019] 300.00
__ Luke Skywalker [AV020] 345.00
__ Luke Skywalker X-Wing Pilot [AV021] 350.00
__ Power Droid 200.00
__ Principessa Leila Organa [AV022].................345.00
__ R5-D4..235.00
__ Sabbipode (Sandpeople) [AV023].................245.00

__ Snaggletooth 200.00
__ Stormtrooper 225.00
__ Walrusman...260.00

Kenner
4-LOM
__ ESB [AV024]...300.00
__ ROTJ [AV025] 60.00
__ Without package, mint, complete [LMC001] 15.00
8D8
__ 8D8 ROTJ [AV026]...45.00
__ Without package, mint, complete [LMC002] ..10.00
A-Wing Pilot
__ POTF [AV027] 100.00
__ Without package, mint, complete [LMC003] 55.00

AV001 AV002 AV003 AV004 AV005 AV006

AV007 AV008 AV009 AV010 AV011

AV012 AV013 AV014 AV015 AV016 AV017

AV018 AV019 AV020 AV021 AV022 AV023

AV024　　　AV025　　　AV026　　　AV027　　　AV028　　　AV029

AV030　　　AV031　　　AV032　　　AV033　　　AV034　　　AV035

AV036　　　AV037　　　AV038　　　AV039　　　AV040　　　AV041

AV042　　　AV043　　　AV044　　　AV045　　　AV046　　　AV047

AV048　　　AV049　　　AV050　　　AV051　　　AV052　　　AV053

AV054

AV055

AV056

AV057

AV058

AV059

AV060

AV061

AV062

AV063

AV064

AV065

AV066

AV067

AV068

AV069

AV070

AV071

AV072

AV073

AV074

AV075

AV076

AV077

AV078

AV079

AV080

AV081

AV082

AV083

AV084　　　　AV085　　　　AV086　　　　AV087　　　　AV088　　　　AV089

AV090　　　　AV091　　　　AV092　　　　AV093　　　　AV094　　　　AV095

AV096　　　　AV097　　　　AV098　　　　AV099　　　　AV100　　　　AV101

AV102　　　　AV103　　　　AV104　　　　AV105　　　　AV106　　　　AV107

AV108　　　　AV109　　　　AV110　　　　AV111　　　　AV112　　　　AV113

AV114

AV115

AV116

AV117

AV118

AV119

AV120

AV121

AV122

AV123

AV124

AV125

AV126

AV127

AV128

AV129

AV130

AV131

AV132

AV133

AV134

AV135

AV136

AV137

AV138

AV139

AV140

AV141

AV142

AV143

Action Figures

AV144

AV145

AV146

AV147

AV148

AV149

AV150

AV151

AV152

AV153

AV154

AV155

AV156

AV157

AV158

AV159

AV160

AV161

AV162

AV163

AV164

AV165

AV166

AV167

AV168

AV169

AV170

AV171

AV172

AV173

AV174

AV175

AV176

AV177

AV178

AV179

AV180

AV181

AV182

AV183

AV184

AV185

AV186

AV187

AV188

AV189

AV190

AV191

AV192

AV193

AV194

AV195

AV196

AV197

AV198

AV199

AV200

AV201

AV202

AV203

AV204

AV205

AV206

AV207

AV208

AV209

AV210

AV211

AV212

AV213

AV214

AV215

AV216

AV217

AV218

AV219

AV220

AV221

AV222

AV223

AV224

AV225

AV226

AV227

AV228

AV229

AV230

AV231

AV232

AV233

Admiral Ackbar
__ ROTJ [AV028] 45.00
__ Without package, mint, complete [LMC004] 8.00
Amanaman
__ POTF [AV029] 260.00
__ Without package, mint, complete [LMC005] 135.00
Anakin Skywalker
__ POTF [AV030] 2,250.00
__ Without package, mint, complete [LMC006] ..40.00
Artoo-Detoo (R2-D2)
__ SW-12 [AV031] 425.00
__ SW 280.00
__ ESB [AV032]....140.00
__ Without package, mint, complete [LMC78] 25.00
Artoo-Detoo (R2-D2) with Sensorscope
__ ESB [AV033]....120.00
__ ROTJ [AV034] 65.00
__ Without package, mint, complete [LMC079] ..25.00
Artoo-Detoo (R2-D2) with Pop-Up Lightsaber
__ POTF [AV035] 175.00
__ Without package, mint, complete [LMC080] ..95.00
AT-AT Commander
__ ESB [AV036]....90.00
__ ROTJ [AV037] 60.00
__ Without package, mint, complete [LMC007] ..10.00
AT-AT Driver ESB
__ ESB [AV038]....115.00
__ ROTJ [AV039] 70.00
__ Without package, mint, complete [LMC008] ..12.00
AT-ST Driver
__ ROTJ [AV040] 40.00
__ POTF [AV041] 85.00
__ Without package, mint, complete [LMC009] ..18.00
B-Wing Pilot
__ ROTJ [AV042] 45.00
__ POTF [AV043] 45.00
__ Without package, mint, complete [LMC010] ..10.00
Barada
__ POTF [AV044] 120.00
__ Without package, mint, complete [LMC011] ..60.00
Ben (Obi-Wan) Kenobi, double telescoping lightsaber
__ SW-12 .... 9,995.00
__ Without package, mint, complete....550.00
Ben (Obi-Wan) Kenobi, gray hair
__ SW-12 [AV045] 710.00
__ SW 190.00
__ ESB [AV046]....125.00
__ ROTJ [AV047] 60.00
__ Without package, mint, complete [LMC012] ..25.00
Ben (Obi-Wan) Kenobi, white hair
__ SW-12 [AV048] 750.00
__ SW 165.00
__ ESB 125.00
__ ROTJ [AV049] 60.00
__ POTF [AV050] 200.00
__ Without package, mint, complete [LMC013] ..25.00
Bespin Security Guard, black
__ ESB [AV051]....65.00
__ ROTJ [AV052] 55.00
__ Without package, mint, complete [LMC014] ..15.00
Bespin Security Guard, white
__ ESB [AV053]....60.00
__ ROTJ [AV054] 55.00
__ Without package, mint, complete [LMC015] ..15.00
Bib Fortuna
__ ROTJ [AV055] 45.00
__ Without package, mint, complete [LMC016] ..15.00
Biker Scout
__ ROTJ [AV056] 85.00
__ POTF [AV057] 110.00
__ Without package, mint, complete [LMC017] ..16.00
Boba Fett
__ Mail-away package....275.00
__ SW [AV058].... 1,650.00
__ ESB [AV059]....500.00
__ ROTJ, desert scene [AV060]....400.00
__ ROTJ, fireball [AV061]....425.00
__ Without package, mint, complete [LMC018] ..35.00
Bossk
__ ESB [AV062]....140.00
__ ROTJ [AV063] 100.00
__ Without package, mint, complete [LMC019] ..10.00
Chewbacca
__ SW-12 [AV064] 375.00
__ SW 250.00
__ ESB [AV065]....215.00
__ ROTJ [AV066] 125.00
__ ROTJ, Endor photo [AV067] 55.00
__ POTF [AV068] 150.00
__ Without package, mint, complete [LMC022] ..12.00
Chief Chirpa
__ ROTJ [AV069] 45.00
__ Without package, mint, complete [LMC023] ..18.00
Cloud Car Pilot
__ ESB [AV070]....130.00
__ ROTJ [AV071] 60.00
__ Without package, mint, complete [LMC024] ..23.00
Darth Vader, double telescoping lightsaber
__ SW-12 .... 8,600.00
__ Without package, mint, complete....470.00
Darth Vader
__ SW-12 [AV072] 850.00
__ SW 300.00
__ ESB [AV073]....125.00
__ ROTJ, lightsaber drawn [AV074]....65.00
__ ROTJ, pointing [AV075] 55.00
__ POTF [AV076] 160.00
__ Without package, mint, complete [LMC025] ..20.00
Death Squad Commander
__ SW-12 [AV077] 330.00
__ SW 160.00
__ ESB [AV078]....125.00
__ Without package, mint, complete [LMC026] ..10.00
Death Star Droid
__ SW [AV079]....230.00
__ ESB [AV080]....160.00
__ ROTJ [AV081] 75.00
__ Without package, mint, complete [LMC027] ..24.00
Dengar
__ ESB [AV082]....95.00
__ ROTJ [AV083] 45.00
__ Without package, mint, complete [LMC028] ..10.00
Emperor
__ ROTJ [AV084] 65.00
__ POTF [AV085] 85.00
__ Without package, mint, complete [LMC029] ..16.00
Emperor's Royal Guard
__ ROTJ [AV086] 85.00
__ Without package, mint, complete [LMC030] ..24.00
EV-9D9
__ POTF [AV087] 245.00
__ Without package, mint, complete [LMC031] ..90.00
FX-7
__ ESB [AV088]....85.00
__ ROTJ [AV089] 75.00
__ Without package, mint, complete [LMC032] ..10.00
Gamorrean Guard
__ ROTJ [AV090] 45.00
__ Without package, mint, complete [LMC033] ..10.00
General Madine
__ ROTJ [AV091] 40.00
__ Without package, mint, complete [LMC034] ..15.00
Greedo
__ SW [AV092]....360.00
__ ESB [AV093]....155.00
__ ROTJ [AV094] 80.00
__ Without package, mint, complete [LMC035] ..14.00
Hammerhead
__ SW [AV095]....270.00
__ ESB [AV096]....120.00
__ ROTJ [AV097] 75.00
__ Without package, mint, complete [LMC036] ..10.00
Han Solo, large head
__ SW-12 [AV098] 1,000.00
__ SW [AV099]....650.00
__ ESB [AV100]....245.00
__ ROTJ, Death Star scene [AV101]....165.00
__ ROTJ, Mos Eisley scene [AV102] 185.00
__ Without package, mint, complete [LMC037] ..25.00
Han Solo, small head
__ SW-12 [AV103] 750.00
__ SW 540.00
__ ESB 300.00
__ Without package, mint, complete [LMC038] ..40.00
Han Solo Bespin
__ ESB [AV104]....145.00
__ ROTJ [AV105] 75.00
__ Without package, mint, complete [LMC039] ..18.00
Han Solo Hoth Battle Gear
__ ESB [AV106]....95.00
__ ROTJ [AV107] 75.00
__ Without package, mint, complete [LMC040] ..15.00
Han Solo in Carbonite Chamber
__ POTF [AV108] 275.00
__ Without package, mint, complete [LMC041] 125.00
Han Solo Trench Coat
__ ROTJ [AV109] 50.00
__ POTF [AV110] 350.00
__ Without package, mint, complete [LMC042] ..22.00
IG-88
__ ESB [AV111]....190.00
__ ROTJ [AV112] 80.00
__ Without package, mint, complete [LMC043] ..10.00
Imperial Commander
__ ESB [AV113]....85.00
__ ROTJ [AV114] 50.00
__ Without package, mint, complete [LMC044] ..10.00
Imperial Dignitary
__ POTF [AV115] 155.00
__ Without package, mint, complete [LMC045] ..70.00
Imperial Gunner
__ POTF [AV116] 165.00
__ Without package, mint, complete [LMC046] ..85.00
Imperial Stormtrooper in Hoth Weather Gear
__ ESB [AV117]....145.00
__ ROTJ [AV118] 60.00
__ Without package, mint, complete [LMC090] ..18.00
Imperial TIE Fighter Pilot
__ ESB [AV119]....130.00
__ ROTJ [AV120] 90.00
__ Without package, mint, complete [LMC094] ..20.00
Jawa, cloth cape
__ SW-12 [AV121] 230.00
__ SW 200.00
__ ESB [AV122]....125.00
__ ROTJ [AV123] 50.00
__ POTF [AV124] 140.00
__ Without package, mint, complete [LMC047] ..18.00
Jawa, plastic cape
__ SW-12 [AV125] 3,500.00
__ Without package, mint, complete....95.00
Klaatu, palace outfit
__ ROTJ [AV126] 50.00
__ Without package, mint, complete [LMC048] ..12.00
Klaatu, skiff outfit
__ ROTJ [AV127] 50.00
__ Without package, mint, complete [LMC049] ..14.00
Lando Calrissian
__ ESB [AV128]....80.00
__ ROTJ [AV129] 45.00
__ Without package, mint, complete [LMC050] ..16.00
Lando Calrissian, no teeth
__ ESB 80.00
__ Without package, mint, complete [LMC051] ..14.00
Lando Calrissian General Pilot
__ POTF [AV130] 145.00
__ Without package, mint, complete [LMC052] ..95.00
Lando Calrissian Skiff Outfit
__ ROTJ [AV131] 45.00
__ Without package, mint, complete [LMC053] ..14.00
Leia Organa Bespin Gown, crew neck
__ ESB, front view [AV132]....185.00
__ ESB, profile 200.00
__ ROTJ (Princess Leia Organa) [AV133] 125.00
__ Without package, mint, complete [LMC073] ..25.00
Leia Organa Bespin Gown, turtle neck
__ ESB, front view [AV134]....190.00
__ ESB, profile [AV135]....195.00
__ ROTJ (Princess Leia Organa) [AV136] 145.00
__ Without package, mint, complete [LMC074] ..25.00
Lobot
__ ESB [AV137]....65.00
__ ROTJ [AV138] 45.00
__ Without package, mint, complete [LMC054] ..10.00
Logray
__ ROTJ [AV139] 60.00
__ Without package, mint, complete [LMC055] ..18.00
Luke Skywalker, double telescoping lightsaber
__ SW-12 .... 4,800.00
__ Without package, mint, complete....225.00
Luke Skywalker, blond hair
__ SW-12 [AV140] 850.00
__ SW 235.00
__ ESB [AV141]....250.00

__ ROTJ [AV142] 240.00
__ ROTJ, Falcon Gunwell [AV143] 180.00
__ Without package, mint, complete [LMC056] ..35.00

Luke Skywalker, brown hair
__ ESB [AV144] 285.00
__ ROTJ [AV145] 290.00
__ Without package, mint, complete [LMC057] ..40.00

Luke Skywalker Battle Poncho
__ POTF [AV146] 170.00
__ Without package, mint, complete [LMC058] ..85.00

Luke Skywalker Bespin Fatigues, blond hair
__ ESB, looking [AV147] 140.00
__ ESB, walking [AV148] 245.00
__ Without package, mint, complete [LMC059] ..25.00

Luke Skywalker Bespin Fatigues, brown hair
__ ESB, looking [AV149] 200.00
__ ESB, walking [AV150] 245.00
__ ROTJ [AV151] 95.00
__ Without package, mint, complete [LMC060] ..20.00

Luke Skywalker Hoth Battle Gear
__ ESB [AV152] 125.00
__ ROTJ [AV153] 80.00
__ Without package, mint, complete [LMC061] ..18.00

Luke Skywalker Jedi
__ ROTJ, blue lightsaber [AV154] 175.00
__ Without package, mint, complete [LMC062] ..40.00

Luke Skywalker Jedi
__ ROTJ, green lightsaber [AV155] 95.00
__ POTF [AV156] 270.00
__ Without package, mint, complete [LMC063] ..55.00

Luke Skywalker Stormtrooper Disguise
__ POTF [AV157] 425.00
__ Without package, mint, complete [LMC064] 165.00

Luke Skywalker X-Wing Pilot
__ SW [AV158] 250.00
__ ESB [AV159] 150.00
__ ROTJ [AV160] 65.00
__ POTF [AV161] 165.00
__ Without package, mint, complete [LMC065] ..15.00

Lumat
__ ROTJ [AV162] 60.00
__ POTF [AV163] 75.00
__ Without package, mint, complete [LMC066] ..55.00

Nien Nunb
__ ROTJ [AV164] 70.00
__ Without package, mint, complete [LMC067] ..10.00

Nikto
__ ROTJ [AV165] 40.00
__ Without package, mint, complete [LMC068] ..20.00

Paploo
__ ROTJ [AV166] 55.00
__ POTF [AV167] 80.00
__ Without package, mint, complete [LMC069] ..34.00

Power Droid
__ SW [AV168] 200.00
__ ESB [AV169] 130.00
__ ROTJ [AV170] 50.00
__ Without package, mint, complete [LMC070] ..15.00

Princess Leia Organa
__ SW-12 [AV171] 675.00
__ SW 260.00
__ ESB [AV172] 295.00
__ ROTJ [AV173] 390.00
__ Without package, mint, complete [LMC071] ..35.00

Princess Leia Combat Poncho
__ ROTJ [AV174] 50.00
__ POTF [AV175] 115.00
__ Without package, mint, complete [LMC076] ..35.00

Princess Leia Hoth
__ ESB [AV176] 160.00
__ ROTJ [AV177] 95.00
__ Without package, mint, complete [LMC072] ..30.00

Princess Leia Organa Boushh Disguise
__ ROTJ [AV178] 60.00
__ Without package, mint, complete [LMC075] ..20.00

Pruneface
__ ROTJ [AV179] 40.00
__ Without package, mint, complete [LMC077] ..14.00

R5-D4
__ SW [AV180] 235.00
__ ESB [AV181] 120.00
__ ROTJ (Arfive-Defour) [AV182] 60.00
__ Without package, mint, complete [LMC081] ..18.00

Rancor Keeper

__ ROTJ [AV183] 40.00
__ Without package, mint, complete [LMC082] ..12.00

Rebel Commander
__ ESB [AV184] 140.00
__ ROTJ [AV185] 50.00
__ Without package, mint, complete [LMC083] ..10.00

Rebel Commando
__ ROTJ [AV186] 50.00
__ Without package, mint, complete [LMC084] ..10.00

Rebel Soldier
__ ESB [AV187] 75.00
__ ROTJ [AV188] 40.00
__ Without package, mint, complete [LMC085] ..12.00

Ree-Yees
__ ROTJ [AV189] 40.00
__ Without package, mint, complete [LMC086] ..10.00

Romba
__ POTF [AV190] 100.00
__ Without package, mint, complete [LMC087] ..55.00

Sandpeople
__ SW-12 [AV191] 390.00
__ SW 170.00
__ ESB [AV192] 120.00
__ ROTJ (Tusken Raider) [AV193] 80.00
__ Without package, mint, complete [LMC095] ..24.00

See-Threepio (C-3PO)
__ SW-12 [AV194] 350.00
__ SW 230.00
__ ESB [AV195] 200.00
__ Without package, mint, complete [LMC020] ..25.00

See-Threepio (C-3PO) with Removable Limbs
__ ESB [AV196] 100.00
__ ROTJ [AV197] 75.00
__ POTF [AV198] 120.00
__ Without package, mint, complete [LMC021] ..10.00

Snaggletooth, blue
__ Without package, mint, complete [LMC088] 180.00

Snaggletooth, red
__ SW [AV199] 200.00
__ ESB [AV200] 160.00
__ ROTJ [AV201] 65.00
__ Without package, mint, complete [LMC089] ..12.00

Squidhead
__ ROTJ [AV202] 45.00
__ Without package, mint, complete [LMC091] ..14.00

Star Destroyer (Death Squad) Commander
__ ESB [AV203] 125.00
__ ROTJ [AV204] 80.00
__ Without package, mint, complete [LMC026] ..14.00

Stormtrooper
__ SW-12 [AV205] 425.00
__ SW 225.00
__ ESB [AV206] 125.00
__ ROTJ [AV207] 65.00
__ POTF [AV208] 260.00
__ Without package, mint, complete [LMC092] ..18.00

Teebo
__ ROTJ [AV209] 50.00
__ POTF [AV210] 200.00
__ Without package, mint, complete [LMC093] ..15.00

Too-Onebee (2-1B)
__ ESB [AV211] 95.00
__ ROTJ [AV212] 50.00
__ Without package, mint, complete [LMC096] ..10.00

Ugnaught
__ ESB [AV213] 80.00
__ ROTJ [AV214] 45.00
__ Without package, mint, complete [LMC097] ..10.00

Walrus Man
__ SW [AV215] 280.00
__ ESB [AV216] 135.00
__ ROTJ [AV217] 65.00
__ Without package, mint, complete [LMC098] ..10.00

Warok
__ POTF [AV218] 125.00
__ Without package, mint, complete [LMC099] ..78.00

Weequay
__ ROTJ [AV219] 40.00
__ Without package, mint, complete [LMC100] ..10.00

Wicket Warrick
__ ROTJ [AV220] 50.00
__ POTF [AV221] 200.00
__ Without package, mint, complete [LMC101] ..26.00

Yak Face

__ POTF 1,995.00
__ Without package, mint, complete [LMC102] 225.00

Yoda
__ ESB, brown snake [AV222] 350.00
__ ESB, orange snake [AV223] 275.00
__ ROTJ [AV224] 175.00
__ POTF [AV225] 585.00
__ Without package, mint, complete with brown snake [LMC103] 40.00
__ Without package, mint, complete with orange snake [LMC104] 35.00

Zuckuss
__ ESB [AV226] 125.00
__ ROTJ [AV227] 60.00
__ Without package, mint, complete [LMC105] ..15.00

Kenner, Australia
__ AT-AT Driver POTF 1,350.00
__ Gamorrean Guard POTF 675.00
__ Nikto POTF 650.00

Kenner, Canada
12 back with Guerre Des Etoiles logo on front.
__ Ben (Obi-Wan) Kenobi [AV228] 575.00
__ C-3PO [AV229] 510.00
__ Darth Vader [AV230] 680.00
__ Jawa [AV231] 510.00
__ R2-D2 [AV232] 550.00
__ Stormtrooper [AV233] 590.00

ESB packaging.
__ 2-1B 82.00
__ AT-AT Driver 79.00
__ Ben (Obi-Wan) Kenobi 55.00
__ Bespin Guard white 66.00
__ Boba Fett 315.00
__ Bossk 135.00
__ C-3PO 92.00
__ Chewbacca 110.00
__ Darth Vader 98.00
__ Death Squad Commander 110.00
__ Death Star Droid 145.00
__ Dengar 71.00
__ FX-7 ....65.00
__ Greedo 125.00
__ Hammerhead 135.00
__ Han Solo Bespin 149.00
__ Han Solo Hoth 114.00
__ Han Solo 245.00
__ IG-88 ....154.00
__ Imperial Commander 64.00
__ Imperial Stormtrooper in Hoth Weather Gear 88.00
__ Jawa 110.00
__ Lando Calrissian, no teeth 66.00
__ Lobot 54.00
__ Luke Skywalker Bespin Fatigues 160.00
__ Luke Skywalker X-Wing Pilot 133.00
__ Luke Skywalker 185.00
__ Power Droid 115.00
__ Princess Leia 165.00
__ Princess Leia Bespin 170.00
__ Princess Leia Hoth 160.00
__ R2-D2 ....85.00
__ R5-D4 ....160.00
__ Rebel Soldier 77.00
__ Sand People 99.00
__ Snaggletooth 136.00
__ Stormtrooper 95.00
__ Ugnaught 46.00
__ Walrus Man 135.00
__ Yoda 135.00

ESB pkg., Sears Canada exclusive.
__ Dengar ....N/V
__ General Veers ....N/V
__ Han Solo (Cloud City Outfit) ....N/V
__ Lobot (Lando's Aid) ....N/V
__ Luke Skywalker (Hoth Outfit) ....N/V
__ R2-D2 with Parascope ....N/V
__ Ugnaught, 3 known to exist ....N/V

ROTJ packaging.
__ C-3PO, ROTJ logo sticker 245.00

__ Luke Skywalker, Jedi Knight Outfit....95.00
__ Princess Leia Organa in Combat Poncho....85.00

Star Wars packaging.
__ Luke Skywalker....575.00

Kenner, Germany
Empire Strikes Back.
__ Han Solo....205.00
__ Han Solo, Bespin outfit....220.00
__ Leia Organa, Bespin gown....205.00
__ Power Droid....75.00
__ Princess Leia Organa....225.00

ESB packaging, double-stem bubbles.
__ Ben (Obi-Wan) Kenobi....215.00
__ Han Solo....175.00
__ Leia Organa, Hoth outfit....195.00
__ Rebel Commander....135.00
__ Stormtrooper....215.00
__ Yoda....275.00

ROTJ packaging, double-stem bubbles.
__ Boba Fett....825.00
__ Luke Skywalker....410.00
__ Luke Skywalker, brown hair....325.00

Lili Ledy, Mexico
ROTJ packaging.
__ 8D8....125.00
__ Admiral Ackbar....195.00
__ Artoo Detoo....332.00
__ AT-ST Driver....150.00
__ B-Wing Pilot....135.00
__ Ben (Obi-Wan) Kenobi....125.00
__ Bib Fortuna....185.00
__ Biker Scout....175.00
__ Boba Fett....415.00
__ C-3PO Removable Limbs....195.00
__ Chewbacca....230.00
__ Chief Chirpa....125.00
__ Cloud Car Pilot....130.00
__ Darth Vader....125.00
__ Emperador....125.00
__ Emperor's Royal Guard....180.00
__ Gamorrean Guard....125.00
__ General Madine....285.00
__ Han Solo, Bespin....135.00
__ Han Solo, Endor....125.00
__ Imperial Commander....125.00
__ Imperial TIE-Fighter Pilot....255.00
__ Jawa, cloth cape....255.00
__ Klaatu Skiff Guard....125.00
__ Klaatu, palace outfit....189.00
__ Lando Calrissian....140.00
__ Lando Calrissian, Skiff Guard....170.00
__ Leia Organa, Bespin....215.00
__ Logray....160.00
__ Luke Skywalker, Bespin....125.00
__ Luke Skywalker, Jedi....125.00
__ Lumat....155.00
__ Nien Numb....165.00
__ Nikto....125.00
__ Paploo....125.00
__ Princess Leia Organa....125.00
__ Princess Leia Organa Disfraz de Boushh....520.00
__ Princess Leia Organa, Endor....125.00
__ Prune Face....125.00
__ Rancor Keeper....125.00
__ Rebel Commander....125.00
__ Ree Yees....184.00
__ See Threepio....155.00
__ Squid Head....150.00
__ Star Destroyer Commander....175.00
__ Stormtrooper....125.00
__ Teebo....125.00
__ Weequay....130.00
__ Wicket W. Warrick....125.00
__ Yoda....125.00
__ Zuckuss....215.00

Meccano, France
L'Empire Contre-Attaque.
__ Conductor AT-AT....325.00
__ FX-7....85.00
__ Garde Bespin....275.00
__ Hoth Stormtrooper....145.00
__ IG-88....190.00
__ Imperial Commander....85.00
__ Lando Calrissian....80.00
__ Rebel Soldier....75.00
__ Ugnaught....80.00
__ Yoda, brown snake....750.00

La Guerre Des Etoiles.
__ Ben Kenobi....265.00
__ Chewbacca....695.00
__ Cispeo (Z-6PO)....525.00
__ Dark Vador....750.00
__ Death Squad Commander....272.00
__ Death Star Droid....370.00
__ Dedeu (D2-R2)....395.00
__ Greedo....475.00
__ Hammerhead....335.00
__ Han Solo....345.00
__ Jawa [AV234]....85.00
__ L'nomme des Sables (Sandpeople)....395.00
__ Luc (Luke Skywalker)....625.00
__ Luke Skywalker X-Wing Pilot....250.00
__ Power Droid....350.00
__ Princess Leia....395.00
__ R5-D4....235.00
__ Snaggle Tooth....495.00
__ Soldat Imperial (Stormtrooper)....375.00
__ Walrus Man....550.00

Le Retour Du Jedi.
__ AT-AT Driver....70.00
__ Biker Scout....85.00
__ Boba Fett....895.00
__ IG-88....125.00
__ Logray....145.00
__ Luc (Tenue Bespin)....95.00
__ Yan (Han) Solo....165.00
__ Yoda....175.00
__ Z6PO....95.00

Palitoy, UK
Empire Strikes Back, double-stem bubbles.
__ Luke Skywalker Hoth....155.00

Empire Strikes Back.
__ 4-LOM....350.00
__ AT-AT Commander....85.00
__ AT-AT Driver....85.00
__ Bespin Guard, black....95.00
__ Bespin Guard, white....95.00
__ Imperial Commander....175.00
__ Imperial TIE Fighter Pilot....110.00
__ Ugnaught....270.00

Return of the Jedi.
__ Boba Fett....250.00
__ Darth Vader....95.00
__ Han Solo Bespin....75.00
__ Rebel Soldier....75.00
__ Stormtrooper....100.00

ROTJ multi-language packaging.
__ Admiral Ackbar....125.00
__ Bespin Guard, black....125.00
__ Bespin Guard, white....195.00
__ Bib Fortuna....50.00
__ Biker Scout....115.00
__ Bossk....70.00
__ Cloud Car Pilot....1,200.00
__ Greedo....165.00
__ Klaatu, palace outfit....50.00
__ Logray....75.00
__ Princess Leia Organa Boushh Disguise....85.00
__ Rebel Commando....70.00
__ Ree Yees....75.00
__ Snaggletooth....125.00
__ Squidhead....60.00

ROTJ tri-logo packaging.
__ 2-1B....110.00
__ 4-LOM....45.00
__ 8D8....165.00
__ A-Wing Pilot....165.00
__ Admiral Ackbar....75.00
__ Amanaman....175.00
__ Anakin Skywalker....145.00
__ Artoo-Detoo (R2-D2) Pop-Up Lightsaber....200.00
__ Artoo-Detoo (R2-D2) with Sensorscope....125.00
__ AT-AT Commander....125.00
__ AT-AT Driver....105.00
__ AT-ST Driver....85.00
__ B-Wing Pilot....85.00
__ Barada....135.00
__ Ben (Obi-Wan) Kenobi....200.00
__ Bespin Security Guard, white....32.00
__ Bib Fortuna....135.00
__ Biker Scout....85.00
__ Boba Fett....635.00
__ Boba Fett; sky blue instead of gray....1,275.00
__ Boba Fett, loose; sky blue instead of gray....170.00
__ Bossk....71.00
__ Boushh....149.00
__ Chewbacca....165.00
__ Chief Chirpa....100.00
__ Darth Vader....125.00
__ Death Squad Commander....64.00
__ Death Star Droid....110.00
__ Dengar....125.00
__ Emperor....135.00
__ Emperor's Royal Guard....80.00
__ EV-9D9....130.00
__ FX-7....85.00
__ Gamorrean Guard....160.00
__ General Madine....2,750.00
__ Hammerhead....60.00
__ Han Solo....125.00
__ Han Solo Bespin....135.00
__ Han Solo Hoth Battle Gear....110.00
__ Han Solo in Carbonite....225.00
__ Han Solo Trench Coat....135.00
__ IG-88....235.00
__ Imperial Commander....125.00
__ Imperial Dignitary....150.00
__ Imperial Gunner....195.00
__ Imperial Stormtrooper in Hoth Battle Gear....195.00
__ Imperial TIE Fighter Pilot....115.00
__ Jawa, cloth cape....350.00
__ Klaatu, Palace Outfit....45.00
__ Klaatu, Skiff Outfit....215.00
__ Lando Calrissian....95.00
__ Lando Calrissian General / Pilot....135.00
__ Lando Calrissian Skiff Outfit....100.00
__ Lando Calrissian, no teeth....150.00
__ Lobot....125.00
__ Logray....65.00
__ Luke Skywalker Battle Poncho....175.00
__ Luke Skywalker Bespin Fatigues, blond hair....365.00
__ Luke Skywalker Bespin Fatigues, brown hair....135.00
__ Luke Skywalker Hoth Battle Gear....34.00
__ Luke Skywalker Imperial Stormtrooper Outfit....400.00
__ Luke Skywalker Jedi Knight Outfit....130.00
__ Luke Skywalker X-Wing Pilot....200.00
__ Luke Skywalker, blonde hair....300.00
__ Luke Skywalker, brown hair....300.00
__ Lumat [AV235]....125.00
__ Max Rebo Band, boxed....118.00
__ Nien Nunb....150.00
__ Nikto....75.00
__ Paploo....150.00
__ Power Droid....60.00
__ Princess Leia Combat Poncho....38.00
__ Princess Leia Organa....200.00
__ Princess Leia Organa Bespin Gown....90.00
__ Princess Leia Organa Hoth Outfit....155.00
__ Pruneface....65.00
__ R5-D4....150.00
__ Rancor Keeper....75.00
__ Rebel Commander....75.00
__ Rebel Commando....235.00
__ Rebel Soldier....100.00
__ Ree-Yees....75.00
__ Romba....125.00
__ See-Threepio (C-3PO) with Removable Limbs....135.00
__ Squidhead....95.00
__ Stormtrooper....280.00

__ Teebo	95.00
__ Tusken Raider	115.00
__ Ugnaught	90.00
__ Walrus Man	84.00
__ Warok	135.00
__ Weequay	135.00
__ Wicket Warrick	95.00
__ Yak Face	485.00
__ Yoda, brown snake	75.00
__ Yoda, orange snake	545.00
__ Zuckuss	150.00

Star Wars.

__ Ben (Obi-Wan) Kenobi	795.00
__ C-3PO	435.00
__ Chewbacca	500.00
__ Darth Vader	580.00
__ Death Squad Commander	185.00
__ Death Star Droid	260.00
__ Greedo	325.00
__ Hammerhead	400.00
__ Han Solo	560.00
__ Jawa	360.00
__ Luke Skywalker X-Wing Pilot	430.00
__ Power Droid	400.00
__ R2-D2	215.00
__ Sand People	285.00
__ Snaggletooth	350.00
__ Stormtrooper	475.00
__ Walrusman	400.00

PBP, Spain

El Imperio Contra ataca.

__ Ben Kenobi	125.00

__ C-3P0	200.00
__ Darth Vader	125.00
__ Lando Calrissian	110.00
__ Luke Skywalker	230.00
__ Luke Skywalker Bespin Outfit	140.00
__ R2-D2	160.00
__ Ugnaught	80.00

El Retorno Del Jedi.

__ Admirante Ackbar	65.00
__ Artoo Detoo with Sensorscope, original card graphic	250.00
__ B-wing Pilot	75.00
__ Chewbacca	125.00
__ Darth Vader	195.00
__ Emperor's Royal Guard	175.00
__ General Madine	55.00
__ Hoth Stormtrooper	145.00
__ Jefe Chirpa	130.00
__ Logray	75.00
__ Luke Skywalker Hoth Battle Gear	125.00
__ Ree-Yees	75.00
__ See Threepio, original card graphic	245.00
__ Snaggletooth	85.00
__ Weequay	175.00
__ Yoda	95.00
__ Zuckuss	125.00

Popy, Japan

__ S 1 Boba Fett [AV236]	1,000.00
__ S 2 Darth Vader [AV237]	400.00
__ S 3 R2-D2 [AV238]	200.00
__ S 4 C-3PO [AV239]	175.00
__ S 5 Luke Skywalker, Bespin [AV240]	275.00

__ S 6 Han Solo, Hoth [AV241]	200.00
__ S 7 Chewbacca [AV242]	185.00
__ S 8 Luke Skywalker [AV243]	375.00
__ S 9 Han Solo [AV244]	350.00
__ S10 Imperial Snowtrooper [AV245]	400.00
__ S11 Death Star Droid [AV246]	225.00
__ S12 Rebel Soldier [AV247]	175.00
__ S13 Luke Skywalker, X-Wing Pilot [AV248]	200.00
__ S14 R5-D4 [AV249]	300.00
__ S15 Stormtrooper [AV250]	400.00

Takara, Japan
Star Wars.

__ Artoo-Detoo	525.00
__ Ben (Obi-Wan) Kenobi	450.00
__ Chewbacca	450.00
__ Darth Vader	550.00
__ Han Solo	700.00
__ Luke Skywalker	600.00
__ Princess Leia	600.00
__ Sandpeople	750.00
__ See-Threepio	445.00
__ Stormtrooper	450.00

Top Toys, Argentina
ROTJ packaging.

__ Chewbacca [AV251]	325.00
__ Darth Vader [AV252]	150.00
__ Logray [AV253]	225.00
__ Luke Skywalker, Jedi	270.00
__ Osito Ewok [AV254]	185.00
__ Stormtrooper [AV255]	150.00
__ Yoda [AV256]	325.00

AV234

AV235

AV236

AV237

AV238

AV239

AV240

AV241

AV242

AV243

AV244

AV245

AV246

AV247

AV248

AV249

AV250

AV251

AV252

AV253

AV254

AV255

AV256

AVM001   AVM002   AVM003   AVM004   AVM005

Action Figures
1978-1986 (Vintage) Multipacks

ROTJ 4-pack, German / French text.
__ AT-AT Commander, C-3PO (removable limbs), Stormtrooper, Emperor's Royal Guard.........400.00
__ Bib Fortuna, Ben Kenobi. Emperor, IG-88....400.00

ROTJ 4-pack, Italian / English text.
__ Darth Vader, Princess Leia Organa (Hoth Outfit), Paploo, Imperial Commander......................350.00
__ Lumat, Emperor, Cloud Car Pilot, Teebo 350.00
__ Rebel Commander, Lando, Lobot, Biker Scout 375.00
__ Squid Head, Emperor's Royal Guard, B-Wing Pilot, AT-ST Driver 350.00

Kenner
__ Sy Snootles / Max Rebo Band [AVM001].....150.00

2-Pack.
__ ROTJ, any 2 random figures [AVM002] 145.00

3-Packs, Empire Strikes Back.
__ Bespin Alliance: Bespin Security Guard, Lando, Luke...560.00
__ Bespin Set 2: C-3PO, Ugnaught, Cloud Car Pilot...485.00
__ Bespin Set: Han Solo Bespin Outfit, Ugnaught, Lobot...575.00
__ Hoth Rebels: Han, Rebel Commander, FX-7550.00
__ Imperial Forces: Bossk, Stormtrooper, IG-88...625.00
__ Imperial Set: Imperial Commander, Dengar, AT-AT Driver 1,600.00
__ Imperial Set: Zuckuss, AT-AT Driver, TIE Fighter Pilot...530.00
__ Rebel Set 2: Princess Leia Hoth Outfit, R2-D2 Sensorscope, Luke Skywalker Hoth Outfit....660.00
__ Rebel Set: 2-1B, Princess Leia Hoth Outfit, Rebel Commander......................................530.00

3-Packs, Star Wars.
__ Android Set: C-3PO, R2-D2, Chewbacca 350.00
__ Creature Set: Hammerhead, Walrus Man, Greedo...1,500.00
__ Droid Set: R5-D4, Death Star Droid, Power Droid 1,250.00
__ Hero Set 1: Han Solo, Princess Leia Organa, Ben Kenobi..700.00
__ Hero Set 2: Luke X-Wing Pilot, Ben Kenobi, Han Solo..680.00
__ Villain Set 2: Sand People, Boba Fett, Snaggle Tooth..3,000.00
__ Villain Set: Stormtrooper, Darth Vader, Death Squad Commander 800.00

6-Packs.
__ AT-AT Driver, Darth Vader, IG-88, Rebel Soldier, Hoth Stormtrooper, Yoda [AVM003].............765.00
__ C-3PO, Darth Vader, Han Solo Hoth Outfit, R2-D2 Sensorscope, Rebel Soldier, Hoth Stormtrooper [AVM004] 670.00

White catalog mailer boxes.
__ 10-pack 39312: Yoda, FX7, Luke Skywalker Bespin Fatiques, Leia Organa Bespin Gown, Lando, Security Guard, Rebel Soldier, Han Solo Hoth Outfit, Imperial Stormtrooper, IG88 ....435.00

__ 3-pack 48-62374: Emperor's Royal Guard, Darth Vader, Boba Fett...275.00
__ 3-pack 49-59033: Admiral Ackbar, General Madine, Rebel Commando...................................150.00
__ 3-pack 49-59041: Gamorrean Guard, Squid Head, Bib Fortuna [AVM005]..................................150.00
__ 3-pack 71740: Darth Vader, The Emperor, Emperor's Royal Guard 150.00
__ 4-pack 38841: C-3PO, R2-D2, Yoda, Luke Skywalker X-Wing Pilot..............................225.00
__ 4-pack 38934: R2D2, Yoda, Luke Skywalker Bespin Fatigues, FX7.................................225.00
__ 4-pack 39550: Greedo, (blue) Snaggletooth, Hammerhead, Walrusman 650.00
__ 4-pack 48-62355: Darth Vader, Boba Fett, Luke Skywalker Bespin Fatigues, Yoda 300.00
__ 4-pack 69712: Han Solo Hoth Outfit, Luke Skywalker X-Wing Pilot, Lando 165.00
__ 7-pack 71660: The Emperor, Klaatu Skiff Guard, Nikto, 8D8, Rancor Keeper, AT-ST Driver, Emperor's Royal Guard...360.00
__ 7-pack 71670: B-Wing Pilot, Princess Leia Organa in Combat Poncho, Wicket W. Warrick, Han Solo in Trench Coat, Prune Face, Teebo, Paploo 360.00
__ 8-pack 49-59228: AT-AT Commander, Luke Hoth, R2D2 Sensorscope, Zuckuss, Cloud Car Pilot, Tie Pilot, Bespin Security Guard (Black), C3PO Removable Limbs 385.00
__ 8-pack 49-59231: IG88, Bespin Security Guard, Luke Skywalker X-Wing Pilot, Cloud Car Pilot, Stormtrooper, Greedo, Ben Kenobi, R2-D2 .385.00
__ 9-pack 49-59035: Luke Skywalker Bespin Fatigues, Leia Organa Bespin Gown, Lando, Security Guard, Rebel Soldier, Han Solo Hoth Outfit, Imperial Stormtrooper, FX7, IG88 ....445.00

Kenner, Canada
3-Packs, bilingual packaging.
__ Creature Set: Hammerhead, Walrus Man, Greedo 1,075.00
__ Droid Set: R5-D4, Death Star Droid, Power Droid 1,075.00
__ Villain Set: Tusken Raider, Boba Fett, Snaggletooth 1,075.00

3-Packs. Empire Strikes Back, Sears exlusives.
__ Imperial TIE Fighter Pilot, Rebel Soldier, Zuckuss 1,850.00
__ R5-D4, R2-D2, Death Star Droid 1,850.00

4-Packs. Include 3 standard carded figures, and one Sears exclusive figure shrink wrapped to card.
__ AT-AT Driver, Dengar, Han Hoth, exclusive R2-D2 with pop-up saber ....N/V
__ Bossk, Luke, Leia, exclusive General Veers.....N/V
__ R2-D2, Leia Bespin, C-3PO, exclusive Han Bespin..N/V
__ Stormtrooper, IG-88, Leia Hoth, exclusive Luke Hoth ....N/V

7-Packs. Include 6 standard carded figures, and one Sears exclusive figure shrink wrapped to card.
__ Bespin Guard (white), Han (large head), Lando (no teeth), Luke (blonde), IG-88, Boba Fett, exclusive Lobot...N/V
__ Death Star Droid, Power Droid, C-3PO, R2-D2, FX-7, R5-D4, exclusive Dengar ....N/V
__ Luke Bespin, Hoth Stormtrooper, Darth Vader, Leia Bespin, Hoth Rebel Soldier, Bossk, exclusive Han Bespin...N/V

__ Luke X-Wing, Death Squad Commander, Han Hoth, Leia, Darth Vader, Stormtrooper, exclusive Tusk from Ugnaught ....N/V
__ Luke, Greedo, Snaggletooth, Walrusman, Jawa, Hammerhead, exclusive Ben Kenobi.............N/V

Kenner, UK
__ Ewok Combat Complete Playpack: 2 Ewoks, 2 Stormtroopers, Catapult, tri-logo 375.00
__ Sy Snootles and the Max Rebo Band 178.00

Parker Bros.
__ 2-Pack, plus accessory 685.00
__ 2-Pack, plus vehicle..................................790.00
__ 3-Pack of figures 1,000.00
__ 4-Pack of figures 575.00

Action Figures
1985-1986 (Vintage Droids)

Glasslite
__ C-3PO..300.00
__ Jord Dusat 250.00
__ Kea Moll 250.00
__ Kez-Iban 250.00
__ R2-D2...250.00
__ Thall Jorban 475.00
__ Vlix 6500.00
__ Vlix, loose 4300.00

Kenner
__ A-Wing Pilot [AVS1001] 250.00
__ Boba Fett [AVS1002] 875.00
__ C-3PO [AVS1003] 200.00
__ Jann Tosh [AVS1004] 65.00
__ Jord Dusat [AVS1005]....................................75.00
__ Kea Moll [AVS1006] 80.00
__ Kez-Iban [AVS1007]..75.00
__ R2-D2 [AVS1008] 150.00
__ Sise Fromm [AVS1009] 275.00
__ Thall Joben [AVS1010].....................................80.00
__ Tig Fromm [AVS1011]....................................165.00
__ Uncle Gundy [AVS1012] 80.00

Kenner, Canada
__ A-Wing Pilot 150.00
__ Boba Fett 1085.00
__ C-3PO 95.00
__ Jann Tosh 65.00
__ Jord Dusat 65.00
__ Kea Moll 65.00
__ Kez-Iban 65.00
__ R2-D2 ....250.00
__ Sise Fromm 175.00
__ Thall Joben 75.00
__ Tig Fromm 165.00
__ Uncle Gundy 55.00

Action Figures
1985-1986 (Vintage Ewoks)

Kenner
__ Dulok Scout [AVS2001] 65.00
__ Dulok Shaman [AVS2002]................................65.00
__ King Gorneesh [AVS2003] 65.00
__ Logray [AVS2004]...65.00
__ Urgah Lady Gorneesh [AVS2005]..................65.00
__ Wicket [AVS2006] 100.00

AVS1001

AVS1002

AVS1003

AVS1004

AVS1005

AVS1006

AVS1007

AVS1008

AVS1009

AVS1010

AVS1011

AVS1012

Kenner, Canada

__ Dulok Scout	40.00
__ Dulok Shaman	40.00
__ King Gorneesh	45.00
__ Lady Ugrah Gorneesh	45.00
__ Logray	40.00
__ Wicket	50.00

Action Figures 1995 (POTF2 Red Card)

Kenner

Ben Kenobi with lightsaber and removable cloak
- __ .00, long saber; close-up photo; brown belt [P3B001] 35.00
- __ .00, long saber; close-up photo; gold belt 35.00
- __ .00, short saber / long tray 1750.00
- __ .01, long saber 35.00
- __ .01, short saber, holo 30.00
- __ .01, short saber; brown belt [P3B002] 15.00
- __ .01, short saber; gold belt 15.00

Boba Fett with sawed-off blaster rifle and jet pack
- __ .00, half circles on hands; "Empire," on bio card 55.00
- __ .01, full circles on hands [P3B003] 15.00
- __ .01, half circles on hands; "Empire." on bio card 50.00
- __ .01, no chest emblem 550.00
- __ .01, no circle on one hand 350.00
- __ .01, no circles or chest emblem 995.00
- __ .01, no shoulder emblem 500.00

C-3PO with realistic metalized body
- __ .00 [P3B004] 8.00

Chewbacca with bowcaster and heavy blaster rifle
- __ .00 [P3B005] 8.00

Darth Vader with lightsaber and removable cape
- __ .00, long saber [P3B006] 15.00
- __ .00, short saber 10.00
- __ .00, short saber / long tray [P3B007] 45.00
- __ .00, tiny saber 10.00

Death Star Gunner w/radiation suit and blaster pistol
- __ .00, col. 1 [P3B008] 10.00

Greedo with Rodarian blaster rifle
- __ .00, col. 1 [P3B009] 10.00

Han Solo with heavy assault rifle and blaster
- __ .00 [P3B010] 6.00

Han Solo in carbonite
- __ .00 with carbonite freezing chamber [P3B011].8.00
- __ .01 in carbonite block [P3B012] 6.00

Han Solo in Hoth gear with blaster pistol and assault rifle
- __ .00, closed right hand [P3B013] 8.00
- __ .00, open right hand [P3B014] 8.00

Jawas with glowing eyes and ionization blasters
- __ .00, col. 2 [P3B015] 18.00

Jedi Knight Luke Skywalker with lightsaber and removable cloak
- __ .00, black vest [P3B016] 12.00
- __ .00, tan vest; indented saber handle 30.00
- __ .00, tan vest; ridged saber handle [P3B017] ..25.00

Lando Calrissian with heavy rifle and blaster pistol
- __ .00 [P3B018] 8.00

Luke Skywalker with grappling hook blaster and lightsaber
- __ .00, long saber [P3B019] 15.00
- __ .00, short saber [P3B020] 8.00
- __ .00, short saber / long tray 700.00

Luke Skywalker in Dagobah fatigues with lightsaber and blaster pistol
- __ .00, long saber [P3B021] 8.00
- __ .00, short saber [P3B022] 8.00
- __ .00, short saber / long tray [P3B023] 15.00
- __ .00, short saber, new bubble, wholesale club ESB 3-pack 8.00
- __ .00, tiny saber 8.00

Luke Skywalker in Stormtrooper disguise with Imperial issue blaster
- __ .00, col. 2, photo [P3B024] 15.00
- __ .00, long saber [P3B025] 8.00

Luke Skywalker in X-wing fighter pilot gear with lightsaber and blaster pistol
- __ .01, long saber 8.00
- __ .01, short saber 8.00
- __ .01, short saber / long tray 15.00

Momaw Nadon "Hammerhead" with double-barreled blaster rifle
- __ .00, col. 2 [P3B026] 12.00

Princess Leia Organa with laser pistol and assault rifle
- __ .00, 2 bands on belt [P3B027] 8.00
- __ .00, 3 bands on belt [P3B028] 8.00

R2-D2 with light-pipe eye port and retractable leg
- __ .00 [P3B029] 10.00

R5-D4 with concealed missile launcher
- __ .00, col. 2, no warning [P3B030] 10.00
- __ .00, col. 2, warning sticker [P3B031] 10.00

Stormtrooper, blaster rifle and heavy infantry cannon
- __ .00, holo [P3B032] 10.00
- __ .00, photo [P3B033] 10.00

Tatooine Stormtrooper with concussion grenade cannon
- __ .00, col. 1 [P3B034] 15.00

AVS2001

AVS2002

AVS2003

AVS2004

AVS2005

AVS2006

P3B001

P3B002

P3B001 long saber

P3B002 short saber

P3B003

P3B004

P3B005

P3B006

P3B007

P3B008

P3B009

P3B010

P3B011

P3B012

carbonite freezing chamber

carbonite block

P3B013 closed right hand

P3B014 open right hand

P3B013

P3B015

P3B016

P3B017

black vest

brown vest

P3B018

P3B019

P3B020

P3B021

P3B022

P3B023 short saber, long tray

Action Figures

TIE Fighter Pilot with Imperial blaster pistol and rifle
__ .00, warning sticker [P3B035] 10.00
__ .01, warning is printed [P3B036] 10.00
__ .02 ....10.00
Tusken Raider with gaderffi stick battle club
__ .00, col. 2 ....10.00
__ .00, col. 2, left hand closed [P3B037] 10.00
Yoda with Jedi trainer backpack and gimer stick
__ .00, holo 20.00
__ .00, photo 10.00
__ .01 [P3B038] 10.00

Kenner, Canada
Red card (square) with image.
__ Ben Kenobi 18.00
__ C-3PO [P3B039] 20.00
__ Chewbacca [P3B040] 20.00
__ Darth Vader [P3B041] 20.00
__ Han Solo [P3B042] 20.00
__ Luke Skywalker [P3B043] 20.00
__ Princess Leia Organa [P3B044] 20.00
__ R2-D2 [P3B045] 20.00
__ Stormtrooper [P3B046] 20.00

Red card with image.
__ Boba Fett [P3B047] 18.00
__ Han Solo in Carbonite [P3B048] 12.00
__ Han Solo in Hoth Gear 14.00
__ Lando Calrissian [P3B049] 9.00
__ Luke Skywalker in Dagobah Fatigues 14.00
__ Luke Skywalker in X-wing Fighter Pilot Gear long
  saber [P3B050] 15.00
__ Luke Skywalker in X-wing Fighter Pilot Gear short

__ saber [P3B051] 15.00
__ Luke Skywalker Jedi Knight THX insert 20.00
__ TIE Fighter Pilot new bubble 18.00
__ TIE Fighter Pilot old bubble 14.00
__ Yoda [P3B052] 18.00

Kenner, Italy
Red card with image.
__ Ben Kenobi long saber [P3B053] 56.00
__ Ben Kenobi short saber [P3B054] 16.00
__ Boba Fett [P3B055] 21.00
__ C1-P8 (R2-D2) [P3B056] 20.00
__ Chewbacca [P3B057] 19.00
__ D-3BO (C-3PO) [P3B058] 14.00
__ Darth Vader long saber [P3B059] 37.00
__ Darth Vader short saber [P3B060] 18.00
__ Han Solo [P3B061] 18.00
__ Han Solo in Hoth Gear [P3B062] 16.00
__ Luke Skywalker [P3B063] 14.00
__ Luke Skywalker in Dagobah Fatigues [P3B064]......16.00
__ Luke Skywalker in X-wing Fighter Pilot Gear
  [P3B065] 16.00
__ Princess Leia Organa 19.00
__ Stormtrooper [P3B066] 24.00
__ TIE Fighter Pilot [P3B067] 13.00
__ Yoda [P3B068] 16.00

Kenner, Mexico
Canadian square red card with image stickered for Mexico.
__ Ben (Obi-Wan) Kenobi [P3B069] 22.00
__ C-3PO [P3B070] 22.00
__ Chewbacca [P3B071] 22.00
__ Darth Vader [P3B072] 22.00

__ Han Solo [P3B073] 22.00
__ Luke Skywalker 22.00
__ Princess Leia Organa 22.00
__ R2-D2 ....22.00
__ Stormtrooper [P3B074] 22.00

Kenner, UK
Red card with image.
__ Boba Fett new bubble 22.00
__ Boba Fett new bubble, sticker on barcode 23.00
__ Boba Fett old bubble 23.00
__ Boba Fett THX insert 24.00
__ C-3PO new bubble 14.00
__ C-3PO old bubble [P3B075] 14.00
__ C-3PO THX insert [P3B076] 22.00
__ Chewbacca new bubble 14.00
__ Chewbacca old bubble [P3B077] 14.00
__ Chewbacca THX insert [P3B078] 24.00
__ Darth Vader new bubble, short saber 14.00
__ Darth Vader new bubble, short saber with sticker
  on barcode 16.00
__ Darth Vader old bubble, long saber
  [P3B079] 18.00
__ Darth Vader old bubble, short saber
  [P3B080] 14.00
__ Darth Vader THX insert, long saber
  [P3B081] 20.00
__ Han Solo [P3B082] 14.00
__ Han Solo THX insert 20.00
__ Han Solo in Hoth Gear [P3B083] 12.00
__ Lando Calrissian [P3B084] 12.00
__ Lando Calrissian THX insert 23.00
__ Luke Skywalker long saber [P3B085] 18.00
__ Luke Skywalker short saber [P3B086] 14.00

P3B024

P3B025

P3B026

P3B027

P3B027 two bands

P3B028 three bands

P3B029

P3B030

P3B030 no warning

P3B031 warning sticker

P3B032

P3B033

P3B034

P3B035

P3B035 warnong sticker

P3B036 pritned warnong

P3B037

P3B038

P3B039

P3B040

P3B041

P3B042

P3B043

P3B044

P3B045

P3B046

P3B047

P3B048

P3B049

P3B050

P3B051

P3B052

P3B053

P3B054

P3B055

P3B056

P3B057

P3B058

P3B059

P3B060

P3B061

P3B062

P3B063

P3B064

P3B065

P3B066

P3B067

P3B068

Action Figures

P3B069

P3B070

P3B071

P3B072

P3B073

P3B074

P3B075

P3B076

P3B077

P3B078

P3B079

P3B080

P3B081

P3B082

P3B083

P3B084

P3B085

P3B086

P3B087

P3B088

P3B089

P3B090

P3B091

P3B092

P3B093

P3B094

P3B095

P3B096

P3B097

P3B098

68

P3C001   P3C002   P3C003   P3C004   P3C005   P3C006

__ Luke Skywalker THX insert [P3B087] 24.00
__ Luke Skywalker, Dagobah [P3B088] 15.00
__ Luke Skywalker in X-wing Fighter Pilot Gear new bubble, short saber.......................................14.00
__ Luke Skywalker in X-wing Fighter Pilot Gear old bubble, long saber..18.00
__ Luke Skywalker in X-wing Fighter Pilot Gear old bubble, short saber.......................................14.00
__ Luke Skywalker in X-wing Fighter Pilot Gear THX insert, long saber..24.00
__ Luke Skywalker in X-wing Fighter Pilot Gear THX insert, short saber.......................................24.00
__ Obi-Wan Kenobi long saber [P3B089].............18.00
__ Obi-Wan Kenobi short saber [P3B090] 14.00
__ Obi-Wan Kenobi THX insert........................24.00
__ Princess Leia Organa new bubble.................14.00
__ Princess Leia Organa old bubble [P3B091]...16.00
__ Princess Leia Organa THX insert [P3B092] 23.00
__ R2-D2 [P3B093]..14.00
__ R2-D2 THX insert [P3B094] 22.00
__ Stormtrooper [P3B095]...............................15.00
__ Stormtrooper THX insert [P3B096] 28.00
__ TIE Fighter Pilot [P3B097]...........................12.00
__ Yoda new bubble.......................................14.00
__ Yoda old bubble [P3B098].............................15.00

Action Figures 1996
(POTF2 Shadows of the Empire)

Kenner
Purple card with image, Shadows of the Empire.
__ Chewbacca in bounty hunter disguise [P3C001] 8.00

__ Dash Rendar with heavy blaster pack [P3C002]...15.00
__ Leia in Boushh disguise [P3C003].................10.00
__ Leia in Boushh disguise, col. 1 [P3C004] 300.00
__ Luke Skywalker in Imperial disguise [P3C005] 12.00
__ Prince Xizor with energy blade shields [P3C006] 12.00

Kenner, Canada
Purple card with foil image, Shadows of the Empire.
__ Chewbacca / Snoova [P3C007]......................14.00
__ Dash Rendar [P3C008] 19.00
__ Luke Skywalker in Imperial Disguise [P3C009]...21.00
__ Prince Xizor [P3C010]..................................9.00
__ Princess Leia in Boushh Disguise [P3C011]...12.00

Kenner, Italy
Orange card with foil image, Shadows of the Empire. Limited to 5,000.
__ Chewbacca / Snoova [P3C012]......................16.00
__ Dash Rendar [P3C013]................................21.00
__ Luke Skywalker in Imperial Disguise 17.00
__ Prince Xizor [P3C014]................................11.00

Kenner, UK
Orange card with foil image, Shadows of the Empire. Limited to 5,000.
__ Chewbacca / Snoova [P3C015].....................30.00
__ Dash Rendar [P3C016] 30.00
__ Luke Skywalker in Imperial Disguise [P3C017]...33.00
__ Prince Xizor [P3C018]................................29.00

Action Figures 1997
(POTF2 Green Carded)

Estrela, Brazil
Green card with foil image.
__ 2-1B [P3D001] 15.00
__ 4-LOM...15.00
__ Admiral Ackbar 15.00
__ ASP-7 Doid 15.00
__ AT-ST Driver 15.00
__ Bib Fortuna 15.00
__ Bossk..15.00
__ Darth Vader...15.00
__ Death Star Gunner 15.00
__ Dengar..15.00
__ Emperor Palpatine 15.00
__ Emperor's Royal Guard 15.00
__ EV-9D9..15.00
__ Gamorrean Guard....................................15.00
__ Garindan..15.00
__ Grand Moff Tarkin.....................................15.00
__ Greedo..15.00
__ Han Solo in Bespin gear 15.00
__ Han Solo in Endor Gear 15.00
__ Hoth Rebel Soldier....................................15.00
__ Jawas...15.00
__ Lando Calrissian in Skiff Disguise 15.00
__ Luke Skywalker in Hoth Gear 15.00
__ Luke Skywalker in Stormtrooper Disguise......15.00
__ Luke Skywalker Jedi Knight.........................15.00
__ Malakili..15.00
__ Momaw Nadon 15.00
__ Nien Nunb..15.00

P3C007   P3C008   P3C009   P3C010   P3C011   P3C012

P3C013   P3C014   P3C015   P3C016   P3C017   P3C018

P3D001

P3D002

P3D003

P3D004

P3D005

P3D006

P3D007

P3D008

P3D009

P3D010

P3D011

P3D012

P3D013

P3D014

P3D015

P3D016

P3D017

P3D018

P3D019

P3D020

standard Darth Vader

SOTE Darth Vader

P3D021

P3D022

P3D023

P3D024

P3D025

P3D026

P3D027

P3D028

P3D029

P3D030

P3D031

P3D032

P3D033

P3D034

P3D035

P3D036

P3D037

P3D038

P3D039

P3D040

P3D041

P3D042

P3D043

P3D044

P3D045

P3D046

P3D047

P3D048

P3D049

P3D050

P3D051

P3D052

P3D053

P3D054

P3D055

P3D056

P3D057

P3D058

Action Figures

Kenner

2-1B Medic Droid with medical diagnostic computer
__ .00, holo, col. 2 [P3D002] 8.00
__ .00, photo, col. 2 ....8.00
__ .01, holo, col. 2, new bubble 8.00

__ .01, holo, col. 2, old bubble 8.00
4-LOM with blaster pistol and blaster rifle
__ .00, holo, col. 2 [P3D003] 10.00
Admiral Ackbar with comlink wrist blaster
__ .00, holo, col. 2 [P3D004] 8.00
ASP-7 Droid with spaceport supply rods
__ .00, holo, col. 2 [P3D005] 8.00
__ .00, photo, col. 2 [P3D006] 8.00
AT-ST Driver with blaster rifle and pistol
__ .00, holo, col. 2 [P3D007] 10.00
__ .00, photo, col. 2 [P3D008] 10.00
__ .02, holo, col. 3, new bubble 8.00
__ .02, holo, col. 3, old bubble 8.00
Ben (Obi-Wan) Kenobi with lightsaber and removable cloak
__ .02, holo, col. 1, short saber, new bubble [P3D009] 8.00

__ .02, holo, col. 1, short saber, old bubble 8.00
__ .02, holo, col. 1 short saber, new bubble 8.00
Bespin Han Solo with heavy assault rifle and blaster
__ .00, holo, col. 1 [P3D010] 10.00
__ .00, photo, col. 1 ....10.00
Bib Fortuna with hold-out blaster
__ .00, holo, col. 1 ....10.00
__ .01, holo, col. 2, new bubble [P3D011] 10.00
__ .01, holo, col. 2, old bubble 10.00
__ .01, photo, col. 2, new bubble [P3D012] 10.00
Boba Fett with sawed-off blaster rifle and jet pack
__ .02, holo, col. 1 ....25.00
__ .03, holo, col. 3 [P3D013] 20.00
__ .03, holo, col. 3 [P3D014] 20.00
Bossk with blaster rifle and pistol
__ .00, holo, col. 2, new bubble 7.00
__ .00, holo, col. 2, old bubble [P3D015] 7.00
__ .00, photo, col. 2 ....7.00
__ .01, holo, col. 2, new bubble 7.00
__ .01, holo, col. 2, old bubble 7.00
C-3PO with realistic metalized body
__ .01, holo, col. 1, new bubble 12.00
__ .01, holo, col. 1, old bubble [P3D016] 12.00
Chewbacca with bowcaster and heavy blaster rifle
__ .01, holo, col. 1, new bubble [P3D017] 10.00
__ .01, holo, col. 1, old bubble 10.00
__ .01, photo, col. 1, new bubble [P3D018] 10.00
Darth Vader with lightsaber and removable cape
__ .01, holo, col. 1 ....10.00
__ .02, holo, col. 3, new bubble [P3D019] 10.00
__ .02, holo, col. 3, old bubble 10.00
__ .02, holo, col. 3, SOTE 2-pack pose [P3D020] 125.00
__ .02, photo, col. 3, new bubble [P3D021] 10.00

P3D059

P3D060

P3D061

P3D062

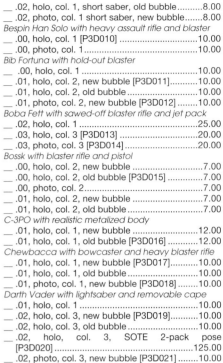

P3D063

P3D064

P3D065

P3D066

printed warning

no warning

P3D067

P3D068

P3D069

P3D070

P3D071

P3D072

P3D073

P3D074

P3D075

P3D076

P3D077

P3D078

P3D079

P3D080

P3D081

P3D082

P3D083

P3D084

P3D085

P3D086

P3D087

P3D088

P3D089

P3D090

P3D091

P3D092

P3D093

P3D094

P3D095

P3D096

P3D097

P3D098

P3D099

P3D100

P3D101

P3D102

P3D103

P3D104

P3D105

P3D106

P3D107

P3D108

P3D109

P3D110

P3D111

P3D112

P3D113

P3D114

P3D115

P3D116

P3D117

P3D118

P3D119

P3D120

Death Star Gunner, Imperial blaster and assault rifle
__ .01, holo, col. 1 [P3D022] 10.00
__ .01, photo, col. 1 [P3D023] 10.00
__ .02, holo, col. 3, new bubble 10.00
__ .02, holo, col. 3, old bubble 10.00
Dengar with blaster rifle
__ .00, holo, col. 2 [P3D024] 12.00
Emperor Palpatine with walking stick
__ .00, holo, col. 1 ....9.00
__ .01, holo, col. 3, new bubble [P3D025] 9.00
__ .01, holo, col. 3, old bubble 9.00
__ .01, photo, col. 3, new bubble [P3D026] 9.00
Emperor's Royal Guard with force pike
__ .00, holo, col. 3 [P3D027] 10.00
__ .00, holo, col. 3 ....10.00
EV-9D9 with datapad
__ .00, holo, col. 2 [P3D028] 8.00
Gamorrean Guard with vibro axe
__ .00, holo, col. 2 [P3D029] 12.00
Garindan (Long Snoot) with hold-out pistol
__ .00, holo, col. 3 [P3D030] 6.00
__ .00, photo, col. 3 [P3D031] 6.00
Grand Moff Tarkin with Imperial issue blaster rifle and pistol
__ .00, holo, col. 2 ....15.00
__ .01, holo, col. 3 [P3D032] 9.00
__ .01, photo, col. 3 [P3D033] 9.00
Greedo with blaster pistol
__ .01, holo, col. 1 [P3D034] 8.00
__ .01, photo, col. 1 ....8.00
Han Solo in carbonite with carbonite block
__ .02, holo, col. 2, new bubble [P3D035] 10.00
__ .02, holo, col. 2, old bubble 10.00
__ .03, holo, col. 1 ....10.00
__ .03, photo, col. 1 ....10.00
Han Solo in Endor gear with blaster pistol
__ .00, holo, col. 1, new bubble [P3D036] 8.00
__ .00, holo, col. 1, old bubble 8.00
__ .00, photo, col. 1, new bubble 8.00
__ .00, photo, col. 1, new bubble, brown pants [P3D037] 8.00
Han Solo with heavy assault rifle and blaster
__ .01, holo, col. 1, new bubble [P3D038] 6.00
__ .01, holo, col. 1, old bubble 6.00
__ .01, photo, col. 1, new bubble 6.00
Hoth Rebel Soldier with survival backpack and blaster rifle
__ .00, holo, col. 2 [P3D039] 8.00
__ .00, photo, col. 2 ....8.00
__ .01, holo, col. 1, new bubble 8.00
__ .01, holo, col. 1, old bubble 8.00

Jawas with glowing eyes and blaster pistols
__ .01, holo, col. 2 [P3D040] 10.00
__ .01, photo, col. 2 ....10.00
__ .02, holo, col. 2, new bubble 10.00
__ .02, holo, col. 2, old bubble 10.00
Lando Calrissian as skiff guard with skiff guard force pike
__ .00, holo, col. 1, new bubble, gold circle 8.00
__ .00, holo, col. 1, old bubble, gold circle [P3D041] 8.00
__ .00, holo, col. 1, silver circle 8.00
Lando Calrissian with heavy rifle and blaster pistol
__ .01, holo, col. 1, wholesale club ESB 3-pack [P3D042] 40.00
Leia in Boushh disguise with blaster rifle and bounty hunter helmet
__ .02, holo, col. 1, new bubble, wholesale club ROTJ 3-pack 12.00
__ .02, holo, col. 1, old bubble [P3D043] 12.00
__ .02, photo, col. 1, old bubble [P3D044] 12.00
Luke Skywalker in cerimonial outfit with medal of valor and blaster pistol
__ .00, holo, col. 2 ....12.00
__ .01, holo, col. 1 [P3D045] 8.00
__ .01, photo, col. 1 ....8.00
Luke Skywalker in Hoth gear with blaster pistol and lightsaber
__ .00, holo, col. 2 [P3D046] 8.00
__ .00, photo, col. 2 [P3D047] 8.00
__ .01, holo, col. 1, new bubble 8.00
__ .01, holo, col. 1, old bubble 8.00
Luke Skywalker in Stormtrooper disguise with Imperial issue blaster
__ .01, holo, col. 2 ....12.00
__ .01, photo, col. 2 ....12.00
__ .02, holo, col. 1, new bubble 12.00
__ .02, holo, col. 1, old bubble [P3D048] 12.00
__ .02, holo, col. 1, new bubble 12.00
Luke Skywalker in X-wing fighter pilot gear with lightsaber and blaster pistol
__ .02, holo, col. 1, new bubble [P3D049] 12.00
__ .02, holo, col. 1, old bubble 12.00
Luke Skywalker Jedi Knight with lightsaber and removable cloak
__ .00, theater edition [P3D050] 75.00
__ .01, holo, col. 2 ....12.00
__ .01, photo, col. 2 ....12.00
__ .02, holo, col. 1 [P3D051] 12.00
__ .02, photo, col. 1 [P3D052] 12.00
Malakili (Rancor Keeper) with long-handled vibro-blade

__ .00, holo, col. 2 [P3D053] 10.00
__ .00, photo, col. 2 [P3D054] 10.00
Momaw Nadon "Hammerhead" with double-barreled blaster rifle
__ .01, holo, col. 2 [P3D055] 10.00
__ .01, photo, col. 2 [P3D056] 10.00
Nien Nunb with blaster pistol and blaster rifle
__ .00, holo, col. 2 [P3D057] 10.00
Ponda Baba with blaster pistol and rifle
__ .00, holo, col. 2, black beard 25.00
__ .00, holo, col. 2, gray beard 60.00
__ .01, holo, col. 3, black beard [P3D058] 8.00
__ .01, holo, col. 3, gray beard 60.00
__ .01, photo, col. 3, black beard [P3D059] 6.00
Princess Leia Organa as Jabba's prisoner
__ .00, holo, col. 1 [P3D060] 8.00
__ .00, photo, col. 1 [P3D061] 8.00
Princess Leia Organa with laser pistol and assault rifle
__ .01, holo, col. 1, new bubble, 2 bands on belt .8.00
__ .01, holo, col. 1, new bubble, 3 bands on belt [P3D062] 8.00
__ .01, holo, col. 1, old bubble 8.00
__ .01, photo, col. 1, new bubble, 3 bands on belt [P3D063] 8.00
R2-D2 with light-pipe eye port and retractable leg
__ .01, holo, col. 1, new bubble [P3D064] 12.00
__ .01, holo, col. 1, old bubble 12.00
R5-D4 with concealed missile launcher
__ .01, holo, col. 2, no warning; hooked firing pin 8.00
__ .01, holo, col. 2, printed warning; hooked firing pin [P3D065] 8.00
__ .01, holo, col. 2, warning sticker; hooked firing pin 8.00
__ .01, photo, col. 2, no warning; hooked firing pin 8.00
__ .01, photo, col. 2, no warning; straight firing pin [P3D066] 8.00
__ .01, photo, col. 2, printed warning; hooked firing pin 8.00
__ .01, photo, col. 2, warning sticker; hooked firing pin 8.00
__ .01, photo, col. 2, warning sticker; straight firing pin 8.00
Rebel Fleet Trooper with blaster pistol and rifle
__ .00, holo, col. 2 ....10.00
__ .01, holo, col. 1 [P3D067] 10.00
Saelt-Marae (Yak face) with battle staff
__ .00, holo, col. 2 [P3D068] 9.00
Sandtrooper with heavy blaster rifle
__ .01, holo, col. 1 ....8.00

74

__ .01, photo, col. 1................................8.00
__ .02, holo, col. 3 [P3D069].............8.00
__ .02, holo, col. 3, old bubble...........8.00
Snowtrooper with Imperial issue blaster rifle
__ .00, holo, col. 3 [P3D070] 8.00
__ .00, holo, col. 3 [P3D071] 8.00
Stormtrooper with blaster rifle and heavy infantry cannon
__ .01, holo, col. 3, new bubble [P3D072].............8.00
__ .01, holo, col. 3, old bubble............8.00
__ .01, photo, col. 3, new bubble.........8.00
TIE Fighter Pilot with Imperial blaster pistol and rifle
__ .03, holo, col. 2 [P3D073] 8.00
__ .04, holo, col. 3, new bubble...........8.00
__ .04, holo, col. 3, old bubble............8.00
Tusken Raider with gaderffii stick
__ .01, holo, col. 2 [P3D074] 8.00
__ .01, photo, col. 2, left hand closed....8.00
__ .02, holo, col. 2, new bubble, wholesale club SW 3-pack................8.00
__ .02, photo, col. 2, new bubble [P3D075] 8.00
Weequay Skiff Guard with force pike and blaster rifle
__ .00, holo, col. 2 ....15.00
__ .01, holo, col. 3 [P3D076] 8.00
Yoda with Jedi trainer backpack and gimer stick
__ .02, holo, col. 2 ....9.00
__ .02, holo, col. 2 ....9.00
__ .03, holo, col. 1, new bubble..........9.00
__ .03, holo, col. 1, old bubble [P3D077] 9.00
__ .03, photo, col. 1, new bubble [P3D078] 9.00

Kenner, Canada
Green card with foil image.
__ 2-1B [P3D079] 12.00
__ 4-LOM [P3D080] 16.00
__ Admiral Ackbar [P3D081].................10.00
__ ASP-7 Doid [P3D082].......................11.00
__ AT-ST Driver [P3D083].....................11.00
__ Bib Fortuna [P3D084] 16.00
__ Bossk [P3D085] 14.00
__ Darth Vader [P3D086].......................11.00
__ Death Star Gunner [P3D087] 12.00
__ Dengar [P3D088]..............................16.00
__ Emperor Palpatine [P3D089] 8.00
__ Emperor's Royal Guard [P3D090].........18.00
__ EV-9D9 [P3D091].............................12.00
__ Gamorrean Guard [P3D092] 9.00
__ Garindan [P3D093]............................7.00
__ Grand Moff Tarkin [P3D094].............8.00
__ Greedo [P3D095] 10.00
__ Han Solo in Bespin gear [P3D096] 7.00

__ Han Solo in Endor Gear................10.00
__ Hoth Rebel Soldier [P3D097]............8.00
__ Jawas [P3D098]..............................15.00
__ Lando Calrissian in Skiff Disguise 9.00
__ Luke Skywalker in Hoth Gear 10.00
__ Luke Skywalker in Stormtrooper Disguise......10.00
__ Luke Skywalker Jedi Knight................9.00
__ Malakili 10.00
__ Momaw Nadon [P3D099] 14.00
__ Nien Nunb [P3D100] 9.00
__ Ponda Baba [P3D101] 9.00
__ Princess Leia as Jabba's Prisoner [P3D102]..10.00
__ R5-D4 [P3D103] 9.00
__ Rebel Fleet Trooper 11.00
__ Saelt-Marae [P3D104].......................10.00
__ Sandtrooper [P3D105].......................16.00
__ Snowtrooper [P3D106] 8.00
__ Stormtrooper [P3D107]......................12.00
__ TIE Fighter Pilot [P3D108]..................12.00
__ Tusken Raider [P3D109]....................14.00
__ Weequay [P3D110] 8.00

Kenner, Italy
Green card with photo image.
__ Bossk [P3D111] 16.00
__ Death Star Gunner [P3D112] 14.00
__ Emperor Palpatine 9.00
__ Greedo [P3D113] 12.00
__ Han Solo in Carbonite [P3D114].........10.00
__ Han Solo in Endor Gear 12.00
__ Luke Skywalker in Hoth Gear [P3D115]..........23.00
__ Ponda Baba [P3D116] 10.00
__ Princess Leia in Boushh Disguise...................20.00
__ Sandtrooper [P3D117].......................10.00
__ Tusken Raider [P3D118]....................14.00

Kenner, Japan
U.S. card with image, Japanese sticker on back.
__ ASP-7 Droid with spaceport supply rods 12.00
__ Bib Fortuna with hold-out blaster 15.00
__ C-3PO, green tinted plastic 17.00
__ Grand Moff Tarkin with Imperial issue blaster rifle and pistol 25.00
__ Greedo with blaster pistol..............................14.00
__ Malakili (Rancor Keeper) with long-handled vibro-blade 15.00
__ Momaw Nadon "Hammerhead" with double-barreled blaster rifle 12.00
__ Tusken Raider with gaderffii stick..................15.00
__ Yoda with Jedi trainer backpack and gimer stick 15.00

Kenner, UK
Green card with FlashBack photo.
__ Luke Skywalker with blaster rifle [P3D119].......8.00
__ R2-D2 with launching lightsaber [P3D120].....14.00

Green card with photo image, with tri-logo.
__ Bossk new bubble 8.00
__ Bossk old bubble [P3D121] 9.00
__ Death Star Gunner [P3D122] 12.00
__ Emperor Palpatine new bubble 12.00
__ Emperor Palpatine new bubble, sticker on barcode.................................12.00
__ Emperor Palpatine old bubble [P3D123] 12.00
__ Greedo [P3D124] 12.00
__ Han Solo in Carbonite new bubble ...12.00
__ Han Solo in Carbonite old bubble [P3D125]...12.00
__ Han Solo in Endor Gear new bubble, blue pants 12.00
__ Han Solo in Endor Gear new bubble, brown pants 17.00
__ Han Solo in Endor Gear old bubble, blue pants [P3D126]...................................12.00
__ Hoth Rebel Soldier...........................12.00
__ Lando Calrissian in Skiff Disguise [P3D127]......................................10.00
__ Luke Skywalker in Hoth Gear new bubble, short saber 12.00
__ Luke Skywalker in Hoth Gear old bubble, short saber [P3D128]............................12.00
__ Luke Skywalker in Stormtrooper Disguise......14.00
__ Luke Skywalker Jedi Knight new bubble, short saber 15.00
__ Luke Skywalker Jedi Knight old bubble, short saber [P3D129].............................13.00

P3D121   P3D122

P3D123   P3D124   P3D125   P3D126   P3D127   P3D128

P3D129   P3D130   P3D131   P3D132   P3D133   P3D134

Action Figures

P3D135 P3D136 P3D137 P3D138 P3D139 P3D140

__ Ponda Baba [P3D130] 13.00
__ Princess Leia as Jabba's Prisoner [P3D131]..19.00
__ Princess Leia in Boushh Disguise [P3D132]...14.00
__ Rebel Fleet Trooper [P3D133] 10.00
__ Sandtrooper new bubble....................................12.00
__ Sandtrooper new bubble, sticker on barcode 12.00
__ Sandtrooper old bubble......................................12.00
__ Tusken Raider [P3D134] 12.00

Green card with photo image, without tri-logo.
__ 4-LOM..17.00
__ Admiral Ackbar [P3D135]..............................14.00
__ Bib Fortuna..11.00
__ Emperor's Royal Guard 13.00
__ Endor Rebel Soldier......................................10.00
__ Ewok 2-pack (Wicket/Logray) [P3D136].........18.00
__ Gamorrean Guard..12.00

__ Grand Moff Tarkin...12.00
__ Han Solo in Bespin Gear [P3D137].................12.00
__ Jawas...17.00
__ Luke Skywalker in Bespin Gear [P3D138].......34.00
__ Momaw Nadon (Hammerhead)........................12.00
__ Snowtrooper [P3D139] 12.00
__ Weequay Skiff Guard [P3D140] 22.00

Action Figures 1998 (POTF2 Freeze Frame)

Kenner
8D8 with droid branding device
__ .00, col. 2 [P3E001]...............................8.00
Admiral Ackbar with comlink wrist blaster
__ .01, col. 2 [P3E002]...............................8.00

AT-AT Driver with Imperial issue blaster
__ .00, col. 3, exclusive to Fan Club [P3E003] 15.00
AT-ST Driver with blaster rifle and pistol
__ .03, col. 3 [P3E004].............................50.00
Bespin Han Solo, heavy assault rifle and blaster pistol
__ .01, col. 1 [P3E005].............................8.00
__ .02, col. 1 ....8.00
Bespin Luke Skywalker, lightsaber and blaster pistol
__ .00, col. 1 [P3E006].............................8.00
__ .01, col. 1 ....8.00
Biggs Darklighter with blaster pistol
__ .00, col. 2 [P3E007].............................12.00
Boba Fett with sawed-off blaster rifle and jet pack
__ .04, col. 3, "Imprisioned" on slide [P3E008]..50.00
C-3PO with realistic metalized body and cargo net
__ .00, col. 1 [P3E009].............................8.00

P3E001 P3E002 P3E003 P3E004 P3E005 P3E006

P3E007 P3E008 P3E009 P3E010 P3E011 P3E012

P3E013 P3E014 P3E015 P3E016 P3E017 P3E018

P3E019

P3E020

P3E021

P3E022

P3E023

P3E024

P3E025

P3E026

P3E027

P3E028

P3E029

P3E030

P3E031

P3E032

P3E033

P3E034

P3E035

P3E036

P3E037

P3E038

P3E039

P3E040

P3E041

P3E042

P3E043

P3E044

P3E045

P3E046

P3E047

P3E048

P3E049

P3E050

P3E051

P3E052

P3E053

P3E054

P3E055

P3E056

Captain Piett
___ .00 blaster rifle and pistol, col. 3 ....20.00
___ .00 blaster pistol and baton, col. 3 [P3E010]..45.00
Chewbacca as Boushh's Bounty with bowcaster
___ .00, col. 1 [P3E011]..8.00
Darth Vader with lightsaber and removable cape
___ .03, col. 3 [P3E012]...12.00
Darth Vader with removable helmet and lightsaber
___ .00, col. 3 [P3E013]...20.00
Death Star Droid with Mouse Droid
___ .00, col. 2, exclusive to Fan Club [P3E014] 10.00
Death Star Trooper with blaster rifle
___ .00, col. 3 [P3E015]...15.00
Emperor Palpatine with walking stick
___ .02, col. 3 [P3E016]...8.00
Emperor's Royal Guard with force pike
___ .01, col. 3 [P3E017]...15.00

Endor Rebel Soldier, survival backpack/blaster rifle
___ .00, col. 1 [P3E018]...8.00
___ .01, col. 1 ....8.00
EV-9D9 with datapad
___ .01, col. 2 [P3E019]...8.00
Ewoks: Wicket and Logray with staff, medicine pouch, and spear
___ .00, col. 2 [P3E020]...15.00
Gamorrean Guard with vibro axe
___ .01, col. 2 [P3E021]...15.00
Garindan with hold-out pistol
___ .01, col. 3 [P3E022]...25.00
Grand Moff Tarkin with Imperial blaster rifle and pistol
___ .02, col. 3 [P3E023]...12.00
Han Solo in carbonite with carbonite block
___ .04, col. 1 [P3E024]...6.00
Han Solo in carbonite with carbonite block
___ .05, col. 1 ....6.00
Han Solo in Endor gear with blaster pistol
___ .01, col. 1 ....8.00
___ .02, col. 1 [P3E025]...8.00
Han Solo with blaster pistol
___ .02, col. 1 [P3E026]...6.00
Hoth Rebel Soldier, survival backpack and blaster rifle
___ .02, col. 1 ....8.00
___ .03, col. 1 [P3E027]...8.00
Ishi Tib with blaster rifle
___ .03, col. 3 [P3E028]...25.00
Lak Sivrak with blaster pistol and vibro blade
___ .00, col. 2 ....10.00
___ .01, col. 2 [P3E029]...10.00
Lando Calrissian as skiff guard, skiff guard force pike
___ .01, col. 1 ....6.00
___ .02, col. 1 [P3E030]...6.00

Lando Calrissian in General's gear with blaster pistol
___ .00, col. 1, 1 sticker on bubble 8.00
___ .00, col. 1, 2 stickers on bubble [P3E031] 8.00
___ .01, col. 1, 1 sticker on bubble 8.00
___ .01, col. 1, 2 stickers on bubble 8.00
Lobot with blaster pistol and transmitter
___ .00, col. 1 [P3E032]...10.00
Luke Skywalker in cerimonial outfit with blaster pistol
___ .01, col. 1 [P3E033]...10.00
Luke Skywalker in Stormtrooper disguise with Imperial blaster
___ .03, col. 1 [P3E034]...10.00
___ .04, col. 1 ....10.00
Luke Skywalker, blast shield helmet and lightsaber
___ .00, col. 1 [P3E035]...10.00
Malakili (Rancor Keeper), long-handled vibro-blade
___ .01, col. 2 [P3E036]...10.00
Mon Mothma with baton
___ .00, col. 1 [P3E037]...10.00
Nien Nunb with blaster pistol and rifle
___ .01, col. 2 [P3E038]...12.00
Obi-Wan (Ben) Kenobi with lightsaber
___ .03, col. 1, short saber [P3E039].......................8.00
___ .04, col. 1, short saber 8.00
Orrimaarko (Prune Face) with blaster rifle
___ .00, col. 1 [P3E040]...8.00
Pote Snitkin with force pike and blaster pistol
___ .00, col. 3, exclusive to Fan Club [P3E041] 25.00
Princess Leia Organa as Jabba's prisoner
___ .01, col. 1 [P3E042]...8.00
___ .02, col. 1 ....8.00
Princess Leia Organa in Ewok celebration outfit
___ .00, col. 1 [P3E043]...8.00
___ .01, col. 1 ....8.00

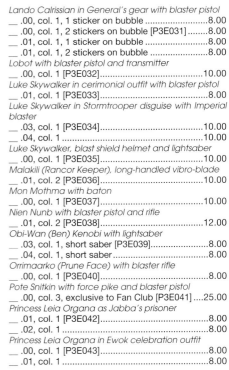

P3E057

P3E058

P3E059

P3E060

P3E061

P3E062

P3E063

P3E064

P3E065

P3E066

P3E067

P3E068

P3E069

P3E070

P3E071

P3E072

P3E073

P3E074

P3E075

P3E076

P3E077

P3E078

P3E079

P3E080

P3E081

P3E082

P3E083

P3E084

P3E085

P3E086

P3E087

P3E088

P3E089

P3E090

P3E091

P3E092

P3E093

P3E094

P3E095

P3E096

P3E097

P3E098

P3F001

P3F002

P3F003

P3F004

P3F005

P3F006

P3F007

P3F008

P3F008 back

P3F009

__ Princess Leia .03, col. 2 [P3F008] 30.00
__ Spacetrooper .03, col. 2 [P3F009]..................30.00

Princess Leia Organa in Hoth gear with blaster pistol
__ .00, col. 3, exclusive to Fan Club [P3E044] 25.00
Princess Leia Organa with blaster rifle and long-barreled pistol
__ .00, col. 1 [P3E045]...8.00
R2-D2 with accessories
__ .00, col. 1, "Death Star Trash Compactor" on freeze frame slide [P3E046]..................................8.00
__ .00, col. 1, "Imperial Trash Compactor" on freeze frame slide 50.00
Rebel Fleet Trooper with blaster pistol and rifle
__ .01, col. 1, .01 sticker....................................10.00
__ .01, col. 1, .01 sticker, FF error [P3E047] 10.00
__ .02, col. 1 ....10.00
Ree-Yees with blaster pistols
__ .00, col. 3 [P3E048].......................................25.00
Saelt-Marae (Yak face) with battle staff
__ .01, col. 2 [P3E049].......................................10.00
Sandtrooper with concussion grenade cannon
__ .03, col. 3 [P3E050].....................................175.00
Snowtrooper with Imperial blaster rifle
__ .01, col. 3 [P3E051].......................................20.00
Stormtrooper with blaster rifle and heavy infantry cannon
__ .02, col. 3 [P3E052].......................................12.00
TIE Fighter Pilot with Imperial blaster pistol and rifle
__ .05, col. 3 [P3E053].......................................50.00
Ugnaughts with tool-kit
__ .00, col. 2 [P3E054].......................................10.00
Weequay Skiff Guard with force pike and blaster rifle
__ .02, col. 3 [P3E055].....................................425.00
Zuckuss with heavy assault blaster rifle
__ .00, col. 3 [P3E056].......................................25.00

Kenner, Canada
Green card with Freeze Frame Action Slide.
__ 8D8 [P3E057]..12.00
__ Admiral Ackbar [P3E058]................................15.00
__ AT-ST Driver [P3E059].....................................58.00
__ Ben (Obi-Wan) Kenobi [P3E060].....................15.00
__ Bespin Han Solo [P3E061]..............................15.00
__ Biggs Darklighter [P3E062].............................20.00
__ Boba Fett [P3E063]...29.00
__ C-3PO / Removable Limbs [P3E064].................12.00
__ Chewbacca as Boushh's Bounty [P3E065]........15.00
__ Darth Vader [P3E066]......................................15.00
__ Emperor Palpatine [P3E067]...........................15.00
__ Emperor's Royal Guard [P3E068].....................26.00
__ Endor Rebel Soldier [P3E069] 8.00
__ EV-9D9 [P3E070] 15.00
__ Ewok 2-Pack (Wicket/Logray) [P3E071].........22.00

__ Gamorrean Guard [P3E072] 17.00
__ Garindan [P3E073]..15.00
__ Grand Moff Tarkin [P3E074] 15.00
__ Han Solo [P3E075]...15.00
__ Han Solo in Endor Gear 15.00
__ Hoth Rebel Soldier [P3E076]...........................15.00
__ Lak Sivrak [P3E077]...18.00
__ Lando Calrissian as General [P3E078].............9.00
__ Lando Calrissian as skiff guard [P3E079].......15.00
__ Lobot [P3E080]..10.00
__ Luke Skywalker in Bespin Gear [P3E081].......11.00
__ Luke Skywalker in Ceremonial Attire [P3E082].9.00
__ Luke Skywalker with Blastshield Helmet [P3E083]..14.00
__ Malakili [P3E084] 15.00
__ MonMothma [P3E085]......................................14.00
__ Nien Nunb [P3E086] 15.00
__ Orrimaarko (Prune Face) [P3E087] 15.00
__ Princess Leia as Jabba's Prisoner [P3E088] ..15.00
__ Princess Leia in Ewok Celebration Dress [P3E089]...9.00
__ Princess Leia Organa New Likeness [P3E090]..15.00
__ R2-D2 with scanner/scomp link/grasp arm/saw [P3E091]...14.00
__ Rebel Fleet Trooper [P3E092].........................15.00
__ Saelt-Marae (Yak Face) [P3E093]....................15.00
__ Snowtrooper [P3E094].....................................10.00
__ Stormtrooper [P3E095].....................................15.00
__ TIE Fighter Pilot [P3E096]...............................55.00
__ Ugnaughts (2-pack) [P3E097]..........................12.00
__ Weequay [P3E098] 45.00

Kenner, Japan
Green card with Freeze Frame Action Slide.
__ Darth Vader with removable helmet and lightsaber .00, col. 3 ....35.00

Action Figures 1998 (POTF2 Expanded Universe)

Kenner
Green card with 3D play scene, Expanded Universe.
__ Clone Emperor Palpatine .02, col. 2 [P3F001]25.00
__ Dark Trooper .01, col. 2 [P3F002].................45.00
__ Grand Admiral Thrawn .02, col. 2 [P3F003]....20.00
__ Imperial Sentinal .01, col. 2 [P3F004] 20.00
__ Kyle Katarn .02, col. 2 [P3F005] 25.00
__ Luke Skywalker .01, col. 2 [P3F006]...............20.00
__ Mara Jade .03, col. 2 [P3F007]......................30.00

Action Figures 1999 (POTF2 Flashback)

Hasbro
Green card with FlashBack photo.
__ Anakin Skywalker with lightsaber .00 [P3G001]..15.00
__ Aunt Beru with service droid .00 [P3G002].....15.00
__ C-3PO with removable arm .00 [P3G003] 10.00

Kenner
Green card with FlashBack photo.
__ Ben (Obi-Wan) Kenobi with lightsaber .00 [P3G004]..10.00
__ Chewbacca with bowcaster rifle .00 [P3G005]..10.00
__ Darth Vader with lightsaber .00 [P3G006] 10.00
__ Emperor Palpatine with Force lightning .00 [P3G007]..15.00
__ Luke Skywalker with blaster rifle and electrobinoculars .00 [P3G008] 10.00
__ Princess Leia in ceremonial dress with medal of honor .00, Queen Amidala w/o make-up on FB [P3G009].. 2000.00
__ Princess Leia in ceremonial dress with medal of honor .01 Padme flashback [P3G010]...........10.00
__ Princess Leia in ceremonial dress with medal of honor .01, Queen Amidala w/o make-up on FB 550.00
__ R2-D2 with launching lightsaber .00, lightsaber on left [P3G011]...10.00
__ R2-D2 with launching lightsaber .00, lightsaber on right [P3G012]...50.00
__ R2-D2 with launching lightsaber .01, lightsaber on left 10.00
__ Yoda with cane and boiling pot .00 [P3G013] 12.00

Kenner, Canada
Green card with FlashBack photo.
__ Anakin Skywalker with Lightsaber [P3G014]..14.00
__ Aunt Beru with Service Droid [P3G015]..........17.00
__ Ben (Obi-Wan) Kenobi with Lightsaber [P3G016]...10.00
__ C-3PO with Removable Arm [P3G017]...........11.00
__ Chewbacca with Bowcaster Rifle [P3G018]...11.00
__ Darth Vader with Lightsaber [P3G019] 16.00
__ Emperor Palpatine with Force Lightning [P3G020]...16.00
__ Luke Skywalker with blaster rifle and electrobinoculars [P3G021] 8.00
__ Princess Leia in Ceremonial Dress [P3G022] ...8.00
__ R2-D2 with Launching Lightsaber [P3G023] ...10.00
__ Yoda with Cane and Boiling Pot [P3G024].....16.00

Action Figures 2000 (CommTech)

Hasbro
Green card with CommTech chip.
__ Admiral Motti with Imperial blaster .0000 [P3H001]..25.00
__ Darth Vader with Imperial interrigation droid .0000, foil chip 10.00
__ Darth Vader with Imperial interrigation droid .0000, white chip [P3H002]......................................10.00
__ Greedo w/blaster .0000, foil chip [P3H003]....10.00

__ Greedo with blaster .0000, white chip 10.00
__ Greedo with blaster .0000, yellow joint pins [P3H004] 10.00
__ Han Solo with blaster pistol and holder .0000, foil chip [P3H005] 8.00
__ Han Solo with blaster pistol and holder .0000, white chip 8.00
__ Jawa and "Gonk" droid .0000, foil chip [P3H006] 10.00
__ Jawa and "Gonk" droid .0000, no pegholes in feet 55.00
__ Jawa and "Gonk" droid .0000, peghole only in one foot 50.00
__ Jawa and "Gonk" droid .0000, white chip 10.00
__ Luke Skywalker with T16 Skyhopper model .0000, foil chip [P3H007]...8.00

__ Luke Skywalker with T16 Skyhopper model .0000, white chip 8.00
__ Princess Leia with sporting blaster .0000 [P3H008] 25.00
__ R2-D2 with holographic Princess Leia .0000, half-moon foot pegs [P3H009]...............................25.00
__ R2-D2 with holographic Princess Leia .0000, round foot pegs [P3H010]....................................100.00
__ Stormtrooper with battle damage and blaster rifle rack .0000, foil chip [P3H011]........................12.00
__ Stormtrooper with battle damage and blaster rifle rack .0000, white chip..................................12.00
__ Wuher with droid detector unit .0000 [P3H012] 18.00
__ Wuher with droid detector unit .0100, white chip 20.00

Hasbro, Canada
Green card with CommTech chip.
__ Admiral Motti with Imperial blaster 32.00
__ Darth Vader with Interrogation Droid [P3H013] 18.00
__ Greedo with blaster [P3H014].........................9.00
__ Han Solo with blaster pistol and holder [P3H015] 8.00
__ Jawa and "Gonk" droid [P3H016]....................8.00
__ Luke Skywalker with T16 Skyhopper model [P3H017] 8.00
__ Princess Leia with sporting blaster................28.00
__ R2-D2 with holographic Princess Leia [P3H018] 185.00
__ Stormtrooper with battle damage and blaster rifle rack [P3H019] 18.00

 P3G001
 P3G002
 P3G003
 P3G004
 P3G005
 P3G006
 P3G007
 P3G008
 P3G009
 P3G010
 P3G011
 P3G012
 P3G013
 P3G014
 P3G015
 P3G016
 P3G017
 P3G018
 P3G019
 P3G020
 P3G021
 P3G022
 P3G023
 P3G024

P3H001

P3H002

P3H003

P3H003 detail (leg pegs)

P3H004 detail (leg pegs)

P3H005

P3H006

P3H007

P3H008

P3H009

R2-D2

P3H009 detail (foot pegs)

R2-D2

P3H010 detail (foot pegs)

P3H011

P3H012

P3H013

P3H014

P3H015

P3H016

P3H017

P3H018

P3H019

P3H020

P3H021

P3H022

CG001

CG002

CG003

CG004

Hasbro, UK

Green card with CommTech chip, tri-language package.
Paper insert in figure bubble.

__ Greedo	10.00
__ Han Solo [P3H020]	10.00
__ Jawa and Gonk [P3H021]	10.00
__ Luke Skywalker [P3H022]	10.00

Action Figures: 1995-2000 (POTF2 Complete Galaxy)

Kenner

__ Dagobah with Yoda [CG001]	20.00
__ Death Star with Darth Vader [CG002]	20.00
__ Endor with Ewok [CG003]	20.00
__ Tatooine with Luke Skywalker [CG004]	25.00

P2S1001

P2S1002

P2S1003

P2S1004

P2S1005

P2S1006

P2S1007

P2S1008

P2S1009

P2S1010

P2S1011

P2S1012

P2S1013

P2S1014

P2S1015

P2S1016

P252001

P252002

P252003

P252004

P252005

P252006

Action Figures: 1995-2000 (POTF2 Deluxe)

Kenner

__ Boba Fett with Wing-Blast Rocketpack .00 ...12.00
__ Boba Fett with Wing-Blast Rocketpack .01 [P2S1001] 12.00
__ Crowd Control Stormtrooper .00...................10.00
__ Crowd Control Stormtrooper .01 [P2S1002] ..10.00
__ Han Solo with Smuggler Flight Pack .00 [P2S1003] 10.00
__ Hoth Rebel Soldier with Radar Laser Gun .00 [P2S1004] 10.00
__ Imperial Probe Droid .00 orange back [P2S1005] 30.00
__ Imperial Probe Droid .01................................10.00

P252007

P252008

P252009

P252010

P2S3001 P2S3002 P2S3003 P2S3004 P2S3005 P2S3006

__ Imperial Probe Droid .02....................................10.00
__ Luke Skywalker with Desert Sport Skiff .00
[P2S1006] 10.00
__ Snowtrooper with E-Web Heavy Repeating Blaster
.00 [P2S1007] 10.00

Kenner, Canada
__ Boba Fett with Wing-Blast Rocketpack
[P2S1008] 14.00
__ Crowd Control Stormtrooper [P2S1009] 14.00
__ Han Solo with Smuggler Flight Pack 9.00
__ Hoth Rebel Soldier with Radar Laser Gun
[P2S1010] 9.00
__ Imperial Probe Droid [P2S1011] 16.00
__ Luke Skywalker with Desert Sport Skiff..........20.00
__ Snowtrooper with E-Web Heavy Repeating Blaster
[P2S1012] 9.00

Kenner, Italy
__ Hoth Rebel Soldier with Radar Laser Gun......15.00
__ Luke Skywalker with Desert Sport Skiff [P2S1013].15.00
__ Snowtrooper with E-Web Heavy Repeating
Blaster..15.00

Kenner, UK
__ Boba Fett with Wing-Blast Rocketpack 15.00
__ Han Solo with Smuggler Flight Pack [P2S1014]...9.00
__ Hoth Rebel Soldier with Radar Laser Gun
[P2S1015] 9.00
__ Luke Skywalker with Desert Sport Skiff [P2S1016].24.00
__ Snowtrooper with E-Web Heavy Repeating
Blaster..9.00

Action Figures 1995-2000 (POTF2 Electronic FX)

Kenner
__ Ben Kenobi .00 [P2S2001]...............................8.00
__ Darth Vader .00 [P2S2002] 10.00
__ Darth Vader .00 signed for Previews 40.00
__ Emperor Palpatine .00 [P2S2003]...................10.00
__ Emperor Palpatine .01 ....10.00
__ Luke Skywalker .00 [P2S2004] 8.00
__ R2-D2 .00...8.00
__ R2-D2 .01...8.00
__ R2-D2 .02 [P2S2005] 8.00

Kenner, Italy
__ Ben (Obi-Wan) Kenobi [P2S2006] 18.00
__ C1-P8 (R2-D2) [P2S2007] 18.00
__ Darth Vader [P2S2008] 18.00
__ Luke Skywalker [P2S2009] 18.00

Kenner, UK
__ Ben (Obi-Wan) Kenobi 12.00
__ Darth Vader [P2S2010] 12.00
__ Luke Skywalker 12.00
__ R2-D2...16.00

Action Figures 1995-2000 (POTF2 Gunner Stations)

Kenner
__ Darth Vader [P2S3001] 15.00

__ Han Solo [P2S3002]..10.00
__ Luke Skywalker [P2S3003] 10.00

Kenner, Canada
__ Darth vader 15.00
__ Han Solo 14.00
__ Luke Skywalker 14.00

Kenner, Italy
__ Darth Vader [P2S3004] 25.00
__ Han Solo [P2S3005]...20.00
__ Luke Skywalker [P2S3006] 20.00

Action Figures 1995-2000 (POTF2 Max Rebo Band)

Kenner
2-packs, Walmart exclusive.
__ Barquin D'an and Droopy McCool .00 ....35.00
__ Barquin D'an and Droopy McCool .01
[P22M001]..35.00
__ Joh Yowza and Sy Snootles .00 [P22M002]...35.00
__ Max Rebo and Bodonawieedo .00
[P22M003]...25.00

Action Figures 1995-2000 (POTF2 Millennium Minted Coins)

Kenner
__ Bespin Han Solo .00..10.00
__ Bespin Han Solo .00, words behind coin
[P2S4001] 25.00

P22M001 P22M002 P22M003 P2S4001 P2S4002

P2S4003 P2S4004 P2S4005 P2S4006 P2S4007

P2M001

P2M002

P2M003

P2M004

P2M005

P2M006

P2M007

___ C-3PO .00 [P2S4002] 12.00
___ Chewbacca .00 [P2S4003] 12.00
___ Chewbacca .00, words behind coin 25.00
___ Emperor Palpatine .00 [P2S4004]...................12.00
___ Endor Leia .00...25.00
___ Endor Leia .01 [P2S4005] 15.00
___ Endor Luke .00 [P2S4006] 25.00
___ Endor Luke .01..15.00
___ Snowtrooper .00 ....12.00
___ Snowtrooper .00, words behind coin [P2S4007] 25.00

Action Figures: 1995-2000 (POTF2 Multipacks)

Hasbro
Cinema Scenes. 3 figures action-posed in a movie scene box. Includes a display base.
___ Cantina Aliens; Labria, Nabrun Leids, Takeel [P2M001]...15.00

___ Jabba's Skiff Guards; Klaatu, Barada, Nikto [P2M002]...12.00
___ Jedi Spirits; Anakin, Yoda, Obi-Wan [P2M003]...25.00
___ Rebel Pilots; Ten Numb, Wedge Antilles, Arvel Crynyd [P2M004] 25.00

Hasbro, Canada
Cinema Scenes.
___ Jedi Spirits; Anakin, Yoda, Obi-Wan 10.00

Kenner
___ 4-Pack Classic [P2M005] 50.00

P2M008

P2M009

P2M010

P2M011

P2M012

P2M013

P2M014

P2M015

P2M016

P2M017

P2M018

P2M019

P2M020

P2M021

P22P001

P22P002

P22P003

P22P004

P22S001

P22S002

2-Packs, Fan Club exclusives.
__ Kabe and Muftak .00 [P2M006] 15.00
__ Oola and Salacious Crumb .00 [P2M007] 25.00

3-Packs, 1997 Hong Kong commemorative. Includes display stand.
__ Boba Fett, Darth Vader, Stormtrooper [P2M008] 75.00
__ C-3PO, Luke Skywalker, Princess Leia [P2M009] 50.00

Cinema Scenes. 3 figures action-posed in a movie scene box. Includes a display base.
__ Cantina Showdown; Ben Kenobi, Dr. Evazan, Ponda Baba .00 [P2M010] 12.00
__ Cantina Showdown; Ben Kenobi, Dr. Evazan, Ponda Baba .01 ....12.00
__ Death Star Escape; Han and Luke in Stormtrooper Disguises, and Chewbacca .00 [P2M011] 30.00
__ Death Star Escape; Han and Luke in Stormtrooper Disguises, and Chewbacca .01 ....30.00
__ Final Jedi Duel; Emperor Palpatine, Luke Skywalker, Darth Vader .00 [P2M012] 25.00
__ Final Jedi Duel; Emperor Palpatine, Luke Skywalker, Darth Vader .01 [P2M013] 25.00
__ Jabba's Dancers; Rystall, Greeta, Lyn Me .00 [P2M014] 12.00
__ Mynock Hunt; Han Solo, Chewbacca, Princess Leia, Mynock Creature .00 ....35.00
__ Purchase of the Droids; Luke Skywalker, Uncle Owen, C-3PO .00 [P2M015] 16.00
__ Purchase of the Droids; Luke Skywalker, Uncle Owen, C-3PO .01 ....15.00

Collectors Packs. 3 individual figures inside one display package.
__ ANH: Stormtrooper Luke, Tusken Raider, Ben Kenobi [P2M016] 30.00

__ ESB: Dagobah Luke, Lando Calrissian, TIE Fighter Pilot [P2M017] 75.00
__ Han Solo, Chewbacca, Lando Calrissian [P2M018] 35.00
__ Luke Skywalker, Ben Kenobi, Darth Vader [P2M019] 35.00
__ R2-D2, C-3PO, Stormtrooper [P2M020] 35.00
__ ROTJ: Jedi Luke, AT-ST Driver, Leia as Boushh [P2M021] 30.00

Kenner, Canada
Cinema Scenes. 3 figures action-posed in a movie scene box. Includes a display base.
__ Mynock Hunt; Han Solo, Chewbacca, Princess Leia, Mynock Creature, tri-logo 65.00

Kenner, Japan
__ 10-Pack: Mos Eisley pop-up Cantina with ten carded action figures [5:340] 220.00

Action Figures: 1995-2000 (POTF2 Princess Collection)

Kenner
Princess Leia and one other character figure.
__ Han Solo .00 [P22P001] 35.00
__ Han Solo .01 ....10.00
__ Luke Skywalker .00 [P22P002] 25.00
__ Luke Skywalker .01 ....10.00
__ R2-D2 .00 [P22P003] 25.00
__ R2-D2 .01 ....10.00
__ Wicket the Ewok .00 [P22P004] 25.00
__ Wicket the Ewok .01 ....10.00

Action Figures: 1995-2000 (POTF2 SOTE 2-Packs)

Kenner
__ Boba Fett vs. IG-88 .00 [P22S001] 25.00
__ Prince Xizor vs. Darth Vader .00 [P22S002] ...20.00

Kenner, UK
__ Boba Fett vs. IG-88 [3:68] 34.00
__ Prince Xizor vs. Darth Vader [5:341] 24.00

Action Figures: 1999-2001 (EPI:TPM)

Hasbro
Adi Gallia with lightsaber
__ .0000, col. 3 [P3001] 8.00
Anakin Skywalker Naboo Pilot with flight simulator
__ .0000, col.1 [P3002] 7.00
Anakin Skywalker Naboo with comlink unit
__ .0000 col. 1 [P3003] 8.00
__ .0100 ....8.00
Anakin Skywalker Tatooine, backpack & grease gun
__ .00, col. 1, blue backpack [P3004] 10.00
__ .00, col. 1, brown backpack 10.00
__ .0100, col. 1 ....7.00
Battle Droid with blaster rifle
__ Clean .00, col. 1 [P3005] 10.00
__ Clean .0100, col. 1 ....10.00
__ Clean .0200, col. 1 ....8.00
__ Dirty .00, col. 1 [P3006] 8.00
__ Dirty .0100, col. 1 ....8.00
__ Dirty .0200, col. 1 ....8.00
__ Shot .00, col. 1 [P3007] 8.00
__ Shot .0100, col. 1 ....8.00
__ Shot .0200, col. 1 ....8.00
__ Sliced .00, col. 1 [P3008] 8.00
__ Sliced .0100, col. 1 ....8.00
__ Sliced .0200, col. 1 ....8.00
Boss Nass with Gungan staff
__ .0000, col. 3 [P3009] 8.00

P3001

P3002

P3003

P3004

P3005

P3006

P3007

P3008

close-up: dirty

close-up: shot

close-up: sliced

P3009

P3010

P3011

P3012

P3013

P3014

P3015

P3016

P3017

P3018

P3019

P3020

P3021

P3022

P3023

P3024

P3025

P3026

P3027

Action Figures

__ .0100, col. 3 ....6.00

C-3PO
__ .00, col. 2 [P3010] 9.00
__ .0100, col. 2 ....8.00

Captain Panaka with blaster rifle and pistol
__ .0000, col. 2 [P3011] 12.00
__ .0000, col. 2, sticker corrects spoken lines 12.00
__ .0100, col. 2 ....12.00

Captain Tarpals with electropole
__ .00, col. 3 ....10.00
__ .0100, col. 3 [P3012] 10.00

Chancellor Valorum with ceremonial staff
__ .00, col. 3 ....10.00
__ .0000, col. 3, printed warning [P3013] 10.00
__ .0000, col. 3, sticker covers printed warning
     [P3014] 10.00

__ .0100 ....9.00
__ .0200 ....9.00

Darth Maul Jedi Duel with double-bladed lightsaber
__ .00, col. 1, new sculpt 10.00
__ .00, col. 1, original sculpt 10.00
__ .0000, col. 1 [P3015] 10.00
__ .0000, col. 1, black vest 200.00
__ .0000, col. 1, white chip 10.00
__ .0100, col. 1 ....10.00

Darth Maul Sith Lord, lightsaber w/removable blade
__ .0000, col. 1 [P3016] 10.00

Darth Maul Tatooine with cloak and lightsaber
__ .0000, col. 1 ....10.00
__ .0100, col. 1 ....10.00
__ .0100, col. 1, white chip [P3017] 10.00

Darth Sidious

P3028

P3029

P3030

P3031

P3032

P3033

P3034

P3035

P3036

P3037

P3038

P3039

P3040

P3041

P3042

P3043

P3044

P3045

P3046

P3047

P3048

P3049

P3050

P3051

P3052

P3053

P3054

P3055

P3056

P3057

P3058

P3059

P3060

P3061

P3062

P3063

P3064

P3065

P3066

P3067

P3068

P3069

P3070

P3071

P3072

P3073

P3074

P3075

P3076

P3077

P3078

P3079

P3080

P3081

P3082

P3083

__ .00, col. 2 [P3018]..9.00
__ .0100, col. 2 ....9.00
Darth Sidious holograph
__ .0000, col. 2 [P3019].......................................30.00
Destroyer Droid
__ .0000, col. 2 [P3020]...7.00
Destroyer Droid battle damaged
__ .0000, col. 1 [P3021].......................................14.00
Gasgano with Pit Droid
__ .0100, col. 3 [P3022]...6.00
__ .0200, col. 3 ....6.00
Jar Jar Binks Naboo swamp with fish
__ .0000, col. 1 [P3023].......................................20.00
Jar Jar Binks with Gungan battle staff
__ .00, col. 1 ....8.00
__ .0100, col. 1 [P3024]...6.00

__ .0200, col. 1 ....6.00
Ki-Adi-Mundi with lightsaber
__ .0000, col. 3 [P3025]...8.00
__ .0100, col. 3 ....6.00
Mace Windu with lightsaber and Jedi cloak
__ .0000, col. 3 [P3026]...8.00
__ .0100, col. 3 ....8.00
__ .0100, col. 3, white chip [P3027] 8.00
Naboo Royal Guard with laser pistol and helmet
__ .0000, col. 2 [P3028].......................................25.00
Naboo Royal Security with blaster pistol and rifle
__ .0000, col. 2 [P3029].......................................10.00
Nute Gunray
__ .0000, col. 2 [P3030].......................................10.00
Obi-Wan Kenobi Jedi Duel with lightsaber
__ .00, col. 1 ....8.00

__ .0100, col. 1 [P3031]...8.00
Obi-Wan Kenobi Jedi Knight with lightsaber and commlink
__ .0000, col. 1 ....8.00
Obi-Wan Kenobi Naboo with lightsaber and handle
__ .0000, col. 1 ....8.00
__ .0100, col. 1 [P3032]...8.00
Ody Mandrell with Otoga 222 pit droid
__ .0000, col. 3 ....8.00
__ .0100, col. 3 [P3033]...8.00
__ .0100, col. 3, white chip 8.00
OOM-9 with blaster and binoculars
__ .0000, col. 3 [P3034]...8.00
__ .0000, col. 3, binoculars in bubble [P3035] 28.00
__ .0000, col. 3, white chip..................................8.00

P3084

P3085

P3086

P3087

P3088

P3089

P3090

P3091

P3092

P3093

P3094

P3095

P3096

P3097

P3098

P3099

P3100

P3101

P3102

P3103

P3104

P3105

P3106

P3107

P3J001   P3J002   P3J003   P3J004   P3J005   P3J006

Padme Naberrie with pod race view screen
__ .00, col. 1 [P3036]............8.00
__ .0100, col. 1 ....8.00

Pit Droids (2-pack)
__ .0000, col. 2 [P3037]............20.00

Queen Amidala Battle with ascension gun
__ .0100, col. 2 [P3038]............45.00

Queen Amidala Coruscant
__ .0100, col. 1 [P3039]............10.00

Queen Amidala Naboo with blaster pistols
__ .00, col. 1 [P3040]............8.00
__ .0100, col. 1 ....8.00

Qui-Gon Jinn Jedi Duel with lightsaber
__ .00, col. 1 [P3041]............6.00
__ .0100, col. 1 ....6.00

Qui-Gon Jinn Jedi Master with lightsaber and comlink
__ .0000, col. 1 [P3042]............8.00

Qui-Gon Jinn Naboo with lightsaber and handle
__ .0100, col. 1 [P3043]............6.00

R2-B1 Astromech Droid with power harness
__ .0000, col. 3 [P3044]............40.00
__ .0100, col. 3 ....35.00

R2-D2 with booster rockets
__ .0000, col. 2 ....8.00
__ .0000, col. 2, small bubble [P3045] 14.00

Ric Olie with helmet and Naboo blaster
__ .00, col. 2 [P3046]............7.00
__ .0100, col. 2 ....7.00
__ .0100, col. 2, closed hand 7.00

Rune Haako
__ .0000, col. 2 [P3047]............9.00

Senator Palpatine with Senate cam droid
__ .00, col. 2 [P3048]............6.00
__ .0100, col. 2 ....6.00

Sio Bibble with blaster pistol
__ .0000, col. 2 [P3049]............30.00

TC-14 protocol droid with serving tray
__ .0000, col. 3 [P3050]............45.00
__ .0100, col. 3 ....40.00

Watto with datapad
__ .00, col. 2 [P3051]............8.00
__ .0100, col. 2 ....8.00

Yoda with Jedi Council chair
__ .0000, col. 2 [P3052]............32.00
__ .0000, col. 2, missing EPI logo [P3053] 9.00

Hasbro, Canada
Tri-language cards.
__ Anakin Skywalker Naboo, col. 1 ....7.00
__ Anakin Skywalker Tatooine, col. 1 [P3054].......7.00
__ Battle Droid (Clean), col. 1 [P3055]............7.00
__ Battle Droid (Dirty), col. 1 [P3056] 12.00
__ Battle Droid (Shot), col. 1............7.00

__ Battle Droid (Sliced), col. 1 ....12.00
__ Boss Nass, col. 3 [P3057]............7.00
__ C-3PO, col. 2 [P3058]............6.00
__ Captain Tarpals, col. 2 [P3059]............8.00
__ Chancellor Valorum, col. 3 [P3060] 12.00
__ Darth Maul Jedi Duel, col. 1 [P3061] 8.00
__ Darth Maul Tatooine, col. 1 [P3062] 9.00
__ Darth Sidious .0100 col. 2 [P3063] 6.00
__ Destroyer Droid, col. 2 [P3064]............14.00
__ Gasgano and Pit Droid .00 col. 3 [P3065] 7.00
__ Jar Jar Binks, col. 1 [P3066]............9.00
__ Ki-Adi-Mundi, col. 3 [P3067]............8.00
__ Mace Windu, col. 3 [P3068]............8.00
__ Nute Gunray, col. 2 [P3069]............7.00
__ Obi-Wan Kenobi Jedi Duel, col. 1 [P3070] 8.00
__ Obi-Wan Kenobi Naboo, col. 1 [P3071] 7.00
__ Ody Mandrell w/Otoga 222 Pit Droid, col. 2.....8.00
__ OOM-9, col. 2 [P3072]............15.00
__ Padme Naberrie .0100 col. 1 [P3073]............6.00
__ Queen Amidala Coruscant, col. 1 [P3074]......11.00
__ Queen Amidala Naboo, col. 1 [P3075]............9.00
__ Qui-Gon Jinn Jedi Duel .0100 col. 1 [P3076]....6.00
__ Qui-Gon Jinn Naboo, col. 1 [P3077]............9.00
__ R2-D2, col. 2 [P3078]............6.00
__ Ric Olie, col. 2 [P3079] 6.00
__ Rune Haako, col. 2 [P3080] 6.00
__ Senator Palpatine .00 col. 2 [P3081] 9.00
__ Watto, col. 2 [P3082]............9.00
__ Yoda, col. 2 [P3083] 7.00

Hasbro, UK
__ Adi Gallia............8.00
__ Anakin Skywalker............9.00
__ Anakin Skywalker Naboo............9.00
__ Anakin Skywalker Naboo pilot [P3084]............9.00
__ Battle Droid (Clean)............9.00
__ Battle Droid (Dirty)............9.00
__ Battle Droid (Shot)............9.00
__ Battle Droid (Sliced)............9.00
__ Boss Nass............9.00
__ C-3PO............8.00
__ Captain Tarpals............10.00
__ Chancellor Valorum............11.00
__ Dark Sidious holograph [P3085]............14.00
__ Darth Maul [P3086]............9.00
__ Darth Maul Sith Lord [P3087] 10.00
__ Darth Maul Tatooine [P3088]............9.00
__ Darth Sidious [P3089]............9.00
__ Destroyer Droid [P3090] 9.00
__ Destroyer Droid Battle Damaged............15.00
__ Gasgano and Pit Droid 9.00
__ Jar Jar Binks [P3091]............8.00

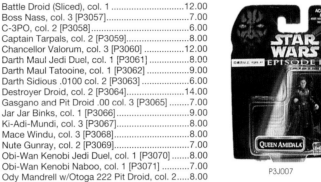

P3J007   P3J008

__ Jar Jar Binks Naboo Swamp 25.00
__ Ki-Adi-Mundi............8.00
__ Naboo Royal Guard [P3092]............13.00
__ Nute Gunray............7.00
__ Obi-Wan Kenobi [P3093]............9.00
__ Obi-Wan Kenobi Jedi Knight [P3094]............9.00
__ Obi-Wan Kenobi Naboo [P3095]............9.00
__ OOM-9............9.00
__ Padme Naberrie [P3096]............9.00
__ Pit Droids [P3097]............16.00
__ Queen Amidala [P3098] 10.00
__ Queen Amidala Coruscant [P3099] 10.00
__ Qui-Gon Jinn [P3100]............9.00
__ Qui-Gon Jinn Jedi Master............9.00
__ Qui-Gon Jinn Naboo [P3101]............9.00
__ R2-D2 with Booster Rockets 10.00
__ Ric Olie [P3102]............9.00
__ Rune Haako............10.00
__ Senator Palpatine [P3103]............9.00
__ Sio Bibble [P3104]............17.00
__ Watto [P3105]............8.00
__ Yoda with Jedi Council Chair [P3106] 9.00

Kenner
__ Mace Windu, mail-away premium [P3107].....15.00

Hasbro
__ 2-pack, Figure Collector, (any 2) [P3L001] 22.00
__ CommTech plus any figure, wholesale clubs [P3L002]............25.00
__ The Final Lightsaber Duel [P3L003]............15.00

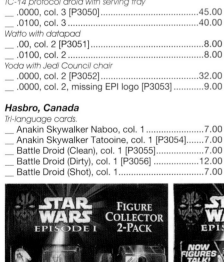

P3L001   P3L002   P3L003   P3L004

ANAKIN SKYWALKER
WITH BONUS PIT DROID

P3T001

DARTH MAUL
WITH BONUS PIT DROID

P3T002

DARTH SIDIOUS
WITH BONUS PIT DROID

P3T003

NABOO ROYAL GUARD
WITH BONUS PIT DROID

P3T004

OBI-WAN KENOBI
WITH BONUS PIT DROID

P3T005

ANAKIN SKYWALKER
WITH BONUS PIT DROID

P3T006

DARTH MAUL
WITH BONUS PIT DROID

P3T007

DARTH SIDIOUS
WITH BONUS PIT DROID

P3T008

NABOO ROYAL GUARD
WITH BONUS PIT DROID

P3T009

OBI-WAN KENOBI
WITH BONUS PIT DROID

P3T010

ANAKIN SKYWALKER
WITH BONUS PIT DROID

P3T011

DARTH MAUL
WITH BONUS PIT DROID

P3T012

DARTH SIDIOUS
WITH BONUS PIT DROID

P3T013

NABOO ROYAL GUARD
WITH BONUS PIT DROID

P3T014

OBI-WAN KENOBI
WITH BONUS PIT DROID

P3T015

ANAKIN SKYWALKER WITH
BONUS BATTLE DROID

P3T016

ANAKIN SKYWALKER WITH
BONUS BATTLE DROID

P3T017

BATTLE DROID WITH
BONUS BATTLE DROID

P3T018

BATTLE DROID WITH
BONUS BATTLE DROID

P3T019

BATTLE DROID WITH
BONUS BATTLE DROID

P3T020

BATTLE DROID WITH
BONUS BATTLE DROID

P3T021

C-3PO WITH
BONUS BATTLE DROID

P3T022

CAPTAIN PANAKA WITH
BONUS BATTLE DROID

P3T023

DARTH MAUL WITH
BONUS BATTLE DROID

P3T024

DARTH MAUL WITH
BONUS BATTLE DROID

P3T025

DARTH MAUL WITH
BONUS BATTLE DROID

P3T026

DARTH SIDIOUS WITH
BONUS BATTLE DROID

P3T027

DESTROYER DROID WITH
BONUS BATTLE DROID

P3T028

JAR JAR BINKS WITH
BONUS BATTLE DROID

P3T029

NABOO ROYAL SECURITY
WITH BONUS BATTLE DROID

P3T030

| P3T031 | P3T032 | P3T033 | P3T034 | P3T035 | P3T036 |

| P3T037 | P3T038 | P3T039 | P3T040 | P3T041 | P3T042 |

Hasbro, Canada
Tri-language packaging.
__ The Final Lightsaber Duel [P3L004]................25.00

Action Figures: 1999-2001 (EPI:TPM 2" Scale)

Hasbro
__ Anakin Skywalker [P3J001] 15.00
__ Battle Droid [P3J002]......................................15.00
__ Darth Maul [P3J003] 15.00
__ Jar Jar Binks [P3J004] 15.00
__ Obi-Wan Kenobi [P3J005].................................15.00
__ Padme Naberrie [P3J006]................................15.00
__ Queen Amidala [P3J007] 15.00
__ Qui-Gon Jinn [P3J008] 15.00

Action Figures: 1999-2001 (EPI:TPM Bonus 2-Packs)

Hasbro
Phantom Menace figure with bonus Pit Droid. 3 colors of Pit Droid available.
__ Brown with Anakin Skywalker col. 1 [P3T001]... 25.00
__ Brown with Darth Maul col. 1 [P3T002] 25.00
__ Brown with Darth Sidious hologram col. 2 [P3T003]... 65.00
__ Brown with Naboo Royal Guard col. 2 [P3T004]65.00
__ Brown with Obi-Wan Kenobi col. 1 [P3T005]...25.00
__ Cream with Anakin Skywalker col. 1 [P3T006]... 25.00
__ Cream with Darth Maul col. 1 [P3T007].............. 25.00
__ Cream with Darth Sidious hologram col. 2 [P3T008]... 65.00
__ Cream with Naboo Royal Guard col. 2 [P3T009]65.00
__ Cream w/Obi-Wan Kenobi col. 1 [P3T010] 65.00
__ Tan with Anakin Skywalker col. 1 [P3T011]..25.00
__ Tan with Darth Maul col. 1 [P3T012].....................25.00
__ Tan with Darth Sidious hologram col. 2 [P3T013]....65.00
__ Tan with Naboo Royal Guard col. 2 [P3T014]..65.00
__ Tan with Obi-Wan Kenobi col. 1 [P3T015] 25.00

Phantom Menace figure with unpainted bonus Battle Droid.
__ Anakin Skywalker col. 1 [P3T016] 20.00
__ Anakin Skywalker Naboo col. 1 [P3T017].......25.00
__ Battle Droid (Clean) col. 1 [P3T018]...............25.00
__ Battle Droid (Dirty) col. 1 [P3T019] 25.00
__ Battle Droid (Shot) col. 1 [P3T020] 25.00
__ Battle Droid (Sliced) col. 1 [P3T021]...............25.00
__ C-3PO col. 2 [P3T022].....................................30.00
__ Capt. Panaka col. 2 [P3T023] 25.00
__ Darth Maul Jedi Duel col. 1 [P3T024] 25.00
__ Darth Maul Jedi Duel, resculpted face col. 1 [P3T025]...25.00
__ Darth Maul Tatooine Battle Droid col. 1 [P3T026]...25.00
__ Darth Sidious col. 2 [P3T027].........................25.00
__ Destroyer Droid col. 2 [P3T028]......................25.00
__ Jar Jar Binks col. 1 [P3T029].........................25.00
__ Naboo Royal Security col. 2 [P3T030]............25.00
__ Nute Gunray col. 2 [P3T031]..........................25.00
__ Obi-Wan Kenobi Jedi Duel col. 1 [P3T032] 25.00
__ Obi-Wan Kenobi Naboo col. 1 [P3T033] 20.00
__ Padme Newberrie col. 1 [P3T034]...................20.00
__ Queen Amidala col. 1 [P3T035] 20.00
__ Queen Amidala Coruscant col. 1 [P3T036].....25.00
__ Qui-Gon Jinn Jedi Duel col. 1 [P3T037] 20.00
__ Qui-Gon Jinn Naboo col. 1 [P3T038]..............20.00

| P3T043 | P3T044 |

__ R2-D2 col. 2 [P3T039] 25.00
__ Ric Olie col. 2 [P3T040] 25.00
__ Rune Haako col. 2 [P3T041]...........................25.00
__ Senator Palpatine col. 2 [P3T042] 30.00
__ Watto col. 2 [P3T043] 30.00
__ Yoda col. 2 [P3T044] 25.00

Action Figures: 1999-2001 (EPI:TPM Cinema Scenes)

Hasbro
Cinema Scenes. 3 figures action-posed in a movie scene box. Includes a display base and CommTech chip.
__ MosEspa Encounter, foil chip [P3M001] 15.00
__ MosEspa Encounter, white chip......................15.00
__ Tatooine Showdown, foil chip [P3M002]........15.00
__ Tatooine Showdown, white chip 15.00
__ Watto's Box, foil chip, foil chip 35.00
__ Watto's Box, white chip [P3M003] 35.00

| P3M001 | P3M002 | P3M003 |

Action Figures

P3Z001   P3Z002   P3Z003   P3Z004   P3Z005   P3Z006

P34001   P34002   P39001   PJ001   PJ002

Action Figures: 1999-2001 (EPI:TPM Deluxe)

Hasbro
□ Darth Maul [P3Z001] 12.00
□ Obi-Wan Kenobi [P3Z002] 12.00
□ Qui-Gon Jinn [P3Z003] 12.00

Hasbro, UK
□ Darth Maul [P3Z004] 12.00
□ Obi-Wan Kenobi [P3Z005] 12.00
□ Qui-Gon Jinn [P3Z006] 12.00

Action Figures: 1999-2001 (EPI:TPM Light-Up)

Hasbro
□ Darth Maul [P34001] 15.00
□ Qui-Gon Jinn [P34002] 15.00

Action Figures: 1999-2001 (EPI:TPM Trophy)

Hasbro
□ Darth Maul with Sith Infiltrator [P39001] 12.00

Action Figures: 2001-2002 (POTJ)

Hasbro
□ Boba Fett, 300th figure .0100 [PJ001] 35.00

□ Boba Fett, 300th figure .0200 [PJ002] 30.00

Episode II: Attack of the Clones. Sneak preview.
□ Clone Trooper [PJ003] 12.00
□ Jango Fett [PJ004] 8.00
□ R3-T7 [PJ005] 8.00
□ Zam Wesell [PJ006] 6.00

Anakin Skywalker Mechanic
□ .0000, col. 1, force file 0000 [PJ007] 8.00
□ .0100, col. 1, force file 0100 ....6.00
Aurra Sing Bounty Hunter
□ .0300, col. 1 [PJ008] 12.00
□ .0400, col. 1 ....12.00
Battle Droid Boomer Damage
□ .0100, col. 1 [PJ009] 10.00
□ .0300, col. 1 ....10.00
□ .0400, col. 1 ....8.00
Battle Droid Security
□ .0000, col. 2 [PJ010] 12.00
□ .0100, col. 2 ....12.00
□ .0400, col. 2 ....12.00
Ben (Obi-Wan) Kenobi Jedi Knight
□ .0100, col. 1 [PJ011] 10.00
Bespin Guard Cloud City Security
□ .0400, col. 2 [PJ012] 10.00
Boss Nass Gungan Sacred Place
□ .0000, col. 2 [PJ013] 10.00
□ .0100, col. 2 ....10.00
Chewbacca Dejarik Champion
□ .0000, col. 2, force file 0000 [PJ014] 10.00
□ .0000, col. 2, force file 0100 ....10.00
□ .0100, col. 2, force file 0100 ....110.00

Chewbacca Millennium Falcon Mechanic
□ .0300, col. 1 [PJ015] 10.00
□ .0400, col. 1 ....10.00
Coruscant Guard
□ .0000, col. 2, force file 0000 [PJ016] 12.00
□ .0100, col. 2, force file 0100 ....12.00
□ .0300, col. 2, force file 0100 ....12.00
□ .0400, col. 2, force file 0100 ....12.00
Darth Maul Final Duel
□ .0000, col. 1 ....10.00
□ .0000, col. 1, sticker on front [PJ017] 10.00
□ .0100, col. 1, sticker on front 10.00
Darth Maul Sith Apprentice
□ .0100, col. 1 ....12.00
□ .0300, col. 1 [PJ018] 12.00
□ .0400, col. 1 ....12.00
Darth Vader Dagobah
□ .0100, col. 1 [PJ019] 10.00
□ .0400, col. 1 ....10.00
Darth Vader Emperor's Wrath
□ .0400, col. 1 [PJ020] 12.00
Ellorrs Madak
□ .0400, col. 2 [PJ021] 10.00
Fode and Beed Podrace Announcer
□ .0100, col. 2 [PJ022] 10.00
□ .0400, col. 2 ....10.00
Gungan Warrior
□ .0000, col. 2 [PJ023] 10.00
□ .0100, col. 2 ....10.00
□ .0300, col. 2 ....10.00
□ .0400, col. 2 ....10.00
Han Solo Bespin Capture
□ .0100, col. 1 [PJ024] 10.00
□ .0300, col. 1 ....10.00
□ .0400, col. 1 ....10.00
Han Solo Death Star Escape
□ .0400, col. 1 [PJ025] 8.00
IG-88 Bounty Hunter
□ .0100, col. 2, closed right claw [PJ026] 10.00
□ .0100, col. 2, open right claw [PJ027] 10.00
□ .0300, col. 2, closed right claw 10.00
Jar Jar Binks Tatooine
□ .0300, col. 2 ....8.00
□ .0400, col. 2 [PJ028] 8.00
Jek Porkins
□ .0000, col. 2 [PJ029] 12.00
□ .0100, col. 2 ....12.00
□ .0300, col. 2 ....12.00
K-3PO Echo Base Protocol Droid
□ .0100, col. 2 [PJ030] 10.00
□ .0300, col. 2 ....10.00
□ .0400, col. 2 ....10.00
Ketwol
□ .0400, col. 2 [PJ031] 8.00

PJ003   PJ004   PJ005   PJ006

PJ007

PJ008

PJ009

PJ010

PJ011

PJ012

PJ013

PJ014

PJ015

PJ016

PJ017

PJ018

PJ019

PJ020

PJ021

PJ022

PJ023

PJ024

PJ025

PJ026

PJ026 detail - closed claw

PJ027 detail - open claw

PJ028

PJ029

PJ030

PJ031

PJ032

PJ033

PJ034

PJ035

PJ036 PJ037 PJ038 PJ039 PJ040 PJ041

PJ042 PJ043 PJ044 PJ045 PJ046 PJ047

PJ048 PJ049 PJ050 PJ050 detail - clean PJ051 detail - shot PJ052

PJ053 PJ054 PJ055 PJ056 PJ057 PJ058

PJ059 PJ060 PJ061 PJ062 PJ063 PJ064

Lando Calrissian Bespin Escape
___ .0300, col. 2 ....10.00
___ .0400, col. 2 [PJ032].............................10.00
Leia Organa Bespin Escape
___ .0300, col. 1 [PJ033].............................10.00
___ .0400, col. 1 ....10.00
Leia Organa General
___ .0000, col. 1 [PJ034]...............................8.00
___ .0100, col. 1 ....8.00
___ .0300, col. 1 ....8.00
___ .0400, col. 1 ....8.00
Luke Skywalker X-Wing Pilot
___ .0400, col. 1 [PJ035]...............................8.00
Mas Amedda
___ .0000, col. 2, force file 0100 [PJ036] 12.00
___ .0100, col. 2, force file 0100 ....12.00
___ .0300, col. 2, force file 0100 ....12.00
___ .0400, col. 2, force file 0100 ....12.00
Mon Calamari Officer
___ .0100, col. 2 [PJ037].............................12.00
___ .0300, col. 2 ....12.00
___ .0400, col. 2 ....10.00
Obi-Wan Kenobi Cold Weather Gear
___ .0300, col. 1 ....12.00
___ .0400, col. 1 [PJ038].............................12.00
___ .0000, col. 1, force file 0100 [PJ039] 8.00
___ .0100, col. 1, force file 0100 ....8.00
Obi-Wan Kenobi Jedi Training Gear
___ .0300, col. 2 ....8.00
___ .0400, col. 2 [PJ040].............................10.00
Plo Koon Jedi Master
___ .0100, col. 2 [PJ041].............................12.00
___ .0300, col. 2 ....12.00
___ .0400, col. 2 ....12.00

PJ065

PJ066

PJ067

PJ068

Queen Amidala Theed Invasion
___ .0100, col. 2 [PJ042].............................12.00
___ .0300, col. 2 ....12.00
___ .0400, col. 2 ....12.00
Qui-Gon Jinn Jedi Training Gear
___ .0400, col. 1 [PJ043].............................10.00
Qui-Gon Jinn Mos Espa Disguise
___ .0000, col. 1, force file 0100 [PJ044] 8.00
___ .0100, col. 1, force file 0100 ....8.00
___ .0400, col. 1, force file 0100 ....10.00
R2-D2 Naboo Escape
___ .0000, col. 1 [PJ045]...............................10.00
___ .0100, col. 1 ....10.00
R2-Q5 Imperial Astromech Droid
___ .0300, col. 2, "Imperial" misspelled 15.00
___ .0400, col. 2, "Imperial" misspelled
[PJ046]...15.00

Sabe Queen's Decoy
___ .0400, col. 2 [PJ047]...............................8.00
Saesee Tiin Jedi Master
___ .0100, col. 2 [PJ048].............................10.00
___ .0300, col. 2 ....10.00
___ .0400, col. 2 ....10.00
Sandtrooper Tatooine Patrol
___ .0300, col. 1 ....15.00
___ .0400, col. 1 ....15.00
Scout Trooper Imperial Patrol
___ .0100, col. 1 [PJ050].............................25.00
___ .0300, col. 1 ....25.00
___ .0400, col. 1, blaster damage [PJ051]............12.00
Sebulba Boonta Eve Challenge
___ .0000, col. 2 ....12.00
___ .0100, col. 2 [PJ052].............................10.00
___ .0400, col. 2 ....10.00

PJ069

PJ070

PJ071

PJ072

PJ073

PJ074

PJ075

PJ076

PJ077

PJ078

PJ079

PJ080

PJ081

PJ082

PJ083

PJ084

PJ085

PJ086

PJ087   PJ088   PJ089   PJ090   PJ091   PJ092

PJ093   PJ094   PJ095   PJ096   PJ097   PJ098

Shmi Skywalker
__ .0400, col. 2 [PJ053] 12.00
Tessek
__ .0300, col. 2 ....10.00
__ .0400, col. 2 [PJ054] 10.00
Tusken Raider Desert Sniper
__ .0000, col. 2 [PJ055] 12.00
__ .0100, col. 2 ....10.00
__ .0300, col. 2 ....10.00
__ .0400, col. 2 ....10.00

Green cards without Force Files.
__ Boshek 0700 [PJ056] 15.00
__ Eeth Koth 0500 [PJ057] 12.00
__ FX-7 Medical Droid 0000 [PJ058] 10.00
__ Imperial Officer 0300 [PJ059] 12.00
__ Queen Amidala Royal Decoy 0100 [PJ060] 8.00
__ R4-M9 and mouse droid 0800 [PJ061] 12.00
__ Rebel Trooper 0200 [PJ062] 10.00
__ Teebo 0600 [PJ063] 10.00
__ Zutton (Snaggletooth) 0400, brown head [PJ064] 15.00
__ Zutton (Snaggletooth) 0400, pink head 15.00

Hasbro, Canada
Episode II: Attack of the Clones. Sneak preview figures. Tri-language.
__ Clone Trooper [PJ065] 15.00
__ Jango Fett [PJ066] 17.00
__ R3-T7 [PJ067] 15.00
__ Zam Wesell [PJ068] 12.00

Tri-language packaging with force file.
__ Anakin Skywalker Mechanic 9.00

__ Aurra Sing Bounty Hunter, tri-language with force file 0000 [PJ069] 9.00
__ Battle Droid Boomer Damage [PJ070] 9.00
__ Bespin Guard [PJ071] 9.00
__ Chewbacca Millennium Falcon Mechanic [PJ072] 9.00
__ Darth Maul Sith Apprentice [PJ073] 9.00
__ Darth Vader Dagobah, secret Luke sticker [PJ074] 35.00
__ Darth Vader Emperors Wrath [PJ075] 9.00
__ Ellors Madak [PJ076] 9.00
__ Han Solo Bespin Capture 9.00
__ Han Solo Death Star Escape [PJ077] 9.00
__ IG-88 [PJ078] 9.00
__ Jar Jar Binks Tatooine 7.00
__ K-3PO [PJ079] 9.00
__ Ketwol [PJ080] 9.00
__ Lando Calrissian Bespin Escape [PJ081] 9.00
__ Leia Organa Bespin Escape [PJ082] 9.00
__ Luke Skywalker X-Wing Pilot [PJ083] 9.00
__ Mon Calamari Officer 9.00
__ Obi-Wan Kenobi Cold Weather Gear [PJ084] 9.00
__ Obi-Wan Kenobi Jedi Knight [PJ085] 9.00
__ Obi-Wan Kenobi Jedi Training Gear [PJ086] 9.00
__ Plo Koon [PJ087] 9.00
__ Queen Amidala Theed Invasion [PJ088] 9.00
__ Qui-Gon Jinn Jedi Training Gear [PJ089] 9.00
__ R2-Q5 Imperial Astromech [PJ090] 9.00
__ Sabe Queen's Decoy [PJ091] 7.00
__ Saesee Tinn [PJ092] 9.00
__ Sandtrooper Tatooine Patrol [PJ093] 9.00
__ Scout Trooper Imperial Patrol [PJ094]..............9.00

__ Scout Trooper Imperial Patrol - dirty boots and blaster damage [PJ095] 9.00
__ Shmi Skywalker [PJ096] 9.00
__ Tessek [PJ097] 9.00

Tri-language packaging.
__ Boba Fett, 300th figure [PJ098] 35.00

Hasbro, Japan
__ Mas Amedda Japan Toy Expo exclusive, 12-09-00, autographed 50.00

Hasbro, UK
Classic trilogy characters. Bi-language with force file.
__ Ben (Obi-Wan) Kenobi Jedi Knight [PJ099] 9.00
__ Darth Vader Dagobah [PJ100] 9.00

Episode I: The Phantom Menace characters. Bi-language with force file.
__ Darth Maul [PJ101] 7.00
__ Obi-Wan Kenobi [PJ102] 7.00
__ Qui-Gon Jinn [PJ103] 7.00

Tomy, Japan
__ Darth Vader Emperors Wrath, 100th figure [PJ104]...35.00

Action Figures: 2001-2002 (POTJ 2-Packs)

Hasbro
__ Masters of the Dark Side, Darth Maul and Darth Vader [PJ2001] 40.00

PJ099   PJ100   PJ101   PJ102   PJ103   PJ104

PJ2001

SSD001

SSD002

SSD003

SSD004

SSD005

SSD006

PJF001

PJF002

PJF003

846480640
Star Wars Figure 4-Pack
PJM001

PJM002

Action Figures: 2001-2002 (POTJ Multi-Packs)

Hasbro
__ 4-pack 846480640, plain white mailer-style package, internet e-tailer offer [PJM001] 25.00

Hasbro, Mexico
__ 4-pack: Vader, Luke, Rebel Trooper, Sandtrooper, Spanish packaging [PJM002] 75.00

Action Figures: 2001-2002 (POTJ Silver Anniversary)

Hasbro
2-pack of figures posed upon a diorama display base.
__ Han Solo and Chewbacca, "Death Star Escape" [PSS001] 18.00
__ Luke and Leia, "Swing to Freedom" [PSS002] 15.00
__ Obi-Wan Kenobi and Darth Vader, "Final Duel" [PSS003] 20.00

Hasbro, Canada
Tri-language packaging.
__ Han Solo and Chewbacca, "Death Star Escape" [PSS004] 18.00
__ Luke and Leia, "Swing to Freedom" [PSS005] 18.00
__ Obi-Wan Kenobi and Darth Vader, "Final Duel" [PSS006] 18.00

Action Figures: 2001-2002 (POTJ Deluxe)

Hasbro
__ Amanaman with Salacious Crumb 0300 [SSD001] 20.00
__ Amanaman with Salacious Crumb 0600 ....12.00
__ Darth Maul with Sith attack droid 0100 [SSD002] ...20.00
__ Darth Maul with Sith attack droid 0500 ....20.00
__ Luke Skywalker in Echo Base bacta tank 0000 [SSD003] 15.00
__ Luke Skywalker in Echo Base bacta tank 0400.......15.00
__ Princess Leia with sail barge cannon 0200 [SSD004] 10.00

Hasbro, Canada
Tri-language packaging.
__ Darth Maul with Sith attack droid [SSD005] 15.00
__ Luke Skywalker in Echo Base bacta tank [SSD006] 15.00

Action Figures: 2001-2002 (POTJ Mega)

Hasbro
Figures are approximately 7" tall.
__ Darth Maul [PJF001] 15.00
__ Destroyer Droid [PJF002] 20.00
__ Obi-Wan Kenobi [PJF003] 15.00

PSS001

PSS002

PSS003

PSS004

PSS005

PSS006

Action Figures: 2002-2004 (Saga 2002)

Hasbro

Blue cards. 1st release with background insert.

__ Anakin Skywalker, Outland Peasant Disguise (02/01) col. 1 [P4A001]......................8.00
__ Battle Droid, Arena Battle (02/11) col. 2, white [P4A002] 10.00
__ Boba Fett, Kamino Escape (02/07) col. 2 [P4A003] 8.00
__ Boba Fett, Kamino Escape (02/07) col. 2, no number on insert card 8.00
__ C-3PO, Protocol Droid (02/04) col. 1 [P4A004] 8.00
__ Captain Typho, Padme's Head of Security (02/09) col. 2 [P4A005]............................8.00
__ Captain Typho, Padme's Head of Security (02/09) col. 2, no number on insert card..............8.00
__ Dexter Jettster, Coruscant Informant (02/16) col. 2, blue tape over "pipe".........................8.00
__ Dexter Jettster, Coruscant Informant (02/16) col. 2, lists pipe accessory 8.00
__ Genosian Warrior (02/15) col. 2 [P4A006].........8.00
__ Jango Fett, Kamino Escape (02/13) col. 1 [P4A007] 8.00
__ Kit Fisto, Jedi Master (02/05) col. 1, With Force Action [P4A008]...............................10.00
__ Obi-Wan Kenobi, Coruscant chase (02/03) col. 1 [P4A009].......................................8.00
__ Padme Amidala, Arena Escape (02/02) col. 1, mole on left cheek, tape on gun [P4A010] 8.00
__ Padme Amidala, Arena Escape (02/02) col. 1, no mole, no tape on gun.........................8.00
__ Padme Amidala, Arena Escape (02/02) col. 1, tape on gun..8.00
__ Plo Koon, Arena Battle (02/12) col. 2 [P4A011] 12.00
__ R2-D2, Coruscant sentry (02/14) col. 1, round shoulder pegs [P4A012].........................12.00
__ Shaak Ti, Jedi Master (02/10) col. 2 [P4A013]..8.00
__ Super Battle Droid (02/06) col. 1, battle damage sticker, dull figure finish 12.00
__ Super Battle Droid (02/06) col. 1, battle damage sticker, glossy figure finish [P4A014]..............12.00
__ Super Battle Droid (02/06) col. 1, no correction sticker over blast apart legs image [P4A015] .12.00
__ Tusken Raider, Female with Tusken child (02/08) col. 2 [P4A016]...............................12.00

Blue cards. Swirl pattern on background.

__ Anakin Skywalker, Hangar Duel (02/22) col. 1, dueling Lightsaber Action [P4A017] 10.00
__ Anakin Skywalker, Hangar Duel (02/22) col. 1, dueling Lightsaber Action, missing "TM" next to "Lightsabers"....................................... 10.00
__ Anakin Skywalker, Hangar Duel (02/22) col. 1, secret Battle Feature [P4A018].....................10.00
__ Anakin Skywalker, Hangar Duel (02/22) col. 1, secret Battle Feature, missing "TM" next to "Lightsabers" 10.00
__ Anakin Skywalker, Hangar Duel (02/22) col. 1, secret Battle Feature, tape over lightsaber 10.00
__ Anakin Skywalker, Outland Peasant Disguise (02/01) col. 1 [P4A019]............................7.00
__ Anakin Skywalker, Outland Peasant Disguise (02/01) col. 1, gun tray has a circular end 7.00
__ Anakin Skywalker, Tatooine Attack (02/43) col. 1, rifle held by bubble tab [P4A020]...............8.00
__ Anakin Skywalker, Tatooine Attack (02/43) col. 1, rifle held by tab...............................8.00
__ Battle Droid, Arena Battle (02/11) col. 2, beige [P4A021]..10.00
__ Battle Droid, Arena Battle (02/11) col. 2, red [P4A022] .15.00
__ Boba Fett, Kamino Escape (02/07) col. 2 [P4A023] 10.00
__ C-3PO, Proto. Droid (02/04) col. 1 [P4A024].......6.00
__ Captain Typho, Padme's Head of Security (02/09) col. 2 [P4A025]...................................6.00
__ Chewbacca, Cloud City Capture (02/38) col. 1 [P4A026]..8.00
__ Clone Trooper (02/17) col. 1, curved bubble, no tab over cannon..................................15.00

__ Clone Trooper (02/17) col. 1, curved bubble, tab over cannon [P4A027]............................. 15.00
__ Clone Trooper (02/17) col. 1, red dots missing from package photo [P4A028]..................... 15.00
__ Clone Trooper (02/17) col. 1, straight bubble over right arm.. 15.00
__ Clone Trooper, Republic Gunship Pilot (02/49) col. 1 [P4A029] 20.00
__ Count Dooku, Dark Lord (02/27) col. 1 [P4A030] 10.00
__ Darth Maul, Sith Training (02/42) col. 1, .3300 kneeling text [P4A031].........................15.00
__ Darth Maul, Sith Training (02/42) col. 1, .6000 corrected text [P4A032].........................15.00
__ Darth Vader, Bespin Duel (02/30) col. 1 [P4A033] 10.00
__ Destroyer Droid, Geonosis Battle (02/48) col. 1 [P4A034].. 10.00
__ Dexter Jettster, Coruscant Informant (02/16) col. 2, blue tape over "pipe" [P4A035]..............8.00
__ Dexter Jettster, Coruscant Informant (02/16) col. 2, pipe accessory listed [P4A036].............8.00
__ Dexter Jettster, Coruscant Informant (02/16) col. 2, pipe accessory removed 8.00
__ Djas Puhr (02/40) col. 2 [P4A037].....................8.00
__ Eeth Koth, Jedi Master (02/56) col. 2 [P4A038]..20.00
__ Endor Rebel Soldier (02/33) col. 2, gun strap loose in bubble [P4A039]............................. 10.00
__ Endor Rebel Soldier (02/33) col. 2, gun strap under bubble.
__ Endor Rebel Soldier without beard (02/33) col. 2, gun strap loose in bubble [P4A040] 12.00

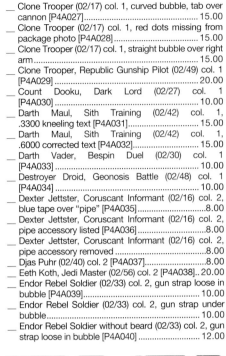

P4A001   P4A002   P4A003   P4A004

P4A005   P4A006   P4A007   P4A008   P4A009   P4A010

P4A011   P4A012   P4A013   P4A014   P4A014 detail   P4A015 detail

P4A016

P4A017

P4A018

P4A019

P4A020

P4A021

P4A022

P4A023

P4A024

P4A025

P4A026

P4A027

P4A027 detail

P4A028 detail

P4A029

P4A030

P4A031 detail

P4A032 detail

P4A031

P4A033

P4A034

P4A035

P4A035 detail

P4A036 detail

P4A036

P4A037

P4A038

P4A039

P4A039 detail

P4A040 detail

Action Figures

P4A040

P4A041

P4A042

P4A043

P4A043 detail

P4A044 detail

P4A045

P4A046

P4A047

P4A048

P4A049

P4A050

P4A051

P4A052

P4A053

P4A054

P4A055 detail

P4A057 detail

P4A056

P4A059

P4A058 detail

P4A060

P4A061

P4A062

P4A063

P4A064

P4A065

P4A066

P4A067

P4A068

__ Endor Rebel Soldier without beard (02/33) col. 2, gun strap under bubble 12.00
__ Ephant Mon, Jabba's Head of Security (02/45) col. 2, bubble curves around left hand [P4A041] ..25.00
__ Ephant Mon, Jabba's Head of Security (02/45) col. 2, bubble shaped under left hand..................25.00
__ Genosian Warrior (02/15) col. 2 [P4A042].......10.00
__ Han Solo, Endor Raid (02/37) col. 1, gray action lever, right arm tray goes to top of bubble [P4A043] .8.00
__ Han Solo, Endor Raid (02/37) col. 1, gray action lever, right arm tray tapers off 8.00
__ Han Solo, Endor Raid (02/37) col. 1, white action lever [P4A044]....................................8.00
__ Imperial Officer (02/55) col. 2, blonde hair [P4A045] 20.00
__ Imperial Officer (02/55) col. 2, brown hair [P4A046] 20.00
__ Jango Fett, Final Battle (02/31) col. 1, accessory angled downward in bubble [P4A047]............8.00
__ Jango Fett, Final Battle (02/31) col. 1, accessory angled upward in bubble [P4A048] 8.00
__ Jango Fett, Kamino Escape (02/13) col. 1, gray armor [P4A049]....................................12.00
__ Jango Fett, Kamino Escape (02/13) col. 1, silver armor 12.00
__ Jango Fett, Slave I Pilot (02/47) col. 1 [P4A050] 8.00
__ Jar Jar Binks, Gungan Senator (02/24) col. 2, bubble ends at right hand [P4A051] 8.00
__ Jar Jar Binks, Gungan Senator (02/24) col. 2, bubble extends to right wrist 8.00
__ Ki-Adi-Mundi, Jedi Master (02/44) col. 2 [P4A052] 8.00
__ Kit Fisto, Jedi Master (02/05) col. 1, With Force Action [P4A053] 12.00
__ Kit Fisto, Jedi Master (02/05) col. 1, With Slashing Lightsaber Action...12.00
__ Lott Dod, Neimodian Senator (02/51) col. 2 [P4A054] 8.00
__ Luke Skywalker, Bespin Duel (02/29) col. 1, bloody hand, magnetic [P4A055] 30.00
__ Luke Skywalker, Bespin Duel (02/29) col. 1, bloody hand, magnetic, no tape on hand [P4A056] ...30.00
__ Luke Skywalker, Bespin Duel (02/29) col. 1, no blood, magnetic...............................10.00
__ Luke Skywalker, Bespin Duel (02/29) col. 1, no blood, pegged [P4A057]................................10.00
__ Luminara Unduli, Jedi Master (02/26) col. 2, "Removable Cloak" listed [P4A058]................8.00
__ Luminara Unduli, Jedi Master (02/26) col. 2, 1 blue tape over "Removable Cloak" [P4A059]...........8.00

__ Luminara Unduli, Jedi Master (02/26) col. 2, 1 blue tape over "Removable" [P4A060] 8.00
__ Luminara Unduli, Jedi Master (02/26) col. 2, 2 blue tapes over "Removable Cloak".........................8.00
__ Mace Windu, Genosian Rescue (02/28) col. 1 [P4A061] 8.00
__ Massiff (02/34) col. 2, bubble covers left front leg 8.00
__ Massiff (02/34) col. 2, bubble exposes left front leg [P4A062]....................................8.00
__ Nikto, Jedi Knight (02/21) col. 2 [P4A063]......15.00
__ Obi-Wan Kenobi Jedi Starfighter Pilot (02/36) col. 1 [P4A064] 8.00
__ Obi-Wan Kenobi, Coruscant chase (02/03) col. 1 [P4A065] 6.00
__ Orn Free Ta (02/35) col. 2, bubble tabs, horns are unsecured [P4A066] 8.00
__ Orn Free Ta (02/35) col. 2, bubble wings, horns are rubber-banded...
__ Padme Amidala, Arena Escape (02/02) col. 1, mole on left cheek 10.00
__ Padme Amidala, Arena Escape (02/02) col. 1, no mole, gun barrel in bubble [P4A067] 10.00
__ Padme Amidala, Arena Escape (02/02) col. 1, no mole, gun barrel in tray 10.00
__ Padme Amidala, Coruscant Attack (02/41) col. 1 [P4A068] 15.00
__ Padme Amidala, Coruscant Attack (02/41) col. 1, original text on back 15.00
__ Padme Amidala, Coruscant Attack (02/41) col. 1, text correction sticker on back [P4A069].......15.00
__ Plo Koon (02/12) col. 2 [P4A070].......................7.00
__ Qui-Gon Jinn (02/32) col. 2 [P4A071] 10.00
__ R2-D2, Coruscant sentry (02/14) col. 1, round shoulder pegs [P4A072]................................12.00
__ R2-D2, Coruscant sentry (02/14) col. 1, star design shoulder pegs [P4A073] 10.00
__ Rebel Trooper, Tantive IV Defender (02/54) col. 2, black hair [P4A074]................................15.00
__ Rebel Trooper, Tantive IV Defender (02/54) col. 2, brown hair [P4A075]................................15.00
__ Royal Guard, Coruscant Security (02/19) col. 2, force pike extends into bubble tray [P4A076]..12.00
__ Royal Guard, Coruscant Security (02/19) col. 2, force pike stays in main bubble......................12.00
__ Saesee Tiin, Jedi Master (02/20) col. 2 [P4A077] 10.00
__ Shaak Ti, Jedi (02/10) col. 2 [P4A078].........12.00
__ Super Battle Droid (02/06) col. 1, battle damage sticker, dull figure finish 10.00

__ Super Battle Droid (02/06) col. 1, battle damage sticker, glossy figure finish 10.00
__ Super Battle Droid (02/06) col. 1, corrected cardback, dull figure finish [P4A079] 10.00
__ Supreme Chancellor Palpatine (02/39) col. 2 [P4A080] 8.00
__ Supreme Chancellor Palpatine (02/39) col. 2, rubber-banded around neck..........................8.00
__ Taun We, Kamino Cloner (02/25) col. 2 [P4A081] 12.00
__ Teebo (02/57) col. 2 [P4A082] 25.00
__ Teemto Pagalies, Pod Racer (02/46) col. 1 [P4A083] 8.00
__ Tusken Raider with Massiff (02/52) col. 2 [P4A084] 8.00
__ Tusken Raider, Female with Tusken child (02/08) col. 2 [P4A085]...............................10.00
__ Watto, Mos Espa Junk Dealer (02/50) col. 2 [P4A086] 8.00
__ Yoda, Jedi High Council (02/53) col. 1 [P4A087] 15.00
__ Yoda, Jedi High Council (02/53) col. 1, tab extends over head [P4A088] 15.00
__ Yoda, Jedi Master (02/23) col. 1, missing "TM" next to lightsaber [P4A089] 10.00
__ Yoda, Jedi Master (02/23) col. 1, no tab over head..10.00
__ Yoda, Jedi Master (02/23) col. 1, tab extends over head..10.00
__ Zam Wesell (02/18) col. 1, Face Reveal Mask [P4A090] 10.00
__ Zam Wesell (02/18) col. 1, Face Reveal Mask, bubble angled above mask [P4A091]...............8.00
__ Zam Wesell (02/18) col. 1, Face Reveal Mask, spoiler picture on back of card [P4A092] 8.00
__ Zam Wesell (02/18) col. 1, Quick Draw Action [P4A093] 8.00

Hasbro, Canada
Blue cards. Swirl pattern on background. Tri-language packaging.
__ Anakin Skywalker Hangar Duel.........................8.00
__ Anakin Skywalker Outland Peasant Disguise...8.00
__ Anakin Skywalker Tatooine Attack 8.00
__ Battle Droid Arena Battle 8.00
__ Boba Fett Kamino Escape 8.00
__ C-3PO Protocol Droid.....................................8.00
__ Captain Typho Padme's Head of Security 8.00
__ Chewbacca Cloud City Capture......................8.00
__ Clone Trooper...8.00
__ Count Dooku Dark Lord..................................8.00

Padmé Amidala

P4A069 detail

P4A070

P4A071

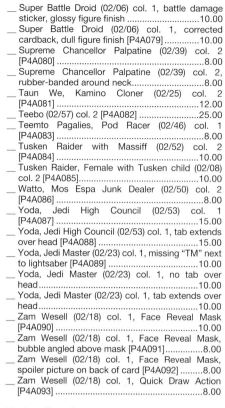

P4A072 detail

P4A073 detail

P4A073

P4A074

P4A074 detail

P4A075 detail

P4A076

P4A077

| P4A078 | P4A079 | | P4A080 | P4A081 | P4A082 | P4A083 |

__ Darth Maul Sith Training 8.00
__ Darth Vader Bespin Duel 8.00
__ Destroyer Droid Arena Battle.............................8.00
__ Dexter Jettster Coruscant Informant 8.00
__ Djas Puhr Alien Bounty Hunter 8.00
__ Eeth Koth Jedi Master 8.00
__ Endor Rebel Soldier...8.00
__ Endor Rebel Soldier without Beard 8.00
__ Ephant Mon Jabba's Head of Security............8.00
__ Geonosian Warrior 8.00
__ Han Solo Endor Raid 8.00
__ Imperial Officer 1st sculpt..................................8.00
__ Imperial Officer 2nd sculpt 8.00
__ Jango Fett Final Battle...8.00
__ Jango Fett Kamino Escape..................................8.00
__ Jango Fett Slave I Pilot.......................................8.00
__ Jar Jar Binks Gungan Senator.........................8.00
__ Ki-Adi-Mundi Jedi Master 8.00
__ Kit Fisto Jedi Master 8.00
__ Lott Dod Neimoidian Senator 8.00
__ Luke Skywalker Bespin Duel 8.00
__ Luminara Unduli Jedi Master.............................8.00
__ Mace Windu Geonosian Rescue 8.00
__ Massiff 8.00
__ Nikto Jedi Master 8.00
__ Obi-Wan Kenobi Coruscant Chase 8.00
__ Obi-Wan Kenobi Jedi Starfighter Pilot.............8.00
__ Orn Free Ta 8.00
__ Padme Amidala Arena Escape 8.00
__ Padme Amidala Coruscant Attack....................8.00
__ Plo Koon Arena Battle...8.00
__ Qui- Gon Jinn Jedi Master..................................8.00
__ R2-D2 Coruscant Sentry 8.00
__ Rebel Fleet Trooper, black hair.........................8.00

__ Rebel Fleet Trooper, brown hair.......................8.00
__ Royal Guard Coruscant Security 8.00
__ SaeSee Tiin Jedi Master.....................................8.00
__ Shaak Ti Jedi Master 8.00
__ Super Battle Droid 8.00
__ Supreme Chancellor Palpatine 8.00
__ Taun We Kamino Cloner......................................8.00
__ Teebo..8.00
__ Teemto Pagalies Pod Racer 8.00
__ Tusken Raider Female with Child Tusken 8.00
__ Tusken Raider with Massiff................................8.00
__ Watto Mos Espa Junk Dealer 8.00
__ Yoda Jedi High Council 8.00
__ Zam Wesell Bounty Hunter 8.00

Action Figures: 2002-2004 (Saga 2003)

Hasbro

Blue cards. Starburst pattern on background.

__ Aayla Secura (03/ 11), col. 2 [P4B001] 12.00
__ Anakin Skywalker, Secret Ceremony (03/ 07), col. 1 [P4B002] 10.00
__ Ashla and Jempa (03/ 16), col. 2, correct UPC 0-76930-84970-5 [P4B003] 8.00
__ Ashla and Jempa (03/ 16), col. 2, rounded UPC correction sticker 8.00
__ Ashla and Jempa (03/ 16), col. 2, square UPC correction sticker 8.00
__ Ashla and Jempa (03/ 16), col. 2, wrong UPC 0-76930-84970-3 [P4B004] 8.00
__ Bariss Offee (03/ 12), col. 2 [P4B005].............12.00
__ Boba Fett, Pit of Carkoon (03/ 08), col. 1, blue [P4B006] 18.00

__ Boba Fett, Pit of Carkoon (03/ 08), col. 1, green [P4B007] 18.00
__ Chewbacca, Mynock Hunt (03/ 14), col. 1 [P4B008] 10.00
__ Darth Tyrannus, Geonosian Escape (03/ 03), col. 1 [P4B009] 15.00
__ Han Solo, Hoth Rescue (03/ 13), col. 1, blue coat, black-and-silver lightsaber handle [P4B010] 10.00
__ Han Solo, Hoth Rescue (03/ 13), col. 1, blue coat, silver lightsaber handle [P4B011] ..10.00
__ Lama Su and Clone Youth (03/ 10), col. 2 [P4B012] 20.00
__ Mace Windu, Arena Confrontation (03/ 02), col. 1 [P4B013] 20.00
__ Obi-Wan, Acklay Battle (03/ 01), col. 1 [P4B014].....15.00
__ Padme Amidala, Droid Factory Chase (03/ 4), col. 2 [P4B015] 20.00
__ R2-D2, Droid Factory Flight (03/ 9), col. 1, long boosters [P4B016] 10.00
__ R2-D2, Droid Factory Flight (03/ 9), col. 1, short boosters 10.00
__ SP-4 and JN-66 (03/ 05), col. 2, SP-4 has long codpiece [P4B017] 12.00
__ SP-4 and JN-66 (03/ 05), col. 2, SP-4 has short codpiece 12.00
__ Tusken Raider, Tatooine Camp Ambush (03/ 6), col. 2 [P4B018] 18.00
__ Tusken Raider, Tatooine Camp Ambush (03/ 6), col. 2, rubber-banded right arm 18.00
__ Yoda and Chian, Padawan Lightsaber Training (03/ 15), col. 2, correct UPC 0-76930-84969-9 ......8.00
__ Yoda and Chian, Padawan Lightsaber Training (03/ 15), col. 2, no. 15, wrong UPC 0-76390-84969-7,

| P4A084 | P4A085 | P4A086 | P4A087 | P4A088 | P4A089 |

| P4A090 | P4A093 | P4A091 detail | P4A092 | P4A092 detail | P4A094 |

P4B001

P4B002

P4B003

P4B004

P4B005

P4B006

P4B007

P4B006 detail

P4B007 detail

P4B008

P4B009

P4B010

long cane tray [P4B019] 8.00
__ Yoda and Chian, Padawan Lightsaber Training (03/ 15), col. 2, rounded UPC sticker, cane tray shortened..8.00
__ Yoda and Chian, Padawan Lightsaber Training (03/ 15), col. 2, square UPC sticker 8.00

Hasbro, Canada
Blue cards. Starburst pattern on background. Tri-language packaging.
__ Anakin Skywalker Secret Ceremony.................8.00
__ Boba Fett The Pitt of Carcoon.........................8.00
__ Chewbacca Mynock Hunt 8.00
__ Clone Trooper Republic Gunship Pilot [P4B020] 8.00
__ Han Solo Hoth Rescue 8.00

__ Mace Windu Arena Confrontation 8.00
__ Obi-Wan Kenobi Ackley Battle 8.00
__ R2-D2 Droid Factory Flight...............................8.00
__ Yoda Jedi Master...8.00

Action Figures: 2002-2004 (Saga 2004)

Hasbro
Gold bar on blue card.
__ Admiral Ozzel (04/16) [P4C001].....................12.00
__ Bossk, Executor Meeting (04/18), wrong image of Tanus Spijek on back of card [P4C002] 12.00
__ Captain Antilles (04/15) [P4C003]..................15.00
__ Dengar, Executor Meeting (04/17) [P4C004]..10.00
__ Dutch Vander (Gold Leader) (04/13)

[P4C005] 15.00
__ General Jan Dodonna (04/12) [P4C006].........10.00
__ General Madine (04/20) [P4C007]...................25.00
__ Han Solo, Endor Strike (04/19) [P4C008] 15.00
__ Hoth Trooper, Hoth Evacuation (04/01) [P4C009] 8.00
__ J'Quille (04/09) [P4C010] 15.00
__ Lando Calrissian, Death Star Attack (04/21) [P4C011] 20.00
__ Lando Calrissian, skiff guard disguise (04/07) [P4C012] 7.00
__ Luke Skywalker, Holographic (04/11) [P4C013] 12.00
__ Luke Skywalker, Hoth Attack (04/03) [P4C014]8.00
__ Luke Skywalker, Jabba's Palace (04/04)

P4B011

P4B010 detail

P4B012 detail

P4B012

P4B013

P4B014

P4B015

P4B016

P4B017

P4B018

P4B019

P4B020

Action Figures

Admiral Ozzel

P4C001

Bossk

P4C002

Captain Antilles

P4C003

Dengar

P4C004

Dutch Vander Gold Leader

P4C005

General Jan Dodonna

P4C006

General Madine

P4C007

Han Solo

P4C008

Hoth Trooper

P4C009

J'Quille

P4C010

Lando Calrissian

P4C011

Lando Calrissian

P4C012

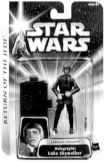

Holographic Luke Skywalker

P4C013

Luke Skywalker

P4C014

Luke Skywalker

P4C015

R-3PO

P4C016

R1-G4

P4C017

R2-D2

P4C018

Rappertunie

P4C019

Tanus Spijek

P4C020

TIE Fighter Pilot

P4C021

Aayla Secura

P4C022

Achk Med-Beq

P4C023

Anakin Skywalker

P4C024

Ashla & Jempa

P4C025

Ayy Vida

P4C026

Bail Organa

P4C027

Barriss Offee

P4C028

Boba Fett

P4C029

C-3PO

P4C030

Coleman Trebor
P4C031

Darth Maul
P4C032

Darth Vader
P4C033

Darth Vader
P4C034

P4C035 detail

P4C036 detail

Elan Sleazebaggano
P4C036

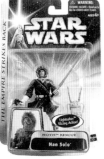
Han Solo
P4C037

Imperial Dignitary
P4C038

Imperial Dignitary
P4C039

Jango Fett
P4C040

Lt. Dannl Faytonni
P4C041

Luke Skywalker
P4C042

Luke Skywalker
P4C043

Luke Skywalker
P4C044

Obi-Wan Kenobi
P4C045

Padmé Amidala
P4C046

Padmé Amidala
P4C047

Princess Leia Organa
P4C048

Snowtrooper
P4C049

Stormtrooper
P4C050

The Emperor
P4C051

WA-7
P4C052

Wat Tambor
P4C053

Yoda & Chian
P4C054

Anakin Skywalker
P4C055

Anakin Skywalker
P4C056

C-3PO
P4C057

C-3PO
P4C058

Chewbacca
P4C059

P4C060

P4C061

P4C062

P4C063

P4C064

P4C065

P4C066

P4C067

P4C068

P4C069

P4C070

P4C071

P4C072

P4C073

[P4C015] 18.00
__ R-3PO, Hoth Evacuation (04/02) [P4C016].....10.00
__ R1-G4 (04/06) [P4C017] 15.00
__ R2-D2, Jabba's Sail Barge (04/05) [P4C018] ...8.00
__ Rappertunie (04/08) [P4C019] 10.00
__ Tanus Spijek (04/10) [P4C020] 12.00
__ TIE Fighter Pilot (04/14) [P4C021]..................12.00

Gold bar on blue card. 2003/2004 transition figures.
__ Aayla Secura (03/11) [P4C022].....................10.00
__ Achk Med-Beq, Coruscant Outlander Club (03/37), col. 2 [P4C023] 10.00
__ Anakin Skywalker, Secret Ceremony (03/07), no col. [P4C024]...8.00
__ Ashla and Jempa (03/16), no col. [P4C025] 8.00
__ Ayy Vida, Outlander Nightclub Patron (03/38), col. 2, no rubber bands in bubble [P4C026]..........10.00
__ Ayy Vida, Outlander Nightclub Patron (03/38), col. 2, rubber band secures arms in bubble..........10.00
__ Bail Organa, Alderaan Senator (03/33), col. 2 [P4C027] 10.00
__ Bariss Offee (03/12), no col. [P4C028] 12.00
__ Boba Fett, Pit of Carkoon (03/08), green [P4C029] 17.00
__ C-3PO, Tatooine Ambush (03/21), col. 1 [P4C030]..20.00
__ Coleman Trebor (03/24), col. 2 [P4C031] 25.00
__ Darth Maul, Theed Hangar Duel (03/25), col. 2 [P4C032] 10.00
__ Darth Maul, Theed Hangar Duel (03/25), col. 2, insert says no. 23...10.00
__ Darth Vader, Death Star Clash (03/32), col. 2 [P4C033] 15.00
__ Darth Vader, Throne Room Duel (03/18), col. 1..20.00

__ Darth Vader, Throne Room Duel (03/18), no col. [P4C034] 20.00
__ Elan Sleazebaggano, Outlander Nightclub Encounter (03/40), col. 2, with ears [P4C035] 15.00
__ Elan Sleazebaggano, Outlander Nightclub Encounter (03/40), col. 2, without ears [P4C036]..............15.00
__ Han Solo, Flight to Alderaan (03/27), col. 2 ......8.00
__ Han Solo, Flight to Alderaan (03/27), col. 2, insert says no. 25..8.00
__ Han Solo, Hoth Rescue (03/13), no col., brown coat [P4C037]..15.00
__ Imperial Dignitary Janus Greejatus, Death Star Procession (03/35), col. 2 [P4C038] 10.00
__ Imperial Dignitary Kren Blista-Vanee, Death Star Procession (03/41), col. 2 [P4C039] 10.00
__ Jango Fett, Kamino Escape (03/20), col. 1, no arrow on back of card...12.00
__ Jango Fett, Kamino Escape (03/20), col. 1, yellow arrow printed on back of card [P4C040] 12.00
__ Jango Fett, Kamino Escape (03/20), col. 1, yellow arrow sticker on back of card.........................12.00
__ Lt. Dannl Faytonni, Coruscant Outlander Club (03/29), col. 2, pink cup [P4C041] 15.00
__ Luke Skywalker, Tatooine Encounter (03/31), col. 2, clear base [P4C042].....................................10.00
__ Luke Skywalker, Throne Room Duel (03/17), col. 1, left hand gloved [P4C043] 30.00
__ Luke Skywalker, Throne Room Duel (03/17), col. 1, right hand gloved [P4C044].............................15.00
__ Luke Skywalker, Throne Room Duel (03/17), no col., right hand gloved 15.00
__ Obi-Wan Kenobi, Outlander Nightclub Encounter (03/39), col. 2 [P4C045] 10.00
__ Padme Amidala, Lars' Homestead (03/36), col. 2 [P4C046] 20.00
__ Padme Amidala, Secret Ceremony (03/22), col. 2 [P4C047] 20.00
__ Padme Amidala, Secret Ceremony (03/22), col. 2, rubber band around left arm..........................20.00
__ Princess Leia Organa, Imperial Captive (03/26), col. 2 [P4C048] 10.00
__ Princess Leia Organa, Imperial Captive (03/26), col. 2, bubble tab around right hip 10.00
__ Snowtrooper, Battle of Hoth (03/19), col. 1 ....15.00
__ Snowtrooper, Battle of Hoth (03/19), no col. [P4C049] 15.00
__ Stormtrooper, concept (03/34), col. 2, fans' choice figure no. 4 [P4C050] 50.00
__ The Emperor, Throne Room (03/30), col. 2 [P4C051] 25.00

__ WA-7 (03/28), col. 2 [P4C052] 12.00
__ Wat Tambor (03/23), col. 2 [P4C053] 18.00
__ Yoda and Chian, Padawan Lightsaber Training (03/15), no col. [P4C054] 8.00

Gold bar on blue card. Hall of Fame asst.
__ Anakin Skywalker, Geonosis Hangar Duel, age warning printed on front [P4C055]................8.00
__ Anakin Skywalker, Geonosis Hangar Duel, age warning sticker on front [P4C056] 8.00
__ C-3PO, Death Star Rescue, clear base [P4C057] 12.00
__ C-3PO, Death Star Rescue, dark base [P4C058] 12.00
__ Chewbacca, Escape from Hoth [P4C059].......8.00
__ Darth Maul, Theed Hangar Duel, clear base...10.00
__ Darth Maul, Theed Hangar Duel, dark base [P4C060] 10.00
__ Darth Vader, Death Star Clash, clear base [P4C061] 10.00
__ Darth Vader, Death Star Clash, dark base [P4C062] 10.00
__ Han Solo, Flight to Alderaan, clear base [P4C063] 10.00
__ Han Solo, Flight to Alderaan, dark base [P4C064] 10.00
__ Luke Skywalker, Tatooine Encounter, clear base [P4C065] 10.00
__ Luke Skywalker, Tatooine Encounter, dark base [P4C066] 10.00
__ Obi-Wan Kenobi, Coruscant Chase [P4C067] 10.00
__ Princess Leia Organa, Death Star Captive, clear base [P4C068] 10.00
__ Princess Leia Organa, Death Star Captive, dark base [P4C069] 10.00
__ R2-D2, clear base [P4C070] 10.00
__ R2-D2, dark base [P4C071]............................10.00
__ Stormtrooper, Death Star Chase [P4C072] 20.00
__ Yoda, Battle of Geonosis [P4C073]................10.00

Hasbro, Canada
Gold bar on blue card. Tri-language.
__ Admiral Ozzel, Executor Assault.....................8.00
__ Anakin Skywalker, Geonosis Hangar Duel 8.00
__ Bossk, Executor Meeting................................8.00
__ C-3PO, Death Star Rescue...............................8.00
__ Captain Antilles, Tantive IV Invasion.................8.00
__ Chewbacca, Escape from Hoth.......................8.00
__ Darth Maul, Theed Hangar Duel 8.00
__ Darth Vader, Death Star Clash 8.00

AFD001

AFD002

AFD003

AFD004

AFD005

AFD006

AFD007

AFD008

AFD009

AFD010

AFD011

AFD012

AFD013

AFD014

AFD015

AFD016

AFD017

AFD018

AFD019

AFD020

AFD021

AFD022

AFD023

AFD024

AFD025

ASM001

ASM002

ASM003

ASM004

ASM005

ASM006

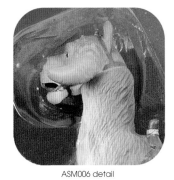

ASM006 detail

ASM007

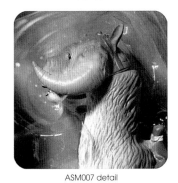

ASM007 detail

ASM008

ASM009

ASM010

ASM011

ASM013

ASM014

ASM012

ASM015

ASM016

ACW001

ACW002

ACW003

ACW004

ACW005

ACW006

ACW007

ACW008

ACW009

ACW010

ACW011

ACW012

ACW012 detail

ACW013 detail

ACW014

ACW015

ACW016

ACW017

ACW018

ACW019

ACW020

ACW021

ACW022

ACW023

ACW024

ACW025

ACW026

ACW027

ACW028

ACW029

Action Figures

CVP001

CVP002

CVP003

CVP004

ACD001

ACD002

ACD003

ACD004

ACD005

__ Dengar, Executor Meeting 8.00
__ Dutch Vander, Gold Leader, Battle of Yavin.....8.00
__ General Jan Dodonna, Battle of Yavin 8.00
__ General Madine, Imperial Shuttle Capture 8.00
__ Han Solo, Endor Strike 8.00
__ Han Solo, Flight to Alderaan...........................8.00
__ Hoth Trooper, Hoth Evacuation.......................8.00
__ J'Quille, Jabba's Sail Barge 8.00
__ Lando Calrissian, Death Star Attack.................8.00
__ Lando Calrissian, Jabba's Sail Barge...............8.00
__ Luke Skywalker, holograph 8.00
__ Luke Skywalker, Hoth Attack...........................8.00
__ Luke Skywalker, Jabba's Palace.......................8.00
__ Luke Skywalker, Tatooine Encounter 8.00
__ Obi-Wan Kenobi Coruscant Chase 8.00
__ Obi-Wan Kenobi Coruscant Chase 8.00
__ Princess Leia Organa, Death Star Captive 8.00
__ R2-D2, Jabba's Sail Barge 8.00
__ R2-D2, Tatooine Mission 8.00
__ Rappertunie, Jabba's Palace............................8.00
__ Stormtrooper, Death Star Chase......................8.00
__ Tanus Spijec, Jabba's Barge............................8.00
__ TIE Fighter Pilot, Battle of Yavin 8.00
__ Yoda, Battle of Geonosis.................................8.00

Action Figures: 2002-2004 (Saga Deluxe / Ultra)

Hasbro

__ Anakin Skywalker with Force-Flipping Attack! [AFD001] 8.00
__ Anakin Skywalker with Lightsaber Slashing Action [AFD002] 7.00
__ C-3PO with Droid Factory Assembly Line [AFD003] 12.00
__ Clone Trooper with Speeder Bike [AFD004] 20.00
__ Darth Tyranus with Force-Flipping Attack! [AFD005] 7.00
__ Flying Geonosian with Attack Pod [AFD006]..15.00
__ Jango Fett with Electronic Jetpack and Snap-On Armor! [AFD007] 8.00
__ Jango Fett with Electronic Jetpack and Snap-On Armor!, no pegholes in feet 35.00
__ Jango Fett, Kamino Showdown [AFD008]......12.00
__ Mace Windu with Blast-Apart (red) Battle Droid, red droid on header card [5:353] 15.00
__ Mace Windu with Blast-Apart (white) Battle Droid, red droid on header card [AFD009] 40.00
__ Mace Windu with Blast-Apart (white) Battle Droid, white droid on header card [AFD010].............10.00

__ Mace Windu with Blast-Apart (white) Battle Droid, white droid on header card, no pegholes in feet...25.00
__ Obi-Wan Kenobi with Force-Flipping Attack! [AFD011] 6.00
__ Obi-Wan Kenobi, Kamino Showdown [AFD012] 12.00
__ Spider Droid [AFD013]..................................20.00
__ Super Battle Droid Builder [AFD014] 15.00
__ Yoda with Force Powers [AFD015]................12.00

Patrons with Cantina Bar Sections. Walmart exclusives.
__ Dr. Evazan [AFD016]...................................125.00
__ Greedo [AFD017] 20.00
__ Kitik Keed'kak [AFD018] 75.00
__ Momaw Nadon [AFD019] 15.00
__ Ponda Baba [AFD020] 15.00
__ Wuher [AFD021]..125.00

Ultra.
__ C-3PO with escape pod [AFD022] 20.00
__ General Reikein with Yavin tactical screen [AFD023] 15.00
__ Jango Fett, Kamino Confrontation [AFD024]..12.00
__ Obi-Wan Kenobi, Kamino Confrontation [AFD025] 16.00

Hasbro, Canada
__ Anakin Skywalker with Force-Flipping Attack!..10.00
__ Anakin Skywalker with Lightsaber Attack.......15.00
__ C-3PO with Droid Factory Assembly Line 15.00
__ Clone Trooper with Speeder Bike...................10.00
__ Darth Tyranus with Force-Flipping Attack! 10.00
__ Flying Geonosian with Attack Pod..................14.00
__ Jango Fett with Electronic Jetpack and Snap-On Armor...15.00
__ Mace Windu with Blast-Apart Battle Droid.....15.00
__ Mace Windu with Blast-Apart Battle Droid, red..10.00
__ Obi-Wan Kenobi with Force Flipping Attack ..10.00
__ Yoda with Force Powers................................15.00

Action Figures: 2002-2004 (Saga Multi-Packs)

Hasbro

__ 4-pack, random figures, exclusive to KB Toys [ASM001] 20.00

__ 4-pack, random figures, age warning sticker, exclusive to KB Toys [ASM002]....................20.00
__ Imperial Forces, exclusive to Toys R Us [ASM003] 40.00
__ Jedi Warriors, exclusive to Toys R Us [ASM004] 30.00
__ Skirmish at at Carkoon, exclusive to Toys R Us [ASM005] 40.00
__ The Battle of Hoth, Tauntaun's horn broken [ASM006] 45.00
__ The Battle of Hoth, Tauntaun's horn not broken [ASM007] 45.00
__ Ultimate Bounty, exclusive to Toys R Us [ASM008] 30.00

Death Star Trash Compactor Scene 2-packs, Walmart exclusives.
__ Luke Skywalker and Han Solo [ASM009] 45.00
__ Princess Leia and Chewbacca [ASM010].......45.00

EPII 2-packs. Clear plastic case with barcode stickers covering Hasbro barcodes, and round Bonus sticker. KMart exclusive.
__ Anakin Duel / Anakin Peasant........................14.00
__ Anakin Skywalker / Obi-Wan Kenobi..............14.00
__ Clone Trooper / Anakin Skywalker 14.00
__ Jango Fett / Yoda [ASM011] 14.00
__ Obi-Wan Kenobi / Jango Fett.........................14.00
__ Yoda / Clone Trooper 14.00

EPII 2-packs. Clear plastic case with barcode stickers covering Hasbro barcodes. BJ's Wholesale Club exclusive.
__ Clone Trooper / Anakin Skywalker - Hangar Duel..18.00
__ Jango Fett - Kamino Escape / C-3PO.............18.00
__ Mace Windu / Jango Fett - Final Battle..........18.00
__ Obi-Wan Kenobi - Super Battle Droid 18.00
__ Obi-Wan Kenobi / Zam Wesell.......................18.00
__ Padme Amidala / Anakin Skywalker - Outland Peasant Disguise 18.00
__ Padme Amidala / Kit Fisto.............................18.00
__ R2-D2 / C-3PO...18.00
__ Yoda / Count Dooku [ASM012] 18.00

Screen Scenes, 3-packs of figures posed.
__ Geonosis War Room 1 [ASM013]....................20.00
__ Geonosis War Room 2 [ASM014]....................20.00
__ Jedi Council 1 [ASM015] 20.00
__ Jedi Council 2 [ASM016] 20.00

ACD006   ACD007   ACD008   ACD009

Action Figures: 2003-2005 (Clone Wars)

Hasbro

ACD010

__ Anakin Skywalker (03/42), glossy painted glove [ACW001]...........10.00
__ Anakin Skywalker (03/42), matte painted glove 10.00
__ ARC Trooper (03/43), blue [ACW002]............25.00
__ ARC Trooper (03/43), red [ACW003] 60.00
__ Asajj Ventress (03/47) [ACW004]...........30.00
__ Clone Trooper (03/50), kneeling [ACW005] 40.00
__ Clone Trooper (03/50), standing [ACW006]....40.00
__ Durge (03/46) [ACW007].................30.00
__ Kit Fisto (03/49) [ACW008].................30.00
__ Mace Windu (03/48) [ACW009].................20.00
__ Obi-Wan Kenobi (03/45) [ACW010] 10.00
__ Saesee Tiin (03/51) [ACW011]...............25.00
__ Yoda (03/44) [ACW012] 10.00
__ Yoda (03/44), top of saber handle unpainted [ACW013]...............10.00

Animation-style figures, Target exclusives.
__ Anakin Skywalker [ACW014] 12.00
__ Asajj Ventress [ACW015] 15.00
__ Clone Trooper [ACW016]...............20.00
__ Count Dooku [ACW017] 10.00
__ Durge [ACW018] 10.00
__ Mace Windu [ACW019]...............12.00
__ Obi-Wan Kenobi [ACW020] 12.00
__ Yoda [ACW021] 25.00

Animation-style figures, Target exclusives. "NEW! Season III" packaging.
__ Anakin Skywalker, duel [ACW022]...............10.00
__ ARC Trooper [ACW023]...............25.00
__ Asajj Ventress [5:355]...............15.00
__ Clone Trooper, blue [ACW024]...............30.00
__ Clone Trooper, red [ACW025] 30.00
__ Clone Trooper, yellow [ACW026]...............30.00
__ Count Dooku [5:355]...............10.00
__ Durge [ACW027] 10.00
__ General Grievous [ACW028] 25.00
__ Mace Windu [ACW029]...............12.00
__ Obi-Wan Kenobi [5:355] 12.00
__ Yoda [5:355]...............25.00

Hasbro, Canada
Animation-style figures, tri-language packaging.
__ Anakin Skywalker...............7.00
__ ARC Trooper...............7.00

__ Clone Trooper, blue...............7.00
__ Clone Trooper, red...............7.00
__ Clone Trooper, yellow...............7.00
__ General Grievous 7.00

Action Figures: 2003-2005 (Clone Wars Deluxe)

Hasbro
Army of the Republic.
__ Clone Trooper with Speeder Bike [CVP001]...20.00

Separatist Forces.
__ Destroyer Droid Battle Launcher [CVP002] 12.00
__ Durge with Swoop Bike [CVP003] 20.00
__ Spider Droid [CVP004]...........15.00

ACD011

Action Figures: 2003-2005 (Clone Wars) Multi-Packs

Hasbro
3-packs.
__ Clone Trooper Army [ACD001] 40.00
__ Clone Trooper Army, blue [ACD002] 50.00
__ Clone Trooper Army, green [ACD003]...........40.00
__ Clone Trooper Army, red [ACD004]...............45.00
__ Clone Trooper Army, yellow [ACD005]...........45.00
__ Droid Army [ACD006] 20.00
__ Jedi Army [ACD007] 30.00
__ Jedi Army, clone side panel [ACD008] 45.00

4-packs. Super articulated clones with limited edition poster. Entertainment Earth exclusives.
__ Blue, green, red, yellow 30.00

AT001   AT002   AT003   AT004

AT005   AT006   AT007   AT008   AT009   AT010

Action Figures

AT011

AT012

AT013

AT014

AT015

AT016

AT017

AT018

AT019

AT020

AT021

AT022

AT023

AT024

AT025

AT026

AT027

AT028

AT029

AT030

AT031

AT032

AT033

AT034

AT035

AT036

AT037

AT038

AT039

AT040

AT041   AT042   AT043   AT044   AT045   AT046

AT047   AT048   AT049   AT050   AT051   AT052

AT053   AT054   AT055   AT056   AT057   AT058

AT059   AT060   AT061   AT062   AT063   AT064

AT065   AT066   AT067   AT068   AT069   AT070

Action Figures

__ Blue, green, red, yellow all battle damaged	40.00
__ White x 4	25.00
__ White x 4 all battle damaged	25.00

Clone Wars figure with bonus Clone Trooper. 2-packs.

__ Anakin Skywalker / Clone Trooper Lieutenant [ACD009]	30.00
__ Arc Trooper / Clone Trooper [ACD010]	30.00
__ Arc Trooper, unpainted right shoulder / Clone Trooper	30.00
__ Yoda / Clone Trooper Commander [ACD011]	25.00

Action Figures: 2004-2005 (Original Trilogy Collection)

Hasbro

__ Bib Fortuna (OTC31) [AT001]	15.00
__ Boba Fett (OTC14) [AT002]	25.00
__ Bossk (OTC28) [AT003]	10.00
__ C-3PO (OTC13) [AT004]	15.00
__ Chewbacca (OTC08) [AT005]	15.00
__ Cloud Car Pilot, Bespin (OTC19) [AT006]	8.00
__ Darth Vader (Death Star) (OTC34) [AT007]	25.00
__ Darth Vader (Hoth) (OTC29) [AT008]	25.00
__ Darth Vader (OTC10) [AT009]	25.00
__ Emperor, Executor Transmission, exclusive to StarWarsShop.com (OTC30) [AT010]	28.00
__ Gamorrean Guard (OTC30) [AT011]	15.00
__ General Madine (OTC36) [AT012]	10.00

__ Greedo (OTC22) [AT013]	20.00
__ Han Solo (AT-ST Driver) (OTC35) [AT014]	25.00
__ Han Solo (OTC07) [AT015]	15.00
__ IG-88 (OTC27) [AT016]	15.00
__ Imperial Trooper (OTC38) [AT017]	20.00
__ Jawas (OTC24) [AT018]	25.00
__ Lando Calrissian (General) (OTC37) [AT019]	15.00
__ Lando Calrissian (Skiff Guard) (OTC32) [AT020]	10.00
__ Lobot, Bespin (OTC20) [AT021]	8.00
__ Luke Skywalker (Bespin Gear) (OTC26) [AT022]	12.00
__ Luke Skywalker, Dagobah (OTC01) [AT023]	12.00
__ Luke Skywalker, Dagobah handstand packaging [AT024]	25.00
__ Luke Skywalker, Jedi (OTC06) [AT025]	15.00
__ Luke Skywalker, X-Wing pilot (OTC05) [AT026]	16.00
__ Obi-Wan Kenobi (OTC15) [AT027]	15.00
__ Obi-Wan Kenobi Spirit, Dagobah (OTC03) [AT028]	15.00
__ Princess Leia (OTC09) [AT029]	20.00
__ Princess Leia (Slave Outfit) (OTC33) [AT030]	12.00
__ Princess Leia, Bespin (OTC18) [AT031]	12.00
__ R2-D2 (OTC12) [AT032]	15.00
__ R2-D2, Dagobah (OTC04) [AT033]	15.00
__ Scout Trooper (OTC11) [AT034]	20.00
__ Snowtrooper (OTC25) [AT035]	20.00
__ Stormtrooper (OTC16) [AT036]	25.00
__ TIE Fighter Pilot (OTC21) [AT037]	20.00
__ Tusken Raider (OTC23) [AT038]	15.00
__ Wedge Antilles, exclusive to StarWarsShop.com	15.00

__ Wicket (OTC17) [AT039]	20.00
__ Yoda, Dagobah (OTC02) [AT040]	10.00

Hasbro, Canada

__ Bib Fortuna	10.00
__ Boba Fett [AT041]	10.00
__ Bossk [AT042]	10.00
__ C-3PO [AT043]	10.00
__ Chewbacca [AT044]	10.00
__ Cloud Car Pilot, Bespin [AT045]	10.00
__ Darth Vader [AT046]	10.00
__ Darth Vader (Hoth)	10.00
__ Gamorrean Guard	10.00
__ General Madine	10.00
__ Greedo [AT047]	10.00
__ Han Solo [AT048]	10.00
__ Han Solo (AT-ST Driver)	10.00
__ IG-88 [AT049]	10.00
__ Imperial Trooper [AT050]	10.00
__ Jawas [AT051]	10.00
__ Lando Calrissian (General)	10.00
__ Lando Calrissian (Skiff Guard) [AT052]	10.00
__ Lobot, Bespin [AT053]	10.00
__ Luke Skywalker, Dagobah [AT054]	10.00
__ Luke Skywalker, Jedi Knight [AT055]	10.00
__ Luke Skywalker, X-Wing pilot [AT056]	10.00
__ Luke Skywalker, Bespin [AT057]	10.00
__ Obi-Wan Kenobi [AT058]	10.00
__ Princess Leia [AT059]	10.00
__ Princess Leia (Slave Outfit)	10.00
__ Princess Leia, Bespin [AT060]	10.00
__ R2-D2 [AT061]	10.00
__ R2-D2, Dagobah [AT062]	10.00
__ Scout Trooper [AT063]	10.00
__ Snowtrooper [AT064]	10.00
__ Spirit Obi-Wan [AT065]	10.00
__ Stormtrooper [AT066]	10.00
__ TIE Fighter Pilot [AT067]	10.00
__ Tusken Raider [AT068]	10.00
__ Wicket [AT069]	10.00
__ Yoda [AT070]	10.00

AOP001

Action Figures: 2004-2005(Original Trilogy Collection Multi-Packs)

Hasbro

__ Bounty Hunter, Diamond excl. [AOP001]	35.00
__ Endor Ambush [AOP002]	40.00
__ Naboo Final Combat [AOP003]	20.00

AOP002

AOP004

AOP005

AOP003

AOP006

AOP007

AOP008

AOP009

Screen Scenes, 3-packs of figures posed.
__ Jedi Council 1 [AOP004]................................35.00
__ Jedi Council 2 [AOP005]................................35.00
__ Jedi Council 3 [AOP006]................................35.00
__ Jedi Council 4 [AOP007]................................35.00
__ MosEisley Cantina 1 [AOP008].......................40.00
__ MosEisley Cantina 2 [AOP009].......................40.00

Action Figures: 2005 (Saga)

Hasbro
__ Chewbacca, Hoth Escape [AT1001]...............12.00
__ Dannik Jerriko, Cantina Encounter [AT1002]..15.00
__ Darth Vader, Death Star Hangar [AT1003]......20.00

__ Feltipern   Trevagg,   Cantina   Encounter
    [AT1004]..14.00
__ Han Solo, Mos Eisley Escape [AT1005]..........10.00
__ Luke Skywalker, Dagobah Training [AT1006].15.00
__ Myo, Cantina Encounter [AT1007]..................12.00
__ Pablo Jill, Geonosis Arena [AT1008]...............24.00
__ Queen   Amidala,   Celebration   Ceremony
    [AT1009]..18.00
__ Rabe, Queen's Chambers [AT1010] 18.00
__ Sandtrooper, Tatooine Search [AT1011]........45.00
__ Scout Trooper, Endor Raid [AT1012]..............25.00
__ Sly Moore, Coruscant Senate [AT1013] 18.00
__ Stormtrooper, Death Star Attack [AT1014].....25.00
__ Yarua, Coruscant Senate [AT1015] 17.00
__ Yoda, Dagobah Training [AT1016]..................16.00

Hasbro, Canada
Black-and-silver cards with starburst background.
__ Pablo Jill, Genonsis Arena 7.00
__ Rabe, Queens Chambers 7.00
__ Sly Moore, Coruscant Senate...........................7.00
__ Yarua, Coruscant Senate.................................7.00

Action Figures: 2005 (Early Bird)

Hasbro
__ Mailer with certificate, limited to 50,000.........45.00
__ Mailer with certificate, extended offer stickers,
    limited to 50,000 [A6T001]..............................45.00
__ Mailer with figures and packaging.................50.00

AT1001

AT1002

AT1003

AT1004

AT1005

AT1006

AT1007

AT1008

AT1009

AT1010

AT1011

AT1012

AT1013

AT1014

AT1015

AT1016

A6T001

Action Figures

Hasbro
____ General Grievous [ATD001] 15.00
____ R4-G9 [ATD002] 15.00
____ Tion Medon [ATD003] 15.00
____ Wookiee Warrior [ATD004] 8.00

Hasbro, Canada
Multi-language packaging.
____ General Grievous 8.00
____ R4-G9 .... 8.00
____ Tion Medon 8.00
____ Wookiee Warrior 8.00

ATD001

ATD002

ATD003

ATD004

AT3001

AT3002

AT3003

AT3004

AT3005

AT3006

AT3007

AT3008

AT3009

AT3010

AT3011

AT3012

AT3013

AT3014

AT3015

AT3016

AT3017

AT3018

AT3019

AT3020

AT3021

AT3022

AT3023

AT3024

AT3025

AT3026

AT3027

AT3028

AT3029

AT3030

AT3031

AT3032

AT3033

AT3034

AT3035

AT3036

AT3037

AT3038

AT3039

AT3040

AT3041

AT3042

AT3043

AT3044

AT3045

AT3046

AT3047

AT3048

AT3049

AT3050

AT3051

AT3052

AT3053

AT3054

AT3055

AT3056

AT3057

AT3058

AT3059

AT3060

AT3061

AT3062

AT3063

AT3064

AT3065

AT3066

AT3067

AT3068

AT3069

AT3070

AT3071

AT3072

AT3073

AT3074

AT3075

AT3076

AT3077

AT3078

AT3079

AT3080

AT3081

AT3082

AT3083

AT3084

Action Figures: 2005 (Episode III)

Hasbro

__ Aayla Secura, Hologram (#67) [AT3001].........15.00
__ Aayla Secura, Jedi Knight (#32) [AT3002].........6.00
__ Agen Kolar, Jedi Master (#20) [AT3003] 6.00
__ Anakin Skywalker, battle damage (#50) [AT3004]..6.00
__ Anakin Skywalker, Lightsaber Attack! (#2) [AT3005]..6.00
__ Anakin Skywalker, Lightsaber Attack! with red Sith lightsaber (#2) [AT3006] 9.00
__ Anakin Skywalker, Lightsaber Attack! with red transparent Sith lightsaber (#2) [AT3007] 10.00
__ Anakin Skywalker, Slashing Attack (#28) [AT3008]..6.00
__ Anakin Skywalker, Slashing Attack with yellow eyes (#28) [AT3009].................................25.00
__ Ask Aak (#46) [AT3010]...................................12.00
__ AT-RT Driver brown and white mask (#54) [AT3011]..8.00
__ AT-RT Driver brown mask (#45) [AT3012] 8.00
__ AT-TE Tank Gunner, Clone Army (#38) [AT3013]..8.00
__ Bail Organa, Republic Senator (#15) [AT3014] .5.00
__ Battle Droid, Separatist Army (#17) [AT3015]...8.00
__ C-3PO, Protocol Droid (#18) [AT3016] 8.00
__ Captain Antilles (#51) [AT3017]........................6.00
__ Cat Miin, Separatist (#62) [AT3018] 8.00
__ Chancellor Palpatine, Supreme Chancellor (#14) [AT3019]..6.00
__ Chewbacca, Wookiee Rage (#5) [AT3020] 6.00
__ Clone Commander, green highlights (#33) [AT3021]..9.00

__ Clone Commander, red highlights (#33) [AT3022]..8.00
__ Clone Pilot black armor (#34) [AT3023] 20.00
__ Clone Pilot white armor (#34) [AT3024] 15.00
__ Clone Trooper super articulated (#41) [AT3025]..8.00
__ Clone Trooper with display case, exclusive to Target [AT3026] 35.00
__ Clone trooper, Quick-Draw Attack (#6) [AT3027]..8.00
__ Clone trooper, Quick-Draw Attack with red and white armor (#6) [AT3028]..............................9.00
__ Commander Bacara (#49) [AT3029] 8.00
__ Commander Bly, Battle Gear white shoulder joints (#57)..8.00
__ Commander Bly, Battle Gear yellow shoulder joints (#57) [AT3030]...8.00
__ Commander Bly, Battle Gear yellow shoulder joints with battle damaged armor (#57).....................8.00
__ Commander Gree, Battle Gear (#59) [AT3031]..8.00
__ Count Dooku (#13) [AT3032] 6.00
__ Darth Vader at Mustafar, Lava Reflection, exclusive to Target [AT3033].............................30.00
__ Darth Vader lava reflection with display case, exclusive to Target [AT3034] 90.00
__ Darth Vader, Lightsaber Attack! (#11) [AT3035]..6.00
__ Destroyer Droid (#44) [AT3036] 8.00
__ Emperor Palpatine, Firing Force Lightning (#12) [AT3037]..6.00
__ Emperor, Holographic, exclusive to Toys R Us [AT3038]..25.00
__ General Grievous (#36) [AT3039] 8.00

__ General Grievous, Four Lightsabers Attack! (#9) [AT3040]..8.00
__ Grievous' Bodyguard silver, Battle Attack! (#60) [AT3041]..15.00
__ Grievous' Bodyguard, Battle Attack! (#8) [AT3042]..6.00
__ Ki-Adi Mundi, Jedi Master (#29) [AT3043]........6.00
__ Kit Fisto, Jedi Master (#22) [AT3044]................8.00
__ Luminara Unduli, Jedi Master (#31) [AT3045]...8.00
__ Mace Windu, Force Combat (#10) [AT3046] 8.00
__ Mas Amedda, Republic Senator (#40) [AT3047]..8.00
__ Meena Tills (#47) [AT3048].............................16.00
__ Mon Mothma, Republic Senator (#24) [AT3049]..6.00
__ Mustafar Sentry (#56) [AT3050] 8.00
__ Neimoidian Commander, Separatist Bodyguard (#63) [AT3051]..8.00
__ Neimoidian Warrior (#42) [AT3052]..................8.00
__ Obi-Wan Kenobi Duel at Mustafar, Lava Reflection, exclusive to Target [AT3053] 30.00
__ Obi-Wan Kenobi, Jedi Kick! (#27) [AT3054] 6.00
__ Obi-Wan Kenobi, pilot gear (#56) [AT3055].......8.00
__ Obi-Wan Kenobi, Slashing Attack (#1) [AT3056]..6.00
__ Padme, Republic Senator (#19) [AT3057]........8.00
__ Palpatine blue lightsaber (#35) [AT3058] 35.00
__ Palpatine red lightsaber (#35) [AT3059]...........8.00
__ Passel Argente, Separatist Leader (#61) [AT3060]..8.00
__ Plo Koon, Hologram (#66) [AT3061] 9.00
__ Plo Koon, Jedi Master (#16) [AT3062] 6.00
__ Polis Massan, Medic (#39) [AT3063] 6.00
__ R2-D2 (#48) [AT3064] 8.00

A4T001

A4T002

A4T003

A4T004

A4T005

A4T006

A4T007

A4T008

A4T009

A4T010

A4T011

A4T012

A4T013

A4T014

A4T015

Action Figures

A5T001

A5T002

A5T003

A8T001

A8T002

__ Tarfful, Firing Bowcaster (#25) [AT3073]...........8.00
__ Tarkin, Govenor (#45) [AT3074] 16.00
__ Utapaun Warrior (#53) [AT3075] 8.00
__ Utapu Shadow Trooper, exclusive to Target..35.00
__ Vader's Medical Droid, Chopper Droid (#37)
[AT3076]..6.00
__ Wookiee Commando, Kashyyyk Battle Bash (#58)
[AT3077]..8.00
__ Wookiee Heavy Gunner (#68) [AT3078].........8.00
__ Wookiee Heavy Gunner (#68) corrected with
sticker 10.00
__ Wookiee Heavy Gunner no. 64 (wrong
number)..10.00
__ Wookiee Warrior brown (#43) [AT3079]............8.00
__ Wookiee Warrior tan (#43) [AT3080]................8.00
__ Yoda, Firing Cannon (#3) [AT3081]..................6.00
__ Yoda, Holographic, exclusive to Toys R Us
[AT3082]...30.00
__ Yoda, Spinning Attack (#26) [AT3083]..............6.00
__ Zett Jukassa (#52) [AT3084] 8.00

__ R2-D2, Droid Attack (#7) [AT3065] 6.00
__ R4-P17 (#64), package number 64 [AT3066] ...8.00
__ R4-P17 (#64), package number 68..................8.00
__ R4-P17 (#64), package stickered as number
64 ....8.00
__ Royal Guard, Senate Security blue (#23)
[AT3067]..8.00

__ Royal Guard, Senate Security red (#23)
[AT3068]..10.00
__ Saesee Tiin, Jedi Master (#30) [AT3069] 6.00
__ Shaak-Ti, Jedi Master (#21) [AT3070]...............6.00
__ Super Battle Droid, Firing Arm Blaster! (#4)
[AT3071]..8.00
__ Tactical Ops Trooper (#65) [AT3072] 8.00

A9T001

A9T002

A9T003

A9T004

A9T005

A9T006

A9T007

A9T008

A9T009

Action Figures: 2005 (Episode III) Action Assortment

Hasbro

__ Anakin Skywalker / Darth Vader [A4T001]......15.00
__ Anakin Skywalker / Darth Vader, accessories in bubble [A4T002]...15.00
__ Clone Trooper with jet pack [A4T003] 15.00
__ Clone Troopers, 3-pack [A4T004]...................20.00
__ Clone Troopers, 3-pack blue.........................30.00
__ Clone Troopers, 3-pack green [A4T005] 30.00
__ Clone Troopers, 3-pack red...........................15.00
__ Crab Droid [A4T006] 15.00
__ Darth Vader with operating table [A4T007].....15.00
__ Emperor Palpatine / Darth Sidious [A4T008]..10.00
__ General Grievous [A4T009]............................15.00
__ Obi-Wan Kenobi and Super Battle Droid [A4T010]..8.00
__ Obi-Wan Kenobi and Super Battle Droid, Super Battle Droid's leg is packed separate [A4T011]..........8.00
__ Spider Droid [A4T012] 15.00
__ Stass Allie with BARC Speed [A4T013] 15.00
__ Vulture Droid (green cockpit)..........................15.00
__ Vulture Droid (red cockpit) [A4T014]...............15.00
__ Yoda with Can Cell [A4T015]..........................12.00

Action Figures: 2005 (Episode III Battle Arena)

Hasbro

__ Anakin Skywalker vs. Count Dooku [A5T001] 12.00
__ Bodyguard vs Obi-Wan [A5T002]....................12.00
__ Sidious vs. Mace [A5T003] 12.00

Action Figures: 2005 (Episode III) Multipacks

Hasbro

__ 9-piece Collector Pack with silver Darth Vader, exclusive to KB Toys [A8T001]......................50.00

Mega Buy 2-packs. Exclusive to Toy R Us.

__ Agen Kolar / Mon Mothma 10.00
__ Ask Aak / Polis Massan 10.00
__ Bail Organa / AT-TE Tank Gunner 10.00
__ Bail Organa / Mon Mothma 10.00
__ Ki-Adi-Mundi / Luminara Unduli 10.00
__ Mas Amedda / Agen Kolar............................10.00
__ Meena Tillis / Bail Organa 10.00
__ Meena Tillis / Mon Mothma 10.00
__ Mon Mothma / Count Dooku...........................10.00
__ Mon Mothma / Luminara Undulli 10.00
__ Polis Massan / Vader's Medical Droid.............10.00
__ R2-D2 / Emperor Palpatine 10.00
__ Saesee Tiin / Plo Koon [A8T002] 10.00
__ Shaak Ti / Agen Kolar 10.00
__ Tarkin / Mon Mothma 10.00

Action Figures: 2005-2007 (Saga2 Battle Packs)

Hasbro

__ Assault on Hoth with sticker correction on warning, exclusive to Toys R Us [A9T001] 45.00
__ Battle Above the Sarlacc [A9T002]................20.00
__ Clone Attack on Coruscant, exclusive to Target [5:361] 50.00

__ Imperial Throne Room, exclusive to K-Mart [A9T003]..55.00
__ Jedi Temple Assault, exclusive to K-Mart [A9T004]..55.00
__ Jedi vs. Darth Sidious [A9T005]......................20.00
__ Jedi vs. Sepratists [A9T006] 20.00
__ Jedi vs. Sith [A9T007] 25.00
__ Mace Windu's Attack Battalion [A9T008].......20.00
__ Rebel vs. Empire [A9T009].............................25.00
__ Sith Lord Attack [A9T010]...............................20.00
__ Skirmish in the Senate, exclusive to Target [A9T011]..25.00
__ The Hunt for General Grievous, exclusive to Toys R Us [A9T012] 40.00

30th anniversary.

__ Ambush at Ilum [A9T013] 20.00
__ ARC-170 Elite squad, exclusive to Target [A9T014]..20.00
__ Battle of Geonosis Jango Fett, Obi-Wan Kenobi, Count Dooku, Aayla Secura, Super Battle Droid [A9T015]..20.00
__ Betrayal on Bespin [A9T016] 20.00
__ Betrayal on Felucia Clone Trooper (x3), Aayla Secura, Clone Commander Bly, exclusive to Target [A9T017]..20.00
__ Capture of Tantive IV [A9T018].......................20.00
__ Clone Attack on Coruscant [A9T019] 20.00
__ Droid Factory Capture [A9T020]....................20.00
__ Jedi Training on Dagobah Yoda, R2-D2, Spirit of Obi-Wan Kenobi, Luke Skywalker, Spirit of Darth Vader [A9T021] 20.00
__ Jedi vs. Darth Sidious Mace Windu, Darth Sidious, Kit Fisto, Agen Kolar, Saesee Tiin [A9T022] ...20.00

A9T010

A9T011

A9T012

A9T013

A9T014

A9T015

A9T016

A9T017

A9T018

A9T019

A9T020

A9T021

A9T022

A9T023

A9T024

__ Jedi vs. Sith Asajj Ventress, Anakin Skywalker, Yoda, General Grievous, General Obi-Wan Kenobi [A9T023]...20.00
__ The Hunt for Grievous [A9T024] 20.00

Action Figures: 2006-2007 (Saga Collection)

Hasbro

__ Anakin Skywalker, ROTS #25 [A3S001] 8.00
__ AT-AT Driver #09 [A3S002]..............................10.00
__ Aurra Sing #70, exclusive to Walmart [A3S003]...8.00
__ Barada #04 [A3S004]...8.00
__ Battle Droids 2-pack #62 [A3S005] 8.00
__ Bib Fortuna #03 [A3S006]...................................6.00
__ Boba Fett, jets in front of bubble #06 [A3S007] 12.00
__ Boba Fett, jets in rear of bubble #06 [A3S008]..14.00
__ C-3PO, Battle of Endor, painted joints #42 [A3S009]..8.00
__ C-3PO, Battle of Endor, unpainted joints #42 [A3S010]..8.00
__ C-3PO, Battle of Geonosis #17 [A3S011] 6.00
__ C-3PO, Battle of Geonosis, battle droid head #17 [A3S012] 6.00
__ Chewbacca, Cloud City Escape #54 [A3S013] 6.00
__ Chewbacca, large shoulder ring connector #05 [A3S014] 6.00
__ Chewbacca, small shoulder ring connector #05 [A3S015] 6.00
__ Chief Chirpa #39 [A3S016] 12.00

__ Clone Commander Appo #64 [A3S017] 8.00
__ Clone Commander Cody #24 [A3S018] 14.00
__ Clone Commander Cody hologram #56 [A3S019] 8.00
__ Clone Trooper 442nd Siege Battalion #57 [A3S020] 6.00
__ Clone Trooper combat engineer #68 [A3S021] 8.00
__ Clone Trooper Fifth Fleet Security #59 [A3S022] 6.00
__ Clone Trooper Sergeant #60 [A3S023]...............6.00
__ Clone Trooper, ROTS #26 [A3S024]..............10.00
__ Darth Maul hologram #48 [A3S025]...................6.00
__ Darth Maul Sith Training #53 [A3S026]...............6.00
__ Darth Vader, Bespin #38 [A3S027]......................8.00
__ Darth Vader, Emperor's Wrath #45 [A3S028] ...6.00
__ Darth Vader, Hoth, lightsaber down #13 [A3S029] 6.00

__ Darth Vader, Hoth, lightsaber up #13 [A3S030] 6.00
__ Death Star Gunner #41 [A3S031] 10.00
__ Dud Bolt and Mars Guo #51 [A3S032] 8.00
__ Elite Corps Clone Trooper #65 dark green visor [A3S033] 8.00
__ Elite Corps Clone Trooper #65 light green visor 8.00
__ Emperor Palpatine #43 [A3S034]....................10.00
__ Firespeeder pilot #22 [A3S035].........................6.00
__ Foul Moudama #29 [A3S036].............................8.00
__ Garindan #34 [A3S037]......................................6.00
__ General Grievous #30 [A3S038]..........................8.00
__ General Grievous, Demise of Grievous [A3S039]...25.00
__ General Rieekan #12 [A3S040].............................6.00
__ General Veers #07 [A3S041]...............................6.00
__ Graga The Grorgmonger #52 [A3S042]...........8.00

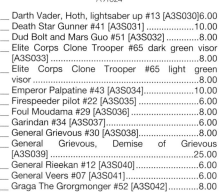

A3S001

A3S002

A3S003

A3S004

A3S005

A3S006

A3S007 detail

A3S008 detail

A3S008

A3S009

A3S009 detail

A3S010 detail

A3S011

A3S012

A3S013

A3S014

A3S014 detail

A3S015 detail

A3S016

A3S017

A3S018

A3S019

A3S020

A3S021

A3S022

A3S023

A3S024

A3S025

A3S026

A3S027

A3S028

A3S029

A3S030

A3S031

A3S032

A3S033

A3S034

A3S035

A3S036

A3S037

Action Figures

GENERAL GRIEVOUS

A3S038

GENERAL GRIEVOUS (HANDS OF WHATEVER)

A3S039

GENERAL RIEEKAN

A3S040

GENERAL VEERS

A3S041

GRAGRA

A3S042

HAN SOLO

A3S043

HAN SOLO

A3S044

HEM DAZON

A3S045

A3S045 detail

A3S046 detail

A3S047 detail

HOLOGRAPHIC OBI-WAN KENOBI

A3S048

JANGO FETT

A3S049

HOLOGRAPHIC KI-ADI-MUNDI

A3S050

KIT FISTO

A3S051

KITIK KEED'KAK

A3S052

LABRIA

A3S053

LUKE SKYWALKER

A3S054

LUKE SKYWALKER

A3S055

LUSHROS DOFINE

A3S056

MAJOR BREN DERLIN

A3S057

MOFF JERJERROD

A3S058

MOMAW NADON

A3S059

NABOO SOLDIER

A3S060

NABRUN LEIDS & KABE

A3S061

OBI-WAN KENOBI

A3S062

OBI-WAN KENOBI

A3S063

PADMÉ AMIDALA

A3S064

POGGLE THE LESSER

A3S065

POWER DROID

A3S066

A3S067

A3S068

A3S069

A3S070

A3S071

A3S072

A3S073

A3S074

A3S075

A3S076

A3S077

A3S078

A3S079

A3S080

A3S081

A3S082

A3S083

A3S084

A3S085

A3S086

A3S087 detail

A3S088 detail

A3S089 detail

A3S089

A3S090

A3S091

A3S092

A3S093

A3S094

A3S095

__ Han Solo #35 [A3S043]....................6.00
__ Han Solo carbonite #02 [A3S044] 6.00
__ Hem Dazon, blue and clear glass #33 [A3S045] 8.00
__ Hem Dazon, blue and white glass #33 [A3S046] 8.00
__ Hem Dazon, clear glass [A3S047] 8.00
__ Holographic Obi-Wan Kenobi #63 dark blue [A3S048] 6.00
__ Holographic Obi-Wan Kenobi #63 light blue....6.00
__ Jango Fett #20 [A3S049] 6.00
__ Ki-Adi-Mundy holographic #27 [A3S050] 8.00
__ Kit Fisto #55 [A3S051] 8.00
__ Kitik Keed'kak #71, exclusive to Walmart [A3S052] 8.00
__ Labria #73, exclusive to Walmart [A3S053]......8.00
__ Luke Skywalker #36 [A3S054] 6.00
__ Luke Skywalker, Endor #44 [A3S055]..............6.00
__ Lushros Dofine #23 [A3S056] 6.00
__ Major Bren Derlin #08 [A3S057] 5.00
__ Moff Jerjerrod #40 [A3S058] 8.00
__ Momaw Nadon, blue and clear glass #31 ....8.00
__ Momaw Nadon, blue and white glass #31 [A3S059] 8.00
__ Momaw Nadon, clear glass #31 ....8.00
__ Naboo Soldier #50 [A3S060] 8.00
__ Nabrun Leids and Kabe #72, exclusive to Walmart [A3S061] 8.00
__ Obi-Wan Kenobi, Naboo #47 [A3S062]............6.00
__ Obi-Wan Kenobi, ROTS #28 [A3S063] 6.00
__ Padme Amidala #67 [A3S064] 8.00
__ Poggle the Lesser #18 [A3S065] 5.00
__ Power Droid #14 [A3S066] 6.00
__ Princess Leia Boushh Disguise #01 [A3S067]..6.00

__ R2-D2 #10 [A3S068] 6.00
__ R4-K5 #67 [A3S069] 8.00
__ R4-M6 #74, exclusive to Walmart [A3S070].....8.00
__ R5-D4 #32 [A3S071] 10.00
__ R5-J2 #58 [A3S072] 6.00
__ Rebel Trooper, black #46 [A3S073].................8.00
__ Rebel Trooper, white #46 [A3S074].................8.00
__ Rep Been #49 [A3S075]...................6.00
__ Sandtrooper #37 [A3S076] 10.00
__ Scorch, Republic Commando #21 [A3S077]..28.00
__ Shadow Stormtrooper, exclusive to StarWarsShop.com [A3S078] 25.00
__ Snowtrooper #11 [A3S079]...............6.00
__ Sora Bulq #15 [A3S080] 6.00
__ Sun Fac #16 [A3S081] 6.00
__ Super Battle Droid #61 [A3S082].....................6.00
__ Yarael Poof #69 [A3S083] 8.00
__ Yoda #19 [A3S084] 6.00

Greatest Battles Collection.

__ 501st Legion Trooper [A3S085].........................8.00
__ AT-TE Tank Gunner [A3S086]...........................8.00
__ C-3PO, corridor base, brown [A3S087]............8.00
__ C-3PO, corridor base, gray [A3S088]...............8.00
__ C-3PO, lava base [A3S089]................8.00
__ Clone Commander [A3S090]...............8.00
__ Count Dooku [A3S091]....................8.00
__ Emperor Palpatine [A3S092]...............8.00
__ Kit Fisto [A3S093]..........................8.00
__ Obi-Wan Kenobi [A3S094]................8.00
__ Padme [A3S095]...........................8.00
__ R2-D2 [A3S096]............................8.00
__ R4-G9 [A3S097]............................8.00
__ Royal Guard [A3S098] 8.00

__ Shocktrooper [A3S099] 8.00
__ Wookiee Warrior [A3S100]................8.00

Heroes and Villains Collection.
__ Anakin Skywalker [A3S101]..............8.00
__ Chewbacca [A3S102].....................8.00
__ Clone Pilot [A3S103]....................15.00
__ Clone Trooper [A3S104]................15.00
__ Commander Bacara [A3S105]..........15.00
__ Darth Vader [A3S106].................12.00
__ Destroyer Droid [A3S107].............10.00
__ General Grievous [A3S108]............10.00
__ Mace Windu [A3S109]....................8.00
__ Obi-Wan Kenobi [A3S110].............8.00
__ R2-D2 [A3S111]..........................8.00
__ Yoda [A3S112]............................8.00

Separation of the Twins.
__ Infant Leia Organa with Bail Organa [A3S113] 25.00
__ Infant Luke Skywalker with Obi-Wan Kenobi [A3S114] 25.00

Ultimate Galactic Hunt. Foil logo, silver holo figure.
__ Anakin Skywalker [A3S115]............................18.00
__ AT-AT Driver [A3S116]....................18.00
__ Boba Fett [A3S117].......................25.00
__ Clone Commander Cody [A3S118] 25.00
__ Darth Vader [A3S119]....................25.00
__ General Grievous [A3S120]..............25.00
__ Han Solo (Carbonite) [A3S121]........18.00
__ Obi-Wan Kenobi [A3S122]..............18.00
__ Scorch (Republic Commando) [A3S123]........36.00
__ Snowtrooper [A3S124]...................16.00

A3S096

A3S097

A3S098

A3S099

A3S100

A3S101

A3S102

A3S103

A3S104

A3S105

A3S106

A3S107

A3S108

A3S109

A3S110

A3S111

A3S112

A3S113

A3S114

A3S115

A3S116

A3S117

A3S118

A3S119

A3S120

A3S121

A3S122

A3S123

A3S124

A3S125

Hasbro, Canada
Black background, tri-language.

__ Anakin Skywalker, ROTS #25	8.00
__ AT-AT Driver #09	10.00
__ Barada #04	8.00
__ Battle Droids 2-pack #62	8.00
__ Bib Fortuna #03	6.00
__ Boba Fett	12.00
__ C-3PO, Battle of Endor #42	6.00
__ C-3PO, Battle of Geonosis #17	6.00
__ C-3PO, Battle of Geonosis, battle droid #17	6.00
__ Chewbacca, Cloud City Escape #54	6.00
__ Chewbacca #05	6.00
__ Chief Chirpa #39	12.00
__ Clone Commander Appo #64	8.00
__ Clone Commander Cody #24	14.00
__ Clone Commander Cody hologram #56	8.00
__ Clone Trooper 442nd Siege Battalion #57	6.00
__ Clone Trooper combat engineer #68	6.00
__ Clone Trooper Fifth Fleet Security #59	6.00
__ Clone Trooper Sergeant #60	6.00
__ Clone Trooper, ROTS #26	10.00
__ Darth Maul hologram #48	6.00
__ Darth Maul Sith Training #53	6.00
__ Darth Vader, Bespin #38	8.00
__ Darth Vader, Emperor's Wrath #45	6.00
__ Darth Vader, Hoth #13	6.00
__ Death Star Gunner #41	10.00
__ Dud Bolt and Mars Guo #51	8.00
__ Elite Corps Clone Trooper #65	8.00
__ Emperor Palpatine #43	10.00
__ Firespeeder pilot #22	6.00
__ Foul Moudama #29	8.00
__ Garindan #34	6.00
__ General Grievous #30	8.00
__ General Rieekan #12	6.00
__ General Veers #07	6.00
__ Graga The Grorgmonger #52	8.00
__ Han Solo #35	6.00
__ Han Solo carbonite #02	6.00
__ Hem Dazon #33	8.00
__ Holographic Obi-Wan Kenobi #63	6.00
__ Jango Fett #20	6.00
__ Ki-Adi-Mundy holographic #27	8.00
__ Kit Fisto #55	8.00
__ Luke Skywalker #36	6.00
__ Luke Skywalker, Endor #44	6.00
__ Lushros Dofine #23	6.00
__ Major Bren Derlin #08	5.00
__ Moff Jerjerrod #40	8.00
__ Momaw Nadon #31	8.00
__ Naboo Soldier #50	8.00

A3T001

A3T002

A3T003

Action Figures

__ Obi-Wan Kenobi, Naboo #47 ....6.00
__ Obi-Wan Kenobi, ROTS #28 ....6.00
__ Padme Amidala #67 ....8.00
__ Poggle the Lesser #18 ....5.00
__ Power Droid #14 ....6.00
__ Princess Leia Boushh Disguise [A3S125]........8.00
__ R2-D2 #10 ....6.00
__ R4-K5 #67 ....8.00
__ R5-D4 #32 ....10.00
__ R5-J2 #58 ....6.00
__ Rebel Trooper, black #46 ....8.00
__ Rebel Trooper, white #46 ....8.00
__ Rep Been #49 ....6.00
__ Sandtrooper #37 ....10.00
__ Scorch, Republic Commando #21 ...28.00
__ Snowtrooper #11 ....6.00
__ Sora Bulq #15 ....6.00
__ Sun Fac #16 ....6.00
__ Super Battle Droid #61 ....6.00
__ Yarael Poof #69 ....8.00
__ Yoda #19 ....6.00

Hasbro, UK
__ General Grievous, Demise of Grievous...........25.00

Action Figures: 2006-2007 (Saga Collection Multipacks)

Hasbro
__ Death Star Briefing Darth Vader, Grand Moff Tarkin, Admiral Motti, General Tagge, Chief Bast, Officer Cass, Colonel Wulff Yularen, exclusive to Previews [A3T001]...........45.00

A4S001   A4S002
A4S003   A4S004
A4S005   A4S006   A4S007   A4S008
A4S009   A4S010   A4S011   A4S012   A4S013   A4S014

__ Republic Commando Delta Squad Boss, Fixer, Sev, Scorch, Geonosian Warrior, Geonosian Warrior with Blaster, Sun Fac [A3T002] 40.00

Hasbro, UK
__ Episode III Gift Pack [A3T003] 65.00

Action Figures: 2007 (30th anniversary)

Hasbro
__ 4-LOM 30-41 [A4S001]...........8.00
__ Airborne Trooper 30-07 [A4S002]...........8.00
__ Anakin Skywalker 30-33 [A4S003]...........8.00
__ Anakin Skywalker, spirit 30-45 [A4S004]...........8.00
__ Biggs Darklighter 30-14 Rebel Pilot [A4S005]..8.00
__ Biggs Darklighter Academy Outfit 30-17 [A4S006]...........8.00
__ Boba Fett animated 30-24 [A4S007]...........8.00
__ C-3PO with Salacious Crumb 30-30 [A4S008].8.00
__ Clone Trooper, 7th legion 30-49 [A4S009] 8.00
__ Clone Trooper, Hawkbat Battalion 30-50 [A4S010]...........8.00
__ Clone Trooper, training fatigues 30-55 [A4S011]...........8.00
__ CZ-4 30-26 [A4S012]...........8.00
__ Darth Malak 30-35 [A4S013]...........8.00
__ Darth Revan 30-34 [A4S014]...........8.00
__ Darth Vader 30-16 [A4S015]...........8.00
__ Darth Vader with coin album 30-01 solid red block on insert [A4S016]...........12.00
__ Darth Vader with coin album 30-01 white stripe on red block on insert [A4S017] 14.00
__ Darth Vader, holographic 30-48 [A4S018]........8.00
__ Death Star Trooper 30-13 [A4S019] 8.00
__ Destroyer Droid 30-59 [A4S020]...........8.00
__ Elis Helrot 30-23 [A4S021]...........8.00
__ Galactic Marine 30-02 [A4S022]...........8.00
__ General McQuarrie 30-40 [A4S023]...........8.00
__ Han Solo 30-11 [A4S024]...........8.00
__ Han Solo, Bespin torture 30-38 [A4S025] 8.00
__ Hermi Odle 30-29 [A4S026]...........8.00
__ Imperial Stormtrooper 30-20 [A4S027]...........8.00
__ Jango Fett 30-57 [A4S028]...........8.00
__ Jawa and LIN Droid 30-19 [A4S029] 8.00
__ Lando Calrissian 30-39 [A4S030] 8.00
__ Luke Skywalker 30-18 [A4S031]...........8.00
__ Luke Skywalker, ceremony outfit 30-12 silver and black lightsaber [A4S032]...........8.00
__ Luke Skywalker, ceremony outfit 30-12 silver lightsaber [A4S033]...........8.00

__ Luke Skywalker, Jedi 30-25 [A4S034]...........8.00
__ M'iiyoom O'nith 30-22 [A4S035]...........8.00
__ Mace Windu 30-06 [A4S036]...........6.00
__ Mustafar Lava Miner 30-03 [A4S037]...........8.00
__ Naboo Soldier, red 30-52 [A4S038]...........8.00
__ Obi-Wan Kenobi 30-05 [A4S039]...........6.00
__ Padme Amidala 30-56 [A4S040]...........8.00
__ Pax Bonkik 30-54 [A4S041]...........8.00
__ Pre-Cyborg Grievous 30-36 [A4S042]...........8.00
__ R2-B1 30-51 [A4S043]...........8.00
__ R2-D2 30-04 [A4S044]...........6.00
__ R2-D2 with cargo net 30-46 [A4S045]...........8.00
__ Rebel Honor Guard 30-10 dark belt, Obi-Wan listed as 30-05 [A4S046]...........8.00
__ Rebel Honor Guard 30-10 light belt, Obi-Wan listed as 30-06 [A4S047]...........8.00
__ Rebel Vanguard 30-53 [A4S048]...........8.00
__ Romba and Graak 30-43 [A4S049]...........8.00
__ Roron Corobb 30-31 [A4S050]...........8.00
__ Super Battle Droid 30-08 [A4S051]...........8.00
__ Tycho Celchu, A-Wing pilot 30-44 name covered by art [A4S052]...........8.00
__ Tycho Celchu, A-Wing pilot 30-44 name not covered [A4S053]...........8.00
__ Umpass-Stay 30-27 [A4S054]...........8.00
__ Voolvif Monn 30-58 [A4S055]...........8.00
__ Yoda and Kybuck 30-32 [A4S056]...........8.00

McQuarrie Concept Series.
__ Boba Fett 30-15 [A4S057]...........25.00
__ Chewbacca 30-21 [A4S058]...........25.00
__ Darth Vader 30-28 [A4S059]...........25.00
__ Han Solo 30-47 [A4S060]...........25.00
__ Rebel Trooper 30-60 [A4S061]...........25.00
__ Snowtrooper 30-42 [A4S062]...........25.00
__ Starkiller Hero 30-37 [A4S063]...........25.00
__ Stormtrooper 30-09 [A4S064]...........25.00

Saga Legends.
__ 501st Clone Trooper [A4S065]...........8.00
__ 501st Clone Trooper, super articulated [A4S066]...........8.00
__ Anakin Skywalker...........8.00
__ Battle Droids 2-pack clean [A4S067]...........8.00
__ Battle Droids 2-pack OOM-9 and clean battle droid [A4S068]...........8.00
__ Battle Droids 2-pack red [A4S069]...........8.00
__ Battle Droids 2-pack shot battle droid and slashed battle droid [A4S070]...........8.00
__ Biker Scout Fans' Choice sticker [A4S071]......8.00
__ Biker Scout no sticker [A4S072]...........8.00

130

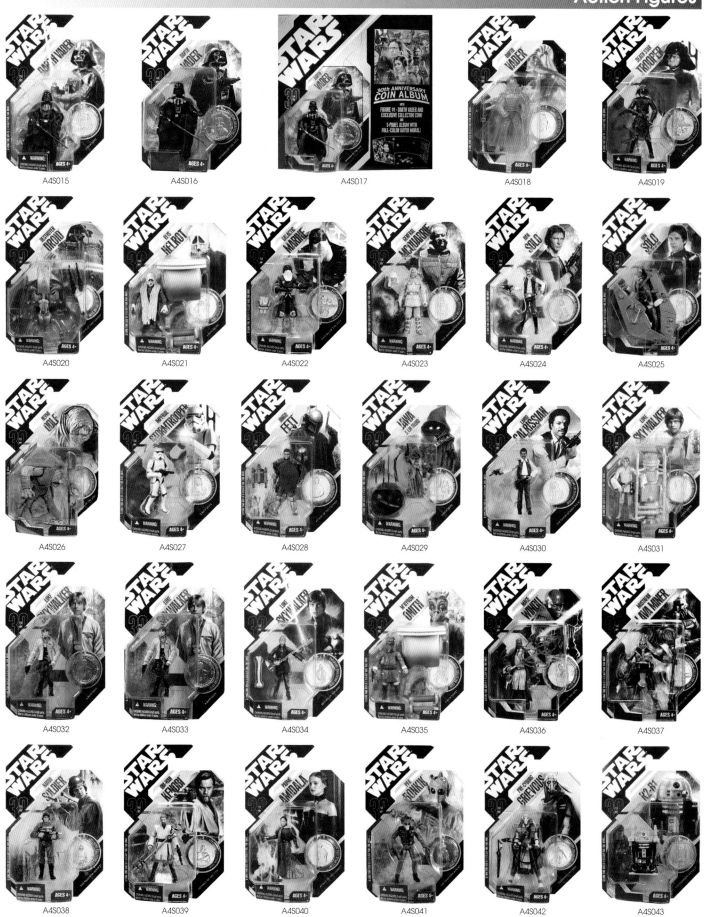

A4S015

A4S016

A4S017

A4S018

A4S019

A4S020

A4S021

A4S022

A4S023

A4S024

A4S025

A4S026

A4S027

A4S028

A4S029

A4S030

A4S031

A4S032

A4S033

A4S034

A4S035

A4S036

A4S037

A4S038

A4S039

A4S040

A4S041

A4S042

A4S043

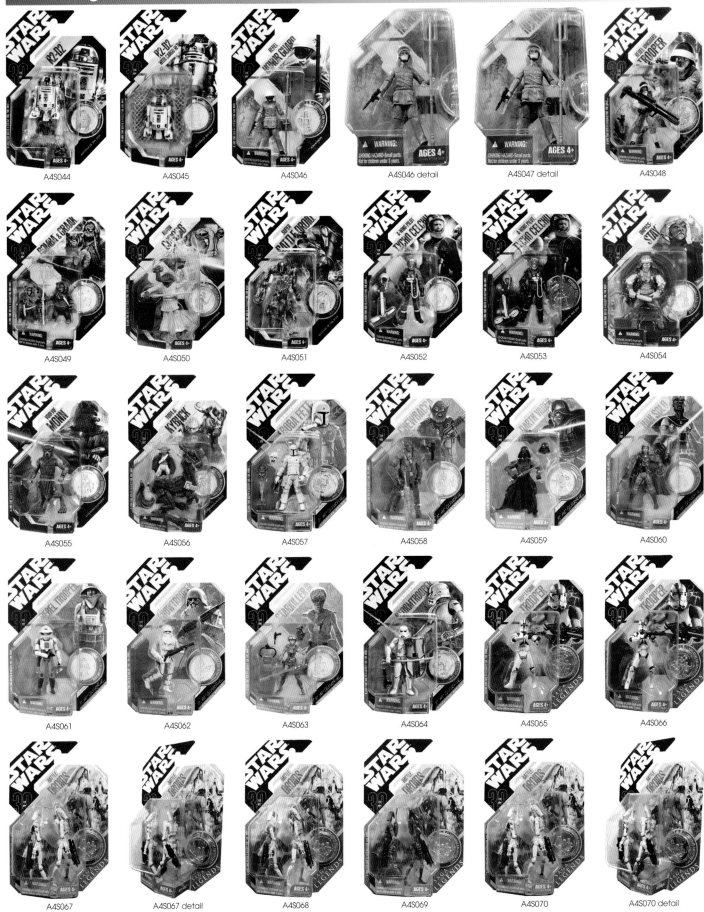

A4S044

A4S045

A4S046

A4S046 detail

A4S047 detail

A4S048

A4S049

A4S050

A4S051

A4S052

A4S053

A4S054

A4S055

A4S056

A4S057

A4S058

A4S059

A4S060

A4S061

A4S062

A4S063

A4S064

A4S065

A4S066

A4S067

A4S067 detail

A4S068

A4S069

A4S070

A4S070 detail

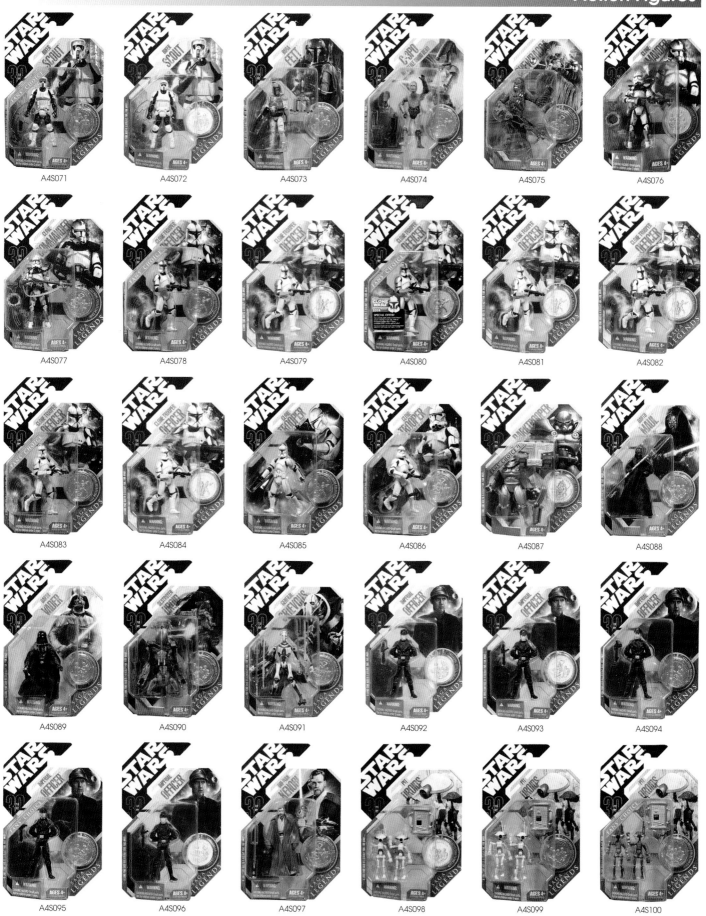

A4S071

A4S072

A4S073

A4S074

A4S075

A4S076

A4S077

A4S078

A4S079

A4S080

A4S081

A4S082

A4S083

A4S084

A4S085

A4S086

A4S087

A4S088

A4S089

A4S090

A4S091

A4S092

A4S093

A4S094

A4S095

A4S096

A4S097

A4S098

A4S099

A4S100

Action Figures

Boba Fett [A4S073].................................8.00
C-3PO [A4S074]....................................8.00
Chewbacca [A4S075]............................8.00
Clone Commander clone trooper rifle, Fans' Choice sticker 8.00
Clone Commander clone trooper rifle, no sticker [A4S076]...8.00
Clone Commander sandtrooper rifle, Fans' Choice sticker 8.00
Clone Commander sandtrooper rifle, no sticker [A4S077]...8.00
Clone Trooper Officer, blue (lieutenant) Fans' Choice sticker [A4S078] 8.00
Clone Trooper Officer, blue (lieutenant) no sticker [A4S079] 8.00
Clone Trooper Officer, green (sergeant) Fans' Choice sticker [A4S080] 8.00
Clone Trooper Officer, green (sergeant) no sticker [A4S081] 8.00
Clone Trooper Officer, red (captain) Fans' Choice sticker 8.00
Clone Trooper Officer, red (captain) no sticker [A4S082] 8.00
Clone Trooper Officer, yellow (commander) Fans' Choice sticker [A4S083] 8.00
Clone Trooper Officer, yellow (commander) no sticker [A4S084]...........................8.00
Clone Trooper, EPII PN 6606725800........8.00
Clone Trooper, EPII PN 6606732400 [A4S085] 8.00
Clone Trooper, EPII PN 6606735900...............8.00
Clone Trooper, EPIII [A4S086]..................8.00
Dark Trooper [A4S087] 8.00
Darth Maul [A4S088] 8.00

Darth Vader [A4S089] 8.00
Destroyer Droid [A4S090]..............................8.00
General Grievous [A4S091].............................8.00
Imperial Officer blonde hair Fans' Choice sticker 8.00
Imperial Officer blonde hair no sticker [A4S092]..8.00
Imperial Officer brown hair Fans' Choice sticker 8.00
Imperial Officer brown hair no sticker [A4S093]..8.00
Imperial Officer brown hair no sticker [A4S094]..8.00
Imperial Officer slim face Fans' Choice sticker [A4S095]......................................8.00
Imperial Officer slim face no sticker [A4S096]..8.00
Obi-Wan Kenobi [A4S097]...............................8.00
Pit Droids 2-pack cream with silver trunk Fans' Choice sticker [A4S098] 8.00
Pit Droids 2-pack cream with silver trunk no sticker [A4S099].................................8.00
Pit Droids 2-pack red with silver trunk Fans' Choice sticker [A4S100] 8.00
Pit Droids 2-pack red with silver trunk no sticker [A4S101].................................8.00
Pit Droids 2-pack tan with silver trunk Fans' Choice sticker [A4S102] 8.00
Pit Droids 2-pack tan with silver trunk no sticker [A4S103].................................8.00
Princess Leia Boushh Disguise [A4S104].........8.00
R2-D2 [A4S105]...8.00
R4-I9 Fans' Choice sticker 8.00
R4-I9 no sticker [A4S106].............................8.00
RA-7 [A4S107]..8.00

Saesee Tiin [A4S108].......................................8.00
Sandtrooper black pauldron / Corporal no dirt [A4S109].......................................8.00
Sandtrooper gray pauldron / Sergeant clean, Fan's Choice sticker................................8.00
Sandtrooper gray pauldron / Sergeant clean, Fans' Choice sticker................................8.00
Sandtrooper gray pauldron / Sergeant dirty, Fan's Choice sticker [A4S110] 8.00
Sandtrooper gray pauldron / Sergeant dirty, Fans' Choice sticker................................8.00
Sandtrooper orange pauldron / squad leader Fan's Choice sticker [A4S111] 8.00
Sandtrooper orange pauldron / squad leader Fans' Choice sticker, no rifle [A4S112].................8.00
Sandtrooper orange pauldron / squad leader Fans' Choice sticker, rifle [A4S113]...........................8.00
Sandtrooper white pauldron / Sergeant no dirt [A4S114].......................................8.00
Shock Trooper [A4S115].................................8.00
TC-14 droid on left [A4S116]........................35.00
TC-14 droid on right [A4S117].......................8.00
Yoda [A4S118]..8.00

Ultimate Galactic Hunt. Foil logo, gold collector coin.
Airborne Trooper [A4S119] 12.00
Biggs Darklighter, Rebel Pilot [A4S120] 12.00
Boba Fett, animated debut [A4S121].........25.00
Boba Fett, McQuarrie concept [A4S122]........25.00
Chewbacca, McQuarrie concept [A4S123] 25.00
Darth Vader [A4S124] 12.00
Galactic Marine [A4S125] 12.00
Han Solo [A4S126]...................................12.00
Luke Skywalker, ceremony outfit [A4S127] 12.00

A4S101

A4S102

A4S103

A4S104

A4S105

A4S106

A4S107

A4S108

A4S109

A4S110

A4S111

A4S112

A4S113

A4S114

A4S115

A4S116

A4S117

A4S118

A4S119　　A4S120　　A4S121　　A4S122　　A4S123　　A4S124

A4S125　　A4S126　　A4S127　　A4S128　　A4S129　　A4S130

__ Mace Windu [A4S128] 12.00
__ R2-D2 [A4S129].............................12.00
__ Stormtrooper, McQuarrie concept [A4S130]..25.00

Hasbro, Canada
Darth Vader background, tri-language package.
__ Airborne Trooper 30-07 [A4S131]....................8.00
__ Anakin Skywalker 30-33 [A4S132]....................8.00
__ Biggs Darklighter 30-13 Rebel Pilot [A4S133]..8.00
__ Biggs Darklighter Academy Outfit 30-17..........8.00
__ Boba Fett animated 30-24 [A4S134]................8.00
__ C-3PO and Salacious Crumb 30-30 [A4S135].8.00
__ CZ-4 30-26 ....8.00
__ Darth Malak 30-35 [A4S136]........................8.00
__ Darth Revan 30-34 [A4S137]........................8.00
__ Darth Vader 30-16 [A4S138]........................8.00
__ Death Star Trooper 30-14 [A4S139] 8.00
__ Elis Helrot 30-23 ....8.00
__ Galactic Marine 30-02 [A4S140]....................8.00
__ Han Solo 30-11 [A4S141]...........................8.00
__ Hermi Odle 30-29 [A4S142] 8.00
__ Jawa and LIN Droid 30-19..........................8.00
__ Luke Skywalker 30-18 ....8.00
__ Luke Skywalker, ceremony outfit 30-12 [A4S143] ..8.00
__ Luke Skywalker, Jedi 30-25.........................8.00
__ M'iiyoom O'nith 30-22 ....8.00
__ Mace Windu 30-03 [A4S144].........................8.00
__ Mustafar Lava Miner 30-06 [A4S145]...............8.00
__ Obi-Wan Kenobi 30-05 [A4S146] 8.00
__ Pre-Cyborg Grievous 30-36 [A4S147]...............8.00
__ R2-D2 30-04 [A4S148]..............................8.00
__ Rebel Honor Guard 30-10 [A4S149].................8.00
__ Roron Corobb 30-31 [A4S150]........................8.00
__ Stormtrooper 30-20 removable helmet [A4S151]..8.00
__ Super Battle Droid 30-08 [A4S152]................8.00
__ Umpass-Stay 30-27 ....8.00
__ Yoda and Kybuck 30-32 [A4S153] 8.00

Darth Vader background card. Tri-language packaging. McQuarrie Concept Series.
__ Boba Fett 30-15 [A4S154] 85.00
__ Chewbacca 30-21 [A4S155]..........................25.00
__ Darth Vader 30 28 ....25.00
__ Starkiller Hero 30-37 [A4S156] 25.00
__ Stormtrooper 30-09 [A4S157] 25.00

Darth Vader background card. Tri-language packaging. Saga Legends.
__ Battle Droids Capt. Rex offer [A4S158] 8.00

__ Biker Scout [A4S159].............................8.00
__ Biker Scout Capt. Rex offer sticker 8.00
__ C-3PO Capt. Rex offer sticker [A4S160] 8.00
__ Chewbacca.....................................8.00
__ Chewbacca Capt. Rex offer sticker................8.00
__ Clone Commander Capt. Rex offer [A4S161]...8.00
__ Clone Trooper Officer, green (sergeant) [A4S162]..8.00
__ Clone Trooper Officer, red (captain) Capt. Rex offer sticker [A4S163]..8.00
__ Clone Trooper Officer, yellow (commander) [A4S164]..8.00
__ Clone Trooper, EPII [A4S165]......................8.00
__ Clone Trooper, EPIII [A4S166] 8.00
__ Darth Maul [A4S167]...............................8.00
__ Darth Maul Capt. Rex offer sticker 8.00
__ Darth Vader...................................8.00
__ Darth Vader Capt. Rex offer sticker [A4S168]..8.00
__ General Grievous [A4S169].........................8.00
__ General Grievous Capt. Rex offer sticker 8.00
__ Obi-Wan Kenobi 8.00
__ Pit Droids cream with tan trunk Capt. Rex offer sticker [A4S170]..8.00
__ Pit Droids red with tan trunk Capt. Rex offer sticker [A4S171]..8.00
__ R2-D2..8.00
__ R2-D2 Capt. Rex offer sticker [A4S172]..........8.00
__ R4-I9 [A4S173]...................................8.00
__ RA-7 [A4S174]...................................8.00
__ Saesee Tiin 8.00
__ Sandtrooper gray pauldron / Sergeant dirty [A4S175]..8.00
__ Shock Trooper [A4S176].............................8.00
__ Shock Trooper Capt. Rex offer sticker 8.00
__ TC-14 [A4S177]...................................8.00
__ Yoda [A4S178]....................................8.00
__ Yoda Capt. Rex offer sticker 8.00

Darth Vader background card. Tri-language packaging. Ultimate Galactic Hunt. Foil logo and gold collector coin.
__ Biggs Darklighter, Rebel Pilot........................12.00
__ Boba Fett animated debut 30-24 ....30.00
__ Chewbacca, McQuarrie concept 30-21 ....35.00
__ Galactic Marine 30-02 [A4S179]...................30.00
__ Han Solo 12.00
__ Luke Skywalker, ceremony outfit....................12.00
__ Mace Windu....................................12.00
__ R2-D2...12.00
__ Stormtrooper, McQuarrie concept 30-09 [A4S180] ..35.00

Hasbro, Japan
Age sticker on front, marketing sticker on back.
__ 4-LOM 30-41 ....8.00
__ Airborne Trooper 30-07 ....8.00
__ Anakin Skywalker 30-33 ....8.00
__ Anakin Skywalker, spirit 30-45 ....8.00
__ Biggs Darklighter 30-13 Rebel Pilot 8.00
__ Biggs Darklighter Academy Outfit 30-17 ....8.00
__ Boba Fett animated 30-24 [A4S181] 8.00
__ C-3PO with Salacious Crumb 30-30 ....8.00
__ Clone Trooper, 7th legion 30-49....................8.00
__ Clone Trooper, Hawkbat Battalion 30-50...........8.00
__ Clone Trooper, training fatigues 30-55.............8.00
__ CZ-4 30-26 ....8.00
__ Darth Malak 30-35 ....8.00
__ Darth Revan 30-34 ....8.00
__ Darth Vader 30-16 ....8.00
__ Darth Vader, holographic 30-48 ....8.00
__ Death Star Trooper 30-14..........................8.00
__ Destroyer Droid 30-59 ....8.00
__ Elis Helrot 30-23 ....8.00
__ Galactic Marine 30-02 ....8.00
__ General McQuarrie 30-40 ....8.00
__ Han Solo 30-11 ....8.00
__ Han Solo, Bespin torture 30-38 ....8.00
__ Hermi Odle 30-29 ....8.00
__ Imperial Stormtrooper 30-20 ....8.00
__ Jango Fett 30-57 ....8.00
__ Jawa and LIN Droid 30-19..........................8.00
__ Lando Calrissian 30-39 ....8.00
__ Luke Skywalker 30-18 ....8.00
__ Luke Skywalker, ceremony outfit 30-12 ....8.00
__ Luke Skywalker, Jedi 30-25.........................8.00
__ M'iiyoom O'nith 30-22 ....8.00
__ Mace Windu 30-03 ....6.00
__ Mustafar Lava Miner 30-06 ....8.00
__ Naboo Soldier, red 30-52 ....8.00
__ Obi-Wan Kenobi 30-05 ....6.00
__ Padme Amidala 30-56 ....8.00
__ Pax Bonkik 30-54 ....8.00
__ Pre-Cyborg Grievous 30-36 ....8.00
__ R2-B1 30-51 ....8.00
__ R2-D2 30-04 ....6.00
__ R2-D2 with cargo net 30-46 ....8.00
__ Rebel Honor Guard 30-10 ....8.00
__ Rebel Vanguard 30-53 ....8.00
__ Romba and Graak 30-43 ....8.00
__ Roron Corobb 30-31 ....8.00
__ Super Battle Droid 30-08 ....8.00
__ Tycho Celchu, A-Wing pilot 30-44..................8.00
__ Umpass-Stay 30-27...............................8.00

A4S131   A4S132   A4S133   A4S134   A4S135   A4S136

A4S137   A4S138   A4S139   A4S140   A4S141   A4S142

A4S143   A4S144   A4S145   A4S146   A4S147   A4S148

A4S149   A4S150   A4S151   A4S152   A4S153   A4S154

A4S155   A4S156   A4S157   A4S158   A4S159   A4S160

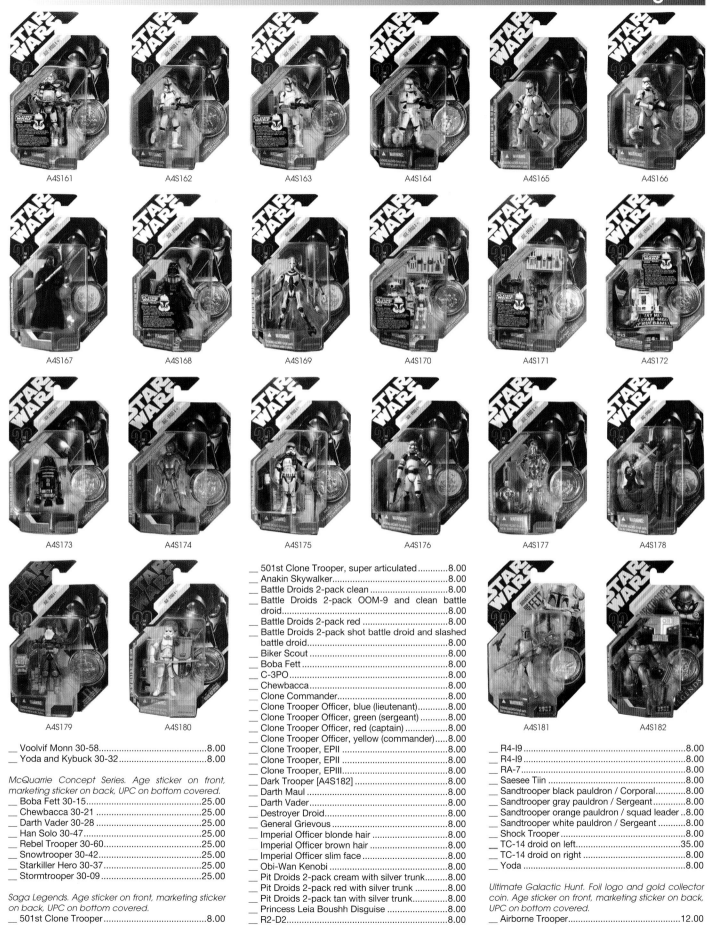

A4S161	A4S162	A4S163	A4S164	A4S165	A4S166
A4S167	A4S168	A4S169	A4S170	A4S171	A4S172
A4S173	A4S174	A4S175	A4S176	A4S177	A4S178
A4S179	A4S180			A4S181	A4S182

__ Voolvif Monn 30-58 .... 8.00
__ Yoda and Kybuck 30-32 .... 8.00

McQuarrie Concept Series. Age sticker on front, marketing sticker on back, UPC on bottom covered.
__ Boba Fett 30-15 .... 25.00
__ Chewbacca 30-21 .... 25.00
__ Darth Vader 30-28 .... 25.00
__ Han Solo 30-47 .... 25.00
__ Rebel Trooper 30-60 .... 25.00
__ Snowtrooper 30-42 .... 25.00
__ Starkiller Hero 30-37 .... 25.00
__ Stormtrooper 30-09 .... 25.00

Saga Legends. Age sticker on front, marketing sticker on back, UPC on bottom covered.
__ 501st Clone Trooper 8.00

__ 501st Clone Trooper, super articulated 8.00
__ Anakin Skywalker 8.00
__ Battle Droids 2-pack clean 8.00
__ Battle Droids 2-pack OOM-9 and clean battle droid 8.00
__ Battle Droids 2-pack red 8.00
__ Battle Droids 2-pack shot battle droid and slashed battle droid 8.00
__ Biker Scout 8.00
__ Boba Fett 8.00
__ C-3PO 8.00
__ Chewbacca 8.00
__ Clone Commander 8.00
__ Clone Trooper Officer, blue (lieutenant) 8.00
__ Clone Trooper Officer, green (sergeant) 8.00
__ Clone Trooper Officer, red (captain) 8.00
__ Clone Trooper Officer, yellow (commander) 8.00
__ Clone Trooper, EPII 8.00
__ Clone Trooper, EPII 8.00
__ Clone Trooper, EPII 8.00
__ Dark Trooper [A4S182] 8.00
__ Darth Maul 8.00
__ Darth Vader 8.00
__ Destroyer Droid 8.00
__ General Grievous 8.00
__ Imperial Officer blonde hair 8.00
__ Imperial Officer brown hair 8.00
__ Imperial Officer slim face 8.00
__ Obi-Wan Kenobi 8.00
__ Pit Droids 2-pack cream with silver trunk 8.00
__ Pit Droids 2-pack red with silver trunk 8.00
__ Pit Droids 2-pack tan with silver trunk 8.00
__ Princess Leia Boushh Disguise 8.00
__ R2-D2 .... 8.00

__ R4-I9 .... 8.00
__ R4-I9 .... 8.00
__ RA-7 .... 8.00
__ Saesee Tiin 8.00
__ Sandtrooper black pauldron / Corporal 8.00
__ Sandtrooper gray pauldron / Sergeant 8.00
__ Sandtrooper orange pauldron / squad leader .. 8.00
__ Sandtrooper white pauldron / Sergeant 8.00
__ Shock Trooper 8.00
__ TC-14 droid on left 35.00
__ TC-14 droid on right 8.00
__ Yoda 8.00

Ultimate Galactic Hunt. Foil logo and gold collector coin. Age sticker on front, marketing sticker on back, UPC on bottom covered.
__ Airborne Trooper 12.00

THE MAX REBO BAND
JABBA'S PALACE ENTERTAINERS

A5S001

THE MAX REBO BAND
JABBA'S PALACE MUSICIANS

A5S002

AT-RT ASSAULT SQUAD
BATTLE PACKS

A5S003

AT-ST WITH STOMPING LEGS!
THE BATTLE OF ENDOR

A5S004

"LASER" TURRET WITH FIRING PROJECTILE
THE BATTLE OF HOTH

A5S005

TREACHERY ON SALEUCAMI
BATTLE PACKS

A5S006

STAR WARS: BATTLEFRONT II CLONE PACK
BATTLEFRONT II

A5S007

COMMEMORATIVE TIN COLLECTION

A5S009

STAR WARS: BATTLEFRONT II DROID PACK
BATTLEFRONT II

A5S008

COMMEMORATIVE TIN COLLECTION

A5S010

COMMEMORATIVE TIN COLLECTION

A5S011

COMMEMORATIVE TIN COLLECTION

A5S012

COMMEMORATIVE TIN COLLECTION

A5S013

A5S014

A5S015

A5S016

A5S017

A5S018

A5S019

A5S020

A5S021

A5S022

A5S023

A5S024

A5S025

A5S026

A5S027

A5S028

A5S029

A5S030

A5S031

A5S032

A5S033

A5S034

A5S036

A5S035

CLONES AND COMMANDERS GIFT PACK

A5S037

___ Biggs Darklighter, Rebel Pilot 12.00
___ Boba Fett, animated debut 25.00
___ Boba Fett, McQuarrie concept 25.00
___ Chewbacca, McQuarrie concept 25.00
___ Darth Vader 12.00
___ Galactic Marine 12.00
___ Han Solo 12.00
___ Luke Skywalker, ceremony outfit 12.00
___ Mace Windu 12.00
___ R2-D2 ....12.00
___ Stormtrooper, McQuarrie concept 25.00

Action Figures: 2007-2008 (30th anniversary Multipacks)

Hasbro

Jabba's Palace, exclusive to Walmart.
___ Entertainers [A5S001] 25.00
___ Musicians [A5S002] 25.00

Battle Packs.
___ AT-RT Assault Squad, exclusive to Target [A5S003] 25.00
___ The Battle of Endor, exclusive to Target [A5S004] ..65.00
___ The Battle of Hoth, exclusive to Target [A5S005] 65.00
___ Treachery On Saleucami [A5S006] 25.00

Battlefront II.
___ Clone Set clone sharpshooter, heavy trooper, clone trooper, clone engineer, galactic marine, jet trooper, exclusive to Previews [A5S007] 45.00
___ Droid Set destroyer droid, 3 battle droids, Grievous' body guard, ammunition droid, exclusive to Previews [A5S008] 45.00

Collector's tin sets.
___ Episode 1: Darth Maul, Obi-Wan Kenobi, Qui-Gon Jinn, R2-R9 1 of 6 [A5S009] 30.00
___ Episode 2: Clone Trooper, Anakin Skywalker, Jango Fett, Count Dooku 2 of 6 [A5S010] 30.00
___ Episode 3: Mace Windu, Yoda, Anakin Skywalker, AT-RT Driver 3 of 6 [A5S011] 30.00
___ Episode 4: Sandtrooper, Princess Leia, Darth Vader, C-3PO 4 of 6 [A5S012] 30.00
___ Episode 5: Snowtrooper, Luke Skywalker, Han Solo, Chewbacca 5 of 6 [A5S013] 30.00
___ Episode 6: Scout Trooper, Darth Vader, Princess Leia, Rebel Commando 6 of 6 [A5S014] 30.00

Collector's tin sets. Exclusive editions.
___ Episode 2: Mace Windu, Sora Bulq, Oppo Rancisis, Zam Wesell, exclusive to K-Mart [A5S015] 45.00
___ Episode 3: Commander Cody, Anakin, General Grievous, Clone Pilot, K-Mart excl. [A5S016].35.00
___ Episode 4: Figrin D'an and the Modal Nodes, exclusive to Walmart [A5S017] 35.00
___ Episode 5: Darth Vader, R5-J2, Biker Scout, Death Star Gunner, exclusive to K-Mart [A5S018]....35.00
___ Episode III, exclusive to K-Mart [A5S019] 35.00
___ Episode IV, exclusive to K-Mart [A5S020] 35.00
___ Episode V, exclusive to K-Mart [A5S021].......35.00

Order 66 2-packs.
___ Anakin Skywalker and Airborne Trooper 5 of 6, exclusive to Target [A5S022] 14.00
___ Darth Vader and Commander Bow 3 of 6, exclusive to Target [A5S023] 14.00
___ Emperor Palpatine & Commander Thire 1 of 6,

exclusive to Target [A5S024] 14.00
___ Mace Windu and Galactic Marine 2 of 6, exclusive to Target [A5S025] 14.00
___ Obi-Wan Kenobi and AT-RT Driver 4 of 6, exclusive to Target [A5S026] 14.00
___ Yoda and Kashyyyk Trooper 6 of 6, exclusive to Target [A5S027] 14.00

Order 66 2-packs. Series 2.
___ Anakin Skywalker and ARC Trooper 2 of 6, exclusive to Target [A5S028] 14.00
___ Emperor Palpatine and Commander Vill 4 of 6, exclusive to Target [A5S029] 14.00
___ Luminara Unduli and AT-RT Driver 5 of 6, exclusive to Target [A5S030] 14.00
___ Master Sev and ARC Trooper 6 of 6, exclusive to Target [A5S031] 16.00
___ Obi-Wan Kenobi and ARC Trooper Commander 1 of 6, exclusive to Target [A5S032] 14.00
___ Tsui Choi and BARC Trooper 3 of 6, exclusive to Target [A5S033] 18.00

Republic Elite Forces.
___ Mandalorians and Clone Troopers 2x Clone Trooper, 2x ARC Trooper, Mij Gilamar, Dred Priest, Isabet Reau, exclusive to Entertainment Earth [A5S034] 40.00
___ Mandalorians and Omega Squad Omega Squad Sergeant, Omega Squad Sniper, Llats Ward, Rav Bralor, B'arin Apma, Omega Squad Demolition, Omega Squad Communications, exclusive to Entertainment Earth [A5S035] 40.00

Hasbro, Canada

Collector's tin sets. Multi-language packaging.
___ Episode 1: Darth Maul, Obi-Wan Kenobi, Qui-Gon Jinn, R2-R9 ....30.00
___ Episode 2: Clone Trooper, Anakin Skywalker, Jango Fett, Count Dooku 30.00
___ Episode 3: Mace Windu, Yoda, Anakin Skywalker, AT-RT Driver 30.00
___ Episode 4: Sandtrooper, Princess Leia, Darth Vader, C-3PO 30.00
___ Episode 5: Snowtrooper, Luke Skywalker, Han Solo, Chewbacca 30.00
___ Episode 6: Scout Trooper, Darth Vader, Princess Leia, Rebel Commando 30.00

Hasbro, Mexico

___ Edicion Especial. Coin folder plus 4 figures, exclusive to Sam's Club [A5S036] 65.00

Hasbro, UK

___ Clones and Commanders gift set [A5S037] ...45.00

Collector's tin sets. Exclusive editions.
___ Clone Wars 35.00

Action Figures: 2008 (30th anniversary)

Hasbro

___ 2-1B Surgical Droid 08-06 [A8A001] 8.00
___ 2-1B Surgical Droid 08-06 Capt. Rex offer sticker 8.00
___ Commander Gree 08-03 [A8A002] 8.00
___ Commander Gree 08-03 Capt. Rex offer 8.00
___ Darth Vader 08-02 [A8A003] 8.00
___ Darth Vader 08-02 Capt. Rex offer sticker 8.00

A8A001

A8A002

A8A003

A8A004

A8A005

A8A006

A8A007

A8A008

A8A009

A8A010

A8A011

A8A012

A8A013

A8A014

A8A015

A8A016

A8A017

A8A018

A8A019

A8A020

A8A021

A8A022

A8A023

A8A024

A8A025

A8A026

A8A027

A8A028

A8A029

A8A030

Action Figures

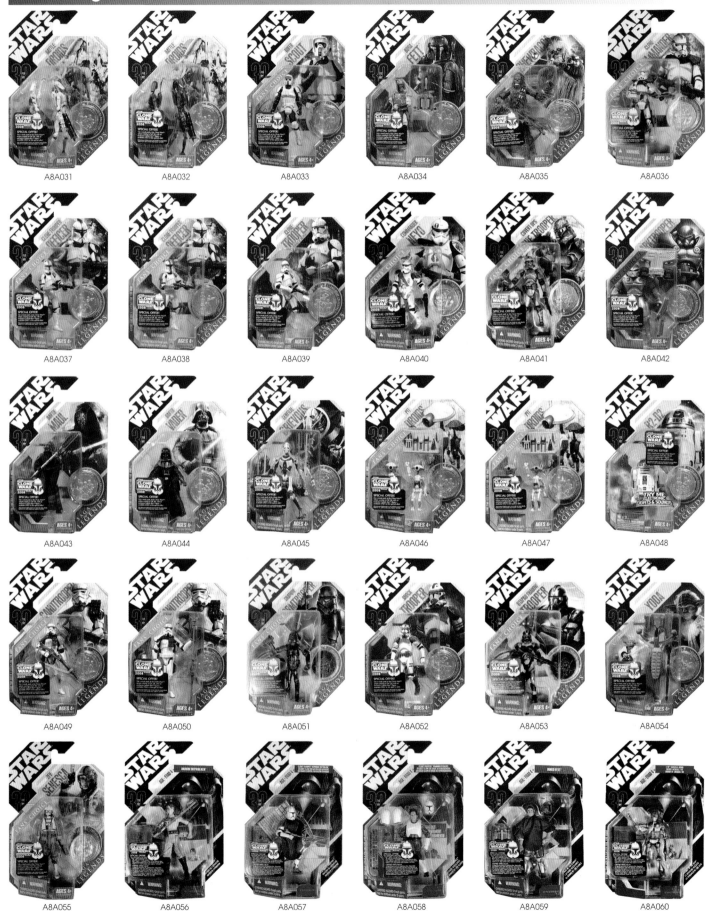

A8A031   A8A032   A8A033   A8A034   A8A035   A8A036

A8A037   A8A038   A8A039   A8A040   A8A041   A8A042

A8A043   A8A044   A8A045   A8A046   A8A047   A8A048

A8A049   A8A050   A8A051   A8A052   A8A053   A8A054

A8A055   A8A056   A8A057   A8A058   A8A059   A8A060

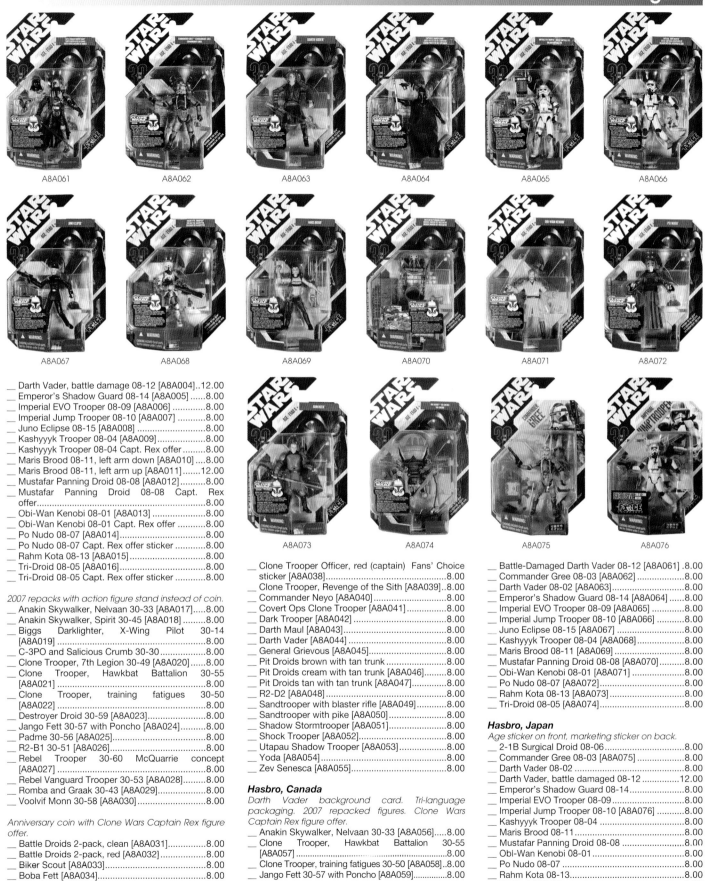

A8A061 A8A062 A8A063 A8A064 A8A065 A8A066

A8A067 A8A068 A8A069 A8A070 A8A071 A8A072

A8A073 A8A074 A8A075 A8A076

__ Darth Vader, battle damage 08-12 [A8A004]..12.00
__ Emperor's Shadow Guard 08-14 [A8A005] 8.00
__ Imperial EVO Trooper 08-09 [A8A006] 8.00
__ Imperial Jump Trooper 08-10 [A8A007] 8.00
__ Juno Eclipse 08-15 [A8A008] 8.00
__ Kashyyyk Trooper 08-04 [A8A009] 8.00
__ Kashyyyk Trooper 08-04 Capt. Rex offer 8.00
__ Maris Brood 08-11, left arm down [A8A010] 8.00
__ Maris Brood 08-11, left arm up [A8A011] 12.00
__ Mustafar Panning Droid 08-08 [A8A012]..........8.00
__ Mustafar Panning Droid 08-08 Capt. Rex offer 8.00
__ Obi-Wan Kenobi 08-01 [A8A013] 8.00
__ Obi-Wan Kenobi 08-01 Capt. Rex offer 8.00
__ Po Nudo 08-07 [A8A014] 8.00
__ Po Nudo 08-07 Capt. Rex offer sticker 8.00
__ Rahm Kota 08-13 [A8A015] 8.00
__ Tri-Droid 08-05 [A8A016] 8.00
__ Tri-Droid 08-05 Capt. Rex offer sticker 8.00

2007 repacks with action figure stand instead of coin.
__ Anakin Skywalker, Nelvaan 30-33 [A8A017].....8.00
__ Anakin Skywalker, Spirit 30-45 [A8A018] 8.00
__ Biggs Darklighter, X-Wing Pilot 30-14 [A8A019] 8.00
__ C-3PO and Salicious Crumb 30-30 ....8.00
__ Clone Trooper, 7th Legion 30-49 [A8A020] 8.00
__ Clone Trooper, Hawkbat Battalion 30-55 [A8A021] 8.00
__ Clone Trooper, training fatigues 30-50 [A8A022] 8.00
__ Destroyer Droid 30-59 [A8A023].....................8.00
__ Jango Fett 30-57 with Poncho [A8A024]..........8.00
__ Padme 30-56 [A8A025].....................................8.00
__ R2-B1 30-51 [A8A026].....................................8.00
__ Rebel Trooper 30-60 McQuarrie concept [A8A027] 8.00
__ Rebel Vanguard Trooper 30-53 [A8A028].........8.00
__ Romba and Graak 30-43 [A8A029]...................8.00
__ Voolvif Monn 30-58 [A8A030] 8.00

Anniversary coin with Clone Wars Captain Rex figure offer.
__ Battle Droids 2-pack, clean [A8A031]...............8.00
__ Battle Droids 2-pack, red [A8A032].................8.00
__ Biker Scout [A8A033].......................................8.00
__ Boba Fett [A8A034]..8.00
__ Chewbacca [A8A035] 8.00
__ Clone Commander [A8A036].............................8.00
__ Clone Trooper Officer, green (sergeant) Fans' Choice sticker [A8A037] 8.00

__ Clone Trooper Officer, red (captain) Fans' Choice sticker [A8A038]................................8.00
__ Clone Trooper, Revenge of the Sith [A8A039]..8.00
__ Commander Neyo [A8A040].............................8.00
__ Covert Ops Clone Trooper [A8A041]................8.00
__ Dark Trooper [A8A042] 8.00
__ Darth Maul [A8A043].......................................8.00
__ Darth Vader [A8A044]......................................8.00
__ General Grievous [A8A045]..............................8.00
__ Pit Droids brown with tan trunk 8.00
__ Pit Droids cream with tan trunk [A8A046]........8.00
__ Pit Droids tan with tan trunk [A8A047].............8.00
__ R2-D2 [A8A048]...8.00
__ Sandtrooper with blaster rifle [A8A049]............8.00
__ Sandtrooper with pike [A8A050].......................8.00
__ Shadow Stormtrooper [A8A051].......................8.00
__ Shock Trooper [A8A052]...................................8.00
__ Utapau Shadow Trooper [A8A053]....................8.00
__ Yoda [A8A054]..8.00
__ Zev Senesca [A8A055]......................................8.00

Hasbro, Canada
Darth Vader background card. Tri-language packaging. 2007 repacked figures. Clone Wars Captain Rex figure offer.
__ Anakin Skywalker, Nelvaan 30-33 [A8A056].....8.00
__ Clone Trooper, Hawkbat Battalion 30-55 [A8A057]...
__ Clone Trooper, training fatigues 30-50 [A8A058]..8.00
__ Jango Fett 30-57 with Poncho [A8A059].............8.00

Darth Vader background card. Tri-language packaging. Clone Wars Captain Rex figure offer.
__ 2-1B Surgical Droid 08-06 [A8A060] 8.00

__ Battle-Damaged Darth Vader 08-12 [A8A061] .8.00
__ Commander Gree 08-03 [A8A062] 8.00
__ Darth Vader 08-02 [A8A063]............................8.00
__ Emperor's Shadow Guard 08-14 [A8A064] 8.00
__ Imperial EVO Trooper 08-09 [A8A065] 8.00
__ Imperial Jump Trooper 08-10 [A8A066] 8.00
__ Juno Eclipse 08-15 [A8A067] 8.00
__ Kashyyyk Trooper 08-04 [A8A068] 8.00
__ Maris Brood 08-11 [A8A069] 8.00
__ Mustafar Panning Droid 08-08 [A8A070]..........8.00
__ Obi-Wan Kenobi 08-01 [A8A071] 8.00
__ Po Nudo 08-07 [A8A072] 8.00
__ Rahm Kota 08-13 [A8A073] 8.00
__ Tri-Droid 08-05 [A8A074] 8.00

Hasbro, Japan
Age sticker on front, marketing sticker on back.
__ 2-1B Surgical Droid 08-06 ....8.00
__ Commander Gree 08-03 [A8A075] 8.00
__ Darth Vader 08-02 ....8.00
__ Darth Vader, battle damaged 08-12 ....12.00
__ Emperor's Shadow Guard 08-14.......................8.00
__ Imperial EVO Trooper 08-09 ....8.00
__ Imperial Jump Trooper 08-10 [A8A076] 8.00
__ Kashyyyk Trooper 08-04 ....8.00
__ Maris Brood 08-11 ....8.00
__ Mustafar Panning Droid 08-08 ....8.00
__ Obl-Wan Kenobi 08-01 ....8.00
__ Po Nudo 08-07 ....8.00
__ Rahm Kota 08-13..8.00
__ Tri-Droid 08-05 ....8.00

A3E001

A3E002

A3E003

A3E004

A3E005

A3E006

A3E007

A3E008

A3E009

A3E010

A3E011

A3E012

A3E013

A3E014

A3E015

A3E016

A3E017

A3E018

A3E019

A3E020

A3E021

A3E022

A3E023

A3E024

A3E025

A3E026

A3E027

A3E028

A3E029

A3E030

A3E031

A3E032

A3E033

A3E034

A3E035

A3E036

Action Figures: 2008-2009 (The Clone Wars)

Hasbro

__ Ahsoka Tano 09 [A3E001] 12.00
__ Ahsoka Tano 09 blue-eyed package [A3E002]..12.00
__ Anakin Skywalker 01 [A3E003] 8.00
__ Anakin Skywalker 01 1st day of issue sticker [A3E004]...10.00
__ Asajj Ventress 15 ....12.00
__ Battle Droid 07 [A3E005] 8.00
__ Battle Droid 07 1st day of issue sticker [A3E006]...10.00
__ C-3PO 16 [A3E007] 12.00
__ Captain Rex, exclusive to mail-in [A3E008]....25.00
__ Captain Rex 04 [A3E009]...................................8.00
__ Captain Rex 04 1st day of issue sticker [A3E010]...10.00
__ Clone Commander Cody 10 [A3E011]............12.00
__ Clone Pilot Oddball 11 [A3E012] 12.00
__ Clone Trooper 05 [A3E013] 8.00
__ Clone Trooper 05 1st day of issue sticker [A3E014]...10.00
__ Clone Trooper, 212th Attack Battalion 19 [A3E015]...12.00
__ Clone Trooper, Space Gear 21 [A3E016] 12.00
__ Clone Trooper. 41st Elite Corps 26 [A3E017].12.00
__ Commander Fox, exclusive to Target [A3E018]...20.00
__ Count Dooku 13 [A3E019] 12.00
__ Destroyer Droid 17 [A3E020] 12.00
__ General Grievous 06 [A3E021].........................8.00
__ General Grievous 06 1st day of issue sticker [A3E022]...10.00
__ General Grievous, Holographic, exclusive to Toys R Us [A3E023] 8.00
__ IG-86 Assassin Droid 18 [A3E024] 12.00
__ Jar Jar Binks 24 [A3E025]..............................12.00
__ Kit Fisto 27 [A3E026] 12.00

__ Magnaguard 22 [A3E027] 12.00
__ Obi-Wan Kenobi 02 [A3E028].........................8.00
__ Obi-Wan Kenobi 02 1st day of issue sticker [A3E029]..10.00
__ Padme Amidala 20 [A3E030] 12.00
__ Plo Koon 14 [A3E031].....................................12.00
__ R2-D2 08 [A3E032]...8.00
__ R2-D2 08 1st day of issue sticker [A3E033] ...10.00
__ R3-S6, "Goldie" 23 [A3E034]..........................12.00
__ Rocket Battle Droid 25 [A3E035].....................12.00
__ Super Battle Droid 12 [A3E036]......................12.00
__ Yoda 03 [A3E037] 8.00
__ Yoda 03 1st day of issue sticker [A3E038] 10.00

Hasbro, Canada

Multi-language packaging.

__ Ahsoka Tano 09..12.00
__ Anakin Skywalker 01.....................................8.00
__ Asajj Ventress 15 ....12.00
__ Battle Droid 07...8.00
__ C-3PO 16 ....12.00
__ Captain Rex 04...8.00
__ Clone Commander Cody 10 ....12.00
__ Clone Pilot Oddball 11..................................12.00
__ Clone Trooper 05...8.00
__ Clone Trooper, 212th Attack Battalion 19 ......12.00
__ Clone Trooper, Space Gear 21 ....12.00
__ Count Dooku 13...12.00

A3E037

A3E038

__ Destroyer Droid 17.......................................12.00
__ General Grievous 06 ....8.00
__ IG-86 Assassin Droid 18 ....12.00
__ Magnaguard 22..12.00
__ Obi-Wan Kenobi 02 ....8.00
__ Padme Amidala 20..12.00
__ Plo Koon 14 ....12.00
__ R2-D2 08...8.00
__ R3-S6, "Goldie" 23 ....12.00
__ Super Battle Droid 12 ....12.00
__ Yoda 03 ....8.00

A4A001

A4A002

A4A003

A4A004

A4A005

A4A006

A4A007

A4A008

Action Figures

Action Figures: 2008-2009 (The Clone Wars) Multipacks

Hasbro
Battle Packs.
- __ AT-TE Assault Squad [A4A001] 35.00
- __ B'Omarr Monastery Assault [A4A002] 35.00
- __ Battle of Christophsis, exclusive to Target [A4A003] 75.00
- __ Jabba's Palace [A4A004]...........................35.00
- __ Jabba's Palace sticker covers age warning on front and chocking hazard text on back [A4A005]..35.00
- __ Obi-Wan Kenobi and 212th Attack Battalion Clone Troopers [A4A006].....................................35.00
- __ Speeder Bike Team Recon [A4A007] 35.00
- __ Yoda and Coruscant Guard [A4A008] 35.00

Action Figures: 2008-2009 (The Legacy Collection)

Hasbro
Droid factory. Each figure includes a piece to collect to build another droid figure.
- __ Ak-rev BD05 R7-ZO left leg 1st day of issue sticker [ALC001] 8.00
- __ Ak-rev BD05 R7-ZO left leg black-eyed package [ALC002] 8.00
- __ Ak-rev BD05 R7-ZO left leg blue-eyed package [ALC003] 8.00
- __ Anakin Skywalker BD50 HK-47 head and rifle [ALC004] 8.00
- __ Anakin Skywalker (EPIII concept) BD48 HK-47 right arm [ALC005] 8.00

- __ ARC Trooper BD53 HK-47 right leg [ALC006]..8.00
- __ Bail Organa BD26 MB-RA7 right arm [ALC007] 8.00
- __ Bane Malar BD07 R7-ZO torso 1st day of issue sticker [ALC008] 8.00
- __ Bane Malar BD07 R7-ZO torso black-eyed package [ALC009] 8.00
- __ Bane Malar BD07 R7-ZO torso blue-eyed package [ALC010] 8.00
- __ Beru Whitesun BD45 HK-47 torso [ALC011]....8.00
- __ Breha Organa BD27 MB-RA7 left leg [ALC012] 8.00
- __ Captain Needa BD40 [ALC013] 8.00
- __ Captain Typho BD47 HK-47 right leg [ALC014] 8.00
- __ Chewbacca BD03 R4-D6 head and center leg [ALC015] 8.00

ALC001

ALC002

ALC003

ALC004

ALC005

ALC006

ALC007

ALC008

ALC009

ALC010

ALC011

ALC012

ALC013

ALC014

ALC015

ALC016

ALC017

ALC018

ALC019

ALC020

ALC021

ALC022

ALC023

ALC024

 ALC025

 ALC026

 ALC027

 ALC028

 ALC029

 ALC030

 ALC031

 ALC032

 ALC033

 ALC034

 ALC035

 ALC036

 ALC037

 ALC038

 ALC039

 ALC040

 ALC041

 ALC042

 ALC043

 ALC044

 ALC045

 ALC046

 ALC047

 ALC048

 ALC049

 ALC050

 ALC051

 ALC052

 ALC053

 ALC054

ALC055

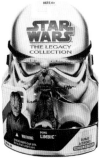

ALC056

ALC057

ALC058

ALC059

ALC060

ALC061

ALC062

ALC063

ALC064

ALC065

ALC066

ALC067

ALC068

ALC069

ALC070

ALC071

ALC072

ALC073

ALC074

ALC075

ALC076

ALC077

ALC078

ALC079

ALC080

ALC081

ALC082

ALC083

ALC084

ALC085

ALC086

ALC087

ALC088

ALC089

ALC090

ALC091

ALC092

ALC093

ALC094

ALC095

ALC096

ALC097

ALC098

ALC099

ALC100

ALC101

ALC102

ALC103

ALC104

ALC105

ALC106

ALC107

ALC108

ALC109

ALC110

ALC111

ALC112

ALC113

ALC114

Chewbacca BD03 R4-D6 head and center leg 1st day of issue sticker [ALC016] 8.00

Clone Pilot BD52 HK-47 left leg [ALC017].......8.00

Clone Trooper BD16 5D6-RA7 head blue-eyed package [ALC018] 8.00

Clone Trooper BD16 R4-J1 right leg black-eyed package [ALC019] 8.00

Clone Trooper, 327th Star Corps BD29 R5-A2 torso [ALC020] 8.00

Clone Trooper, Coruscant Landing Platform BD17 5D6-RA7 torso [ALC021] 8.00

Commander Faie BD24 MB-RA7 torso [ALC022] 8.00

Commander Faie BD24 R5-A2 left leg 8.00

Count Dooku, Holographic BD21 5D6-RA7 right arm [ALC023] 8.00

Darth Vader BD08 5D6-RA7 right leg blue-eyed package [ALC024] 8.00

Darth Vader BD08 R7-ZO head and center leg 1st day of issue sticker [ALC025] 8.00

Darth Vader BD08 R7-ZO head and center leg black-eyed package [ALC026] 8.00

Emperor Palpatine BD39 [ALC027].............8.00

FX-6 BD28 MB-RA7 right leg [ALC028].......8.00

General Grievous BD25 MB-RA7 head 8.00

General Grievous BD25 R5-A2 right leg [ALC029] 8.00

Han Solo BD01 R4-D6 left leg 1st day of issue sticker [ALC030] 8.00

Han Solo BD01 R4-D6 left leg black-eyed package [ALC031] 8.00

Han Solo BD01 R4-D6 left leg blue-eyed package [ALC032] 8.00

Han Solo (stormtrooper disguise) BD31 R5-A2 right leg blue-eyed package [ALC033] 8.00

Hoth Rebel Trooper BD42 with beard [ALC034] 8.00

Hoth Rebel Trooper without beard BD42 ....8.00

IG Lancer Droid BD13 R4-J1 torso [ALC035]...8.00

Imperial Engineer BD22 5D6-RA7 left arm [ALC036] 8.00

Jango Fett BD51 HK-47 torso [ALC037] 8.00

Jawa with WED Treadwell Droid BD33 R5-A2 torso blue-eyed package [ALC038] 8.00

Jodo Kast BD18 5D6-RA7 head [ALC039] 8.00

Leektar and Nippet BD04 R4-D6 torso 1st day of issue sticker [ALC040] 8.00

Leektar and Nippet BD04 R4-D6 torso black-eyed package [ALC041] 8.00

Leektar and Nippet BD04 R4-D6 torso blue-eyed package [ALC042] 8.00

Luke Skywalker BD02 R4-D6 right leg 1st day of issue sticker [ALC043] 8.00

Luke Skywalker BD02 R4-D6 right leg black-eyed package [ALC044] 8.00

Luke Skywalker BD02 R4-D6 right leg blue-eyed package [ALC045] 8.00

Luke Skywalker BD02 R5-A2 head and center leg blue-eyed package [ALC046] 8.00

Luke Skywalker BD38 [ALC047]......................8.00

Luke Skywalker (stormtrooper disguise) BD30 R5-A2 left leg blue-eyed package [ALC048] 8.00

Mon Calamari Warrior BD14 R7-T1 torso [ALC049] 8.00

Obi-Wan Kenobi BD09 5D6-RA7 torso blue-eyed package [ALC050] 8.00

Obi-Wan Kenobi BD09 R4-J1 left leg black-eyed package [ALC051] 8.00

Obi-Wan Kenobi BD34 R2-N6 left leg blue-eyed package [ALC052] 8.00

Obi-Wan Kenobi BD44 HK-47 head and rifle [ALC053] 8.00

Owen Lars BD46 HK-47 left leg [ALC054]........8.00

Padme Amidala BD12 R7-T1 left leg [ALC055] 8.00

Pons Limbic BD35 R2-N6 right leg blue-eyed package [ALC056] 8.00

Princess Leia BD41 [ALC057].........................8.00

Quarren Soldier BD15 R7-T1 head and center leg [ALC058] 8.00

Saesee Tiin BD11 R7-T1 right leg [ALC059].....8.00

Saleucami Clone Trooper BD20 5D6-RA7 left leg [ALC060] 8.00

Scuba Trooper BD10 R4-J1 head and center leg [ALC061] 8.00

Space Trooper BD32 R5-A2 head and center leg

A8B001

A8B002

A8B003

A8B004

A8B005

A8B006

A8B007

A8B008

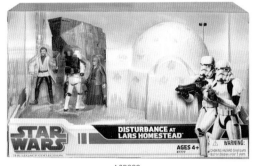

A8B009

A8B010

A8B011

blue-eyed package [ALC062] 8.00
__ Stass Allie BD23 MB-RA7 left arm [ALC063]....8.00
__ Tarados Gon BD49 HK-47 left arm [ALC064]...8.00
__ Trinto Duaba and Dice Ibegon BD37 R2-N6 torso
    blue-eyed package [ALC065] 8.00
__ Ugnaught BD43 blue smock [ALC066]............8.00
__ Wioslea BD36 R2-N6 head and center leg blue-
    eyed package [ALC067].....................................8.00
__ Yaddle and Evan Piell BD19 5D6-RA7 right leg
    [ALC068] 8.00
__ Yarna D'Al'Gargan BD06 R7-ZO right leg 1st day of
    issue sticker [ALC069] 8.00
__ Yarna D'Al'Gargan BD06 R7-ZO right leg black-
    eyed package [ALC070]....................................8.00
__ Yarna D'Al'Gargan BD06 R7-ZO right leg blue-eyed
    package [ALC071] 8.00

*Greatest hits with droid factory. Repacked figures
include a piece to collect to build another droid
figure.*
__ Commander Gree GH01 1st day of issue sticker
    [ALC072] 8.00
__ Commander Gree GH01 black-eyed package
    [ALC073] 8.00
__ Commander Gree GH01 5D6-RA7 left leg blue-
    eyed package [ALC074]....................................8.00
__ Darth Vader, battle damaged GH03 1st day of issue
    sticker [ALC075] 8.00
__ Darth Vader, battle damaged GH03 R4-D6 head
    and center leg black-eyed package [ALC076]..8.00
__ Darth Vader, battle damaged GH03 R4-D6 head
    and center leg blue-eyed package [ALC077] ...8.00
__ Imperial EVO Trooper GH04 1st day of issue sticker
    [ALC078] 8.00
__ Imperial EVO Trooper GH04 black-eyed package
    [ALC079] 8.00
__ Imperial EVO Trooper GH04 5D6-RA7 left arm blue-
    eyed package [ALC080]....................................8.00
__ Kashyyyk Scout Trooper GH02 1st day of issue
    sticker [ALC081] 8.00
__ Kashyyyk Scout Trooper GH02 black-eyed package
    [ALC082] 8.00
__ Kashyyyk Scout Trooper GH02 5D6-RA7 right arm
    blue-eyed package [ALC083] 8.00

Saga Legends. Each figure includes clone gear.
__ 501st Trooper SL16 [ALC084] 8.00
__ Arc Trooper SL19 black-eyed package
    [ALC085] 8.00
__ Arc Trooper SL19 blue-eyed package
    [ALC086] 8.00

__ Arc Trooper Commander SL23 [ALC087].........8.00
__ Barc Trooper SL18 black-eyed package
    [ALC088] 8.00
__ Barc Trooper SL18 blue-eyed pkg. [ALC089]...8.00
__ Battle Droid 2-pack SL20 red [ALC090] 8.00
__ Battle Droid 2-pack SL20 white [ALC091]........8.00
__ C-3PO SL06 [ALC092]......................................8.00
__ Clone Trooper SL05 [ALC093]..........................8.00
__ Clone Trooper Officer SL12 blue [ALC094] 8.00
__ Clone Trooper Officer SL12 green [ALC095]......8.00
__ Clone Trooper Officer SL12 red [ALC096].........8.00
__ Clone Trooper Officer SL12 yellow [ALC097]...8.00
__ Darth Maul SL14 [ALC098] 8.00
__ Darth Vader SL13 [ALC099]..............................8.00
__ Darth Vader (Anakin) SL03 [ALC100]...............8.00
__ Destroyer Droid SL11 [ALC101].......................8.00
__ General Grievous SL07 [ALC102].....................8.00
__ Jango Fett SL15 [ALC103]................................8.00
__ Luke Skywalker SL22 [ALC104].......................8.00
__ Mace Windu SL08 [ALC105].............................8.00
__ Obi-Wan Kenobi SL04 [ALC106].......................8.00
__ Plo Koon SL09 [ALC107].................................8.00
__ R2-D2 SL01 [ALC108].......................................8.00
__ Saesee Tiin SL26 [ALC109].............................8.00
__ Sandtrooper SL21 [ALC110].............................8.00
__ Shock Trooper SL17 [ALC111].........................8.00
__ Super Battle Droid SL10 [ALC112]...................8.00
__ Tri-Droid SL24 [ALC113]...................................8.00
__ Yoda and Kybuck SL02 [ALC114] 8.00

Hasbro, Canada
*Droid factory. Each figure includes a piece to
collect to build another droid figure. Multi-language
packaging.*
__ Ak-rev BD05 R7-ZO left leg............................8.00
__ Bane Malar BD07 R7-ZO torso.......................8.00
__ Chewbacca BD03 R4-D6 head 8.00
__ Clone Trooper BD16 R4-J1 right leg 8.00
__ Corucsant Clone Trooper BD17 ....8.00
__ Count Dooku, Holographic BD21 ....8.00
__ Darth Vader BD08 R7-ZO head 8.00
__ Han Solo BD01 R4-D6 left leg.........................8.00
__ IG Lancer Droid BD13 R4-J1 torso..................8.00
__ Imperial Engineer BD22 ....8.00
__ Jodo Kast BD18..8.00
__ Leektar and Nippet BD04 R4-D6 torso 8.00
__ Luke Skywalker BD02 R4-D6 right leg 8.00
__ Mon Calamari Warrior BD14 R7-T1 torso........8.00
__ Obi-Wan Kenobi BD09 R4-J1 left leg...............8.00
__ Padme Amidala BD12 R7-T1 left leg...............8.00
__ Quarren Soldier BD15 R7-T1 head..................8.00

__ Saesee Tiin BD11 R7-T1 right leg 8.00
__ Saleucami Clone Trooper BD20.......................8.00
__ Scuba Trooper BD10 R4-J1 head 8.00
__ Yaddle and Evan Piell BD19 ....8.00
__ Yarna D'Al'Gargan BD06 R7-ZO right leg 8.00

*Greatest hits with droid factory. Repacked figures
include a piece to collect to build another droid
figure. Multi-language packaging.*
__ Commander Gree GH01 ....8.00
__ Darth Vader, battle damaged GH03 ....8.00
__ Imperial EVO Trooper GH04 ....8.00
__ Kashyyyk Scout Trooper GH02 ....8.00

*Saga Legends. Each figure includes clone gear. Multi-
language packaging.*
__ 501st Trooper SL16 ....8.00
__ Arc Trooper SL19 ....8.00
__ Barc Trooper SL18 ....8.00
__ C-3PO SL06...8.00
__ Clone Trooper SL05..8.00
__ Clone Trooper, EPII red SL12 ....8.00
__ Darth Maul SL14 ....8.00
__ Darth Vader SL13 ....8.00
__ Darth Vader (Anakin) SL03 ....8.00
__ Destroyer Droid SL11 ....8.00
__ General Grievous SL07 ....8.00
__ Jango Fett SL15 ....8.00
__ Mace Windu SL08 ....8.00
__ Obi-Wan Kenobi SL04 ....8.00
__ Plo Koon SL09 ....8.00
__ R2-D2 SL01 ....8.00
__ Shock Trooper SL17 ....8.00
__ Super Battle Droid SL10 ....8.00
__ Yoda and Kybuck SL02 ....8.00

Action Figures: 2008-2009 (The Legacy Collection Multipacks)

Hasbro
__ Battlefront II: Clone Pack [A8B001] 35.00
__ Battlefront II: Droid Pack [A8B002]................35.00
__ Crimson Empire 6-pack, exclusive to Previews
    [A8B003] 35.00
__ Joker Squad, exclusive to Entertainment Earth
    [A8B004] 40.00
__ Legends of the Saga 5-pack Darth Maul, Darth
    Vader, Boba Fett, Luke Skywalker, Obi-Wan
    Kenobi, exclusive to K-Mart [A8B005]...........35.00

A8B012

A8B013

A8B014

A8B015

A8B016

A8B017

Battle Packs.
__ Attack on Kashyyyk, Target excl. [A8B007]....25.00
__ Battle at Sarlacc Pit, exclusive to Target [A8B008] 75.00
__ Battle On Mygeeto [A8B009] 25.00
__ Disturbance at Lars' Homestead, exclusive to Toys R Us [A8B010] 50.00
__ Hoth Patrol, excl. to Toys R Us [A8B011].......25.00
__ Hoth Recon Patrol [A8B012]...........................25.00
__ Hoth Speeder Bike Patrol [A8B013] 25.00
__ Jedi Training on Dagobah [A8B014]................25.00
__ Scramble on Yavin [A8B015] 25.00
__ Shield Generator Assault [A8B016] 25.00
__ STAP Attack, exclusive to Toys R Us [A8B006]...25.00
__ Training on the Falcon Ben holding helmet in hand..25.00
__ Training on the Falcon Ben holding helmet under arm [A8B017] 25.00

Droid Factory 2-packs. Each includes an additional piece to build C-3PX. Walmart exclusives.
__ Darth Vader and K-3PX, 2 of 6, C-3PX's left arm [A8B018] 18.00
__ Han Solo Hoth and R-3PO, 3 of 6, C-3PX's left leg [A8B019] 18.00
__ Kit Fisto and R4-H5, 4 of 6, C-3PX's torso [A8B020] 18.00
__ Luke Skywalker / R2-D2, C-3PX's right arm [A8B021] 18.00
__ Plo Kloon and R4-F5 1 of 6 C-3PX's right leg [A8B022] 18.00
__ Watto and R2-T0 5 of 6 C-3PX's head [A8B023] 18.00

A8B018

A8B019

A8B020

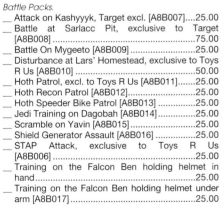

A8B021

A8B022

A8B023

Action Figures: 2009-2010 (The Clone Wars)

Hasbro

__ 4A-7 CW13 [A4E001].......................................8.00
__ AAT Driver Battle Droid CW33 [A4E002] 8.00
__ Aayla Secura CW40 [A4E003] 8.00
__ Admiral Yularen CW07 [A4E004] 8.00
__ Ahsoka Tano CW23 [A4E005].........................8.00
__ Anakin Skywalker CW18 [A4E006] 8.00
__ Anakin Skywalker CW21 [A4E007] 8.00
__ Anakin Skywalker CW42 [A4E008] 8.00
__ ARF Trooper CW10 [A4E009] 8.00
__ Cad Bane CW22 [A4E010]..............................8.00
__ Captain Argyus CW31 [A4E011].....................8.00
__ Captain Rex CW24 [A4E012]...........................8.00
__ Captain Rex (Cold Assault Gear) CW50 [A4E013].......................................8.00
__ Clone Commander Stone CW44 [A4E014].......8.00
__ Clone Commander Thire CW32 [A4E015] 8.00
__ Clone Tank Gunner CW36 [A4E016] 8.00
__ Clone Trooper Denal CW20 [A4E017] 8.00
__ Clone Trooper Echo CW17 [A4E018] 8.00
__ Clone Trooper Jek CW38 [A4E019].................8.00
__ Clone Trooper w/space gear CW02 [A4E020]..8.00
__ Clone Trooper, 41st Elite Corps. CW04 [A4E021].......................................8.00
__ Commander Bly CW39 [A4E022].....................8.00
__ Commander Gree CW09 [A4E023]...................8.00
__ Commander Ponds, exclusive to Toys R Us [A4E024].....................................10.00
__ Commander TX-20 CW46 [A4E025].................8.00
__ Commando Droid CW16 [A4E026]...................8.00

__ Darth Sidious CW45 [A4E027].........................8.00
__ Firefighter Droid CW47 [A4E028].....................8.00
__ General Grievous CW01 [A4E029]....................8.00
__ Hondo Ohnaka CW41 [A4E030].......................8.00
__ Jawas 2-pack CW08 [A4E031].........................8.00
__ Kit Fisto CW05 [A4E032].................................8.00
__ Luminara Unduli CW30 [A4E033].....................8.00
__ Mace Windu CW06 [A4E034]...........................8.00
__ MagnaGuard (with Cape) CW49.......................8.00
__ Matchstick CW34 [A4E035].............................8.00
__ Obi-Wan Kenobi CW12 [A4E036].....................8.00
__ Obi-Wan Kenobi CW19 [A4E037].....................8.00
__ Obi-Wan Kenobi (Cold Weather Gear) CW48 [A4E038].......................................8.00
__ Padme Amidala CW35 [A4E039] 8.00
__ Rocket Battle Droid CW03 [A4E040].................8.00
__ Super Battle Droid, heavy assault CW11 [A4E041].......................................8.00
__ Thi-Sen CW43 [A4E042].................................8.00
__ Whorm Loathsome CW15 [A4E043]..................8.00
__ Yoda CW14 [A4E044]......................................8.00
__ Ziro's Assassin Droid CW37 [A4E045]..............8.00

Hasbro, UK

__ Qui-Gon Jinn and Eopie special offer sticker...8.00
__ CW18 Qui-Gon Jinn and Eopie special offer sticker. 8.00
__ 4A-7 CW13 ....8.00
__ 4A-7 CW13 Qui-Gon Jinn and Eopie special offer sticker. 8.00
__ AAT Driver Battle Droid CW33.........................8.00
__ Aayla Secura CW40 ....8.00
__ Admiral Yularen CW07 ....8.00

__ Admiral Yularen CW07 Qui-Gon Jinn and Eopie special offer sticker.......................................8.00
__ Ahsoka Tano CW23 ....8.00
__ Ahsoka Tano CW23 Qui-Gon Jinn and Eopie special offer sticker. [A4E046] 8.00
__ Anakin Skywalker CW18.......................................8.00
__ Anakin Skywalker CW21.......................................8.00
__ Anakin Skywalker CW21 Qui-Gon Jinn and Eopie special offer sticker. [A4E047] 8.00
__ Anakin Skywalker CW42.......................................8.00
__ ARF Trooper CW10 ....8.00
__ ARF Trooper CW10 Qui-Gon Jinn and Eopie special offer sticker.......................................8.00
__ Cad Bane CW22 ....8.00
__ Cad Bane CW22 Qui-Gon Jinn and Eopie special offer sticker. [A4E048]........................8.00
__ Capatain Rex CW24 ....8.00
__ Captain Argyus CW31 ....8.00
__ Captain Rex (Cold Assault Gear) CW50 ....8.00
__ Clone Commander Stone CW44 ....8.00
__ Clone Commander Thire CW32.........................8.00
__ Clone Tank Gunner CW36...............................8.00
__ Clone Trooper Denal CW20...............................8.00
__ Clone Trooper Denal CW20 Qui-Gon Jinn and Eopie special offer sticker. 8.00
__ Clone Trooper Echo CW17...............................8.00
__ Clone Trooper Echo CW17 Qui-Gon Jinn and Eopie special offer sticker.......................................8.00
__ Clone Trooper Jek CW38 ....8.00
__ Clone Trooper with space gear CW02 ....8.00
__ Clone Trooper with space gear CW02 Qui-Gon Jinn and Eopie special offer sticker. 8.00
__ Clone Trooper, 41st Elite Corps. CW04 ....8.00

A4E001

A4E002

A4E003

A4E004

A4E005

A4E006

A4E007

A4E008

A4E009

A4E010

A4E011

A4E012

A4E013

A4E014

A4E015

A4E016

A4E017

A4E018

CLONE TROOPER JEK

A4E019

CLONE TROOPER

A4E020

CLONE TROOPER

A4E021

COMMANDER BLY

A4E022

COMMANDER GREE

A4E023

COMMANDER PONDS

A4E024

TX-20

A4E025

DROID

A4E026

DARTH SIDIOUS

A4E027

DROID

A4E028

GRIEVOUS

A4E029

HONDO OHNAKA

A4E030

JAWAS

A4E031

KIT FISTO

A4E032

LUMINARA UNDULI

A4E033

MACE WINDU

A4E034

MATCHSTICK

A4E035

KENOBI

A4E036

KENOBI

A4E037

KENOBI

A4E038

PADMÉ AMIDALA

A4E039

BATTLE DROID

A4E040

SUPER BATTLE DROID

A4E041

THI-SEN

A4E042

LOATHSOM

A4E043

YODA

A4E044

ASSASSIN DROID

A4E045

AHSOKA TANO

A4E046

SKYWALKER

A4E047

CAD BANE

A4E048

A6A001

A6A002

A6A003

A6A004

A6A005

A6A006

A6A007

A6A008

A6A009

A6A010

A6A011

A6A012

LEGENDS OF THE CLONE WARS

A5A001

ANAKIN SKYWALKER & R2-D2

A5A002

SKYWALKER & R2-D2

A5A003

REX & FIVES

A5A004

CODY & TROOPER

A5A005

CLONE COMMANDER CODY vs. BATTLE DROID

A5A006

CODY & ECHO

A5A007

GENERAL GRIEVOUS & BATTLE DROID

A5A008

GENERAL GRIEVOUS & BATTLE DROID

A5A009

LIEUTENANT THIRE & RYS

A5A010

OBI-WAN KENOBI vs. BATTLE DROID

A5A011

YODA & CLONE TROOPER JEK

A5A012

AMBUSH AT ABREGADO

A5A013

AMBUSH ON THE VULTURE'S CLAW

A5A014

GELAGRUB PATROL

A5A015

GEONOSIS ASSAULT

A5A016

HOLOCRON HEIST

BATTLE PACKS

A5A017

JEDI SHOWDOWN

BATTLE PACKS

A5A018

RISHI MOON OUTPOST ATTACK

BATTLE PACKS

A5A019

COMMEMORATIVE TIN COLLECTION

COUNT DOOKU   ASAJJ VENTRESS   OBI-WAN KENOBI   CAPTAIN REX

A5A020

Action Figures: 2009-2010 (The Clone Wars Deluxe)

Hasbro

__ 212th Battalion Clone Trooper and Jet Backpacks [A6A001] 35.00
__ Anakin Skywalker and Can-Cell [A6A002] 30.00
__ AT-RT with ARF Trooper [A6A003] 30.00
__ BARC Speeder with Clone Commander Cody [A6A004] 30.00
__ Battle Droid and Armored Scout Tank [A6A005] 30.00
__ Clone Trooper and BARC Speeder Bike [A6A006] 30.00
__ Count Dooku and Speederbike [A6A007].......30.00
__ Crab Droid [A6A008]..................................20.00
__ Freeco Speeder and Obi-Wan Kenobi [A6A009] 30.00
__ Speeder Bike with Scout Trooper, exclusive to Toys R Us [A6A010]...30.00
__ STAP with Battle Droid [A6A011]...................30.00
__ Turbo Tank Support Squad [A6A012].............35.00

Hasbro, UK

__ AT-RT with ARF Trooper 30.00

Action Figures: 2009-2010 (The Clone Wars Multipacks)

Hasbro

__ Legends of the Clone Wars [A5A001].............35.00

ARC TROOPER
ALD003

AT-AT DRIVER
ALD004

BIKER SCOUT
ALD005

BOBA FETT
ALD006

2-Packs.

__ Anakin Skywalker and R2-D2 [A5A002]..........15.00
__ Anakin Skywalker and R2-D2 1 of 3 [A5A003] 15.00
__ Captain Rex and Clone Trooper Fives, exclusive to Walmart [A5A004] 15.00
__ Clone Commander Cody and Clone Trooper 3 of 3 [A5A005] 15.00
__ Clone Commander Cody vs. Battle Droid [A5A006]...15.00
__ Clone Trooper Echo and Commander Cody, exclusive to Walmart [A5A007].......................15.00
__ General Grievous and Battle Droid [A5A008] .15.00
__ General Grievous and Battle Droid 2 of 3 [A5A009] 15.00
__ Lieutenant Thire and Clone Trooper Rys 2 of 2 [A5A010] 15.00
__ Obi-Wan Kenobi vs. Battle Droid [A5A011]....15.00
__ Yoda and Clone Trooper Jek 1 of 2 [A5A012] 15.00

Battle Packs.

__ Ambush at Abregado [A5A013] 35.00
__ Ambush on the Vulture's Claw [A5A014]........35.00
__ Gelagrub Patrol [A5A015] 35.00
__ Geonosis Assault [A5A016] 35.00
__ Holocron Heist [A5A017] 35.00
__ Jedi Showdown [A5A018]..............................35.00
__ Rishi Moon Outpost Attack [A5A019].............35.00

Collector's tin sets.

__ Count Dooku, Asajj Ventress, Obi-Wan Kenobi, Captain Rex, exclusive to Toys R Us [A5A020] 30.00

Action Figures: 2009-2010 (The Legacy Collection)

Hasbro

Droid factory. Each figure includes a piece to collect to build another droid figure.

__ Agen Kolar BD43 [ALD001] 8.00
__ Anakin Skywalker BD14 [ALD002]....................8.00
__ ARC Trooper BD26 [ALD003] 8.00
__ AT-AT Driver BD49 [ALD004]...........................8.00
__ Biker Scout BD12 [ALD005] 8.00
__ Boba Fett BD36 [ALD006] 8.00
__ Chewbacca BD31 [ALD007].............................8.00
__ Clegg Holdfast BD11 [ALD008] 8.00
__ Clone Commander Bacara BD47 [ALD009] 8.00

AGEN KOLAR
ALD001

SKYWALKER
ALD002

CHEWBACCA
ALD007

CLEGG HOLDFAST
ALD008

Action Figures

BACARA

ALD009

CODY

ALD010

DEVISS

ALD011

SCUBA TROOPER

ALD012

WING GUARD

ALD013

WING GUARD

ALD014

DARK TROOPER

ALD015

DARTH MAUL

ALD016

DARTH SIDIOUS

ALD017

EWOKS

ALD018

GIRAN

ALD019

WARRIOR

ALD020

HAN SOLO

ALD021

HAN SOLO

ALD022

KAL FAS

ALD023

IG-88

ALD024

SCANNING CREW

ALD025

JACEN SOLO

ALD026

JAINA SOLO

ALD027

JANGO FETT

ALD028

JAWA

ALD029

JAWA

ALD030

COLTON

ALD031

K'KRUHK

ALD032

KI-ADI-MUNDI

ALD033

LEESUB SIRLN

ALD034

SKYWALKER

ALD035

LUKE SKYWALKER

ALD036

SKYWALKER

ALD037

MAJOR PANNO

ALD038

MALAKILI

ALD039

NIEN NUNB

ALD040

GUNNER

ALD041

OBI-WAN KENOBI

ALD042

KENOBI

ALD043

PADMÉ AMIDALA

ALD044

PLO KOON

ALD045

PRINCESS LEIA

ALD046

QUEEN AMIDALA

ALD047

R2-D2

ALD048

R2-X2

ALD049

RUM SLEG

ALD050

TROOPER

ALD051

SHAAK TI

ALD052

SNOWTROOPER

ALD053

SPACETROOPER

ALD054

SPACETROOPER

ALD055

STORMTROOPER

ALD056

UGNAUGHT

ALD057

UTAI

ALD058

WILLROW HOOD

ALD059

ZUCKUSS

ALD060

TROOPER

ALD061

C-3PO

ALD062

CHEWBACCA

ALD063

CHEWBACCA

ALD064

CLONE TROOPER

ALD065

CLONE TROOPER

ALD066

DARTH MAUL

ALD067

DARTH VADER

ALD068

ALD069

ALD070

ALD071

ALD072

ALD073

ALD074

ALD075

ALD076

ALD077

ALD078

ALD079

ALD080

__ Clone Commander Cody BD44 [ALD010] 8.00
__ Clone Commander Deviss BD37 [ALD011] 8.00
__ Clone Scuba Trooper BD27 [ALD012].............8.00
__ Cloud City Wing Guard (Sgt. Edian) BD50
[ALD013] 8.00
__ Cloud City Wing Guard (Utris M'Toc) BD50
[ALD014] 8.00
__ Dark Trooper Phase I BD56 [ALD015] 8.00
__ Darth Maul BD05 [ALD016]............................8.00
__ Darth Sidious hologram BD10 [ALD017] 8.00
__ Ewoks BD18 [ALD018]...................................8.00
__ Giran BD21 [ALD019].....................................8.00
__ Gungan Warrior BD07 [ALD020].....................8.00
__ Han Solo BD30 [ALD021] 8.00
__ Han Solo, stormtrooper disguise BD02
[ALD022]...8.00
__ Hrchek Kal Fas BD33 [ALD023].......................8.00
__ IG-88, concept art BD40 [ALD024]..................8.00
__ Imperial Scanning Crew BD32 [ALD025]...........8.00
__ Jacen Solo BD59 [ALD026].............................8.00
__ Jaina Solo BD60 [ALD027] 8.00
__ Jango Fett BD15 [ALD028]..............................8.00
__ Jawa and Security Droid BD39 [ALD029].........8.00
__ Jawa with WED Treadwell Droid BD04
[ALD030]...8.00
__ Jeremoch Colton BD42 [ALD031].....................8.00
__ K'kruhk BD57 [ALD032]...................................8.00
__ Ki-Adi-Mundi, concept art BD38 [ALD033] 8.00
__ Leesub Sirln BD34 [ALD034]...........................8.00
__ Luke Skywalker BD16 [ALD035].......................8.00
__ Luke Skywalker, snowspeeder pilot BD51
[ALD036]...8.00
__ Luke Skywalker, stormtrooper disguise BD01
[ALD037]...8.00

__ Major Panno BD20 [ALD038]...........................8.00
__ Malakili BD22 [ALD039].................................8.00
__ Nein Nunb BD19 [ALD040].............................8.00
__ Nikto Gunner BD23 [ALD041]..........................8.00
__ Obi-Wan Kenobi BD06 [ALD042].....................8.00
__ Obi-Wan Kenobi BD13 [ALD043].....................8.00
__ Padme Amidala BD35 [ALD044]......................8.00
__ Plo Koon BD45 [ALD045]................................8.00
__ Princess Leia BD17 [ALD046]..........................8.00
__ Queen Amidala BD08 [ALD047].......................8.00
__ R2-D2 BD29 [ALD048]....................................8.00
__ R2-X2 BD52 [ALD049]....................................8.00
__ Rum Sleg BD09 [ALD050]...............................8.00
__ Saleucami Clone Trooper BD25 [ALD051] 8.00
__ Shaak Ti BD61 [ALD052] 8.00
__ Snowtrooper, concept art BD48 [ALD053].......8.00
__ Spacetrooper BD03 [ALD054] 8.00
__ Spacetrooper BD58 [ALD055] 8.00
__ Stormtrooper BD46 [ALD056]..........................8.00
__ Ugnaught BD28 [ALD057] 8.00
__ Utai BD41 [ALD058].......................................8.00
__ Willrow Hood BD53 [ALD059]..........................8.00
__ Zuckuss BD54 [ALD060].................................8.00

Saga Legends. Each figure includes clone gear.
__ 501st Legion Trooper SL08 [ALD061] 8.00
__ C-3PO SL18 [ALD062] 8.00
__ Chewbacca, combed fur SL15 [ALD063] 8.00
__ Chewbacca, wind blown fur SL15 [ALD064] 8.00
__ Clone Trooper, AOTC SL04 [ALD065] 8.00
__ Clone Trooper, ROTS SL12 [ALD066] 8.00
__ Darth Maul SL07 [ALD067] 8.00
__ Darth Vader SL02 [ALD068]............................8.00
__ Darth Vader SL06 [ALD069]............................8.00

__ Han Solo SL16 [ALD070] 8.00
__ Luke Skywalker, X-Wing Pilot SL17 [ALD071]..8.00
__ Obi-Wan Kenobi SL03 [ALD072] 8.00
__ Obi-Wan Kenobi, Pilot SL19 [ALD073] 8.00
__ Plo Koon SL13 [ALD074] 8.00
__ R2-D2 SL01 [ALD075] 8.00
__ Saesee Tiin SL11 [ALD076] 8.00
__ Sandtrooper SL10 [ALD077]...........................8.00
__ Shocktrooper SL14 [ALD078] 8.00
__ Super Battle Droid SL05 [ALD079] 8.00
__ Yoda SL09 [ALD080] 8.00

Hasbro, UK

Droid factory. Each figure includes a piece to collect to build another droid figure. Multi-language packaging.
__ Agen Kolar BD43 ....8.00
__ Anakin Skywalker BD14.................................8.00
__ ARC Trooper BD26...8.00
__ AT-AT Driver BD49 ....8.00
__ Biker Scout BD12 ....8.00
__ Boba Fett BD36 ....8.00
__ Chewbacca BD31...8.00
__ Clegg Holdfast BD11.....................................8.00
__ Clone Commander Bacara BD47 ....8.00
__ Clone Commander Cody BD44 ....8.00
__ Clone Commander Deviss BD37 ....8.00
__ Clone Scuba Trooper BD27.............................8.00
__ Cloud City Wing Guard (Sgt. Edian) BD50 ....8.00
__ Cloud City Wing Guard (Utris M'Toc) BD50 .....8.00
__ Dark Trooper Phase I BD56.............................8.00
__ Darth Maul BD05 ....8.00
__ Darth Sidious hologram BD10 ....8.00
__ Ewoks BD18 ....8.00

ALD081

ALD082

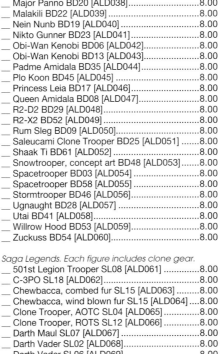
ALD083

ALD084

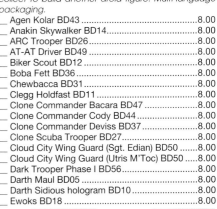
ALD085

ALD086

CLONE TROOPER SQUAD

A9B001

A9B002

A9B003

A9B004

A9B005

A9B006

A9B007

A9B008

A9B009

A9B010

A9B011

A9B012

BATTLE FOR ENDOR

A9B013

BIRTH OF DARTH VADER

A9B014

DUEL ON MUSTAFAR

A9B015

A9B016

A9B017

A9B018

A9B019

__ General Grievous BD24 ....8.00
__ Giran BD21 ....8.00
__ Gungan Warrior BD07 ....8.00
__ Han Solo BD30 ....8.00
__ Han Solo, stormtrooper disguise BD02 ....8.00
__ Hrchek Kal Fas BD33 ....8.00
__ IG-88, concept art BD40 ....8.00
__ Imperial Scanning Crew BD32 ....8.00
__ Jacen Solo BD59 ....8.00
__ Jaina Solo BD60 ....8.00
__ Jango Fett BD15 ....8.00
__ Jawa and Security Droid BD39 ....8.00
__ Jawa with WED Treadwell Droid BD04 ....8.00
__ Jeremoch Colton BD42 ....8.00
__ K'kruhk BD57 ....8.00
__ Ki-Adi-Mundi, concept art BD38 ....8.00
__ Leesub Sirln BD34 ....8.00
__ Luke Skywalker BD16 ....8.00
__ Luke Skywalker, snowspeeder pilot BD51 ....8.00
__ Luke Skywalker, stormtrooper disguise BD01 .8.00
__ Major Panno BD20 ....8.00
__ Malakili BD22 ....8.00
__ Nein Nunb BD19 ....8.00
__ Nikto Gunner BD23 ....8.00
__ Obi-Wan Kenobi BD06 ....8.00
__ Obi-Wan Kenobi BD13 ....8.00
__ Padme Amidala BD35...8.00
__ Plo Koon BD45 ....8.00
__ Princess Leia BD17 ....8.00
__ Queen Amidala BD08 ....8.00
__ R2-D2 BD29..8.00
__ R2-X2 BD52..8.00
__ Rum Sleg BD09 ....8.00
__ Saleucami Clone Trooper BD25 ....8.00
__ Shaak Ti BD61 ....8.00
__ Snowtrooper BD46 ....8.00
__ Snowtrooper, concept art BD48 ....8.00
__ Spacetrooper BD03 ....8.00
__ Spacetrooper BD58 ....8.00
__ Ugnaught BD28 ....8.00
__ Utai BD41 ....8.00
__ Willrow Hood BD53 ....8.00
__ Zuckuss BD54 ....8.00

Saga Legends. Each figure includes clone gear. Multi-language packaging.
__ 501st Legion Trooper SL08 [ALD081] 8.00
__ C-3PO SL18 [ALD082]..8.00
__ Chewbacca SL15 ....8.00
__ Clone Trooper SL04...8.00

__ Clone Trooper SL12...8.00
__ Darth Maul SL07 ....8.00
__ Darth Vader SL02 [ALD083]...............................8.00
__ Darth Vader SL06 ....8.00
__ Han Solo SL16 ....8.00
__ Luke Skywalker, X-Wing Pilot SL17 ....8.00
__ Luke Skywalker, X-Wing Pilot SL17 ....8.00
__ Obi-Wan Kenobi SL03 [ALD084]........................8.00
__ Obi-Wan Kenobi, Pilot SL19..............................8.00
__ Plo Koon SL13 ....8.00
__ R2-D2 SL01 [ALD085]..8.00
__ Saesee Tiin SL11 ....8.00
__ Sandtrooper SL10 ....8.00
__ Shock Trooper SL14 [ALD086].........................8.00
__ Super Battle Droid SL05 ....8.00
__ Yoda SL09 ....8.00

Hasbro
__ Clone Trooper Squad, exclusive to K-Mart [A9B001] 25.00

2-packs. Droid factory. Includes an additional piece to build Dark Trooper Phase II. Walmart exclusives.
__ Anakin Skywalker and Cortosis Battle Droid [A9B002] 18.00
__ Boba Fett and BL-17 [A9B003] 18.00
__ Corran Horn and Whistler [A9B004] 18.00
__ Darth Maul and I-5YQ [A9B005] 18.00
__ General Grievous and CB-3D [A9B006] 18.00

A9B020

A9B021

A7A001

A7A002

A7A003

A7A004

A7A005

A7A006

A7A007

A7A008

A7A009

A7A010

A7A011

A7A012

A7A013

A7A014

A7A015

A7A016

A7A017

A7A018

A7A019

A7A020

A7A021

A7A022

A7A023

A7A024

A7A025

A7A026

A7A027

A7A028

A7A029

A7A030

Action Figures

A7A031

A7A032

A7A033

A7A034

A7A035

A7A036

A7A037

A7A038

A7A039

A7A040

A7A041

A7A042

A6B001

A6B002

A6B003

A6B004

A6B005

A6B006

A6B007

A6B008

A6B009

A7B001

A7B002

A7B003

A7B004

A7B005

A7B006

A7B007

A7B008

A7B009

A7B010

A7B011

A7B012

Action Figures

A7B013

A7B014

A7B015

COMMANDO SQUAD
A7B016

A7B017

A7B018

A7B019

2-packs. Geonosis Battle Area. Target exclusives.
__ Coleman Trebor and Jango Fett [A9B007] 16.00
__ Joclad Danva and Battle Droid [A9B008] 16.00
__ Kit Fisto and Geonosis Warrior [A9B009] 16.00
__ Mace Windu and Battle Droid Commander
[A9B010] 16.00
__ Roth Del Masona and Super Battle Droid
[A9B011] 16.00
__ Yoda and Destroyer Droid A9B012] 16.00

Battle Packs.
__ Battle For Endor [A9B013] 35.00
__ Birth of Darth Vader [A9B014] 35.00
__ Duel on Mustafar [A9B015]...........................35.00
__ Geonosis Assault [A9B016] 35.00
__ Kamino Conflict [A9B017]..............................35.00
__ Resurgence of the Jedi [A9B018] 35.00
__ Tatooine Desert Ambush [A9B019] 35.00

McQuarrie concept figures. Toys R Us exclusives.
__ Set 1 [A9B020]...65.00
__ Set 2 [A9B021]...65.00

Action Figures: 2010-2011 (The Clone Wars)

Hasbro
__ Ahsoka CW44 [A7A001] 8.00
__ Ahsoka Tano CW17 [A7A002] 8.00
__ Anakin Skywalker CW45 [A7A003] 8.00
__ Anakin Skywalker, Space Suit CW07
[A7A004] 8.00
__ Aqua Droid CW46 [A7A005] 8.00
__ ARF Trooper CW18 [A7A006] 8.00
__ ARF Trooper Kamino CW56 ....8.00
__ Asajj Ventress CW15 [A7A007].......................8.00
__ Aurra Sing CW11 [A7A008].............................8.00
__ Barriss Offee CW50 [A7A009]..........................8.00
__ Battle Droid CW19 [A7A010] 8.00
__ Boba Fett CW32 [A7A011]...............................8.00
__ Cad Bane CW13 [A7A012] 8.00
__ Cad Bane and TODO-360 CW42 [A7A013]......8.00
__ Captain Rex CW01 [A7A014]...........................8.00
__ Captain Rex with jet pack CW62 ....8.00
__ Cato Parasitti CW37 [A7A015].........................8.00
__ Chewbacca CW63 ....8.00
__ Clone Captain Lock, exclusive to K-Mart
[A7A016] 20.00
__ Clone Commander Colt CW52 [A7A017] 8.00
__ Clone Commander Wolffe CW48 [A7A018]......8.00
__ Clone Pilot Odd Ball CW14 [A7A019] 8.00
__ Clone Trooper Draa CW35 [A7A020].................8.00
__ Clone Trooper Hevy CW41 [A7A021] 8.00

__ Commander Cody CW03 [A7A022].................8.00
__ Commander Gree CW21 [A7A023]..................8.00
__ Count Dooku CW06 [A7A024] 8.00
__ Eeth Koth CW51 [A7A025]...............................8.00
__ El-Les CW47 [A7A026] 8.00
__ Embo CW33 [A7A027].....................................8.00
__ Even Piell CW58 ....8.00
__ Jar Jar Binks CW65 ....8.00
__ Kit Fisto Cold Weather Gear CW60 ....8.00
__ Kul Teska, exclusive to Toys R Us [A7A028]..15.00
__ Mandalorian Police Officer CW09 [A7A029].....8.00
__ Mandalorian Warrior CW29 [A7A030]...............8.00
__ Nikto Guard, exclusive to Toys R Us
[A7A031] 12.00
__ Obi-Wan Kenobi CW02 [A7A032]....................8.00
__ Obi-Wan Kenobi CW40 [A7A033]....................8.00
__ Plo Koon Cold Weather Gear CW53 ....8.00
__ Pre Vizsla CW08 [A7A034]..............................8.00
__ Quinlan Vos CW36 [A7A035]...........................8.00
__ R4-P17 CW30 [A7A036] 8.00
__ R7-A7 CW43 [A7A037]....................................8.00
__ R7-D4 CW64 ....8.00
__ Riot Control Clone Trooper CW49 [A7A038]....8.00
__ Saesee Tiin CW54 ....8.00
__ Savage Opress CW55 ....8.00
__ Savage Opress armored CW59........................8.00
__ Seripas CW61 ....8.00
__ Shaak Ti CW31 [A7A039].................................8.00
__ Stealth Clone Trooper CW57...........................8.00
__ Super Battle Droid CW16 [A7A040]..................8.00
__ Undead Geonosian CW34 [A7A041] 8.00
__ Yoda CW05 [A7A042].......................................8.00

Action Figures: 2010-2011 (The Clone Wars Deluxe)

Hasbro
__ Armored Scout Tank with Tactical Droid
[A6B001]..24.00
__ Assassin Spider Droid and Clone Troopers....24.00
__ AT-RT with ARF Trooper Boil [A6B002]..........24.00
__ AT-RT with Clone Captain Keeli 24.00
__ BARC Speeder with Clone Trooper Buzz........24.00
__ Barc Speeder Bike with Clone Trooper Jesse
[A6B003]..24.00
__ Barc Speeder Bike with Obi-Wan Kenobi
[A6B004]..24.00
__ Freeco Speeder with Clone Trooper [A6B005]..24.00
__ Freeco Speeder with Obi-Wan Kenobi 24.00
__ Mandalorian Speeder with Mandalorian Warrior
[A6B006]..24.00
__ Naboo Star Skiff /Anakin Skywalker [A6B007].........24.00

__ Pirate Speeder Bike with Cad Bane
[A6B008]..24.00
__ Speeder Bike with Plo Koon
[A6B009]..24.00
__ Y-Wing Bomber with Clone Pilot 24.00

Action Figures: 2010-2011 (The Clone Wars Multipacks)

Hasbro
2-Packs.
__ ARF Trooper Waxer and Battle Droid, exclusive to
Target [A7B001]......................................20.00
__ Cad Bane and IG-86, exclusive to Target
[A7B002] 20.00
__ Senate Guard and Senate Commander, exclusive
to Target [A7B003]..................................20.00
__ Special Ops Clone Trooper and Geonosian Drone,
exclusive to Target [A7B004].........................20.00

Battle Packs with DVD.
__ Hostage Crisis, exclusive to Target [A7B005] 35.00
__ The Hidden Enemy, exclusive to Target
[A7B006] 35.00

Battle Packs.
__ Anti-Hailfire Droid Squad [A7B007] 35.00
__ Battle of Orto Plutonia [A7B008]....................35.00
__ Clone Commando Squad [A7B009] 35.00
__ Clone Troopers and Droids [A7B010].............35.00
__ Holocron Heist [A7B011] 35.00
__ Invasion of Utapu [A7B012] 35.00

Clone Wars DVD set 2-packs.
__ 1 Rising Malevolence Plo Koon and Ahsoka
[A7B013]..25.00
__ 2 Shadow of Malevolence Anakin Skywalker and
Matchstick [A7B014]..25.00
__ 3 Destroy Malevolence Obi-Wan Kenobi and
General Grievous [A7B015] 25.00

Hasbro, Canada
Battle Packs.
__ Clone Commando Squad [A7B016] 35.00

Hasbro, UK
3-Packs.
__ Captain Rex, Anakin Skywalker, Cad Bane
[A7B017] 35.00
__ Commander Cody, Obi-Wan Kenobi, General
Grievous [A7B018]..35.00
__ Lieutenant Thire, Yoda, Destroyer Droid
[A7B019] 35.00

Action Figures: 2010-2011 (The Legacy Collection)

Hasbro

__ Jodo Kast, exclusive to K-Mart [ALE001].......12.00

Saga Legends. Each figure includes secret weapons.

__ 501st Legion Trooper SL19 [ALE002]..............8.00
__ Battle Droids SL20 [ALE003] 8.00
__ Boba Fett SL30..8.00
__ Bossk SL01 [ALE004] 8.00
__ C-3PO SL17 [ALE005] 8.00
__ Chewbacca SL18 [ALE006] 8.00
__ Clone Trooper, EPII SL10 [ALE007]..................8.00
__ Clone Trooper, EPIII SL16 [ALE008].................8.00
__ Darth Maul SL08 [ALE009]..............................8.00

__ Death Star Trooper SL27 ....8.00
__ Darth Vader SL06 [ALE010]............................8.00
__ Darth Vader, Sith Apprentice SL11 [ALE011] ...8.00
__ Destroyer Droid SL31 ....8.00
__ General Grievous SL09 [ALE012] 8.00
__ Greedo SL04 [ALE013] 8.00
__ Han Solo, Hoth SL22 [ALE014]........................8.00
__ IG-88 SL02 [ALE015] 8.00
__ Jango Fett SL05 [ALE016] 8.00
__ Leia, Boushh Disguise SL07 [ALE017] 8.00
__ Luke, Snowspeeder Pilot SL21 [ALE018] 8.00
__ Mace Windu SL29 ....8.00
__ Obi-Wan Kenobi, EPIII SL24...........................8.00
__ Obi-Wan Kenobi SL12 lightsaber in left hand..8.00
__ Obi-Wan Kenobi SL12 lightsaber in right

hand [ALE019] 8.00
__ R2-D2 SL14 [ALE020]....................................8.00
__ Shocktrooper SL15 [ALE021] 8.00
__ Snowtrooper SL23 [ALE022] 8.00
__ Space Trooper SL32.....................................14.00
__ Stormtrooper SL25 ....8.00
__ Super Battle Droid, EPIII SL28........................8.00
__ Yoda SL13 [ALE023]......................................8.00
__ Zuckuss SL03 [ALE024].................................8.00

Action Figures: 2010-2011 (The Legacy Collection) Multipacks

Hasbro

__ Battlefields of Naboo, Target exclusive..........35.00
__ Hoth Assault [ALF001]....................................35.00

ALE001

ALE002

ALE003

ALE004

ALE005

ALE006

ALE007

ALE008

ALE009

ALE010

ALE011

ALE012

ALE013

ALE014

ALE015

ALE016

ALE017

ALE018

ALE019

ALE020

ALE021

ALE022

ALE023

ALE024

Action Figures

ALF001

ACP001

ACP002

ACP003

ACP004

ACP005

ACP006

ACP007

ACP008

ACP009

ACP010

ACP011

ACP012

ACP013

ACP014

ACP015

ACP016

ACP017

ACP018

ACP019

ACP020

ACP021

ACP022

ACP023

ACP024

ACP025

ACP026

ACP027

ACP028

ACP029

ACP030

ACP031   ACP032   ACP033   ACP034   ACP035   ACP036   ACP037

ACP038   ACP039   ACP040   ACP041   ACP042   ACP043   ACP044

ACP045   ACP046   ACP047   ACP048   ACP049   ACP050   ACP051

ACP052   ACP053   ACP054   ACP055   ACP056   ACP057   ACP058

ACP059   ACP060   ACP061   ACP062   ACP063   ACP064   ACP065

Action Figures

__ Pad Racer Pilots, Target exclusive.................35.00
__ Search for Luke Skywalker..............................35.00

Action Figures: Comic Packs

Hasbro
2007-2008. Black package with red numbers.
__ 01 Kir Kanos and Carnor Jax Crimson Empire, exclusive to Entertainment Earth [ACP001]....25.00
__ 02 Darth Vader and Rebel Officer Star Wars bright blue highlights [ACP002].............................25.00
__ 02 Darth Vader and Rebel Officer Star Wars dim blue highlights..................................25.00
__ 03 Governor Tarkin and Stormtrooper Star Wars blue deco [ACP003]...............................25.00
__ 03 Governor Tarkin and Stormtrooper Star Wars no blue deco [ACP004]..........................25.00
__ 04 Chewbacca and Han Solo (stormtrooper disguise) Star Wars blue deco [ACP005]........25.00
__ 04 Chewbacca and Han Solo (stormtrooper disguise) Star Wars no blue deco [ACP006]...27.00
__ 05 Quinlan Vos and Vilmarh Grahrk Star Wars Tales [ACP007]...25.00
__ 06 Luke Skywalker (stormtrooper disguise) and R2-D2 Star Wars blue deco [ACP008]............25.00
__ 06 Luke Skywalker (stormtrooper disguise) and R2-D2 Star Wars no blue deco [ACP009]...........27.00
__ 07 Obi-Wan Kenobi and ARC Trooper Alpha Star Wars Republic [ACP010] 25.00
__ 08 A'sharad Hett and Dark Woman Hunt for Aurra Sing [ACP011]..25.00
__ 09 Princess Leia and Darth Vader Infinities [ACP012]...25.00
__ 10 Luke Skywalker and Mara Jade Heir to the Empire Mara's lightsaber is blue [ACP013] 25.00
__ 10 Luke Skywalker and Mara Jade Heir to the Empire Mara's lightsaber is green [ACP014]..30.00
__ 11 Anakin Skywalker and A-Series assassination droid Republic [ACP015] 25.00
__ 12 Baron Soonter Fel and Hobbie Klivian X-Wing Rogue Squadron [ACP016] 25.00
__ 13 Koffi Arana and Bultar Swan Purge [ACP017]...25.00
__ 14 Lt. Jundland (Luke) and Lt. Shan Empire [ACP018]...25.00
__ 15 Mouse and Able Empire [ACP019] 25.00
__ 16 Republic Commando and Super Battle Droid Star Wars Tales [ACP020] 25.00
__ Anakin Skywalker and Count Dooku Revenge of the Sith, exclusive to Walmart [ACP021]..............25.00
__ Boba Fett and RA-7 Droid Star Wars, exclusive to Walmart [ACP022]..........................25.00
__ Commander Keller and Galactic Marine Republic, exclusive to Walmart [ACP023] 25.00
__ Kashyyyk Trooper and Wookiee Trooper Revenge of the Sith, exclusive to Walmart [ACP024]....25.00

__ Lando Calrissian and Stormtrooper Star Wars, exclusive to Walmart [ACP025] 25.00
__ Obi-Wan Kenobi and Bail Organa with twins Revenge of the Sith, exclusive to Walmart [ACP026]...25.00

2008. White package with blue header.
__ 01 Asajj Ventress and Tol Skorr [ACP027]......25.00
__ 02 Anakin Skywalker and Durge [ACP028].....25.00
__ 02 Darth Talon and Cade Skywalker Legacy [ACP029]...25.00
__ 03 Anakin Skywalker and Assassin droid Republic [ACP030]...25.00
__ 05 Antares Draco and Ganner Krieg Legacy [ACP031]...25.00
__ 06 Fenn Shysta and Dengar [ACP032]...........25.00
__ 07 Princess Leia and Tobbi Dalk [ACP033]....25.00
__ 07 Tobbi Dala and Princess Leia [ACP034]....25.00
__ 08 Leia Organa and Prince Xizor [ACP035] 25.00
__ 09 Grand Admiral Thrawn and Talon Karrde Heir to the Empire [ACP036].......................................25.00
__ 10 Darth Vader and Grand Moff Trachta Empire [ACP037]...25.00
__ 11 Darth Vader and Princess Leia Infinities [ACP038]...25.00
__ 12 Emperor Palpatine Clone and Luke Skywalker Dark Empire II [ACP039] 25.00
__ 13 Commander Fae and Quinlan Vos Star Wars #82 [ACP040]...25.00
__ Ibtisam and Nrin Vakil X-Wing Rogue Squadron #19, exclusive to Walmart [ACP041] 25.00
__ Janek Sunber and Amanin Empire #16, exclusive to Walmart [ACP042] 25.00
__ Machook, Keoulkeech, and Kettch Star Wars #94, exclusive to Walmart [ACP043] 25.00

2009-2010. White package with red header.
__ 01 Darth Vader and Rebel Officer Star Wars #1 [ACP044]...25.00
__ 02 Chewbacca and Han Solo [ACP045]........25.00
__ 03 Yuzzhan Vong and Kyle Katarn Star Wars Tales #21 [ACP046]...25.00
__ 04 Borsk Fey'lya and Wedge Antilles X-Wing Rogue Squadron #32 [ACP047] 25.00
__ 05 Luke Skywalker and Deena Shan Rebellion #3 [ACP048]...25.00
__ 06 Ki-Adi-Mundi and Sharad Hett Star Wars #11 [ACP049]...25.00
__ 07 Lumiya and Luke Skywalker Star Wars #96 [ACP050]...25.00
__ 08 Darth Krayt and Sigel Dare Legacy #22 [ACP051]...25.00
__ 09 Clone Trooper and Clone Commander Republic #84 [ACP052]...25.00
__ 10 Clone Trooper Lieutenant and Clone Trooper Routine Valor [ACP053] 25.00

__ 11 Exar Kun and Ulic Quel Droma Tales of the Jedi #6 [ACP054]..25.00
__ 12 Jedi Master Tholme and Jedi Master T'ra Saa Republic #65 [ACP055]...................................25.00
__ 13 Stormtrooper and Blackhole Hologram Classic Star Wars #1 [ACP056]...................................25.00
__ 15 Jarael and Rohlan Dyre Knights of the Realm #6, exclusive to Entertainment Earth [ACP057]....25.00
__ 16 Delia Blue and Darth Nihl Legacy #7, exclusive to Entertainment Earth [ACP058]..................25.00
__ 17 Baron Soontir Fel and Ysanne Isard Rogue Squadron #29, exclusive to EE [ACP059].......25.00
__ 18 Jaster Mereel and Montross Jango Fett: Open Seasons #2, exclusive to Entertainment Earth [ACP060]...25.00
__ Dllr Nep and Plourr Ilo Rogue Squadron #1, exclusive to Walmart [ACP061] 25.00
__ IG97 and Rom Mohc Star Wars Tales #4, exclusive to Walmart [ACP062]..........................25.00
__ Storm Commando and General Weir X-Wing Rogue Leader #2, Walmart excl. [ACP063] 25.00

2010. Convention exclusives.
__ Camie and Fixer Empire, exclusive to Star Wars Celebration V [ACP064] 35.00
__ Darth Maul and Owen Lars Star Wars Visionaries, exclusive to San Diego Comic-Con [ACP065]...35.00

Action Figures: Commemorative Multipacks

Hasbro
Classic Trilogy, The Saga Collection.
__ A New Hope [C3P001]...................................35.00
__ Empire Strikes Back [C3P002]......................35.00
__ Return of the Jedi [C3P003] 35.00

Classic Trilogy.
__ A New Hope [C3P004]...................................35.00
__ Empire Strikes Back [C3P005]......................35.00
__ Return of the Jedi [C3P006] 35.00

Clone Wars 3D.
__ Clone Trooper, Anakin Skywalker, R2-D2, exclusive to Walmart [C3P007]...................................30.00
__ General Grievous, Obi-Wan Kenobi, Battle Droid, exclusive to Walmart [C3P008]....................30.00

Clone Wars.
__ I: Jedi Forces: Obi-Wan, Anakin, ARC Trooper [C3P009]..50.00
__ I: Sith Attack Pack: Asajj Ventress, General Grievous, Durge [C3P010] 50.00
__ II: Anakin Skywalker, Saesee Tiin, Clone Trooper [C3P011]...50.00
__ II: Clone Commander Cody, Obi-Wan Kenobi,

C3P001

C3P002

C3P003

C3P004

C3P005

C3P006

C3P007

C3P008

C3P009   C3P010   C3P011   C3P012

C3P013   C3P014   C3P015   C3P016

C3P017   C3P018   C3P019   C3P020

General Grievous [C3P012] 50.00

Episode III: Revenge of the Sith.
__ Anakin Skywalker, Mace Windu, Obi-Wan Kenobi [C3P013] 25.00
__ Clone Troopers [C3P014] 25.00
__ Emperor Palpatine, Darth Vader, Count Dooku [C3P015] 25.00

The Force Unleashed.
__Darth Vader with Incinerator Troopers [C3P016]...........30.00
__ Emperor Palpatine with Shadow Stormtroopers [C3P017] 30.00

The Force Unleashed. Commemorative Collection.
__ Darth Vader with Incinerator Troopers [C3P018].....30.00
__ Emperor Palpatine with Shadow Stormtroopers [C3P019]..30.00

The Force Unleashed. Legacy Collection.
__ Darth Vader with Incinerator Troopers [C3P020].....30.00
__ Emperor Palpatine with Shadow Stormtroopers.....30.00

Hasbro, Canada
Classic Trilogy.
__ A New Hope...35.00

__ Empire Strikes Back 35.00
__ Return of the Jedi 35.00

Action Figures: Evolutions

Hasbro
2005. Revenge of the Sith.
__ Anakin to Darth Vader [A7T001] 25.00
__ Clone Trooper (yellow) to Stormtrooper, "Republic" error 35.00
__ Clone Trooper (yellow) to Stormtrooper, "Republic"

A7T001   A7T002

A7T003   A7T004

A7T005

A7T006

A7T007

A7T008

A7T009

A7T010

A7T011

A7T012

A7T013

A7T014

A7T015

A7T016

A7T017

A7T018

A7T019

A7T020

corrected 30.00
__ Clone Trooper to Stormtrooper [A7T002].......30.00
__ Sith Lords [A7T003] 30.00

2007. 30th anniversary packaging.
__ Anakin Skywalker to Darth Vader [A7T004]....30.00
__ Clone Trooper to Stormtrooper [A7T005].......30.00
__ The Fett Legacy Mandalore, Jango Fett, Boba Fett
[A7T006]...30.00
__ The Jedi Legacy Bultar Swan, Qui-Gon Jinn, Luke
Skywalker [A7T007].............................30.00
__ The Sith Darth Maul, Count Dooku, Emperor
Palpatine [A7T008].............................30.00
__ The Sith Legacy Darth Nihilus, Darth Bane, Darth
Maul [A7T009]..................................30.00
__ Vader's Secret Apprentice [A7T010] 30.00

2008. Legacy collection, blue text.
__ Imperial Pilot Legacy Clone Wars, Revenge of the
Sith, Darklighter / Empire [A7T011] 30.00
__ Rebellion Pilot Legacy Dorovio Bold, Wes Janson,
Ten Numb [A7T012]...........................30.00
__ Rebellion Pilot Legacy series II Cesi Eirriss, Kesin
Ommis, Keyan Farlander [A7T013].................30.00
__ The Fett Legacy Mandalore, Jango Fett, Boba Fett
[A7T014]...30.00
__ The Fett Legacy Mandalore, Jango Fett, Boba Fett
Boba missing chest emblem 30.00
__ The Padme Amidala Legacy Queen Amidala, Senator
of Naboo, Mother of Heroes [A7T015]............30.00
__ The Sith Legacy Darth Bane, Darth Nihilus, Darth
Maul [A7T016]..................................30.00
__ Vader's Secret Apprentice Secret Apprentice, Sith
Lord, Jedi Knight [A7T017]............................30.00

2009. Legacy collection, red text.
__ Clone Commandos Alpha, Fi Skirata, Storm
Commando, exclusive to Walmart [A7T018] ..30.00
__ Imperial Pilot Legacy series II Clone Pilot (gunship),
Clone Pilot (v-wing), Imperial Pilot, exclusive to
Walmart [A7T019] 30.00
__ Rebel Pilot Legacy series III John Branon, Shira Brie,
Jake Farrell, exclusive to Walmart [A7T020]...30.00

Action Figures: Exclusives

Big Alley
Custom figures to promote celebrity signings.
__ Merceedes Ngoh, Aug 19, 2000.....................50.00
__ Peter Mayhew, July 1, 2000 ....50.00
__ Ray Park, Oct 7, 2000....................................50.00

Hasbro
__ 501st Legion join-up figure, exclusive to Walmart
[AFE001] 30.00

1998 Strategic Partners Meeting.
__ Battle Droid on STAP, sneak preview...........125.00

*2007 Star Wars weekends. Unnamed cantina band
members with musical base.*
__ (Figrin D'an) [AFE002] 25.00
__ (Ickabel) [AFE003]..25.00
__ (Nalan) [AFE004] 25.00
__ (Tech) [AFE005]...25.00
__ (Tedn) [AFE006] 25.00

Astromech droid 5-pack. Entertainment Earth exclusives.
__ Series I: R3-T6, R3-T2, R2-C4, R4-A22, R2-Q2
[AFE007]......................................35.00

__ Series II: R3-Y2, R2-M5, R2-A6, R4-E1, R2-X2
[AFE008]......................................35.00

ComicCon exclusives.
__ 2005 Princess Leia, Holographic [AFE009] 20.00
__ 2006 501st Stormtrooper "Comic-Con exclusive"
on package [AFE010]...........................45.00
__ 2006 501st Stormtrooper unmarked pkg. 45.00
__ 2007 Concept Obi-Wan and Yoda [AFE011]..45.00
__ 2007 R2-KT benefits Make-A-Wish foundation
[AFE012] 65.00
__ 2007 Shadow Scout, Speederbike [AFE013]..45.00
__ 2008 Clone Senate Security [AFE014]............30.00
__ 2008 Disturbance in the Force Darth Vader and
Hologram Emperor [AFE015]......................35.00
__ 2009 Luke Skywalker pilot [AFE016] 30.00
__ 2009 Stormtrooper Commander [AFE017].....30.00

Commemorative.
__ 500th Darth Vader [AFE018] 15.00

Disney exclusives, Star Tours.
__ Ambush at Star Tours....................................50.00
__ Droid Pack R2-D2, C-3PO, WEG-1618, RX-24
"Rex", DL-X2 [AFE019].......................35.00
__ Jedi Training Academy [AFE020]...................40.00
__ Star Tours Boarding Party [AFE021]...............65.00
__ Star Tours Travel Agency 50.00

*Disney exclusives. Disney characters dressed up as
Star Wars characters. Special editions.*
__ Donald Duck as Shadow Trooper, exclusive to Star
Wars Celebration V [AFE022] 40.00

Action Figures

AFE001

AFE002

AFE003

AFE004

AFE005

AFE006

AFE007

AFE008

AFE009

AFE010

AFE011

AFE012

AFE013

AFE014

AFE015

AFE016

AFE017

AFE018

AFE019

AFE020

174

STAR TOURS Boarding Party

Limited Edition of 15,000

STAR TOURS Officer · Kaink · Teek · Ree-Yees · Chewbacca

AFE021

AFE022

AFE023

AFE024

AFE025

AFE026

AFE027

AFE028

AFE029

AFE030

AFE031

AFE032

AFE033

AFE034

AFE035

AFE036

AFE037

AFE038

AFE039

AFE040

AFE041

AFE042

AFE043

AFE044

AFE045

AFE046

Action Figures

AFE047

AFE048

AFE049

AFE050

AFE051

AFE052

AFE053

AFE054

AFE055

AFE056

AFE057

AFE058

AFE059

AFE060

AFE061

AFE062

AFE063

AFE064

AFE065

AFE066

AFE067

AFE068

AFE069

AFE070

AFE071

AFE072

AFE073

AFE074   AFE075   AFE076   AFE077   AFE078   AFE079

AFE080   AFE081   AFE082   AFE083   AFE084   AFE085

AFE086   AFE087   AFE088   AFE089

__ Stitch as Emperor Palpatine Hologram [AFE023] 40.00

Series 1.
__ Donald Duck as Han Solo [AFE024] 15.00
__ Goofy as Darth Vader [AFE025].....................15.00
__ Mickey Mouse as Luke Skywalker [AFE026]...15.00
__ Minnie Mouse as Princess Leia [AFE027].......15.00
__ Stitch as Emperor Palpatine [AFE028]............15.00

Series 2.
__ Donald Duck as Darth Maul [AFE029] 15.00
__ Goofy as Jar Jar Binks [AFE030] 15.00
__ Mickey Mouse as Anakin Skywalker [AFE031] 15.00
__ Minnie Mouse as Queen Amidala [AFE032]....15.00
__ Stitch as Yoda [AFE033] 15.00

Series 3.
__ Chip and Dale as Ewoks [AFE034] 25.00
__ Donald Duck as Stormtrooper [AFE035] 15.00
__ Goofy as Chewbacca [AFE036].....................15.00
__ Mickey Mouse as Luke Skywalker Pilot [AFE037] 15.00
__ Minnie Mouse as Princess Leia (slave) [AFE038] 25.00
__ Minnie Mouse as Slave Leia [AFE039]...........75.00

Series 4.
__ Bad Pete as Boba Fett [AFE040] 25.00
__ Donald Duck as Han Solo in Carbonite [AFE041] 15.00
__ Goofy as C-3PO [AFE042]..............................15.00
__ Mickey Mouse as Luke Skywalker Jedi Knight [AFE043] 15.00
__ Minnie Mouse as Princess Leia in Boushh disguise [AFE044] 15.00

AFE090   AFE091   AFE092

Disney exclusives. Disney characters dressed up as Star Wars characters. 2-packs.
__ Jedi Mickey and Yoda; Yoda has a blue lightsaber [AFE045] 65.00
__ Jedi Mickey and Yoda [AFE046].....................40.00

Disney exclusives. Droids from Star Tours.
2002. POTJ style cardback.
__ DL-X2 [AFE047] 10.00
__ G2-4T [AFE048] 10.00
__ R3-D3 [AFE049] 20.00
__ R4-M9 [AFE050] 15.00
__ RX-24 REX [AFE051].......................................20.00
__ WEG-1618 [AFE052].......................................15.00
2003. Saga style cardback.
__ G2-9T [AFE053] 15.00
__ R5-D2 [AFE054] 25.00

__ SK-Z38 [AFE055] 20.00
2004. Saga style cardback. Not officially released.
__ 3T-RNE [AFE056]..20.00
__ G3-5LE [AFE057] 20.00
__ MSE-IT [AFE058] 20.00
2004. Original Trilogy Collection style cardback.
__ 3T-RNE [AFE059]..25.00
__ G3-5LE [AFE060] 25.00
__ MSE-1T [AFE061] 25.00

Game pre-sale premiums.
__ Biker Scout [AFE062].......................................35.00
__ Biker Scout, "Not for resale" [AFE063]...........25.00
__ Biker Scout, sticker covers "Not for Resale" [AFE064] 50.00
__ Stormtrooper Commander, exclusive to Electronic Boutique [AFE065]...35.00

Action Figures

Holiday Editions.
__ 2002 C-3PO and R2-D2, exclusive to Walmart [AFE066] 45.00
__ 2003 Yoda, exclusive to Fan Club [AFE067] ..25.00
__ 2004 Jawas, exclusive to Entertainment Earth [AFE068] 20.00
__ 2005 Darth Vader, Fan Club excl. [AFE069] ...15.00
__ 2007 Father's Day Darth Vader and Luke [AFE070] 50.00

OTC figures. Cardback is invitation to Media DVD event.
__ Darth Vader..75.00
__ Han Solo 75.00
__ Luke Skywalker, X-Wing Pilot.........................75.00
__ Princess Leia 75.00

Shop.StarWars.com
__ Concept Grievous [AFE071] 25.00
__ Covert Ops Clone Trooper [AFE072] 35.00
__ Lucas Collector's Set [AFE073] 45.00

Silver colored figures.
__ 2002 Darth Vader, Toy Fair NYC [AFE074]...135.00
__ 2002 R2-D2 25th anniversary, exclusive to Toys R Us [AFE075] 30.00
__ 2003 Boba Fett, conventions [AFE076] 25.00
__ 2003 Boba Fett, MexiCon pkg [AFE077] 20.00
__ 2003 Clone Trooper, exclusive to Toys R Us [AFE078] 25.00
__ 2004 Darth Vader, exclusive to Toys R Us [AFE079] 25.00
__ 2004 Sandtrooper, conventions [AFE080]......25.00

Star Wars Celebrations.
__ 2002 Jorg Sacul, Celebration II [AFE081].......85.00
__ 2005 Darth Vader, electronic, Celebration III [AFE082] 60.00
__ 2007 C-3PO and R2-D2 McQuarrie concept, Celebration Europe [AFE083] 65.00
__ 2007 C-3PO and R2-D2 McQuarrie concept C-3PO and R2-D2 cardback, Celebration IV [AFE084] 20.00
__ 2007 C-3PO and R2-D2 McQuarrie concept Luke Skywalker cardback, Star Wars Celebration IV..20.00
__ 2007 Luke Skywalker McQuarrie concept, Celebration IV [AFE085]................................25.00
__ 2007 Luke Skywalker McQuarrie concept, Celebration Europe..45.00

Toy fare.
__ 2005 Anakin Skywalker / Darth Vader [AFE086] 350.00

Hasbro, France
Star Wars Reunions.
__ 2005 Anakin Skywalker, limited to 2,000, exclusive to Reunion [AFE087] 85.00
__ 2007 C-3PO and R2-D2 McQuarrie concept, exclusive to Reunion II..................................55.00

Hasbro, Germany
Jedi-Con.
__ 2001 C-3PO, limited to 2,000 [AFE088]..........55.00
__ 2004 2-pack, limited to 2,500 [AFE089] 85.00
__ 2008 Shadow Troopers Order 66 2-pack, limited to 2,000..65.00

ATV001

ATV002

ATV003

ATV004

ATV005

ATV006

ATV007

ATV008

ATV009

ATV010

ATV011

ATV012

ATV013

ATV014

ATV015

ATV016

ATV017

ATV018

ATV019

ATV020

ATV021

ATV022

ATV023

ATV024

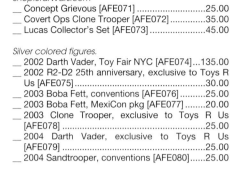
ATV025

| ATV026 | ATV027 | ATV028 | ATV029 | ATV030 | ATV031 |

| ATV032 | ATV033 | ATV034 | ATV035 | ATV036 | ATV037 |

| ATV038 | ATV039 | ATV040 | ATV041 | ATV042 | ATV043 |

| ATV044 | ATV045 | ATV046 | ATV047 | ATV048 | ATV049 |

| ATV050 | ATV051 | ATV052 | ATV053 | ATV054 | ATV055 |

Action Figures

ATV056

ATV057

ATV058

ATV059

ATV060

ATV061

ATV062

ATV063

ATV064

ATV065

ATV066

ATV067

ATV068

ATV069

ATV070

ATV071 back

ATV072

ATV073

ATV074

ATV075

ATV076

ATV077

ATV078

ATV079

ATV080

ATV081

ATV082

ATV083

ATV084

ATV085

Hasbro, Japan
ComicCon exclusives.
__ 2008 Disturbance in the Force Darth Vader and Hologram Emperor, exclusive to World Characters Convention..35.00

McQuarrie concept figures relabeled for Japanese market.
__ C-3PO and R2-D2 ....35.00
__ Luke Skywalker..25.00
__ Obi-Wan and Yoda 45.00

Hasbro, UK
Star Wars Celebrations.
__ 2007 C-3PO and R2-D2 McQuarrie concept Celebration Europe coin 65.00
__ 2007 Luke Skywalker McQuarrie concept Celebration Europe coin 65.00

Japan Tour
__ Aurra Sing 45.00
__ Boba Fett 45.00
__ Greedo 45.00
__ Mas Amedda 45.00
__ Rune Haako 45.00

Mexico City Conventions, Mexico
2002, June 28-30. 2-packs.
__ Han Solo and Chewbacca [AFE090]............190.00
__ Obi-Wan Kenobi and Darth Vader [AFE091].190.00

2004. 2-pack.
__ Luke Skywalker's Encounter with Yoda [AFE092] 70.00

2008, August 8-10.
__ Commander Bow and Airborne Trooper Order 66 2-pack..85.00

Philadelphia Toy Expo
__ Bib Fortuna 65.00
__ Boba Fett 75.00
__ Chewbacca 75.00
__ R2-D2 ....75.00

Red Mercury
Custom figures to promote celebrity signings.
__ David Prowse, April 28, 2000 ....80.00
__ Jerome Blake, April 28, 2000..........................65.00
__ Peter Mayhew, June 30, 2000 ....80.00

Action Figures: Modern Vintage Packaging

Hasbro
2004-2007. Vintage style cardback in clamshell case.
__ Biker Scout, ROTJ [ATV001]............................20.00
__ Boba Fett, ROTJ [ATV002] 20.00
__ Bossk [ATV003] 25.00
__ C-3PO, ESB [ATV004] 30.00
__ Chewbacca, ROTJ [ATV005] 20.00
__ Darth Vader, ESB [ATV006] 30.00
__ George Lucas, Stormtrooper Disguise, exclusive to mail-in [ATV007]...45.00
__ Greedo, SW [ATV008].....................................12.00
__ Han Solo (Hoth Outfit) [ATV009] 25.00
__ Han Solo, ROTJ [ATV010]................................15.00
__ Han Solo, SW [ATV011]...................................20.00

__ Han Solo, SW missing disclaimer on back.....20.00
__ IG-88 [ATV012] 25.00
__ Lando Calrissian, ESB [ATV013]......................20.00
__ Luke Skywalker (Bespin Fatigues) [ATV014]....25.00
__ Luke Skywalker X-Wing Pilot, SW [ATV015]...15.00
__ Luke Skywalker, SW [ATV016]..........................20.00
__ Obi-Wan Kenobi, SW [ATV017].........................10.00
__ Obi-Wan Kenobi, SW missing disclaimer on back 10.00
__ Princess Leia (Combat Poncho) [ATV018]......25.00
__ Princess Leia, SW [ATV019] 20.00
__ Princess Leia, SW missing disclaimer on back 20.00
__ R2-D2, ROTJ [ATV020]....................................15.00
__ Sand People, SW [ATV021] 12.00
__ Stormtrooper (Hoth Battle Gear) [ATV022] 25.00
__ Stormtrooper, ROTJ [ATV023]..........................20.00
__ Yoda, ESB [ATV024] 15.00

2010-2011. Vintage style cardback.
__ 2-Pack: 4-LOM and Zuckuss sticker over UPC, exclusive to JediCon [ATV025].......................45.00
__ 4-LOM VC10 [ATV026] 12.00
__ Admiral Ackbar VC22 [ATV027].......................12.00
__ Anakin Skywalker VC13 [ATV028] 12.00
__ Anakin Skywalker VC32 [ATV029] 12.00
__ Anakin Skywalker (Darth Vader) VC13 [ATV030]...12.00
__ ARC Trooper VC54 ....12.00
__ AT-AT Commander VC05 [ATV031] 12.00
__ AT-RT VC46 [ATV032] 12.00
__ Barriss Offee VC51 ....12.00
__ Boba Fett VC09 [ATV033]................................14.00
__ Bom Vimdin VC53...12.00
__ Clone Commander Cody VC19 [ATV034].......12.00
__ Clone Trooper VC15 [ATV035].........................12.00
__ Clone Trooper, 212th Battalion VC38 [ATV036]...12.00
__ Clone Trooper (AOTC) VC45 [ATV037].............12.00
__ Commander Gree VC43 [ATV038]..................12.00
__ Dak Ralter VC07 [ATV039]...............................10.00
__ Darth Sidious VC12 [ATV040]..........................12.00
__ Darth Vader VC08 [ATV041] 12.00
__ Dengar VC01 [ATV042] 12.00
__ Fi-Ek Sirch (Jedi Knight) VC49 [ATV043] 12.00
__ Gamorrean Guard VC21 [ATV044]..................12.00
__ General Grievous VC17 [ATV045]...................15.00
__ General Lando Calrissian VC47 [ATV046] 12.00
__ Han Solo Yavin Ceremony VC42 [ATV047] ..12.00
__ Han Solo (Echo Base Outfit) VC03 [ATV048]..12.00
__ Han Solo (Bespin Outfit) VC50 ....12.00
__ Jango Fett VC34 [ATV049] 12.00
__ Kit Fisto VC29 [ATV050]...................................12.00
__ Leia (Hoth Outfit) VC02 [ATV051] 12.00
__ Logray VC55 ....12.00
__ Luke Skywalker VC39 [ATV052]........................12.00
__ Luke Skywalker (Bespin) VC04 [ATV053] 12.00
__ Luke Skywalker (Dagobah) VC44 [ATV054]....12.00
__ Luke Skywalker (Jedi Knight outfit) VC23 [ATV055] 12.00
__ Mace Windu VC35 [ATV056]............................12.00
__ MagnaGuard VC18 [ATV057]..........................12.00
__ Obi-Wan Kenobi VC16 [ATV058]....................12.00
__ Obi-Wan Kenobi VC31 [ATV059]....................12.00
__ Padme Amidala VC33 [ATV060].....................12.00
__ Ponda Baba VC70 ....12.00
__ R2-D2, full card (back) VC25 ....40.00
__ R2-D2, head shot (back) VC25 [ATV061].......12.00
__ R5-D4 VC40 [ATV062] 12.00

__ Rebel Commando VC26 [ATV063] 12.00
__ Rebel Fleet Trooper VC52 ....12.00
__ Sandtrooper VC14 [ATV064]...........................12.00
__ See-Threepio (C-3PO) VC06 [ATV065]...........12.00
__ Senate Security Guard VC36 [ATV066] 12.00
__ Senate Security Guard VC36 close-up photo [ATV067]..35.00
__ Stormtrooper VC41 [ATV068] 12.00
__ Super Battle Droid VC37 [ATV069].................12.00
__ Twin-Pod Cloud Car Pilot VC11 [ATV070]......12.00
__ Wedge Antilles, full card (back) VC28 [ATV071]..125.00
__ Wedge Antilles, head shot (back) VC28 ....50.00
__ Weequay (Skiff Master) VC48 [ATV072].........12.00
__ Wicket VC27 [ATV073]....................................12.00
__ Wooof VC24 [ATV074]....................................12.00
__ Yoda VC20 [ATV075] 12.00
__ Zam Wesell VC30 [ATV076].............................12.00

2010-2011. Vintage style cardback. Ultimate galactic hunt packaging.
__ Anakin Skywalker VC13 [ATV077]....................15.00
__ Boba Fett VC09 [ATV078]................................15.00
__ Clone Trooper VC15 [ATV079].........................15.00
__ Clone Trooper VC15 [ATV080].........................15.00
__ General Grievous VC17 [ATV081]...................15.00
__ Luke Skywalker Bespin VC04 [ATV082] 15.00
__ Obi-Wan Kenobi VC16 [ATV083]....................15.00
__ Sandtrooper VC14 [ATV084]...........................15.00

2012. Vintage style cardback. Revenge of the Jedi.
__ Admiral Ackbar VC22 ....20.00
__ Boba Fett VC09 ....20.00
__ Darth Vader VC08 ....20.00
__ Endor Rebel Commando VC26 ....20.00
__ Luke Skywalker VC23 ....20.00
__ R2-D2 VC25 ....20.00
__ Stormtrooper VC41 ....20.00
__ Wicket VC27 ....20.00

Hasbro, Canada
2010-2011. Vintage style cardback.
__ 4-LOM VC10 ....12.00
__ Anakin Skywalker VC32 ....12.00
__ AT-AT Commander VC05 ....12.00
__ AT-RT Driver VC46 ....12.00
__ Clone Commander Cody VC19 ....12.00
__ Clone Trooper, 212th Battalion VC38 ....12.00
__ Clone Trooper, EPII VC45................................12.00
__ Commander Gree VC43 ....12.00
__ Dak Ralter VC07 ....12.00
__ Darth Vader VC08 ....12.00
__ Dengar VC01 ....12.00
__ Fi-Ek Sirch VC49..12.00
__ General Lando Calrissian VC47......................12.00
__ Han Solo Yavin Ceremony VC42 ....12.00
__ Han Solo Echo base outfit VC03 ....12.00
__ Jango Fett VC34 ....12.00
__ Kit Fisto VC29 ....12.00
__ Leia Hoth outfit VC02 ....12.00
__ Luke Skywalker Dagobah Landing VC44 ....12.00
__ Luke Skywalker Death Star Escape VC39......12.00
__ Luke Skywalker Bespin fatigues VC04 ....12.00
__ Mace Windu VC35...12.00
__ MagnaGuard VC18 ....12.00
__ Obi-Wan Kenobi VC31 ....12.00
__ Padme Amidala VC33 ....12.00
__ R5-D4 VC40 ....12.00
__ See-Threepio (C-3PO) VC06 ....12.00

ATW001

ATW002

ATW003

ATW004

Action Figures

STAR WARS
REBEL TROOPER BUILDER SET

STAR WARS
REBEL TROOPER BUILDER SET
PROOF OF PURCHASE

0 76930 26816 2

Made in China

P2S7001

STORMTROOPER
TROOP BUILDER SET

STORMTROOPER
TROOP BUILDER SET
PROOF OF PURCHASE

0 76930 32519 3

Made in China

P2S7002

P2S7003 (box not shown)

SKU # 69736
MADE IN CHINA
AGES 4 & UP

P2S7004 figure and box

P2S7005 (box not shown)

P2S7006 figure and box

STAR WARS
TRILOGY
SPECIAL EDITION

NO. 00000

P2S7007

__ Senate Security Guard, close-up VC36 ....35.00
__ Senate Security, Guard full front VC36 ....12.00
__ Stormtrooper VC41 ....12.00
__ Super Battle Droid VC37 ....12.00
__ Twin-Pod Cloud Car Pilot VC11 ....12.00
__ Wedge Antilles, full card (back) VC28 ....125.00
__ Wedge Antilles, head shot (back) VC28 ....50.00
__ Weequay Skiff Master VC48 ....12.00
__ Zam Wesell VC30 ....12.00

2010-2011. Vintage style cardback. Ultimate galactic hunt packaging.
__ Anakin Skywalker VC13 ....15.00
__ Boba Fett VC09 ....15.00
__ Clone Trooper VC15 ....15.00
__ Darth Sidious VC12 ....15.00
__ General Grievous VC17 ....15.00

__ Luke Skywalker Bespin fatigues VC04 ....15.00
__ Obi-Wan Kenobi VC16 ....15.00
__ Sandtrooper VC14 ....15.00

Hasbro, UK
2004-2007. Vintage style cardback in clamshell case.
__ Darth Vader, ESB, exclusive to Woolworths
[ATV085] 35.00

Action Figures: Modern Vintage Packaging Multipacks

Hasbro
3-Packs.
__ Hero Set: Luke X-Wing Pilot, Ben Kenobi, Han Solo,
exclusive to Target [ATW001] 25.00

__ Rebel Set: 2-1B, Leia (Hoth Outfit), Rebel
Commander, exclusive to Target [ATW002] ...25.00
__ Villain Set: Stormtrooper, Darth Vader, Death Squad
Commander, exclusive to Target [ATW003] ...25.00

9-Packs.
__ Imperial Set, Hoth Rebels, Bespin Alliance: 4-LOM,
AT-AT Driver, Imperial TIE Fighter Pilot, Han Solo,
Hoth Rebel Trooper, FX-7, Bespin Wing guard,
Lando Calrissian, Luke Skywalker, exclusive to
Target [ATW004] 60.00

Action Figures: Special Offer

Hasbro
Troop Builder Sets. 4-packs or 'army builder' figures.
__ Endor Rebel Soldiers 20.00
__ Rebel Trooper [P2S7001] 25.00
__ Sandtroopers 20.00
__ Stormtroopers [P2S7002] 45.00

Kenner
__ B'Omarr Monk [P2S7003] 15.00
__ Ben Kenobi Spirit, "Made in" sticker
[P2S7004] 10.00
__ Ben Kenobi Spirit, "Made" sticker 10.00
__ Ben Kenobi Spirit, Printed warning 10.00
__ Cantina Band Member, printed warning
[P2S7005] 15.00
__ Cantina Band Member, warning sticker 15.00
__ Han Solo in Stormtrooper Disguise 20.00
__ Han Solo in Stormtrooper Disguise, no tabs inside
of helmet [P2S7006] 20.00

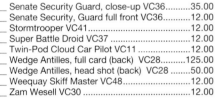
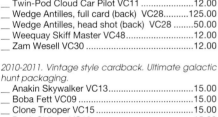

BAH001   BAH002   BAH003   BAH004   BAH005   BAH006   BAH007   BAH008

BAH009   BAH010   BAH011   BAH012   BAH013   BAH014   BAH015

BAH016 front, side, and package

Kenner, UK
__ Obi-Wan Kenobi spirit, limited to 40,000, numbered [P2S7007] 40.00

Action Figures: Unlicensed 1977-1986 (Vintage)

__ 3-pack, "Space Figures", 3 licensed figures in generic package [2:66] 275.00
__ Darth Vader, approx. 6" tall with flashing lightsaber [2:66] 17.00
__ Stormtrooper on Star Wars hanger card, approx. 16" 41.00

2-Pack on ROTJ hanger card, figures are approximately 4" in height.
__ C-3PO and Darth Vader.................................48.00
__ C-3PO and R2-D2...51.00
__ Chewbacca and Darth Vader........................45.00
__ Darth Vader and Darth Vader 50.00

Mexico.
__ Chewbacca..35.00
__ Gamorrean Guard..35.00

Mexico. Comic art cardback.
__ Darth Vader...45.00
__ Klaatu, palace 35.00
__ Klaatu, skiff 35.00

Mexico. Modern bootleg of vintage figures.
__ Admiral Ackbar [BAH001] 12.00
__ Bib Fortuna [BAH002]....................................12.00
__ Bossk [BAH003]...12.00
__ Chewbacca [BAH004].....................................12.00
__ Emperor [BAH005]..12.00
__ Emperor's Royal Guard [BAH006]...................12.00
__ Gamorrean Guard [BAH007].........................25.00
__ Greedo [BAH008]..12.00
__ Imperial TIE Pilot [BAH009]............................12.00
__ Klaatu (Palace) [BAH010]...............................12.00
__ Klaatu (Skiff) [BAH011] 12.00
__ Logray [BAH012]..12.00
__ Luke Skywalker [BAH013]..............................25.00
__ Princess Leia 25.00
__ R5-D4..25.00
__ See-Threepio [BAH013]..................................15.00
__ Ugnaught [BAH014]..12.00
__ Weequay [BAH015]..12.00
__ Yoda 25.00

ModelTrem, Brazil
Lead figures. Aventura Na Galaxia, cardboard box packaging. Limbs attached using screw-in fasteners.
__ 2-1B ....N/V
__ Ben Kenobi, lead lightsaber [3:433]................N/V
__ Ben Kenobi, plastic lightsaber blue [3:433] ......N/V
__ Ben Kenobi, plastic lightsaber yellow [3:433]...N/V
__ Bespin Guard...N/V
__ Bib Fortuna ....N/V
__ Biker Scout ....N/V
__ Bossk..N/V
__ Chewbacca..N/V
__ Cloud Car Pilot ....N/V
__ Darth Vader, lead lightsaber ....N/V
__ Darth Vader, plastic lightsaber ....N/V
__ Death Squad Commander...............................N/V
__ Emperor Palpatine ....N/V
__ Gamorrean Guard ....N/V
__ Han Solo..N/V
__ Han Solo, Hoth ....N/V
__ Hoth Soldier...N/V
__ IG-88...N/V
__ Imperial TIE Figher Pilot.................................N/V
__ Lando Calrissian ....N/V
__ Lobot..N/V
__ Luke Skywalker, Hoth [BAH016]......................N/V
__ Luke Skywalker, Jedi ....N/V
__ Luke Skywalker, lead lightsaber yellow ....N/V
__ Luke Skywalker, plastic lightsaber blue............N/V
__ Luke Skywalker, X-Wing Pilot..........................N/V
__ Princess Leia ....N/V
__ Princess Leia, Hoth ....N/V
__ Sand People ....N/V
__ See-Threepio ....N/V
__ Snaggletooth ....N/V
__ Snowtrooper ....N/V
__ Stormtrooper ....N/V
__ Wicket..N/V
__ Yoda ....N/V

Uzay
__ AT Driver [2:66] 300.00
__ Blue Stars [2:66] 950.00
__ C-3PO, alone on card [2:66] 300.00
__ C-3PO, card shows 2nd droid.......................414.00
__ Chewbacca, close-up card...........................750.00
__ Chewbacca, vegitation card [2:66] 425.00
__ Darth Vader [2:66] 735.00
__ Death Star Droid 650.00
__ Emperor's Royal Guard, with cloak 475.00
__ Emperor's Royal Guard, without cloak........475.00
__ Head Man ....N/V
__ Imperial Gunner [2:66] 800.00
__ Imperial Stormtrooper (Snowtrooper).......1150.00
__ MLC-3 Mini Rig..325.00
__ MTV-7 Mini Rig..325.00
__ R5-D4...650.00
__ Stormtrooper [2:66]..310.00
__ TIE Pilot...325.00

Action Figures: Unlicensed 1995-1999 (POTF2)

__ AT-AT Driver on "Plastic Toys" header card 125.00
__ Darth Vader and Stormtrooper, each driving a Sport Skiff...12.00

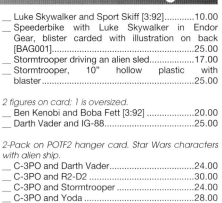

__ Luke Skywalker and Sport Skiff [3:92]...........10.00
__ Speederbike with Luke Skywalker in Endor Gear, blister carded with illustration on back [BAG001]..25.00
__ Stormtrooper driving an alien sled................17.00
__ Stormtrooper, 10" hollow plastic with blaster 25.00

2 figures on card; 1 is oversized.
__ Ben Kenobi and Boba Fett [3:92] 20.00
__ Darth Vader and IG-88...................................25.00

2-Pack on POTF2 hanger card. Star Wars characters with alien ship.
__ C-3PO and Darth Vader...............................24.00
__ C-3PO and R2-D2...30.00
__ C-3PO and Stormtrooper..............................24.00
__ C-3PO and Yoda..28.00
__ Darth Vader and Dagobah Luke 14.00
__ Darth Vader and R2-D2 [BAG002].................30.00

Bagged on a Landspeeder header card.
__ Darth Vader and C-3PO driving a Landspeeder...18.00
__ Two Sport Skiffs 11.00

Characters come in red, black, white. Figures are approximately 2" in height. Sold loose.
__ C-3PO [BAG003] 5.00
__ Darth Vader [BAG004] 3.00
__ Luke Skywalker [BAG005] 3.00

Deluxe Han Solo card.
__ Deluxe Han 5.00
__ Deluxe Luke [3:92] 5.00
__ Deluxe Stormtrooper 5.00
__ Speeder Bike and Scout 16.00
__ Swoop Bike and Rider 5.00

Deluxe Stormtrooper card.
__ Deluxe Han 5.00
__ Deluxe Luke 5.00
__ Swoop Bike Rider 14.00

La Guerra De Las Galaxias.
__ Darth Vader and Stormtrooper 15.00
__ Darth Vader and Stormtrooper with a Sport Skiff..21.00

POTF2 AT-ST Driver oversized card, figures approximately 5" in height.
__ AT-ST Driver [3:92] 8.00
__ Hoth Luke 8.00
__ Hoth Rebel Soldier [BAG006] 8.00
__ Imperial Gunner 9.00

POTF2 C-3PO card.
__ Chewbacca..5.00
__ Darth Vader 5.00
__ Dash Rendar 5.00
__ Han Solo 5.00
__ Han Solo in Hoth Gear 5.00
__ Obi-Wan Kenobi 5.00
__ Princess Leia [BAG007] 5.00
__ R2-D2 [BAG008]..11.00
__ Stormtrooper 5.00
__ TIE Fighter Pilot 5.00
__ Yoda 5.00

BAG001

BAG002

BAG003

BAG004

BAG005

Action Figures

BAG006

BAG007

BAG008

BAG009

BAG010

BAG011

BAG012

BAG013

BAG014

BAG015

BAG016

BAG017

BAG018

BAG019

BAG020

BAG021

BAG022

BAG023

BAG024

BAG025

BAG026

BAG027

BAG028

BAG029

BAG030

BAG031

BAG032

BAG033

BAG034

BAG035

POTF2 Chewbacca card, figures approximately 6" in height.
__ Bespin Luke [3:92] 11.00
__ Lando as Skiff Guard 9.00

POTF2 Chewbacca card. Random figures cast from unlicensed vintage molds.
__ 3-packs, any characters [BAG009] 45.00

POTF2 Darth Vader card.
__ Stormtroopers resembling Applause PVC figures 15.00

POTF2 Endor Han card.
__ C-3PO [3:92] 5.00
__ R2-D2 ....6.00
__ Yoda 6.00

POTF2 Luke Dagobah card.
__ Boba Fett 15.00
__ C-3PO 5.00
__ Chewbacca 5.00
__ Darth Vader 5.00
__ Han Hoth 5.00
__ Han Solo 5.00
__ Lando 5.00
__ Luke Dagobah 5.00
__ Luke Skywalker 7.00
__ Luke X-Wing Pilot 6.00
__ R2-D2 ....5.00
__ Yoda [3:92] 7.00

POTF2 Luke in Stormtrooper Disguise card.
__ 2-1B 5.00
__ AT-ST Driver 5.00
__ Ben Kenobi [BAG010] 5.00
__ Bossk 5.00
__ C-3PO [BAG011] 5.00
__ Darth Vader 5.00
__ Darth Vader bendy 12.00
__ Death Star Gunner 12.00
__ Greedo [BAG012] 6.00
__ Han Solo bendy [BAG013] 12.00
__ Hoth Rebel Soldier 5.00
__ Imperial Gunner 6.00
__ Jawas 5.00
__ Leia Boushh 5.00
__ Luke Hoth 5.00
__ Luke Skywalker [BAG014] 5.00
__ Luke Stormtrooper 5.00
__ Princess Leia [BAG015] 5.00

__ R5-D4 ....7.00
__ Sandtrooper 5.00
__ Stormtrooper [BAG016] 5.00
__ Tusken Raider 5.00

POTF2 Luke Jedi card.
__ C-3PO [BAG017] 5.00
__ Chewbacca [BAG018] 5.00
__ Chewbacca / Snoova [BAG019] 5.00
__ Han Solo, brown belt 5.00
__ Han Solo, silver belt 5.00
__ Leia / Boushh [BAG020] 5.00
__ Luke in Imperial Guard Disguise 9.00
__ Luke Skywalker 7.00
__ Obi-Wan Kenobi [BAG021] 5.00
__ Princess Leia, red belt [BAG022] 5.00
__ Princess Leia, white belt 5.00
__ R2-D2 [BAG023] 6.00
__ Stormtrooper 5.00
__ Tie Pilot [BAG024] 5.00
__ Yoda [BAG025] 5.00

POTF2 Luke Jedi oversized card, figures approximately 5" in height.
__ Chewbacca / Snoova 8.00
__ Darth Vader 8.00
__ Dash Rendar 8.00
__ Han Carbonite 8.00
__ Han Hoth 8.00
__ Lando 8.00
__ Luke Jedi 8.00
__ Momaw Nadon 8.00
__ TIE Fighter Pilot 8.00
__ Yoda 8.00

POTF2 Luke Skywalker card.
__ Ben Kenobi [BAG026] 5.00
__ Boba Fett [BAG027] 15.00
__ C-3PO [BAG028] 5.00
__ Chewbacca 5.00
__ Darth Vader [BAG029] 5.00
__ Han Hoth [BAG030] 5.00
__ Han Solo [BAG031] 5.00
__ Luke Jedi 6.00
__ Luke Skywalker [BAG032] 7.00
__ Luke X-Wing Pilot [BAG033] 6.00
__ Obi-Wan Kenobi 5.00
__ Princess Leia 5.00
__ R2-D2 [BAG034] 5.00
__ Stormtrooper, on Star Hero card [3:93] 10.00
__ Yoda [BAG035] 5.00

POTF2 Sandtrooper oversized card, figures approximately 5" in height.
__ AT-ST Driver 8.00
__ Hoth Luke 8.00
__ Hoth Rebel Soldier 8.00
__ Imperial Gunner [BAG036] 9.00

POTF2 Sandtrooper oversized card, figures are approximately 5" in height.
__ Luke Stormtrooper [3:93] 8.00
__ Stormtrooper 8.00

Spirit figures from Japan.
__ Anakin Skywalker 65.00
__ Ben Kenobi 50.00
__ Yoda 85.00

Star Warrs
__ X-Wing similar to Galoob Micromachine with 2 micro-pilots and 2" figures: Luke, C-3PO and Vader 27.00

Thunderforce figures, approximately 11" in height.
__ Darth Vader [BAG037] 35.00
__ Stormtrooper [BAG038] 18.00

Galaxy Empire
Figures are approximately 6" in height.
__ Boba Fett [BAG039] 12.00
__ Chewbacca [BAG040] 9.00
__ Chewbacca / Snoova [BAG041] 6.00
__ Darth Vader [BAG042] 9.00
__ Han Solo [BAG043] 9.00
__ Luke Jedi [BAG044] 9.00
__ Stormtrooper [BAG045] 9.00

Galaxy Heroes
__ Darth Vader mask with Vader figure, approx 5" 4.00

Industrial Argentina
__ Darth Vader 18.00
__ Stormtrooper 18.00

Space Power Warrior
Darth Vader character figures, approximately 8" in height.
__ Black armor [3:93] 26.00
__ Black armor, Lost in Space Robot on package [BAG046] 28.00
__ White armor 19.00

BAG036

BAG037

BAG038

BAG039

BAG040

BAG041

BAG042

BAG043

BAG044

BAG045

BAG046

Action Figures

BAG047

BAG048

BAG049

BAG050

BAG051

BAG052

BAG053

BAG054

BAG055

BAG056

BAG057

BAG058

BAG059

BAG060

BAG061

BAG062

Star Warrio

SOTE card, AT-ST Driver.
__ Ben Kenobi [BAG047].......................................5.00
__ C-3PO [BAG048] 5.00
__ Chewbacca [BAG049] 5.00
__ Darth Vader [BAG050].....................................5.00
__ Han Solo [BAG051]..5.00
__ Luke in Imperial Disguise [BAG052] 5.00
__ Luke Skywalker [BAG053] 5.00
__ Princess Leia [BAG054] 5.00
__ Princess Leia / Boushh [BAG055].....................5.00
__ R2-D2 [BAG056]..5.00
__ Stormtrooper [BAG057] 5.00
__ Yoda [BAG058]...7.00

SOTE card, Stormtrooper.
__ Biker Scout 34.00

__ Deluxe Han 8.00
__ Deluxe Luke 8.00
__ Han Solo in Carbonite....................................14.00
__ Luke 10.00
__ Luke Jedi 10.00
__ Stormtrooper 12.00
__ Swoop Rider 10.00
__ TIE Fighter Pilot 5.00

Vs 2-Pack

2-Pack, figures approximately 5" in height.
__ Dash Rendar vs. Carbonite Han 16.00
__ Imperial Guard Luke vs. Boba Fett [BAG059] 16.00
__ Lando vs. Momaw Nadon [BAG060] 19.00
__ Leia / Boushh vs. Hoth Han [BAG061] 16.00
__ Prince Xizor vs. Jedi Luke [BAG062] 16.00

Anakin Skywalker cardback with fake CommTech chip.
__ Darth Maul [BAF001].......................................9.00

C-3PO card with fake CommTech chip.
__ C-3PO [BAF002] 7.00
__ Darth Sidious [BAF003] 7.00
__ Ric Olie [BAF004]..7.00
__ Senator Palpatine [BAF005]............................7.00
__ Watto [BAF006]...7.00

Correct card with fake CommTech chip.
__ Anakin Skywalker..7.00
__ Darth Maul 7.00
__ Jar Jar Binks 7.00
__ Obi-Wan Kenobi 7.00
__ Padme (Darth Maul card)..................................7.00
__ Queen Amidala 7.00
__ Qui-Gon Jinn...7.00

Darth Maul card with fake CommTech chip.
__ Darth Maul [BAF007].......................................6.00

Darth Maul card with full-card bubble, figures are approximately 8" in height.
__ Anakin Skywalker [BAF008]..............................8.00
__ Darth Maul [BAF009].....................................12.00
__ Jar Jar Binks [BAF010] 9.00
__ Obi-Wan Kenobi [BAF011]...............................8.00
__ Qui-Gon Jinn [BAF012]....................................8.00

BAF001

BAF002

BAF003

BAF004

BAF005

BAF006

BAF007

BAF008

BAF009

BAF010

BAF011

BAF012

BAF013

BAF014

BAF015

BAF016

BAF017

BAF018

BAF019

BAF020

BAF021

BAF022

BAF023

BAF024

BAF025

BAF026

BAF027

BAF028

BAF029

BAF030

BAF031

BAF032

Action Figures

AFX001

AFX002

AFX003

AFX004

AFX005

AFX006

Darth Maul card, figures are approximately 6" in height.
__ Anakin Skywalker [BAF013]...............................8.00
__ C-3PO [BAF014]..8.00
__ Darth Maul [BAF015]..12.00
__ Obi-Wan Kenobi [BAF016]................................8.00
__ Queen Amidala [BAF017]..................................8.00
__ Qui-Gon Jinn [BAF018].....................................8.00

Darth Maul Space Wars card.
__ 2-pack: Darth Maul and Ric Olie [BAF019].....20.00
__ 2-pack: Darth Sidious and C-3PO [BAF020]..20.00
__ 2-pack: Senator Palpatine and Mace Windu
[BAF021] 20.00
__ 4-pack: Qui-Gon, Watto, Padme, Chancellor
Velorum [BAF022]...30.00
__ 5-pack: Mace Windu, Ric Ollie, Pit Droid, Gasgano,
Ki-Adi-Mundi [BAF023].................................35.00

Figures are bagged with header card.
__ Darth Maul 8.00
__ Yoda 9.00

Queen Amidala card.
__ Anakin Skywalker [BAF024].............................7.00
__ Battle Droid (gold) [BAF025] 20.00
__ Boss Nass..9.00
__ C-3PO 7.00
__ Chancellor Valorum 7.00
__ Darth Maul [BAF026].......................................9.00
__ Darth Sidious 7.00
__ Gasgano and Pit Droid 10.00
__ Jar Jar Binks [BAF027]....................................7.00
__ Ki-Adi-Mundy...7.00
__ Mace Windu 7.00

__ Obi-Wan Kenobi [BAF028]...............................7.00
__ Padme [BAF029]..7.00
__ Queen Amidala [BAF030].................................7.00
__ Qui-Gon Jinn [BAF031]....................................7.00
__ Ric Olie 7.00
__ Senator Palpatine 7.00
__ Watto 7.00

TPM card with classic trilogy art.
__ Darth Sidious [BAF032] 15.00

Action Figures: Unlicensed 2002-2004 (Saga)

__ Clone Trooper [AFX001] 15.00
__ Jango Fett [AFX002] 15.00
__ Obi-Wan Kenobi [AFX003].............................15.00

2-packs.
__ Jango Fett and Count Dooku 45.00
__ Jango Fett and Obi-Wan Kenobi 45.00

3-packs.
__ Count Dooku, Jango Fett, Anakin Skywalker .45.00
__ Count Dooku, Jango Fett, Obi-Wan Kenobi...45.00

5-packs.
__ Obi-Wan, Anakin, Mace Windu, Jango Fett, Count
Dooku, carded horizontal 45.00
__ Obi-Wan, Anakin, Mace Windu, Jango Fett, Count
Dooku, carded vertical...................................45.00

6-packs.
__ Clone Trooper, Han, Jango, Yoda, Vader, Obi-Wan
[AFX004] 65.00

10-packs.
__ Clone Troopers, helmets not attached 25.00
__ Clonetroopers: 5 marching, 5 firing bagged...55.00

Attack of the Clones. Approx. 5 inches tall.
__ Darth Sidious [AFX005]...................................15.00
__ Mace Windu [AFX006] 15.00

Action Fleet Battle Packs

Galoob
__ #1: Rebel Alliance: Speeder Bikes, Lando,
Luke, Leia, Rebel Trooper, Echo base Trooper
[MMB001] 15.00

__ #1: Rebel Alliance: Speeder Bikes, Lando, Luke, Leia,
Rebel Trooper, Echo base Trooper, Yoda......25.00
__ #2: Galactic Empire: AT-ST, AT-ST Pilot,
Scout Trooper, Darth Vader, Sandtrooper
[MMB002] 15.00
__ #2: Galactic Empire: AT-ST, AT-ST Pilot, Scout
Trooper, Darth Vader, Sandtrooper, Royal
Guard..25.00
__ #3: Aliens and Creatures: Bantha, Tusken Raider,
Gamorrean Guard, Bib Fortuna, Brea Tonnika
[MMB003] 8.00
__ #3: Aliens and Creatures: Bantha, Tusken Raider,
Gamorrean Guard, Bib Fortuna, Brea Tonnika,
Ponda Baba [MMB004] 25.00
__ #4: Galactic Hunters: Dewback, Sandtrooper, Boba
Fett, Greedo, Bossk [MMB005] 8.00
__ #4: Imperial Hunters: Dewback, Sandtrooper, Boba
Fett, Greedo, Bossk, IG-88............................25.00
__ #5: Shadows of the Empire: Swoops, Dash
Rendar, Prince Xizor, Guri, LE-BO2D9, Jix
[MMB006] 20.00
__ #5: Shadows of the Empire: Swoops, Dash
Rendar, Prince Xizor, Guri, LE-BO2D9, Jix,
Chewbacca...25.00
__ #5: Shadows of the Empire: Swoops, Dash Rendar,
Prince Xizor, Guri, LE-BO2D9, Jix, Skahtul ...25.00
__ #6: Dune Sea Pack: Desert Skiff, Boba Fett, Nikto,
Chewbacca, Han, Luke, Barada [MMB007] ...25.00
__ #6: Dune Sea: Desert Skiff, Boba Fett, Nikto,
Chewbacca, Han, Luke [MMB008].................20.00
__ #7: Droid Escape: Escape Pod, R2-D2, Obi-
Wan Kenobi, C-3PO, Sandtrooper, Darth Vader
[MMB009] 20.00
__ #7: Droid Escape: Escape Pod, R2-D2, Obi-Wan
Kenobi, C-3PO, Sandtrooper, Darth Vader, Avon
Canada exclusive, white box [MMB010] 28.00
__ #7: Rebel Escape: Escape Pod, R2-D2, Obi-Wan
Kenobi, C-3PO, Sandtrooper, Darth Vader, EG6
Power Droid..25.00
__ #8: Desert Palace: Jabba the Hutt, Ishi Tib, Princess
Leia (Boushh), Lando, Sy Snootles, Salacious
Crumb [MMB011] 15.00
__ #8: Desert Palace: Jabba the Hutt, Ishi Tib, Princess
Leia (Boushh), Lando, Sy Snootles, Weequay,
Salacious Crumb [MMB012]...........................27.00
__ #9: Endor Adventure: Hang Glider, Speeder Bike,
Luke, Scout Trooper, Wicket, Rebel Trooper, Ewok
[MMB013] 15.00
__ #10: Mos Eisley Spaceport: Ronto, Luke, Ben,
Jawa, Dr. Evazan, Garindan [MMB014]..........15.00
__ #11: Cantina Encounter: Landspeeder, C-3PO,
Ben, Figrin D'an, Muftak, Han [MMB015].........8.00

MMG001

MMG002

MMB001

MMB002

MMB003

MMB004

MMB005

MMB006

MMB007

MMB008

MMB009

MMB010

MMB011

MMB012

MMB013

MMB014

MMB015

MMB016

MMB017

MMB018

MMB019

MMB020

MMG003

MMB021

MMB022

MMB023

MMM001

MMM002

MMM003

MMM004

MMM005

MMM006

__ #12: Cantina Smugglers and Spies: Lak Sivrak, Duros, Labria, Momaw Nadon, Arcona, Wuher, Nabrun Leids, Advozsec [MMB016] 30.00

__ #13: Hoth Attack: Tauntaun, General Veers, Wampa, Han Solo with tauntaun, Luke, Snowtrooper [MMB017] 22.00

__ #14: Death Star Escape: General Tagge, Admiral Motti, Princess Leia, Han, Ben, Darth Vader, R2-D2, Luke [MMB018] 20.00

__ #15: Endor Victory: Yoda (Glow-In-The-Dark), Obi-Wan (GITD), Anakin (GITD), Luke, Leia, Han, Chewbacca, Ewok [MMB019] 20.00

__ #16: Lars Family Homestead: Landspeeder, Owen Lars, Beru Lars, Luke, EG-6, Jawa [MMB020] 20.00

__ #17: Imperial Troops: Speeder Bike, Scout Troopers, Stormtrooper, Snowtrooper, Sandtrooper [MMB021] 20.00

__ #18: Rebel Troops: Echo Base Troopers, Rebel Troopers, Endor Trooper, X-Wing Pilot, Y-Wing Pilot, Y-Wing Gunner [MMB022] 18.00

Galoob / Gigi, Italy

__ #08: Il Palazzo del Deserto: Jabba the Hutt, Ishi Tib, Princess Leia (Boushh), Lando, Sy Snootles, Salacious Crumb [MMB023].........................25.00

Action Fleet Classic Duels

Galoob

__ Millennium Falcon vs. Tie Interceptor, exclusive to Toys R Us [MMG001] 36.00

__ X-Wing Fighter vs. TIE Fighter, exclusive to Toys R Us [MMG002]..36.00

__ X-Wing Fighter vs. TIE Fighter pewter colored, limited to 4,800, exclusive to Zaap [MMG003]...200.00

Action Fleet Flight Controllers

Galoob

__ Darth Vader's TIE Fighter [MMM001] 15.00

__ Darth Vader's TIE Fighter with bonus X-Wing fighter targets [MMM002] 65.00

__ Tie Interceptor [MMM003] 30.00

__ X-Wing Fighter [MMM004].............................15.00

__ X-Wing Fighter with bonus TIE fighter targets [MMM005]..65.00

__ Y-Wing Fighter [MMM006].............................30.00

Action Fleet Mini Scenes

Galoob

Play scene with micro-sized figures included. First edition packaging.

__ #1 STAP Invasion...10.00

__ #2 Destroyer Droid Ambush 10.00

__ #3 Gungan Assault 10.00

__ #4 Sith Pursuit 10.00

Play scene with micro-sized figures included.

__ #1 STAP Invasion [MMO001]...........................8.00

__ #2 Destroyer Droid Ambush [MMO002] 8.00

MMO001

MMO002

MMO003

MMO004

MMO005

MMO006

MMO007

MMO008

MMO009

MMO010

MMO011

MMO012

MNP001

MNP002

MNP003

MNP004

MNP005

MNP006

__ #3 Gungan Assault [MMO003]..........................8.00
__ #4 Sith Pursuit [MMO004].................................8.00
__ #5 Trade Federation Raid [MMO005] 15.00
__ #6 Throne Room Reception [MMO006]..........15.00
__ #7 Watto's Deal [MMO007] 15.00
__ #8 Generator Core Duel [MMO008]................20.00

Hasbro
__ Dune Sea Ambush [MMO009] 20.00
__ Imperial Endor Pursuit [MMO010] 20.00
__ Mos Eisley Encounter [MMO011] 20.00
__ Tatooine Droid Hunter [MMO012] 20.00

Action Fleet Playsets

Galoob
Classic trilogy, gold logo.
__ Ice Planet Hoth [MNP001] 25.00
__ The Death Star [MNP002].............................25.00
__ Yavin Rebel Base [MNP003]...........................25.00

Classic trilogy, silver logo.
__ Ice Planet Hoth 34.00
__ Ice Planet Hoth with two additional figures, exclusive to BJ's Warehouse [MNP004].........95.00
__ The Death Star..34.00

__ The Death Star with two additional pilots, exclusive to BJ's Warehouse [MNP005] 95.00

Episode I: The Phantom Menace.
__ Naboo Hangar, Final Combat [MNP006]........18.00

MMR001

MMR002

MMR003

MMR004

MMR005

MMR006

MMR007

MMR008

MMR009

MMR010

MMR011

MMR012

MMA001

MMA002

MMA003

MMA004

MMA005

MMA006

MMA007

MMA008

MMA009

MMA010

MMA011

MMA012

MMA013

MMA014

MMA015

Action Fleet Series Alpha

Galoob
__ B-Wing Fighter [MMR001] 10.00
__ Imperial AT-AT 17.00
__ Imperial AT-AT, includes Topps trading card [MMR002] 25.00
__ Imperial Shuttle [MMR003] 17.00
__ Imperial Shuttle, includes Topps trading card [MMR004] 25.00
__ Snowspeeder [MMR005] 17.00
__ Snowspeeder, includes Topps trading card... 25.00
__ Twin-Pod Cloud Car [MMR006] 20.00
__ X-Wing Starfighter [MMR007] 17.00
__ X-Wing Starfighter, incl. Topps trading card .. 25.00
__ X-Wing Starfighter, includes Topps trading card, white parts 38.00
__ Y-Wing Fighter [MMR008] 20.00

Hasbro
__ Naboo Fighter [MMR009] 125.00
__ Royal Starship [MMR010] 100.00
__ Sith Infiltrator [MMR011] 135.00
__ Trade Federation Droid Fighter [MMR012] 80.00

Action Fleet Vehicles

Galoob
Episode I: The Phantom Menace.
__ Anakin's Pod Racer [MMA001] 10.00
__ Fambaa with remote control [MMA002] 15.00
__ Flash Speeder [MMA003] 20.00
__ Gungan Sub [MMA004] 30.00
__ Mars Guo's Pod Racer [MMA005] 25.00
__ Naboo Fighter [MMA006] 15.00
__ Republic Cruiser [MMA007] 12.00
__ Sebulba's Pod Racer [MMA008] 10.00
__ Trade Federation Droid Fighter [MMA009] 10.00
__ Trade Federation Landing Ship [MMA010] 30.00
__ Trade Federation MTT [MMA011] 10.00
__ Trade Federation Tank with remote control [MMA012] 25.00

Release 1: Silver logo, limited edition sticker.
__ 2-Pack: Luke's Landspeeder / AT-ST, exclusive to KB Toys 35.00
__ A-Wing Starfighter with C-3PO and Rebel Pilot 30.00
__ Darth Vader's TIE Fighter with Darth Vader and Imperial Pilot 29.00
__ Imperial AT-AT with Imperial Driver and Stormtrooper (Note: actually includes Driver and Snowtrooper.) 29.00
__ Imperial Shuttle Tydirium with Han Solo and Chewbacca 30.00
__ Luke's X-Wing Starfighter with Luke Skywalker and R2-D2 .... 25.00
__ Rebel Snowspeeder with Luke Skywalker and Rebel Gunner 27.00

Release 2: Silver logo.
__ 2-Pack: Luke's Landspeeder / AT-ST, exclusive to KB Toys [MMA013] 25.00
__ A-Wing Starfighter with C-3PO and Rebel Pilot 20.00
__ Darth Vader's TIE Fighter with Darth Vader and Imperial Pilot (battle damage, large) 19.00
__ Darth Vader's TIE Fighter with Darth Vader and Imperial Pilot (no battle damage, small).......... 25.00
__ Imperial AT-AT with Imperial Driver and Snowtrooper 24.00
__ Imperial Shuttle Tydirium with Han Solo and Chewbacca 26.00
__ Luke's X-Wing Starfighter with Luke Skywalker and R2-D2 .... 19.00
__ Rebel Snowspeeder with Luke Skywalker and Rebel Gunner 25.00

Release 3: Silver logo, box marked 'Display Stand Included'.
__ A-Wing Starfighter with C-3PO and Rebel Pilot (battle damage, old hinge) 20.00
__ A-Wing Starfighter with C-3PO and Rebel Pilot (battle damage) 18.00
__ A-Wing Starfighter with C-3PO and Rebel Pilot (no battle damage) [MMA014] 24.00
__ Darth Vader's TIE Fighter with Darth Vader and Imperial Pilot (battle damage, small).............. 24.00
__ Darth Vader's TIE Fighter with Darth Vader and Imperial Pilot (no battle damage, large) [MMA015] 19.00
__ Darth Vader's TIE Fighter with Darth Vader and Imperial Pilot (no battle damage, small).......... 17.00
__ Imperial AT-AT with Imperial Driver and Snowtrooper (battle damage) 19.00
__ Imperial AT-AT with Imperial Driver and Snowtrooper (no battle damage) [MMA016] 22.00
__ Imperial Shuttle Tydirium with Han Solo and Chewbacca (battle damage, old hinge) 20.00
__ Imperial Shuttle Tydirium with Han Solo and Chewbacca (battle damage).......................... 24.00
__ Imperial Shuttle Tydirium with Han Solo and Chewbacca (no battle damage) [MMA017] 26.00
__ Jawa Sandcrawler with Jawa and Scavenger Droid [MMA018] 45.00
__ Luke's X-Wing Starfighter with Luke Skywalker and R2-D2 (battle damage).................................. 15.00
__ Luke's X-Wing Starfighter with Luke Skywalker and R2-D2 (no battle damage) 24.00
__ Rebel Snowspeeder with Luke Skywalker and Rebel Gunner (battle damage)....................... 16.00
__ Rebel Snowspeeder with Luke Skywalker and Rebel Gunner (no battle damage) [MMA019] 22.00
__ Slave I with Boba Fett and Han Solo [MMA020] 17.00
__ Tie Interceptor with 2 Imperial Pilots 26.00
__ Tie Interceptor with 2 Imperial Pilots (dark blue) [MMA021] 18.00
__ Y-Wing Starfighter with Gold Leader and R2 Unit 14.00
__ Y-Wing Starfighter with Rebel Pilot and R2 Unit 17.00

Release 4: Gold logo. No window.
__ AT-AT, remote control 2-button, exclusive to KB Toys [MMA022].. 15.00

Release 4: Gold logo.
__ A-Wing Starfighter with C-3PO and Rebel Pilot (battle damage) [MMA023] 18.00
__ A-Wing with Mon Mothma and Pilot, green [MMA024] 18.00
__ A-Wing with Mon Mothma and Pilot, green missing emblem 25.00
__ AT-AT, remote control 2-button, full window box, exclusive to KB Toys [MMA025] 15.00
__ B-Wing Starfighter with Rebel Pilot and Admiral Ackbar [MMA026] 15.00
__ Bespin Cloud Car with Cloud Car Pilot and Lobot [MMA027] 12.00
__ Darth Vader's TIE Fighter with Darth Vader and Imperial Pilot (battle damage, small) [MMA028] 17.00
__ E-Wing Starfighter with Rebel Pilot and R7 Droid [MMA029] 150.00
__ Imperial AT-AT with Imperial Driver and Snowtrooper (battle damage) [MMA030] 17.00
__ Imperial Landing Craft with Sandtrooper and Imperial Officer [MMA031] 50.00
__ Imperial Shuttle Tydirium with Han Solo and Chewbacca [MMA032] 18.00
__ Incom T-16 Skyhopper with Biggs Darklighter and Luke Skywalker [MMA033] 25.00
__ Jabba's Sail Barge with Saelt-Marae (Yak Face) and R2-D2 [MMA034] 60.00
__ Jawa Sandcrawler with Jawa and Scavenger Droid [MMA035] 30.00
__ Luke's X-Wing Starfighter with Luke Skywalker and R2-D2 [MMA036] 12.00
__ Millennium Falcon with Han Solo and Chewbacca [MMA037] 45.00
__ Rancor with Gamorrean Guard and Luke Skywalker [MMA038] 30.00
__ Rebel Blockade Runner with Princess Leia and Rebel Trooper [MMA039]................................ 30.00
__ Rebel Snowspeeder (Rogue Two colors) with Rebel Pilots and Rebel Gunner (battle damage) [MMA040] 18.00
__ Rebel Snowspeeder with Luke Skywalker and Rebel Gunner (battle damage) [MMA041] 12.00
__ Slave I with Boba Fett and Han Solo [MMA042] 15.00
__ Tie Bomber with Imperial Pilot and Imperial Naval Trooper [MMA043] 15.00
__ Tie Defender with Imperial TIE Pilot and Moff Jerjerrod [MMA044] 150.00
__ TIE Fighter with Imperial Pilot and Grand Moff Tarkin [MMA045]... 15.00
__ Tie Interceptor with 2 Imperial Pilots [MMA046] 18.00
__ Virago with Prince Xizor and Guri [MMA047].. 48.00
__ X-Wing with Jek Porkins and R2-Unit [MMA048] 18.00
__ X-Wing with Wedge Antillies and R2 Unit [MMA049] 18.00
__ Y-Wing Starfighter with Blue Leader and R2 Unit [MMA050] 15.00
__ Y-Wing Starfighter with Gold Leader and R2 Unit [MMA051] 12.00
__ Y-Wing Starfighter with Rebel Pilot and R2 Unit [MMA052] 15.00

Special boxed exclusives.
__ AT-AT, remote control 3-button, exclusive to JC Penney [MMA053] 95.00
__ Darth Vader's TIE Fighter, exclusive to Avon [MMA054] 14.00
__ Luke's X-Wing Starfighter, exclusive to Avon [MMA055] 14.00
__ X-Wing from Dagobah Swamp, exclusive to Toy Fair [MMA056] 20.00

Galoob, Canada
Episode I: The Phantom Menace.
__ Republic Cruiser 12.00
__ Sebulba's Pod Racer 16.00
__ Trade Federation MTT 12.00

Gold logo, Main Event Toys, bi-language package.
__ Imperial Landing Craft with Sandtrooper and Imperial Officer 55.00
__ Millennium Falcon with Han Solo and Chewbacca 70.00
__ Rebel Snowspeeder with Rebel Pilots and Rebel Gunner 55.00

Galoob, UK
Episode I: The Phantom Menace.
__ Naboo Fighter 18.00
__ Republic Cruiser 12.00
__ Sebulba's Pod Racer 16.00
__ Trade Federation MTT 12.00

Galoob / Gigi, Italy
__ Rancor 35.00
__ Sandcrawler 35.00
__ Slave I [MMA057] 35.00

Hasbro
Episode I: The Phantom Menace.
__ Royal Starship [MMA058] 95.00
__ Sith Infiltrator [MMA059] 95.00
__ Trade Federation Droid Control Ship [MMA060] 95.00
__ Trade Federation Tank [MMA061] 75.00

Star Wars Saga, classic trilogy.
__ AT-AT [MMA062] 30.00
__ Luke Skywalker's Snowspeeder [MMA063] ... 30.00
__ Millennium Falcon [MMA064] 20.00
__ TIE Advanced x1 [MMA065] 15.00
__ X-Wing Fighter [MMA066] 15.00

Star Wars Saga, prequel trilogy.
__ AT-TE [MMA067] 20.00
__ Jango Fett's Slave I [MMA068] 20.00
__ Naboo N-1 Fighter [MMA069] 15.00
__ Republic Assault Ship [MMA070] 40.00
__ Republic Gunship [MMA071] 40.00
__ Solar Sailor [MMA072] 20.00

Titanium Ultra series.
__ Anakin's Jedi Starfighter [MMA073] 25.00
__ ARC-170 [MMA074] 25.00
__ AT-AT [MMA075] 25.00

MMA016

MMA017

MMA018

MMA019

MMA020

MMA021

MMA022

MMA023

MMA024

MMA025

MMA026

MMA027

MMA028

MMA029

MMA030

MMA031

MMA032

MMA033

MMA034

MMA035

MMA036

MMA037

MMA038

MMA039

MMA040

MMA041

MMA042

MMA043

MMA044

MMA045

MMA046

MMA047

MMA048

MMA049

MMA050

MMA051

MMA052

195

Action Fleet Vehicles

MADE IN CHINA

MMA053

MMA054

MMA055

MMA056

MMA057

MMA058

SITH INFILTRATOR
Featuring Darth Maul

MMA059

TRADE FEDERATION
DROID CONTROL SHIP
Featuring Neimoidian Commander

MMA060

MMA061

MMA062

MMA063

MMA064

MMA065

MMA066

MMA067

MMA068

MMA069

MMA070

MMA071

MMA072

MMA073

MMA074

MMA075

MMA076

MMA077

MMA078

MMA079

MMA080

MMA081

MMA082

MMA083

MMA084

MMA085

MMA086

Action Fleet Vehicles

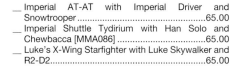

__ Darth Vader's TIE Advanced X1 [MMA076]....25.00
__ Droid Tri-Fighter [MMA077].........................25.00
__ Millennium Falcon [MMA078]........................25.00
__ Republic gunship [MMA079]..........................25.00
__ Republic gunship (Clone Wars) [MMA080].....25.00
__ Slave I, Boba Fett [MMA081]........................20.00
__ Snowspeeder [MMA082] 20.00
__ TIE Fighter [MMA083]..................................25.00
__ X-Wing fighter [MMA084] 25.00
__ X-Wing Starfighter [MMA085].......................25.00

Ideal, UK
Silver logo.

__ A-Wing Starfighter with C-3PO and Rebel Pilot...65.00
__ Darth Vader's TIE Fighter with Darth Vader and Imperial Pilot..65.00

__ Imperial AT-AT with Imperial Driver and Snowtrooper...65.00
__ Imperial Shuttle Tydirium with Han Solo and Chewbacca 65.00
__ Luke's X-Wing Starfighter with Luke Skywalker and R2-D2..65.00

Action Masters

Kenner

__ C-3PO [MMD001] 9.00
__ C-3PO, Gold, mail-in exclusive 22.00
__ Darth Vader [MMD002] 12.00
__ Luke Skywalker [MMD003]............................8.00
__ R2-D2 [MMD004].......................................10.00
__ Stormtrooper [MMD005].............................10.00

4-packs.

__ C-3PO, Princess Leia, R2-D2, Obi-Wan Kenobi [MMD006] 30.00
__ C-3PO, Princess Leia, R2-D2, Obi-Wan Kenobi; POTF style pkg. [MMD007].........................33.00

6-Packs.

__ Boba Fett, Han, Chewbacca, Darth Vader, Luke, Stormtrooper [MMD008]................................36.00
__ Boba Fett, Han, Chewbacca, Darth Vader, Luke, Stormtrooper; POTF style pkg. [MMD009].....45.00

Kenner, UK

__ 4-pack: C-3PO, Princess Leia, R2-D2, Obi-Wan Kenobi [MMD010]..33.00
__ 6-pack: Boba Fett, Han, Chewbacca, Darth Vader, Luke, Stormtrooper [MMD011]......................45.00

MMD001　　　MMD002　　　MMD003　　　MMD004　　　MMD005

MMD006　　　　　　MMD007　　　　　　MMD008

MMD009　　　　　MMD010　　　　　MMD011

AVQ001　　　MMD012　　　MMD013　　　　　BTY001

SBB001   SBB002   SBB003 side 1 and side 2

SBB004   SBB005   SBB006   SBB007   SBB008

SBB009   SBB010   SBB011   BHB001   BHB002

BHB003   BHB004 side 1 and side 2

Packaged individually.
__ Darth Vader [MMD012] 7.00
__ R2-D2 [MMD013] 7.00

Action Value Pack

Spectra Star
__ Star Wars kite, frisbee, and yo-yo [AVQ001] 17.00

Balancing Toys

Galoob
__ Balance of Power, exclusive to Fan Club [BTY001] 19.00

Balls

Disney / MGM
__ Soccer ball, mini Star Wars with characters [SBB001] 10.00

Kellytoy
__ Football, characters [SBB002] 6.00

Mondo, Italy
Episode I, 8" inflated.
__ Anakin / Podracing [SBB003] 8.00
__ Darth Maul / Tatooine Duel 8.00

Party Express
__ Darth Vader [SBB004] 4.00
__ Yoda and Darth Vader [SBB005] 5.00

Rand International
Mini basketball hoop sets.
__ Clone Trooper, exclusive to Dollar Tree [SBB006] 5.00
__ Darth Vader, exclusive to Dollar Tree [SBB007] 5.00

Tapper Candies
__ Super Bounce balls, 4-pack [SBB008] 4.00

The Promotions Factory, Australia
Mega bounce balls. Classic trilogy.
__ C-3PO [SBB009] 5.00
__ Darth Vader 5.00
__ Luke Skywalker [SBB010] 5.00
__ Stormtrooper [SBB011] 5.00
Mega bounce balls. EPIII: ROTS.
__ Anakin 5.00
__ Clone Trooper 5.00
__ Darth Vader 5.00
__ Yoda 5.00

Balls, Beach

__ 20th anniversary with net 45.00
__ Star Wars: EPIII, 16" [BHB001] 8.00
__ Star Wars: EPIII, 20" [BHB002] 10.00

Star Wars Celebration V
__ Star Wars Celebration V [BHB003] 16.00

Target
__ Darth Vader, gold and black [BHB004] 15.00

Balls, Hopper

HPB001

HPB002

HPB003

PGB001

BSB001

BSB002

BSB003 image 1

BSB003 image 2

BSB003 image3

BIN001

BSB004 image 1

BSB004 image 2

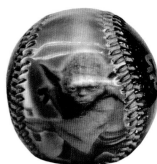
BSB004 image 3

Balls, Hopper

__ Yoda, Clone Wars [HPB001]..........................18.00

Hedstrom
__ Clone Wars [HPB002].....................................10.00

Kellytoy
__ Darth Vader [HPB003] 10.00
__ Yoda 10.00

Balls, Punching

__ Clone Wars [PGB001].......................................5.00

Baseball Equipment

__ Clone Wars soft bat and ball set [BSB001]...35.00
__ Yoda mitt and ball [BSB002] 25.00

Disney / MGM
__ Star Tours, silver and black [BSB003]............19.00
__ Yoda and Darth Vader with logo [BSB004] 16.00

Binoculars

Tiger Electronics
__ Darth Maul binoculars with listening device [BIN001]...38.00

Bobble Heads

__ Darth Vader [BBH001] 25.00
__ Yoda [BBH002]..25.00

Episode III: Revenge of the Sith. Mini.
__ Darth Vader [BBH003] 15.00
__ Yoda [BBH004] 15.00

Cards, Inc., UK
Episode III: Revenge of the Sith.
__ C-3PO [4:29]...25.00
__ Clone Trooper [4:29] 25.00
__ Darth Vader [4:29]..25.00
__ General Grievous [4:29] 25.00
__ R2-D2 [4:29]..25.00
__ Yoda [4:29]...25.00

Disney Theme Park Merchandise
__ Yoda, Must Be At Least This Tall... [BBH005]..35.00

Mini bobble heads.
__ Donald Trooper [BBH006] 15.00
__ Goofy Vader [BBH007] 15.00
__ Mickey Jedi (brown robe) [BBH008]...............15.00
__ Mickey Pilot [BBH009].....................................15.00
__ Minnie Princess [BBH010] 15.00

__ 5-pack: Mickey Jedi (white robe), Mickey pilot, Goofy Vader, Minnie princess, Donald trooper silver bases with words, limited to 500 [BBH011]..125.00

Funko
7" Bobble ships.
__ Darth Vader's TIE fighter [BBH012] 25.00
__ Luke Skywalker's X-Wing fighter [BBH013]....25.00

Sitters, talking.
__ Boba Fett [BBH014]..12.00
__ Darth Vader [BBH015].....................................12.00
__ Yoda [BBH016]..12.00

Vinyl Pop!
__ Chewbacca [BBH017] 20.00
__ Darth Vader [BBH018] 20.00
__ Greedo..55.00
__ Han Solo [BBH019]...20.00
__ Princess Leia [BBH020] 20.00
__ Stormtrooper [BBH021] 20.00
__ Yoda [BBH022] 20.00

Wacky Wobblers, ultra-stylized.
__ Boba Fett [BBH023]...20.00
__ Chewbacca [BBH024] 20.00
__ Clone Trooper, 501st, exclusive to San Diego Comic-Con [BBH025] 55.00
__ Darth Vader [BBH026] 20.00
__ Stormtrooper [BBH027] 20.00
__ Yoda [BBH028] 20.00

Wacky Wobblers.
__ 4-LOM [BBH029] 14.00
__ Ahsoka [BBH030]..14.00
__ Anakin Skywalker [BBH031] 14.00
__ Anakin Skywalker chrome base variant..........25.00
__ Battle Droid [BBH032] 14.00

BBH001

BBH002

BBH003

BBH004

BBH005

BBH006

BBH007

BBH008

BBH009

BBH010

BBH011

BBH012

BBH013

BBH014

BBH015

BBH016

BBH017

BBH018

BBH019

BBH020

BBH021

BBH022

BBH023

BBH024

BBH025

BBH026

BBH027

BBH028

Bobble Heads

4-LOM BOBBLE-HEAD	AHSOKA TANO BOBBLE-HEAD	ANAKIN SKYWALKER BOBBLE-HEAD	BATTLE DROID BOBBLE-HEAD	BOBA FETT BOBBLE-HEAD	BOBA FETT BOBBLE-HEAD	BOSSK BOBBLE-HEAD	C-3PO BOBBLE-HEAD	CAPTAIN REX BOBBLE-HEAD
BBH029	BBH030	BBH031	BBH032	BBH033	BBH034	BBH035	BBH036	BBH037
CHEWBACCA BOBBLE-HEAD	CLONE TROOPER BOBBLE-HEAD	CLONE TROOPER DENAL BOBBLE-HEAD	CLONE TROOPER DENAL BOBBLE-HEAD	UTAPAU CLONE TROOPER BOBBLE-HEAD	COMMANDER GREE BOBBLE-HEAD	DARTH MAUL BOBBLE-HEAD	DARTH VADER BOBBLE-HEAD	DARTH VADER HOLOGRAM BOBBLE-HEAD
BBH038	BBH039	BBH040	BBH041	BBH042	BBH043	BBH044	BBH045	BBH046
EMPEROR PALPATINE BOBBLE-HEAD	GAMORREAN GUARD BOBBLE-HEAD	GENERAL GRIEVOUS BOBBLE-HEAD	GREEDO BOBBLE-HEAD	HAN SOLO BOBBLE-HEAD	HAN SOLO BOBBLE-HEAD	JANGO FETT BOBBLE-HEAD	JAWA BOBBLE-HEAD	K-3PO BOBBLE-HEAD
BBH047	BBH048	BBH049	BBH050	BBH051	BBH052	BBH053	BBH054	BBH055
LUKE SKYWALKER BOBBLE-HEAD	LUKE SKYWALKER X-WING PILOT LIMITED EDITION	LUKE SKYWALKER BOBBLE-HEAD	LUKE SKYWALKER BOBBLE-HEAD	OBI-WAN KENOBI BOBBLE-HEAD	OBI-WAN KENOBI BOBBLE-HEAD	PRINCESS LEIA BOBBLE-HEAD	PRINCESS LEIA BOBBLE-HEAD
BBH056	BBH057	BBH058	BBH059	BBH060	BBH061	BBH062	BBH063
R2-D2 BOBBLE-HEAD	R2-R9 BOBBLE-HEAD	R2-X2 BOBBLE-HEAD	SHOCK TROOPER BOBBLE-HEAD	STORMTROOPER BOBBLE-HEAD	SHADOW STORMTROOPER BOBBLE-HEAD	TC-14 BOBBLE-HEAD	TUSKEN RAIDER BOBBLE-HEAD	YODA BOBBLE-HEAD
BBH064	BBH065	BBH066	BBH067	BBH068	BBH069	BBH070	BBH071	BBH072

| BBH073 | BBH074 | BBH075 | BBH076 | BBH077 | BBH078 | BBH079 |

| BBH080 | BBH081 | BBH082 | BBH083 | BBH084 | BBH085 | BBH086 |

__ Boba Fett [BBH033]...14.00
__ Boba Fett, holiday special, exclusive to Entertainment Earth [BBH034]......................60.00
__ Bossk [BBH035]...14.00
__ C-3PO [BBH036] 14.00
__ Captain Rex [BBH037]....................................14.00
__ Chewbacca [BBH038]....................................14.00
__ Clone Trooper [BBH039] 14.00
__ Clone Trooper chrome base variant 25.00
__ Clone Trooper Denal, exclusive to Walmart [BBH040]...14.00
__ Clone Trooper Denal chrome base variant, exclusive to Walmart [BBH041]......................................25.00
__ Clone Trooper, Utapau, exclusive to Action Figure Xpress [BBH042] 35.00
__ Commander Gree [BBH043]...........................14.00
__ Darth Maul [BBH044].....................................14.00
__ Darth Vader [BBH045] 14.00
__ Darth Vader chrome base variant 25.00
__ Darth Vader, holographic, limited to 2,500, exclusive to San Diego Comic-Con [BBH046] 35.00
__ Emperor Palpatine [BBH047].........................14.00
__ Gamorrean Guard [BBH048] 14.00
__ General Grievous [BBH049]...........................14.00
__ General Grievous chrome base variant 25.00
__ Greedo [BBH050]...14.00
__ Greedo chrome base variant 25.00
__ Han Solo [BBH051]...14.00
__ Han Solo, Stormtrooper Disguise [BBH052]...14.00
__ Jango Fett [BBH053]......................................14.00
__ Jawa [BBH054]...14.00
__ Jawa chrome base variant 25.00
__ K-3PO, limited to 1,500 [BBH055].................18.00
__ Luke Skywalker [BBH056] 14.00

__ Luke Skywalker as X-Wing pilot Limited Edition sticker [BBH057]...14.00
__ Luke Skywalker as X-Wing pilot Toys R Us sticker [BBH058]...14.00
__ Luke Skywalker in Stormtrooper Disguise, limited to 1,500, exclusive to San Diego Comic-Con [BBH059]...14.00
__ Obi-Wan Kenobi [BBH060]............................14.00
__ Obi-Wan Kenobi, Clone Wars [BBH061] 14.00
__ Princess Leia [BBH062] 14.00
__ Princess Leia as Jabba's prisoner [BBH063] .14.00
__ R2-Q2, exclusive to Entertainment Earth [BBH064]...20.00
__ R2-R9, exclusive to Entertainment Earth [BBH065]...20.00
__ R2-X2, exclusive to Entertainment Earth [BBH066]...20.00
__ Shock Trooper, limited to 1,003, exclusive to San Diego Comic-Con [BBH067]..........................55.00
__ Stormtrooper [BBH068] 14.00
__ Stormtrooper, shadow, limited to 1,500, exclusive to Action Figure Xpress [BBH069].................14.00
__ Stormtrooper, shadow chrome base variant, exclusive to Action Figure Xpress..................25.00
__ TC-14, limited to 480, exclusive to Comicon [BBH070]..45.00
__ Tusken Raider [BBH071] 14.00
__ Tusken Raider chrome base variant 25.00
__ Yoda [BBH072]...14.00
__ Yoda chrome base variant..............................25.00

Wacky Wobblers. Christmas editions. 2008.
__ Jawa [BBH073]...15.00
__ Yoda [BBH074]...15.00

Wacky Wobblers. Christmas editions. 2009.
__ C-3PO [BBH075] 15.00
__ Darth Vader [BBH076] 15.00
__ Yoda [BBH077] 15.00

Wacky Wobblers. Family Guy - Blue Harvest.
__ Chewbrian [BBH078] 16.00
__ Darth Stewie 20.00
__ Darth Stewie, full mask 20.00
__ Quag-3PO [BBH079] 16.00

Wacky Wobblers. Halloween editions. 2010.
__ Chewbacca as werewolf [BBH080] 8.00
__ Darth Vader as Dr. Frankenstein's monster [BBH081]...8.00
__ Stormtrooper as skeleton [BBH082]................8.00
__ Yoda as vampire [BBH083] 8.00

Wizards of the Coast
Collection 1, limited edition of 4,000.
__ Boba Fett [BBH084]......................................28.00
__ C-3PO with R2-D2 [BBH085] 28.00
__ Darth Vader [BBH086] 28.00

Bop Bags

UK. Inflatable bop bags.
__ Darth Vader / Yoda [YB001] 20.00

Baleno, Hong Kong
Episode III.
__ Darth Vader..35.00
__ Yoda 35.00

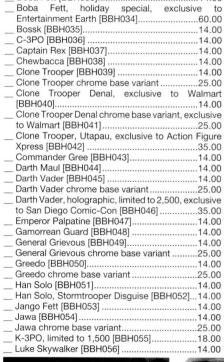

| YB001 | YB002 | YB003 | YB004 | YB005 |

Bop Bags

YB006　　　　　　YB007　　　　　　YB008　　　　　　YB009

Character Games, Ltd.
__ Darth Vader with sound FX [YB002] 35.00

Clipper, Netherlands
__ Darth Vader...230.00

Hedstrom
__ Clone Wars [YB003].......................................15.00

Intex Recreation Corp.
__ Darth Maul [YB004].......................................12.00

Kenner
__ Chewbacca [YB005] 185.00
__ Darth Vader [YB006] 125.00
__ Jawa [YB007]..225.00
__ R2-D2 [YB008]..125.00

Building Brick Toys and Figures

Cube Dudes. Numbered. Convention exclusives..
__ 5-pack: R2-D2, C-3PO, Yoda, Capt. Rex, Obi-Wan
Kenobi, Star Wars Celebration V [LO001] 135.00
__ 5-pack: Zuckuss, Dengar, Boba Fett, IG-88, Bossk,
San Diego Comic Con [LO002].....................85.00

__ Obi-Wan Kenobi, numbered, Star Wars
Celebration V [LO003]....................................35.00

Lego / Pepsi / Lays / Target
Guess and Win promotion displays.
__ R2-D2, exclusive to Target 75.00
__ Yoda, exclusive to Target [LO004] 75.00

Lego / Walmart
__ Clone Building Event clone trooper box 93 with
helmets, 52 without helmets [LO005] 330.00

The LEGO Group
__ 3 in 1 Super Pack 66341 Republic Swamp Speeder,
Clone Walker battle pack, and Assassin Droids
battle pack [LO006] 100.00
__ A-wing fighter 6207 [LO007]...........................45.00
__ A-Wing Fighter 7134 [LO008].........................44.00
__ Ahsoka's Starfighter and Vulture Droid 7751
[LO009] 40.00
__ Anakin's and Sebulba's Podracers 7962
[LO010] 80.00
__ Anakin's Jedi Starfighter 7669 [LO011] 20.00
__ Anakin's Podracer 7131 [LO012]....................35.00
__ Anakin's Y-Wing Starfighter 8037 [LO013].......60.00
__ ARC-170 Fighter 7259 [LO014].......................40.00
__ ARC-170 Starfighter 8088 [LO015].................60.00
__ Armored Assault Tank 8018 [LO016]...............50.00
__ Assassin Droids Battle pack 8015 [LO017] 14.00
__ AT-AP Walker 7671 [LO018]...........................40.00
__ AT-AT 4483 [LO019] 135.00
__ AT-AT Walker 8129 [LO020] 115.00
__ AT-ST 7657 [LO021] 20.00
__ AT-TE 4482 [LO022] 70.00
__ AT-TE Walker 7675 [LO023]...........................90.00
__ B-Wing at Rebel Control Center 7180
[LO024] 55.00
__ B-Wing fighter 6208 [LO025]..........................45.00
__ Battle Droid Carrier 7126 [LO026]..................24.00
__ Battle For Geonosis 7869 [LO027] 40.00
__ Battle of Endor 8038 [LO028] 100.00
__ Battle of Naboo 7929 [LO029] 25.00

__ Boba Fett's Slave I 6209 [LO030] 45.00
__ Bounty Hunter Assault Gunship 7930
[LO031]...50.00
__ Bounty Hunter Pursuit 7133 [LO032]...............30.00
__ Cad bane's Speeder 8128 [LO033] 50.00
__ Clone Scout Walker 7250 [LO034] 10.00
__ Clone Trooper Battle Pack 7913 [LO035].......12.00
__ Clone Troopers Battle Pack 7655 [LO036].....10.00
__ Clone Turbo Tank 7261 [LO037]......................90.00
__ Clone Turbo Tank 8098 [LO038]....................120.00
__ Clone Walker Battle Pack 8014 [LO039] 14.00
__ Corporate Alliance Tank Droid 7748 [LO040].25.00
__ Count Dooku's Solar Sailer 7752 [LO041]......55.00
__ Darth Maul's Sith Infiltrator 7961 [LO042] 50.00
__ Darth Vader Transformation 7251 [LO043].......7.00
__ Darth Vader's TIE Fighter 8017 [LO044] 35.00
__ Desert Skiff 7104 [LO045]...............................12.00
__ Droid Escape 7106 [LO046]............................14.00
__ Droid Fighter 7111 [LO047] 14.00
__ Droid Gunship 7678 [LO048] 35.00
__ Droid Tri-Fighter 7252 [LO049].......................15.00
__ Droid Tri-Fighter 8086 [LO050] 12.00
__ Droids Battle Pack 7654 [LO051] 10.00
__ Echo Base 7749 [LO052]................................25.00
__ Emperor Palpatine's Shuttle 8096 [LO053] 60.00
__ Episode III Collector's Set 65771 [LO054]......75.00
__ Ewok Attack 7139 [LO055]..............................16.00
__ Ewok Attack 7956 [LO056] 25.00
__ Final Duel I 7200 [LO057]...............................10.00
__ Final Duel II 7201 [LO058]...............................25.00
__ Flash Speeder 7124 [LO059] 18.00
__ Freeco Speeder 8085 [LO060]........................12.00
__ General Grievous Chase 7255 [LO061] 20.00
__ General Grievous Starfighter 7656 [LO062]....40.00
__ General Grievous' Starfighter 8095 [LO063]...50.00
__ Geonosian Fighter 4478 [LO064].....................20.00
__ Geonosian Starfighter 7959 [LO065]...............25.00
__ Gungan Patrol 7115 [LO066] 15.00
__ Gungan Sub 7161 [LO067] 45.00
__ Hailfire Droid 4481 [LO068] 50.00
__ Hailfire Droid and Spider Droid 7670
[LO069] 20.00
__ Home One Mon Calamari Star Cruiser 7754
[LO070] 120.00
__ Hoth Echo Base 7879 ....40.00
__ Hoth Rebel Base 7666 [LO071] 65.00
__ Hoth Wampa Cave 8089 [LO072]...................40.00
__ Hyena Droid Bomber 8016 [LO073] 25.00
__ Imperial AT-ST 7127 [LO074]..........................16.00
__ Imperial Dropship 7667 [LO075].....................10.00
__ Imperial Inspection 7264 OTC packaging
[LO076] 50.00
__ Imperial Landing Craft 7659 [LO077]..............50.00
__ Imperial Shuttle 7166 [LO078] 42.00
__ Imperial Star Destroyer 6211 [LO079] 100.00
__ Imperial Star Destroyer 8099 [LO080] 40.00
__ Imperial V-wing Starfighter 7915 [LO081].......20.00
__ Jabba's Message 4475 [LO082].......................20.00
__ Jabba's Palace 4480 [LO083].........................30.00
__ Jabba's Prize 4476 [LO084]............................20.00
__ Jabba's Sail Barge 6210 [LO085] 75.00
__ Jango Fett's Slave I 7153 [LO086]...................50.00
__ Jango Fett's Slave I with bonus cargo case 65153 /
7153 [LO087] 50.00
__ Jedi Defense 7203 [LO088] 10.00
__ Jedi Defense II 7204 [LO089]..........................10.00
__ Jedi Duel 7103 [LO090] 10.00
__ Jedi Starfighter 7143 [LO091].........................18.00

LO001

LO002

LO003

LO004

LO005

LO006

LO007

LO008

LO009

LO010

LO011

LO012

LO013

LO014

LO015

LO016

LO017

LO018

LO019

Building Brick Toys and Figures

LO020

LO021

LO022

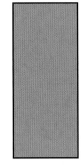

LO023

LO024

LO025

LO026

LO027

LO028

LO029

LO030

LO031

LO032

LO033

LO034

LO035

LO036

LO037

LO038

LO039

LO040

LO041

LO042

LO043

LO044

LO045

LO046

LO047

207

LO048

LO049

LO050

LO051

LO052

LO053

LO054

LO055

LO056

LO057

LO058

LO059

LO060

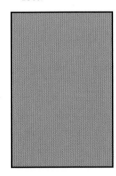

LO061

LO062

LO063

LO064

LO065

LO066

LO067

LO068

LO069

LO070

LO071

LO072

LO073

LO074

LO075

LO076

LO077

Building Brick Toys and Figures

LO078

LO079

LO080

LO081

LO082

LO083

LO084

LO085

LO086

LO087

LO088

LO089

LO090

LO091

LO092

LO093

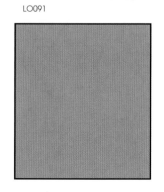

LO094

LO095

LO096

LO097

LO098

LO099

LO100

LO101

LO102

LO103

LO104

LO105

LO106

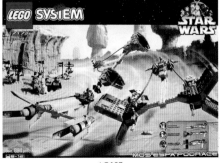

LO107

LO108

LO109

LO110

LO111

LO112

LO113 side 1 and side 2

LO114

LO115

LO116

LO117

LO118

LO119

LO120

LO121

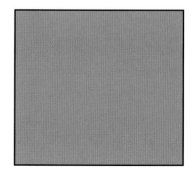

LO122

LO123

LO124

LO125

LO126

LO127

LO128

LO129

LO130

LO131

LO132

LO133

LO134

LO135

LO136

LO137

LO138

LO139

LO140

LO141

LO142

LO143

LO144

LO145

LO146

LO147

LO148

LO149

LO150

LO151

LO152

LO153

LO154

LO155

LO156

LO157

LO158

LO159

LO160

LO161

LO162

LO163

LO164

LO165

LO166

LO167

LO168

Building Brick Toys and Figures

LO169

LO170

LO171

LO172

LO173

LO174

LO175

LO176

LO177

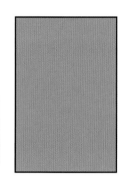

LO178

LO179

LO180

LO181

LO182

LO183

LO184

LO185

LO186

216

LO187

LO188

LO189

LO190

LO191

LO192

LO193

LO194

LO195

LO196

LO197

LO198

LO199

LO200

LO201

LO202

LO203

LO204

LO205

LO206

LO207

LO208

LO209

LO210

LO211

LO212

LO213

LO214

LO215

LO216

LO217

LO218

LO219

LO220

LO221

LO222

LO223

LO224

LO225

LO226

LO227

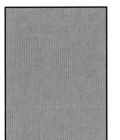

LO228

LO229

LO230

LO231

LO232

LO233

LO234

LO235

LO236

LO237

LO238

LO239

__ Jedi Starfighter and Vulture Droid 7256 [LO092] 20.00
__ Jedi Starfighter with Hyperdrive Booster Ring 7661 [LO093] 50.00
__ Landspeeder 7110 [LO094] 12.00
__ Lightsaber Duel 7101 [LO095] 17.00
__ Luke's Landspeeder 8092 [LO096] 25.00
__ Mace Windu's Jedi Starfighter 7868 [LO097] 40.00
__ Magna Guard Starfighter 7673 [LO098] 50.00
__ Mandalorian Battle Pack 7914 [LO099] 12.00
__ Millennium Falcon 4504 [LO100] 50.00
__ Millennium Falcon 4504 OTC packaging [LO101] 50.00
__ Millennium Falcon 7190 [LO102] 125.00
__ Millennium Falcon 7778 [LO103] 40.00
__ Millennium Falcon 7965 [LO104] 140.00
__ Mos Eisley Cantina 4501 [LO105] 30.00
__ Mos Eisley Cantina 4501 OTC packaging [LO106] 30.00
__ MosEspa Podrace 7171 [LO107] 85.00
__ Naboo Fighter 7141 [LO108] 30.00
__ Naboo Fighter 7877 ....40.00
__ Naboo Starfighter with Vulture Droid 7660 [LO109] 30.00
__ Naboo Swamp 7121 [LO110] 15.00
__ Pirate Tank 7753 [LO111] 40.00
__ Plo Koon's Jedi Starfighter 8093 [LO112] 25.00
__ Pod Race Brick 7159 [LO113] 24.00
__ Rebel Scout Speeder 7668 [LO114] 10.00
__ Rebel Snowspeeder 4500 [LO115] 50.00
__ Rebel Snowspeeder 4500 OTC packaging [LO116] 50.00
__ Rebel Trooper Battle Pack 8083 [LO117] 12.00
__ Republic Attack Shuttle 8019 [LO118] 60.00
__ Republic Cruiser 7665 [LO119] 90.00
__ Republic Frigate 7964 [LO120] 120.00
__ Republic Gunship 7163 [LO121] 39.00
__ Republic Gunship 7676 [LO122] 120.00
__ Republic Swamp Speeder 8091 [LO123] 30.00
__ Rogue Shadow 7672 [LO124] 50.00
__ Separatist's Shuttle 8036 [LO125] 30.00
__ Sith Infiltrator 7151 [LO126] 30.00
__ Sith Infiltrator 7663 [LO127] 65.00
__ Sith Nightspeeder 7957 [LO128] 25.00
__ Slave I 7144 [LO129] 40.00
__ Slave I 8097 [LO130] 80.00
__ Snow Speeder 7130 [LO131] 40.00
__ Snowtrooper Battle Pack 8084 [LO132] 12.00
__ Speeder Bikes 7128 [LO133] 12.00
__ Star Wars Advent Calendar 7958 ....40.00
__ T-16 Skyhopper 4477 [LO134] 15.00
__ T-6 Jedi Shuttle 7931 [LO135] 60.00
__ Tie Bomber 4479 [LO136] 40.00
__ TIE Crawler 7664 [LO137] 50.00
__ TIE Defender 8087 [LO138] 50.00
__ TIE Fighter 7146 [LO139] 24.00
__ TIE Fighter 7263 OTC packaging [LO140] 20.00
__ TIE Fighter and Y-Wing 7150 [LO141] 65.00
__ TIE interceptor 6206 [LO142] 25.00
__ Trade Federation AAT 7155 [LO143] 20.00
__ Trade Federation MTT 7184 [LO144] 25.00
__ Trade Federation MTT 7662 [LO145] 100.00
__ Tusken Raider Encounter 7113 [LO146] 10.00
__ Twin-Pod Cloud Car 7119 [LO147] 12.00
__ Ultimate Lightsaber Duel 7257 [LO148] 30.00
__ Ultimate Space Battle 7283, exclusive to Target [LO149] 75.00
__ V-19 Torrent Starfighter 7674 [LO150] 55.00
__ V-wing fighter 6205 [LO151] 45.00
__ Value Pack: Gungan Sub and Naboo Swamp 7161 / 7121, exclusive to Toys R Us [LO152] 65.00
__ Venator-class Republic Attack Cruiser 8039 [LO153] 120.00
__ Watto's Junk Yard 7186 [LO154] 35.00
__ Wookiee Attack 7258 [LO155] 30.00
__ Wookiee Catamaran 7260 [LO156] 50.00
__ X-Wing Dagobah scene 4502 [LO157] 50.00
__ X-Wing Dagobah scene 4502 OTC packaging [LO158] 50.00
__ X-Wing Fighter 6212, exclusive to Toys R Us [LO159] 50.00
__ X-Wing Fighter 7140 [LO160] 42.00
__ Y-wing Fighter 7658 [LO161] 40.00

Mindstorm developer kits.
__ Darkside Developer [LO162] 95.00
__ Droid Developer [LO163] 95.00

Mini Building Sets.
__ AAT 30052, exclusive to Brickmaster [LO164] 6.00
__ Anakin and Sebulba's Podracers 4485 [LO165] 10.00
__ ARC-170 6967 [LO166] 15.00
__ AT-AT 20018, exclusive to Brickmaster [LO167] 10.00
__ AT-AT 4489 [LO168] 10.00
__ AT-ST 30054, exclusive to Brickmaster [LO169] 6.00
__ AT-ST and Snowspeeder 4486 [LO170] 10.00
__ AT-TE 4495 [LO171] 10.00
__ AT-TE Walker 20009, exclusive to Brickmaster [LO172] 10.00
__ Battle Droid on STAP 30004, exclusive to Daily Mirror [LO173] 15.00
__ Battle Droid on STAP 80004 ....8.00
__ Bounty Hunter Assault Ship 20021, exclusive to Brickmaster [LO174] 14.00
__ Clone Turbo Tank 20006, exclusive to Brickmaster [LO175] 10.00
__ General Grievous' Starfighter 8033 [LO176] 6.00
__ Imperial Shuttle 20016, exclusive to Brickmaster [LO177] 10.00
__ Imperial Shuttle 4494 [LO178] 10.00
__ Imperial Speeder Bike 30005, exclusive to Daily Mirror [LO179] 15.00
__ Jedi Starfighter 6966 [LO180] 15.00
__ Jedi Starfighter and Slave I 4487 [LO181] 10.00
__ Millennium Falcon 4488 [LO182] 25.00
__ MTT 4491 [LO183] 10.00
__ Republic Attack Shuttle 30050 [LO184] 6.00
__ Republic Gunship 20010, exclusive to Brickmaster [LO185] 10.00
__ Republic Gunship 4490 [LO186] 10.00
__ Republic Star Destroyer 20007, exclusive to Brickmaster [LO187] 10.00
__ Sith Infiltrator 4493 [LO188] 10.00
__ Slave I 20019, exclusive to Brickmaster [LO189] 12.00
__ Star Destroyer 30053, exclusive to Brickmaster [LO190] 6.00
__ Star Destroyer 4492 [LO191] 10.00
__ TIE Advanced and X-Wing Fighter 4484 [LO192] 10.00
__ TIE Fighter 3219, exclusive to Lego Club [LO193] 25.00
__ TIE Fighter with club mailer packaging 3219, exclusive to Lego Club [LO194] 45.00
__ TIE Interceptor 6965 [LO195] 10.00
__ V-19 Torrent 8031 [LO196] 6.00
__ Vulture Droid 30055, exclusive to Brickmaster [LO197] 6.00
__ X-Wing 30051 [LO198] 6.00

Mini Building Sets. Japan. Distributed by Kabaya.
__ 1 X-Wing Fighter [LO199] 15.00
__ 2 Slave I [LO200] 15.00
__ 3 TIE Interceptor [LO201] 15.00

Prebuilt statues.
__ Darth Vader, exclusive to FAO Schwarz [LO202] 9,500.00

Promotional brick sets.
__ Star Wars Brickmaster, limited to 500, numbered, exclusive to Comicon [LO203] 225.00

Promotional bricks.
__ Darth Vader Transformation 7251 2005 VIP Gala February 19, 2005 [LO204] 75.00
__ Embossed with SW logo and April 20-May 1 2005 [LO205] 35.00
__ Embossed with SW logo and TPM Lego characters; distributed at the SW Celebration in Denver CO, limited to 7,000 [LO206] 28.00

Promotional dioramas.
__ Ahsoka Tano, Mace Windu, Clone Trooper, limited to 900, numbered, exclusive to Comicon [LO207] 150.00
__ Clone Trooper, Obi-Wan, Anakin, limited to 1,250, numbered, exclusive to Comicon [LO208] ...100.00
__ Vader Arrives, limited to 500, exclusive to Star Wars Celebration IV 150.00

Technics.
__ Battle Droid 8001 [LO209] 30.00
__ C-3PO (8007) 8007 [LO210] 50.00
__ Darth Vader 8010 [LO211] 55.00
__ Destroyer Droid 8002 [LO212] 50.00
__ Jango Fett 8011 [LO213] 30.00
__ Pit Droid 8000 [LO214] 45.00
__ R2-D2 8009 [LO215] 20.00
__ Stormtrooper 8008 [LO216] 50.00
__ Super Battle Droid 8012 [LO217] 35.00

Ultimate Collector series.
__ AT-AT Walker 10178 [LO218] 130.00
__ AT-ST 10174 [LO219] 135.00
__ Cloud City 10123 [LO220] 200.00
__ Darth Maul 10018 [LO221] 175.00
__ Darth Vader's TIE Advanced 10175 [LO222] 100.00
__ Death Star II 10143 [LO223] 325.00
__ General Grievous 10186 [LO224] 60.00
__ Imperial Shuttle 10212 [LO225] 260.00
__ Imperial Star Destroyer 10030 [LO226] 285.00
__ Millennium Falcon 10179 [LO227] 500.00
__ Naboo Starfighter 10026 [LO228] 50.00
__ Obi-Wan's Jedi Starfighter 10215 [LO229] 90.00
__ Rebel Blockade Runner 10019 [LO230] 175.00
__ Rebel Snowspeeder 10129 [LO231] 125.00
__ Republic Dropship with AT-OT 10195 [LO232] 275.00
__ Sandcrawler 10144 OTC packaging [LO233] .75.00
__ Super Star Destroyer 10221 ....180.00
__ Tantive IV 10198 [LO234] 150.00
__ TIE Collection 10131 OTC packaging [LO235] 95.00
__ Tie Interceptor 7181 [LO236] 135.00
__ X-Wing 7191 [LO237] 135.00
__ Y-wing Attack Starfighter 10134 OTC packaging [LO238] 135.00
__ Yoda 7194 [LO239] 95.00

Cameras*

Tiger Electronics

Picture plus cameras.
__ Darth Maul with background [CAM01] 35.00
__ Darth Maul without background [CAM02] 25.00

CAM01

CAM01 detail

CAM02 detail

CNT01

**Non-toy edition contains additional items in this category*

Canteens

Hunter Leisure
__ Darth Vader [CNT01]....................................35.00

Coins: Action Figure

Hasbro
30th anniversary exclusives.
__ 30th anniversary, exclusive to San Diego Comic-Con 15.00
__ 30th anniversary black box, exclusive to Toy Fair [C001] 65.00
__ Celebration Europe Ziplock baggie, exclusive to Star Wars Celebration Europe.......................12.00
__ Celebration IV Ziplock baggie, exclusive to Star Wars Celebration IV [C002]...........................10.00

30th anniversary.
__ 4-LOM 30-41 [C003]..5.00
__ A-Wing Pilot 30-44 [C004]...............................5.00
__ Airborne Trooper 30-07 [C005]..........................5.00
__ Anakin Skywalker 30-33 [C006]........................5.00
__ Anakin Skywalker, Spirit 30-45 [C007] 5.00
__ Biggs Darklighter Academy Outfit 30-17 [C008]..5.00
__ Biggs Darklighter, Rebel Pilot 30-13 [C009].....5.00
__ Boba Fett, animated 30-24 [C010] 5.00
__ C-3PO 30-30 [C011]..5.00
__ Clone Trooper, 7th legion 30-49 [C012] 5.00
__ Clone Trooper, Hawkbat Battalion 30-50 [C013] 5.00
__ Clone Trooper, training fatigues 30-55 [C014] .5.00
__ CZ-4 30-26 [C015]...5.00
__ Darth Malak 30-35 [C016]................................5.00
__ Darth Revan 30-34 [C017] 5.00
__ Darth Vader 30-01 from binder pack [C018] 5.00
__ Darth Vader 30-16 [C019]................................5.00
__ Darth Vader, holographic 30-48 [C020]...........5.00
__ Death Star Trooper 30-14 [C021] 5.00
__ Destroyer Droid 30-59 [C022]..........................5.00
__ Elis Helrot 30-23 [C023]...................................5.00
__ Galactic Marine 30-02 [C024]..........................5.00
__ General McQuarrie 30-40 [C025].....................5.00
__ Han Solo 30-11 [C026] 5.00
__ Han Solo, Bespin 30-38 [C027] 5.00
__ Hermi Odle 30-29 [C028].................................5.00
__ Jango Fett 30-57 [C029]..................................5.00
__ Jawa 30-19 [C030]..5.00
__ Lando Calrissian 30-39 [C031] 5.00
__ Lava Miner 30-06 [C032] 5.00
__ Luke Skywalker 30-18 [C033]..........................5.00
__ Luke Skywalker, ceremony outfit 30-12 [C034] 5.00
__ Luke Skywalker, Jedi 30-25 [C035] 5.00
__ M'iiyoom O'nith 30-22 [C036]..........................5.00
__ Mace Windu 30-03 [C037]...............................5.00
__ Naboo Soldier 30-52 [C038]............................5.00
__ Obi-Wan Kenobi 30-05 [C039] 5.00
__ Padme Amidala 30-56 [C040]...........................5.00
__ Pax Bonkik 30-54 [C041]..................................5.00
__ Qymaen jai Sheelal 30-36 [C042] 5.00
__ R2-B1 30-51 [C043]...5.00
__ R2-D2 30-04 [C044]..5.00
__ R2-D2, Endor 30-46 [C045]..............................5.00
__ Rebel Honor Guard 30-10 [C046]....................5.00
__ Rebel Vanguard 30-53 [C047] 5.00
__ Romba and Graak 30-43 [C048]......................5.00
__ Roron Corobb 30-31 [C049] 5.00
__ Stormtrooper 30-20 [C050]...............................5.00
__ Super Battle Droid 30-08 [C051] 5.00
__ Umpass-Stay 30-27 [C052] 5.00
__ Voolvif Monn 30-58 [C053] 5.00
__ Yoda 30-32 [C054]..5.00

30th anniversary. McQuarrie concept figures.
__ Boba Fett 30-15 [C055] 5.00
__ Chewbacca 30-21 [C056] 5.00
__ Darth Vader 30-28 [C057]..................................5.00
__ Han Solo 30-47 [C058] 5.00
__ Luke Skywalker, exclusive to HasbroToyShop.com [C059] 10.00
__ Obi-Wan and Yoda 15.00
__ Obi-Wan and Yoda, exclusive to HasbroToyShop.com [C060] 10.00
__ R2-D2 and C-3PO, exclusive to Star Wars Celebration IV [C061].....................................15.00
__ Rebel Trooper 30-60 [C062] 5.00
__ Snowtrooper 30-42 [C063] 5.00
__ Starkiller Hero 30-37 [C064] 5.00
__ Stormtrooper 30-09 [C065]...............................5.00

30th anniversary. Saga Legends.
__ Episode I [C066] 3.00
__ Episode II [C067]...3.00
__ Episode III [C068]..3.00
__ Episode IV [C069] 3.00
__ Episode V [C070] 3.00
__ Episode VI [C071] 3.00
__ Expanded universe [C072]................................5.00

30th anniversary. Ultimate Galactic Hunt gold colored coins from chase figures.
__ Airborne Trooper [C073] 4.00
__ Biggs Darklighter [C074]...................................4.00
__ Boba Fett, animated debut [C075] 4.00
__ Boba Fett, McQuarrie concept [C076].............8.00
__ Chewbacca, McQuarrie concept [C077] 5.00
__ Darth Vader [C078] 4.00
__ Expanded universe 10.00
__ Galactic Marine [C079] 4.00
__ Han Solo [C080]..4.00
__ Luke Skywalker [C081] 4.00
__ Mace Windu [C082] 4.00
__ R2-D2 [C083] 4.00
__ Stormtrooper, McQuarrie concept [C084]......12.00

Galactic Hunt mail away coins. Sent as a complete set during mail-in promotion.
__ Bossk 10.00
__ Han Solo Hoth 10.00
__ IG-88..10.00
__ Imperial Snowtrooper 10.00
__ Luke Skywalker Bespin...................................10.00
__ Princess Leia Organa Endor 10.00
__ Set of 7, boxed 45.00

JusToys
Bend-Ems premiums.
__ Millennium Falcon [4:108] 10.00
__ TIE Fighter [4:108]..10.00
__ X-Wing Fighter [4:108] 10.00

Kenner
Droids (vintage).
__ A-Wing Pilot [C085] 35.00
__ Boba Fett [C086]..65.00
__ C-3PO [C087] 12.00
__ Jann Tosh [C088]..10.00
__ Jord Dusat [C089]..10.00
__ Kea Moll [C090] 10.00
__ Kez-Iban [C091] 10.00
__ RD-D2 [C092]...12.00
__ Sise Fromm [C093] 10.00
__ Thall Joben [C094]...10.00
__ Tig Fromm [C095] 10.00
__ Uncle Gundy [C096]..10.00

Ewoks (vintage).
__ Dulok Scout [C097]...10.00
__ Dulok Shaman [C098]......................................10.00
__ King Gorneesh [C099]......................................10.00
__ Logray [C100] 17.00
__ Urgah Lady Gorneesh [C101] 10.00
__ Wicket [C102] 17.00

Power of the Force 2 (modern). From the Millennium Minted Coin (MMC) series of action figures.
__ C-3PO [C103] 15.00
__ Chewbacca [C104] 5.00
__ Emperor Palpatine [C105].................................5.00
__ Han Solo [C106]..5.00
__ Luke Skywalker [C107] 5.00
__ Princess Leia [4:108]..5.00
__ Snowtrooper (Hoth Stormtrooper) [C108] 15.00

Power of the Force (vintage).
__ 2-1B [C109]...135.00
__ A-Wing Pilot [C110] 10.00
__ Amanaman [C111] 25.00
__ Anakin Skywalker [C112].............................120.00
__ AT-AT [C113] 65.00
__ AT-ST Driver [C114]...45.00
__ B-Wing Pilot [C115] 30.00
__ Barada [C116] 10.00
__ Bib Fortuna [C117]...175.00
__ Biker Scout [C118]...25.00
__ Boba Fett [C119]...350.00
__ C-3PO [C120] 35.00
__ Chewbacca [C121] 35.00
__ Chief Chirpa [C122] 135.00
__ Creatures [C123]...300.00
__ Darth Vader [C124] 20.00
__ Droids (R5-D4 and Power Droid) [C125] 200.00
__ Emperor [C126]...40.00
__ Emperor's Royal Guard [C127].....................125.00
__ EV-9D9 [C128] 15.00
__ FX-7 [C129]..130.00
__ Gamorrean Guard [C130] 55.00
__ Greedo [C131] 200.00
__ Han Solo, Carbon Freeze [C132]....................15.00
__ Han Solo, Rebel [C133] 40.00
__ Han Solo, Rebel Fighter [C134] 125.00
__ Han Solo, Rebel Hero [C135]........................185.00
__ Hans Solo, Rebel (misspelling / error) [4:109]..700.00
__ Hoth Stormtrooper [C136] 250.00
__ Imperial Commander [C137].........................130.00
__ Imperial Dignitary [C138] 10.00
__ Imperial Gunner [C139]...................................15.00
__ Jawas [C140] 25.00
__ Lando Calrissian, Rebel General (Cloud City) [4:109]...125.00
__ Lando Calrissian, Rebel General (Falcon) [C141] 15.00
__ Logray [C142] 50.00
__ Luke Skywalker, Jedi Knight [C143] 35.00
__ Luke Skywalker, Jedi Knight on Dagobah [C144] 240.00
__ Luke Skywalker, Jedi with X-Wing [C145]......35.00
__ Luke Skywalker, Rebel Leader (Landspeeder) [4:109]...115.00
__ Luke Skywalker, Rebel Leader (Scout Bike) [C146] 18.00
__ Luke Skywalker, Rebel Leader (Stormtrooper armor, no eyes) [4:109] 500.00
__ Luke Skywalker, Rebel Leader (Stormtrooper armor) [C147]...70.00
__ Luke Skywalker, Rebel Leader (Tauntaun) [C148] 200.00
__ Lumat [C149] 30.00
__ Millenium Falcon (misspelling) [4:109] 345.00
__ Millennium Falcon [C150] 100.00
__ Obi-Wan Kenobi [C151]...................................35.00
__ Paploo [C152] 20.00
__ Princess Leia, Boushh [C153].......................175.00
__ Princess Leia, Rebel Leader (Endor Fatigues) [C154] 25.00
__ Princess Leia, Rebel Leader (R2-D2) [C155] 500.00
__ R2-D2 [C156] 18.00
__ Romba [C157]...12.00
__ Sail Barge [4:109]..300.00
__ Sail Skiff [C158] 350.00
__ Sail Skiff without Star Wars logo (error) [4:109]...500.00
__ Star Destroyer Commander [C159] 78.00
__ Stormtrooper [C160].......................................35.00
__ Teebo [C161] 10.00
__ TIE Fighter Pilot [C162]...................................50.00
__ Tusken Raider [C163] 150.00
__ Warok [C164] 15.00
__ Wicket [C165] 20.00
__ Yak Face [C166] 100.00
__ Yoda [C167]...70.00
__ Zuckuss [C168]...165.00

__ 63rd: Jedi Knight, prototype only, aluminum or bronze finish [4:109]......................................750.00

Toy Fair
__ Darth Vader, exclusive to Toy Fair..................25.00

Coins: Action Figure

C001 C002 C003 C004 C005 C006
C007 C008 C009 C010 C011 C012
C013 C014 C015 C016 C017 C018
C019 C020 C021 C022 C023 C024
C025 C026 C027 C028 C029 C030
C031 C032 C033 C034 C035 C036
C037 C038 C039 C040 C041 C042

222

C043

C044

C045

C046

C047

C048

C049

C050

C051

C052

C053

C054

C055

C056

C057

C058

C059

C060

C061

C062

C063

C064

C065

C066

C067

C068

C069

C070

C071

C072

C073

C074

C075

C076

C077

C078

C079

C080

C081

C082

C083

C084

C085

C086

C087

C088

C089

C090

C091

C092

C093

C094

C095

C096

C097

C098

C099

C100

C101

C102

C103

C104

C105

C106

C107

C108

C109

C110

C111

C112

C113

C114

C115

C116

C117

C118

C119

C120

C121

C122

C123

C124

C125

C126

C127

C128

C129

C130

C131

C132

C133

C134

C135

C136

C137

C138

C139

C140

C141

C142

C143

C144

C145

C146

C147

C148

C149

C150

C151

C152

C153

C154

C155

C156

C157

C158

C159

C160

C161

C162

C163

C164

C165

C166

C167

C168

YC001

YC002

YC003

AFC001

AFC002

AFC003

Collector Fleet Toys

Kenner
__ Imperial Star Destroyer [YC001] 95.00
__ Rebel Blockade Runner [YC002] 75.00
__ Super Star Destroyer [YC003] 290.00

Containers, Figural

Applause
__ Darth Maul, PVC [AFC001] 18.00
__ R2-D2, PVC [AFC002].....................................18.00

Kelloggs, Malaysia
Collectible Jars.
__ R2-D2 [AFC003]..35.00

Kelloggs
__ C-3PO [AFC004]..10.00
__ Darth Vader [AFC005]...................................10.00
__ R2-D2 [AFC006]..10.00

Cork Boards

Manton Cork
__ AT-AT, glow-in-dark dome [CK001] 18.00
__ Boba Fett, Darth Vader, Stormtroopers [CK002]...26.00
__ C-3PO and R2-D2, 2-piece set [CK003].........28.00
__ C-3PO and R2-D2, glow-in-dark dome [CK004]...18.00
__ C-3PO, Chewbacca, Han, Leia, Luke, R2-D2 [CK005] 24.00

__ Chewbacca, glow-in-dark dome [CK006] 18.00
__ Chewbacca, glow-in-dark dome round "glows" sticker [CK007] 18.00
__ Darth Vader [CK008]....................................24.00
__ Darth Vader and Luke Skywalker Duel [CK009] 18.00
__ Darth Vader, glow-in-dark dome [CK010] 18.00
__ Darth Vader, helmet and shoulders [CK011] ..24.00
__ Ewok Hut [CK012] 18.00
__ Jabba the Hutt [CK013] 18.00
__ Jabba's Palace [CK014] 18.00
__ Luke on Tauntaun [CK015] 24.00
__ Luke on Tauntaun, glow-in-dark dome [CK016] 18.00
__ Max Rebo Band [CK017]...............................18.00
__ Millennium Falcon "May The Force Be With You" 23.00

AFC004

AFC005

AFC006

CK001

CK002

CK003

CK004

CK005

CK006

CK007

CK008

CK009

CK010

CK011

CK012

CK013

CK014

CK015

CK016

CK017

CK018

CK019

CK020

CK021

CK022

FK001

FK002

__ Paploo, Wicket, C-3PO and R2-D2 [CK018] ..18.00
__ Star Wars logo, Millennium Falcon, TIE Fighters, X-Wing [CK019] 22.00
__ Yoda [CK020]...24.00
__ Yoda, glow-in-dark [CK021] 25.00
__ Yoda, glow-in-dark dome [CK022] 18.00

Crafts: Art Kits

Germany.
__ Clone Wars Commander Fox, Captain Rex, Anakin, Yoda, Obi-Wan 10.00

Australia. Velvet art sets.
__ C-3PO and R2-D2 [FK001] 8.00

Animations
__ Clone Wars activity Case ruler, eraser, markers, pencil sharpener, sticker sheet, sketchbook, colored pencils, carry case [FK002] 20.00
__ Deluxe Activity Set ruler, eraser, markers, pencil sharpener, sticker sheet, sketchbook, colored pencils, tracing desk [FK003] 20.00

Funtastic Pty. Ltd.
__ C-3PO art kit [FK004] 8.00
__ Darth Maul color and paint center [FK005]...24.00

Hasbro
__ R2-D2 Art Center [FK006]..............................14.00
__ Star Wars Ultimate Art Kit [FK007] 9.00

FK003

FK004

FK005

FK006

FK007

FK008

FK009

FK010

FK011

FK012

FK013

FK014

Hunter Leisure, Ltd., Australia
__ Combo pack 6 crayons, 6 markers, 6 colored pencils and an eraser [FK008] 8.00

Q-Stat, UK
__ Jar Jar Binks textured case, 5 pencils, 5 pens, eraser, sharpener, ruler [FK009] 15.00

Rose Art Industries
__ A New Hope Sand Art [FK010] 9.00
__ Activity Case, ANH [FK011] 10.00
__ Star Wars Fun Kit with stickers, pens, scissors [FK012]..8.00

Episode III: Revenge of the Sith.
__ Activity Case [FK013]....................................10.00
__ Fuzzy t-shirt kit [FK014]..................................10.00

Crafts: Clip-Alongs

Craft Master
__ Compass with crayon, R2-D2 [VCL001].........12.00
__ Crayon holder and sharpener [VCL002] 12.00
__ Wicket magnifying glass [VCL003] 16.00

Crafts: Coloring Sets

Argentina.
__ Colorear Stickers [COL001]............................25.00

Animations
__ Jedi coloring set stickers, stampers, stamp pad, markers, sketchpad, crayons, coloring sheet, stencils [COL002]...20.00

Craft House
Star Wars Mega-Fuzz coloring sets.
__ AT-AT [COL003]..7.00
__ Darth Vader [COL004].....................................7.00
__ Death Star Battle [COL005] 5.00
__ Luke and Leia [COL006] 7.00

Craft Master
__ Color N' Clean Machine, 50" roll of reusable scenes to color, four crayons and wipe cloth [4:124] .35.00

Crayola
__ 3-D Comic Maker [COL007] 18.00
__ Color Explosion 18 Clone Wars scenes, 6 markers, stencil sheet, 2 sticker sheets [COL008] 16.00
__ Color Surge 18 scenes, 18 blank pages, 8 markers [COL009]...16.00

VCL001

VCL002

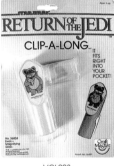

VCL003

COL001

COL002

COL003

COL004

COL005

COL006

COL007

COL008

COL009

COL010

COL011

COL012

COL013

COL014

COL015

COL016

COL017

COL018

COL019

COL020

DOD001

DOD002

DOD003

DOD004

DOD005

DOD006

__ Giant Coloring Pages 20 Clone Wars pages [COL010]...12.00
__ ReColoritz 10 Clone Wars scenes, 6 markers, 1 sponge, pop-out frame [COL011]....................15.00
__ ReColoritz Black 10 Clone Wars scenes, 6 markers, 1 sponge, pop-out frame [COL012]................15.00

Hunter Leisure, Ltd., Australia
__ Colouring Set coloring pages, stickers and colored pencils [COL013] 10.00

Rose Art Industries
__ A New Hope: Crayon by Number [COL014].....7.00
__ Deluxe Light-Up Drawing Desk [COL015] 18.00
__ Designer Desk [COL016] 16.00
__ Droid Factory [COL017] 12.00
__ Light Up Drawing Desk [COL018]...................12.00

Episode III: Revenge of the Sith.
__ Activity Roller Desk [COL019]........................25.00
__ Lite Up Tracing Desk [COL020] 15.00

Crafts: Doodle Kits

Trends International Corp.
Episode I.
__ 3-D Doodle Kit [DOD001] 6.00
__ Doodle Bag [DOD002] 8.00
__ Doodle Clings with 6 Markers [DOD003]..........8.00
__ Jar Jar Binks Velvet Doodle 11"x15" plus 6 color pens [DOD004] 7.00
__ Podrace doodle poster, six markers, bonus magnet, bonus full-color movie poster [DOD005] 14.00

Episode II.
__ Doodles with six markers [DOD006].................6.00

Crafts: Figure Makers

Flair Leisure Products Plc., UK
Clone Wars.
__ Plaster Creations [FGM001]...........................25.00
__ Shaker Maker [FGM002]................................25.00

Hasbro, UK
__ Star Wars [FGM003] 15.00

Hasbro
__ Creepy Crawler Character-Maker [FGM004]..35.00

Humbrol, UK
__ 3D Plaster Mold and Paint Set, EPII [FGM005] 15.00
__ Badge and Magnet figure molding set, EPII [FGM006] 30.00

Kenner
Figure maker kits.
__ Droids [FGM007]...6.00
__ Jedi [FGM008] 6.00
__ Millennium Falcon [FGM009] 10.00
__ Slave I [FGM010] 15.00
__ Space Creatures [FGM011] 6.00

Mako, France
Plaster character casting sets.
__ 5 classic trilogy characters [FGM012] 25.00

FGM001

FGM002

FGM003

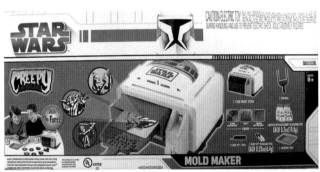

FGM004

FGM005

FGM006

FGM007

FGM008

FGM009

FGM010

FGM011

FGM012

FGM013

FGM014

FGM015

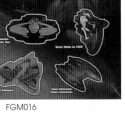

FGM016

FGM017

FGM018

CRL001   CRL002   CRL003   CRL004   CRL005

CRP001   CRP002   CRP003   CRP004   CRP005

__ 8 classic trilogy characters [FGM013] 35.00
__ Darth Vader [FGM014] 8.00
__ Luke Skywalker [FGM015] 8.00

Supercast, UK
__ Badge and Magnet molding set [FGM016].....27.00
__ Heroes 3D plaster molding set [FGM017] 24.00
__ Villains 3D plaster molding set [FGM018].......24.00

Crafts: Latchhook Kits

Leewards Creative Crafts
__ C-3PO and R2-D2 rug 24"x36" 225.00
__ C-3PO rug..175.00
__ Chewbacca rug, 20"x27"............................325.00
__ Darth Vader pillow, 15"x15" [CRL001]..........275.00
__ Darth Vader rug, 20"x27"............................175.00
__ R2-D2 pillow, 15"x15" [CRL002] 275.00
__ R2-D2 rug, 20"x27" [CRL003] 175.00
__ Stormtrooper rug 24"x36" [CRL004] 450.00
__ Yoda rug 20"x27" [CRL005] 175.00

Crafts: Paint-By-Number

Craft House
Star Wars acrylic paint-by-number kit.
__ AT-ST and Speeder Bike [CRP001]..................5.00

__ Darth Vader and Boba Fett [CRP002]...............6.00
__ Luke and Han [CRP003] 3.00

Craft Master
__ Battle on Hoth [CRP004] 16.00
__ Boba Fett [CRP005].......................................16.00

CRP006   CRP007   CRP008

CRP009   CRP010   CRP011   CRP012   CRP013

CRP014   CRP015   CRP016   CRP017   CRP018   CRP019

CRF001

CRF002

CRF003

CRF004

CRF005

CRF006

CRF007

CRF008

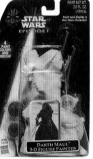

CRF009

CRF010

CRF011

CRA001

CRA002

CRA003

CRA004

CRA005

CRA006

CRA007

CRA008

CRA009

CRA010

CRA011

CRA012

CRA013

CRA014

CRA015

CRA016

CRA017

CRK001

__ C-3PO and R2-D2 [CRP006] 16.00
__ Chase Through Asteroids [CRP007].............16.00
__ Darth Vader [CRP008] 16.00
__ Ewok Gliders [CRP009] 16.00
__ Ewok Village [CRP010] 16.00
__ Han Solo and Princess Leia [CRP011] 16.00
__ Jabba the Hutt [CRP012]...........................16.00
__ Lando Calrissian and Boushh [CRP013] 16.00
__ Luke Skywalker [CRP014] 16.00
__ Max Rebo band [CRP015] 16.00
__ Wicket and Baga [CRP016] 16.00
__ Yoda [CRP017] 16.00

Rose Art Industries
__ A New Hope [CRP018] 8.00
__ Revenge of the Sith [CRP019] 10.00

Crafts: Paintable Figures

Craft Master
Empire Strikes Back.
__ Boba Fett [CRF001] 20.00
__ Han Solo [CRF002] 20.00
__ Luke on Tauntaun [CRF003] 20.00
__ Princess Leia [CRF004] 20.00
__ Yoda [CRF005] 20.00

Return of the Jedi.
__ Admiral Ackbar [CRF006] 20.00
__ C-3PO and R2-D2 [CRF007] 20.00
__ Wicket [CRF008] 20.00

Hasbro
3D Figure Painters.
__ Darth Maul [CRF009] 9.00
__ Obi-Wan Kenobi [CRF010] 9.00
__ Qui-Gon Jinn [CRF011]...............................9.00

Lili Ledy, Mexico
__ Admiral Ackbar 45.00
__ C-3PO and R2-D2 ....45.00
__ Wicket the Ewok [4:125] 45.00

Crafts: Poster Art Kits

Craft Master
__ Dagobah and Yoda / Battle on Hoth [CRA001]...65.00
__ Darth Vader 3D [CRA002].............................85.00

__ Darth Vader Lives / May The Force Be With You [CRA003]...65.00
__ Galactic dogfight / Forces of Good and Evil [CRA004]...65.00
__ Heroes and Villains / Cantina and Aliens [CRA005]...65.00

Kenner
__ Playnts, 5-poster set [CRA006] 50.00

Merlin Publishing Internat'l Ltd.
__ Star Wars, 4 posters with crayons 11"x17" [CRA007]..12.00

Q-Stat, UK
Episode I: The Phantom Menace.
__ Anakin Skywalker [CRA008] 10.00
__ Darth Maul [CRA009] 10.00
__ Queen Amidala [CRA010] 10.00

Rose Art Industries
__ A New Hope, 4 Exciting Scenes to Color [CRA011]...8.00

Episode III: Revenge of the Sith Fuzzy poster art 6"x9" with 3 pens.
__ Darth Vader [CRA012] 5.00
__ Droids [CRA013] 5.00

Episode III: Revenge of the Sith.
__ Fuzzy posters 11"x15" [CRA014] 8.00
__ Fuzzy posters 16"x20"........................12.00
__ Fuzzy super value set [CRA015]....................20.00

Takara, Japan
Poster art kits.
__ Forces of Good and Evil / Galactic dogfight [CRA016]......................................175.00
__ Vader and Heroes / Battle over Yavin [CRA017]......................................175.00

Crafts: Sewing Kits

Craft Master
__ Wicket and Friends Sew 'N Show Cards [CRK001]...17.00

Crafts: Sun Catcher Kits

Fundimensions
Makeit and Bakeit kits.
__ Darth Vader [CRS001] 16.00
__ Gamorrean Guard [CRS002].........................16.00
__ Jabba the Hutt [CRS003]...........................16.00
__ R2-D2 [CRS004] 16.00

Leewards Creative Crafts
__ C-3PO [CRS005]..35.00
__ Darth Vader [CRS006] 35.00
__ Darth Vader, head [CRS007] 35.00
__ IG-88 [CRS008]..35.00
__ Luke on Tauntaun [CRS009].........................35.00
__ Luke Skywalker [CRS010] 40.00
__ Millennium Falcon [CRS011].........................40.00
__ Princess Leia [CRS012] 35.00

CRS001 CRS002 CRS003 CRS004

CRS005 CRS006 CRS007 CRS008 CRS009 CRS010

CRS011 CRS012 CRS013 CRS014 CRS015 CRS016

233

FT001

FT002

FT003

FT004

FT005

WPS001

WPS002

DSP001

DSP002

DSP003

DSP004   DSP005

__ R2-D2 and Yoda [CRS013]............................35.00
__ Snowspeeder [CRS014] 35.00
__ Stormtrooper [CRS015]................................35.00
__ X-Wing Fighter [CRS016]..............................40.00

Crafts: Watercolor Paint Sets

Craft House
__ Star Wars [WPS001] 8.00

Fundimensions
__ Ewok 18.00
__ Ewok Glider 18.00
__ Ewok Village...18.00

Kenner
__ Dip Dots paint set [WPS002] 50.00

Dart Boards

Gentle Giant
__ Princess Leia 200.00

Decision Making Toys

Hasbro
__ Ask The Force [FT001]...................................12.00
__ Ask Yoda, 24 phrases [FT002].......................24.00

Original Trilogy Collection.
__ Ask Yoda, 24 phrases [FT003].......................20.00

Revenge of the Sith.
__ Call Upon Yoda [FT004]...............................25.00

Kenner
__ Yoda the Jedi magic answer [FT005] 85.00

Dispensers: Candy

Cap Candy
__ Jango Fett gum dispenser [DSP001]................6.00
__ Naboo Fighter Skittles dispenser [DSP002] 8.00
__ R2-D2 dispenser with M&Ms [DSP003]............8.00

Masterfoods USA
__ M&M Minis, blue light-up saber [DSP004]........3.00

__ M&M Minis, red light-up saber [DSP005] 3.00

Toy & Pogo mini M&M dispensers, boxed. Asia exclusive.
__ C-3PO [DSP006]...8.00
__ Death Star [DSP007]...8.00
__ Storm Trooper [DSP008] 8.00
__ Yoda [DSP009] 8.00

Toy & Pogo mini M&M dispensers, cardback.
__ Anakin Skywalker [DSP010].............................5.00
__ C-3PO [DSP011]...5.00
__ Death Star [DSP012]...5.00
__ Obi-Wan [DSP013]..5.00
__ Storm Trooper [DSP014] 5.00
__ Yoda [DSP015] 5.00

DSP006

DSP007

DSP008

DSP009

DSP010

DSP011

DSP012

DSP013

DSP014

DSP015

DC001 - DC003

RND001

RND002

RND003

RND004

RND005

RND006

RND007

RND008

RND009

RND010

RND011

RND012

RND013

RND014

RND015

Dolls: Collector

Dolls: Collector

Madame Alexander
8" dolls, limited to 1,000. FAO Schwarz exclusive.
__ Han Solo [DC001] 175.00
__ Luke Skywalker [DC002]..............................175.00
__ Princess Leia [DC003] 175.00

Dolls: Nesting

Hot Toys
Chubbys. 3 nested dolls.
__ C-3PO [RND001] 18.00

__ Darth Vader [RND002] 18.00
__ Ewoks [RND003]..18.00
__ General Grievous [RND004]..........................18.00
__ Jango and Boba Fett [RND005].....................18.00
__ Luke Skywalker [RND006] 18.00
__ Obi-Wan Kenobi [RND007]............................18.00
__ Princess Leia [RND008] 18.00
__ Rebel Pilots [RND009] 18.00
__ Shadow Troopers [RND010].........................45.00
__ Sith [RND011] 18.00
__ Stormtrooper [RND012].................................18.00
__ Wookiees [RND013]..18.00

Chubbys. Jumbo.
__ Darth Vader 220 cm tall. [RND014].................65.00
__ Jango Fett [RND015] 65.00

Electronic Toys

Disney Theme Park Merchandise
Hot Buttons. Speaks three phrases.
__ C-3PO [TES001] 12.00
__ Chewbacca [TES002] 12.00
__ Darth Vader [TES003] 12.00
__ Princess Leia [TES004] 12.00
__ Yoda [TES005] 12.00

Gemmy Industries
Dashboard drivers, series 1.
__ C-3PO [TES006] 10.00
__ Darth Vader [TES007] 10.00
__ Yoda [TES008] 10.00

TES001

TES002

TES003

TES004

TES005

TES006

TES007

TES008

TES009

TES010

TES011

TES012

TES013

TES014

TES015

TES016

TES017

TES018

TES019

TES020

TES021

TES022

TES023

236

TES024

TES025

TES026

TES027

TES028

TES029

TES030

TES031

TES032

TES033

TES034

TES035

TES036

TES037

TES038

TES039

TES040

TES041

TES042

TES043

TES044

TES045

TES046

TES047

Electronic Toys

Dashboard drivers, series 2.
__ C-3PO [TES009] 10.00
__ Chewbacca 10.00
__ Stormtrooper [TES010] 10.00

Gemmy Industries, Australia
Dashboard drivers.
__ Chewbacca [TES011] 10.00
__ Stormtrooper [TES012] 10.00

Hasbro
"Deformed" palm talkers.
__ Boba Fett [TES013] 20.00
__ C-3PO [TES014] 15.00
__ C-3PO, green tint with golden limbs 15.00
__ Chewbacca [TES015] 15.00
__ Darth Vader [TES016] 15.00
__ R2-D2 [TES017] 12.00
__ Stormtrooper [TES018] 15.00

Episode III: Revenge of the Sith "deformed" palm talkers.
__ Boba Fett [TES019]..........................25.00
__ C-3PO [TES020] 25.00
__ Chewbacca [TES021] 25.00
__ Darth Maul [TES022]........................25.00
__ Darth Vader [TES023] 25.00
__ R2-D2 [TES024] 25.00
__ Stormtrooper [TES025] 25.00
__ Yoda [TES026] 25.00

Force Link starships.
__ Anakin Skywalker's Speeder [TES027]...........15.00

__ Jango Fett's Slave I [TES028].........................15.00
__ Obi-Wan Kenobi's Jedi Starfighter [TES029]................................15.00
__ Zam Wesell's Speeder [TES030] 15.00

Oregon Scientific
Learning laptops.
__ Clone Trooper [TES031] 40.00
__ Clone Trooper Jr. [TES032] 30.00
__ Darth Vader [TES033] 50.00
__ R2-D2 [TES034] 25.00
__ The Clone Wars [TES035]...................40.00

Tiger Electronics
__ Interactive Yoda [TES036] 39.00

Tomy, Japan
Classic trilogy "deformed" palm talkers.
__ Boba Fett [TES037]..........................35.00
__ C-3PO [TES038] 35.00
__ C-3PO, green tint with golden limbs [TES039] 35.00
__ Chewbacca [TES040] 35.00
__ Darth Vader [TES041] 35.00
__ Stormtrooper [TES042] 35.00

Episode I: The Phantom Menace "deformed" palm talkers.
__ Battle Droid [TES043] 45.00
__ Darth Maul [TES044]........................45.00
__ Jar Jar Binks [TES045].....................45.00
__ R2-D2 [TES046] 45.00
__ Yoda [TES047] 45.00

Figures: Attacktix

Hasbro
__ Exclusive Battle Pack: 6 figures plus Republic gunship [FTX001]..45.00

Battle masters.
__ AT-RT, s1 #37 [FTX002]....................35.00
__ Boga, s1 #36 [FTX003]......................35.00
__ Jabba the Hutt, s3 #31 [FTX004]....................45.00
__ Republic Gunship, s2 #31 [FTX005] 18.00
__ Republic Gunship, Clone Wars s4 #23 [FTX006]..35.00
__ Wampa, s5 [FTX007]........................50.00

Booster packs.
__ Series 1 [FTX008]............................50.00
__ Series 2 [FTX009]............................50.00
__ Series 3, Han Solo vs. Stormtrooper [FTX010]..35.00
__ Series 3, Luke vs. Tusken Raider [FTX011] 35.00
__ Series 3, Obi-Wan vs. Darth Vader [FTX012]..35.00
__ Series 4...10.00

Intergalactic showdown packs.
__ Starter set 65.00

Series 1 promo figures.
__ Clone Lieutenant, Separatist #12 [FTX013] 12.00
__ Clone Trooper, Republic #04.........................12.00
__ Commander Bly, Republic #15...................12.00
__ Count Dooku, Sith #11 ....20.00

FTX001   FTX002   FTX003   FTX004

FTX005   FTX006   FTX007

FTX008 side 1, side 2, side 3   FTX009 side 1, side 2, side 3   FTX010   FTX011   FTX012

FTX013

FTX014

FTX015

FTX016

FTX017

FTX018

FTX019

FTX020

FTX021

FTX022

FTX023 chrome base variant

FTX0123

FTX024

FTX025

FTX026

FTX027

FTX028

FTX029

FTX030

FTX031

FTX032

FTX033

FTX034

FTX035

Special thanks to "Malform" from http://attacktix.wikia.com
for contributing Attacktix figure photography

239

Figures: Attacktix

FTX036

FTX037

FTX038

FTX039

FTX040

FTX041

FTX042

FTX043

FTX044

FTX045

FTX046

FTX047

FTX048

FTX049

FTX050

FTX051

FTX052

FTX053

FTX054

FTX055

FTX056

FTX057

FTX058

FTX059

*Special thanks to "Malform" from http://attacktix.wikia.com
for contributing Attacktix figure photography*

FTX060

FTX061

FTX062

FTX063

FTX064

FTX065

FTX066

FTX067

FTX068

FTX069

FTX070

FTX071

FTX072

FTX073

FTX074

FTX075

FTX076

FTX077

FTX078

FTX079

FTX080

*Special thanks to "Malform" from http://attacktix.wikia.com
for contributing Attacktix figure photography*

241

FTX081

FTX082

FTX083

FTX084

FTX085

FTX086

FTX087

FTX088

FTX089

FTX090

FTX091

FTX092

FTX093

FTX094

FTX095

FTX096

FTX097

FTX098

FTX099

FTX100

FTX101

FTX102

FTX103

*Special thanks to "Malform" from http://attacktix.wikia.com
for contributing Attacktix figure photography*

FTX104

FTX105

FTX106

FTX107

FTX108

FTX109

FTX110

FTX111

FTX112

FTX113

FTX114

FTX115

FTX116

FTX117

FTX118

FTX119

FTX120

FTX121

FTX122

FTX123

FTX124

Special thanks to "Malform" from http://attacktix.wikia.com for contributing Attacktix figure photography

FTX125

FTX126

FTX127

FTX128

FTX129

FTX130

FTX131

FTX132

FTX133

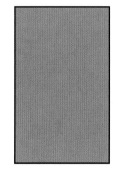

FTX134

FTX135

FTX136

FTX137

FTX138

FTX139

FTX140

Special thanks to "Malform" from http://attacktix.wikia.com
for contributing Attacktix figure photography

244

__ Neimodian Guard, Separatist #14 [FTX014] 5.00
__ Padme Amidala, Republic #06 .....9.00
__ Plo Koon, Jedi #07 .....15.00
__ Super Battle Droid, Droid Army #02 .....12.00
__ V-Wing Pilot, Separatist #10 .....7.00
__ Wookiee Commando, Wookiee #09 .....9.00
__ Wookiee Scout, Wookiee #03 .....5.00

Series 1.
__ Agen Kolar, Jedi #23 [FTX015] 15.00
__ Anakin Skywalker, Jedi #26 [FTX016] 15.00
__ Bail Organa, Republic #08 [FTX017] 10.00
__ Battle Droid, Droid Army #01 [FTX018] 5.00
__ Chewbacca, Wookiee #22 [FTX019] 8.00
__ Clone Commander, Separatist #34 starter set [FTX020] 15.00
__ Clone Lieutenant, Separatist #12 [FTX021] 12.00
__ Clone Sergeant, Republic #35 Battle Case exclusive [FTX022] 15.00
__ Clone Trooper, Republic #04 [FTX023] 5.00
__ Clone Trooper, Separatist #05 [FTX024] 5.00
__ Commander Bly, Republic #15 [FTX025] 9.00
__ Commander Gree, Republic #21 [FTX026] 15.00
__ Count Dooku, Sith #11 [FTX027] 20.00
__ Darth Vader #32 starter set [FTX028] 25.00
__ Darth Vader, Sith #16 [FTX029] 20.00
__ Emperor, Sith #24 [FTX030] 20.00
__ General Grievous, Droid Army #28 [FTX031] ..25.00
__ Grievous Bodyguard, Droid #13 [FTX032] 10.00
__ Ki Adi Mundi, Jedi #18 [FTX033] 19.00
__ Mace Windu, Jedi #19 [FTX034] 15.00
__ Neimodian Guard, Separatist #14 [FTX035] 5.00
__ Nute Gunray, Separatist #25 [FTX036] 10.00
__ Obi Wan Kenobi, Jedi #31 starter set [FTX037] 15.00
__ Obi-Wan Kenobi, Jedi #27 [FTX038] 10.00
__ Padme Amidala, Republic #06 [FTX039] 9.00
__ Palpatine, Separatist #17 [FTX040] 25.00
__ Plo Koon, Jedi #07 [FTX041] 15.00
__ Shaak Ti, Jedi #20 [FTX042] 30.00
__ Super Battle Droid, Droid Army #02 [FTX043] 12.00
__ Tarfful, Wookiee #29 [FTX044] 12.00
__ V-Wing Pilot, Separatist #10 [FTX045] 7.00
__ Wookiee Commando, Republic #33 starter set [FTX046] 10.00
__ Wookiee Commando, Wookiee #09 [FTX047] ..9.00
__ Wookiee Scout, Wookiee #03 [FTX048] 5.00
__ Yoda, Jedi #30 [FTX049] 50.00

Series 2.
__ ARC Pilot #05 [FTX050] 3.00
__ Battle Droid Commander #12 [FTX051] 7.00
__ Boba Fett #30 [FTX052] 13.00
__ Bossk #13 [FTX053] 4.00
__ Chewbacca #23 [FTX054] 5.00
__ Clone Captain #09 [FTX055] 5.00
__ Clone Commander #08 [FTX056] 12.00
__ Clone Trooper #03 [FTX057] 3.00
__ Darth Maul #26 [FTX058] 35.00
__ Darth Sidious #25 [FTX059] 13.00
__ Darth Vader #17 [FTX060] 15.00
__ Destroyer Droid #19 [FTX061] 20.00
__ General Grievous #24 [FTX062] 30.00
__ Grievous Bodyguard #06 [FTX063] 8.00
__ Han Solo #28 [FTX064] 5.00
__ Jango Fett #15 [FTX065] 20.00
__ Jedi Knight #01 [FTX066] 6.00
__ Kit Fisto #27 [FTX067] 20.00
__ Luke Skywalker #29 [FTX068] 5.00
__ Mace Windu #16 [FTX069] 20.00
__ Medic Droid #20 [FTX070] 15.00
__ Neimoidian Captain #10 [FTX071] 3.00
__ Obi-Wan Kenobi #18 [FTX072] 18.00
__ Princess Leia #14 [FTX073] 4.00
__ R2-D2 #21 [FTX074] 25.00
__ Royal Guard #07 [FTX075] 12.00
__ Scout Trooper #04 [FTX076] 3.00
__ Tion Medon #22 [FTX077] 4.00
__ Utapau Warrior #02 [FTX078] 6.00
__ Wookiee Captain #11 [FTX079] 5.00

Series 3.
__ Biggs Darklighter #26 [FTX080] 4.00
__ Boba Fett #18 .....14.00
__ Bossk #07 [FTX081] 4.00
__ C-3PO #25 [FTX082] 15.00
__ Captain Antilles #12 [FTX083] 5.00
__ Chewbacca #15 [FTX084] 6.00
__ Darth Vader #23 [FTX085] 12.99
__ Death Star Gunner #08 [FTX086] 3.00
__ Greedo #11 [FTX087] 5.00
__ Hammerhead #16 [FTX088] 20.00
__ Han Solo #22 [FTX089] 10.00
__ Han Solo as Stormtrooper #29 [FTX090] 5.00
__ Heavy Stormtrooper #17 [FTX091] 4.00
__ Imperial Officer #09 [FTX092] 3.00
__ Jawa #10 [FTX093] 5.00
__ Jawa Warlord #24 [FTX094] 13.00
__ Luke as Stormtrooper #28 [FTX095] 6.00
__ Luke Skywalker #21 [FTX096] 9.00
__ Obi-Wan Kenobi #20 [FTX097] 12.00
__ Princess Leia #14 [FTX098] 5.00
__ R2-Q5 #30 [FTX099] 15.00
__ Rebel Trooper #04 [FTX100] 4.00
__ Sandtrooper #06 [FTX101] 5.00
__ Stormtrooper #01 [FTX102] 4.00
__ TIE Pilot #02 [FTX103] 4.00
__ Tusken Raider #03 [FTX104] 4.00
__ Tusken Sniper #13 [FTX105] 7.00
__ Tusken Warlord #19 [FTX106] 12.00
__ Wedge #27 [FTX107] 3.00
__ X-Wing Pilot #05 [FTX108] 4.00

Series 4.
__ Admiral Ackbar #14 [FTX109] 5.00
__ AT-ST Driver #06 [FTX110] 3.00
__ Biker Scout #01 [FTX111] 4.00
__ Boba Fett #21 starter set [FTX112] 7.00
__ Boba Fett with flight #10 [FTX113] 15.00
__ Chewbacca #19 starter set [FTX114] 7.00
__ Chief Chirpa #17 [FTX115] 9.00
__ Clone Pilot #24 .....7.00
__ Darth Vader #11 [FTX116] 13.00
__ Endor Scout #02 [FTX117] 3.00
__ Grand Moff Tarkin #16 [FTX118] 6.00
__ Greedo #22 starter set [FTX119] 7.00
__ Han Solo #12 [FTX120] 8.00
__ Han Solo #20 starter set [FTX121] 7.00
__ IG-88 #15 [FTX122] 15.00
__ Imperial Officer #08 [FTX123] 4.00
__ Logray #07 [FTX124] 12.99
__ Luke Skywalker #13 [FTX125] 9.00
__ Princess Leia #18 [FTX126] 18.00
__ Royal Guard #05 [FTX127] 3.00
__ Sandtrooper #09 [FTX128] 6.00
__ Stormtrooper #04 [FTX129] 4.00
__ Wicket #03 [FTX130] 6.00

Series 5.
__ AT-AT Driver #05 .....3.00
__ Battle Droid #04 .....3.00
__ Dengar #11 .....3.00
__ Emperor #17 .....3.00
__ Gamorrean Guard #06 .....3.00
__ Hoth Soldier #01 .....3.00
__ Imperial Cadet #03 .....3.00
__ Kit Fisto #18 .....3.00
__ Lando Calrissian #09 .....3.00
__ Luke Skywalker #08 .....3.00
__ Plo Koon #14 .....3.00
__ Ponda Baba #07 .....3.00
__ Qui-Gon Jinn #15 .....3.00
__ R5-D4 #16 .....3.00
__ Red Leader #13 .....3.00
__ Snowtrooper #02 .....3.00
__ Yoda #10 .....3.00
__ Zuckuss #12 .....3.00

Star Wars vs. Transformers.
__ AT-RT SVT2 .....10.00
__ Darth Vader SVT4 .....3.00
__ Luke Skywalker SVT3 .....3.00

Starter sets.
__ Series 1 with starter CD Wookiee Commando, Obi-Wan Kenobi, Clone Commander, Darth Vader, secret figure [FTX131] 35.00
__ Series 2 General Grievous, Super Battle Droid, Clone Captain, Obi-Wan Kenobi, secret figure [FTX132] 40.00
__ Series 2 Wookiee Warrior, Mace Windu, Clone Captain, Anakin Skywalker, secret figure [FTX133] 15.00
__ Series 3 Luke Skywalker, Rebel Trooper, Imperial Officer, Darth Vader, secret figure [FTX134] ...25.00
__ Series 4 Han Solo, Chewbacca, Boba Fett, Greedo [FTX135] 25.00
__ Series 4 Han Solo, Chewbacca, Boba Fett, Greedo, bonus extra battle figure [FTX136] 35.00
__ Series 5 Han Solo (Hoth), Chewbacca, Darth Vader, Heavy Stormtrooper 150.00

Storage case.
__ With exclusive Clone Sergeant [FTX137] 25.00

Hasbro, Germany
Booster packs.
__ Series 4. [FTX138] 30.00

Hasbro, UK
Starter sets.
__ Series 4 Han Solo, Chewbacca, Boba Fett, Greedo [FTX139] 35.00
__ Series 5 Han Solo (Hoth), Chewbacca, Darth Vader, Heavy Stormtrooper [FTX140] 120.00

Figures: Bend-Ems

JusToys
__ Admiral Ackbar, 20 back, Lando card [TYB001] 12.00
__ Admiral Ackbar, 20 back, Mon Cal card, square bubble [TYB002] 8.00
__ Admiral Ackbar, 20 back, trench card, square bubble [TYB003] 10.00
__ Bib Fortuna, 20 back, Bib card, square bubble [TYB004] 15.00
__ Boba Fett, 20 back, Luke / Leia card, square bubble [TYB005] 35.00
__ C-3PO, 08 back 14.00
__ C-3PO, 08 back, C-3PO card [TYB006] 11.00
__ C-3PO, 08 back, C-3PO card, micro-name, age warning on card corner [TYB007] 13.00
__ C-3PO, 08 back, C-3PO card, micro-name, age warning under bubble [TYB008] 14.00
__ C-3PO, 12 back, C-3PO card, square bubble [TYB009] 7.00
__ Chewbacca, 08 back [TYB010] 16.00
__ Chewbacca, 08 back, Chewbacca card [TYB011] 13.00
__ Chewbacca, 08 back, Chewbacca card, micro-name, age warning on card corner [TYB012] 15.00
__ Chewbacca, 08 back, Chewbacca card, micro-name, age warning under bubble [TYB013] ...16.00
__ Chewbacca, 12 back, galaxy card, square bubble [TYB014] 7.00
__ Emperor's Royal Guard, 20 back, ERG card [TYB015] 9.00
__ Emperor's Royal Guard, 20 back, Luke / Leia card, square bubble [TYB016] 11.00
__ Gamorrean Guard, 20 back, Gamorrean card, square bubble [TYB017] 18.00
__ Han Solo, 08 back, Han card [TYB018] 11.00
__ Han Solo, 08 back, Han card with transitional "trading card" sticker [TYB019] 18.00
__ Han Solo, 12 back, galaxy card [TYB020] 14.00
__ Han Solo, 12 back, Gamorrean card [TYB021] 16.00
__ Han Solo, 12 back, Han card, square bubble [TYB022] 12.00
__ Han Solo, 20 back, Chewbacca card, large head [TYB023] 14.00
__ Han Solo, 20 back, DSII card, square bubble, large head [TYB024] 14.00
__ Lando Calrissian, 20 back, DSII card, square bubble [TYB025] 9.00
__ Lord Darth Vader, 08 back [TYB026] 14.00
__ Lord Darth Vader, 08 back, Vader card [TYB027] 11.00
__ Lord Darth Vader, 08 back, Vader card, micro-name [TYB028] 14.00
__ Lord Darth Vader, 08 back, Vader card, micro-name, age warning in corner 13.00

TYB001

TYB002

TYB003

TYB004

TYB005

TYB006

TYB007

TYB008

TYB009

TYB010

TYB011

TYB012

TYB013

TYB014

TYB015

TYB016

TYB017

TYB018

TYB019

TYB020

TYB021

TYB022

TYB023

TYB024

TYB025

TYB026

TYB027

TYB028

TYB029

TYB030

TYB031

TYB032

TYB033

TYB034

TYB035

TYB036

TYB037

TYB038

TYB039

TYB040

TYB041

TYB042

TYB043

TYB044

TYB045

TYB046

TYB047

TYB048

TYB049

TYB050

TYB051

TYB052

TYB053

TYB054

TYB055

TYB056

TYB057

TYB058

TYB059

TYB060

TYB061

TYB062

TYB063

TYB064

TYB065

TYB066

TYB067

TYB068

TYB069

TYB070

TYB071

TYB072

TYB073

TYB074

TYB075

TYB076

TYB077

TYB078

TYB079

FEB01

__ Lord Darth Vader, 12 back, Vader card, square bubble [TYB029]..8.00

__ Luke Skywalker X-Wing Pilot, 12 back, DSII card, square bubble..26.00

__ Luke Skywalker X-Wing Pilot, 20 back, pilot card, square bubble [TYB030]........................24.00

__ Luke Skywalker, 08 back [TYB031].................14.00

__ Luke Skywalker, 08 back, Luke card..............11.00

__ Luke Skywalker, 08 back, Luke card, micro-name [TYB032]..14.00

__ Luke Skywalker, 08 back, Luke card, micro-name, age warning in corner...........................12.00

__ Luke Skywalker, 12 bk, Luke card [TYB033]..10.00

__ Obi-Wan Kenobi, 08 back [TYB034]...............14.00

__ Obi-Wan Kenobi, 08 back, Obi-Wan card [TYB035]...11.00

__ Obi-Wan Kenobi, 12 back, Obi-Wan card, square bubble [TYB036]..9.00

__ Princess Leia, 08 back [TYB037]....................15.00

__ Princess Leia, 08 back, Leia card [TYB038]...12.00

__ Princess Leia, 08 back, Leia card, micro-name [TYB039]..14.00

__ Princess Leia, 12 back, galaxy card, square bubble..12.00

__ Princess Leia, 20 back, galaxy card, square bubble [TYB040]...10.00

__ Princess Leia, 20 back, trench battle card, square bubble..12.00

__ R2-D2, 08 back [TYB041]................................15.00

__ R2-D2, 08 back, R2-D2 card 12.00

__ R2-D2, 12 back, R2-D2 card [TYB042] 10.00

__ R2-D2, 20 back, galaxy card, square bubble [TYB043]..8.00

__ Stormtrooper, 08 back [TYB044]....................15.00

__ Stormtrooper, 08 back, Stormtrooper card [TYB045]...12.00

__ Stormtrooper, 08 back, Stormtrooper card, micro-name [TYB046] 14.00

__ Stormtrooper, 08 back, Stormtrooper card, micro-name, age warning in corner [TYB047]...........12.00

__ Stormtrooper, 20 back, Bib card, square bubble [TYB048]...14.00

__ The Emperor, 12 back, emperor card.............12.00

__ The Emperor, 12 back, galaxy card, square bubble [TYB049]...14.00

__ The Emperor, 12 back, trench battle card [TYB050]...14.00

__ The Emperor, 12 back, trench battle card, square bubble..12.00

__ Tusken Raider, 20 back, galaxy card, square bubble [TYB051] 15.00

__ Tusken Raider, 20 back, pilot card [TYB052]...13.00

__ Tusken Raider, 20 back, tusken card [TYB053]...15.00

__ Wicket an Ewok, 8 back, galaxy card [TYB054]...35.00

__ Wicket the Ewok, 12 back, galaxy card [TYB055]...14.00

__ Wicket the Ewok, 20 back, Ewok card, square bubble [TYB056]..12.00

__ Yoda the Jedi Master, 08 back [TYB057]...14.00

__ Yoda the Jedi Master, 08 back, Yoda card [TYB057]...9.00

__ Yoda the Jedi Master, 08 back, Yoda card, micro-name [TYB058]......................................12.00

__ Yoda the Jedi Master, 20 back, DSII card, square bubble..12.00

10-piece gift set.

__ Ackbar, Bib Fortuna, Chewbacca, Darth Vader, Royal Guard, Han, Leia, Luke, R2-D2, Stormtrooper, brass collectors coin, with bonus trading card [TYB059]....................................45.00

4-piece gift sets.

__ C-3PO, Darth Vader, R2-D2, Stormtrooper [TYB060]...25.00

__ C-3PO, Darth Vader, R2-D2, Stormtrooper, with bonus trading card [TYB061]........................25.00

__ C-3PO, Han, Leia, Obi-Wan, with bonus trading card [TYB062]...25.00

__ Chewbacca, Stormtrooper, Wicket, Yoda.......25.00

__ Chewbacca, Stormtrooper, Wicket, Yoda, with bonus trading card [TYB063]......................25.00

__ Darth Vader, Emperor, Luke Skywalker, R2-D2, with bonus trading card [TYB064].................25.00

4-piece movie gift sets.

__ A New Hope Chewbacca, Luke Skywalker, R2-D2, Tusken Raider, brass collectors coin, with bonus trading cards [TYB065].............................35.00

__ Empire Strikes back brass collectors coin, with bonus trading cards................................35.00

__ Return of the Jedi Admiral Ackbar, Bib Fortuna, Boba Fett, Wicket, brass collectors coin, with bonus trading cards [TYB066].......................35.00

6-piece gift sets.

__ Admiral Ackbar, Chewbacca, Darth Vader, Emperor's Royal Guard, Lando Calrissian, Stormtrooper with bonus trading cards [TYB067].......................35.00

8-piece gift sets.

__ Darth Vader, Luke, C-3PO, Emperor, Stormtrooper, R2-D2, Leia, Wicket [TYB068].......................35.00

__ Darth Vader, Luke, C-3PO, R2-D2, Obi-Wan, Stormtrooper, Leia, Wicket............................35.00

__ Darth Vader, Luke, C-3PO, Yoda, Stormtrooper, R2-D2, Leia, Wicket......................................35.00

JusToys, Canada

No Bend-Ems logo, or trading card callout. International age symbol.

__ C-3PO, 12 back, Galaxy card.........................24.00

__ Chewbacca, 12 back, Galaxy card.................24.00

__ Han Solo, 12 back, Galaxy card....................24.00

__ Han Solo, 12 back, Galaxy card, square bubble [TYB069]...24.00

__ Lord Darth Vader, 12 back, Galaxy card........24.00

__ Luke Skywalker, 12 back, Galaxy card...........24.00

__ Princess Leia, 12 back, Galaxy card..............24.00

__ R2-D2, 12 back, Galaxy card 24.00

__ Stormtrooper, 12 back, Galaxy card..............24.00

__ The Emperor, 12 back, Galaxy card...............24.00

__ Wicket the Ewok, 12 back, Galaxy card.........24.00

__ Yoda the Jedi Master, 12 back, Galaxy card .24.00

JusToys, UK

No Bend-Ems logo, or trading card callout. CE and international age symbol.

__ Admiral Ackbar, 20 back, Galaxy card, square bubble..24.00

__ C-3PO, 20 back, Galaxy card........................24.00

__ Chewbacca, 20 back, Galaxy card.................24.00

__ Chewbacca, 20 back, Galaxy card, square bubble..24.00

__ Han Solo, 20 back, Galaxy card....................24.00

__ Han Solo, 20 back, Galaxy card, square bubble..24.00

__ Lord Darth Vader, 20 back, Galaxy card........24.00

__ Lord Darth Vader, 20 back, Galaxy card, square bubble..24.00

__ Luke Skywalker, 20 back, Galaxy card...........24.00

__ Luke Skywalker, 20 back, Galaxy card, square bubble..24.00

__ Obi-Wan Kenobi, 20 back, Galaxy card..........24.00

__ Princess Leia, 20 back, Galaxy card..............24.00

__ R2-D2, 20 back, Galaxy card, square bubble 24.00

__ Tusken Raider, 20 back, Galaxy card.............24.00

__ Tusken Raider, 20 back, Galaxy card, square bubble..24.00

__ Wicket the Ewok, 20 back, Galaxy card.........24.00

__ Yoda the Jedi Master, 20 back, Galaxy card .24.00

ZPF001

ZPF002

ZPF003

ZPF004

ZPF005

ZPF006

ZPF007

ZPF008

ZPF009

ZPF010

ZPF011

ZPF012

ZPF013

Figures: Bend'Ems

JusToys / GiGi, Italy

__ Assaltatore Imperiale 12 back, Galaxy card [TYB070] 25.00
__ C1-P8 12 back, Galaxy card [TYB071]...........25.00
__ Chewbacca 12 back, Galaxy card [TYB072] 25.00
__ D-3B0 12 back, Galaxy card [TYB073].............25.00
__ Ewok 12 back, Galaxy card [TYB074] 25.00
__ Han Solo 12 back, Galaxy card 25.00
__ Kenobi 12 back, Galaxy card [TYB075].........25.00
__ L'Imperatore 12 back, Galaxy card [TYB076] 25.00
__ Lord Darth Vader 12 back, Galaxy card 25.00
__ Luke Skywalker 12 back, Galaxy card [TYB077] 25.00
__ Principessa Leia Organa 12 back, Galaxy card [TYB078] 25.00
__ Yoda 12 back, Galaxy card [TYB079].............25.00

Figures: Epic Battles

Hasbro
Characters.
__ Anakin Skywalker................................10.00
__ Captain Rex..10.00
__ General Grievous 10.00
__ Obi-Wan Kenobi [FEB01].............................10.00

Vehicles.
__ AAT 10.00
__ Obi-Wan's Jedi Starfighter 10.00

Figures: Epic Force

Hasbro
__ Darth Maul [ZPF001].......................................15.00
__ Obi-Wan Kenobi [ZPF002].................................45.00
__ Qui-Gon Jinn [ZPF003] 15.00

Kenner
__ 3-Pack: Ben Kenobi, Chewbacca, Han Solo, exclusive to FAO Schwarz [ZPF004] 120.00
__ Ben Kenobi, exclusive to FAO Schwarz [ZPF005] 35.00
__ Boba Fett [ZPF006]......................................20.00
__ C-3PO [ZPF007] 12.00
__ Chewbacca, exclusive to FAO Schwarz [ZPF008] 35.00
__ Darth Vader [ZPF009] 20.00
__ Han Solo, exclusive to FAO Schwarz [ZPF010] 35.00
__ Luke Skywalker, Bespin fatigues [ZPF011] 12.00
__ Princess Leia [ZPF012] 12.00
__ Stormtrooper [ZPF013] 20.00

Figures: Force Battlers

Hasbro
Approx. 7" scale.
__ Anakin Skywalker, Lightsaber attack! [F1A001].......................................10.00
__ Chewbacca, Boulder-launching backpack [F1A002].......................................10.00

__ Chewbacca, Water firing blaster! [F1A003].......................................10.00
__ Clone Trooper, Quick-draw blasting action! [F1A004].......................................15.00
__ Darth Vader #2 [F1A005].......................................15.00
__ Darth Vader, Slashing attack! [F1A006].......................................10.00
__ Emperor Palpatine [F1A007].............................10.00
__ General Grievous, Ballistic buzz-disc [F1A008].......................................10.00
__ General Grievous, Multiple lightsaber attack! [F1A009].......................................10.00
__ Han Solo [F1A010].......................................10.00
__ Jango Fett, Clamping claw [F1A011]..............15.00
__ Luke Skywalker [F1A012] 10.00
__ Mace Windu, Firing Jedi gauntlet! [F1A013]...10.00
__ Obi-Wan Kenobi, Lightsaber attack! [F1A014].......................................10.00
__ Obi-Wan Kenobi, Slashing lightsaber attack [F1A015].......................................10.00
__ Yoda [F1A016].......................................10.00

Approx. 7" scale. Clone Wars.
__ Anakin Skywalker [F1A017] 15.00
__ Captain Rex [F1A018].......................................15.00
__ General Grievous [F1A019].......................................15.00

Hasbro, Canada
Approx. 7" scale, tri-language package.
__ Anakin Skywalker, Lightsaber attack!.............10.00
__ Darth Vader, Slashing attack! 10.00
__ General Grievous, Four-arm attack! 10.00
__ Obi-Wan Kenobi, Quick-draw attack!.............10.00

F1A001   F1A002   F1A003   F1A004   F1A005   F1A006   F1A007

F1A008   F1A009   F1A010   F1A011   F1A012   F1A013

F1A014   F1A015   F1A016   F1A017   F1A018   F1A019

Figures: Galactic Heroes

Hasbro

2004 2-packs. Blue logo with green oval.
__ 4-LOM and Bossk [P1A001] 10.00
__ C-3PO and Chewbacca [P1A002] 6.00
__ Dengar and Boba Fett [P1A003].....................12.00
__ Dengar and Boba Fett insert shows characters reversed [P1A004] 6.00
__ IG-88 and Zuckuss [P1A005].............................6.00
__ Jango Fett and Obi-Wan Kenobi [P1A006] 6.00
__ Jawa and Tusken Raider [P1A007]...................6.00
__ Jedi Luke Skywalker and Gamorrean Guard [P1A008] 12.00
__ Luke Skywalker and R2-D2 [P1A009]..............6.00
__ Obi-Wan Kenobi and Darth Vader [P1A010] 6.00
__ Padme Amidala and Anakin Skywalker [P1A011] 6.00
__ Princess Leia and Han Solo [P1A012] 6.00
__ Skiff Guard and Lando Calrission [P1A013] 6.00
__ Stormtroopers [P1A014] 6.00
__ Yoda and Clone Trooper [P1A015]...................6.00

2005 2-packs. Orange logo.
__ 4-LOM and Bossk [P1A016] 8.00
__ Anakin Skywalker and Count Dooku [P1A017] 6.00

__ C-3PO and Chewbacca [P1A018] 6.00
__ Chewbacca and Clone Trooper [P1A019] 6.00
__ Dark Side Anakin and Clone Trooper [P1A020]6.00
__ Darth Vader and Holographic Emperor Palpatine [P1A021] 8.00
__ Dengar and Boba Fett [P1A022] 6.00
__ Emperor Palpatine and Yoda [P1A023] 6.00
__ IG-88 and Zuckuss [P1A024] 8.00
__ Kit Fisto and Mace Windu [P1A025] 6.00
__ Luke Skywalker and Gamorrean Guard [P1A026] 6.00
__ Luke Skywalker and R2-D2 [P1A027]..............6.00
__ Obi-Wan Kenobi and Clone Trooper [P1A028].8.00
__ Obi-Wan Kenobi and Darth Vader [P1A029] 6.00
__ Obi-Wan Kenobi and General Grievous [P1A030] 6.00
__ Princess Leia and Han Solo [P1A031] 6.00
__ Super Battle Droid and R2-D2 [P1A032] 6.00
__ Tusken Raider and Jawa [P1A033]...................6.00
__ Yoda and Kashyyyk Trooper [P1A034].............8.00

2006 2-packs. Blue logo with orange oval.
__ Battle Droid and Clone Trooper [P1A035] 8.00
__ Emperor Palpatine and Shock Trooper [P1A036] 6.00
__ Greedo and Han Solo [P1A037].......................6.00
__ IG-88 and Zuckuss orange Star Wars on insert [P1A038] 6.00

__ Luke Skywalker (Hoth) and Han Solo (Hoth) [P1A039] 10.00
__ Luke Skywalker and Han Solo in Stormtrooper disguises painted helmet brow - Han only [P1A040] 6.00
__ Luke Skywalker and Han Solo in Stormtrooper disguises painted helmet brows [P1A041] 6.00
__ Luke Skywalker and Han Solo in Stormtrooper disguises unpainted helmet brows [P1A042] ...6.00
__ Luke Skywalker and Han Solo in Stormtrooper disguises unpainted helmet brows, warning over "R" on cardback [P1A043]..................................6.00
__ Obi-Wan Kenobi and Darth Maul [P1A044] 6.00
__ Sandtrooper and Obi-Wan painted helmet brow, sticker on bottom covers safety certification [P1A045] 6.00
__ Sandtrooper and Obi-Wan unpainted helmet brow [P1A046] 6.00
__ Speederbike with Luke Skywalker [P1A047] 8.00
__ Speederbike with Scout Trooper [P1A048] 8.00
__ Wedge and TIE Pilot [P1A049].........................6.00
__ Wedge and TIE Pilot warning over "R" on cardback [P1A050]..6.00
__ Yoda and Kashyyyk Trooper [P1A051].............6.00

2007 2-packs. White logo.
__ Anakin Skywalker and Clone Trooper [P1A052] 10.00

 P1A001
 P1A002
 P1A003
 P1A004
 P1A005
 P1A006
 P1A007
 P1A008
 P1A009
 P1A010
 P1A011
 P1A012
 P1A013
 P1A014
 P1A015
 P1A016

P1A017

P1A018

P1A019

P1A020

P1A021

P1A022

P1A023

P1A024

P1A025

P1A026

P1A027

P1A028

P1A029

P1A030

P1A031

P1A032

P1A033

P1A034

P1A035

P1A036

P1A037

P1A038

P1A039

P1A040

P1A040 - P1A042 helmet paint detail view

P1A041

P1A042

P1A043

P1A044

P1A045

P1A046

P1A047

P1A048

P1A049

P1A050

P1A051

P1A052

P1A053

P1A054

P1A055

P1A056

P1A057

P1A058

P1A059

P1A060

P1A061

P1A062

P1A063

P1A064

P1A065

P1A066

P1A067

P1A068

P1A069

P1A070

P1A071

P1A072

P1A073

P1A074

P1A075

P1A076

P1A077

P1A078

P1A079

P1A080

P1A081

P1A082

P1A083

P1A084

P1A085

P1A086

P1A087

P1A088

P1A089

P1A090

P1A091

P1A092

P1A093

P1A094

P1A095

P1A096

P1A097

P1A098

P1A099

P1A100

P1A101

P1A102

P1A103

P1A104

P1A105

P1A106

P1A107

P1A108

P1A109

P1A110

P1A111

P1A112

P1A113

P1A114

P1A115

P1A116

P1A117

P1A118

P1A119

P1A120

P1A121

P1A122

P1A123

P1A124

P1A125

P1A126

P1A127

P1A128

P1A129

P1A130

P1A131

P1A132

P1A133

P1A134

P1A135

P1A136

P1A137

P1A138

P1A139

P1A140

P1A141

P1A142

P1A143

P1A144

P1A145

P1A146

P1A147

P1A148

P1A149

P1A150

__ Rebel Trooper and Snow Trooper [P1A073].....6.00
__ Royal Guard and Imperial Gunner [P1A074].....6.00
__ Saesee Tiin and Agen Kolar [P1A075]..............6.00
__ Sandtrooper and Obi-Wan Kenobi [P1A076]....6.00
__ Scout Trooper and Speeder Bike [P1A077]......6.00
__ Snow Trooper and Rebel Trooper insert shows characters reversed, sticker on bottom covers safety certifications [P1A078] 6.00
__ Tarfful and Commander Gree [P1A079] 6.00
__ Wedge and TIE Pilot [P1A080]........................6.00
__ Weequay and Barada [P1A081].......................6.00

2008 2-packs. Blue logo helmet shaped.
__ Anakin Skywalker and Clone Trooper [P1A082]........6.00
__ Chewbacca and C-3PO [P1A083] 6.00
__ Jango Fett and Obi-Wan Kenobi [P1A084] 6.00
__ Jar Jar Binks and Destroyer Droid [P1A085] ...6.00
__ Kit Fisto and General Grievous [P1A086] 6.00
__ Luke Skywalker and Darth Vader [P1A087]......6.00
__ Luke Skywalker and R2-D2 [P1A088].............6.00
__ Obi-Wan Kenobi and Clone Trooper [P1A089].6.00
__ Plo Koon and Captain Jag [P1A090] 6.00
__ Princess Leia and Darth Vader 6.00
__ Princess Leia in Boushh Disguise and Han Solo [P1A091] 6.00
__ R2-D2 and Super Battle Droid [P1A092] 6.00
__ Shaak Ti and Magna Guard [P1A093] 6.00

2008 2-packs. Blue logo with stripe.
__ Ahsoka Tano and Captain Rex [P1A094] 6.00
__ Anakin Skywalker and STAP [P1A095]..............6.00
__ Asajj Ventress and Count Dooku [P1A096] 6.00
__ Clone Trooper / Mace Windu [P1A097]..........10.00
__ Clone Trooper and Dwarf Spider Droid [P1A098] 10.00
__ Duros / Garindan [P1A099]..........................10.00
__ Obi-Wan Kenobi and Clone Commander Cody [P1A100] 6.00
__ Padme Amidala / Jar Jar Binks [P1A101].......10.00
__ Padme Amidala and Clone Trooper [P1A102]..6.00
__ Plo Koon and Captain Jag [P1A103] 6.00
__ Ponda Baba and Snaggletooth [P1A104].......10.00
__ R2-D2 with serving tray and Princess Leia, Jabba's slave [P1A105] 6.00

__ Anakin Skywalker and Count Dooku [P1A053].6.00
__ AT-AT Commander and AT-AT Driver [P1A054] 6.00
__ Chewbacca and Clone Trooper [P1A055] 6.00
__ Chewbacca and Disassembled C-3PO sticker on bottom covers safety certification [P1A056].....6.00
__ Commander Bly and Aayla Secura [P1A057] ...6.00
__ Darth Maul and Sith Speeder [P1A058]..........10.00
__ Death Star Trooper and Imperial Officer [P1A059] 6.00
__ Duros and Garindan [P1A060] 6.00
__ Figrin D'an and Hammerhead [P1A061] 6.00
__ Grand Moff Tarkin and Imperial Officer [P1A062] 6.00
__ Han Solo and Logray 6.00

__ Ki-Adi-Mundi and Comm. Bacara [P1A063].....6.00
__ Luke Skywalker and Darth Vader [P1A064]......6.00
__ Luke Skywalker and Han Solo in Stormtrooper disguises painted helmet brows 6.00
__ Luke Skywalker and Lando Calrissian [P1A065]........6.00
__ Luke Skywalker with Yoda and Spirit of Obi-Wan Kenobi [P1A066] 6.00
__ Obi-Wan Kenobi and Darth Maul [P1A067]......6.00
__ Obi-Wan Kenobi and Durge [P1A068]............10.00
__ Ponda Baba and Snaggletooth [P1A069].........6.00
__ Princess Leia and Darth Vader sticker on bottom covers safety certification [P1A070] 6.00
__ Princess Leia and Rebel Commando [P1A071]6.00
__ Princess Leia in Boushh Disguise and Han Solo [P1A072] 6.00

P1A151

P1A152

P1A153

P1A154

__ Super Battle Droid and Luminara Unduli [P1A106] 10.00

2009 2-packs. Red logo.
__ Ahsoka Tano and R3-S6 (Goldie) [P1A107] 10.00
__ Anakin Skywalker and ARF Trooper

[P1A108] 10.00
__ Anakin Skywalker and Clone Trooper [P1A109] 6.00
__ Chewbacca, Death Star Droid and Mouse Droid [P1A110] 12.00
__ Clone Gunner and Rocket Battle Droid

[P1A111] 10.00
__ Clone Trooper and Dwarf Spider Droid [P1A112] 12.00
__ Clone Trooper and Mace Windu [P1A113] 6.00
__ Han Solo and Logray [P1A114] 10.00
__ IG-86 and Clone Commander Thire [P1A115] 10.00

P1A155

P1A156

P1A157

P1A158

P1A159

P1A160

P1A161

P1A162

P1A163

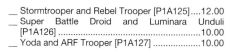

P1A164

__ Kit Fisto and General Grievous [P1A116] 10.00
__ Kit Fisto and General Grievous translucent lightsabers [P1A117].......................................10.00
__ Luke Skywalker and Lando Calrissian [P1A118] 6.00
__ Nein Nunb and Admiral Ackbar [P1A119].......14.00

__ Obi-Wan Kenobi and Commander Fil [P1A120] 10.00
__ Padme Amidala and Jar Jar Binks [P1A121]..10.00
__ Princess Leia and Darth Vader [P1A122]..........6.00
__ R2-D2 and two Jawas [P1A123]....................12.00
__ Stormtrooper and Darth Vader [P1A124]........10.00

__ Stormtrooper and Rebel Trooper [P1A125]....12.00
__ Super Battle Droid and Luminara Unduli [P1A126] 10.00
__ Yoda and ARF Trooper [P1A127] 10.00

2010 2-packs. Blue logo.

P1A165

P1A166

P1A167

P1A168

P1A169

P1A170

P1A171

P1A172

P1A173

P1A174

__ Ahsoka and Anakin Skywalker [P1A128]........10.00
__ Anakin Skywalker and ARF Trooper [P1A129] 10.00
__ Anakin Skywalker and Clone Trooper [P1A130] 10.00
__ Anakin Skywalker and STAP [P1A131]...........10.00

__ Aqua Battle Droid and Senate Commando [P1A132] 10.00
__ Barriss Offee and Quinlan Voss [P1A133] 10.00
__ Cad Bane and Aurra Sing [P1A134] 10.00
__ Commando Droid and Count Dooku [P1A135] 10.00

__ Emperor Palpatine and Darth Vader [P1A136] 10.00
__ Kit Fisto and General Grievous [P1A137] 10.00
__ Luke Skywalker and Darth Vader [P1A138]....10.00
__ Luke Skywalker and Speeder bike [P1A139]..10.00

P1A175

P1A176

P1A177

P1A178

P1A179

P1A180

P1A181

P1A182

P1A183

P1A184

__ Mandalorian Warrior and Pre Vizsla [P1A140] 10.00
__ Obi-Wan Kenobi and Commander Fil [P1A141] 10.00
__ Obi-Wan Kenobi and Darth Maul [P1A142]....10.00
__ Padme Amidala and Senate Security Clone Trooper [P1A143] 10.00
__ Republic Commando Fixer and Republic Commando Boss [P1A144] 10.00
__ Sergeant Bric and Clone Trooper Echo [P1A145] 10.00
__ Super Battle Droid and Clone Trooper Bomb Squad [P1A146] 10.00

3-packs stocking stuffers.
__ Boba Fett, Darth Vader, Stormtrooper [P1A147] 10.00
__ Han Solo, C-3PO, Chewbacca [P1A148] 10.00
__ Luke Skywalker, Yoda, R2-D2 [P1A149] 10.00
__ Shock Trooper, Anakin Skywalker, Obi-Wan Kenobi [P1A150] 10.00

Cinema scenes.
__ Assault on the Death Star [P1A151] 30.00
__ Battle for Naboo [P1A152].............................25.00

__ Battle on Mustafar, exclusive to Target [P1A153] 25.00
__ Cantina Band, exclusive to Walmart [P1A154] 25.00
__ Cantina Encounter, exclusive to Walmart [P1A155] 25.00
__ EPII: Battle of Geonosis [P1A156] 25.00
__ EPIII: Jedi Vs. Sith [P1A157] 25.00
__ EPIV: Death Star Escape [P1A158].................25.00
__ EPV: Vader's Bounty Hunters [P1A159] 25.00
__ Escape from Mos Eisley [P1A160]..................25.00
__ Geonosis Battle Arena [P1A161].....................25.00
__ Jabba's Palace, exclusive to Target [P1A162] 30.00
__ Speeder Bike Chase, exclusive to Target [P1A163] 25.00
__ The Battle of Hoth, exclusive to Toys R Us [P1A164] 25.00

Cinema scenes. Blue and white packaging.
__ Anakin Skywalker's Jedi Starfighter [P1A165]30.00
__ Battle on Kashyyyk, exclusive to Toys R Us [P1A166] 30.00
__ Darth Vader's TIE Fighter [P1A167]................30.00
__ Escape from Mos Eisley 30.00

__ Geonosis Arena Battle #2...............................30.00
__ Hoth Snowspeeder Assault [P1A168].............30.00
__ Jabba's Palace [P1A169]................................30.00
__ Jabba's Skiff [P1A170] 30.00
__ Jedi Starfighter [P1A171] 30.00
__ Rancor Pit, exclusive to Toys R Us [P1A172].30.00
__ X-Wing Dagobah Landing [P1A173]...............30.00

Cinema scenes. Red and white packaging.
__ Assault on Ryloth [P1A174] 30.00
__ Attack on the Invisible Hand [P1A175] 30.00
__ Endor Attack [P1A176] 30.00
__ Escape from Kamino [P1A177].......................30.00
__ Hoth Snowspeeder Assault [P1A178].............30.00
__ Jabba's Sail Barge [P1A179] 30.00
__ Kamino Showdown, exclusive to Toys R Us [P1A180] 30.00
__ Millennium Falcon, Return of the Jedi [P1A181] 40.00
__ Obi-Wan Kenobi's Jedi Starfighter [P1A182] .30.00
__ Purchase of the Droids, exclusive to Toys R Us [P1A183] 30.00
__ Shadow Squadron Y-Wing [P1A184] 30.00
__ Slave I and Boba Fett [P1A185].....................30.00

P1A185

P1A186

P1A187

P1A188

P1A189

P1A190

P1A191

P1A192

P1A193

P1A194

P1A195

P1A196

P1A197

P1A198

P1A199

P1A200

P1A201

P1A202

P1A203

P1A204

P1A205

P1A206

P1A207

P1A208

P1A209

P1A210

P1A211

P1A212

P1A213

P1A214

P1A215

P1A216

P1A217

P1A218

P1A219

P1A220

P1A221

P1A222

Individually packaged 2007.
__ Battle Droid [P1A186] 5.00
__ Bossk [P1A187] 5.00
__ C-3PO [P1A188] 5.00
__ Chewbacca [P1A189] 5.00
__ Clone Trooper green (sergeant) [P1A190] 5.00
__ Darth Vader [P1A191] 5.00
__ Han Solo Hoth [P1A192] 5.00
__ Luke Skywalker [P1A193] 5.00

Individually packaged 2008.
__ Bossk [P1A194] 5.00
__ C-3PO [P1A195] 5.00
__ Chewbacca [P1A196] 5.00
__ Darth Vader [P1A197] 5.00
__ Han Solo [P1A198] 5.00
__ Luke Skywalker [P1A199] 5.00

Individually packaged 2009.
__ Anakin Skywalker [P1A200] 5.00
__ Battle Droid [P1A201] 5.00
__ Clone Trooper [P1A202] 5.00
__ Darth Maul [P1A203] 5.00
__ Darth Vader [P1A204] 5.00
__ Destroyer Droid [P1A205] 5.00
__ General Grievous [P1A206] 5.00
__ Obi-Wan Kenobi [P1A207] 5.00
__ R2-D2 [P1A208] 5.00

Individually packaged.
__ Scout Trooper, exclusive to Comicon [P1A209] 10.00

Vehicles.
__ 2-in-One Landspeeder Desert Crawler [P1A210] 40.00

__ 2-in-One X-Wing Racer [P1A211]..................40.00
__ AT-AT [P1A212] 50.00
__ AT-ST [P1A213] 175.00
__ Millennium Falcon [P1A214] 125.00
__ Millennium Falcon [P1A215] 150.00
__ X-Wing [P1A216].......................................55.00

Hasbro, UK
Individual figures sold blind-packed with stat card and puzzle piece. Stat card is in Spanish and Italian.
__ Anakin Skywalker.......................................5.00
__ Battle Droid (Maroon)...............................5.00
__ Boba Fett 5.00
__ C-3PO..5.00
__ Chewbacca...5.00
__ Count Dooku...5.00
__ Darth Maul 5.00
__ Darth Vader 5.00
__ Durge...5.00
__ General Grievous 5.00
__ Han Solo 5.00
__ Jango Fett..5.00
__ Jar Jar Binks 5.00
__ Luke Skywalker 5.00
__ Luke Skywalker Hoth Gear 5.00
__ Obi-Wan Kenobi 5.00
__ Padme Amidala..5.00
__ Qui-Gon Jinn...5.00
__ R2-D2..5.00
__ Stormtrooper 5.00
__ Super Battle Droid 5.00
__ The Emperor 5.00
__ Utapau Clone Trooper 5.00
__ Yoda 5.00

Vehicles.
__ AT-AT..50.00

Playskool
__ Arena Adventure [P1A217]...........................35.00
__ Duel with Darth Maul [P1A218].....................35.00
__ Fast Through the Forest 0100 original Luke text [P1A219] 65.00
__ Fast Through the Forest 0100 sticker correcting Luke text 65.00
__ Fast Through the Forest 0500 corrected Luke text..65.00
__ Millennium Falcon Adventure [P1A220]........125.00
__ The Stompin' Wampa [P1A221] 65.00
__ X-Wing Adventure [P1A222] 35.00

Hasbro
__ Anakin Skywalker with Jedi Pod sticker corrects asst number [P2A001] 12.00
__ Anakin Skywalker with Rescue Glider [P2A002] 10.00
__ C-3PO and R2-D2 [P2A003]..........................10.00
__ C-3PO and R2-D2 with hook on card 10.00
__ Chewbacca with Wookiee Action Tool [P2A004] 10.00
__ Chewbacca with Wookiee Scout Flyer sticker corrects asst number [P2A005]...................10.00
__ Darth Vader with Imperial Claw Droid, clear lightsaber [P2A006]..................................10.00
__ Darth Vader with Imperial Claw Droid, red lightsaber no hook on card [P2A007]...............25.00
__ Darth Vader with Imperial Claw Droid, red lightsaber with hooked card [P2A008] 10.00
__ Han Solo with Jet Bike sticker corrects asst number [P2A009] 10.00
__ Luke Skywalker hoverboard [P2A010]............10.00
__ Luke Skywalker with Jedi Jet Pack [P2A011].10.00
__ Mace Windu with purple lightsaber and Jedi grappling hook [P2A012] 10.00
__ Yoda with Swamp Stomper [P2A013] 10.00

Creatures.
__ Obi-Wan Kenobi with Boga [P2A014].............70.00

First 50, Hasbro COA, eBay exclusives.
__ Chewbacca..75.00
__ Darth Vader..75.00
__ Luke Skywalker...75.00

P2A001

P2A002

P2A003

P2A004

P2A005

P2A006

P2A007

P2A008

P2A009

P2A010

P2A011

P2A012

P2A013

P2A014

P2A015

P2A016

P2A017

P2A018

P2A019

P2A020

__ R2-D2 and C-3PO 75.00

Vehicles.
__ Luke Skywalker with Speederbike [P2A015] ..45.00
__ Luke Skywalker with Speederbike clear lightsaber [P2A016] 20.00
__ Luke Skywalker with Speederbike green lightsaber [P2A017] 20.00
__ Luke Skywalker with Speederbike yellow flight suit [P2A018] 25.00
__ X-Wing Fighter [P2A019] 40.00
__ X-Wing Fighter 100.00
__ X-Wing Fighter eBay exclusive (color variation) [P2A020] 50.00

Figures: Kubrick and Bearbrick

Kubricks. 400% scale, boxed.
__ C-3PO 140.00
__ TC-14 ....140.00

Tomy, Japan
Bearbricks.
__ Wicket Chase figure from series 7 ....175.00

Bearbricks. 400% scale, boxed.
__ Darth Vader...190.00
__ Imperial logo [P1B001] 150.00
__ Paploo...145.00
__ Teebo...150.00
__ Wicket...180.00

Bearbricks. Boxed sets.
__ 2-Pack: Wicket and Paploo, exclusive to Star Wars Celebration Japan [P1B002]............................75.00
__ 5-Pack: Ewoks Paploo, Teebo, Lumat, Romba, Chief Chirpa [P1B003] 95.00

Bearbricks. Pepsi Nex premiums.
__ Boba Fett [P1B004] 4.00
__ C-3PO [P1B005] 4.00
__ Chewbacca [P1B006] 4.00
__ Clone Trooper (EP2) [P1B007]...........................4.00
__ Clone Trooper (EP3) [P1B008].........................4.00
__ Darth Maul [P1B009]...4.00
__ Darth Vader [P1B010].......................................4.00
__ Imperial Logo [P1B011] 4.00
__ Jango Fett [P1B012]..4.00
__ Jawa [P1B013]...4.00
__ R2-D2 [P1B014]..4.00
__ Rebel Alliance Logo [P1B015] 4.00
__ Stormtrooper [P1B016].....................................4.00
__ TIE Fighter Pilot [P1B017]..................................4.00

__ Wicket [P1B018] 4.00
__ Yoda [P1B019] 4.00

Kubricks, carded 6-packs.
__ Boba Fetts: Black-and-White prototype, Droids, Holiday Special, McQuarrie and Johnson concept, McQuarrie concept, Vintage Kenner, exclusive to Tokyo Toys Exhibition...................................250.00
__ Bounty Hunters: 4-LOM, Boba Fett (ROTJ), Bossk, Dengar, IG-88, Zuckuss, exclusive to Medicom Toy Exhibition [P1B020] 225.00
__ Series 2: Sandtrooper, Han Solo, Cantina Band Member, Obi-Wan Kenobi, Greedo, Tusken Raider, limited to 1,000, exclusive to Medicom Toy Exhibition 175.00

Kubricks, carded.
__ Artoo Detoo, Wonder Festival '04 [P1B022]..........150.00
__ Boba Fett animated, Wonder Festival 2004 [P1B023]...200.00
__ Boba Fett, Mediacom Toy Expo '03 [P1B024] 550.00
__ Chewbacca, exclusive to Wonder Festival Summer [P1B025]...60.00
__ Commander Jorg Sacul, Medicom Toy Expo '06 [P1B026]...350.00
__ Darth Vader lightsaber sticks through bubble, exclusive to Medicom Toy Exhibition [P1B027] 150.00
__ Darth Vader, Medicom Toy Expo '05 [P1B028]....325.00
__ Han Solo in Carbonite coin on package is a sticker, exclusive to Medicom Toy Exhibition 220.00
__ Luke Skywalker [P1B029] 150.00
__ Princess Leia hologram, World Characters Convention 19, limited to 500 [P1B030] 100.00
__ R2-D2 from Droids TV series, limited to 2004, exclusive to Medicom Toy Exhibition 140.00
__ Sandtrooper, Medicon Toy Expo 2004 at Parco, Tokyo Japan [P1B031]...................................350.00
__ Shadow Stormtrooper, limited to 2006, exclusive to World Characters Convention 70.00

Kubricks.
__ Blue Star Snowtrooper, limited to 2,007 ....35.00
__ Darth Maul with Sith Speeder, limited to 2,007 [P1B032]...35.00
__ Imperial Speederbike with Scout Trooper [P1B033] 45.00

Kubricks. 400% scale, boxed.
__ Boba Fett [P1B034] 225.00
__ Boba Fett ESB [P1B035] 275.00
__ Darth Vader, limited to 4,000 [P1B036] 125.00
__ Han Solo in stormtrooper disguise, limited to 2,000 [P1B037]...150.00
__ Luke Skywalker in stormtrooper disguise, limited to 2,000 [P1B038] 150.00

Kubricks. Boxed sets.
__ 2-Pack: Jango Fett and Boba Fett, exclusive to Medicom Online [P1B039]............................120.00
__ 4-Pack: Droopy McCool, Sy Snootles, Max Rebo, Doda Bodonawieedo, limited to 2,005 [P1B040]..150.00
__ 5-Pack: Luke Skywalker (Ceremonial outfit), K-3PO, R5-A1, Ten Nunb, and Romba, exclusive to Toys R Us [P1B041] 85.00
__ 5-Pack: Luke Skywalker (Dagobah with Yoda), C-3PO, Snowtrooper, B-Wing Pilot, 2-1B, exclusive to mail-in [P1B042] 275.00
__ 5-Pack: Spirit of Obi-Wan, Han Solo (Bespin), Paploo, R5-D4, R2 Imperial Droid, exclusive to Toys R Us Japan [P1B043]............................95.00
__ 5-Pack: Super Battle Droid, TC-14, Jango Fett (Second Jetpack), Clone Trooper/Shock Trooper, Padme Amidala, exclusive to mail-in [P1B044]...350.00
__ 5-Pack: Y-Wing Pilot, Hoth Chewbacca, Holographic Darth Vader, R2-B5, Mace Windu, exclusive to mail-in [P1B045] 225.00
__ Speekerbike with Luke Skywalker and Princess Leia [P1B046] 135.00

Kubricks.
__ Early Bird Kit: Luke, Leia, Chewbacca, R2-D2 [P1B047] 250.00

Kubricks. Series 1.
__ 4-LOM [P1B048] 15.00
__ Boba Fett [P1B049] 10.00
__ Boba Fett / secret variation 125.00
__ Bossk [P1B050] 10.00
__ Dengar [P1B051]..15.00
__ IG-88 [P1B052] 10.00
__ Zuckuss [P1B053]...15.00

Kubricks. Series 2.
__ Cantina Band member [P1B054]....................10.00
__ Cantina Band member, alt. Instrument...........10.00
__ Greedo [P1B055] 25.00
__ Han Solo [P1B056] 10.00
__ Indiana Jones (Han Solo box)......................175.00
__ Obi-Wan Kenobi [P1B057]...............................25.00
__ Sandtrooper, orange pauldron [P1B058]........10.00
__ Sandtrooper, white pauldron 45.00
__ Tusken Raider [P1B059] 25.00

Kubricks. Series 3.
__ AT-AT Driver [P1B060].....................................10.00
__ Han Solo in Carbonite [P1B061].......................10.00
__ Han Solo released from Carbonite 45.00
__ Jawa [P1B062]...10.00
__ Lando Calrissian [P1B063] 10.00

P1B001

P1B002

P1B003

P1B004

P1B005

P1B006

P1B007

P1B008

P1B009

P1B010

P1B011

P1B012

P1B013

P1B014

P1B015

P1B016

P1B017

P1B018

P1B019

P1B020

P1B021

P1B022

P1B023

P1B024

P1B025

P1B026

P1B027

P1B028

P1B029

P1B030

P1B031

P1B032

P1B033

P1B034

P1B035

P1B036

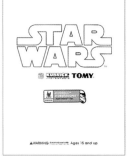

P1B037

P1B038

P1B039

P1B040

P1B041

P1B042

P1B043

P1B044

P1B045

P1B046

P1B047

P1B048

P1B049

P1B050

P1B051

P1B052

P1B053

P1B054

P1B055

P1B056

P1B057

P1B058

P1B059

P1B060

P1B061

P1B062

P1B063

P1B064

P1B065

Figures: Kubricks and Bearbricks

P1B066

P1B067

P1B068

P1B069

P1B070

P1B071

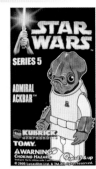
P1B072

P1B073

P1B074

P1B075

P1B076

P1B077

P1B078

P1B079

P1B080

P1B081

P1B082

P1B083

P1B084

P1B085

P1B086

P1B087

P1B088

P1B089

P1B090

P1B091

P1B092

P1B093

P1B094

P1B095

P1B096

P1B097

P1B098

P1B099

P1B100

P1B101

P1B102

P1B103

P1B104

P1B105

P1B106

P1B107

P1B108

P1B109

P1B110

P1B111

P1B112

P1B113

P1B114

P1B115

__ See Threepio [P1B064] 10.00
__ Wicket [P1B065] 10.00

Kubricks. Series 4.
__ Darth Vader with removable helmet 10.00
__ Darth Vader [P1B066] 10.00
__ Emperor Palpatine [P1B067] 10.00
__ Han Solo, Hoth [P1B068] 10.00
__ Luke Skywalker, Bespin [P1B069] 10.00
__ Nien Numb [P1B070] 10.00
__ Stormtrooper [P1B071] 10.00
__ Stormtrooper / Han 100.00
__ Stormtrooper / Luke 100.00

Kubricks. Series 5.
__ Admiral Ackbar [P1B072]................................10.00
__ Death Star Gunner [P1B073] 10.00
__ Luke Skywalker, Jedi [P1B074] 10.00
__ Princess Leia, captive [P1B075] 10.00
__ Snaggletooth [P1B076]...................................10.00
__ Yoda [P1B077]...10.00

Kubricks. Series 6.
__ Death Star Trooper [P1B078] 10.00
__ Luke Skywalker, X-Wing Pilot [P1B079] 10.00
__ R4-M9 [P1B080] 10.00
__ RA-7 (Death Star Droid) 10.00
__ Rebel Fleet Trooper 10.00
__ TIE Fighter Pilot [P1B081]..............................10.00

Kubricks. Series 7.
__ Anakin Skywalker...120.00
__ Emperor's Royal Guard [P1B082]...................10.00
__ Gamorrean Guard...10.00
__ Lando Calrissian as Skiff Guard [P1B083]......10.00
__ Leia Boushh Disguise [P1B084]......................10.00

__ Saelt Marae Yakface....................................120.00
__ Scout Trooper [P1B085] 10.00
__ Senate Guard..45.00
__ Spirit of Anakin Skywalker [P1B086] 10.00

Kubricks. Series 8.
__ Anakin Skywalker [P1B087] 10.00
__ Aurra Sing 150.00
__ Battle Droid [P1B088] 10.00
__ C-3PO (EPI) [P1B089].....................................10.00
__ Darth Maul [P1B090]......................................10.00
__ Jar Jar Binks 70.00
__ Queen Amidala [P1B091]................................10.00
__ Qui-Gon Jinn [P1B092] 10.00

Kubricks. Series 9.
__ Anakin Skywalker [P1B093] 10.00
__ Clone Commander..35.00
__ Clone Trooper [P1B094]..................................10.00
__ Count Dooku [P1B095]....................................10.00
__ Jango Fett [P1B096].......................................10.00
__ Obi-Wan Kenobi [P1B097]..............................10.00
__ Shaak Ti 150.00
__ Yoda [P1B098]...10.00

Kubricks. Series 10.
__ Anakin Skywalker (EP3) [P1B099] 10.00
__ Clone Trooper (EP3) [P1B100].........................10.00
__ Commander Gree 35.00
__ Darth Sidious (EP3) [P1B101] 10.00
__ Darth Vader (EP3) [P1B102] 10.00
__ General Grievous [P1B103] 10.00
__ General Grievous, 4 arms 150.00
__ Tion Medon..130.00

Kubricks. Series 11; deluxe series 1.
__ Amanaman...45.00
__ Bib Fortuna 35.00
__ C-3PO and Salacious Crumb [P1B104]..........15.00
__ Chewbacca [P1B105] 15.00
__ Jabba the Hutt bonus figure 95.00
__ Luke Skywalker [P1B106] 15.00
__ R2-D2 with serving tray [P1B107].................15.00

Kubricks. Series 12; deluxe series 2.
__ AT-ST bonus vehicle....................................125.00
__ Chewbacca [P1B108] 15.00
__ Han Solo, Hoth [P1B109] 15.00
__ Luke Skywalker, Hoth [P1B110] 15.00
__ Princess Leia, Hoth.......................................40.00
__ R-3PO..40.00
__ Snowtrooper Commander [P1B111] 15.00

Kubricks. Series 13; deluxe series 3.
__ Garindan 35.00
__ Landspeeder bonus vehicle..........................120.00
__ Luke Skywalker..15.00
__ Obi-Wan Kenobi 15.00
__ R5-D4...35.00
__ Sandtrooper..15.00
__ Tusken Raider..15.00

Kubricks. Special series, "Boba Fett".
__ Boba Fett, black-and-white [P1B112] 12.00
__ Boba Fett, Droids [P1B113].............................15.00
__ Boba Fett, holiday special [P1B114]...............15.00
__ Boba Fett, McQuarrie concept 15.00
__ Boba Fett, McQuarrie alternate sculpt 15.00
__ Boba Fett, vintage era [P1B115].....................20.00

Figures: Metal

Figures: Metal

Hasbro
Titanium.
__ Boba Fett [FT1001].................................25.00
__ Boba Fett vintage finish [FT1002].................30.00
__ Bossk [FT1003]..................................20.00
__ Bossk vintage finish [FT1004]...................30.00
__ Darth Vader [FT1005]............................20.00
__ Darth Vader vintage finish [FT1006]..............30.00
__ Sandtrooper [FT1007]............................20.00
__ Sandtrooper vintage finish......................30.00

Titanium. Color packaging.
__ Boba Fett......................................25.00
__ Boba Fett vintage finish [FT1008]................30.00
__ C-3PO [FT1009].................................25.00

__ Clone Trooper [FT1010]..........................30.00
__ Clone Trooper vintage finish [FT1011]............30.00
__ Darth Maul [FT1012].............................25.00
__ Darth Vader [FT1013]............................25.00
__ Darth Vader vintage finish......................30.00
__ Darth Vader Mustafar armor, exclusive to Target
[FT1014]..30.00
__ General Grievous [FT1015].......................25.00
__ IG-88 [FT1016].................................30.00
__ IG-88 vintage finish [FT1017]....................30.00
__ Jango Fett [FT1018].............................35.00
__ Luke Skywalker, snowspeeder pilot...............25.00

Tomy, Japan
8" Real action figures.
__ Boba Fett [FT1019]............................100.00
__ Darth Vader [FT1020]..........................100.00

Figures: Mighty Beanz

Moose Enterprise Pty Ltd.
__ 01 Luke Skywalker (Tatooine) [FMB001].........3.00
__ 02 Han Solo [FMB002]...........................3.00
__ 03 Princess Leia [FMB003]......................3.00
__ 04 Darth Vader [FMB004]........................3.00
__ 05 R2-D2 [FMB005].............................3.00
__ 06 Obi-Wan Kenobi (Old) [FMB006]..............3.00
__ 07 Yoda [FMB007]..............................3.00
__ 08 Chewbacca [FMB008].........................3.00
__ 09 Jabba the Hutt [FMB009].....................3.00
__ 10 Battle Droid [FMB010].......................3.00
__ 11 C-3PO [FMB011].............................3.00
__ 12 Clone Tooper [FMB012].......................3.00
__ 13 501st Legion [FMB013].......................3.00
__ 14 Commander Cody [FMB014]....................3.00

FT1001

FT1002

FT1003

FT1004

FT1005

FT1006

FT1007

FT1008

FT1009

FT1010

FT1011

FT1012

FT1013

FT1014

FT1015

FT1016

FT1017

FT1018

FT1019

FT1020

FMB001

FMB002

FMB003

FMB004 front and back

FMB005

FMB006

FMB007

FMB008

FMB009

FMB010

FMB011

FMB012

FMB013

FMB014

FMB015

FMB016

FMB017

FMB018

FMB019

FMB020

FMB021

FMB022

FMB023

FMB024

FMB025

FMB026

FMB027

FMB028

FMB029

FMB030

FMB031

FMB032

FMB033

FMB034

FMB035

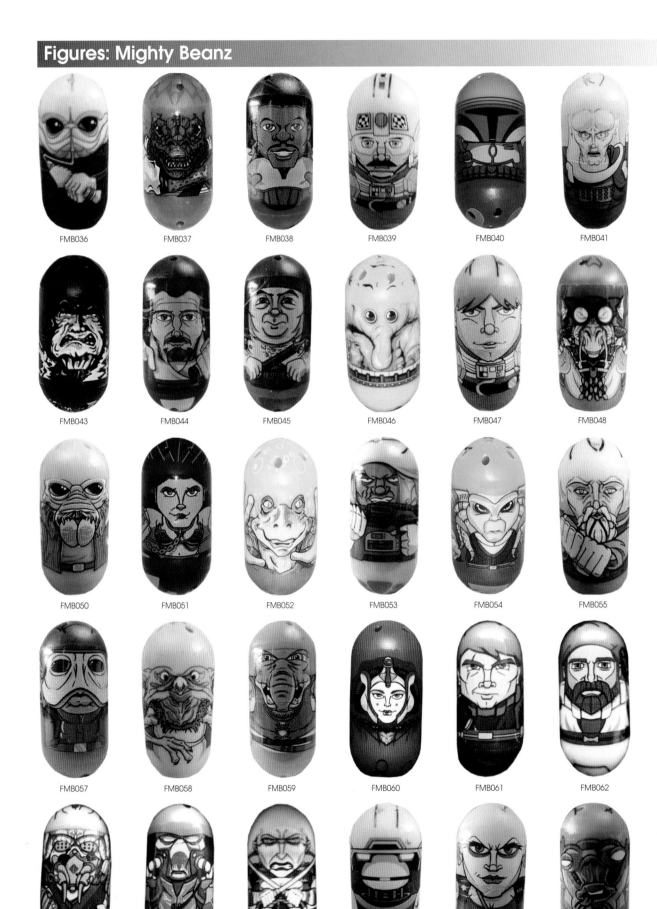

FMB036 FMB037 FMB038 FMB039 FMB040 FMB041 FMB042

FMB043 FMB044 FMB045 FMB046 FMB047 FMB048 FMB049

FMB050 FMB051 FMB052 FMB053 FMB054 FMB055 FMB056

FMB057 FMB058 FMB059 FMB060 FMB061 FMB062 FMB063

FMB064 FMB065 FMB066 FMB067 FMB068 FMB069 FMB070

FMB071 front and back   FMB072   FMB073   FMB074   FMB075   FMB076

FMB077   FMB078   FMB079   FMB080   FMB081   FMB082   FMB083

FMB084   FMB085   FMB086

__ 69 Asajj Ventress [FMB066]..............................4.00
__ 71 TX-20 [FMB067]..6.00
__ 72 Aurra Sing [FMB068].................................5.00
__ 73 Zombie Geonosian [FMB069].....................4.00
__ 74 Nahdar Vebb [FMB070] 5.00
__ 80 Darth Vader (with lightsaber) [FMB071].......3.00
__ 81 Luke Skywalker (Jedi) [FMB072]..................3.00
__ 82 R2-Q5 [FMB073]..50.00
__ 83 K-3PO [FMB074]..50.00
__ 84 R5-D4 [FMB075].......................................50.00
__ 85 R4-P44 [FMB076]......................................50.00
__ 86 Pit Droid [FMB077] 50.00
__ 87 Han Solo [FMB078]....................................3.00
__ 88 Chewbacca [FMB079]................................3.00
__ 89 Darth Sidious [FMB080].............................3.00
__ 90 Luke Skywalker (Bespin) [FMB081] 3.00
__ 92 Imperial Gunner [FMB082].........................3.00
__ 93 Grand Moff Tarkin [FMB083].......................3.00

Unopened packages.
__ 4-Pack [FMB084]..7.00
__ 4-Pack includes Clone Wars character, exclusive to Walmart [FMB085]...8.00
__ 4-Pack includes Clone Wars character [FMB086] 8.00

Moose Enterprise Pty Ltd.
Flip tracks. Lightsaber shaped with exclusive beanz included.
__ Bespin Luke Skywalker [FMBA001]................15.00
__ Darth Sidious [FMBA002] 15.00

__ 15 Stormtrooper [FMB015]...............................3.00
__ 16 Admiral Ackbar [FMB016]...........................3.00
__ 17 Gamorrean Guard [FMB017] 3.00
__ 18 Count Dooku [FMB018] 3.00
__ 19 Boba Fett [FMB019]....................................3.00
__ 20 Greedo [FMB020].......................................3.00
__ 21 Sand Trooper [FMB021] 3.00
__ 22 Anakin Skywalker (Tatooine) [FMB022] 3.00
__ 23 Mace Windu [FMB023] 3.00
__ 24 AT-AT Driver [FMB024]................................3.00
__ 25 General Grievous [FMB025].........................3.00
__ 26 TIE Pilot [FMB026].....................................3.00
__ 27 Snow Trooper [FMB027]..............................3.00
__ 28 Wicket [FMB028] 3.00
__ 29 Jawa [FMB029]..3.00
__ 30 Tusken Raider [FMB030] 3.00
__ 31 Padme Amidala [FMB031]...........................3.00
__ 32 Darth Maul [FMB032]..................................3.00
__ 33 Anakin Skywalker (Jedi) [FMB033] 3.00
__ 34 2-1B [FMB034]...3.00
__ 35 Han Solo (carbonite) [FMB035]...................3.00
__ 36 Cantina Musician [FMB036].........................3.00
__ 37 Bossk [FMB037]...3.00
__ 38 Lando Calrissian [FMB038].........................3.00
__ 39 Biggs Darklighter [FMB039].........................3.00
__ 40 Jango Fett [FMB040] 3.00
__ 41 Bib Fortuna [FMB041].................................3.00
__ 42 IG-88 [FMB042] 3.00
__ 43 Emperor Palpatine [FMB043]........................3.00
__ 44 Qui-Gon Jinn [FMB044]...............................3.00
__ 45 Rancor Keeper [FMB045].............................3.00
__ 46 Max Rebo [FMB046]....................................3.00
__ 47 Luke Rebel Pilot [FMB047]..........................3.00
__ 48 Sebulba [FMB048].....................................3.00

__ 49 Rancor [FMB049]..3.00
__ 50 Ponda Baba [FMB050].................................3.00
__ 51 Princess Leia (captive) [FMB051] 3.00
__ 52 Jar Jar Binks [FMB052]...............................3.00
__ 53 Dengar [FMB053]..3.00
__ 54 Kit Fisto [FMB054]......................................3.00
__ 55 Ki-Adi-Mundi [FMB055]...............................3.00
__ 56 Jek Porkins [FMB056]................................25.00
__ 57 Nien Nunb [FMB057] 3.00
__ 58 Salacious Crumb [FMB058]..........................3.00
__ 59 Watto [FMB059]..3.00
__ 60 Queen Amidala [FMB060].............................3.00
__ 61 Anakin Skywalker (Clone Wars) [FMB061]...3.00
__ 63 Obi-Wan Kenobi (Clone Wars) [FMB062] 3.00
__ 65 Captain Rex [FMB063].................................4.00
__ 66 Plo Koon [FMB064].....................................3.00
__ 68 Cad Bane [FMB065] 3.50

FMBA001   FMBA002   FMBA003   FMBA004   FMBA005

Figures: Mighty Beanz Accessories

Storage case.

__ Darth Vader, beanz shaped with exclusive Luke Skywalker and Darth Vader beanz [FMBA003] 20.00
__ Death Star with exclusive Grand Moff Tarkin and Imperial Gunner beanz [FMBA004].................25.00
__ Millennium Falcon with exclusive Han Solo and Chewbacca beanz, exclusive to Toys R Us [FMBA005].................................25.00
__ Millennium Falcon with exclusive Han Solo and Chewbacca beanz [FMBA005] 25.00

Figures: Mighty Muggs

Hasbro

__ Admiral Ackbar, excl. to Previews [FMM001].20.00

__ Anakin Skywalker [FMM002] 10.00
__ Asajj Ventress [FMM003]..................................10.00
__ Biggs Darklighter, exclusive to Target [FMM004]..10.00
__ Boba Fett [FMM005]...10.00
__ Bossk, exclusive to Target [FMM006] 10.00
__ C-3PO, exclusive to Target [FMM007] 10.00
__ Captain Rex, exclusive to Target [FMM008]...10.00
__ Chewbacca [FMM009]..10.00
__ Clone Commander Cody, exclusive to Target [FMM010]..10.00
__ Commander Gree, exclusive to San Diego Comic-Con [FMM011] 50.00
__ Count Dooku [FMM012] 10.00
__ Darth Maul [FMM013]...10.00
__ Darth Revan [FMM014].......................................10.00
__ Darth Vader [FMM015]..10.00

__ Darth Vader, two dots each eye [FMM016] 40.00
__ Darth Vader (removable helmet) [FMM017]....10.00
__ Emperor Palpatine [FMM018] 10.00
__ Gamorrean Guard [FMM019]...........................25.00
__ General Grievous [FMM020].............................10.00
__ Grand Moff Tarkin [FMM021].............................10.00
__ Han Solo [FMM022]..10.00
__ Han Solo (Hoth) [FMM023] 10.00
__ Imperial Guard [FMM024]..................................10.00
__ Jango Fett [FMM025]..10.00
__ Lando Calrissian [FMM026]...............................10.00
__ Luke Skywalker [FMM027] 10.00
__ Luke Skywalker, Bespin [FMM028] 10.00
__ Mace Windu [FMM029].......................................10.00
__ Obi-Wan Kenobi [FMM030]................................10.00
__ Plo Koon [FMM031] 10.00
__ Princess Leia [FMM032].....................................10.00

FMM001

FMM002

FMM003

FMM004

FMM005

FMM006

FMM007

FMM008

FMM009

FMM010

FMM011

FMM012

FMM013

FMM014

FMM015

FMM016

FMM017

FMM018

FMM019

FMM020

FMM021

FMM022

FMM023

FMM024

jango fett
FMM025

lando calrissian
FMM026

luke skywalker
FMM027

luke skywalker
FMM028

mace windu
FMM029

obi-wan kenobi
FMM030

plo koon
FMM031

princess leia
FMM032

qui-gon jinn
FMM033

shadow stormtrooper
FMM034

shock trooper
FMM035

snowtrooper
FMM036

stormtrooper
FMM037

teebo
FMM038

wampa
FMM039

wicket
FMM040

__ Qui-Gon Jinn [FMM033] 10.00
__ Shadow Stormtrooper, exclusive to Previews
   [FMM034]...20.00
__ Shock Trooper, Target exclusive [FMM035]...10.00
__ Snowtrooper, Target exclusive [FMM036]......10.00
__ Stormtrooper [FMM037]................................10.00
__ Teebo, exclusive to Target [FMM038] 10.00
__ Wampa [FMM039]..10.00
__ Wicket [FMM040]...10.00
__ Yoda [FMM041] 10.00

Mini Mugg 3-packs, exclusive to Target.
__ Bossk, Boba Fett, IG-88 [FMM042]...............30.00
__ Cad Bane, General Grievous, Captain Rex
   [FMM043]...30.00
__ Yoda, Darth Vader, Stormtrooper [FMM044]..30.00

Hasbro, Japan
__ Commander Gree Japanese sticker on bottom
   with San Diego Comic Convention sticker on
   front, limited to 200, exclusive to World Characters
   Convention...50.00

yoda
FMM041

bossk / boba fett / ig-88
FMM042

Figures: Mini

__ R2-D2 trinket with loop [TYF001] 3.00

Caricature style, 2" tall.
__ Anakin Skywalker [TYF002] 3.00
__ Battle Droid [TYF003] 3.00
__ Boss Nass [TYF004] 3.00
__ Darth Maul [TYF005].......................................3.00

cad bane / general grievous / captain rex
FMM043

yoda / darth vader / stormtrooper
FMM044

TYF001

TYF002

TYF003

TYF004

TYF005

TYF006

TYF007

TYF008

TYF009

TYF010

TYF011

TYF012

TYF013

TYF014

TYF015

TYF016

TYF017

TYF018

TYF019

TYF020

TYF021

TYF022

TYF023

TYF024

TYF025

TYF026

TYF027

TYF028

TYF029

TYF030

TYF031

TYF032   TYF033   TYF034   TYF035   TYF036   TYF037   TYF038   TYF039

TYF040   TYF041   TYF042

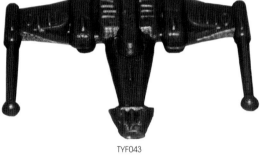

TYF043   TYF044   TYF045   TYF046

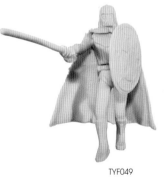

TYF047   TYF048   TYF049

TYF050   TYF051   TYF052   TYF053

TYF054

TYF055

TYF056

TYF057

TYF058

TYF059

TYF060

TYF061

TYF062

TYF063

TYF064

TYF065

TYF066

TYF067

TYF068

TYF069

TYF070

TYF071

TYF072

TYF073

TYF074

TYF075

TYF076

TYF077

TYF078

TYF079

TYF080

TYF081

TYF082

TYF083

TYF084

TYF085

TYF086

TYF087

TYF088

TYF089

TYF090

TYF091

TYF092

TYF093

TYF094

TYF095

TYF096

TYF097

TYF098

TYF099

TYF100

Han Solo

TYF101

Stormtrooper

TYF102

Chewbacca

TYF103

C-3PO

TYF104

TYF105

TYF106

TYF107

TYF108

TYF109

TYF110

Package for TYF111-TYF128

TYF111

TYF112

TYF113

TYF114

TYF115

TYF116

TYF117

TYF118

TYF119

TYF120

TYF121

TYF122

TYF123

TYF124

TYF125

TYF126

TYF127

TYF128

TYF129

TYF130

TYF131

TYF132

TYF133

TYF134

TYF135

TYF136

TYF137

TYF138

TYF139

TYF140

TYF141

TYF142

TYF143

TYF144

TYF145

TYF146

TYF147

TYF148

TYF149

TYF150

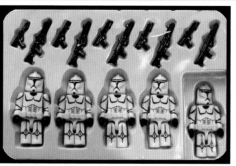

TYF151

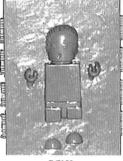

TYF152

TYF153

TYF154

TYF155

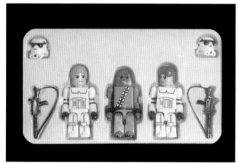

TYF156

TYF157

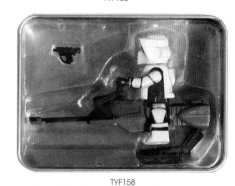

TYF158

__ Darth Sidious [TYF006].....................................3.00
__ Darth Vader [TYF007] 3.00
__ Jabba the Hutt [TYF008].................................3.00
__ Jar Jar Binks [TYF009]....................................3.00
__ Qui-Gon Jinn [TYF010] 3.00
__ Yoda [TYF011] 3.00

Caricature style, 2" tall. Glossy painted ceramic.
__ Anakin Skywalker [TYF012] 3.00
__ Battle Droid [TYF013] 3.00
__ Boss Nass [TYF014] 3.00
__ Darth Maul [TYF015].......................................3.00
__ Darth Sidious [TYF016]...................................3.00
__ Darth Vader [TYF017] 3.00
__ Jabba the Hutt [TYF018].................................3.00
__ Jar Jar Binks [TYF019]....................................3.00
__ Qui-Gon Jinn [TYF020] 3.00
__ Yoda [TYF021] 3.00

Caricature style, 2" tall. Glow-in-the-dark features.
__ Anakin Skywalker [TYF022] 3.00
__ Battle Droid [TYF023] 3.00
__ Boss Nass [TYF024] 3.00
__ Darth Maul [TYF025] 3.00
__ Darth Sidious [TYF026]...................................3.00
__ Darth Vader [TYF027] 3.00
__ Jabba the Hutt [TYF028].................................3.00
__ Jar Jar Binks [TYF029]....................................3.00
__ Qui-Gon Jinn [TYF030] 3.00
__ Yoda [TYF031] 3.00

*Episode I: The Phantom Menace. Approximately 3"
tall, round textured base, with removable weapons.*
__ Anakin Skywalker with backpack and grease gun
[TYF032]...5.00
__ Battle Droid with blaster [TYF033]...................5.00

__ Darth Maul with attached lightsaber
[TYF034]..5.00
__ Jar Jar Binks with Gungan staff [TYF035] 5.00
__ Obi-Wan with blue lightsaber [TYF036]............5.00
__ Padme with podrace viewscreen [TYF037] 5.00
__ Queen Amidala with long pistol [TYF038].........5.00
__ Qui-Gon Jinn with green lightsaber and Naboo
pistol [TYF039]..5.00

*Episode I: The Phantom Menace. Approximately
3" tall.*
__ Darth Maul [TYF040] 3.00

Look-alike starships. Hard plastic.
__ Millennium Falcon [TYF041] 15.00
__ TIE Fighter [TYF042] 10.00
__ X-Wing Fighter [TYF043]................................10.00

TYF159

TYF160

TYF161

TYF162

TYF163

TYF164

TYF165

TYF166

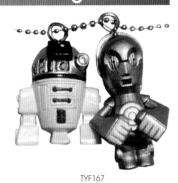

TYF167

TYF168

TYF169

Japan. Mascots.
__ Darth Vader, exclusive to Star Wars Celebration
Japan [TYF044]...15.00
__ Obi-Wan Kenobi, exclusive to Star Wars Celebration
Japan [TYF045]...15.00

Malaysia. Push together toys with accessories.
"Modern and Elegant in Fashion."
__ C-3PO, EPI [TYF046] 12.00
__ Chewbacca in battle armor with bowcaster
[TYF047]...12.00
__ Clone Trooper with rifle [TYF048] 12.00
__ Darth Vader with lightsaber and star shield
[TYF049]...12.00
__ Mace Windu with lightsaber [TYF050] 12.00
__ R2-D2 with amazing head crane [TYF051].....12.00
__ Yoda with lightsaber [TYF052].........................12.00

Applause
__ 4-Pack: Anakin Skywalker, Destroyer Droid, Jar Jar
Binks, Queen Amidala [TYF053] 12.00
__ 4-Pack: Darth Maul, Obi-Wan Kenobi, Qui-Gon Jinn,
battle droid ground commander [TYF054] 12.00
__ 5-Pack [TYF055] 16.00
__ 5-Pack with bonus 6th figure, Blockbuster exclusive
[TYF056]...23.00
__ 6-Pack with display base [TYF057] 26.00
__ 7-Pack, includes exclusive Boba Fett
[TYF058]...24.00
__ Admiral Ackbar [TYF059].................................4.00
__ Anakin Skywalker (Tatooine) [TYF060] 3.00
__ Boba Fett [TYF061]..4.00
__ Bossk [TYF062]..4.00
__ C-3PO [TYF063]...4.00
__ C-3PO and R2-D2 on platform [TYF064]..........6.00

__ Chewbacca [TYF065] 4.00
__ Darth Maul [TYF066]..5.00
__ Darth Vader [TYF067]......................................4.00
__ Destroyer Droid [TYF068]................................4.00
__ Emperor Palpatine [TYF069]............................4.00
__ Greedo [TYF070]..4.00
__ Han Solo [TYF071]...4.00
__ Han Solo and Jabba the Hutt [TYF072]...........7.00
__ Jar Jar Binks [TYF073].....................................4.00
__ Lando Calrissian [TYF074]...............................4.00
__ Luke Skywalker [TYF075].................................4.00
__ Obi-Wan [TYF076]..5.00
__ Obi-Wan Kenobi [TYF077]...............................4.00
__ Obi-Wan Kenobi, spirit [TYF078] 4.00
__ Pit Droid [TYF079]..4.00
__ Princess Leia [TYF080] 4.00
__ Queen Amidala (Naboo) [TYF081] 3.00
__ Qui-Gon [TYF082]...5.00
__ R2-D2 [TYF083]..4.00
__ Snowtrooper [TYF084]......................................4.00
__ Stormtrooper [TYF085].....................................4.00
__ TIE Fighter Pilot [TYF086]...............................4.00
__ Tusken Raider [TYF087]...................................4.00
__ Wedge Antillies [TYF088].................................4.00
__ Yoda [TYF089]...4.00

Bimbo, Mexico
Potmetal figures, approx. 1.5" in height.
__ Anakin Skywalker..8.00
__ Chewbacca...8.00
__ Count Dooku...8.00
__ Darth Vader..8.00
__ General Grievous 8.00
__ Obi-Wan Kenobi 8.00

TYF170

TYF171

TYF172

TYF173

TYF174

TYF175

TYF176

TYF177

TYF178

TYF179

TYF180   TYF181   TYF182   TYF183   TYF184

TYF185 package and opened   TYF186   TYF187

__ Palpatine 8.00
__ Yoda 8.00

Potmetal figures, approx. 1.5" in height. Chase figures, gold in color.
__ Anakin Skywalker..16.00
__ Chewbacca 16.00
__ Count Dooku 16.00
__ Darth Vader..16.00
__ General Grievous 16.00
__ Obi-Wan Kenobi 16.00
__ Palpatine 16.00
__ Yoda 16.00

Comics Spain
__ C-3PO [TYF090]...12.00
__ C-3PO, all gold colored [TYF091]...................35.00
__ Chief Chirpa [TYF092]...................................10.00
__ Dulok [TYF093]...12.00
__ Kez-Iban [TYF094]...10.00
__ Kneesa [TYF095]...12.00
__ Latara [TYF096] 10.00
__ R2-D2 [TYF097]..12.00
__ Teebo [TYF098]...10.00
__ Wicket [TYF099]..10.00

DeAgostini
__ 01 Darth Vader..20.00
__ 02 Han Solo [TYF100].....................................20.00
__ 03 Stormtrooper and Yoda [TYF101].............40.00
__ 04 Luke Skywalker 20.00
__ 05 Chewbacca [TYF102] 20.00
__ 06 TIE Advanced..20.00
__ 07 C-3PO [TYF103]...20.00
__ 08 Obi-Wan Kenobi 20.00
__ 09 Darth Maul..20.00
__ 10 Princess Leia 20.00
__ 11 Anakin Skywalker.......................................20.00
__ 11 R2-D2..20.00
__ 12 Admiral Ackbar 20.00
__ 13 X-Wing Fighter 20.00
__ 14 Count Dooku 20.00
__ 15 Wicket the Ewok 20.00
__ 16 Jabba the Hutt 20.00
__ 17 Grand Moff Tarkin 20.00
__ 18 Imperial Royal Guard 20.00
__ 19 Anakin Skywalker.......................................20.00
__ 20 Emperor 20.00
__ 21 Padme Amidala 20.00
__ 22 Boba Fett..20.00
__ 23 Clone Trooper 20.00

__ 24 Tion Medon...20.00
__ 25 Bib Fortuna 20.00
__ 26 Jango Fett...20.00
__ 27 Lando Calrissian 20.00
__ 28 AT-AT...20.00
__ 29 General Grievous 20.00
__ 30 Greedo 20.00
__ 31 Jawa 20.00
__ 32 IG-88 ....20.00
__ 33 Mace Windu 20.00
__ 34 Tusken Raider 20.00
__ 35 Millennium Falcon 20.00
__ 36 Wedge Antilles 20.00
__ 37 Landspeeder 20.00
__ 38 Imperial Shuttle 20.00
__ 39 Grievous' Bodyguard 20.00
__ 40 Aayla Secura 20.00
__ 41 Gamorrean Guard 20.00
__ 42 Qui-Gon Jinn 20.00
__ 43 Snowtrooper 20.00
__ 44 Boushh 20.00
__ 45 Oola 20.00
__ 46 TIE Fighter Pilot 20.00
__ 47 Super Battle Droid 20.00
__ 48 Zam Wesell 20.00
__ 49 Shaak Ti 20.00
__ 50 Watto 20.00
__ 51 Max Rebo 20.00
__ 52 Hoth Rebel Trooper 20.00
__ 53 Scout Trooper 20.00
__ 54 Zuckuss 20.00
__ 55 Lobot 20.00
__ 56 4-LOM 20.00
__ 57 Bossk 20.00
__ 58 Dengar 20.00
__ 59 Y-Wing 20.00
__ 60 Slave I 20.00

Disney / MGM
__ Artoo Detoo [TYF104] 8.00
__ Chewbacca [TYF105] 8.00
__ Darth Vader [TYF106] 8.00
__ See Threepio [TYF107] 8.00
__ Stormtrooper [TYF108] 8.00
__ Wicket the Ewok [TYF109].................................8.00
__ Yoda [TYF110] 8.00

Series 4 Collector Packs. Blind packed in packets of three.
__ Boba Fett [TYF111]...3.00
__ C-3PO [TYF112]..3.00

__ Captain Rex [TYF113]..3.00
__ Chewbacca [TYF114] 3.00
__ Darth Maul [TYF115]..3.00
__ Darth Vader [TYF116]...3.00
__ Ewok [TYF117]...3.00
__ Jabba the Hutt [TYF118].....................................3.00
__ Jar Jar Binks [TYF119] 3.00
__ Jedi Mickey [TYF120] 3.00
__ Mickey Mouse as Luke Skywalker [TYF121] 3.00
__ Millennium Falcon [TYF122] 3.00
__ Minnie Mouse as Princess Leia [TYF123]........3.00
__ R2-D2 [TYF124] 3.00
__ Star Tours Starspeeder 3000 [TYF125] 3.00
__ Stormtrooper [TYF126] 3.00
__ X-Wing Fighter [TYF127] 3.00
__ Yoda [TYF128] 3.00

Series 9 Collector Packs. Blind packed in packets of three.
__ Admiral Ackbar [TYF129] 3.00
__ AT-AT [TYF130] 3.00
__ Clone Trooper [TYF131].....................................3.00
__ Clone Trooper colored (secret) [TYF132]........10.00
__ Darth Vader [TYF133]...3.00
__ Darth Vader's TIE Fighter [TYF134] 3.00
__ Death Star [TYF135] 3.00
__ DL-X2 Attraction Droid [TYF136].........................3.00
__ Donald Duck as Darth Maul [TYF137] 3.00
__ Goofy as Darth Vader [TYF138]..........................3.00
__ Greedo [TYF139]...3.00
__ Imperial Royal Guard [TYF140]............................3.00
__ Jango Fett [TYF141] 3.00
__ Jawa [TYF142] 3.00
__ Star Destroyer [TYF143] 3.00
__ Star Tours Cast Member [TYF144] 3.00
__ Stitch as Emperor [TYF145]................................3.00
__ Teek [TYF146]..3.00
__ Tusken Raider [TYF147] 3.00
__ Unopened package [TYF148].............................9.00

Kamiru
__ Boba Fett with tin storage cylinder [TYF149]...15.00
__ Boba Fett, single figure promotion 18.00
__ Clone Set 1: 4 clones, clone commander [TYF150]..50.00
__ Clone Set 1: 4 clones, clone pilot [TYF151]....50.00
__ Han in Carbonite Block, single figure promotion [TYF152]...16.00
__ Set 1, ANH: R2-D2, C-3PO. Princess Leia, Ben Kenobi [TYF153] 45.00
__ Set 2, ESB: Stormtrooper, Han, Chewbacca, Boba Fett [TYF154] 52.00
__ Set 3, ROTJ: Darth Vader, Luke, Yoda, Emperor [TYF155]..45.00
__ Set 4: Death Star Escape: Luke and Han in Stormtrooper disguise, Chewbacca [TYF156]...45.00
__ Set 5, EPI: Qui-Gon Jinn and Darth Maul [TYF157]..25.00
__ Speederbike trooper and speederbike with storage tin [TYF158]...35.00
__ Stormtrooper 10.00

Kotobukiya, Japan
One coin figures.
__ Han Solo chase figure from Indiana Jones series 35.00

Lego
Episode III.
__ Anakin Skywalker with light-up lightsaber, 2004 gift [TYF159].....................25.00

Maruka, Japan
__ 50-piece multipack 125.00
__ C-3PO 9.00
__ Darth Vader's TIE Fighter [TYF160] 9.00
__ Landspeeder 9.00
__ Millennium Falcon [TYF161] 9.00
__ R2-D2 ....9.00
__ X-Wing Fighter [TYF162].................................9.00
__ Y-Wing Fighter [TYF163] 9.00

Takara Tomy Arts, Japan
2-pack of Touma figures connected by ball chain.
__ Anakin Skywalker and Han Solo (secret) [TYF164]...20.00
__ Boba Fett and Han Solo [TYF165]..................12.00
__ Princess Leia and Luke Skywalker [TYF166]..12.00
__ R2-D2 and C-3PO [TYF167] 12.00
__ Stormtrooper and Darth Vader [TYF168].......12.00
__ Wicket and Yoda [TYF169] 12.00

Tomy, Japan
__ Anakin and Sebulba [TYF170] 4.00
__ Anakin and Watto [TYF171] 4.00
__ Battle Droid on Stap [TYF172]..........................4.00
__ Darth Maul on Sith Speeder [TYF173] 4.00
__ Destroyer Droid [TYF174] 5.00
__ Nute Gunray and Senator Palpatine [TYF175]...4.00
__ Obi-Wan and Darth Maul [TYF176]...................4.00
__ Obi-Wan and TC-14 [TYF177]..........................4.00
__ Qui-Gon and Jar Jar Binks [TYF178].................4.00
__ Qui-Gon with lightsaber and Jar Jar Binks [TYF179]...4.00

Mini deformed figures. Series 1.
__ Boba Fett [TYF180] 6.00
__ C-3PO [TYF181]...6.00
__ Darth Vader [TYF182] 6.00
__ K-3PO (secret) 24.00
__ R2-D2 [TYF183] 6.00
__ R2-Q5 (secret) [TYF184] 20.00
__ Shadow Trooper, exclusive to Hyper Hobby [TYF185]..50.00
__ Stormtrooper [TYF186].....................................6.00
__ Yoda [TYF187] 6.00

The LEGO Group
__ A-Wing Pilot...3.00
__ Aldar Beedo 3.00
__ Anakin Skywalker Naboo pilot..........................3.00
__ Anakin Skywalker no cape................................3.00
__ Anakin Skywalker podracer 3.00
__ Anakin Skywalker with cape 3.00
__ AT-AT Driver 3.00
__ B-Wing Pilot..3.00
__ Battle Droid blue pilot......................................3.00
__ Battle Droid no backpack 3.00
__ Battle Droid red security 3.00
__ Battle Droid with backpack 3.00
__ Battle Droid yellow commander 3.00
__ Bib Fortuna 3.00
__ Biggs Darklighter 3.00
__ Boba Fett 3.00
__ Boba Fett detailed 3.00
__ Boba Fett young 3.00
__ C-3PO 3.00
__ Captain Tarpals..3.00
__ Chewbacca 3.00
__ Clone Trooper 3.00
__ Count Dooku..3.00
__ Dack Ralter 3.00
__ Darth Maul 3.00
__ Darth Vader removable helmet 3.00
__ Echo Base trooper..3.00
__ Emperor Palpatine black hands........................3.00
__ Emperor Palpatine yellow hands 3.00
__ Emperor's Royal Guard 3.00
__ EV-9D9...3.00
__ Flash speeder pilot 3.00
__ Gamorrean Guard 3.00
__ Gasgano 3.00
__ Geonosian pilot..3.00
__ Geonosian warrior 3.00
__ Greedo 3.00
__ Han Solo blue pants with vest 3.00
__ Han Solo brown pants no vest 3.00
__ Han Solo brown pants with vest.......................3.00
__ Han Solo in carbonite 3.00
__ Hoth rebel soldier 3.00
__ Imperial Officer 3.00
__ Imperial Pilot 3.00
__ Jabba the Hutt..5.00
__ Jango Fett 3.00
__ Jar-Jar Binks..3.00

__ Jedi 3.00
__ Kaadu...3.00
__ Lando Calrissian 3.00
__ Lobot...3.00
__ Luke Skywalker Bespin.....................................3.00
__ Luke Skywalker Dagobah 3.00
__ Luke Skywalker jedi Endor 3.00
__ Luke Skywalker jedi hood up, yellow hand 3.00
__ Luke Skywalker jedi no hood, black hand........3.00
__ Luke Skywalker pilot...3.00
__ Luke Skywalker Tatooine 3.00
__ Mechanic, A-Wing 3.00
__ Mechanic, X-Wing/B-Wing 3.00
__ Obi-Wan Kenobi (OT)..3.00
__ Obi-Wan Kenobi (PT) no hood..........................3.00
__ Obi-Wan Kenobi (PT) no hood, headset...........3.00
__ Obi-Wan Kenobi (PT) with hood 3.00
__ Padme Naberrie 3.00
__ Paploo 3.00
__ Pit Droid brown 3.00
__ Pit Droid brown and white 3.00
__ Pit Droid white 3.00
__ Princess Leia 3.00
__ Princess Leia Bespin..3.00
__ Princess Leia Jabba's captive 3.00
__ Qui-Gon Jinn..3.00
__ R2 unit red 3.00
__ R2-D2 ....3.00
__ Sandtrooper..3.00
__ Scout Trooper 3.00
__ Sebulba 3.00
__ Snowtrooper 3.00
__ Stormtrooper 3.00
__ Super Battle Droid 3.00
__ T-16 Skyhopper Pilot 3.00
__ TIE Fighter Pilot 3.00
__ Tusken Raider 3.00
__ Watto 3.00
__ Wicket 3.00
__ Y-Wing Pilot...3.00
__ Yoda 3.00
__ Zam Wesell / Clawdite......................................3.00

Mini-figure 3-packs.
__ #1 Emperor, Darth Vader, Darth Maul (3340) [T1F001]...25.00
__ #2 Han, Luke, Boba Fett (3341) [T1F002].......25.00
__ #3 Chewbacca, two biker scout troops (3342) [T1F003]...25.00
__ #4 OOM-9, two battle droids (3343) [T1F004]...25.00

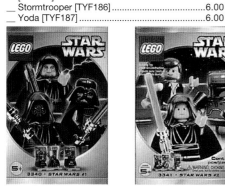
T1F001

T1F002

T1F003

T1F004

T1F005

T1F006

T1F007

T1F008

T1F009

T2F001

T2F002

T2F003

T2F004

T2F005

T2F006

T2F007

T2F008

Promotional.
__ Boba Fett, concept [T1F005] 35.00
__ C-3PO, gold, limited to 10,000 [T1F006] 190.00
__ Darth Vader, chromed [T1F007] 35.00
__ Shadow ARF Trooper [T1F008] 35.00
__ Stormtrooper, chromed [T1F009] 35.00

Figures: Mpire

Hasbro
2-packs with stands.
__ Chewbacca and Master Windu [T2F001] 10.00
__ Dooku and Maul [T2F002] 10.00
__ Emperor and Anakin [T2F003] 10.00
__ Grievous and Kenobi [T2F004] 10.00

__ Luke and Leia [T2F005] 10.00
__ Queen Amidala, R2-D2, and C-3PO [T2F006] 10.00
__ Solo and Boba Fett [T2F007] 12.00
__ Stormtrooper and Vader [T2F008] 12.00

2-packs with stands. Special Collector's Edition.
__ Dooku and Maul 15.00
__ Luke and Leia 15.00
__ Queen Amidala, R2-D2, and C-3PO 15.00
__ Solo and Boba Fett..15.00

Figures: Plastic / Resin / Vinyl

Deformed figures, approx. 3" tall. No articulation.
__ Anakin Skywalker [FG001] 5.00

__ Battle Droid [FG002] 5.00
__ C-3PO [FG003] 5.00
__ Darth Maul [FG004] 5.00
__ Darth Maul, hooded [FG005] 5.00
__ Jar Jar Binks [FG006] 5.00
__ Mace Windu [FG007] 5.00
__ Obi-Wan Kenobi [FG008] 5.00
__ Qui-Gon Jinn [FG009] 5.00
__ Sebulba [FG010] 5.00

Deformed style figures, approximately 4" tall. No articulation.
__ Anakin Skywalker [FG011] 6.00
__ Darth Maul [FG012]...6.00
__ Sebulba, swivels at neck [FG013]....................6.00
__ Watto, swivels at waist [FG014].......................6.00

FG001

FG002

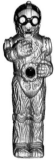

FG003

FG004

FG005

FG006

FG007

FG008

FG009

FG010

FG011

FG012

FG013

FG014

FG015

FG016

FG017　　　　FG018　　　　FG019　　　　FG020　　　　FG021　　　　FG022　　　　FG023

FG024　　　　FG025　　　　FG026　　　　FG027　　　　FG028　　　　FG029　　　　FG030　　　　FG031

FG032　　　　FG033　　　　FG034　　　　FG035　　　　FG036　　　　FG037　　　　FG038　　　　FG039

FG040　　　　FG041　　　　FG042　　　　FG043　　　　FG044　　　　FG045

FG046　　　　FG047　　　　FG048　　　　FG049　　　　FG050

FG051

FG052

FG053

FG054

FG055

FG056

FG057

FG058 side 1

FG058 side 2

FG058 side 3

FG059

FG060

FG061

FG062

FG063

FG064

FG065

FG066

FG067

FG068

FG069

FG070

FG071

FG072   FG073   FG074   FG075   Package for FG076-FG083

FG076   FG077   FG078   FG079   FG080

FG081   FG082   FG083   FG084

FG085   FG086   FG087   FG088   FG089

FG090   FG091   FG092   FG093   FG094   FG095   FG096

Figures: Plastic / Resin / Vinyl

FG097   FG098   FG099   FG100   FG101   FG102

FG103   FG104   FG105   FG106   FG107

FG108   FG109   FG110   FG111

Argentina.
__ Chewbacca..12.00

Belgium.
__ Darth Vader [FG015] 15.00

Applause
__ Darth Vader with removable helmet 24.00

Classic trilogy characters.
__ Boba Fett [FG016] 30.00
__ C-3PO [FG017] 15.00
__ Chewbacca w/ C-3PO in cargo net [FG018] ..18.00
__ Darth Vader [FG019] 23.00
__ Darth Vader with removable dome, limited edition
[FG020] 48.00
__ Darth Vader, cloth cape [FG021] 18.00
__ Dash Rendar [FG022] 10.00
__ Emperor Palpatine [FG023] 18.00
__ Greedo [FG024] 18.00
__ Han Solo in Stormtrooper disguise [FG025]...18.00
__ Lando Calrissian in Skiff disguise [FG026] 18.00
__ Leia as Jabba's Prisoner [FG027]...................24.00
__ Luke Skywalker in Pilot Gear [FG028] 35.00
__ Luke Skywalker, Jedi Training with glow-in-dark
lightsaber [FG029] 17.00
__ Luke with Yoda in backpack [FG030]...............12.00
__ Luke with Yoda in backpack, pewter colored plastic
[FG031] 24.00
__ Obi-Wan Kenobi [FG032]..................................18.00
__ Obi-Wan Kenobi, glow-in-dark [FG033] 20.00
__ Prince Xizor [FG034]...26.00
__ Princess Leia and R2-D2 ....22.00
__ Princess Leia, Endor outfit [FG035]................18.00
__ R2-D2 [FG036]..18.00
__ TIE Fighter Pilot [FG037]..................................18.00
__ Tusken Raider [FG038] 18.00

__ Wedge Antillies [FG039] 20.00

Episode I: The Phantom Menace. "Collectible Character," approximately 10" tall.
__ Darth Maul [FG040]..11.00
__ Obi-Wan Kenobi [FG041]...............................11.00
__ Queen Amidala [FG042] 11.00
__ Qui-Gon Jinn [FG043] 11.00

Episode I: The Phantom Menace. "Mega Collectible," approx 14" with lighted saber in numbered package.
__ Darth Maul [FG044]..50.00
__ Obi-Wan Kenobi [FG045]...............................50.00
__ Qui-Gon Jinn [FG046] 50.00

Episode I: The Phantom Menace. Approximately 7" tall. Some articulation
__ Anakin Skywalker [FG047]..............................8.00
__ Darth Maul with binoculars [FG048] 8.00
__ Jar Jar Binks [FG049] 8.00
__ Watto [FG050]..8.00

Daft Productions Ltd.
Daft Ducks.
__ Luke, part of a larger non-Star Wars series
[FG051] 15.00

Decopac
Episode I: The Phantom Menace Cake top figures.
__ Jar Jar Binks..4.00
__ Watto 9.00

Episode II: Attack of the Clones cake top figures.
__ Darth Vader [FG052]......................................6.00
__ Jango Fett [FG053] 6.00

__ Obi-Wan Kenobi [FG054]...............................6.00

Episode III: Revenge of the Sith cake top figures.
__ Yoda with light-up saber 8.00

Disney Theme Park Merchandise
Collectible figures.
__ 6-Pack Collectible Figures Jango Fett, Battle Droid,
Clone Trooper, Darth Maul, General Grievous, Jar
Jar Binks [FG055] 35.00
__ 6-Pack Collectible Muppet Figures Kermit,
Miss Piggy, Beaker, Gonzo, Rizzo, Fozzy Bear
[FG056] 35.00
__ 8-Pack Collectible Figures Yoda, Chewbacca,
Boba Fett, C-3PO, Wicket, Stormtrooper, R2-D2,
Darth Vader [FG057] 35.00

Bathtub toys.
__ 7-Pack of soft figures Yoda, C-3PO, R2-D2,
Chewbacca, Stormtrooper, Boba Fett, Darth Vader
[FG058] 50.00

Vinylmation.
__ Boba Fett [FG059] 18.00
__ C-3PO [FG060] 18.00
__ Chewbacca [FG061] 18.00
__ Darth Vader [FG062] 18.00
__ Han Solo [FG063] 18.00
__ Lando Calrissian [FG064] 18.00
__ Luke Skywalker [FG065] 18.00
__ Obi-Wan Kenobi chase figure [FG066]..........65.00
__ Obi-Wan Kenobi spirit super chase figure
[FG067] 135.00
__ Princess Leia [FG068].....................................18.00
__ R2-D2 [FG069]..18.00

290

FG112   FG113   FG114   FG115   FG116

__ Stormtrooper [FG070].....................................18.00
__ Yoda [FG071]..18.00

Gentle Giant Studios
Kustomz. Rotocast vinyl with certificate of authenticity.
__ Darth Vader on Imperial Star Destroyer..........75.00
__ Jawas in Sandcrawler......................................75.00
__ Scout Trooper on Speeder Bike 75.00
__ TIE Pilot with TIE Fighter................................75.00
__ TIE Pilot with TIE Fighter, red, exclusive to Star Wars Celebration Japan 75.00

Hasbro
__ Anakin Skywalker [FG072]..............................12.00
__ Darth Vader [FG073].....................................12.00
__ Jango Fett [FG074] 12.00
__ Mace Windu [FG075] 12.00

Itrangers Lab
Ciboy Star Wash (parody).
__ Dark Vapor (Darth Vader) [FG076] 20.00
__ Sh-it (Darth Maul) [FG077] 20.00
__ Skywasher (Luke) [FG078] 20.00
__ Soapie (Chewie) [FG079] 20.00
__ Wash Trooper (stormtrooper) [FG080]...........20.00
__ Washer Master (Yoda) [FG081]......................20.00
__ WC30 (C-3PO) [FG082] 20.00
__ WC30, silver (C-3PO; chase figure) [FG083] 25.00

Jack Candy, Argentina
__ Robot 1 (C-3PO) 34.00
__ Robot 2 (R2-D2)...34.00

Kinder
Hippo Star Wars parody figure accessories.
__ Blue Star diorama play scene.........................35.00
__ Hippo Landspeeder [FG084] 25.00
__ Millennium Hippo, limited edition, numbered [FG085] 4.00

Hippo Star Wars parody figures.
__ Aubacca [FG086]..4.00
__ Dark Laser [FG087]..4.00
__ Dark Laser, black [FG088]................................65.00
__ ER2WO Hippo [FG089]......................................4.00
__ H-IPO [FG090] 4.00
__ Happy Han [FG091] 4.00
__ Hippoda [FG092] 4.00
__ Jango Jett [FG093] 4.00
__ Luke Eiwalker [FG094] 4.00
__ Obi-Wan Hippobi [FG095] 4.00
__ Prinzessin Hippeia [FG096]..............................4.00

Kurt S. Adler, Inc.
Christmas figures. 2005.
__ C-3PO wrapped in lights [FG097]...................20.00
__ R2-D2 with presents [FG098].........................20.00
__ Santa Yoda [FG099] 20.00

Christmas figures. 2006.
__ Darth Vader building Death Star in snow [FG100]...20.00
__ Santa Yoda [FG101] 20.00

Christmas figures. 2007.
__ Boba Fett, Christmas delivery [FG102]...........30.00
__ C-3PO with wreath [FG103]...........................30.00
__ Darth Vader building Death Star from Snow ..30.00

__ Jawas with Christmas toys [FG104] 30.00
__ R2-D2 with presents [FG105] 30.00
__ Santa Yoda [FG106] 20.00

M&M World
Approx. 6" tall with removable base. Limited to 2,500 each.
__ Boba Fett [FG107] 45.00
__ Darth Maul [FG108].......................................45.00
__ Darth Vader [FG109].....................................45.00
__ Luke Skywalker [FG110]................................45.00
__ Princess Leia [FG111]....................................45.00

Medicom, Japan
Vinyl Collectible Dolls, oversized.
__ Darth Vader, limited to 600 ....200.00

Vinyl Collectible Dolls.
__ 501st Clone Trooper, exclusive to Comicon [FG112] 95.00
__ Black Hole Stormtrooper, limited to 1,000, exclusive to San Diego Comic-Con [FG113]................100.00
__ Black Hole Stormtrooper 75.00
__ Boba Fett ESB [FG114] 65.00
__ Boba Fett, World Character Convention 18, limited to 2,004...175.00
__ C-3PO 75.00
__ C-3PO 75.00
__ Clone Trooper, limited to 2,006 [FG115] 75.00
__ Darth Maul 75.00
__ Darth Vader...75.00
__ Imperial Royal Guard, limited to 2,007 ....75.00
__ Jawa 85.00
__ R2-D2..75.00

FG117   FG118   FG119   FG120   FG121   FG122   FG123   FG124   FG125

FG126   FG127   FG128   FG129   FG130   FG131

__ Shadow Guard	100.00
__ Stormtrooper [FG116]	75.00
__ TC-14	120.00
__ TIE Pilot	75.00
__ Wicket	120.00
__ Yoda	75.00
__ Yoda	75.00

Out of Character

__ C-3PO [FG117]	19.00
__ Chewbacca [FG118]	17.00
__ Darth Vader [FG119]	18.00
__ Han Solo [FG120]	17.00
__ Luke Skywalker, Jedi [FG121]	17.00
__ Luke Skywalker, X-wing pilot [FG122]	24.00
__ Obi-Wan Kenobi [FG123]	18.00
__ Princess Leia [FG124]	17.00

__ R2-D2 [FG125]	19.00
__ Stormtrooper [FG126]	18.00

Super7

__ Super Shogun StormTrooper 24" tall, spring-loaded firing fist, metallic stickers in English and Japanese, numbered [FG127] 350.00

Takara, Japan

__ C-3PO [FG128]	245.00
__ Chewbacca [FG129]	245.00
__ Darth Vader [FG130]	245.00
__ Stormtrooper [FG131]	245.00

__ Anakin Skywalker [AFU001]	45.00
__ Darth Maul [AFU002]	85.00
__ Darth Sidious [AFU003]	35.00
__ Darth Tyrannus [AFU004]	50.00
__ Darth Vader [AFU005]	100.00
__ Darth Vader (removable helmet) [AFU006]	265.00
__ Jango Fett and Boba Fett [AFU007]	60.00
__ Luke Skywalker, Jedi [AFU008]	70.00
__ Mace Windu [AFU009]	40.00
__ Obi-Wan Kenobi [AFU010]	40.00
__ Padme Amidala [AFU011]	70.00
__ Princess Leia [AFU012]	120.00

Color package.

__ Aayla Secura [AFU013]	40.00
__ Anakin Skywalker, EPIII [AFU014]	48.00

Figures: Unleashed

AFU001

AFU002

AFU003

AFU004

AFU005

AFU006

AFU007

AFU008

AFU009

AFU010

AFU011

AFU012

AFU013

AFU014

AFU015

AFU016

AFU017

AFU018

AFU019

AFU020

AFU021

AFU022

AFU023

AFU024

| AFU025 | AFU026 | AFU027 | AFU028 | AFU029 | AFU030 |

| AFU031 | AFU032 | AFU033 | AFU034 | AFU035 | AFU036 |

| AFU037 | AFU038 | AFU039 | AFU040 | AFU041 | AFU042 |

| AFU043 | AFU044 | AFU045 | AFU054 | AFU046 | AFU047 |

| AFU048 | AFU049 | AFU050 | AFU051 | AFU052 | AFU053 |

Figures: Unleashed

___ Asajj Ventress [AFU015] 15.00
___ Aura Sing [AFU016] 30.00
___ Boba Fett [AFU017] 120.00
___ Bossk [AFU018] 20.00
___ Chewbacca [AFU019] 40.00
___ Chewbacca on Kashyyyk [AFU020] 30.00
___ Clone Commander [AFU021] 25.00
___ Clone Trooper [AFU022] 20.00
___ Count Dooku [AFU023].................................50.00
___ Darth Sidious [AFU024] 40.00
___ Darth Vader (removable helmet) [AFU025] 60.00
___ Darth Vader, EPIII [AFU026] 20.00
___ General Grievous [AFU027] 25.00
___ Han Solo [AFU028] 80.00
___ Han Solo in Stormtrooper outfit [AFU029]...20.00
___ IG-88 [AFU030] 30.00
___ Luke Skywalker [AFU031] 60.00
___ Luke Skywalker, pilot [AFU032]....................40.00
___ Mace Windu [AFU033]..................................40.00
___ Obi-Wan Kenobi [AFU034] 40.00
___ Obi-Wan Kenobi, EPIII [AFU035] 15.00
___ Princess Leia [AFU036]................................70.00
___ Shock Trooper [AFU037] 20.00
___ Stormtrooper [AFU038]................................80.00
___ Tusken Raider [AFU039] 20.00
___ Yoda [AFU040]...100.00
___ Yoda vs. Palpatine [AFU041] 35.00

Cylinder-shaped package.
___ Anakin Skywalker, ROTS..............................30.00
___ ARC heavy gunner, exclusive to internet
    [AFU042]..30.00
___ Boba Fett, exclusive to Target [AFU043]........30.00

___ Darth Vader, excl. to Best Buy [AFU044]........50.00
___ Darth Vader, excl. to Walmart [AFU045].........30.00
___ General Grievous, exclusive to Target
    [AFU046]..30.00
___ Luke Skywalker, exclusive to Walmart
    [AFU047]..30.00
___ Obi-Wan Kenobi, ROTS [AFU048]..................30.00
___ Shadow Stormtrooper [AFU049] 45.00

Unused cardbacks. ComicCon 2004 exclusive.
___ Aayla Secura 10.00
___ Bossk 10.00
___ Tusken Raider 10.00

Hasbro, Canada
Blue package.
___ Darth Maul [AFU050] 20.00
___ Jango Fett and Boba Fett [AFU051] 20.00

No SW Unleashed logo on cardback.
___ Anakin Skywalker [AFU052]..........................25.00
___ Darth Vader [AFU053] 35.00
___ Padme Amidala [AFU054]............................35.00

Figures: Unleashed Battle Packs

Hasbro
___ Commander Bly [A1U001] 3.00
___ Darth Vader [A1U002].....................................3.00
___ Darth Vader (Anakin) [A1U003] 3.00
___ Han Solo [A1U004]...3.00
___ Luke Skywalker [A1U005]................................3.00

___ Mace Windu [A1U006]....................................3.00
___ Obi-Wan Kenobi [A1U007] 3.00
___ Shock Trooper [A1U008] 3.00
___ Stormtrooper [A1U009]...................................3.00

4-packs, black and silver packaging.
___ Aayla Secura's Star Corps [A1U010].............10.00
___ Attack Battalion, standing trooper is on
    right...10.00
___ Attack Battalion, standing trooper second from left
    [A1U011]..10.00
___ Battle Droids, battle droid on left [A1U012]....10.00
___ Battle Droids, destroyer droid on left.............10.00
___ Commanders [A1U013] 10.00
___ Imperial Encounter [A1U014]........................10.00
___ Imperial Invasion [A1U015]...........................10.00
___ Imperial Snowtroopers [A1U016]...................10.00
___ Jedi Masters [A1U017] 10.00
___ Kashyyyk and Felucia Heroes [A1U018].........10.00
___ Rebel Alliance Troopers [A1U019]..................10.00
___ Shock Trooper Battalion [A1U020].................10.00
___ Snowtrooper Battalion [A1U021]...................10.00
___ The New Empire [A1U022]............................10.00
___ Utapaun Warriors, kneeling warrior on left
    [A1U023]..10.00
___ Utapaun Warriors, kneeling warrior on right...10.00
___ Vader's 501st Legion [A1U024] 10.00
___ Wampa Assault [A1U025]..............................10.00
___ Wookiee Warriors [A1U026]...........................10.00
___ Yoda's Elite Corps [A1U027] 10.00

4-packs, blue and white packaging.
___ 501st Legion [A1U028] 10.00
___ ARC Troopers [A1U029] 10.00

A1U001 A1U002 A1U003 A1U004 A1U005 A1U006

A1U007 A1U008 A1U009 A1U010 A1U011

A1U012 A1U013 A1U014 A1U015 A1U016

A1U017

A1U018

A1U019

A1U020

A1U021

A1U022

A1U023

A1U024

A1U025

A1U026

A1U027

A1U028

A1U029

A1U030

A1U031

A1U032

A1U033

A1U034

A1U035

A1U036

A1U037

A1U038

A1U039

A1U040

A1U041

A1U042

A1U043

A1U044

A1U045

A1U046

A1U047

A1U048

A1U049

A1U050

A1U051

A1U052

A1U053

A1U054

A1U055

A1U056

A1U057

A1U058

A1U059

A1U060

A1U061

A1U062

A1U063

A1U064

A1U065

A1U066

A1U067   A1U068   A1U069

A1U070   A1U071

___ Battle Droid Factory [A1U030] 10.00
___ Battle Droids [A1U031] 10.00
___ Clone Troopers [A1U032] 10.00
___ Clone Troopers (Battle Front II) [A1U033].......10.00
___ Commanders [A1U034] 10.00
___ Jedi Generals [A1U035] 10.00
___ Jedi Heroes [A1U036] 10.00
___ Jedi vs. Sith [A1U037] 10.00
___ Shock Trooper Battalion [A1U038] 10.00
___ Theed Battle Heroes [A1U039] 10.00
___ Vader's Bounty Hunters [A1U040] 10.00
___ Yoda's Elite Clone Troopers [A1U041] 10.00

4-packs, color packaging.
___ 187th Legion Troopers [A1U042] 10.00
___ A New Empire [A1U043] 10.00
___ Aayla Secura's 327th Star Corps [A1U044]....10.00
___ Battle Droid Factory [A1U045] 10.00
___ Battle Droids [A1U046] 10.00

___ Cantina Encounter [A1U047] 10.00
___ Commanders (Tantive IV) [A1U048]................10.00
___ Commanders (Utapau) [A1U049]......................10.00
___ Imperial and Rebel Commanders [A1U050] ...10.00
___ Imperial and Rebel Pilots [A1U051] 10.00
___ Imperial Troopers [A1U052] 10.00
___ Imperial Troops [A1U053] 10.00
___ Jawas and Droids [A1U054] 10.00
___ Jedi Masters [A1U055] 10.00
___ Mygeeto Clone Battalion [A1U056] 10.00
___ Rebel Blockade Troopers [A1U057] 10.00
___ Sandtrooper Search [A1U058] 10.00
___ Shock Trooper Battalion [A1U059] 10.00
___ Stormtrooper Boarding Party [A1U060]..........10.00
___ The Empire [A1U061]......................................10.00
___ The Streets of Mos Eisley [A1U062] 10.00
___ Tusken Raiders [A1U063] 10.00
___ Unleashed Warriors [A1U064] 10.00
___ Vader's 501st Legion [A1U065] 10.00

___ Yoda's Elite Clone Troopers [A1U066] 10.00

Deluxe.
___ Evacuation at Echo Base [A1U067]................12.00
___ Snowspeeder Assault [A1U068] 12.00

Ultimate battle packs.
___ Droid Invasion Battle of Kashyyyk
[A1U069]...20.00
___ Imperial Invasion Battle of Hoth
[A1U070]...20.00
___ The Clone Wars Battle of Geonosis
[A1U071]...20.00

Fingerboards

Germany. Clone Wars fingerboard skatepark ramp and rail accessories.
___ Obi-Wan deck / Yoda ramp [FGR001]............30.00
___ Obi-Wan ramp / Yoda ramp [FGR002] 30.00
___ Yoda Ramp / Clone Trooper high rail
[FGR003]...30.00
___ Yoda Ramp / Clone Wars rail
[FGR004]...30.00

Flight Simulators

Kenner
___ X-Wing Flight Simulator, electronic lights and sounds [YJ001] 30.00

FGR001   FGR002

FGR003   FGR004   YJ001

Flying Discs

Flying Discs

Burger King
__ Darth Vader [FRI001] 25.00

KFC
__ Battle Droid flying bucket topper [FRI002] 4.00
__ Jar Jar Binks flying bucket topper [FRI003]......4.00

Pine-Sol
Line art and logo. Mail-in premiums.
__ C-3PO [FRI004]...35.00
__ Chewbacca [FRI005] 35.00
__ Darth Vader [FRI006] 35.00
__ R2-D2 [FRI007] 35.00
__ Stormtrooper [FRI008] 35.00

__ X-Wing Fighter [FRI009]...............................35.00

Rand International
__ Mini Flying Space Discs, 3-pack [FRI010]........5.00

Splash Discs.
__ Clone Trooper [FRI011].................................5.00
__ Jedi Starfighter, exclusive to Dollar Tree [FRI012]..5.00

Spectra Star
__ Star Wars logo above raised images of Star Destroyer and Millennium Falcon [FRI013].....10.00

Worlds Apart, UK
__ Darth Maul E.Pix flying disc, glows in the dark [FRI014]..11.00

__ Whizza Performance Disc, Star Wars logo and X-wings on colored sticker 20.00

Skimmer discs.
__ Imperial Fighter [FRI015]..............................12.00
__ Stormtrooper [FRI016] 12.00

Games: Board

Argentina.
__ Fureza Jedi vs. Sepratistas [NB001]...............50.00
__ Sorry-like party game [NB002] 10.00

Greece.
__ Return of the Jedi 170.00

Spain.
__ La Guerre Des Etoiles 65.00

20th Century Fox
__ EPII Dice scoring game with cloth storage pouch, promotional..25.00

Avalon Hill
__ The Queens Gambit [NB003].........................60.00

Character Games, Ltd.
__ Jango Fett: Journey to Geonosis water maze [NB004] 10.00
__ Rescue on Geonosis [NB005].........................25.00

EG
__ Star Wars The Game 45.00

FRI001

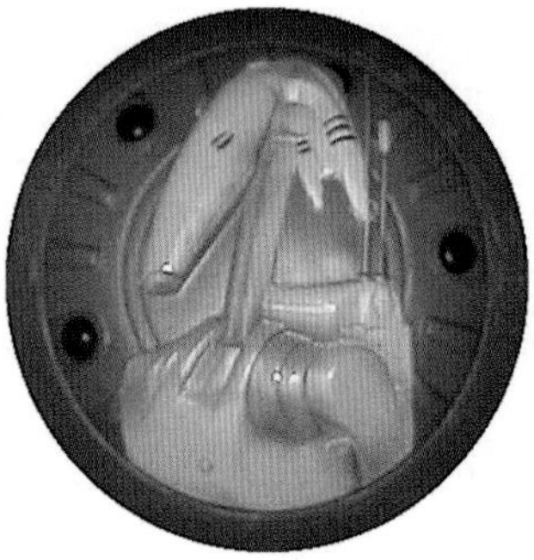

FRI002

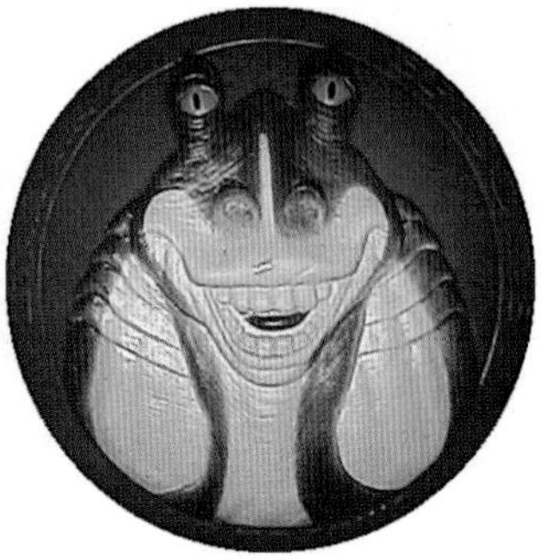

FRI003

FRI004

FRI005

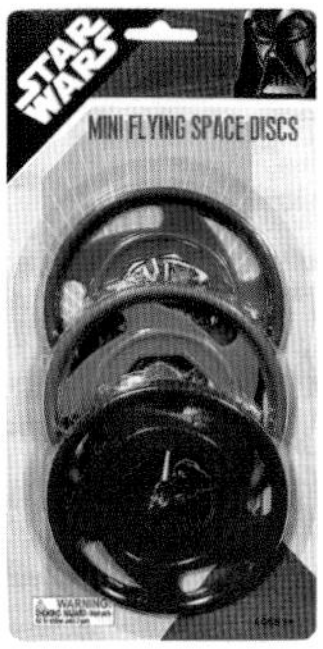

FRI010

FRI011

FRI012

FRI006

FRI007

FRI013

FRI014

FRI008

FRI009

FRI015

FRI016

NB001

NB002

NB003

NB004

NB005

NB006

NB007

NB008

Gamma Two
__ Star Wars [NB006] 55.00

Hasbro
__ AAT Attack [NB007] 30.00
__ Battle for Naboo 3D action game [NB008] 20.00
__ Galactic Battle, Episode I, electronic [NB009]35.00

__ Jar Jar Binks 3-D adventure game [NB010] ...15.00
__ Lightsaber Duel battle game [NB011].............20.00
__ R2-D2 is in Trouble 15.00
__ Simon space battle game [NB012] 34.00
__ Star Wars Monopoly, Episode I edition
   [NB013] 35.00

Horn Abbott International, Australia
__ Trivial Pursuit, Star Wars Bite Size
   [NB014] 25.00

IMC Toys, UK
__ Clone 4 [NB015] 25.00

NB009

NB010

NB011

NB012

NB013

NB014

NB015

NB016

NB017

NB018

NB019

NB020

NB021

NB022

NB023

__ R2-D2 Repair [NB016] 20.00
__ Star Cruiser Attack [NB017]............................30.00

Kenner
__ Adventures of R2-D2 [NB018] 25.00
__ Destroy Death Star [NB019] 55.00
__ Escape from Death Star [NB020]....................40.00
__ Hoth Ice Planet adventure [NB021] 40.00
__ Yoda the Jedi Master [NB022].......................75.00

Kinder
__ Nine Men's Morris, SW hippo [NB023]...........20.00

Kirjalito, Finland
__ Naboon Valloitus [NB024]..............................30.00

Milton Bradley
__ Fighting Figures, Darth Vader vs. Luke Skywalker
[NB025]...16.00
__ Guess Who? [NB029] 25.00

Galactic Heroes.
__ Anakin Skywalker vs. Count Dooku [NB026]..25.00
__ Clone vs. Super Battle Droid [NB027] 25.00
__ Obi-Wan vs. General Grievous [NB028] 25.00

Episode II: Attack of the Clones.
__ Battle Ship [NB030] 25.00
__ Epic Duels [NB031].......................................15.00
__ Jedi Unleashed [NB032] 12.00
__ Life [NB033] 25.00
__ Stratego [NB034] 25.00

Episode III: Revenge of the Sith.
__ Stratego, exclusive to Toys R Us [NB035]......25.00

Montecarlo, Mexico
__ El Regresodel Jedi (Return of the Jedi)
[NB036]..24.00

__ Star Wars El Imperio Contr Ataca (Star Wars)
[NB037]..24.00
__ Star Wars Una Nueva Esperanza (Empire Strikes
Back) [NB038]..18.00

Montenegro, Serbia
__ Star Wars [NB039] 25.00

Palitoy, UK
__ Escape from Death Star 45.00

Parker Bros.
__ Adventures of R2-D2, bi-language 25.00
__ Battle at Sarlacc's Pit [NB040] 35.00
__ Battle at Sarlacc's Pit, bi-language 35.00

NB024

NB025

NB026

NB027

NB028

NB029

NB030

NB031

NB032

NB033

NB034   NB035   NB036

NB037   NB038   NB039

__ Death Star Assault [NB041] 15.00
__ Escape the Death Star [NB042] 15.00
__ La Guerre des Etoiles (Star Wars video board
   game) 25.00
__ Risk: Classic Trilogy edition [NB043] 25.00
__ Risk: Clone Wars edition [NB044] 25.00

__ Star Wars [NB045] 30.00
__ Star Wars Monopoly, classic trilogy edition
   [NB046] 28.00
__ Star Wars Monopoly, classic trilogy edition, Original
   Trilogy Collection [NB047] 40.00
__ Star Wars Monopoly, Clone Wars edition

__ [NB048] 25.00
__ Star Wars Monopoly, collectors edition
   [NB049] 55.00
__ Star Wars Monopoly, Saga edition [NB050] ...25.00
__ Star Wars The Game (Escape from Death
   Star) 50.00

NB040   NB041   NB042

NB043   NB044   NB045

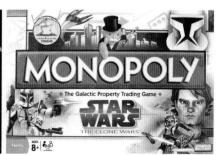

NB046   NB047   NB048

__ Star Wars video board game [NB051]............25.00
__ The Ewoks save the trees [NB052].................45.00
__ Trivial Pursuit, limited edition bonus DVD, exclusive
to Star Wars Celebration III [NB053]...............10.00
__ Trivial Pursuit, Saga edition [NB054] 50.00
__ Trivial Pursuit, Saga edition with (random) bonus
figure, exclusive to BJ's Warehouse...............50.00
__ Trivial Pursuit, Saga edition with collector's tin,
exclusive to Toys R Us 60.00
__ Trivial Pursuit, Star Wars edition [NB055].......55.00
__ Trivial Pursuit, Star Wars edition promo
cards 5.00
__ Wicket the Ewok [NB056] 20.00

NB049

NB050

Parker Bros., Canada
__ Star Wars The Game (Escape from Death Star)......65.00

Parker Bros., Germany
__ Kreig der Sterne...65.00

Parker Bros., Spain
__ Star Wars video board game 30.00

Scholastic
__ Star Wars Episode I: Adventures, Clone Trooper
case [NB057] 18.00
__ Star Wars Episode I: Adventures, Darth Maul case

__ [NB058] 8.00
__ Star Wars Missions [NB059] 16.00

Takara, Japan
__ Escape from Death Star [NB060].................190.00
__ Star Wars [NB061] 65.00

NB051

NB052

NB053

NB054

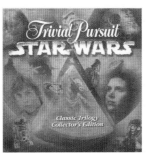

NB055

NB056

NB057

NB058

NB059

NB060

NB061 front and back

NB062

NB063

NB064

NB065

NB066

NB067

NB068

NB069

NB070

NB071

NB072

NB073

NB074

NB075

TGA, UK
__ The Clone Wars 4-in-a-Row [NB062] 50.00

Tiger Electronics
__ Escape from Naboo [NB063] 18.00
__ Galactic Battle, electronic [NB064] 43.00

Toltoys
__ Star Wars The Game (Escape from Death Star) 17.00

Tomy, Japan
Episode III: Revenge of the Sith packaging.
__ Rocketing Darth Vader 40.00

Saga packaging.
__ R2-D2 launching lightsaber game, talking [NB065] 65.00
__ Rocketing Darth Vader [NB066] 40.00

Tsukuda, Japan
__ Death Star 45.00
__ Endor [NB067] 45.00
__ Hoth 45.00

Uzay
__ "Yildiz Savaslari" (Star Wars) [NB068] 27.00

Waddington, UK
__ Star Wars Monopoly, Episode I edition [NB069] 34.00
__ Star Wars Monopoly, Episode II [NB070] 45.00

West End Games
__ Assault on Hoth 30.00
__ Battle for Endor [NB071] 30.00
__ Escape from the Death Star [NB072] 26.00
__ Lightsaber dueling pack [NB073] 10.00
__ Star Warriors - starfighter combat 25.00

__ Starfighter battle book [NB074] 10.00

West End Games, Germany
__ Angriff Auf Hoth [NB075] 32.00

__ Playing cards, Vader images [NC001] 8.00

Argentina.
__ Burako [NC002] 20.00
__ Domino [NC003] 35.00
__ La Venganza De Los Sith [NC004]..................15.00
__ Loteria Infantil 20.00

Brazil.
__ Domino (flat cardboard) [NC005] 20.00
__ Memotest [NC006]..20.00

Hungary.
__ Return of the Jedi (matching) 23.00

Cartamundi
__ 3-Card Match [NC007] 12.00
__ Happy Families [NC008] 12.00

Character Games, Ltd.
__ Feel the Force Hidden Powers Game [NC009] .. 24.00

Copag, Brazil
__ Uno [NC010].. 25.00

Cromy
__ El Regresodel Jedi (Return of the Jedi) [NC011] 45.00

Crown Products, UK
__ Fish, Clone Wars [NC012]...............................15.00

__ Fish, Star Wars [NC013] 15.00
__ Snap [NC014] 15.00

Decipher
__ Empire Strikes Back 2 player introductory game 15.00
__ Episode I Customizable Card Game, 160 cards in 4 decks plus rules................................14.00
__ First Anthology Collectible Card Game 19.00
__ Official Tournament Sealed Deck 43.00
__ Star Wars 2 player introductory game............20.00
__ Young Jedi Collectible Card Game (CCG) 40 Card Sample Pack (2 sample decks) 'Not For Sale' .5.00

Hasbro
__ Clash of the Lightsabers [NC015]....................8.00

Heraclio Fournier
Spain
__ Droids / Ewoks..60.00

Nick Trost
__ Star Wars Card Trick 30.00

Parker Bros.
__ Ewoks: Favorite Five [NC016] 25.00
__ Ewoks: Paw Pals [NC017] 20.00
__ Ewoks: Say "Cheese" [NC018] 20.00
__ Return of the Jedi: Play for Power [NC019]....15.00
__ Top Trumps [NC020] 7.00

Ravensburger, Germany
__ Attack of the Clones, 110 cards and 25 pogs 25.00

Ravensburger, UK
Clone Wars.
__ Giant card games [NC021] 25.00
__ Memory [NC022]..15.00

NC001

NC002

NC003

NC004

NC005

NC006

NC007

NC008

NC009

NC010

NC011

NC012

NC013

NC014

NC015

NC016

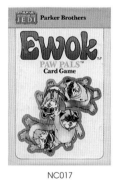

NC017

NC018

NC019

NC020

NC021

NC022

NC023

NC024　　　NC025　　　NC026　　　NC027　　　NC028

NC029　NC030　NC031　NC032　NC033　NC034　NC035

Schmid, Germany
__ Krieg der Sterne [NC023]...............................30.00

Vintage Sports Cards
__ Collectible Card Game, box of 14 CCG expansion packs [NC024] 25.00

Winning Moves
__ Top Trumps Tournament [NC025] 45.00

Premium cards.
__ Biggs Darlighter, exclusive to pre-order 2.00
__ Chancellor Palpatine, exclusive to Star Wars Celebration Europe...8.00
__ Gamorrean Guard, exclusive to pre-order........2.00
__ Grand Moff Tarkin, exclusive to pre-order........2.00
__ Logray, exclusive to pre-order.........................2.00

__ TIE Fighter Pilot, exclusive to pre-order 2.00
__ Top Trumps promo pack, exclusive to pre-order 2.00

Top Trumps decks, super mini.
__ Clone Wars [NC026] 7.00

Top Trumps decks.
__ Clone Wars Obi-Wan, Yoda, Anakin, Captain Rex cover [NC027]...20.00
__ Clone Wars Yoda and Obi-Wan cover [NC028] 20.00
__ Rise of the Bounty Hunters [NC029]...............12.00
__ Star Wars Episodes I-III Darth Vader cover [NC030]..12.00
__ Star Wars Episodes I-III Epic Duel cover [NC031]..12.00

__ Star Wars Episodes IV-VI Heroes cover [NC032]..12.00
__ Star Wars Episodes IV-VI Star Destroyer cover [NC033]..12.00
__ Star Wars Starships [NC034].........................12.00

Winning Moves, Germany
Top Trumps decks.
__ Star Wars Starships [NC035].........................12.00

Games: Chess

A La Carte
__ Sculpted plastic pieces, red box [ND001] 65.00
__ Sculpted plastic pieces, yellow box [ND002]..85.00

ND001　　　　　ND002　　　　　ND003

ND004　　　　　ND005　　　　　ND006

ND007

ND008

ND009

ND010

Character Games, Ltd.
__ Clone Wars [ND003] 35.00
__ EPII: Pewter and Bronze Effect [ND004].........50.00
__ Episode III [ND005] 35.00

Danbury Mint
__ Star Wars, pewter w/chess board [ND006] ..980.00

Gentle Giant Studios
__ Star Wars 600.00

Parker Bros.
__ Episode II [ND007]...35.00
__ Episode III [ND008].......................................35.00

Really Useful
__ Episode I chess [ND009] 65.00

Tiger Electronics
__ Galactic Chess, electronic [ND010]................79.00

Games: Electronic

__ Episode I, handheld 8.00
__ Star Wars, handheld 8.00

Hasbro
Episode I: The Phantom Menace.
__ Sith Droid Attack Game [NE001] 22.00

Giga pets. Japan.
__ R2-D2 [NE002]...15.00

Jakks Pacific, Inc.
Super gamekey combo packs.
__ Darth Vader...35.00

TV Games. 5 games in one controller.
__ Classic Trilogy Edition 25.00
__ Darth Vader [NE003] 25.00
__ General Grievous, exclusive to Walmart.........25.00
__ R2-D2 [NE004]...25.00
__ Yoda [NE005]..25.00

TV Games. Super Value Power Packs. 5 games in one controller, game key, AC transformer.
__ Yoda, exclusive to Sam's Club [NE006] 50.00

Wireless 2-piece sets.
__ Darth Vader...45.00

Kenner
__ Electronic Battle Command [NE007]..............55.00
__ Laser Battle [NE008] 85.00
__ X-Wing Aces target game [NE009] 995.00

Learning Path
Didj cartridges.
__ Math 1st-3rd grades [NE010] 30.00

Leapster cartridges.
__ Jedi Math [NE011] 15.00

NE001

NE002

NE003

NE004

NE005

NE006

NE007

NE008

NE009

NE010 NE011 NE012 NE013 NE014

NE015 NE016 NE017 NE018 NE019 NE020 NE021

NE022 NE023 NE024 NE025

Leapster.
__ Clone Wars [NE012]...15.00
__ Jedi Reading [NE013] 15.00
__ Leapster 2 Jedi Math special edition exclusive Star Wars design, exclusive to Target [NE014]......30.00

Micro Games of America
__ Shakin' Pinball [NE015]...................................35.00
__ Star Wars Intimidator, talking [NE016].............54.00

Handheld games.
__ Empire Strikes Back, silver logo, blue control..25.00
__ Empire Strikes Back, silver logo, yellow control..25.00
__ Return of the Jedi, silver logo, blue control....25.00
__ Return of the Jedi, stormtrooper art, red control [NE017] 25.00
__ Star Wars, character collage, yellow control ..25.00
__ Star Wars, droid art, yellow control 25.00
__ Star Wars, silver logo, red control 25.00
__ Star Wars, silver logo, yellow control 25.00

LCD electronic games, boxed, character art with red controls.
__ Empire Strikes Back, Yoda...........................26.00
__ Return of the Jedi, Stormtrooper and AT-AT..26.00
__ Star Wars, C-3PO / R2-D2 ....26.00

Palm games. Grey and white with black controllers.
__ 2-in-1 Star Wars game with Medallion [NE018] 25.00
__ Empire Strikes Back 20.00
__ Return of the Jedi 20.00
__ Star Wars [NE019] 20.00

NE026 NE027

NE028 NE029 NE030 NE031 NE032 NE033

NE034

NE035

NE036

NE037

NE038

NE039

NE040

NE041

NE042

NE043

NE044

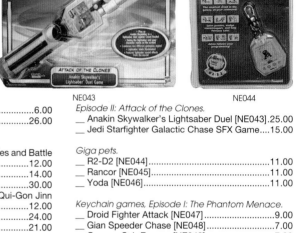

Star Wars Wizard games.
__ 2-in-1 [NE020]...15.00
__ 3-in-1 [NE021]...17.00

Palitoy, UK
__ Destroy Death Star [NE022]..........................185.00

Thinkway
Episode I: The Phantom Menace.
__ Dancing Jar Jar Binks [NE023] 18.00

Tiger Electronics
__ Clone Wars Blaster TV Game [NE024] 60.00
__ Death Star Escape [NE025] 12.00
__ Galactic Laser Pinball [NE026] 63.00
__ Imperial Assault with Darth Vader joystick [NE028] 12.00
__ Lightsaber Battle [NE027] 35.00
__ Millennium Falcon "Sounds of the Force" 18.00
__ Millennium Falcon Challenge LCD game........16.00
__ Quiz Whiz [NE029] 11.00
__ R2-D2 Ditto Droid 14.00

__ R2-D2, clip-on [NE030]...................................6.00
__ Rebel Forces Laser Game 26.00

Episode I: The Phantom Menace.
__ Battle of Naboo game with Capt. Tarples and Battle Droid joysticks [NE031]...................................12.00
__ Battle Tank Attack game [NE032]...................14.00
__ Destroyer Droid game [NE033] 30.00
__ Jedi Hunt game with Darth Maul and Qui-Gon Jinn joysticks [NE034] 12.00
__ Lightsaber Duel game [NE035] 24.00
__ Naboo Defense game [NE036] 21.00
__ Naboo Escape game [NE037]..........................12.00
__ Naboo Fighter game with exclusive Anakin Pilot figure (figure on center of card) 15.00
__ Naboo Fighter game with exclusive Anakin Pilot figure (figure on right of card) [NE038]...........15.00
__ Podrace Challenge game [NE039].................15.00
__ Podrace game [NE040]...................................24.00
__ Sith Speeder game with Darth Maul action figure [NE041] 15.00
__ Underwater Race to Theed game [NE042].....16.00

Episode II: Attack of the Clones.
__ Anakin Skywalker's Lightsaber Duel [NE043].25.00
__ Jedi Starfighter Galactic Chase SFX Game....15.00

Giga pets.
__ R2-D2 [NE044]...11.00
__ Rancor [NE045]...11.00
__ Yoda [NE046]...11.00

Keychain games, Episode I: The Phantom Menace.
__ Droid Fighter Attack [NE047] 9.00
__ Gian Speeder Chase [NE048] 7.00
__ Gungan Sub Escape [NE049] 7.00

Pen games, Episode I: The Phantom Menace.
__ Lightsaber Duel [NE050] 9.00
__ Sith Infiltrator [NE051] 9.00

R-Zone game consoles.
__ Headgear with Millennium Falcon Challenge .18.00
__ Xtreme pocket game with Jedi Adventure [NE052] 24.00

NE045

NE046

NE047

NE048

NE049

NE050

NE051

NE052

NE053

NE054

NE055

NE056

NE057

GFZ001

GSI001

GSI002

PG001

PG002

PG003

PG004

AGP001

AGP002

AGP003

AGP004

R-Zone xtreme pocket game cartridges.
__ Imperial Assault [NE053] 8.00
__ Jedi Adventure [NE054] 8.00
__ Millennium Falcon Challenge [NE055] 8.00
__ Millennium Falcon Challenge with super screen
   attachment [NE056] 8.00
__ Rebel Forces [NE057] 8.00

Tsukuda, Japan
__ Star Wars 44.00

Games: Foosball

Sportcraft
__ EPIII: ROTS Foosball [GFZ001] 75.00

Games: Midway

Playhut
__ 3 'N 1 Sports Center [GSI001] 40.00
__ Hot Shot Jr. [GSI002] 35.00

Games: Pachinko

Star Wars Jedi Knights, handheld.
__ Blue [PG001] 35.00
__ Red [PG002] 35.00

Sankyo Co., Ltd., Japan
__ Star Wars classic trilogy [PG003] 1,650.00
__ Star Wars prequel / clone wars [PG004] .. 2,150.00

Games: Pinball

Australia.
__ EPIII, free standing..150.00
__ Star Wars, tabletop [AGP001]..........................35.00

Arco Falc
__ Star Wars, 13"x24" [AGP002] 175.00

Funrise
__ Darth Vader, tabletop [AGP003] 35.00

IMC Toys, UK
__ Episode III battery operated 50.00

Super Pinball, tabletop.
__ Clone Wars battery operated..........................35.00

Super Pinball.
__ Darth Vader battery operated [AGP004].........35.00

Helmets, Miniature

Riddell
__ Boba Fett [HN001]...175.00
__ C-3PO [HN002]..35.00
__ Darth Vader [HN003].......................................50.00
__ Stormtrooper [HN004]....................................150.00
__ X-Wing Pilot [HN005]....................................125.00

Tomy, Japan
Wave 1.
__ C-3PO [HN006]..10.00
__ Darth Vader [HN007].......................................10.00
__ Rebel Trooper [HN008]....................................10.00

HN001

HN002

HN003

HN004

HN006

HN007 dome on

HN007 dome off

HN008

HN009

HN010

HN005

HN011

HN012

HN013

HN014

HN015

HN016

HN017   HN018

HN019

HN020

ITN001

KI005

KI012

KI014

__ Stormtrooper [HN009] 10.00
__ Tie Pilot [HN010]...10.00
__ X-Wing Pilot [HN011]....................................10.00
__ X-Wing Pilot Wedge / chase [HN012].............25.00

Wave 2.
__ AT-AT Driver [HN013] 10.00
__ Biker Scout [HN014] 10.00
__ Boba Fett [HN015]..10.00
__ Boushh [HN016]..10.00
__ Imperial Gunner [HN017] 10.00
__ Jango Fett / chase [HN018]...........................25.00
__ Kashyyyk Trooper / chase [HN019] 25.00
__ Skiff Guard [HN020]......................................10.00

Inflatable Toys

Takara, Japan
__ Inflatable X-Wing [ITN001].............................325.00

Kites

General Mills
__ Star Wars delta-wing flyer, mail-in premium [2:287]19.00
__ Star Wars diamond flyer, mail-in premium [3:281]...19.00

Go Fly A Kite
Delta kites.
__ Captain Rex [KI001]..6.00

KI001

KI002

KI003

KI004

KI006

KI007

KI008   KI009

KI010   KI011   KI013   KI015   KI016   KI017   KI018   KI019   KI020   KI021

Stunt kites.
__ Darth Maul 35.00
__ Darth Vader 40.00

Jakks Pacific, Inc.
3D deluxe vehicle kites.
__ Darth Vader's TIE Fighter [KI002] 25.00
__ Han Solo's Millennium Falcon [KI003] 25.00
__ Luke Skywalker's X-Wing Fighter [KI004].......25.00

Palitoy, UK
__ Wing shaped kite with X-Wing and TIE Fighter 42.00

Spectra Star
__ Darth Vader Parasail Kite...............................12.00
__ Speeder Bike 50 ft dragon kite [KI005]..........22.00
__ Wacky Winder in Darth Vader pkg...................5.00

Box kites.
__ Characters [KI006] 17.00
__ ROTJ Characters [KI007] 17.00

Delta wing kites.
__ Characters [KI008] 8.00
__ Darth Vader 11.00
__ Death Star Trench [4:170] 8.00

Diamond kites.
__ Boba Fett 6.00
__ Darth Vader 16.00
__ Luke Skywalker vs Darth Vader.......................8.00
__ Millennium Falcon...16.00

Figure kites.
__ Darth Vader [KI009]..14.00
__ Luke Skywalker [KI010].....................................14.00
__ Wicket the Ewok [KI011] 12.00

Streamer Kites.
__ Darth Vader [KI012]...8.00
__ Darth Vader [KI013]...8.00
__ Droids [KI014] 12.00
__ Ewoks on Gliders [6:268] 10.00

The Kite Factory
__ Darth Vader character art diamond kite [KI015]..12.00
__ Darth Vader figure kite 34"x33" [KI016]..........12.00
__ Luke vs. Vader character art 49" delta wing [KI017]..12.00
__ X-Wing fighter figure kite [KI018]....................12.00

Worlds Apart, UK
__ C-3PO and R2-D2 pocket kite [KI019] 12.00
__ Jar Jar Binks delta wing [KI020] 8.00
__ Naboo Fighter stunt kite [2:287] 8.00
__ ROTJ: Darth Vader [KI021] 12.00

Hasbro
__ Captain Tarpals with Kaadu [KB001]................9.00
__ Jar Jar Binks [KB002] 9.00
__ Sebulba [KB003]...9.00
__ Watto [KB004]..9.00

Hasbro
__ 10 Sheets from SW Trilogy, and 8 freeform sheets with bonus pegs [LBR001]...............................5.00
__ 12 Sheets from SW Trilogy, and 8 freeform sheets [LBR002] 6.00
__ Picture refill set, 8 characters [LBR003] 8.00

Jakks Pacific, Inc.
Marbles: Clone Wars
__ Ahsoka Tano #2 [MRB001]..................................4.00
__ Anakin Skywalker #1 [MRB002] 4.00
__ Asajj Ventress #8 [MRB003] 4.00
__ Battle Droid #10 [MRB004]..................................4.00
__ C-3PO and R2-D2 #11 [MRB005]........................4.00
__ Clone Captain Rex #6 [MRB006]........................4.00
__ Count Dooku #7 [MRB007]..................................4.00
__ Jabba the Hutt #9 [MRB008] 4.00
__ Obi-Wan #4 [MRB009]...4.00
__ Twilight #5 shooter [MRB010] 4.00
__ Yoda #3 [MRB011]...4.00
__ Ziro the Hutt #12 platinum colored [MRB012]..4.00

Marbles: Episode 4.
__ Chewbacca #13 [MRB013] 4.00
__ Darth Vader 1#8 [MRB014]..................................4.00
__ Darth Vader vs. Obi-Wan #24 platinum colored [MRB015]..4.00
__ Grand Moff Tarkin #20 [MRB016]......................4.00
__ Greedo #21 [MRB017] 4.00

KB001   KB002   KB003   KB004   LBR001   LBR002   LBR003

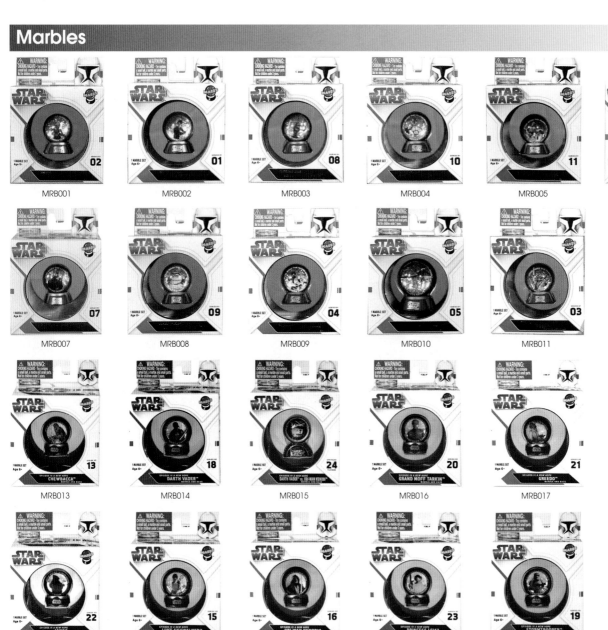

MRB001   MRB002   MRB003   MRB004   MRB005   MRB006

MRB007   MRB008   MRB009   MRB010   MRB011   MRB012

MRB013   MRB014   MRB015   MRB016   MRB017   MRB018

MRB019   MRB020   MRB021   MRB022   MRB023   MRB024

MRB025   MRB026   MRB027   MRB028   MRB029   MRB030

MRB031   MRB032   MRB033   MRB034   MRB035   MRB036

MRB037

MRB038 front*

MRB038 back*

__ X-Wing and TIE Fighter no. 12 [MRB035].......24.00
__ Yoda no. 8 [MRB036] 24.00

__ Limited edition set of Starbles, plastic padded case [MRB037]...325.00

Starbles, 1.75" diameter. Front shows character or movie scene, back has collector information. 1982.
__ Yoda* [MRB038] 350.00

Micro Collection

Kenner

__ Bespin Control Room [TYM001]....................35.00
__ Bespin Freeze Chamber [TYM002].................75.00
__ Bespin Gantry [TYM003]..............................35.00
__ Bespin World [TYM004]................................195.00
__ Death Star Compactor [TYM005]...................75.00
__ Death Star Escape [TYM006] 75.00
__ Death Star World [TYM007]...........................175.00
__ Hoth Generator Attack [TYM008] 35.00
__ Hoth Ion Cannon [TYM009].........................65.00
__ Hoth Turret Defense [TYM010] 35.00
__ Hoth Wampa Cave [TYM011] 45.00
__ Hoth World [TYM012]....................................120.00
__ Imperial TIE Fighter [TYM013]......................85.00
__ Imperial TIE Fighter, crash features [TYM014]...85.00
__ Imperial TIE Fighter, crash features, Special offer...110.00
__ Imperial TIE Fighter, Special offer.................100.00
__ Millennium Falcon, exclusive to Sears [TYM015]...410.00

__ Han Solo #14 [MRB018] 4.00
__ Jawas #22 [MRB019] 4.00
__ Luke Skywalker #15 [MRB020].........................4.00
__ Obi-Wan Kenobi #16 [MRB021] 4.00
__ Princess Leia #23 [MRB022]............................4.00
__ Stormtrooper #19 [MRB023] 4.00
__ X-Wing Fighter #17 shooter [MRB024]..............4.00

Marbles: Episode 5.
__ AT-AT shooter...10.00
__ Boba Fett 10.00
__ C-3PO and R2-D2 ....10.00
__ Han Solo / Tauntaun 10.00
__ Han Solo in Carbonite platinum colored.........10.00
__ Lando Calrissian 10.00
__ Lobot...10.00
__ Luke on Dagobah 10.00
__ Princess Leia 10.00

__ Snowtrooper 10.00
__ Wampa..10.00
__ Yoda 10.00

Marble Vision

Starbles, 1.75" diameter. Front shows character or movie scene, back has collector information. 1997.
__ C-3PO and R2-D2 no. 7 [MRB025] 24.00
__ Chewbacca no. 2 [MRB026].........................24.00
__ Darth Vader no. 3 [MRB027].........................24.00
__ Emperor Palpatine no. 5 [MRB028] 24.00
__ Han Solo no. 6 [MRB029].............................24.00
__ Jabba the Hutt no. 9 [MRB030] 24.00

__ Luke Skywalker no. 11 [MRB031]...................24.00
__ Princess Leia no. 4 [MRB032] 24.00
__ Princess Leia and R2-D2 no. 10 [MRB033]....24.00
__ Wicket Warrick no. 1 [MRB034].....................24.00

TYM001

TYM002

TYM003

TYM004

TYM005

TYM006

TYM007

TYM008

TYM009

TYM010

Special thanks to Henry Rembish for contributing photography

TYM011

TYM012

TYM013

TYM014

TYM015

TYM016

TYM017

TYM018

__ Snowspeeder, exclusive to JC Penney [TYM016]...200.00
__ X-Wing Fighter [TYM017]...............................85.00
__ X-Wing Fighter, crash features [TYM018].......75.00
__ X-Wing Fighter, Special offer..........................95.00

Micro Collection Figures

Kenner
Bespin Control Room.
__ Darth Vader lightsaber held ready [FMC001] ...5.00
__ Darth Vader right arm fully extended [FMC002] 5.00
__ Luke Skywalker landing with lightsaber [FMC003] 5.00
__ Luke Skywalker with gun raised [FMC004].......5.00

Bespin Freeze Chamber.
__ Boba Fett [FMC005] 14.00
__ Darth Vader hands on hips [FMC006] 5.00
__ Han Solo in Carbonite [FMC007]....................10.00
__ Han Solo in cuffs [FMC008]..............................5.00

__ Lando Calrissian with cape [FMC009]..............5.00
__ Lobot [FMC010]...5.00
__ Stormtrooper gun pointing up [FMC011]..........5.00
__ Stormtrooper with gun at waist [FMC012]........5.00

Bespin Gantry.
__ Darth Vader left arm extended [FMC013].........5.00
__ Darth Vader with cape blowing [FMC014].........5.00
__ Luke Skywalker lunging with lightsaber [FMC015] 5.00
__ Luke Skywalker missing hand [FMC016]..........5.00

Build Your Armies mail away.
__ Snowtrooper crawling [FMC017] 5.00
__ Snowtrooper kneeling [FMC018] 5.00
__ Snowtrooper with laser cannon [FMC019].......6.00
__ Soldier, gun pointing straight [FMC020]...........5.00
__ Soldier, gun tilted down [FMC021] 5.00
__ Soldier, gun tilted up [FMC022] 5.00

Death Star Compactor.
__ Darth Vader holding lightsaber to left [FMC023] 5.00

__ Han Solo in stormtrooper disguise [FMC024] ..5.00
__ Luke Skywalker in stormtrooper disguise [FMC025] 5.00
__ Obi-Wan Kenobi [FMC026]...............................5.00
__ Princess Leia firing rifle [FMC027]...................5.00
__ Stormtrooper firing forward [FMC028].............5.00
__ Stormtrooper firing up [FMC029].....................5.00
__ Stormtrooper standing shot [FMC030]..............5.00

Death Star Escape.
__ Chewbacca [FMC031] 5.00
__ Darth Vader right arm straight [FMC032].........5.00
__ Luke Skywalker [FMC033] 5.00
__ Princess Leia firing pistol [FMC034] 5.00
__ Stormtrooper advancing [FMC035] 5.00
__ Stormtrooper kneeling [FMC036] 5.00

Hoth Generator Attack.
__ Darth Vader walking [FMC037].........................5.00
__ Snowtrooper crawling and firing [FMC038]......5.00
__ Snowtrooper firing from hip [FMC039].............5.00
__ Snowtrooper kneeling and firing [FMC040].......5.00
__ Snowtrooper standing and firing [FMC041]......5.00

FMC001

FMC002

FMC003

FMC004

FMC005

FMC006

FMC007

FMC008

FMC009

FMC010

FMC011

FMC012

FMC013

FMC014

FMC015

FMC016

FMC017

FMC018

FMC019

FMC020

FMC021

FMC022

FMC023

FMC024

FMC025

FMC026

FMC027

FMC028

FMC029

FMC030

FMC031

FMC032

FMC033

FMC034

FMC035

FMC036

FMC037

FMC038

FMC039

FMC040

FMC041

FMC042

FMC043

FMC044

FMC045

FMC046

FMC047

FMC048

FMC049

FMC050

FMC051

FMC052

FMC053

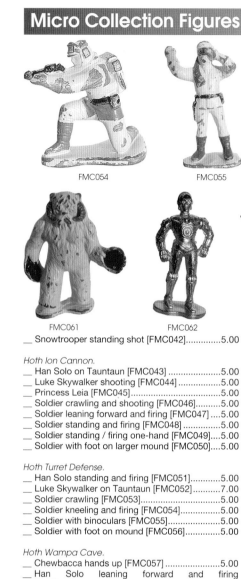

FMC054 FMC055 FMC056 FMC057 FMC058 FMC059 FMC060

FMC061 FMC062 FMC063 FMC064 FMC065 FMC066 FMC067

__ Snowtrooper standing shot [FMC042].............5.00

Hoth Ion Cannon.
__ Han Solo on Tauntaun [FMC043] 5.00
__ Luke Skywalker shooting [FMC044] 5.00
__ Princess Leia [FMC045].................................5.00
__ Soldier crawling and shooting [FMC046]..........5.00
__ Soldier leaning forward and firing [FMC047] 5.00
__ Soldier standing and firing [FMC048] 5.00
__ Soldier standing / firing one-hand [FMC049]....5.00
__ Soldier with foot on larger mound [FMC050]....5.00

Hoth Turret Defense.
__ Han Solo standing and firing [FMC051]............5.00
__ Luke Skywalker on Tauntaun [FMC052]...........7.00
__ Soldier crawling [FMC053]..............................5.00
__ Soldier kneeling and firing [FMC054]................5.00
__ Soldier with binoculars [FMC055]....................5.00
__ Soldier with foot on mound [FMC056].............5.00

Hoth Wampa Cave.
__ Chewbacca hands up [FMC057].......................5.00
__ Han Solo leaning forward and firing
   [FMC058]..5.00
__ Luke Skywalker dangling [FMC059] 5.00
__ Probot [FMC060] 3.00

__ Wampa [FMC061] 7.00

Millennium Falcon.
__ C-3PO [FMC062] 12.00
__ Chewbacca with tool [FMC063] 12.00
__ Han Solo with gun pointing up [FMC064].......12.00
__ Lando Calrissian no cape [FMC065] 12.00
__ Luke Skywalker sitting relaxed [FMC066].......12.00
__ R2-D2 [FMC067]..18.00

Snowspeeder.
__ Gunner kneeling..25.00
__ Pilot waving 25.00

Tie Fighter.
__ Pilot..25.00

X-Wing Fighter.
__ Pilot..25.00

Galoob
Classic trilogy, "space" card.
__ Imperial AT-AT [MCM001] 7.00

__ Imperial Star Destroyer [MCM002] 20.00
__ Millennium Falcon [MCM003] 7.00
__ TIE Fighter [MCM004]......................................7.00
__ X-wing Starfighter [MCM005] 7.00

Classic trilogy, striped card.
__ A-wing Starfighter [MCM006] 5.00
__ Darth Vader's TIE Fighter [MCM007].................5.00
__ Death Star II [MCM008] 5.00
__ Imperial AT-AT 7.00
__ Imperial Star Destroyer...................................20.00
__ Landspeeder [MCM009] 7.00
__ Millennium Falcon 7.00
__ Slave I [MCM010] 7.00
__ Snowspeeder [MCM011] 7.00
__ Super Star Destroyer Executor
   [MCM012] 7.00
__ TIE Bomber [MCM013] 9.00
__ TIE Fighter 7.00
__ X-wing Starfighter 7.00
__ Y-wing Starfighter [MCM014] 7.00

Classic trilogy.
__ Millennium Falcon, bagged premium for Suncoast
   Video...12.00

MCM001

MCM002

MCM003

MCM004

MCM005

MCM006

MCM007

MCM008

MCM009

MCM010

MCM011

MCM012

MCM013

MCM014

MCM015

MCM016

MCM017

MCM018

MCM019

MCM020

MCM021

MCM022

Episode I: The Phantom Menace, boxed.
__ Anakin's Podracer [MCM015]............................5.00
__ Gasgano's Podracer [MCM016] 5.00
__ Gungan Sub (Bongo) [MCM017] 5.00
__ Mars Guo's Podracer [MCM018]....................10.00
__ Naboo Fighter [MCM019] 10.00
__ Sebulba's Podracer [MCM020] 10.00

__ Sith Infiltrator [MCM021]..................................5.00
__ Trade Federation MTT [MCM022] 10.00

Galoob, Japan
2-packs: 1 vehicle, 1 figure; gray striped cards.
__ Bespin Twin-Pod Cloud Car / Lando Calrissian
[MCM023] 16.00

__ Escape Pod / R2-D2 [MCM024] 16.00
__ Imperial AT-AT / Stormtrooper [MCM025]......16.00
__ Imperial AT-ST / Imperial Driver [MCM026].....16.00
__ Imperial Star Destroyer / Vader [MCM027].....16.00
__ Millennium Falcon / Han Solo [MCM028] 16.00
__ Rebel Blockade Runner / Princess Leia
[MCM029] 16.00

MCM023

MCM024

MCM025

MCM026

MCM027

MCM028

MCM029

MCM030

MCM031

MCM032

MCM033

MCM034

MCM035

MME001

MME002

MME003

MME004

__ Shuttle Tydirium / Chewbacca [MCM030]......16.00
__ Slave I / Boba Fett [MCM031] 16.00
__ Snowspeeder / Rebel Pilot [MCM032] 16.00
__ TIE Fighter / Imperial Pilot [MCM033].............16.00
__ X-Wing Starfighter / Luke Skywalker [MCM034] 16.00

Galoob / Gigi, Italy
Classic trilogy, striped card.
__ Y-Wing Starfighter [MCM035] 25.00

Micro Machines: Adventure Gear

Galoob
__ Luke's Binoculars / Yavin Rebel Base, 1st release with Topps trading card [MME001] 20.00

__ Luke's Binoculars / Yavin Rebel Base, 1st release without Topps trading card 15.00
__ Luke's Binoculars / Yavin Rebel Base, 2nd release without Topps trading card [MME002] 12.00
__ Vader's Lightsaber / Death Star Trench, 1st release with Topps trading card [MME003] 20.00
__ Vader's Lightsaber / Death Star Trench, 1st release without Topps trading card 14.00
__ Vader's Lightsaber / Death Star Trench, 2nd release without Topps trading card [MME004] 12.00

Micro Machines: Boxed Sets

20th Century Fox, Germany
Bronze colored promotional vehicles.
__ Imperial Star Destroyer 25.00
__ TIE Starfighter 25.00
__ X-Wing Starfighter 25.00

20th Century Fox, Mexico
__ 10-pack of pewter colored ships, given away with trilogy video sets [MMF001] 35.00

Galoob
__ 11-Piece Collector's Gift Set, exclusive to KB Toys 10.00
__ 3-pack: Micro, SW:SE premiere and Toy Fair exclusive 15.00
__ Collector's Gift Set, bronze colored, exclusive to Toys R Us [MMF002] 24.00
__ Droids [MMF003] 10.00

__ Galaxy Battle Collector's Set 1st edition with limited edition vehicle and 2 figures, limited edition sticker, exclusive to K-Mart [MMF004] 10.00
__ Galaxy Battle Collector's Set 2nd edition, exclusive to K-Mart [MMF005]...10.00
__ Imperial Forces Gift Set 1st edition with exclusive Emperor figure, exclusive to Target [MMF006] .. 10.00
__ Imperial Forces Gift Set 2nd edition, exclusive to Target [MMF007]...10.00
__ Master Collector's Edition 19-piece, exclusive to Toys R Us [MMF008] 25.00
__ Master Collector's Edition 40-piece, exclusive to Toys R Us [MMF009] 60.00
__ Rebel Forces Gift Set 2nd edition, exclusive to Target [MMF010] 10.00
__ Rebel Forces Gift Set with exclusive Admiral Ackbar figure, exclusive to Target [MMF011]................15.00
__ Rebel vs. Imperial Gift Set introducing new Imperial Royal Guard with limited edition sticker [MMF012]...... 10.00

2-packs.
__ Darth Vader / Star Destroyer, limited to 68,000, exclusive to Fan Club [MMF013] 10.00
__ Han Solo / Millennium Falcon, limited to 26,000, exclusive to Fan Club [MMF014] 10.00

3-packs. Mini Micro Machines.
__ Millennium Falcon / Boba Fett's Slave I, Death Star II, exclusive to internet [MMF015]...................10.00

Collector's Editions, pewterized with limited edition sticker.
__ A New Hope [MMF016] 7.00
__ Empire Strikes Back [MMF017] 7.00

MMF001

MMF002

MMF003

MMF004

MMF005

MMF006

MMF007

MMF008

MMF009

MMF010

MMF011

MMF012

MMF013

MMF014

MMF015

MMF016

MMF017

MMF018

MMF019

MMF020

MMF021

MMF022

BMF023

319

Micro Machines: Boxed Sets

MMJ001

MMJ002

MMJ003

MMJ004

MMJ005

MMJ006

Galoob / Gigi, Italy
Collector's Editions, pewterized with limited edition sticker.
__ A New Hope..35.00
__ Empire Strikes Back 35.00
__ Return of the Jedi 35.00

Galoob / Ideal
__ Imperial Forces gift set [MMF022] 20.00
__ Rebel Forces gift set [MMF023] 20.00

__ Return of the Jedi [MMF018] 7.00

Galoob, UK
__ 16-pack, Trilogy Select Set [MMF019] 25.00
__ 3-pack: AT-AT, snowspeeder, X-wing, bronze

colored [MMF020]..20.00
__ 3-pack: Star Destroyer, TIE Fighter, Millennium
Falcon, bronze colored [MMF021].................20.00

Micro Machines: Epic Collections

Galoob
__ Heir to the Empire [MMJ001].......................5.00
__ Jedi Search [MMJ002].................................5.00
__ Truce at Bakura [MMJ003] 5.00

MMK001

MMK002

MMK003

MMK004

MMK005

MMK006

MMK007

MMK008

MMK009

MMK010

MMK011

MMK012

MMK013

MMK014

MMK015

MMK016

Foreign exclusives.
__ Dark Apprentice [MMJ004]..............................90.00
__ Dark Force Rising [MMJ005].........................90.00
__ The Courtship of Princess Leia [MMJ006]......90.00

Micro Machines: Figures

Galoob

1994. Cards are dark blue and show rebel pilot, imperial pilot, stormtrooper, and ewok along with Micro machines logo.
__ Ewoks [MMK001]...18.00

__ Imperial Pilots [MMK002]..............................18.00
__ Imperial Stormtroopers [MMK003]................18.00
__ Rebel Pilots [MMK004]..................................18.00

1995. Cards show x-wing fighter with prominent Micro Machines Space logo.
__ Echo Base Troops [MMK005].........................12.00

MMK017

MMK018

MMK019

MMK020

MMK021

MMK022

MMK023

MMK024

MMK025

MMK026

MMK027

MMK028

MMK029

MMK030

MMK031

MMK032

MMK033

MMK034

MMK035

MMK036

MA7001

M3M001

M3M002

M3M003

M3M004

M3M005

M3M006

M3M007

M3M008

__ Ewoks [MMK006]..14.00
__ Imperial Officers [MMK007]........................12.00
__ Imperial Pilots [MMK008].............................12.00
__ Imperial Stormtroopers [MMK009] 14.00
__ Jawas [MMK010]...12.00
__ Rebel Pilots [MMK011] 12.00

1996. Cards show x-wing with prominent Star Wars logo.
__ Classic Characters [MMK012] 10.00
__ Echo Base Troops [MMK013].........................10.00
__ Ewoks [MMK014]...18.00
__ Imperial Naval Troopers [MMK015] 10.00
__ Imperial Officers [MMK016] 10.00
__ Imperial Pilots [MMK017]..............................10.00
__ Imperial Stormtroopers [MMK018] 10.00
__ Jawas [MMK019]...10.00
__ Rebel Fleet Troopers [MMK020]....................10.00
__ Rebel Pilots [MMK021] 10.00
__ Tusken Raiders [MMK022] 10.00

1997. Cards are black and gray striped with orange background.
__ Bounty Hunters [MMK023] 18.00
__ Classic Characters [MMK024] 14.00
__ Classic Characters (revised) [MMK025]..........11.00
__ Echo Base Troops [MMK026]...........................7.00
__ Endor Rebel Strike Team [MMK027] 20.00
__ Imperial Naval Troopers [MMK028] 7.00
__ Imperial Officers [MMK029] 7.00
__ Imperial Pilots [MMK030]................................7.00
__ Imperial Scout Troopers [MMK031]................20.00
__ Imperial Stormtroopers [MMK032] 10.00
__ Jawas [MMK033] 7.00
__ Rebel Fleet Troopers [MMK034]......................7.00

__ Rebel Pilots [MMK035] 7.00
__ Tusken Raiders [MMK036] 7.00

Galoob / Gigi, Italy
1997. Guerre Stellari. Cards are black and gray striped with orange background.
__ Assaltori Imperiali 15.00
__ Personaggi Classici 15.00

Ideal
1997. Cards are black and gray striped with orange background.
__ Bounty Hunters...11.00
__ Classic Characters..11.00
__ Classic Characters 2......................................11.00
__ Echo Base Troops 11.00
__ Endor Rebel Strike Team 11.00
__ Ewoks 11.00
__ Imperial Naval Troopers.................................11.00
__ Imperial Officers 11.00
__ Imperial Pilots 11.00
__ Imperial Scout Troopers 11.00
__ Imperial Stormtroopers..................................11.00
__ Jawas 11.00
__ Rebel Fleet Troopers 11.00
__ Rebel Pilots 11.00
__ Tusken Raiders 11.00

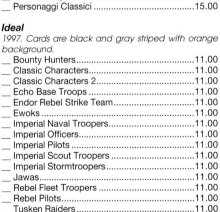

Micro Machines: Mega-Deluxe Playsets

Galoob
__ Trade Federation MTT / Naboo Battlefield
[MA7001]...38.00

Micro Machines: Micro Vehicles

Hasbro
2 vehicles and 2 figures.
__ AT-RT and BARC Speeder with Clone Trooper and
Chewbacca [M3M001].......................................8.00
__ Darth Vader's TIE fighter and an X-wing with Darth
Vader and Luke Skywalker [M3M002] 8.00
__ Jedi Starfighter and ARC-170 with Obi-Wan Kenobi
and Clone Pilot [M3M003] 8.00
__ Jedi Starfighter and Droid Tri-Fighter with Anakin
Skywalker and Battle Droid [M3M004] 8.00
__ Millennium Falcon and B-Wing with Han Solo and
Chewbacca [M3M005]..8.00
__ Sand Crawler and Landspeeder with Sandtrooper
and Luke Skywalker [M3M006] 8.00
__ Shuttle Tydirium and Slave I with Emperor and
Boba Fett [M3M007]..8.00
__ Snowspeeder and Imperial AT-AT walker with
Snowtrooper and Luke Skywalker....................8.00
__ TIE Fighter and A-Wing with TIE Fighter Pilot and
A-Wing Pilot [M3M008].....................................8.00

Micro Machines: Mini-Action Sets

Galoob
First release on 'space' card.
__ I: Boba Fett, Admiral Ackbar, Gamorrean Guard
[MMN001] ....
__ II: Nien Nunb, Greedo, Tusken Raider
[MMN002] 5.00
__ III: Jawa, Yoda, Princess Leia as Boushh
[MMN003] 5.00
__ IV: Bib Fortuna, Figrin D'an, Scout Trooper
[MMN004] 5.00

Second release on black and gray bars card.
__ I: Boba Fett, Admiral Ackbar, Gamorrean Guard
[MMN005] 5.00
__ II: Nien Nunb, Greedo, Tusken Raider
[MMN006] 5.00
__ III: Jawa, Yoda, Princess Leia as Boushh
[MMN007] 5.00
__ IV: Bib Fortuna, Figrin D'an, Scout Trooper
[MMN008] 5.00
__ V: Bossk, Duros, Sandtrooper [MMN009] 40.00
__ VI: 2-1B, Weequay, Emperor's Royal Guard
[MMN010] 40.00
__ VII: 4-LOM, Rebel Pilot, Snowtrooper
[MMN011] 125.00

MMN001

MMN002

MMN003

MMN004

MMN005

MMN006

MMN007

MMN008

MMN009

MMN010

MMN011

MMN012

__ VIII: Wampa, Wicket, TIE Fighter Pilot 40.00
__ IX: Salacious Crumb, Jabba the Hutt, AT-AT Driver
[MMN012] 40.00

Individually bagged. Distributed through Pizza Hut.
__ 2-1B [MMN013] 7.50
__ Bossk [MMN014] 7.50
__ Duros [MMN015] 7.50
__ Imperial AT-AT Assault Pilot [MMN016] 7.50
__ Jabba The Hut [MMN017] 7.50

__ Royal Guard [MMN018] 7.50
__ Salacious Crumb [MMN019] 7.50
__ Stormtrooper [MMN020] 7.50
__ TIE Fighter Pilot [MMN021] 7.50
__ Wampa [MMN022] 7.50
__ Weequay [MMN023] 7.50
__ Wicket W. Warrick [MMN024] 7.50

Mail-in exclusives.
__ C-3PO, exclusive to Walmart [MMN025] 14.00

Mini-Action, boxed. 7 Figure Heads.
__ C-3PO Set, foreign exclusive [MMN026] 295.00
__ Yoda with trading card [MMN027] 12.00

Galoob / Gigi, Italy
1997. Italian. Gray bar packaging.
__ I: Boba Fett, Admiral Ackbar, Gamorrean 8.00
__ II: Nien Nunb, Greedo, Tusken Raider
[MMN028] 8.00
__ III: Jawa, Yoda, Boushh [MMN029] 8.00

MMN013

MMN014

MMN015

MMN016

MMN017

MMN018

MMN019

MMN020

MMN021

MMN022

MMN023

MMN024

MMN025 closed and opened

MMN026

MMN027

MMN028

MMN029

MMN030

MMN031

__ IV: Bib Fortuna, Figrin D'an, Scout Trooper......8.00
__ IX: Salacious Crumb, Jabba the Hutt, AT-AT Driver 8.00
__ V: Bossk, Duros, Sandtrooper..........................8.00
__ VI: 2-1B, Weequay, Emperor's Royal Guard 8.00
__ VII: 4-LOM, Rebel Pilot, Snowtrooper 8.00
__ VIII: Wampa, Wicket, TIE Fighter Pilot..............8.00

1997. Italian. Space packaging.
__ I: Boba Fett, Admiral Ackbar, Gamorrean Guard [MMN030] 6.00
__ II: Nien Nunb, Greedo, Tusken Raider [MMN031] 6.00
__ III: Jawa, Yoda, Princess Leia as Boushh.........6.00
__ IV: Bib Fortuna, Figrin D'an, Scout Trooper......6.00

Ideal
1997. UK. Gray bar packaging.
__ I: Gamorrean Guard, Boba Fett, Admiral Ackbar...8.00

__ II: Tusken Raider, Greedo, Nien Nunb 8.00
__ III: Yoda, Jawa, Princess Leia as Boushh.........8.00
__ IV: Figrin D'an, Scout Trooper, Bib Fortuna......8.00

Micro Machines: Platform Action Sets

Galoob
__ Galactic Dogfight [MA4001]...........................12.00
__ Galactic Senate: Coruscant Taxi, Senator Palpatine, Chancellor Valorum [MA4002] 12.00
__ Naboo Temple Ruins: Gungan guard, Boss Nass, Gian Speeder [MA4003]................................12.00
__ Pod Race Arena: Flagman, Aldar Beedo's Pod Racer, Jabba the Hutt [MA4004] 20.00
__ Tatooine Desert: Royal Starship, Qui-Gon Jinn, Qui-Gon Jinn on Eopie [MA4005]..................12.00
__ Theed Rapids: Gungan Sub (Bongo), Qui-Gon Jinn, Obi-Wan Kenobi [MA4006]............................12.00

Micro Machines: Playsets

Galoob
1st release, space / grid packaging.
__ Death Star [MMP001] 15.00
__ Death Star Deluxe...38.00
__ Endor Planetary Power Station [MMP002] 10.00
__ Ice Planet Hoth [MMP003]............................10.00
__ Millennium Falcon carry playset [MMP004]....30.00
__ Millennium Falcon carry playset, 24k gold Falcon offer [MMP005] 30.00
__ Millennium Falcon carry playset, 24k gold Star Destroyer offer [MMP006].............................30.00
__ Millennium Falcon carry playset, Try Me feature [MMP007] 25.00
__ Planet Dagobah [MMP008]...........................10.00
__ Planet Tatooine [MMP009] 10.00

MA4001

MA4002

MA4003

MA4004

MA4005

MA4006

324

MMP001

MMP002

MMP003

MMP004

MMP005

MMP006

MMP007

MMP008

MMP009

MMP010

MMP011

MMP012

MMP013

MMP014

MMP015

2nd release, gray and black bar packaging.
___ Cloud City [MMP010].......................................14.00
___ Death Star [MMP011]..15.00
___ Endor Planetary Power Station [MMP012] 15.00
___ Ice Planet Hoth [MMP013]..............................10.00
___ Millennium Falcon carry playset [MMP014]....25.00
___ Planet Dagobah [MMP015]..............................10.00
___ Planet Tatooine [MMP016] 15.00
___ Rebel Transport [MMP017]..............................20.00

Episode I: The Phantom Menace.
___ Gian Speeder and Theed Palace Action Fleet playset (Episode I Sneak Preview) [MMP018] 10.00
___ Mos Espa Market [MMP019] 15.00
___ Mos Espa Market, first edition........................15.00

___ Otoh Gunga [MMP020]...................................60.00
___ Pod Racer Hangar Bay 20.00
___ Pod Racer Hangar Bay, first edition [MMP021] 20.00
___ Royal Starship Repair [MMP022]...................25.00
___ Theed Palace [MMP023]..............................60.00
___ Theed Palace Assault [MMP024]................150.00

Galoob, Australia
Space / grid packaging. Micromachine poster offer sticker on front of box.
___ Endor [MMP025]...15.00
___ Ice Planet Hoth [MMP026]..............................15.00
___ Planet Dagobah 15.00
___ Planet Tatooine 15.00
___ The Death Star [MMP027] 15.00

Ideal
1st release, space / grid packaging.
___ Death Star..18.00
___ Endor Planetary Power Station.....................18.00
___ Hoth Base..18.00
___ Planet Dagobah 18.00
___ Planet Tatooine...18.00

2nd release, gray and black bar packaging.
___ Cloud City 25.00
___ Death Star 20.00
___ Endor Planetary Power Station.....................20.00
___ Hoth Base..20.00
___ Planet Dagobah 20.00
___ Planet Tatooine...20.00
___ Rebel Transport 25.00

MMP016

MMP017

MMP018

MMP019

MMP020

MMP021

MMP022

MMP023

MMP024

MMP025

MMP026

MMP027

MMDT001

MMDT002

MA2001

MA2002

MA2005

MA2006

MA2003

MA2004

MA2007

MA2009

MA2008

MA2010

MA2011

MA2012

MA2013

MA2014

MA2016

MA2015

MA2017

MA2018

MA2019

MA2020

MA2021

Micro Machines: Playsets, Double Takes

Galoob
__ Death Star [MMDT001] 45.00
__ Death Star, 24k gold Death Star offer
[MMDT002] 95.00

Ideal
__ Death Star..55.00

Micro Machines: Pod Racers

Galoob
Build Your Own Pod Racer sets.
__ Blue [MA2001] 9.00
__ Red [MA2002] 7.00
__ Teal [MA2003] 7.00
__ Yellow [MA2004] 7.00

Pod racer packs.
__ I : Anakin Skywalker / Ratts Tyerell [MA2005] ..7.00
__ I : Anakin Skywalker / Ratts Tyerell first edition
packaging 9.00
__ II : Sebulba / Clegg Holdfast [MA2006] 7.00
__ II : Sebulba / Clegg Holdfast first edition
packaging 9.00
__ III : Dud Bolt / Mars Guo [MA2007]...................7.00
__ III : Dud Bolt / Mars Guo first edition
packaging 9.00
__ IV : Boles Roor / Neva Kee [MA2008] 7.00
__ IV : Boles Roor / Neva Kee first edition
packaging 9.00

Racing sets.
__ Arch Canyon Adventure, includes Dud Bolt's and
Clegg Holdfast's podracers [MA2009]............16.00
__ Beggars Canyon Challenge, includes Mars Guo's
and Ratts Tyrell's podracers [MA2010] 16.00
__ Boonta Eve Challenge, includes Anakin Skywalker's
and Sebulba's podracers [MA2011] 24.00

Turbo pod racers.
__ 2-pack: Gasgano / Teemto [MA2012] 25.00
__ Gasgano [MA2013] 12.00
__ Gasgano first edition packaging 12.00
__ Ody Mandrell [MA2014] 12.00
__ Ody Mandrell first edition packaging..............12.00

Galoob, UK
Pod racer packs.
__ I : Anakin Skywalker / Ratts Tyerell [MA2015] ..7.00
__ II : Sebulba / Clegg Holdfast..............................7.00
__ III : Dud Bolt / Mars Guo 7.00
__ IV : Boles Roor / Neva Kee 7.00

Racing sets.
__ Arch Canyon Adventure, includes Dud Bolt's and
Clegg Holdfast's podracers [MA2016]............16.00
__ Beggars Canyon Challenge, includes Mars Guo's
and Ratts Tyrell's podracers [MA2017] 16.00

Hasbro
Build Your Own Pod Racer sets.
__ Black [MA2018]...7.00
__ Crystal blue [MA2019] 8.00
__ Orange [MA2020] 7.00
__ Yellow [MA2021] 7.00

Micro Machines: Transforming Action Sets

Galoob
1st release, space / grid packaging.
__ Boba Fett / Cloud City 25.00
__ Boba Fett / Cloud City with Topps trading
card...25.00
__ C-3PO / Cantina [MMS001] 19.00
__ Chewbacca / Endor [MMS002] 16.00
__ Darth Vader / Bespin [MMS003] 19.00
__ R2-D2 / Jabba's Desert Palace [MMS004].....19.00
__ Rebel Pilot / Hoth...16.00
__ Rebel Pilot / Hoth with Topps trading card G1
[MMS005] 24.00
__ Royal Guard / Death Star II [MMS006] 16.00
__ Stormtrooper / Death Star [MMS007].............16.00
__ Tie Pilot / Academy [MMS008] 16.00

2nd release, gray and black bar packaging.
__ Boba Fett / Cloud City [MMS009] 16.00
__ C-3PO / Cantina 16.00
__ Darth Vader / Bespin [MMS010] 16.00
__ Jabba / Mos Eisley Space Port [MMS011].....14.00
__ Luke Skywalker / Hoth [MMS012] 16.00
__ R2-D2 / Jabba's Desert Palace [MMS013].....16.00
__ Royal Guard / Death Star II [MMS014] 16.00
__ Slave I / Tatooine [MMS015] 16.00
__ Star Destroyer / Space Fortress [MMS016]....16.00
__ Stormtrooper / Death Star [MMS017].............16.00
__ TIE Fighter Pilot / Academy [MMS018]...........16.00
__ Yoda / Dagobah [MMS019] 16.00

Episode I: The Phantom Menace.
__ Battle Droid / Trade Federation Control Ship
[MMS020]...17.00
__ Darth Maul / Theed Generator
[MMS021]...28.00
__ Gungan Sub / Otoh Gunga [MMS022] 28.00
__ Jar Jar / Naboo [MMS023] 17.00

Galoob, UK
Episode I: The Phantom Menace.
__ Gungan Sub / Otoh Gunga [MMS024] 28.00
__ Jar Jar / Naboo [MMS025] 17.00

Hasbro
Episode III: Revenge of the Sith Battle Sets.
__ Kashyyyk Assault [MMS026] 15.00
__ Mustafar Duel [MMS027] 15.00
__ Sith Attack [MMS028]......................................15.00

MMS001

MMS002

MMS003

MMS004

MMS005

MMS006

MMS007

MMS008

MMS009

MMS010

MMS011

MMS012

MMS013

MMS014

MMS015

MMS016

MMS017

MMS018

MMS019

MMS020

MMS021

MMS022

MMS023

MMS024

MMS025

MMS026

MMS027

MMS028

MMS029

MMS030

330

MMS031

MMS032

MMS033

MMS034

MMS035

MMS036

MMS037

MMS038

Ideal

1st release, space / grid packaging, silver logo.

__ Boba Fett / Cloud City [MMS029] 18.00
__ C-3PO / Bar [MMS030]...................................18.00
__ Darth Vader / Bespin [MMS031]....................18.00
__ Rebel Pilot / Hoth [MMS032]..........................18.00
__ Stormtrooper / Death Star [MMS033].............18.00

__ 1 Franc Bonus package add to any set
[MMS034] 7.00

2nd release, space / grid packaging, gold logo.

__ Boba Fett / Cloud City 18.00
__ Chewbacca / Endor [MMS035].......................18.00
__ R2-D2 / Jabba's Desert Palace [MMS036].....18.00

3rd release, gray and black bar packaging.

__ Jabba / Mos Eisley Space Port [MMS037].....18.00
__ Royal Guard / Death Star II [MMS038] 18.00
__ TIE Fighter Pilot / Academy 18.00
__ Yoda / Dagobah...18.00

Micro Machines: Vehicle / Figure Collections

Galoob

Episode I: The Phantom Menace.

__ Collection 01: Anakin's Pod Racer, Anakin, Flash
Speeder, Sio Bibble [MA3001].........................7.00
__ Collection 01: Anakin's Pod Racer, Anakin, Flash
Speeder, Sio Bibble, first edition 14.00
__ Collection 02 Gungan Sub, Boss Nass, Federation
Tank AAT, Nute Gunray [MA3002]...................7.00
__ Collection 02 Gungan Sub, Boss Nass, Federation
Tank AAT, Nute Gunray first edition 14.00
__ Collection 03: Gasgano's Pod Racer, Gasgano,
Fambaa, Jar Jar Binks [MA3003].....................7.00
__ Collection 03: Gasgano's Pod Racer, Gasgano,
Fambaa, Jar Jar Binks, first edition 14.00
__ Collection 04: Coruscant Taxi, Ki-Adi Mundi, Sith
Infiltrator, Darth Sidious [MA3004]...................7.00
__ Collection 04: Coruscant Taxi, Ki-Adi Mundi, Sith
Infiltrator, Darth Sidious, first edition 14.00

__ Collection 05: Gungans 7.00
__ Collection 05: Gungans, first edition
[MA3005]...14.00
__ Collection 06: Battle Droids............................7.00
__ Collection 06: Battle Droids, first edition
[MA3006]...14.00
__ Collection 07: Sebulba, Sebulba's Pod Racer,
Kitster, Eopie [MA3007] 15.00
__ Collection 08: Darth Maul, Sith Speeder with Darth
Maul, Naboo Fighter, Naboo Pilot [MA3008]..15.00
__ Collection 09: Jar Jar Binks, Falumpaset with
Cart, Mars Guo, Mars Guo's Pod Racer
[MA3009]...15.00
__ Collection 10: Battle Droid, Trade Federation MTT,
Rune Haako, Gian Speeder [MA3010]............15.00

SOTE.

__ I: IG-2000, Guri, Darth Vader, ASP, Stinger......9.00
__ II: Virago, Xizor, Emperor, Swoop with Rider....9.00
__ III: Outrider, Dash Rendar, Luke Skywalker, LE-
BO2D9, Hound's Tooth 9.00

MA3001

MA3002

MA3003

MA3004

MA3005

MA3006

MA3007

MA3008

MA3009

MA3010

MA3011

MA3012

MA3013

MA3014

MA3015

MA3016

SOTE. Exclusive Micro Comic Inside.
__ I: IG-2000, Guri, Darth Vader, ASP, Stinger
[MA3011]...11.00
__ II: Virago, Xizor, Emperor, Swoop with Rider
[MA3012]...11.00
__ III: Outrider, Dash Rendar, Luke Skywalker, LE-
BO2D9, Hound's Tooth [MA3013].................11.00

SOTE. Sticker covering Exclusive Micro Comic text.
__ I: IG-2000, Guri, Darth Vader, ASP, Stinger....11.00
__ II: Virago, Xizor, Emperor, Swoop with Rider..11.00
__ III: Outrider, Dash Rendar, Luke Skywalker, LE-
BO2D9, Hound's Tooth 11.00

Episode I: The Phantom Menace.
__ Collection 01: Anakin's Pod Racer, Anakin, Flash
Speeder, Sio Bibble.................................7.00
__ Collection 02: Gungan Sub, Boss Nass, Federation
Tank AAT, Nute Gunray 7.00
__ Collection 03: Gasgano's Pod Racer, Gasgano,

Fambaa, Jar Jar Binks.............................7.00
__ Collection 04: Coruscant Taxi, Ki-Adi Mundi, Sith
Infiltrator, Darth Sidious 7.00
__ Collection 05: Gungans 7.00
__ Collection 06: Battle Droids.........................7.00
__ Collection 07: Sebulba, Sebulba's Pod Racer,
Kitster, Eopie 7.00
__ Collection 08: Darth Maul, Sith Speeder with Darth
Maul, Naboo Fighter, Naboo Pilot 7.00
__ Collection 09: Jar Jar Binks, Falumpaset with Cart,
Mars Guo, Mars Guo's Pod Racer 7.00
__ Collection 10: Battle Droid, Trade Federation MTT,
Rune Haako, Gian Speeder 7.00

Hasbro
Episode I: The Phantom Menace.
__ Collection 11: Obi-Wan, Republic Cruiser, Gungan
Warrior, Kaadu and Rider [MA3014]...............35.00
__ Collection 12: Ratts Tyerell, Ratts Tyerell's Podracer,
Queen Amidala, Royal Starship [MA3015]......35.00
__ Collection 13: Naboo Security [MA3016]........35.00

Micro Machines: Vehicle Collections

Galoob
1993. One set of vehicles per classic trilogy movie with holofoil logo.
__ Empire Strikes Back: TIE Fighter, AT-AT,
Snowspeeder [MMT001]...........................8.00
__ Return of the Jedi: AT-ST, Jabba's Sail Barge,
B-Wing [MMT002].................................8.00
__ Star Wars: X-Wing, Millennium Falcon, Star
Destroyer [MMT003] 8.00

1994. Cards show different ships in background.
__ I: Tie Interceptor, Star Destroyer, Blockade Runner
[MMT004]...14.00
__ II: Landspeeder, Millennium Falcon, Jawa
Sandcrawler [MMT005]............................14.00
__ III: Darth Vader's TIE Fighter, Y-Wing, X-Wing
[MMT006]...14.00

MMT001

MMT002

MMT003

MMT004

MMT005

MMT006

MMT007

MMT008

MMT009

MMT010

MMT011

MMT012

MMT013

MMT014

MMT015

MMT016

MMT017

MMT018

MMT019

MMT020

MMT021

MMT022

MMT023

MMT024

MMT025

MMT026

MMT027

MMT028

MMT029

MMT030

MMT031

MMT032

MMT033

MMT034

MMT035

MMT036

MMT037

MMT038

MMT039

MMT040

MMT041

MMT042

MMT043

MMT044

MMT045

MMT046

MMT047

MMT048

MMT049

MMT050

MMT051

MMT052

MMT053

MMT054

MMT055

MMT056

MMT057

MMT058

MMT059

MMT060

MMT061

MMT062

MMT063

MMT064

MMT065

MMT066

MMT067

MMT068

MMT069

MMT070

MMT071

MMT072

MMT073

MMT074

MMT075

__ IV: Probot, AT-AT, Snowspeeder [MMT007] ..14.00
__ IX: Executor, B-Wing, A-Wing [MMT008] 14.00
__ V: Rebel Transport, Tie Bomber, AT-ST [MMT009]..14.00
__ VI: Escort Frigate, Slave I, Twin-Pod Cloud Car [MMT010]..14.00
__ VII: Mon Calamari Star Cruiser, Jabba's Sail Barge, Speeder Bike with Rebel [MMT011] 14.00
__ VIII: Speeder Bike with Imperial, Shuttle Tydirium, TIE Fighter [MMT012] 14.00

1994. Two sets of vehicles per classic trilogy movie.
__ Empire Strikes Back: Slave I, Twin-Pod Cloud Car, Tie Bomber [MMT013]...8.00
__ Empire Strikes Back: TIE Fighter, AT-AT, Snowspeeder [MMT014]....................................8.00
__ Return of the Jedi: AT-ST, Jabba's Sail Barge, B-Wing [MMT015]..8.00
__ Return of the Jedi: Speeder Bike with Rebel, Shuttle Tydirium, A-Wing [MMT016]..........................8.00
__ Star Wars: Blockade Runner, Sand Crawler, Y-Wing [MMT017]..8.00
__ Star Wars: X-Wing, Millennium Falcon, Star Destroyer [MMT018] 8.00

1995. Cards show x-wing fighter with prominent Micro Machines Space logo.
__ I: Tie Interceptor, Star Destroyer, Blockade Runner [MMT019]..12.00
__ II: Landspeeder, Millennium Falcon, Jawa Sandcrawler [MMT020]...............................12.00
__ III: Darth Vader's TIE Fighter, Y-Wing, X-Wing [MMT021]..12.00
__ IV: Probot, AT-AT, Snowspeeder [MMT022] ..12.00
__ IX: Executor, B-Wing, A-Wing [MMT023] 14.00
__ V: Rebel Transport, Tie Bomber, AT-ST [MMT024]..12.00
__ VI: Escort Frigate, Slave I, Twin-Pod Cloud Car [MMT025]..12.00
__ VII: Mon Calamari Star Cruiser, Jabba's Sail Barge, Speeder Bike with Rebel [MMT026] 12.00
__ VIII: Speeder Bike with Imperial, Shuttle Tydirium, TIE Fighter [MMT027] 15.00
__ X: T-16 Skyhopper, Lars Family Landspeeder, Death Star II [MMT028] 12.00
__ XI: Cloud City, Mon Calamari Rebel Cruiser, Escape Pod [MMT029]..12.00

1996. Cards show x-wing fighter with prominent Star Wars logo.
__ I: Tie Interceptor, Star Destroyer, Blockade Runner [MMT030]..10.00
__ II: Landspeeder, Millennium Falcon, Jawa Sandcrawler [MMT031]...............................10.00

__ III: Darth Vader's TIE Fighter, Y-Wing, X-Wing [MMT032]..10.00
__ IV: Probot, AT-AT, Snowspeeder [MMT033] ..10.00
__ IX: Executor, B-Wing, A-Wing [MMT034] 10.00
__ V: Rebel Transport, Tie Bomber, AT-ST [MMT035]..10.00
__ VI: Escort Frigate, Slave I, Twin-Pod Cloud Car [MMT036]..10.00
__ VII: Mon Calamari Star Cruiser, Jabba's Sail Barge, Speeder Bike with Rebel [MMT037] 10.00
__ VIII: Speeder Bike with Imperial, Shuttle Tydirium, TIE Fighter [MMT038] 15.00
__ X: T-16 Skyhopper, Lars Family Landspeeder, Death Star II [MMT039]..10.00
__ XI: Cloud City, Mon Calamari Rebel Cruiser, Escape Pod [MMT040]..12.00
__ XII: Battle damaged A-Wing, battle damaged TIE Fighter, battle damaged Y-Wing [MMT041] ...12.00
__ XIII: Battle damaged X-Wings (Red, Blue, Green) [MMT042]..12.00

1997. Cards are black and gray striped with orange background.
__ I: Tie Interceptor, Star Destroyer, Blockade Runner [MMT043]..8.00
__ II: Landspeeder, Millennium Falcon, Jawa Sandcrawler [MMT044].................................8.00
__ III: Darth Vader's TIE Fighter, Y-Wing, X-Wing [MMT045]..8.00
__ IV: Probot, AT-AT, Snowspeeder [MMT046] 8.00
__ IX: Super Star Destroyer Executor, B-Wing Starfighter, A-Wing Starfighter [MMT047] 8.00
__ V: Rebel Transport, Tie Bomber, AT-ST [MMT048]..8.00
__ VI: Escort Frigate, Slave I, Twin-Pod Cloud Car [MMT049]..8.00
__ VII: Mon Calamari Star Cruiser, Jabba's Sail Barge, Speeder Bike with Rebel [MMT050] 8.00
__ VIII: Speeder Bike with Imperial, Shuttle Tydirium, TIE Fighter [MMT051] 25.00
__ X: T-16 Skyhopper, Lars Family Landspeeder, Death Star II [MMT052] 8.00
__ XI: Cloud City, Mon Calamari Rebel Cruiser, Escape Pod [MMT053]..20.00
__ XII: A-Wing, TIE Fighter, Y-Wing, all battle damaged [MMT054]..8.00
__ XIII: Battle Damaged X-Wings (Red, Blue, Green) [MMT055]..8.00
__ XIV: Landing Craft, Death Star, S-Swoop [MMT056]..16.00
__ XV: Outrider, Tibanna Refinery, V-35 Landspeeder [MMT057]..18.00

Galoob / Gigi, Italy
1997. Italian. Cards are black and gray striped with orange background.
__ I: Tie Interceptor, Star Destroyer, Blockade Runner [MMT058]..15.00
__ II: Landspeeder, Millennium Falcon, Jawa Sandcrawler [MMT059].................................15.00
__ III: Darth Vader's TIE Fighter, Y-Wing, X-Wing [MMT060]..15.00
__ IV: Probot, AT-AT, Snowspeeder [MMT061] ..15.00
__ IX: Super Star Destroyer Executor, B-Wing Starfighter, A-Wing Starfighter [MMT062] 15.00
__ V: Rebel Transport, Tie Bomber, AT-ST [MMT063]..15.00
__ VI: Escort Frigate, Slave I, Twin-Pod Cloud Car [MMT064]..15.00
__ VII: Mon Calamari Star Cruiser, Jabba's Sail Barge, Speeder Bike with Rebel [MMT065] 15.00
__ VIII: Speeder Bike with Imperial, Shuttle Tydirium, TIE Fighter [MMT066] 15.00
__ X: T-16 Skyhopper, Lars Family Landspeeder, Death Star II [MMT067]..15.00
__ XI: Cloud City, Mon Calamari Rebel Cruiser, Escape Pod [MMT068]..15.00
__ XII: A-Wing, TIE Fighter, Y-Wing, all battle damaged [MMT069]..15.00
__ XIII: Battle Damaged X-Wings (Red, Blue, Green) [MMT070]..15.00

One set of vehicles per classic trilogy movie with holofoil logo.
__ Empire Strikes Back: TIE Fighter, AT-AT, Snowspeeder [MMT071]................................25.00
__ Return of the Jedi: AT-ST, Jabba's Sail Barge, B-Wing...25.00
__ Star Wars: X-Wing, Millennium Falcon, Star Destroyer 25.00

Ideal
1997. Cards are black and gray striped with orange background.
__ I: Tie Interceptor, Star Destroyer, Blockade Runner 9.00
__ II: Landspeeder, Millennium Falcon, Jawa Sandcrawler 9.00
__ III: Darth Vader's TIE Fighter, Y-Wing, X-Wing...9.00
__ IV: Probot, AT-AT, Snowspeeder.....................9.00
__ IX: Executor, B-Wing, A-Wing [MMT072] 9.00
__ V: Rebel Transport, Tie Bomber, AT-ST 9.00
__ VI: Escort Frigate, Slave I, Twin-Pod Cloud Car 9.00
__ VII: Mon Calamari Star Cruiser, Jabba's Sail Barge, Speeder Bike with Rebel [MMT073] 9.00

__ VIII: Speeder Bike with Imperial, Shuttle Tydirium, TIE Fighter......................9.00

__ X: T-16 Skyhopper, Lars Family Landspeeder, Death Star II......................9.00

__ XI: Cloud City, Mon Calamari Rebel Cruiser, Escape Pod [MMT074]......................9.00

__ XII: A-Wing, TIE Fighter, Y-Wing [MMT075] 9.00

__ XIII: Battle Damaged X-Wings (Red, Blue, Green)......................9.00

__ XIV: Landing Craft, Death Star, Speeder Swoop......................9.00

__ XV: Outrider, Tibanna Refinery, V-35 Landspeeder......................9.00

Vehicles from classic trilogy movies with holofoil logo.

__ Empire Strikes Back: TIE Fighter, AT-AT, Snowspeeder......................24.00

__ Return of the Jedi: AT-ST, Jabba's Sail Barge, B-Wing......................24.00

__ Star Wars: X-Wing, Millennium Falcon, Star Destroyer......................24.00

Micro Machines: Vehicles

Galoob

24k prizes, limited to 30 of each.

__ Imperial Star Destroyer [MMZ001]...............250.00

__ Millennium Falcon......................250.00

Classic trilogy. 10-packs with X-ray shuttle.

__ Gold logo, JCPenney exclusive [MMZ002].....50.00

__ Silver logo, JCPenney exclusive [MMZ003] ...50.00

__ A-Wing Fighter [MMZ004] 70.00

__ Death Star [MMZ005] 24.00

__ Executor with Star Destroyer [MMZ006] 15.00

__ Imperial Star Destroyer [MMZ007]...................7.00

__ Landspeeder [MMZ008] 25.00

__ Millennium Falcon [MMZ009]......................7.00

__ Slave I [MMZ010]......................65.00

__ Snowspeeder [MMZ011] 125.00

__ Tie Bomber [MMZ012]......................60.00

__ TIE Fighter [MMZ013]......................7.00

__ X-Wing Fighter [MMZ014]......................7.00

__ Y-Wing Fighter [MMZ015] 7.00

Classic trilogy. 'Special display stand' printed on bottom.

__ A-Wing Fighter......................70.00

__ Death Star......................24.00

__ Executor with Star Destroyer......................15.00

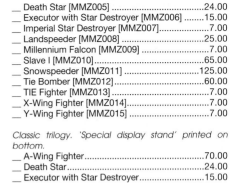
MMZ001

MMZ002

MMZ003

MMZ004

MMZ005

MMZ006

MMZ007

MMZ008

MMZ009

MMZ010

MMZ011

MMZ012

MMZ013

MMZ014

MMZ015

MMZ016

MMZ017

MMZ018

MMZ019

MMZ020

MMZ021

MMZ022

MMZ023

MMZ024

MMZ025

MMZ026

MMZ027

MMZ028

MMZ029

MMZ030

MMZ031

MMZ032

MMZ033   MMZ034   MMZ035   MMZ040

MMZ036

MMZ037

MMZ038

MMZ039

__ Landspeeder..25.00
__ Slave I..65.00
__ Snowspeeder..125.00
__ Tie Bomber..60.00

Classic trilogy. 24k gold plated 2-packs.
__ Imperial Logo / Shuttle Tydirium [MMZ016] ...75.00
__ Millennium Falcon and Darth Vader's TIE Fighter
   [MMZ017]..90.00
__ X-Wing and Slave I [MMZ018] 90.00

Classic trilogy. Round header with round bubble.
__ Imperial Star Destroyer [MMZ019]....................8.00
__ Jawa Sandcrawler [MMZ020] 8.00
__ Millennium Falcon [MMZ021] 8.00
__ TIE Fighter [MMZ022]......................................8.00
__ X-Wing Starfighter [MMZ023]...........................8.00
__ Y-Wing Starfighter [MMZ024]..........................8.00

Episode I: The Phantom Menace.
__ Gian Speeder [MMZ025]...................................6.00
__ Republic Cruiser [MMZ026]............................40.00
__ Royal Starship [MMZ027] 6.00
__ Sebulba's Pod Racer [MMZ028]......................50.00
__ Sith Infiltrator [MMZ029].................................65.00
__ Trade Federation Battleship [MMZ030]..............6.00
__ Trade Federation Droid Starfighter [MMZ031]..6.00
__ Trade Federation Tank [MMZ032] 40.00

Episode I: The Phantom Menace. First edition.
__ Gian Speeder..15.00
__ Royal Starship..15.00
__ Trade Federation Battleship 15.00
__ Trade Federation Droid Starfighter 15.00

Galoob, Australia
__ 7-pack, boxed X-Wing, Tie-Fighter, Death Star,
   Millennium Falcon, Y-Wing, Star Destroyer,
   Sandcrawler [MMZ033] 65.00

Galoob, Canada
__ 7-pack, boxed: X-Wing, TIE-Fighter, Death Star,
   Millennium Falcon, Y-Wing, Star Destroyer,
   Sandcrawler [MMZ034] 65.00

Galoob / Gigi, Italy
1997. Italian. Gray bar packaging.
__ Jawa Sandcrawler [MMZ035] 15.00

Hasbro
*Titanium series 5-packs with raw metal vehicle.
Walmart exclusives.*
__ Anakin's Jedi Starfighter, Republic Gunship, AT-RT
   (rm), Droid Tri-Fighter, Obi-Wan's Jedi Starfighter
   [MMZ036]..35.00
__ Slave I, ARC-170, TIE Bomber(rm), X-Wing Fighter,
   Clone Swamp Speeder [MMZ037] 35.00
__ TIE Advanced, AT-AT, Death Star(rm), Star
   Destroyer, Imperial Shuttle [MMZ038]...........35.00
__ TIE Fighter, Landspeeder, Millennium Falcon(rm),
   X-Wing Fighter, Y-Wing Fighter [MMZ039].....35.00

Titanium series. Buy 1 Get 1 Free packaging.
__ ARC-170 / X-Wing Fighter..............................35.00
__ AT-RT / Slave I...35.00
__ Millennium Falcon / Republic Gunship
   [MMZ040]..35.00
__ TIE Fighter / Anakin's Jedi Starfighter 35.00

Titanium series. Convention exclusives.
__ 2006 Darth Vader's TIE Fighter gold, exclusive to
   Comicon [MMZ041] 65.00

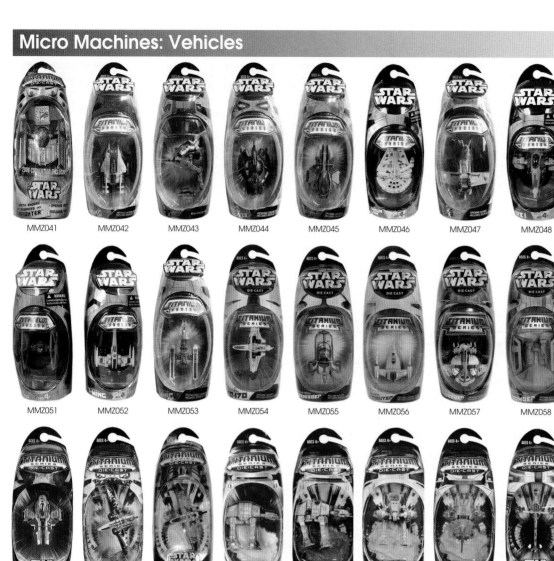

MMZ041 MMZ042 MMZ043 MMZ044 MMZ045 MMZ046 MMZ047 MMZ048 MMZ049 MMZ050

     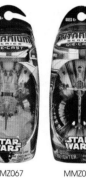  

MMZ051 MMZ052 MMZ053 MMZ054 MMZ055 MMZ056 MMZ057 MMZ058 MMZ059 MMZ060

        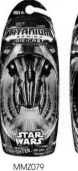 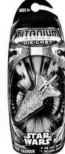

MMZ061 MMZ062 MMZ063 MMZ064 MMZ065 MMZ066 MMZ067 MMZ068 MMZ069 MMZ070

MMZ071 MMZ072 MMZ073 MMZ074 MMZ075 MMZ076 MMZ077 MMZ078 MMZ079 MMZ080

MMZ081 MMZ082 MMZ083 MMZ084 MMZ085 MMZ086 MMZ087 MMZ088 MMZ089 MMZ090

  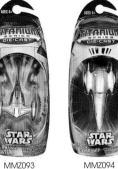      

MMZ091　　MMZ092　　MMZ093　　MMZ094　　MMZ095　　MMZ096　　MMZ097　　MMZ098　　MMZ099

  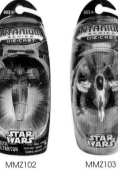     

MMZ100　　MMZ101　　MMZ102　　MMZ103　　MMZ104　　MMZ105　　MMZ106　　MMZ107　　MMZ108

        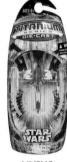

MMZ109　　MMZ110　　MMZ111　　MMZ112　　MMZ113　　MMZ114　　MMZ115　　MMZ116　　MMZ117

MMZ118　　MMZ119　　MMZ120　　MMZ121　　MMZ122　　MMZ123　　MMZ124　　MMZ125　　MMZ126

       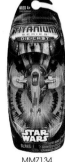 

MMZ127　　MMZ128　　MMZ129　　MMZ130　　MMZ131　　MMZ132　　MMZ133　　MMZ134　　MMZ135

341

MMZ136	MMZ137	MMZ138
MMZ139	MMZ140	MMZ141
MMZ142	MMZ143	MMZ144
MMZ145	MMZ146	MMZ147
MMZ148	MMZ149	MMZ150
MMZ151	MMZ152	MMZ153
MMZ154	MMZ155	MMZ156
MMZ157	MMZ158	MMZ159
MMZ160	MMZ161	MMZ162
MMZ163	MMZ164	MMZ165
MMZ166	MMZ167	MMZ168
MMZ169	MMZ170	MMZ171
MMZ172	MMZ173	MMZ174
MMZ175	MMZ176	MMZ177
MMZ178	MMZ179	MMZ180

| MMZ181 | MMZ182 | MMZ183 | MMZ184 | MMZ185 | MMZ186 | MMZ187 | MMZ188 | MMZ189 |

| MMZ190 | MMZ191 | MMZ192 | MMZ193 | MMZ194 | MMZ195 | MMZ196 | MMZ197 | MMZ198 |

| MMZ199 | MMZ200 | MMZ201 | MMZ202 | MMZ203 | MMZ204 | MMZ205 | MMZ206 | MMZ207 |

| MMZ208 | MMZ209 | MMZ210 | MMZ211 | MMZ212 | MMZ213 | MMZ214 | MMZ215 | MMZ216 |

| MMZ217 | MMZ218 | MMZ219 | MMZ220 | MMZ221 | MMZ222 | MMZ223 | MMZ224 | MMZ225 |

MMZ226

MMZ227

MMZ228

MMZ229

MMZ230

MMZ231

__ X-Wing Fighter, gold Celebration 3 giveaway, limited to 250 ....350.00

Titanium series. Package style 1: Star Wars logo on top. Exclusive to Walmart.
__ A-Wing Fighter [MMZ042] 10.00
__ AT-RT [MMZ043] 10.00
__ Droid Tri-Fighter [MMZ044] 10.00
__ Jedi Starfighter [MMZ045] 10.00
__ Millennium Falcon [MMZ046] 10.00
__ Republic Gunship [MMZ047] 10.00
__ Slave I [MMZ048] 10.00
__ Snow Speeder [MMZ049] 10.00
__ Star Destroyer [MMZ050] 10.00
__ TIE Fighter [MMZ051] 10.00
__ X-Wing [MMZ052] 10.00
__ Y-Wing Fighter [MMZ053] 10.00

Titanium series. Package style 2: Star Wars logo and 'Diecast' on top. Exclusive to Walmart.
__ ARC-170 [MMZ054] 15.00
__ Landspeeder [MMZ055] 15.00
__ Naboo Fighter [MMZ056]................................15.00
__ Swamp Speeder [MMZ057]..............................15.00
__ TIE Bomber [MMZ058]....................................15.00

Titanium series. Package style 3: Titanium logo on top, chrome Star Wars logo at bottom.
__ A-Wing Starfighter blue [MMZ059].........8.00
__ Amidala's Star Skiff [MMZ060] 15.00
__ Amidala's Star Skiff dirty finish......................15.00
__ Anakin's Starfighter, exclusive to Walmart [MMZ061]...15.00
__ ARC-170 Clone Wars deco [MMZ062] 8.00
__ ARC-170 Starfighter gray [MMZ063]...............8.00
__ AT-AT Walker [MMZ064] 8.00
__ AT-AT, Endor [MMZ065] 8.00
__ AT-ST [MMZ066] 8.00
__ AT-TE [MMZ067]...8.00
__ B-Wing Fighter [MMZ068] 8.00
__ B-Wing Starfighter orange [MMZ069].............10.00
__ Clone Turbo Tank [MMZ070]...........................8.00
__ Clone Turbo Tank snow deco [MMZ071] 8.00
__ Darth Maul's Sith Speeder [MMZ072] 20.00
__ Darth Vader's Sith Starfighter [MMZ073].........8.00
__ Darth Vader's TIE Advanced x1 Starfighter [MMZ074]...8.00
__ Death Star [MMZ075] 25.00
__ Dewback with Stormtrooper [MMZ076] 15.00
__ Executor [MMZ077]..10.00
__ Firespray Interceptor [MMZ078] 15.00
__ General Grievous' Starfighter [MMZ079]........10.00

__ Imperial Attack Cruiser [MMZ080] 8.00
__ Imperial Shuttle, packaged nose forward [MMZ081]...8.00
__ Imperial Shuttle, packaged top up [MMZ082]...8.00
__ Invisible Hand [MMZ083]................................10.00
__ Jabba's Sail Barge [MMZ084] 60.00
__ Jedi Starfighter, Anakin's Modified [MMZ085] .8.00
__ Jedi Starfighter, Mace Windu's [MMZ086] 8.00
__ Jedi Starfighter, Obi-Wan Kenobi's [MMZ087].8.00
__ Jedi Starfighter, Obi-Wan's [MMZ088].............8.00
__ Jedi Starfighter, Obi-Wan's hyperspace ring [MMZ089]...8.00
__ Jedi Starfighter, Plo Koon's [MMZ090]...........12.00
__ Millennium Falcon, Battle-Ravaged, exclusive to Walmart [MMZ091].........................15.00
__ Millennium Falcon, Episode III [MMZ092].......12.00
__ Naboo Patrol Fighter [MMZ093] 18.00
__ Naboo Royal Starship, exclusive to Walmart [MMZ094]...12.00
__ Rebel Blockade Runner [MMZ095].................10.00
__ Republic Attack Cruiser [MMZ096].................12.00
__ Republic Cruiser [MMZ097]...........................15.00
__ Republic Gunship command deco [MMZ098]..8.00
__ Republic Gunship, packaged nose down [MMZ099]...12.00
__ Republic Gunship, packaged nose up [MMZ100]...12.00
__ Sandcrawler [MMZ101].................................12.00
__ Sith Infiltrator [MMZ102].............................30.00
__ Slave I Jango Fett [MMZ103].........................10.00
__ Speeder Bike [MMZ104].................................8.00
__ Speeder Bike, Leia's [MMZ105] 8.00
__ Speeder Bike, Luke Skywalker's [MMZ106].....8.00
__ Speeder Bike, Paploo [MMZ107]....................10.00
__ Swamp Speeder [MMZ108] 8.00
__ TIE Fighter gray [MMZ109] 8.00
__ TIE Fighter white [MMZ110]..........................18.00
__ TIE Fighter white Titanium logo on wing.......150.00
__ TIE Interceptor [MMZ111]............................15.00
__ TIE Interceptor, Royal Guard [MMZ112].........25.00
__ Trade Federation AAT [MMZ113] 8.00
__ V-Wing Starfighter [MMZ114].........................10.00
__ Vulture Droid [MMZ115]................................12.00
__ Wookiee Flyer, exclusive to Walmart [MMZ116]...8.00
__ X-Wing, Dagobah [MMZ117]...........................8.00

Titanium series. Package style 4: Titanium logo on top, white Star Wars logo at bottom.
__ A-Wing, green [MMZ118]................................8.00
__ Anakin's Podracer [MMZ119] 15.00

__ AT-AP [MMZ120] 8.00
__ AT-AT, Shadow [MMZ121] 12.00
__ AT-OT [MMZ122] 8.00
__ AT-RT camouflaged deco [MMZ123] 8.00
__ AT-ST (Hoth) [MMZ124]................................10.00
__ Darth Vader's TIE Advanced x1 Starfighter white [MMZ125]...8.00
__ Jabba's Desert Skiff [MMZ126] 10.00
__ Jedi Starfighter red / orange [MMZ127] 20.00
__ Jedi Starfighter, Kit Fisto's [MMZ128] 15.00
__ Jedi Starfighter, Mace Windu's [MMZ129] 10.00
__ Jedi Starfighter, Saesee Tiin's [MMZ130] 15.00
__ Millennium Falcon [MMZ131] 8.00
__ Mon Calamari Star Cruiser [MMZ132]............15.00
__ Rogue Shadow [MMZ133]..............................10.00
__ Slave I [MMZ134] 8.00
__ Speeder Bike, Kashyyyk [MMZ135].................8.00
__ T-16 Skyhopper [MMZ136].............................12.00
__ Tantive IV [MMZ137]....................................12.00
__ TIE Interceptor, Baron Fel's [MMZ138]...........25.00
__ Trade Federation AAT [MMZ139] 8.00
__ Trade Federation Battleship [MMZ140]............8.00
__ V-Wing Starfighter, Imperial [MMZ141] 16.00
__ X-Wing, Luke Skywalker's Red Five [MMZ142]..8.00

Titanium series. Package style 5: Blue Star Wars logo with foil background on top. First day releases.
__ ARC-170 Starfighter [MMZ143] 20.00
__ ARC-170 Starfighter Lucky Lekku [MMZ144].20.00
__ AT-AP [MMZ145] 20.00
__ AT-OT [MMZ146] 20.00
__ AT-TE [MMZ147]...20.00
__ Cloud Car [MMZ148] 20.00
__ Jedi Starfighter with Hyperdrive [MMZ149]....20.00
__ Republic Attack Cruiser [MMZ150].................20.00
__ Republic Gunship [MMZ151] 20.00
__ Trade Federation AAT [MMZ152] 20.00
__ Vulture Droid [MMZ153]................................20.00
__ XP-34 Landspeeder [MMZ154].......................20.00

Titanium series. Package style 6: Blue Star Wars logo with black background on top.
__ A-Wing [MMZ155]...8.00
__ ARC-170 Starfighter [MMZ156] 8.00
__ ARC-170 Starfighter Lucky Lekku [MMZ157].12.00
__ AT-AP [MMZ158] 8.00
__ AT-OT [MMZ159] 8.00
__ AT-RT [MMZ160] 8.00
__ AT-TE [MMZ161]...8.00
__ B-Wing Starfighter, Dagger Squadron [MMZ162]..15.00

__ C-9979 Landing Craft [MMZ163].....................25.00
__ Cloud Car [MMZ164]...12.00
__ Imperial Landing Craft [MMZ165].................18.00
__ Jabba's Desert Skiff [MMZ166] 10.00
__ Jedi Starfighter with Hyperdrive [MMZ167]......8.00
__ Jedi Starfighter, Aayla Secura's [MMZ168] 25.00
__ Jedi Starfighter, Anakin Skywalker's [MMZ169]...........8.00
__ P-38 Starfighter [MMZ170] 12.00
__ Rebel Transport [MMZ171]................................10.00
__ Republic Attack Cruiser [MMZ172].................10.00
__ Republic Fighter Tank [MMZ173] 16.00
__ Republic Gunship 8.00
__ Republic Gunship, Lucky Lekku [MMZ174]....10.00
__ Sandspeeder [MMZ175].....................................12.00
__ Shadow Trooper Gunship [MMZ176] 15.00
__ Speeder Bike, Shadow Scout [MMZ177] 15.00
__ TIE Defender [MMZ178].....................................30.00
__ TIE Fighter, Ecliptic Evader [MMZ179] 20.00
__ Trade Federation AAT [MMZ180] 10.00
__ Trade Federation MTT [MMZ181]....................10.00
__ V-19 Torrent Fighter..12.00
__ Vulture Droid [MMZ182].....................................12.00
__ X-Wing Fighter, Wedge Antilles [MMZ183].....10.00
__ X-Wing Starfighter, Biggs Darklighter's Red Three [MMZ184]................................10.00
__ XP-34 Landspeeder [MMZ185].......................14.00
__ Y-Wing Fighter, green [MMZ186]....................15.00
__ Z-95 Headhunter [MMZ187] 15.00

Titanium series. Package style 7: Raised blue Star Wars logo on top.
__ ARC-170 Starfighter [MMZ188] 12.00

__ BARC Speeder [MMZ189] 15.00
__ IG-2000 [MMZ190]..25.00
__ Jedi Starfighter with Hyperdrive Ring [MMZ191]...10.00
__ Jedi Starfighter, Anakin's [MMZ192] 10.00
__ Jedi Starfighter, Anakin's with Hyperspace Ring [MMZ193]..10.00
__ Jedi Starfighter, Obi-Wan's [MMZ194]...........10.00
__ Neimoidian Shuttle [MMZ195]..........................16.00
__ Republic Attack Shuttle [MMZ196]..................15.00
__ The Twilight [MMZ197] 18.00
__ Virago [MMZ198] 25.00
__ X-Wing Starfighter, Red Leader's Red One [MMZ199]..10.00
__ Y-Wing, Gold Leader [MMZ200]......................18.00

Titanium series. Package style 8: White Star Wars logo with black background on top.
__ Anakin's Pod Racer [MMZ201]........................14.00
__ Dengar's Punishing One [MMZ202].................25.00
__ Droid Gunship [MMZ203] 20.00
__ Hailfire Droid [MMZ204]....................................20.00
__ Hound's Tooth [MMZ205]..................................30.00
__ Hyena Droid Bomber [MMZ206].......................18.00
__ Imperial Shuttle, Emperor's Hand [MMZ207] .20.00
__ Jedi Starfighter with Hyperdrive Ring [MMZ208]..10.00
__ Jedi Starfighter, Mace Windu's [MMZ209] 10.00
__ Malevolence [MMZ210].....................................18.00
__ Mist Hunter [MMZ211].......................................20.00
__ Nebulon-B Escort Frigate [MMZ212]..............20.00
__ Outrider [MMZ213] 35.00
__ Rebel Transport [MMZ214]...............................14.00

__ Republic Fighter Tank [MMZ215] 12.00
__ Republic Gunship [MMZ216].........................10.00
__ Sebulba's Pod Racer [MMZ217].....................20.00
__ TIE Interceptor, Baron Fel's [MMZ218]...........15.00
__ V-Wing Starfighter, Republic [MMZ219]..........10.00
__ X-Wing Fighter, Luke Skywalker's Red 5 [MMZ220]...10.00
__ X-Wing Starfighter, John Branon's Red Four [MMZ221]................................10.00
__ Xanadu Blood [MMZ222]..................................16.00
__ Y-Wing Fighter, Davish Krail's Gold Five [MMZ223].................................16.00
__ Y-Wing, Anakin's [MMZ224] 12.00
__ Z-95 Headhunter [MMZ225] 14.00

Titanium series. Ultimate Galactic Hunt.
__ Slave I...20.00

Hasbro, UK
Episode I: The Phantom Menace.
__ Gian Speeder [MMZ226]...................................11.00
__ Republic Cruiser [MMZ227]..............................30.00
__ Royal Starship [MMZ228]..................................11.00
__ Sebulba's Pod Racer [MMZ229]......................20.00
__ Sith Infiltrator [MMZ229]...................................50.00
__ Trade Federation Battleship [MMZ230] 11.00
__ Trade Federation Droid Starfighter [MMZ231]..30.00

Ideal
1997. Gray bar packaging.
__ Jawa Sandcrawler [5:423] 12.00

MMX001   MMX002   MMX003

MMX004   MMX005   MMX006

MMX007   MMX008   MMX009

TMS001

TMS002

TMS003

Micro Machines: X-Ray Fleet

Galoob
First release. Space cardback.

Misc. Toys

MOP001

MOP002

MOP003

MOP004

MOP005

MOP006

MOP007

MOP008

MOP009

MOP010

MOP011

MOP012

MOP013

MOP014

MOP015

MOP016

MOP017

MOP018

MOP019

MOP020

MOP021

MOP022

MOP023

MOP024

MOP025

MOP026

MOP027

MOP028

MOP029

MOP030

MOP031

MOP032

MOP033

MOP034

MOP035

MOP036

UK. Star Wars Episode III flip phones.
__ Obi-Wan...16.00
__ Padme [TMS002] 16.00

Disney / MGM
__ Robot Claw, C-3PO packaging [TMS003]......18.00

Izzy Bonkers
Crazy Bones.
__ Leia look-alike [4:412].....................2.00

Models: Plastic

Airfix
__ AT-AT, ESB [4:185].........................29.00
__ Luke Skywalker's Snowspeeder, ESB [4:185]24.00
__ Slave I, ESB [4:185] 75.00

AMT/Ertl
__ 3-Piece Set: B-Wing, X-Wing, Tie Interceptor, ROTJ Snap-together [MOP001]....25.00
__ A-Wing Fighter, ROTJ Snap-together [MOP002]....22.00
__ AT-AT, ROTJ.................................20.00
__ AT-AT, Snap-Fast [MOP003].................8.00
__ AT-ST, Snap-Fast [MOP004].................8.00
__ B-Wing Fighter, ROTJ limited edition gold [MOP005]....36.00

__ Battle on Ice Planet Hoth, ESB [MOP006]......15.00
__ Cantina Action Scene [MOP007] 24.00
__ Darth Vader, SW 12.00
__ Darth Vader's TIE Fighter, SW.................12.00
__ Darth Vader's TIE Fighter, SW flight display [MOP008]....22.00
__ Darth Vader's TIE Fighter, SW flight display with free Shaowds of the Empire comic [MOP009].......27.00
__ Darth Vader's TIE Fighter, SW with paint [MOP010]....17.00
__ Death Star [MOP011]........................28.00
__ Encounter with Yoda on Dagobah, ESB [MOP012]....16.00
__ Imperial TIE Fighters........................14.00
__ Jabba's Throne Room, ROTJ [MOP013]....15.00
__ Luke Skywalker's Snowspeeder, ESB............16.00
__ Millennium Falcon, ROTJ.....................18.00
__ Millennium Falcon, ROTJ cutaway [MOP014]....35.00
__ Rancor, Collector's Edition [MOP015]............65.00
__ Rebel base, ESB..............................18.00
__ Shuttle Tydirium, ROTJ [MOP016]................15.00
__ Slave I, ESB [MOP017] 16.00
__ Speeder Bike, ROTJ..........................20.00
__ Speederbike with flight display.................16.00
__ Star Destroyer, ESB [4:186]..................12.00
__ Star Destroyer, ESB with fiber optic lights [MOP018]....75.00
__ Tie Interceptor, ROTJ limited edition gold [MOP019]....45.00

__ Tie Interceptor, ROTJ Snap-together [MOP020]....16.00
__ X-Wing Fighter, Electronic [MOP021].............24.00
__ X-Wing Fighter, ROTJ.......................12.00
__ X-Wing Fighter, ROTJ flight display.............20.00
__ X-Wing Fighter, ROTJ limited edition gold [MOP022]....35.00
__ X-Wing Fighter, ROTJ with paint 15.00
__ X-Wing Fighter, Snap-together [MOP023]......12.00
__ Xizor's Virago, SOTE [MOP024] 20.00

2005 rereleases.
__ AT-AT Walker [MOP025]......................14.00
__ AT-ST Walker [MOP026]......................14.00
__ B-Wing Fighter..............................14.00
__ Darth Vader's TIE-Fighter 17.00
__ Death Star [MOP027]........................25.00
__ Millennium Falcon [MOP028]................25.00
__ Naboo Starfighter............................14.00
__ Slave I 17.00
__ Snowspeeder [MOP029]......................14.00
__ Speeder Bike...............................17.00
__ Star Destroyer...............................25.00
__ TIE Interceptor 14.00
__ X-Wing 17.00
__ X-Wing snap together [MOP030]..............14.00

Episode I: The Phantom Menace.
__ Anakin's Pod Racer [MOP031] 12.00

MOP037

MOP038

MOP039

MOP040

Box: MOP041-045

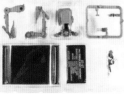
MOP041

MOP042

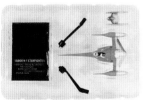
MOP043

MOP044

MOP045

Box: MOP046-051

MOP046

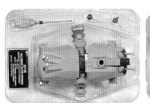
MOP047

MOP048

MOP049

MOP050

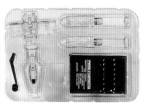
MOP051

| MOP052 | MOP053 | MOP054 | MOP055 | MOP056 |

| MOP057 | MOP058 | MOP059 | MOP060 | MOP061 | MOP062 |

__ Droid Fighters (3 in kit) [MOP032].................14.00
__ Gungan Sub [MOP033].............................39.00
__ Naboo Fighter [MOP034].........................12.00
__ STAP [MOP035]......................................16.00
__ Trade Federation Battle Tank [MOP036] 18.00

Episode I: TPM. Snapfast mini models.
__ Landing Ship 5 parts [MOP037] 6.00
__ Large Transport 8 parts [MOP038] 5.00
__ Republic Cruiser 7 parts [MOP039].................6.00
__ Sith Infiltrator 5 parts [MOP040] 7.00

Episode III: Revenge of the Sith.
__ Corporate Alliance Droid 44.00
__ Jedi Starfighter 32.00

Clipper, Netherlands
__ R2-D2...35.00

F-Toys, Japan
Vehicle Collection. Series 1. 1/144 scale. Set of 5 plus 1 secret.
__ AT-ST [MOP041]...12.00
__ ETA-2 Jedi Starfighter [MOP042] 12.00
__ Naboo N-1 Starfighter [MOP043] 12.00
__ TIE Fighter [MOP044] 12.00
__ X-Wing Starfighter [MOP045] 12.00

Vehicle Collection. Series 2. 1/144 scale. Set of 5 plus 1 secret.
__ AT-AT [MOP046]...15.00
__ AT-TE [MOP047]...15.00
__ Snowspeeder [MOP048]...............................15.00
__ TIE Advanced X1 Starfighter [MOP049] 15.00
__ Y-Wing Starfighter orange [MOP050]...........25.00
__ Y-Wing Starfighter yellow [MOP051].............15.00

Fine Molds, Japan
__ Jedi Starfighter with hyperspace ring [MOP052]..34.00
__ Millennium Falcon.......................................165.00
__ Slave I [MOP053]...34.00
__ TIE Fighter [MOP054] 34.00
__ TIE Interceptor [MOP055] 34.00
__ X-Wing Fighter 34.00

Original Trilogy Collection style packaging.
__ TIE Fighter...35.00
__ TIE Interceptor 35.00
__ X-Wing Fighter [MOP056]..............................35.00
__ X-Wing Fighter, free 1:72 painted brass C-3PO 40.00

Harbert, Italy
__ Caccia T.I.E. [MOP057]...............................25.00

Heller, France
Rapid kits Episode I: The Phantom Menace.
__ Republic Cruiser [MOP058] 25.00
__ Sith Infiltrator [MOP059] 25.00
__ Trade Federation Landing Ship [MOP060] 25.00
__ Trade Federation Large Transport [MOP061]..25.00

Kenner, UK
__ R2-D2, SW [4:187]...45.00

Lili Ledy, Mexico
__ Darth Vader's TIE Fighter [MOP062] 75.00
__ Luke Skywalker's X-Wing Fighter [MOP063]..75.00

Meccano, France
__ Z-6PO (C-3PO) [4:187] 45.00

MPC
__ A-Wing Fighter, ROTJ Snap-together [MOP064]..22.00
__ AT-AT, ESB [MOP065]...................................35.00
__ AT-ST, ROTJ [MOP066]...................................35.00
__ AT-ST, ROTJ commerative edition sticker [4:187]..15.00
__ B-Wing Fighter, ROTJ Snap-together [MOP067]..35.00

| MOP063 | MOP064 | MOP065 | MOP066 |

| MOP067 | MOP068 | MOP069 | MOP070 | MOP071 | MOP072 |

| MOP073 | MOP074 | MOP075 | MOP076 |

MOP077

MOP078

MOP079

MOP080

MOP081

MOP082

MOP083

MOP084

MOP085

MOP086

MOP087

MOP088

MOP089

MOP090

__ Battle on Ice Planet Hoth, ESB [MOP068]......36.00
__ C-3PO, ROTJ [MOP069]................................15.00
__ C-3PO, SW 48.00
__ C-3PO, SW reduced box [MOP070].............35.00
__ C-3PO, SW with ESB sticker [4:187] 95.00
__ Darth Vader, SW with Glo-Light saber [MOP071]...55.00
__ Darth Vader, SW with Glo-Light saber, commemorative edition [4:187] 20.00
__ Darth Vader, SW action model [MOP072] 75.00
__ Darth Vader's TIE Fighter, SW [4:187]...........45.00
__ Darth Vader's TIE Fighter, SW reduced box [MOP073]..35.00
__ Darth Vader's TIE Fighter, SW reduced box commemorative edition sticker [4:187]...........25.00
__ Encounter with Yoda on Dagobah, ESB [MOP074]...50.00
__ Jabba the Hutt Throne Room, ROTJ [MOP075] 43.00
__ Luke Skywalker's Snowspeeder, ESB [MOP076].40.00
__ Luke Skywalker's Snowspeeder, ESB commemorative edition sticker [4:187].........30.00
__ Luke Skywalker's X-Wing Fighter, SW [4:187]..45.00
__ Luke Skywalker's X-Wing Fighter, SW reduced box [MOP077]............................35.00
__ Millennium Falcon, ROTJ [MOP078]...............65.00
__ Millennium Falcon, ROTJ commemorative edition sticker [4:188] 45.00

__ Millennium Falcon, SW with lights [MOP079]...125.00
__ R2-D2, ROTJ [MOP080] 22.00
__ R2-D2, SW [MOP081].................................35.00
__ Rebel base, ESB [MOP082].........................35.00
__ Rebel base, ESB commemorative edition sticker [4:188]...24.00
__ Shuttle Tydirium, ROTJ [MOP083]................38.00
__ Slave I, ESB [MOP084] 75.00
__ Speeder Bike, ROTJ [MOP085].....................28.00
__ Star Destroyer, ESB [MOP086].....................35.00
__ TIE Fighter, ROTJ 18.00
__ Tie Interceptor, ROTJ Snap-together [MOP087]..20.00
__ Van, Darth Vader, SW Snap-together [MOP088]..50.00

__ Van, Luke Skywalker, SW Snap-together [MOP089]..50.00
__ Van, R2-D2, SW Snap-together [MOP090]..50.00
__ X-Wing Fighter, ROTJ [MOP091]...................20.00
__ X-Wing Fighter, ROTJ Snap-together [MOP092]..20.00
__ Y-Wing Fighter, ROTJ [MOP093]...................50.00

Mirr-a-Kits, ROTJ.
__ AT-ST [MOP094]...16.00
__ Shuttle Tydirium [MOP095].............................16.00
__ Speeder Bike [MOP096] 16.00
__ Tie Interceptor...16.00
__ X-Wing Fighter...16.00
__ Y-Wing Fighter [MOP097].............................16.00

MOP091

MOP092

MOP093

MOP094

MOP095

MOP096

MOP097

MOP098

MOP099

MOP100

MOP101

MOP102

MOP103

MOP104

MOP105

MOP106

Models: Plastic

MTR001

MTR002

MTR003

ORG001

BPT001

BPT002

BPT003

BPT004

Structor wind-ups, ROTJ.
__ AT-AT [MOP098]..27.00
__ AT-ST [MOP099]..27.00
__ C-3PO [MOP100]..27.00

MPC/Ertl
__ 3-Piece Set: B-Wing, X-Wing, Tie Interceptor, ROTJ
   Snap-together..36.00
__ A-Wing Fighter, ROTJ Snap-together 17.00
__ AT-AT, ROTJ [MOP101]................................20.00
__ AT-ST, ROTJ..10.00
__ Darth Vader, SW...15.00
__ Darth Vader's TIE Fighter, SW......................15.00
__ Luke Skywalker's Snowspeeder, ESB............20.00
__ Millennium Falcon, ROTJ................................20.00
__ Rebel base, ESB...15.00
__ Shuttle Tydirium, ROTJ...................................17.00
__ Speeder Bike, ROTJ 18.00
__ Star Destroyer, ESB..15.00

__ Tie Interceptor, Snap-together [MOP102] 14.00
__ X-Wing Fighter, ROTJ....................................12.00
__ X-Wing Fighter, ROTJ Snap-together
   [MOP103]..12.00
__ Y-Wing Fighter, ROTJ....................................35.00

Polydata
1/6 scale, pre-painted, limited to 9,000.
__ Ben Kenobi [2:308] 75.00
__ Lando Calrissian [2:308] 75.00
__ Luke Skywalker [2:308]..................................75.00
__ Princess Leia [2:308]......................................75.00
__ Tusken Raider [2:308] 75.00

1/6 scale, pre-painted.
__ Ben Kenobi [4:188] 25.00
__ Lando Calrissian [4:188] 27.00
__ Luke Skywalker [4:188]..................................25.00
__ Princess Leia [4:188]......................................25.00
__ Tusken Raider [4:188] 33.00

Takara, Japan
__ R2-D2 [MOP104] 75.00
__ TIE Fighter [MOP105] 150.00
__ X-Wing [MOP106]...150.00

Motorcycle Toys

Hasbro
Star Wars Customs.
__Imperial Chopper with Darth Vader, facing left
[MTR001]..25.00
__Imperial Chopper with Darth Vader, facing right...........25.00
__Outlaw Chopper with Boba Fett, facing left [MTR002] 25.00
__Outlaw Chopper with Boba Fett, facing right [4:412]....25.00
__Rebel Chopper with Luke Skywalker, facing left
[MTR003]..25.00
__Rebel Chopper with Luke Skywalker, facing right
[4:412]..25.00

Organizers, Electronic

Tiger Electronics
__ Jedi Dex [ORG001] 25.00

Parachute Toys

Unlicensed
2" figures with parachutes, various colors.
__ C-3PO [BPT001] 3.00
__ Chewbacca [BPT002] 3.00
__ Greedo [BPT003] 3.00
__ Leia, Hoth 3.00

YD001

YD002

YD003

YD004

YD005

YD006

YD007

YD008

YD009   YD010   PYH001   PYH002

__ Luke / X-Wing pilot 3.00
__ Stormtrooper [BPT004]....................................3.00

Clone Wars stampers with Galactic Heroes figures.
__ Ahsoka and Anakin [YD009] 8.00
__ Obi-Wan and R2-D2 [YD010] 8.00

Applause
__ Jar Jar Binks 12" 12.00
__ Jar Jar Binks 18" [TYN003]............................29.00
__ Jar Jar Binks 48" [TYN004]............................95.00
__ R2-D2 [TYN005]...18.00
__ Watto 12" 12.00
__ Watto 18" 29.00
__ Wicket the Ewok 13" tall [TYN006] 75.00
__ Yoda 18" [TYN007] 40.00
__ Yoda 24" [TYN008] 350.00

Play-Doh Sets

Kenner
Vintage.
__ Attack the Death Star [YD001].....................210.00
__ Empire Strikes Back action set: Ice Planet Hoth
  [YD002] 125.00
__ Empire Strikes Back action set: Yoda [YD003] 125.00
__ Return of the Jedi: Jabba the Hutt
  [YD004] 85.00
__ Star Wars action set [YD005].......................145.00
__ Wicket the Ewok [YD006] 160.00

Palitoy, UK
Vintage.
__ Star Wars Adventure Modeling Set 155.00

Parker, Canada
Vintage.
__ Empire Strikes Back action set: Ice Planet
  Hoth 125.00
__ Return of the Jedi: Jabba the Hutt 85.00
__ Star Wars action set 145.00
__ Wicket the Ewok..180.00

Playskool
__ Clone Wars activity kit [YD007] 20.00
__ R2-D2 Playset [YD008] 30.00

Play Houses

__ Magic Pop Up tent [PYH001] 35.00

ERO Industries
__ EPI:TPM 40"x30"x44" [PYH002] 25.00

Playhut
Clone Wars.
__ Adventure Hut [PYH003]................................30.00
__ AT-TE Hide 'N Fun [PYH004].........................20.00
__ Control Center [PYH005] 30.00
__ Control Center 30.00
__ Hide 'N Fun Elite [PYH006]............................20.00
__ Hideaway [PYH007]..30.00

Worlds Apart, UK
__ Pop'n'Fun Pop-Out Play Tunnel with Episode I
  Space Battle Scenes [PYH008] 37.00
__ Pop'n'Fun Pop-Up Naboo Fighter [PYH009]..54.00

Plush Toys and Dolls

__ Desert scavenger...14.00
__ Yoda [TYN001]..12.00
__ Yoda. sitting with hood [TYN002]...................12.00

Big Dog
Dog Wars, parody.
__ Bark Maul [TYN009].......................................14.00
__ Luke Skybarker [TYN010] 14.00

Build-A-Bear Workshop, Inc.
__ Anakin Skywalker Read Teddy [TYN011] 40.00
__ Captain Rex Pawsome Panda [TYN012]........38.00
__ Darth Vader Dimples Teddy [TYN013]............37.00
__ Jedi Knight Champ A Champion Fur Kids
  [TYN014]..40.00
__ Slumber Style Scruffy Puppy [TYN015]..........35.00

Outfits only.
__ Anakin Skywalker 3-piece belted tunic, red pants
  and plush lightsaber 15.00
__ Clone Captain Rex 3-piece detailed top, pants and
  soft mask 15.00
__ Darth Vader 5-piece black top, belted pants, cape,
  mask, helmet and plush lightsaber.................15.00
__ Jedi Knight 4-piece brown belted tunic, hooded brown
  robe, brown pants and plush lightsaber.........15.00
__ Star Wars pajamas 2-piece Star Wars design
  pajama tee with matching pants.....................12.00

PYH003   PYH004   PYH005

PYH006   PYH007   PYH008   PYH009

Plush Toys and Dolls

Celebrity Bears
___ Star Wars [TYN016] 12.00

Comic Images
___ Yoda, full-sized, limited to 500, exclusive to Star Wars Celebration IV 75.00

Collector plush, 18" to 22". Display stand included.
___ Chewbacca [TYN017] 50.00
___ Darth Vader [TYN018] 50.00
___ R2-D2 [TYN019] 50.00
___ Yoda 50.00

Deformed style figures, approximately 4" tall.
___ Ahsoka [TYN020] ....,.......15.00
___ Anakin Skywalker [TYN021] 15.00
___ Boba Fett [TYN022] 15.00
___ Captain Rex [TYN023] 15.00
___ Chewbacca [TYN024] 15.00
___ Darth Maul [TYN025] 15.00
___ Darth Vader [TYN026] 15.00
___ Darth Vader, Santa hat [TYN027] 20.00
___ General Grievous [TYN028] 15.00
___ Jawa [TYN029] 15.00
___ Obi-Wan Kenobi [TYN030] 15.00
___ R2-D2 [TYN031] 15.00
___ Shock Trooper [TYN032] 15.00
___ Stormtrooper [TYN033] 15.00
___ Wicket [TYN034] 15.00
___ Yoda [TYN035] 15.00
___ Yoda [TYN036] 15.00
___ Yoda, Santa hat and candy cane [TYN037]....20.00

Poseable plush, 11" to 14".
___ Chewbacca [TYN038] 40.00

___ Darth Vader [TYN039] 40.00
___ Yoda [TYN040] 40.00

Disney / MGM
___ Ewok, dark brown with pink cowl, Ewoks tag [TYN041]...15.00
___ Ewok, dark brown with pink cowl, Mousketoys tag [TYN042]..12.00
___ Ewok, light brown with green cowl, Ewoks tag........18.00
___ Ewok, light brown with green cowl, Mousketoys tag [TYN043]...15.00
___ Ewok, pink cowl [TYN044].............................20.00
___ Yoda, 18" latex [TYN045]..............................45.00

Star Wars Weekends.
___ 2004 Jedi Mickey, limited to 3,000 [TYN046]..........25.00
___ 2005 Vader Mickey [TYN047]...............................25.00
___ 2006 Vader Goofy [TYN048]..............................30.00
___ 2007 Mickey Luke and Minnie Leia [TYN049]...35.00

Disney Theme Park Merchandise
Approx. 7" scale.
___ Jedi Mickey [TYN050]....................................20.00

Frito Lay
___ Ewok 3' SW: SE promotion [TYN051]...................335.00

Galerie Chocolates
___ Darth Vader with jellybeans [TYN052] 10.00

Hasbro
___ Jar Jar Binks, exclusive to FAO Schwarz [TYN053]22.00
___ Jar Jar Binks Hungry Hero [TYN054] 24.00
___ Watto, exclusive to FAO Schwarz [TYN055]............22.00

Battle buddys.
___ C-3PO..10.00
___ Chewbacca [TYN056] 10.00
___ Clone [TYN057]...10.00
___ R2-D2 ....10.00
___ Yoda 10.00

Buddies. Episode I: The Phantom Menace.
___ Darth Maul [TYN058] 21.00
___ Jar Jar Binks [TYN059].................................15.00
___ Obi-Wan Kenobi [TYN060] 15.00
___ Padme Naberrie [TYN061].............................15.00
___ Qui-Gon Jinn [TYN062]................................15.00
___ Watto [TYN063]..21.00

Clone Wars 9" talking plush characters.
___ Captain Rex 25.00
___ Clone Trooper 25.00
___ R2-D2 ....25.00
___ Yoda [TYN064]...25.00

Lightsabers.
___ Blue [TYN065]..12.00
___ Green [TYN066]..12.00
___ Red [TYN067]..12.00

Mpire buddies.
___ Anakin Skywalker 10.00
___ Boba Fett..15.00
___ Chewbacca [TYN068] 10.00
___ Count Dooku 12.00
___ Darth Maul..12.00
___ Darth Vader [TYN069].....................................10.00
___ Emperor [TYN070]..10.00

TYN001 TYN002 TYN003 TYN004 TYN005 TYN006

TYN007 TYN008 TYN009 TYN010 TYN011 TYN012

TYN013 TYN014 TYN015 TYN016 TYN017 TYN018

TYN019

TYN020

TYN021

TYN022

TYN023

TYN024

TYN025

TYN026

TYN027

TYN028

TYN029

TYN030

TYN031

TYN032

TYN033

TYN034

TYN035

TYN036

TYN037

TYN038

TYN039

TYN040

TYN041

TYN042

TYN043

TYN044

TYN045

Plush Toys and Dolls

TYN046   TYN047   TYN048   TYN049

TYN050   TYN051   TYN052   TYN053   TYN054   TYN055

__ General Grievous	10.00
__ Han [TYN071]	10.00
__ Luke [TYN072]	10.00
__ Mace Windu	10.00
__ Obi-Wan [TYN073]	12.00
__ Princess Leia [TYN074]	10.00
__ Queen Amidala	10.00
__ R2-D2	10.00
__ Stormtrooper [TYN075]	10.00

Original Trilogy Collection (OTC)
__ C-3PO [TYN076]	10.00
__ Chewbacca [TYN077]	10.00
__ R2-D2 [TYN078]	10.00
__ Wicket [TYN079]	10.00
__ Yoda [TYN080]	10.00

Wrestling Buddy.
__ Darth Vader [TYN081]	30.00
__ R2-D2	35.00

Idea Factory
Farce Wars.
__ Anteater Dirtwalker [TYN082]	7.00
__ Dark Gator [TYN083]	7.00
__ Dark Mole [TYN084]	7.00
__ Goata [TYN085]	7.00
__ Queen Armadillo [TYN086]	7.00
__ Slabba the Mutt [TYN087]	7.00

Kenner
__ Chewbacca [TYN088]	275.00
__ R2-D2 [TYN089]	65.00

Buddies. Classic trilogy.
__ C-3PO [TYN090]	10.00
__ Chewbacca, black bandolier [TYN091]	10.00
__ Chewbacca, brown bandolier [TYN092]	22.00
__ Figrin D'An [TYN093]	10.00
__ Jabba the Hutt [TYN094]	8.00
__ Jawa [TYN095]	20.00
__ Max Rebo [TYN096]	8.00
__ R2-D2 [TYN097]	10.00
__ Salacious Crumb [TYN098]	10.00
__ Wampa [TYN099]	10.00
__ Wicket the Ewok [TYN100]	9.00
__ Yoda [TYN101]	25.00

Ewoks.
__ Latara	29.00

TYN056   TYN057   TYN058   TYN059   TYN060

TYN061   TYN062   TYN063   TYN064   TYN065 TYN066 TYN067

TYN068

TYN069

TYN070

TYN071

TYN072

TYN073

TYN074

TYN075

TYN076

TYN077

TYN078

TYN079

TYN080

TYN081

TYN082

TYN083

TYN084

TYN085

TYN086

TYN087

TYN088

TYN089

TYN090

Plush Toys and Dolls

__ Paploo..85.00
__ Princess Kneesaa 185.00
__ Wicket...25.00

Woklings.
__ Gwig..40.00
__ Malani 40.00
__ Mookiee 40.00
__ Nippet 40.00
__ Wiley 40.00

Kenner, Canada
__ The Ewok 190.00

Kenneth Feld
__ Yoda, Plastic head, 12" tall............................135.00

Kinder
Approximately 5.5" in height.
__ Aubacca [TYN102].......................................18.00
__ Hippoda [TYN103] 18.00

Masterfoods USA
M&Ms 12" mail-in premiums.
__ Darth Vader...35.00
__ Emperor [TYN104] 35.00
__ Luke 35.00

Palitoy, UK
Ewoks, boxed.
__ Leeni the Ewok 175.00
__ Mookie the Ewok 175.00
__ Princess Kneesa 175.00

Pepsi Cola
__ Yoda, includes hoverchair [TYN105] 125.00
__ Yoda, standing with cane [TYN106] 125.00

Quiron
__ Kneesa, bagged..240.00
__ Wicket, bagged..240.00
__ Wicket, boxed..335.00

Regal
__ Chewbacca, 15" 675.00
__ Chewbacca, 4' 725.00
__ Jawa, 12" 340.00

Snap Toys
__ Artoo-Detoo, talking [TYN107]........................35.00

 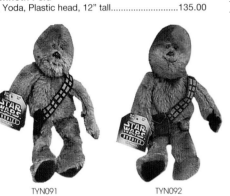   

| TYN091 | TYN092 | TYN093 | TYN094 | TYN095 |

| TYN096 | TYN097 | TYN098 | TYN099 | TYN100 |

| TYN101 | TYN102 | TYN103 | TYN104 |

| TYN105 | TYN106 | TYN107 | TYN108 | TYN109 |

TYN110

TYN111

TYN112

TYN113

TYN114

TYN115

TYN116

TYN117

TYN118

TYN119

TYN120

TYN121

TYN122

TYN123

TYN124

TYN125

TYN126

Star Wars Celebration III
__ Yoda same as Pepsi Yoda but without hover chair., limited to 500, exclusive to Star Wars Celebration III [TYN108] 185.00

Star Wars Celebration V
__ Wampa with removable arm, exclusive to Star Wars Celebration V [TYN109] 50.00

Super Live Adventure, Japan
__ Yoda [TYN110]...115.00

Takara, Japan
Oversized comic-style head, gold hang string. Approximately 7" tall.
__ C-3PO [TYN111] 25.00
__ Chewbacca [TYN112] 25.00
__ Darth Vader [TYN113] 30.00
__ Luke Skywalker [TYN114]................................25.00
__ R2-D2, 5" [TYN115] 25.00

Tomy, Japan
Approximately 15" in height.
__ Ewok [TYN116] 45.00
__ Jawa [TYN117]..45.00
__ Yoda 45.00

Underground Toys
15" talking character plush.
__ Chewbacca [TYN118]......................................40.00
__ Darth Vader [TYN119] 40.00

9" talking character plush.
__ Artoo Detoo [TYN120].....................................18.00
__ Artoo Detoo 18.00
__ Chewbacca [TYN121] 18.00
__ Chewbacca [TYN122] 18.00
__ Darth Vader [TYN123] 18.00
__ Darth Vader [TYN124] 18.00
__ Yoda [TYN125]...18.00
__ Yoda [TYN126]...18.00

Pool Toys

Aqua Fun, Australia
Floaters.
__ R2-D2...85.00

Frito Lay
__ Yoda, "May the Fun be with you" [IPT001].....25.00

Episode I game card prizes.
__ Pod Racer [IPT002]......................................130.00
__ Sith Macrobinoculars....................................75.00

Intex Recreation Corp.
__ Anakin's Pod Racer Lounge [IPT003].............20.00
__ Gungan Sub Ride-In [IPT004]............................9.00
__ Jar Jar 2 Person Ride-In [IPT005]..................14.00
__ Landspeeder Boat Lounge [IPT006]...............20.00
__ Millennium Falcon Island/River Raft [IPT007].20.00

IPT001

IPT002

IPT003

IPT004

IPT005

Pool Toys

IPT006

IPT007

IPT008

IPT009

IPT010

IPT011

IPT012

IPT013

IPT014

__ Naboo Starfighter Ride-In..............................12.00
__ Naboo Starfighter Ride-On [IPT008]..............14.00
__ Trade Fed Droid Starfighter Ride-In [IPT009] .12.00
__ Trade Federation Droid Starfighter Ride-On [IPT010]..14.00

Jakks Pacific, Inc.
Inflatable ride-ons.
__ Anakin Skywalker's Jedi Starfighter, deluxe [IPT011]..40.00
__ Luke Skywalker's X-Wing, deluxe [IPT012] 40.00
__ Millennium Falcon [IPT013].............................30.00
__ Obi-Wan's Jedi Starfighter [IPT014] 30.00

Sport Fun, Inc.
__ Space Battle Waterslide 16ft classic trilogy [6:375] 15.00

Premiums

Episode I: The Phantom Menace. Talking tip-overs.
__ Darth Maul 5.00
__ Jar Jar Binks..5.00

__ Obi-Wan Kenobi 5.00
__ Qui-Gon Jinn..5.00

Barcel, Mexico
__ Battle Droid..5.00
__ Clone Trooper 5.00
__ Count Dooku...5.00
__ Darth Sidious 5.00
__ Darth Vader...5.00
__ Darth Vader (Anakin) 5.00
__ General Grievous 5.00
__ Grievous' Bodyguard..5.00

Bimbo, Mexico
Shooters target game pieces.
__ Anakin Skywalker..5.00
__ Count Dooku...5.00
__ Darth Sidious 5.00
__ Mace Windu 5.00
__ Obi-Wan Kenobi 5.00
__ Princess Leia 5.00
__ Qui-Gon Jinn...5.00
__ R2-D2..5.00
__ Yoda 5.00

Burger King
EPIII: Revenge of the Sith. Series I. Special.
__ Darth Vader...15.00

EPIII: Revenge of the Sith. Series I. Image Viewers.
__ C-3PO 5.00
__ Darth Maul 5.00
__ Luke Skywalker [PCT001]...................................5.00
__ Mace Windu 5.00
__ Obi-Wan Kenobi 5.00
__ Princess Leia Organa...5.00

EPIII: Revenge of the Sith. Series I. Plush.
__ Boga 5.00
__ Chewbacca..5.00
__ Jawa 5.00
__ Tarfful 5.00
__ Wampa 5.00
__ Wicket 5.00

EPIII: Revenge of the Sith. Series I. Pullbacks.
__ Darth Vader's TIE fighter...................................5.00
__ Jedi Starfighter 5.00
__ Landspeeder..5.00

PCT001

PCT002

PCT003

PCT004

PCT005

PCT006

PCT006

PCT007

PCT008

__ Millennium Falcon [PCT002] 5.00
__ Podracer 5.00
__ X-Wing fighter [PCT003] 5.00

EPIII: Revenge of the Sith. Series I. Water Squirters.
__ Boba Fett 5.00
__ Emperor Palpatine 5.00
__ Jabba the Hutt [PCT004] 5.00
__ Jar Jar Binks 5.00
__ R2-D2 [PCT005]...5.00
__ Super Battle Droid 5.00

EPIII: Revenge of the Sith. Series I. Wind-Ups.
__ Clone Trooper 5.00
__ General Grievous 5.00
__ Han Solo [PCT006] 5.00
__ Padme Amidala...5.00

__ Watto 5.00
__ Yoda [PCT007]..5.00

EPIII: Revenge of the Sith. Series II. Special.
__ Darth Vader, breathing sound [PCT008]...........5.00

EPIII: Revenge of the Sith. Series II. Cosmic Cruisers.
__ ARC Clone Fighter 5.00
__ Naboo Starfighter 5.00
__ Snowspeeder 5.00
__ Vulture Droid 5.00

EPIII: Revenge of the Sith. Series II. Galactic Spinners.
__ Anakin Skywalker..5.00
__ Chewbacca 5.00
__ Emperor Palpatine 5.00
__ Luke Skywalker 5.00

EPIII: Revenge of the Sith. Series II. Jedi Wisdom.
__ Kit Fisto...5.00
__ Mace Windu..5.00
__ Obi-Wan Kenobi 5.00
__ Yoda 5.00

EPIII: Revenge of the Sith. Series II. Shadow Casters.
__ Bail Organa 5.00
__ Queen Amidala 5.00
__ R2-D2 ....5.00
__ Stormtrooper 5.00

Burger King, Argentina
Episode III: Revenge of the Sith.
__ C-3PO 10.00
__ Chewbacca...10.00
__ Darth Vader..10.00
__ R2-D2...10.00

Burger King, UK
__ C-3PO 8.00
__ Chewbacca...8.00
__ Darth Vader..8.00
__ Millennium Falcon...8.00
__ R2-D2...8.00
__ Yoda 8.00

Felfont, Argentina
Super Jack chocolate egg premiums. Non-articulated. Weapons and accessories are removable.
__ Aayla Secura [PCT009] 8.00
__ Ahsoka Tano [PCT010] 8.00
__ Anakin Skywalker [PCT011]...............................8.00

PCT009 PCT010 PCT011 PCT012 PCT013
PCT014 PCT015 PCT016 PCT017 PCT018 PCT019
PCT020 PCT021 PCT022 PCT023 PCT024 PCT025
PCT026 PCT027 PCT028 PCT029 PCT030 PCT031 PCT032

359

Premiums

PCT033

PCT034

PCT035

PCT036

PCT037

PCT038

PCT039

PCT040

PCT041

PCT042

PCT043

__ Asajj Ventress [PCT012] 8.00
__ C-3PO [PCT013] 8.00
__ Cad Bane [PCT014] 8.00
__ Clone Trooper [PCT015] 8.00
__ Commander Cody [PCT016] 8.00
__ Commander Ponds [PCT017] 8.00
__ Count Dooku [PCT018] 8.00
__ Darth Sidious [PCT019] 8.00
__ Jabba the Hutt [PCT020] 8.00
__ Jedi Starfighter, Anakin's [PCT021] 8.00
__ Jedi Starfighter, Obi-Wan's [PCT022] 8.00
__ Kit Fisto [PCT023] 8.00
__ Luminara Unduli [PCT024] 8.00
__ Mace Windu [PCT025] 8.00
__ Magna Guard [PCT026] 8.00
__ Obi-Wan Kenobi [PCT027] 8.00
__ Padme Amidala [PCT028].................................8.00

__ Plo Koon [PCT029] 8.00
__ R2-D2 [PCT030]..8.00
__ Super Battle Droid [PCT031] 8.00
__ Yoda [PCT032]..8.00

Frito Lay
3D Star Pics. Cheetos premiums. Red, blue, green, purple variations.
__ Anakin Skywalker [PCT033]...............................1.00
__ Clone Trooper, yellow only [PCT034] 3.00
__ Count Dooku [PCT035]....................................1.00
__ Jango Fett [PCT036]..1.00
__ Mace Windu [PCT037]......................................1.00
__ Obi-Wan Kenobi [PCT038] 1.00
__ Padme Amidala [PCT039]..................................1.00
__ R2-D2 and C-3PO [PCT040]...............................1.00
__ Yoda [PCT041]...1.00

__ Zam Wesell [PCT042] 1.00

Gamesa
Mini figures.
__ Ben Kenobi [PCT043] 2.00
__ C-3PO [PCT044]..2.00
__ Chewbacca [PCT045].......................................2.00
__ Darth Vader [PCT046]......................................2.00
__ Han Solo [PCT047]...2.00
__ Luke Skywalker [PCT048]..................................2.00
__ Princess Leia [PCT049]....................................2.00

Hungry Jacks
EPIII: Revenge of the Sith Darth Vader assembly.
__ Part 1 ....3.00
__ Part 2 ....3.00
__ Part 3 ....3.00
__ Part 4 ....3.00

EPIII: Revenge of the Sith finger puppets.
__ Anakin 5.00
__ Darth Sidious 5.00
__ Obi-Wan 5.00
__ Yoda 5.00

Kelloggs
__ Box of 6, promotional [PCT050] 45.00
__ Blue - Naboo space battle [PCT051]...............5.00
__ Green - Gungan army [PCT052] 5.00
__ Orange - Podrace [PCT053]...........................5.00
__ Purple - Jedi vs. Sith [PCT054]......................5.00
__ Red - Jedi [PCT055].....................................5.00
__ Yellow - Battle droids [PCT056]......................5.00

PCT044

PCT045

PCT046

PCT047

PCT048

PCT049

Rebel Rocket from Kelloggs C-3PO's cereal.
__ C-3PO and Darth Vader [PCT057]...................35.00
__ Chewbacca and Stormtrooper [PCT058]...25.00
__ Luke Skywalker and R2-D2 [PCT059] 25.00

Kelloggs, Germany
Mini-statue scene viewers.
__ Anakin Skywalker [PCT060].............................4.00
__ C-3PO and R2-D2 [PCT061]............................4.00
__ Darth Vader [PCT062]......................................4.00
__ Jango Fett [PCT063]...4.00
__ Obi-Wan Kenobi [PCT064] 4.00
__ Padme Amidala [PCT065].................................4.00

Kelloggs, Thailand
Gyros cereal premiums. Available in blue, red, yellow, green, purple, and pink.
__ Anakin Skywalker [PCT066]..............................4.00
__ Clone Trooper [PCT067] 4.00
__ Darth Sidious [PCT068] 4.00
__ Darth Vader [PCT069]..4.00
__ General Grievous [PCT070]................................4.00
__ Obi-Wan Kenobi [PCT071] 4.00
__ R2-D2 and C-3PO [PCT072]..............................4.00
__ Yoda [PCT073]..4.00

Kelloggs, UK
Episode III: Revenge of the Sith Cereal and Milk bars sticker dispensers.
__ Anakin Skywalker..8.00
__ Darth Maul [PCT074] 8.00
__ Darth Vader...8.00
__ Luke Skywalker [PCT075].................................8.00

__ Princess Leia [PCT076]....................................8.00
__ Yoda 8.00

Episode III: Revenge of the Sith. Glow-in-the-dark lightsaber maze games.
__ Anakin, blue 8.00
__ Darth Vader, red 5.00
__ Luke, green 5.00
__ Mace Windu, purple...5.00
__ Obi-Wan, blue 5.00
__ Yoda, green 5.00

Statue with mini-scroll.
__ 10-piece set, boxed [PCT077] 45.00
__ Anakin Skywalker [PCT078]..............................4.00
__ Boss Nass [PCT079] 4.00
__ C-3PO [PCT080] 4.00
__ Darth Maul [PCT081] 4.00
__ Darth Sidious [PCT082] 4.00
__ Jar Jar Binks [PCT083]......................................4.00
__ Obi-Wan Kenobi [PCT084] 4.00
__ Queen Amidala [PCT085] 4.00
__ Qui-Gon Jinn [PCT086].......................................4.00
__ R2-D2 [PCT087]..4.00

KFC
__ AT-AT with snowtrooper on door [PCT088] 5.00
__ AT-ST with walking action [PCT089] 5.00
__ Balancing TIE fighter and X-wing fighter [PCT090]....4.00
__ Death Star shooter [PCT091]............................4.00
__ Sandcrawler with R2 [PCT092]..........................4.00
__ Vader head spinner [PCT093]............................4.00

Episode I: The Phantom Menace.
__ Anakin Skywalker's Naboo fighter [PCT094]....3.00
__ Boss Nass squirter [PCT095]............................3.00
__ Gungan Sub Squirter [PCT096] 3.00
__ Jar Jar Binks Squirter [PCT097] 3.00
__ Naboo ground battle [PCT098]...........................3.00
__ Opee Sea Creature Chaser [PCT099]...............3.00
__ Planet Naboo [PCT100] 3.00
__ Queen Amidala's Hidden Identity [PCT101] 3.00
__ Swimming Jar Jar Binks [PCT102] 3.00
__ Trade Federation droid fighter [PCT103] 3.00

KFC, Mexico
__ Collapsible Pit Droid [PCT104] 6.00
__ Darth Maul's sith speeder with ripcord [PCT105]......3.00
__ Watto jumping, suction and spring [PCT106] 6.00
__ Yoda / Anakin illusion cube 4.00

PCT050

PCT051

PCT052

PCT053

PCT054

PCT055

PCT056

PCT057 rocket and decals

PCT058 decals

PCT059 decals

PCT060

PCT061

PCT062

PCT063

PCT064

PCT065

361

Premiums

PCT066

PCT067

PCT068

PCT069

PCT070

PCT071

PCT072

PCT073

McDonalds

Clone Wars bobble head characters in vehicles.

___ Ahsoka Tano / freighter, light-up [PCT107] 2.00
___ Anakin Skywalker / Jedi Starfighter, pullback [PCT108]...2.00
___ Asajj Ventress / droid fighter, light-up [PCT109] ...2.00
___ Boba Fett / Slave I, rolling [PCT110] 2.00
___ C-3PO / landspeeder, rolling [PCT111] 2.00
___ Captain Rex / Republic gunship, pullback [PCT112]...2.00
___ Chewbacca / AT-ST, walking [PCT113] 2.00
___ Darth Vader / TIE Fighter X1 Advanced, sounds [PCT114]...2.00
___ General Grievous / starfighter, light-up [PCT115] .2.00
___ Han Solo / Millennium Falcon, pullback [PCT116]2.00
___ Luke Skywalker / X-Wing fighter, pullback [PCT117]...2.00

___ Obi-Wan Kenobi / Jedi starfighter, pullback [PCT118]...2.00
___ Padme Amidala / royal starship, rolling [PCT119].2.00
___ Princess Leia / blockade runner, rolling [PCT120]2.00
___ R2-D2 / Naboo starfighter, sounds [PCT121]...2.00
___ Stormtrooper / AT-AT, walking [PCT122]..............2.00
___ Wicket the Ewok / Speederbike, pullback [PCT123]...2.00
___ Yoda / Republic gunship, sounds [PCT124] 2.00

Fingerboard skateboards. Package includes 1 fingerboard and 1 tattoo.

___ #1 Anakin Skywalker Cad Bane tattoo 7.00
___ #2 Captain Rex Anakin Skywalker tattoo 7.00
___ #3 Obi-Wan Kenobi General Grievous tattoo ...7.00

___ #4 Yoda Asajj Ventress tattoo 7.00
___ #5 General Grievous Yoda tattoo 7.00
___ #6 Cad Bane Commander Cody tattoo............7.00
___ #7 Commander Cody Obi-Wan Kenobi tattoo .7.00
___ #8 Mace Windu Captain Rex tattoo 7.00
___ #9 Asajj Ventress Mace Windu tattoo...............7.00

McDonalds, Belgium

Clone Wars.

___ Darth Maul Lightsaber 12.00
___ Darth Vader..12.00
___ Jedi Starfighter 12.00
___ Lightsaber..12.00
___ R2-D2..12.00
___ Yoda 12.00

PCT074

PCT075

PCT076

PCT077

PCT078

PCT079

PCT080

PCT081

PCT082

PCT083

PCT084

PCT085

PCT086

PCT087

PCT088

PCT089

PCT090

PCT091

PCT092

PCT093

PCT094

PCT095

PCT096

PCT097

PCT098

PCT099

PCT100

PCT101

PCT102

PCT103

PCT104

PCT105

PCT106

PCT107

PCT108

PCT109

PCT110

PCT111

PCT112

PCT113

PCT114

PCT115

PCT116

PCT117

PCT118

PCT119

PCT120

PCT121

PCT122

PCT123

PCT124

PCT125

PCT126

PCT127

PCT128

PCT129

PCT130

PCT131

PCT132

PCT133

PCT134

PCT135

PCT136

PCT137

PCT138

PCT139

PCT140

PCT141

PCT142

PCT143

PCT144

PCT145

PCT146

PCT147

PCT148

PCT149

PCT150

PCT151

PCT152

PCT153

PCT154

PCT155

PCT156

PCT157

PCT158

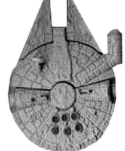
PCT159

PCT160

PCT161

PCT162

PCT163

PCT164

PCT165

PCT166

PCT167

PCT168

PCT169

McDonalds, Malaysia

Clone Wars.

__ Anakin Skywalker	8.00
__ Darth Vader	8.00
__ Jedi Starfighter	8.00
__ Millennium Falcon	8.00
__ R2-D2	8.00
__ Republic Gunship	8.00
__ X-Wing Fighter	8.00
__ Yoda	8.00

Petroglyph

__ Death Star desktop ball, pre-order for Empire at War game [PCT125].........8.00

Pizza Hut

Episode I: The Phantom Menace.

__ Darth Maul's Sith Infiltrator	3.00
__ Jar Jar Binks Squishy [PCT126]	3.00
__ Lott Dod Walking Throne [PCT127]	3.00
__ Planet Coruscant	3.00
__ Queen Amidala's Starship [PCT128]	3.00
__ R2-D2	3.00
__ Sith Holoprojector	3.00
__ Yoda Jedi Destiny [PCT129]	3.00

Pizza Hut, UK

__ Death Star 3D puzzle [PCT130]	6.00
__ Han in Carbonite sliding puzzle [PCT131]	6.00
__ Millennium Falcon navigating asteroid field game [PCT132]	6.00
__ R2-D2 and C-3PO magnetic droid factory puzzle [PCT133]	6.00

Quick, France

__ Yoda magnetic maze game [PCT134] 8.00

Sonrics, Mexico

Clone Wars game card holder with marker coin.

__ Captain Rex [PCT135]	10.00
__ R2-D2 [PCT136]	10.00

Taco Bell

Episode I: The Phantom Menace.

__ Anakin Transforming Bank	3.00
__ Anakin Viewer [PCT137]	3.00
__ Anakin's Podracer [PCT138]	3.00
__ Darth Maul's Sith Speeder [PCT139]	3.00
__ Hovering Watto	3.00
__ Joking Jar Jar [PCT140]	3.00
__ Levitating Queen's ship [PCT141]	3.00
__ Planet Tatooine [PCT142]	3.00
__ Sebulba's Podracer [PCT143]	3.00
__ Sith Probe Viewer	3.00
__ Walking Sebulba [PCT144]	3.00

Star Wars Special Edition / Feel the Force.

__ Balancing Boba Fett	3.00
__ Exploding Death Star [PCT145]	6.00
__ Floating Cloud City	4.00
__ Folding Picture Cube, Special Edition scenes..3.00
__ Illusion Cube [PCT146]	4.00
__ Millennium Falcon with zip chord	4.00
__ R2-D2 3-piece playset	4.00
__ Yoda figure	5.00

Tambola

__ AT-AT [PCT147].................4.00

__ AT-AT Attack, puzzle [PCT148]	6.00
__ C-3PO [PCT149]	5.00
__ Chewbacca [PCT150]	5.00
__ Darth Vader [PCT151]	5.00
__ Darth Vader on Bespin, puzzle [PCT152]	6.00
__ Darth Vader's TIE Fighter [PCT153]	4.00
__ Dogfight Above Death Star II, puzzle [PCT154]	6.00
__ Han Solo [PCT155]	5.00
__ Heroes on Hoth, puzzle [PCT156]	6.00
__ Imperial Shuttle [PCT157]	4.00
__ Luke Skywalker [PCT158]	5.00
__ Millennium Falcon [PCT159]	4.00
__ Princess Leia [PCT160]	5.00
__ R2-D2 [PCT161]	5.00
__ Stormtrooper [PCT162]	5.00
__ TIE Fighter [PCT163]	4.00
__ X-Wing Fighter [PCT164]	4.00
__ Yoda [PCT165]	5.00
__ Yoda, Puzzle [PCT166]	6.00

Walkers, UK

Jar Jar Binks Sticky Tongue Toys.

__ Glow in dark [PCT167]	11.00
__ Mail-in package [PCT168]	12.00
__ Regular [PCT169]	11.00

Preschool Toys

Kenner

Ewoks.

__ Family Hut [PST001]	85.00
__ Fire Cart [PST002]	135.00
__ Music Box Radio [PST003]	22.00
__ Talking Telephone [PST004]	45.00
__ Teaching Clock [PST005]	75.00
__ Woodland Wagon [PST006]	95.00

Playskool

Mr. Potato Heads, Disney Star Tours exclusives.

__ C-3PotatO [PST007]	20.00
__ Chipbacca [PST008]	20.00
__ Darth Mash [PST009]	20.00
__ Luke Frywalker [PST010]	20.00
__ Mashter Yoda [PST011]	20.00
__ Princess Tater [PST012]	20.00
__ Spuda Fett [PST013]	20.00
__ Yam Solo [PST014]	20.00

Mr. Potato Heads.

__ Artoo-Potatoo [PST015] 10.00

PST001

PST002

PST003

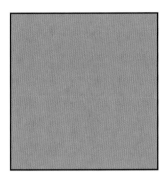

PST004

PST005

PST006

PST007

PST008

PST009

PST010

PST011

PST012

PST013

PST014

PST015

PST016

PST017

PST018

PST019

PST020

PST021

367

Preschool Toys

__ Artoo-Potatoo, white packaging [PST016] 10.00
__ Darth Tater [PST017] 15.00
__ Darth Tater, white packaging [PST018] 10.00
__ SpudTrooper [PST019] 20.00
__ SpudTrooper, white packaging [PST020] 10.00
__ Tater Trio set, exclusive to Costco [PST021] .35.00

Playskool, Australia
__ Darth Tater / Spud Trooper collector 2-pk. 50.00

Projectors / Viewers

UK.
__ Clone Wars multi projector [TYV001] 14.00

UK. Projection torches with interchangeable lenses.
__ Clone Wars [TYV002] 20.00
__ Star Wars [TYV003] 20.00

Banpresto, Japan
Night projectors.
__ R2-D1 (red) 12cm [TYV004] 20.00
__ R2-D2 (blue) 12cm [TYV005] 20.00
__ R3-A2 (black) 12cm 20.00

Chad Valley
__ Slide Projector Set 375.00

Harbert, Italy
__ Star Wars movie strip viewer 250.00

Kenner
__ Movie Viewer with "May The Force Be With You"
Cassette [TYV006] 200.00

Give-a-Show Projectors.
__ ESB [TYV007] 295.00
__ ESB with Scooby Doo Special Offer 2,450.00
__ SW [TYV008] 245.00
__ Wicket the Ewok 175.00

TYV001

TYV002

TYV003

TYV004

TYV005

TYV006

TYV007

TYV008

TYV009

TYV010

TYV011

TYV012

TYV013-TYV015 package

TYV013

TYV014

TYV015

Movie Viewer cartridges.
__ Assault on Death Star [TYV009] 150.00
__ Battle in Hyperspace [TYV010].....................150.00
__ Danger at the Cantina [TYV011] 150.00
__ Destroy Death Star [TYV012].......................150.00

Meccano, France
__ Minicinex...185.00
__ Star Wars Cinevue 325.00
__ Star Wars movie-frame cassette 45.00

Smith's Snackfood
__ 50 frames, binder, flashlight projector 165.00

Tiger Electronics
__ Lightsaber Image Projector 16.00

Toltoys
__ Give-A-Show projector 225.00

Tomy, Japan
Mini-frame projectors.
__ Boba Fett [TYV013]...12.00
__ Darth Maul [TYV014]..12.00
__ Darth Vader...12.00
__ Yoda [TYV015] 12.00

Punch-Out Activities

Frito Lay
Build-a-droids.
__ C-3PO [PRC001]...4.00
__ R2-D2 [PRC002] 4.00

General Mills
Punch-out spaceships, cereal premiums.
__ Landspeeder [PRC003]....................................11.00
__ Millennium Falcon [PRC004]...........................11.00
__ TIE Fighter [PRC005].......................................11.00
__ X-Wing Fighter [PRC006]................................11.00

Paizo Publishing / Fan Club
__ Fan Club 2003 membership mini-standee [PRC007]...5.00

Puppets

Applause
__ Jar Jar Binks, latex [YE001].............................20.00
__ Yoda, latex [YE002] 20.00

Disney / MGM
__ Ewok, green hood [YE003] 26.00

Kenner
__ Yoda hand puppet [YE004]..............................65.00

Palitoy, UK
__ Yoda hand puppet...65.00

Regal
__ Chewbacca hand puppet 850.00

Tiger Electronics, UK
Finger Forces, electronic talking finger puppets.
__ Anakin Skywalker...20.00
__ Battle Droid [YE005] 20.00

__ Darth Maul [YE006]...20.00
__ Jar Jar Binks [YE007] 20.00
__ Obi-Wan Kenobi [YE008]................................20.00
__ Qui-Gon Jinn [YE009] 20.00

Puzzles

__ Star Wars: Special Edition logo, 300 extra-large pieces, 2'x3' [TYP001]....................................12.00

La Guerra de la Galaxias.
__ Millennium Falcon cockpit 20.00

Argentina.
__ Episodio I 23.5cm x 33cm [TYP002]...............22.00
__ Forest Rancor [TYP003]...................................25.00
__ Princess Leia [TYP004] 25.00
__ The Clone Wars, paper [TYP005] 5.00

Argentina. 40 piece bagged puzzles.
__ The Empire Strikes Back characters. [TYP006] 12.00
__ The Empire Strikes Back scenes. [TYP007] ...12.00

Argentina. 8 pieces each.
__ Darth Maul [TYP008].......................................10.00
__ Jango Fett [TYP009] 10.00

Australia. Clone Wars tray puzzles.
__ Ahsoka [TYP010]...15.00
__ Anakin [TYP011]...15.00
__ Obi-Wan [TYP012]..15.00
__ Yoda [TYP013]..15.00

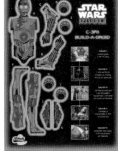
PRC001

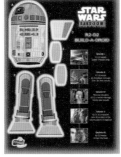
PRC002

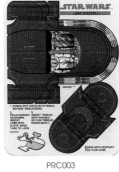
PRC003

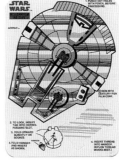
PRC004

PRC005

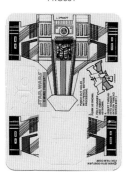
PRC006

PRC007

YE001

YE002

YE003

YE004

YE005

YE006

YE007 standing

YE007 opened

YE008

YE009

Puzzles

TYP001

TYP002

TYP003

TYP004

TYP005

Germany.
__ Yoda puzzle sculpture [TYP014].....................30.00

UK. 3D sculpture puzzles.
__ Anakin's Jedi Starfighter 505 pieces [TYP015] 25.00

Borras, Spain
Guerra De Las Galaxias. 150 pieces.
__ Millennium Falcon cockpit 51x36 cm [TYP016] 12.00

Cardinal
__ 3 Puzzle pack: Anakin, Capt. Rex, Ahsoka; Anakin and Ahsoka; Capt. Rex and Obi-Wan 100 pieces each [TYP017]..24.00
__ 3' floor puzzle, Captain Rex and Jedi 46 pieces [TYP018] 25.00

100 pieces, lenticular.
__ Darth Vader [TYP019] 10.00
__ Death Star trench [TYP020] 10.00

100 pieces.
__ Darth Vader [TYP021] 10.00
__ Empire Strikes Back characters [TYP022]......10.00

48 pieces, lenticular.
__ Capt. Rex, Anakin, Obi-Wan [TYP023].............6.00
__ Yoda and Jedi [TYP024] 6.00

48 pieces.
__ Anakin and clone troopers [TYP025] 5.00
__ Clone commanders [TYP026]...........................5.00

__ General Grievous [TYP027] 5.00
__ Jedi [TYP028]...5.00
__ Sith [TYP029] 5.00

Collectors puzzle sets in storage tin.
__ ESB Characters foil puzzle, saga character poster puzzle [TYP030] 28.00

Character Games, Ltd.
__ 4 in 1 Puzzle bumper pack 2x200 pcs., 2x42 pcs. [TYP031] 8.00
__ Darth Vader picture sculpture puzzle [TYP032] 25.00
__ Heroes and Villains on Reflection Puzzle [TYP033] 15.00
__ Xtra Dimension 3D w/glasses [TYP034] 18.00

42 chunky pieces.
__ Darth Vader [TYP035].....................................15.00
__ Wookiees and Clones [TYP036] 15.00

Episode II: AOTC.
__ Double Vision [TYP037] 12.00

Clementoni, France
__ 250 pieces, Qui-Gon Jinn [TYP038] 18.00
__ 500 pieces, Episode I [TYP039].....................18.00

Craft Master
__ B-Wing Fighters, 170 pieces [TYP040]..........10.00
__ Battle on Endor, 170 pieces [TYP041]............10.00
__ Death Star, 70 pieces [TYP042].......................8.00
__ Ewok Leaders, 170 pieces [TYP043]..............10.00
__ Ewoks: Fishing, 35 pieces 7.00

__ Ewoks: Lessons..7.00
__ Ewoks: Swimming Hole, 35 pieces 7.00
__ Jabba's Henchmen, 70 pieces [TYP044]..........8.00
__ Jabba's Throne Room, 70 pieces [TYP045].....8.00
__ Luke Inspects Droids 8.00

Tray puzzles.
__ Darth Vader [TYP046] 6.00
__ Ewok Gliders [TYP047] 6.00
__ Ewok Village [TYP048] 6.00
__ Gamorrean Guard [TYP049] 6.00
__ Princess Kneesaa and Baga [TYP050] 6.00
__ Princess Leia and Wicket [TYP051]..................6.00
__ R2-D2 and Wicket [TYP052]............................6.00
__ Wicket the Ewok [TYP053] 6.00

Cromy
El Regreso del Jedi.
__ C-3PO and R2-D2 [TYP054]...........................45.00
__ Jabba's Palace 45.00
__ Luke Skywalker...45.00
__ Rebel Hangar..45.00

Crown Products, UK
__ Darth Vader 300 pieces, 35x49cm [TYP055]..10.00
__ Four in One frame tray puzzles [TYP056] 12.00
__ Wookiees 48 pieces [TYP057] 6.00

Disney Theme Park Merchandise
__ 4 Poster puzzles [TYP058].............................35.00
__ The Muppets, 2-side puzzle [TYP059]............25.00

Hallmark
__ Jumbo coloring puzzle 12 pieces [TYP060] ...10.00

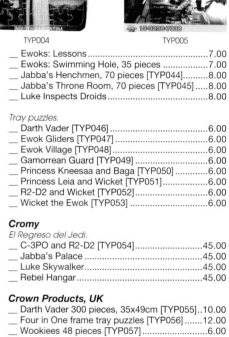

TYP006

TYP007

TYP008

TYP009

TYP010

TYP011

TYP012

TYP013

TYP014

TYP015

TYP016

TYP017

TYP018

TYP019

TYP020

TYP021

TYP022

TYP023

TYP024

TYP025

TYP026

TYP027

TYP028

TYP029

TYP030

TYP031

TYP032

TYP033

TYP034

TYP035

TYP036

TYP037

TYP038

TYP039

TYP040

TYP041

TYP042

TYP043

TYP044

TYP045

TYP046

TYP047

TYP048

TYP049

TYP050

TYP051

TYP052

TYP053

TYP054

TYP055

TYP056

TYP057

TYP058

TYP059

TYP060

TYP061

TYP062

TYP063

TYP064

TYP065

TYP066

TYP067

TYP068

TYP069

TYP070

TYP071

TYP072

TYP073

TYP074

TYP075

Puzzles

TYP076

TYP077

TYP078

TYP079

TYP080

TYP081

TYP082

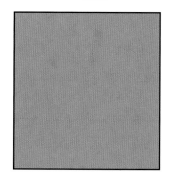

TYP083

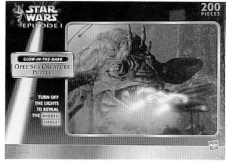
TYP084

TYP085

TYP086

TYP087

TYP088

TYP089

Hasbro

__ Death Star sphere puzzle 60 pieces [TYP061] 18.00
__ TPM: Movie Teaser Poster, 300 extra-large pieces [TYP062] 8.00

Clone Wars 100 pieces, free Galactic Heroes figure.
__ Obi-Wan Kenobi [TYP063]................................6.00
__ Yoda [TYP064]..6.00

Clone Wars 100 pieces.
__ Yoda, Obi-Wan, Anakin, Y-Wing Starfighters [TYP065] 15.00

EPI: The Phantom Menace 100 piece shaped puzzle, includes theme shaped pieces.
__ Darth Maul [TYP066].......................................5.00

__ Jar Jar Binks [TYP067] 5.00
__ R2-D2 [TYP068]...5.00
__ Yoda [TYP069]...5.00

EPI: The Phantom Menace 50 piece mini-puzzle.
__ Jedi vs. Sith [TYP070].....................................2.00
__ Pit Droids [TYP071]...2.00
__ Queen Amidala [TYP072]..................................2.00
__ Sebulba [TYP073]...2.00

EPI: The Phantom Menace 540 pieces, movie mazes.
__ No. 1 of 2 [TYP074].......................................15.00
__ No. 2 of 2 [TYP075]......................................15.00

EPI: The Phantom Menace 750 pieces, puzzle printed on front and back.
__ Bravo Squadron Assault [TYP076] 7.00

__ Gungan Sub Escape [TYP077] 7.00
__ Podrace Challenge [TYP078]...........................7.00

EPI: The Phantom Menace Slivers.
__ Anakin Skywalker [TYP079].............................8.00
__ Darth Maul [TYP080].......................................8.00
__ Jar Jar Binks [TYP081] 8.00

EPI: The Phantom Menace. 200 pieces, hidden image glows in the dark.
__ Jedi vs. Sith [TYP082]......................................7.00
__ Mos Espa Podrace [TYP083]............................7.00
__ Opee Sea Creature [TYP084] 7.00

EPI: The Phantom Menace. 3D mini-puzzles.
__ Gungan Sub 66 pieces [TYP085].......................9.00
__ Sith Infiltrator 73 pieces [TYP086] 9.00

TYP090

TYP091

TYP092

TYP093

TYP094

TYP095

TYP096

TYP097

TYP098

TYP099

TYP100

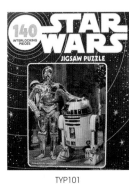

TYP101

TYP102

TYP103

TYP104

TYP105

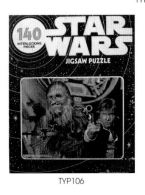

TYP106

TYP107

TYP108

TYP109

TYP110

TYP111

TYP112

TYP113

TYP114

TYP115

TYP116

TYP117

TYP118

TYP119

TYP120

TYP121

TYP122

TYP123

TYP124

TYP125

TYP126

TYP127

TYP128

TYP129

TYP130

TYP131

TYP132

TYP133

TYP134

TYP135

TYP136

TYP137

TYP138

TYP139

TYP140

TYP141

TYP142

TYP143

TYP144

TYP145

TYP146

TYP147

TYP148

TYP149

377

TYP150

TYP151

TYP152

TYP153

TYP154

TYP155

TYP156

TYP157

TYP158

TYP159

TYP160

TYP161

TYP162

TYP163

TYP164

TYP165

TYP166

TYP167

TYP168

TYP169

TYP170

TYP171

TYP172

EPII: Attack of the Clones 500 piece puzzle in tin storage box.
__ Bounty Hunters...15.00
__ Heroes...15.00
__ Vehicles...15.00
__ Villains..15.00

Hasbro, Canada
EPI: The Phantom Menace 100 piece shaped puzzle, includes theme shaped pieces. Bi-language.
__ Darth Maul..5.00
__ Jar Jar Binks [TYP087].......................................5.00
__ R2-D2...5.00
__ Yoda [TYP088]..5.00

Hasbro, Mexico
EPI: The Phantom Menace 50 piece mini-puzzle, 5"x7".
__ Jedi vs. Sith...2.00
__ Pit Droids...2.00
__ Queen Amidala..2.00
__ Sebulba..2.00

Hasbro, UK
EPI: The Phantom Menace. 30 pieces.
__ Movie poster art 51x36 cm [TYP089].............15.00

IN
Tray puzzles. Episode III: Revenge of the Sith.
__ Clone Trooper [TYP090].....................................8.00
__ Darth Vader [TYP091]...8.00
__ Darth Vader / Epic Duel [TYP092].....................8.00
__ Epic Duel / Yoda [TYP093]................................8.00

__ General Grievous and Darth Vader [TYP094]...8.00
__ General Grievous and Yoda [TYP095].............8.00
__ Revenge of the Sith collage [TYP096].............8.00
__ Yoda [TYP097]..8.00

Karnan
EPI TPM. 50 pieces.
__ Jedi Duel [TYP098]...25.00

Kenner
__ Aboard The Millennium Falcon, 1000 pieces [TYP099]...24.00
__ Artoo-Detoo / See-Three Pio, 140 pieces, black box [TYP100]..15.00
__ Artoo-Detoo / See-Three Pio, 140 pieces, blue box [TYP101]...24.00
__ Bantha, 140 pieces [TYP102].........................10.00
__ Corridor of Lights, 1500 pieces [TYP103].......26.00
__ Darth Vader and Obi-Wan Duel, 500 pieces [TYP104]...10.00
__ Han and Chewbacca, 140 pieces, black box [TYP105]...15.00
__ Han and Chewbacca, 140 pieces, blue box [TYP106]...24.00
__ Hildebrandt Movie Poster Art, 1000 pieces [TYP107]...17.00
__ Hildebrandt Movie Poster Art, 1000 pieces Kenner logo in bar...20.00
__ Jawas Capture R2-D2 [TYP108].....................10.00
__ Luke and Leia, 500 pieces [TYP109].............10.00
__ Luke Meets R2-D2, 140 pieces [TYP110].......15.00
__ Luke Skywalker, 500 pieces, black box [TYP111]...15.00

__ Luke Skywalker, 500 pieces, purple box [TYP112]...12.00
__ Millennium Falcon, 1500 pieces [TYP113]......24.00
__ Purchase of the Droids, 500 pieces [TYP114]12.00
__ Sandtroopers in Mos Eisley, 140 pieces [TYP115]...8.00
__ Space Battle, 500 pieces, black box [TYP116]........15.00
__ Space Battle, 500 pieces, purple box [TYP117]......24.00
__ The Cantina Band, 500 pieces [TYP118]..................12.00
__ Trapped in the Trash Compactor, 140 pieces, black box [TYP119]...8.00
__ Tusken Raider, 140 pieces [TYP120]................8.00
__ Victory Celebration, 500 pieces [TYP121]......10.00
__ Victory Celebration, 500 pieces, wrong image, correction sticker [TYP122]............................65.00
__ X-Wing Hangar tight view, 500 pieces [TYP123]...10.00
__ X-Wing Hangar wide view, 500 pieces [TYP124]...10.00

Kinder
__ 150 pieces, Hippo landspeeder scene...........10.00

King International
__ 1000 pieces, scenes from the classic trilogy [TYP125]...24.00

Kinder (Lili Ledy)
Lili Ledy, Mexico
__ Darth Vader, tray..35.00

Mastertrade, Germany
1000 piece puzzles.
__ Coruscant [TYP126].......................................20.00

TYP173 TYP174 TYP175 TYP176 TYP177 TYP178 TYP179

TYP180 TYP181 TYP182 TYP183 TYP184

TYP185 side 1 and side 2   TYP186 side 1 and side 2

TYP187

TYP188

TYP189

TYP190

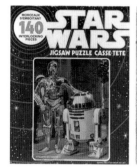

TYP191

TYP192

TYP193

TYP194

TYP195

TYP196

TYP197

TYP198

TYP199

TYP200

TYP201

TYP202

TYP203

TYP204

TYP205

TYP206

TYP207

TYP208

TYP209

TYP210   TYP211   TYP212   TYP213   TYP214 package and puzzle

TYP215   TYP216   TYP217

TYP218   TYP219   TYP220

TYP221   TYP222   TYP223   TYP224

TYP225   TYP226   TYP227   TYP228   TYP229

TYP230

TYP231

TYP232

TYP233

TYP234

TYP235

TYP236

TYP237

TYP238

TYP239

TYP240

TYP241

TYP242

TYP243

TYP244

TYP245

TYP246

TYP247

TYP248

TYP249

TYP250

TYP251

TYP252

TYP253

TYP254

TYP255

TYP256

TYP257

__ Jedi Starfighters [TYP127] 20.00
__ Padme's legacy [TYP128] 20.00
__ Saga Edition, main characters [TYP129] 20.00

Milton Bradley
100 piece classic trilogy.
__ C-3PO and R2-D2 in desert [TYP130] 8.00
__ C-3PO, Chewbacca, Han, and Leia in Shuttle Tydirium [TYP131] 8.00
__ Darth Vader [TYP132] 8.00
__ Jabba's Dias [TYP133] 14.00

100 piece classic trilogy. POTF style packaging.
__ Classic Trilogy [TYP134] 12.00
__ Empire Strikes Back [TYP135] 12.00
__ Return of the Jedi [TYP136] 12.00
__ Star Wars [TYP137] 12.00

100 piece Clone Wars puzzles, 10"x13".
__ Anakin and Ahsoka [TYP138] 15.00
__ Anakin Skywalker [TYP139] 15.00
__ Captain Rex [TYP140] 15.00
__ Obi-Wan Kenobi [TYP141] 15.00

200 piece classic trilogy puzzles. POTF style packaging. Reflective image.
__ Empire Strikes Back 12.00
__ Return of the Jedi [TYP142] 12.00
__ Star Wars [TYP143] 12.00

221 piece mural puzzles.
__ Scene 1: A New Hope [TYP144] 6.00
__ Scene 2: Empire Strikes Back [TYP145] 6.00
__ Scene 3: Return of the Jedi [TYP146] 6.00
__ Scene 4: Trilogy [TYP147] 6.00

3D sculpture puzzles.
__ Darth Vader, tri-language 35.00

__ Darth Vader [TYP148] 35.00
__ Imperial Star Destroyer 35.00
__ Jar Jar Binks [TYP149] 25.00
__ Jedi Starfighter [TYP150] 20.00
__ Millennium Falcon [TYP151] 35.00
__ R2-D2 with electronic sounds [TYP152] 35.00

500 pieces, in shaped tin.
__ Captain Rex [TYP153] 15.00
__ Stormtrooper 15.00

550 pieces with foil highlights.
__ Return of the Jedi [TYP154] 12.00
__ Star Wars: A New Hope [TYP155] 12.00
__ The Empire Strikes Back [TYP156] 12.00

60 piece classic trilogy puzzles.
__ A New Hope [TYP157] 15.00
__ Empire Strikes Back 15.00
__ Return of the Jedi [TYP158] 15.00

Episode II: Attack of the Clones 50 piece mini-puzzle, 5"x7".
__ Anakin Skywalker [TYP159] 3.00
__ C-3PO and R2-D2 [TYP160] 3.00
__ Darth Vader [TYP161] 3.00
__ Jango Fett [TYP162] 3.00
__ Mace Windu [TYP163] 3.00
__ Obi-Wan Kenobi [TYP164] 3.00
__ Padme Amidala [TYP165] 3.00
__ Zam Wesell [TYP166] 3.00

Episode II: Attack of the Clones. 100 pieces.
__ Anakin Skywalker [TYP167] 8.00
__ Boba and Jango Fett [TYP168] 8.00
__ Obi-Wan Kenobi [TYP169] 8.00
__ Padme Amidala and Princess Leia [TYP170] ...8.00

Episode II: Attack of the Clones. 150 Metallix pieces.
__ Anakin Skywalker [TYP171] 9.00
__ Count Dooku 9.00
__ Mace Windu [TYP172] 9.00
__ Obi-Wan Kenobi 9.00

Episode III: Revenge of the Sith 50 piece mini-puzzle, 5"x7".
__ Anakin [TYP173] 3.00
__ C-3PO and R2-D2 [TYP174] 3.00
__ Darth Vader [TYP175] 3.00
__ General Grievous [TYP176] 3.00
__ Obi-Wan [TYP177] 3.00
__ Padme [TYP178] 3.00
__ Palpatine [TYP179] 3.00
__ Yoda [TYP180] 3.00

Episode III: Revenge of the Sith. 100 pieces.
__ Anakin vs. Obi-Wan [TYP181] 10.00
__ Darth Vader / Anakin [TYP182] 10.00
__ Space Battle [TYP183] 10.00
__ Wookiees [TYP184] 10.00

Episode III: Revenge of the Sith. 500 pieces in tin storage box, 2-sided.
__ Emperor, General Grievous, and clone troopers / Anakin, Obi-Wan, Yoda and Mace Windu [TYP185] 15.00

__ Obi-Wan Kenobi and Yoda / Darth Vader, Emperor, Count Dooku and Anakin Skywalker [TYP186] 15.00

Nathan, France
Episode III: Revenge of the Sith.
__ Clone Trooper, 150 pieces [TYP187]..............14.00
__ Jedi Starfighter, 100 pieces [TYP188] 14.00

Parker Bros.
__ Bantha, 140 pieces [TYP189] 35.00
__ Battle above Death Star, 500 pieces [TYP190] 35.00
__ C-3PO and R2-D2, 140 pieces [TYP191] 35.00
__ Death Star II, 70 pieces [TYP192].....................8.00
__ Jabba's Henchmen, 70 pieces [TYP193] 8.00
__ Light Saber Duel, 500 pieces [TYP195]..........35.00
__ Luke Meets R2-D2, 140 pieces [TYP196].......35.00
__ Luke Skywalker, 500 pieces [TYP197]............35.00
__ Rebel Base, 500 pieces [TYP199] 35.00
__ Sandtroopers in Mos Eisley, 140 pieces [TYP200] 8.00
__ Selling of Droids, 500 pieces [TYP201] 35.00
__ Stormtroopers, 140 pieces [TYP194] 35.00
__ Trash Compactor, 140 pieces [TYP198]........35.00
__ Victory, 500 pieces [TYP202].......................35.00

Kreig der Sterne mini-puzzles.
__ Battle over Death Star [TYP203] 18.00
__ C-3PO and R2-D2 [TYP204] 18.00
__ Death Star Assault, art 18.00
__ Han and Chewbacca [TYP205].......................18.00
__ Imperial Star Destroyer [TYP206] 18.00
__ Obi-Wan Kenobi 18.00
__ Princess Leia and R2-D2 ....18.00
__ Stormtroopers [TYP207].................................18.00
__ Tusken Raider...18.00
__ Vader confronts Leia [TYP208] 18.00

Tray puzzles.
__ Princess Kneesa and Bagga...........................8.00

Party Express
__ 5 pieces, Darth Vader, 8-pack [TYP209] 5.00

Pizza Hut
Get Into It! Episode I Puzzle Games.
__ Blue border 5.00
__ Red border [TYP210] 5.00

Pizza Hut, Mexico
Get Into It! Episode I Puzzle Games.
__ Blue border [TYP211] 5.00
__ Red border [TYP212] 5.00

Get Into It! Pieces stored in mini-pizza box.
__ Blue border [TYP213] 20.00
__ Red border [TYP214] 20.00

Ravensburger, France
Ewoks.
__ Ewoks, 100 pieces...25.00
__ Ewoks, 3x49 ....25.00

Ravensburger, UK
__ 3 Puzzle pack: Jedi, Bounty Hunters, Clones [TYP215] 25.00
__ Captain Rex and Jedi 100 pieces [TYP216] ...15.00
__ Classic Trilogy 500 pieces [TYP217] 25.00
__ Clone Wars 100 pieces [TYP218] 15.00
__ Clone Wars 60 pieces [TYP219] 15.00
__ Saga, panorama 1,000 pieces [TYP220] 35.00

Puzzle balls.
__ Clone Wars 96 pieces [TYP221] 15.00
__ Star Wars 240 pieces [TYP222] 25.00

Really Useful
3D miniature sculpture puzzles.
__ Anakin Skywalker [TYP223] 14.00
__ Darth Maul, color [TYP224]...........................25.00
__ Darth Vader [TYP225]....................................14.00
__ Jar Jar Binks [TYP226] 32.00
__ Obi-Wan Kenobi [TYP227].............................14.00
__ Qui-Gon Jinn [TYP228].................................14.00

Rose Art Industries
100 pieces.
__ Luke and Leia [TYP229]..................................8.00
__ Star Wars poster art [TYP230].........................8.00

550 pieces.
__ Empire Strikes Back 8.00
__ Return of the Jedi 8.00
__ Star Wars 8.00

Schmid, Germany
Return of the Jedi 2-in-1.
__ Darth Vader / Tyderium Cockpit [TYP231] 36.00
__ Jabba the Hutt and Luke in Jabbas Court......36.00

Springbok
__ Empire Strikes Back, 1000 pieces [TYP232] ..24.00
__ Star Wars, 1500 pieces [TYP233]...................24.00

T. Theophanides and Son
__ Mini-Puzzles, 63 pieces, 14x18cm, eight different pictures, each [TYP234]................................24.00

Takara, Japan
60 pieces.
__ C-3PO and R2-D2 [TYP235]...........................35.00
__ Chewbacca and Han Solo [TYP236] 35.00
__ Darth Vader..35.00
__ Luke Skywalker [TYP237]..............................35.00
__ Space Battle [TYP238]..................................35.00
__ Star Wars 35.00

Any of six scenes.
__ 100 pieces 45.00
__ 500 pieces 50.00
__ 700 pieces 50.00

Plastic framed tray puzzles.
__ R2-D2..45.00
__ Victory Celebration 45.00

Tomy, Japan
__ Anakin Skywalker, 56 pieces [TYP239] 15.00

Mini puzzles in tins.
__ C-3PO and R2-D2 [TYP240] 7.00
__ Darth Maul [TYP241].......................................7.00
__ Yoda [TYP242]..7.00

Visual Echo
__ Star Wars 3D 210 pieces [TYP243] 8.00

Waddington, UK
150 pieces.
__ C-3PO and R2-D2 [TYP244] 25.00
__ Chewbacca and Han [TYP245].......................25.00
__ Darth Vader [TYP246] 16.00
__ Entering Mos Eisley [TYP247]........................25.00
__ Ewoks at home 14.00
__ Ewoks in woods...14.00
__ Ewoks sledding..14.00
__ Ewoks swimming 14.00
__ Inside the Millennium Falcon [TYP248]...........25.00
__ Jabba's Throne Room 16.00
__ Luke with blaster..16.00

PZB001

PZB002

PZB003

PZB004

PZB005

PZB006

PZB007

PZB008

ANAKIN SKYWALKER
PZB009

C-3PO
PZB010

DARTH MAUL
PZB011

JAR JAR BINKS
PZB012

OBI-WAN KENOBI
PZB013

QUEEN AMIDALA
PZB014

PZB015

350 pieces. Action figure scenes.
__ Land Speeder [TYP249].................................65.00
__ Land Speeder, X-Wing and TIE Fighter [TYP250] 65.00

Waddington / Capiepa, France
Guerre de Etoiles.
__ D2 R2 et Z6 PO [TYP251]...............................36.00
__ Entree Dans la Ville [TYP252] 36.00
__ Yan Solo et Chiktabba [TYP253] 36.00

Wrebbit
3D sculpture puzzles.
__ Anakin's Jedi Starfighter [TYP254] 35.00
__ Millennium Falcon [TYP255] 35.00
__ R2-D2 [TYP256]...35.00
__ Star Destroyer [TYP257] 35.00

Puzzles: Block

Argentina. Classic trilogy.
__ Boba Fett [PZB001] 10.00
__ Darth Vader [PZB002]....................................10.00
__ Han Solo [PZB003] 10.00
__ Luke Skywalker [PZB004]...............................10.00
__ Princess Leia [PZB005]...................................10.00
__ Yoda [PZB006]...10.00

Craft Master
__ Ewoks [PZB007] 12.00
__ Return of the Jedi characters [PZB008] 12.00

Pepsi Cola
The Phantom Menace 36 piece promotional puzzles.
__ Anakin Skywalker [PZB009]..............................7.00

__ C-3PO [PZB010]...7.00
__ Darth Maul [PZB011]......................................7.00
__ Jar Jar Binks [PZB012] 7.00
__ Obi-Wan Kenobi [PZB013] 7.00
__ Queen Amidala [PZB014] 7.00

Takara, Japan
__ C-3PO and R2-D2 ....45.00
__ Character art...45.00
__ Darth Vader...45.00
__ Han Solo and Chewbacca [PZB015] 45.00
__ Yavin Ceremony 45.00
__ Yavin Hangar 45.00

Puzzles: Twisting

Harry N. Abrams, Inc.
__ Dressing a Galaxy puzzle cube, book premium...18.00

Hasbro
__ Darth Maul Rubik's Cube Puzzle [PZ001].........7.00

Kelloggs, Canada
Episode II: Attack of the Clones. Cereal premium. Character sculpted on front and rear.
__ Anakin Skywalker / Darth Vader [PZ002]..........6.00
__ C-3PO/ R2-D2 [PZ003]...................................6.00
__ Count Dooku / Darth Sidious [PZ004] 6.00
__ Jango Fett / Clone trooper [PZ005] 6.00
__ Obi-Wan Kenobi / Ben Kenobi [PZ006]............6.00
__ Princess Leia / Padme Amidala [PZ007] 6.00

PZ001

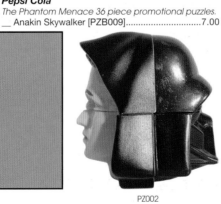
PZ002

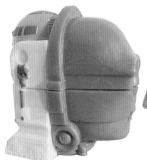
PZ003

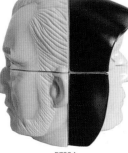
PZ004

PZ005

PZ006

PZ007

385

RBO001
RBO002
RBO003
RBO004
RBO005

RBO006
RBO007
RBO008
RBO009
RBO010

RBO011
RBO012
YF001
YF002

R2-D2 Misc. Toys

Disney Theme Park Merchandise
__ R2-D2 light spinner Star Tours [RBO001].......35.00

Hasbro
Interactive R2-D2.
__ EPIII packaging with bonus poster [RBO002] 200.00
__ Industrial Automation packaging [RBO003] .135.00
__ Legacy packaging [RBO004] 135.00
__ Saga Collection packaging [RBO005] 250.00

Kinder
__ R2-Hippo, pull-back friction [RBO006]...........16.00

Micro Games of America
__ Talking R2-D2, says four different phrases [RBO007] 14.00

Palitoy, UK
__ Talking R2-D2, says four different phrases [RBO008] 895.00

Takara, Japan
__ Bump-and-Go battery powered R2-D2 [RBO009] 264.00
__ Missile Firing R2-D2, die cast metal [RBO010] 285.00
__ Missile Firing R2-D2, plastic [RBO011] 175.00
__ Missile Firing R2-D2, plastic in window box [RBO012] 175.00

Racing Sets

Fundimensions
__ Duel at Death Star [YF001] 125.00
__ Duel at Death Star, white box with line-art only [YF002]...165.00

Racing Vehicles

Action / Revell
__ 1/18 scale "standard limited edition" racing car..45.00
__ 1/18 scale racing car, limited to 1,500 ....100.00
__ 1/18 scale racing car, limited to 4,000 ....250.00

YL001

YL002

YL003

YL004

YL005

YL006

YL007

YL008

YL009

YL010

YL011

YL012

YL019

YL013

YL014

YL020

YL015

YL016

YL021

YL017

YL018

YL022

YL023

YL024

YL025

YL027

YL028

YL029

YL030

YL031

YL032

YL026

__ 1/24 scale "clear window bank" racing car, 8.3" long, limited to 10,000 ....75.00
__ 1/24 scale "Elite" racing car 26.00
__ 1/24 scale "standard limited edition" racing car..24.00
__ 1/24 scale racing car, limited to 12,500 [YL001]...36.00
__ 1/24 scale racing car, 8.3" long, limited to 3,500...42.00
__ 1/43 scale racing car, limited to 5,500 [YL003]...44.00
__ 1/64 scale diecast racing car, 3.1" long, limited to 15,000 [YL002]...14.00
__ 1/64 scale racing car, limited to 20,000 [YL004]...8.00
__ "Pedal car bank " with trailer, 6.2" long, limited to 2,500...55.00

Episode III: Revenge of the Sith.
__ M&M 1/24 scale Elliott Sadler white gold, limited to 25 ....250.00

Disney Theme Park Merchandise
__ Darth Vader carry case with 15 racers including 4 exclusive: TC-14, Shadow Trooper, Shadow Guard, Wedge Antilles, exclusive to Star Tours [YL005]..95.00

1/64 scale die cast metal body race cars.
__ AT-AT, exclusive to Star Tours [YL006]..........15.00
__ Battle Droid, exclusive to Star Tours..............15.00
__ Boba Fett, exclusive to Star Tours [YL007] 15.00
__ C-3PO, exclusive to Star Tours 15.00
__ Clone Trooper, exclusive to Star Tours 15.00
__ Darth Maul, exclusive to Star Tours [YL008] ..15.00

__ Darth Vader, exclusive to Star Tours [YL009].15.00
__ General Grievous, exclusive to Star Tours [YL010]..15.00
__ Imperial Guard, exclusive to Star Tours [YL011]..15.00
__ Jango Fett, exclusive to Star Tours [YL012]...15.00
__ Jawa, exclusive to Star Tours [YL013]............15.00
__ Jedi Master Plo Koon, exclusive to Star Tours...15.00
__ Lando Calrissian, exclusive to Star Tours [YL014]..15.00
__ Luke Skywalker X-Wing Pilot, exclusive to Star Tours [YL015]..15.00
__ R2-D2, exclusive to Star Tours [YL016]..........15.00
__ Stormtrooper, exclusive to Star Tours............15.00
__ Tusken Raider, exclusive to Star Tours [YL017]..15.00

YL033

YL034

YL035

YL036

YL037

YL038

__ Watto, exclusive to Star Tours [YL018] 15.00
__ Yoda, exclusive to Star Tours.........................15.00

Disney Theme Park Merchandise, UK
1/64 scale die cast metal body race cars.
__ 3-pack: Luke pilot, Darth Maul, Darth Vader..35.00

General Mills
Mail-away premiums. Car 43, 1/64 scale.
__ Classic Trilogy [YL019] 15.00
__ Episode I [YL020]..15.00
__ Episode II [YL021]...15.00

Greenlight
1/64 scale die cast metal body race cars.
__ Clone Wars, Marco Andretti [YL022] 15.00

Hasbro
EPI: The Phantom Menace Winner's Circle series.
__ 1/64 scale racing car with Jeff Gordon trading card [YL023]...12.00
__ Pit Row [YL024] 17.00

Ripcord racers action sets.
__ Assault on General Grievous [YL025] 25.00
__ Hyperspace Challenge [YL026] 25.00

Ripcord racers with lightsaber launcher.
__ Slave I [YL033] 14.00

Ripcord racers.
__ Anakin's Jedi Starfighter [YL027] 10.00
__ General Grievous' Starfighter [YL028] 10.00
__ Magnaguard Fighter [YL029] 10.00

__ Obi-Wan's Jedi Starfighter [YL030]................10.00
__ Republic Gunship [YL031]...............................10.00
__ Y-Wing Bomber [YL032]..................................10.00

Kenner
__ Power Racing Speeder Bike [YL034].............12.00

SSP vans.
__ 2 Vans, cones, obstacles [YL035]..................995.00
__ Darth Vader [YL036]..150.00
__ Luke Skywalker [YL037] 150.00

Team Caliber
__ 1/24 scale 2002 John Andretti Star Wars Episode II Dark Chrome car, limited to 450....................75.00
__ 1/64 scale 2002 John Andretti Star Wars Episode II car [YL038]..12.00

 YG001
 YG002
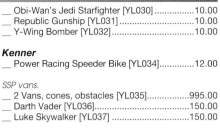 YG003 YG004
 YG007
 YG008
 YG005
 YG006
 YG009
 YG010
 YG011
 YG012
 YG013
 YG014

Radio Controlled

YG015

YG016

YG017

YG018

YH001

YH002

YH003

YH004

Radio Controlled Toys

__ Cobot (R2-D2 robot with Coca-Cola can body) [YG001] 395.00

Foodland
__ Mr. Grocer, licensed variation on the Cobot 185.00

Hasbro
__ Hailfire Droid [YG002] 60.00

Astromech droids, control is lightsaber shaped.
__ R2-D2, exclusive to Target [YG003] 20.00
__ R2-Q5, exclusive to Target [YG004] 20.00
__ R5-D4, exclusive to Target [YG005] 20.00
__ R5-X2, exclusive to Target [YG006]..............20.00

Flying vehicles with charging controllers.
__ Millennium Falcon [YG007]...........................45.00
__ Obi-Wan's Jedi Starfighter [YG008] 35.00
__ Republic Gunship [YG009] 35.00

Hitari
__ Darth Vader [YG010]......................................75.00

Kenner
__ Imperial Speeder Bike [YG011]......................50.00
__ Speederbike with Luke Skywalker [YG012]....70.00

Vintage.
__ R2-D2 [YG013]..165.00
__ R2-D2 with obstacle course 3850.00

Kenner, Canada
__ R2-D2...165.00

Palitoy, UK
__ R2-D2...165.00

Takara, Japan
__ R2-D2, fires toy discs and top of body turns [YG014] 425.00

Tomy, Japan
Astromech droids, control is lightsaber shaped.
__ R2-D2 [YG015]...25.00
__ R2-D2, clear, exclusive to Star Wars Celebration Japan [YG016]...35.00
__ R2-D2, weathered [YG017]...........................35.00
__ R2-Q5 [YG018]..35.00
__ R4-P17...35.00
__ R5-D4..35.00
__ R5-X2..35.00

Remote Controlled Toys

Banpresto, Japan
__ Millennium Falcon [YH001] 23.00
__ R2-D2 [YH002]..18.00

Hasbro
__ R2-D2 [YH003]..40.00

Kenner
__ R2-D2 [YH004]..20.00

Role Playing Game

TSR Hobbies
__ Gamemaster Screen [4:272] 10.00

West End Games
Adventure journals. Star Wars element on cover.
__ 01 B-Wing [RPG001] 17.00
__ 02 Rancor [RPG002] 14.00
__ 03 Stormtrooper [RPG003] 15.00
__ 04 Royal Guard [RPG004] 12.00
__ 05 2-1B [RPG005]..12.00
__ 06 Millennium Falcon [RPG006] 12.00
__ 07 X-Wing and TIE Fighter [RPG007] 12.00
__ 08 Santa Yoda [RPG008].................................12.00
__ 09 Bounty hunters [RPG009] 12.00
__ 10 Hoth battle [RPG010]................................12.00
__ 11 Speederbike [RPG011] 12.00
__ 12 Mos Eisley [RPG012] 12.00
__ 13 Star Destroyer [RPG013] 12.00
__ 14 Y-Wing [4:272] 15.00
__ 15 Luke in X-Wing gear [RPG014].................15.00

West End Games, Brazil
Adventure supplements.
__ Batalla por el Sol Dorado [4:272]....................15.00

West End Games
Adventure supplements.
__ Battle for the Golden Sun [RPG015]...............12.00
__ Black Ice 12.00
__ Black Sands of Socorro [RPG016] 14.00

West End Games, Brazil
Adventure supplements.
__ Caceria humana en Tatooine [4:272]..............15.00

West End Games
Adventure supplements.
__ Classic Adventures [4:272] 16.00
__ Classic Adventures II [4:272] 15.00
__ Classic Adventures III [RPG017] 16.00
__ Classic Adventures IV [RPG018] 15.00

West End Games, Brazil
Adventure supplements.
__ Comando Shantipole [4:272] 15.00

West End Games
Adventure supplements.
__ Crisis on Cloud City......................................12.00
__ Darkstryder Campaign [RPG019] 14.00
__ Darkstryder Campaign: Endgame [4:272] 17.00
__ Darkstryder Supplement: Kathol Rift.............18.00
__ Death in the Undercity 12.00
__ Domain of Evil..12.00

West End Games, Brazil
Adventure supplements.
__ Espacio paralelo [4:272] 15.00
__ Estrella Rendida [4:272].................................15.00

West End Games
Adventure supplements.
__ Flashpoint: Brak Sector 13.00
__ Goroth [RPG020] 12.00
__ Graveyard of Alderaan...................................12.00
__ Imperial Double-Cross [4:272] 18.00
__ Instant Adventures [4:272].............................14.00
__ Isis Coordinates 12.00
__ Live Action Adventures [4:272] 20.00
__ Mission to Lianna 12.00
__ No Disintegrations 20.00
__ Otherspace [4:272] 12.00
__ Otherspace II: Invasion [4:272] 12.00
__ Planet of the Mists 12.00
__ Riders of the Maelstrom [4:272] 12.00
__ Scavenger Hunt [RPG021]..............................12.00
__ Secrets of the Sisar Run [4:272] 14.00
__ Starfall..12.00
__ Strike Force: Shantipole [4:272] 12.00
__ Supernova [RPG022]......................................13.00
__ Tapanu Sector - Instant Adventures [4:272]....18.00
__ Tatooine Manhunt [RPG023].........................12.00
__ The Abduction 14.00
__ The Game Chambers of Questal [RPG024]....12.00
__ The Politics of Contraband [4:272] 12.00
__ Twin Stars of Kira 13.00

    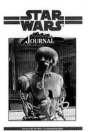  

RPG001   RPG002   RPG003   RPG004   RPG005   RPG006   RPG007

RPG008   RPG009   RPG010   RPG011   RPG012   RPG013   RPG014

West End Games, Brazil
Adventure supplements.
__ Ultimo Juego [4:272]..15.00

West End Games
Background books.
__ Cracken's Rebel Field Guide [RPG025]..........18.00
__ Cracken's Rebel Operatives [4:272]...............18.00
__ Creatures of the Galaxy [4:272] 18.00
__ Death Star Technical Companion [RPG026] ..18.00
__ Droids [RPG027]..16.00
__ Galladinium's Fantastic Technology...............18.00
__ Hideouts and Strongholds [4:272]..................18.00
__ Operation: Elrod [4:272]..................................12.00
__ Pirates and Privateers.....................................18.00
__ Planets of the Galaxy Vol. I [4:272].................18.00
__ Planets of the Galaxy Vol. II [4:272]................18.00
__ Planets of the Galaxy Vol. III [4:272]..............18.00
__ Platt's Starpost Guide 25.00
__ Shadows of the Empire Planets Guide
[RPG028]...18.00
__ Star Wars Planet Collection............................25.00
__ Wanted by Cracken 18.00
__ Wretched Hives of Scum and Villainy
[RPG029]...17.00

Galaxy guides.
__ #01 A New Hope [4:272]................................14.00

__ #02 Yavin and Bespin [RPG030] 14.00
__ #03 The Empire Strikes Back [4:272] 14.00
__ #04 Alien Races...14.00
__ #05 Return of the Jedi [4:272] 14.00
__ #06 Tramp Freighters [RPG031] 14.00
__ #07 Mos Eisley..14.00
__ #08 Scouts [4:272]..14.00
__ #09 Fragments from the Rim 14.00
__ #10 Bounty Hunters...14.00
__ #11 Criminal Organizations.............................14.00
__ #12 Aliens 14.00

Gamemaster equipment.
__ Gamemasters Handbook, 2nd edition [4:272]24.00
__ Gamemasters Kit [4:272] 18.00
__ Gamemasters Screen [4:272]............................8.00
__ Gamemasters Screen for 2nd Edition [4:272]...8.00
__ Gamemasters Screen handbook [4:272]........24.00

Rule books.
__ Introductory game rule book [4:272] 24.00
__ Star Wars: The Role Playing Game primary, 2nd
edition [4:272]..20.00
__ Star Wars: The Role Playing Game, companion 18.00
__ Star Wars: The Role Playing Game, primary
[4:272] 22.00

Sourcebooks.
__ Classic Campaigns [4:272] 14.00
__ Dark Empire [4:272] 17.00
__ Dark Force Rising [4:272] 17.00
__ Han Solo and the Corporate Sector [4:272] ...17.00
__ Heir to the Empire [4:272]...............................17.00
__ Imperial [4:272]...17.00
__ Last Command [4:272] 17.00
__ Movie Trilogy 17.00
__ Rebel Alliance [4:272].....................................17.00
__ Shadows of the Empire 25.00
__ Star Wars [4:272] 17.00
__ The Truce at Bakura [4:272] 15.00

RPG015   RPG016

RPG017   RPG018   RPG019   RPG020   RPG021   RPG022   RPG023

RPG024   RPG025   RPG026   RPG027   RPG028   RPG029   RPG030

RPG031 RPG032 RPG033 RPG034 RPG035 RPG036 RPG037

RPG038 RPG039 RPG040 RPG041 RPG042 RPG043 RPG044

RPG045 RPG046 RPG047 RPG048 RPG049 RPG050 RPG051

Wizards of the Coast

__ Alien Anthology [RPG032]	27.00
__ Arms and Equipment Guide [RPG033]	22.00
__ Character Record Sheets [RPG034]	10.00
__ Core Rulebook [RPG035]	35.00
__ Core Rulebook, revised [RPG036]	40.00
__ Coruscant and the Core Worlds [RPG037]	30.00
__ Galactic Campaign Guide [RPG038]	30.00
__ Galaxy of Intrigue by Rodney Thompson, published: January 19, 2010	30.00
__ Game Master's Screen [RPG039]	10.00
__ Geonosis and the Outer Rim Worlds [RPG040]	30.00
__ Hero's Guide [RPG041]	30.00
__ Invasion of Theed Adventure Game [4:272]	35.00
__ Invasion of Theed Adventure Game, action figure in cover window [4:272]	75.00
__ Living Force Campaign Pack [RPG042]	20.00
__ New Jedi Order Sourcebook [4:272]	30.00
__ Power of the Jedi Sourcebook [4:272]	27.00
__ Rebellion Era Sourcebook [RPG043]	30.00
__ Secrets of Tatooine Campaign Pack [RPG044]	22.00
__ Star Wars Roleplaying Game [4:272]	35.00
__ Starships of the Galaxy 1st edition [RPG045]	22.00
__ Starships of the Galaxy 2nd edition [4:272]	35.00
__ Tempest Feud [4:272]	25.00
__ The Dark Side Sourcebook [RPG046]	30.00
__ The Secrets of Naboo Campaigns [4:272]	20.00
__ The Unknown Regions	30.00
__ Ultimate Adversaries [RPG047]	30.00
__ Ultimate Alien Anthology [RPG048]	40.00

Ultimate Missions for miniatures game.

__ Clone Strike [RPG049]	25.00
__ Rebel Storm [RPG050]	25.00
__ Revenge of the Sith [RPG051]	25.00

Role Playing Miniatures

West End Games
Blister packed figures and blister packed vehicles.

__ Aliens of the Galaxy	8.00

__ Aliens of the Galaxy #2 [RPM001]	8.00
__ Aliens of the Galaxy #3	8.00
__ AT-AT	12.00
__ AT-PT	9.00
__ Bantha and Rider	8.00
__ Bounty Hunters #1 [RPM002]	8.00
__ Bounty Hunters #2	8.00
__ Bounty Hunters #3	8.00
__ Darkstryder #1	12.00
__ Darkstryder #2 [RPM003]	12.00
__ Darkstryder #3	12.00
__ Darth Vader, Leia, and Luke	8.00
__ Denizens of Cloud City [RPM004]	8.00
__ Denizens of Tatooine [RPM005]	8.00
__ Droids [RPM006]	8.00
__ Emperor	8.00
__ Encounter on Hoth [RPM007]	12.00
__ Ewoks	8.00
__ Gamorrean Guards [RPM008]	12.00
__ Heir to the Empire Villains	8.00
__ Heroes #1: Luke, C-3PO, R2-D2	8.00
__ Heroes #2: Chewbacca, Han, Leia	8.00
__ Hoth Rebels [RPM009]	8.00
__ Imperial Army Troopers #1	8.00
__ Imperial Army Troopers #2	8.00
__ Imperial Crew with Heavy Blaster	8.00
__ Imperial Navy Troopers #1	8.00
__ Imperial Navy Troopers #2	8.00
__ Imperial Officers	8.00
__ Imperial Speederbikes [RPM010]	12.00
__ Imperial Troop Pack	18.00
__ Jabba the Hutt	12.00
__ Jabba's Servants	10.00
__ Jedi Knights	8.00
__ Landspeeder [RPM011]	10.00
__ Mon Calamari [RPM012]	8.00
__ Mos Eisley Cantina	11.00
__ Mos Eisley Cantina Aliens #1	8.00
__ Mos Eisley Cantina Aliens #2	8.00
__ Mos Eisley Space Station	10.00
__ Nogri [RPM013]	8.00
__ Pilots and Gunners	8.00
__ Pirates [RPM014]	9.00

__ Rebel Commanders #1	8.00
__ Rebel Commanders #2	8.00
__ Rebel Commandos #1	8.00
__ Rebel Commandos #2	8.00
__ Rebel Operatives	8.00
__ Rebel Speeder Bikes	10.00
__ Rebel Troop Pack	18.00
__ Rebel Troopers #1 [RPM015]	8.00
__ Rebel Troopers #2 [RPM016]	8.00
__ Rebel Troopers #3	8.00
__ Rebel Troopers #4	8.00
__ Sandtroopers	8.00
__ Scout Troopers	8.00
__ Skywalkers [RPM017]	8.00
__ Snowspeeder	10.00
__ Snowtroopers	8.00
__ Storm Skimmers [RPM018]	10.00
__ Stormtroopers #1	8.00
__ Stormtroopers #2	8.00
__ Stormtroopers #3	8.00
__ Stormtroopers #4	8.00
__ Taun-Taun and Rider	8.00
__ Users of the Force	8.00
__ Wookiees [RPM019]	8.00
__ Zero G Troopers [RPM020]	8.00

Boxed figures.

__ A New Hope [RPM021]	15.00
__ Bounty Hunters [RPM022]	15.00
__ Empire Strikes Back [RPM023]	15.00
__ Heroes of the Rebellion [RPM024]	15.00
__ Imperial Forces [RPM025]	15.00
__ Imperial Troopers [RPM026]	15.00
__ Jabbas Palace [RPM027]	15.00
__ Mos Eisley Cantina [RPM028]	15.00
__ Rancor Pit [RPM029]	15.00
__ Rebel Characters [RPM030]	15.00
__ Rebel Troopers [RPM031]	15.00
__ Return of the Jedi [RPM032]	15.00
__ Stormtroopers [RPM033]	15.00
__ Zero G Assault Troopers [RPM034]	15.00

Guide books.
__ Star Wars Miniatures Battles [4:274] 18.00
__ Star Wars Miniatures Battles Companion [4:274]...............15.00

Starter sets.
__ Miniature Battles................35.00
__ Mos Eisley................35.00
__ Vehicles [4:274]................35.00

Wizards of the Coast
__ Cerean Jedi [RPM035]................5.00
__ Cerean Noble [RPM036]................5.00
__ Female Human Fringer [RPM037]................5.00
__ Female Human Handmaiden................5.00
__ Female Human Scoundrel................5.00
__ Female Human Scout [RPM038]................5.00
__ Female Human Soldier................5.00
__ Female Twi'lek Jedi................5.00
__ Gungan Scout................5.00
__ Male Human Fringer................5.00
__ Male Human Jedi................5.00
__ Male Human Scout................5.00
__ Male Human Soundrel [RPM039]................5.00
__ Male Twi'lek Scoundrel [RPM040]................5.00
__ Roadian Soldier................5.00
__ Rodian Scout [RPM041]................5.00
__ Wookiee Scout................5.00

Blind packed booster packs.
__ 2-pack: Rebels and Imperials [RPM042] 5.00

Convention exclusives.
__ Snowtrooper with E-Web blaster square base and embossed Star Wars logo, exclusive to Star Wars Celebration IV................35.00

Miniatures Game.
__ AT-AT Imperial Walker Colossal Pack, 18"x14"x7" [RPM043]................65.00
__ Attack on Endor. Includes an AT-ST, 3 stormtroopers, 4 maps, abbreviated scenario book...............50.00
__ Battle of Hoth scenario pack, exclusive to Target................60.00
__ Galaxy Tiles customizable terrain.................16.00
__ Rancor Attack!................35.00

Miniatures Game. Alliance and Empire.
__ Admiral Piett 24 (R)................3.00
__ Advance Agent, Officer 58 (UC)................0.50
__ Advance Scout 59 (C)................0.25
__ Aurra Sing, Jedi Hunter 02 (VR)................20.00
__ Biggs Darklighter 03 (VR)................6.00
__ Boba Fett, Enforcer 38 (VR)................25.00
__ C-3PO and R2-D2 05 (R)................5.00
__ Chadra-Fan Pickpocket 39 (UC)................0.25
__ Chewbacca, Enraged Wookiee 04 (R)................3.00
__ Darth Vader, Imperial Commander 25 (VR)......8.00
__ Death Star Gunner 26 (UC)................1.25
__ Death Star Trooper 27 (C)................0.50
__ Duro Explorer 40 (C)................0.25
__ Elite Hoth Trooper 06 (C)................0.25
__ Ephant Mon 41 (VR)................8.00
__ Ewok Hang Glider 42 (R)................5.00
__ Ewok Warrior 43 (C)................0.75

__ Gamorrean Guard 44 (C)................0.25
__ Han Solo in Stormtrooper Armor 08 (R)............5.00
__ Han Solo on Tauntaun 09 (VR)................8.00
__ Han Solo, Rogue 07 (R)................2.50
__ Heavy Stormtrooper 28 (UC)................1.25
__ Human Force Adept 45 (C)................0.25
__ Imperial Governor Tarkin 29 (R)................3.00
__ Imperial Officer 30 (UC)................1.00
__ Ithorian Commander 10 (UC)................0.75
__ Jabba, Crime Lord 46 (VR)................25.00
__ Jawa on Ronto 47 (VR)................12.00
__ Jawa Trader 48 (UC)................1.25
__ Lando Calrissian, Dashing Scoundrel 49 (R) 2.50
__ Luke Skywalker, Champion of the Force 11 (VR)................25.00
__ Luke Skywalker, Hero of Yavin 12 (R)................3.00
__ Luke's Landspeeder 13 (VR)................18.00
__ Mara Jade, Jedi 37 (R)................10.00
__ Mon Calamari Tech Specialist 14 (C) 0.10
__ Nikto Soldier 50 (C)................0.25
__ Obi-Wan Kenobi, Force Spirit 15 (VR) 18.00
__ Princess Leia 16 (R)................3.00
__ Quinlan Vos, Infiltrator 01 (VR)................20.00
__ Rampaging Wampa 51 (VR)................18.00
__ Rebel Commando 17 (C)................0.25
__ Rebel Commando Strike Leader 18 (UC) 0.75
__ Rebel Leader 19 (UC)................0.25
__ Rebel Pilot 20 (C)................0.25
__ Rebel Trooper 21 (UC)................0.75
__ Rodian Scoundrel 52 (UC)................0.25
__ Scout Trooper 31 (UC)................1.00
__ Snivvian Fringer 53 (C)................0.10
__ Snowtrooper 32 (C)................0.75

RPM001　RPM002　RPM003　RPM004　RPM005　RPM006　RPM007

RPM008　RPM009　RPM010　RPM011　RPM012　RPM013　RPM014

RPM015　RPM016　RPM017　RPM018　RPM019　RPM020

RPM021

RPM022

RPM023

RPM024

RPM025

RPM026

RPM027

RPM028

RPM029

RPM030

RPM031

RPM032

RPM033

RPM034

__ Storm Commando 33 (R) 18.00
__ Stormtrooper 34 (C) 1.25
__ Stormtrooper Officer 35 (UC) 1.00
__ Stormtrooper on Repulser Sled 36 (VR) 20.00
__ Talz Spy 54 (UC) 0.25
__ Transdoshan Mercenary 55 (UC) 1.25
__ Tusken Raider 56 (C) 0.50
__ Twi'lek Rebel Agent 22 (UC) 0.25
__ Wicket 57 (R) 6.00
__ Wookiee Freedom Fighter 23 (C) 0.25
__ Yomin Carr 60 (R) 5.00

Miniatures Game. Bounty Hunters.
__ 4-LOM, Bounty Hunter 32 (R) 7.00
__ Aqualish Assassin 15 (C) 0.40
__ Ayy Vida 16 (R) 4.50
__ Basilisk War Droid 54 (U) 5.50
__ Bib Fortuna 17 (R) 5.00
__ Bith Black Sun Vigo 18 (U) 0.70
__ Boba Fett, Bounty Hunter 19 (V) 45.00
__ Boshek 20 (R) 4.25
__ Bossk, Bounty Hunter 21 (R) 7.00
__ Boushh 22 (R) 7.00
__ Calo Nord 23 (R) 6.50
__ Chewbacca with C-3PO 6 (V) 15.00
__ Commerce Guild Homing Spider Droid 2 (U) ...4.75
__ Corellian Pirate 24 (U) 1.00
__ Corporate Alliance Tank Droid 3 (U) 3.50
__ Dannik Jerriko 25 (V) 11.00
__ Dark Hellion Marauder on Swoop Bike 26 (U) ..1.25
__ Dark Hellion Swoop Gang Member 27 (C) 0.50
__ Defel Spy 28 (C) 0.50
__ Dengar Bounty Hunter 29 (R) 5.00
__ Djas Puhr 30 (R) 4.00
__ Droid Starfighter in Walking Mode 4 (R) 8.00
__ E522 Assassin Droid 31 (U) 1.00
__ Gamorrean Thug 33 (C) 0.50
__ Garindan 34 (R) 10.00
__ Han Solo Scoundrel 7 (V) 18.00
__ Huge Crab Droid 5 (R) 2.50
__ Human Blaster-for-Hire 35 (C) 0.50
__ IG-88, Bounty Hunter 36 (V) 21.00
__ ISP Speeder 1 (R) 5.50
__ Jango Fett, Bounty Hunter 37 (V) 34.00
__ Klatooinian Hunter 38 (C) 0.50
__ Komari Vosa 39 (R) 9.75
__ Lord Vader 13 (U) 25.00
__ Luke Skywalker of Dagobah 8 (R) 12.50
__ Mandalore the Indomitable 55 (V) 32.00
__ Mandalorian Blademaster 56 (U) 1.50
__ Mandalorian Commander 57 (U) 1.25

__ Mandalorian Soldier 58 (C) 0.70
__ Mandalorian Supercommando 59 (U) 1.50
__ Mandalorian Warrior 60 (C) 0.70
__ Mistryl Shadow Guard 40 (U) 1.50
__ Mustafarian Flea Rider 41 (R) 5.00
__ Mustafarian Soldier 42 (C) 0.70
__ Nikto Gunner on Desert Skiff 43 (V) 30.00
__ Nym 44 (V) 15.00
__ Princess Leia Hoth Commander 9 (R) 11.00
__ Quarren Bounty Hunter 45 (C) 0.50
__ Rebel Captain 10 (U) 1.00
__ Rebel Heavy Trooper 11 (U) 1.25
__ Rebel Snowspeeder 12 (U) 7.25
__ Rodian Hunt Master 46 (U) 0.70
__ Talon Karrde 14 (V) 13.00
__ Tamtel Skreej (Lando Calrissian) 47 (V) 18.00
__ Tusken Raider Sniper 48 (C) 0.50
__ Utapaun on Dactillion 49 (R) 3.50
__ Weequay Leader - Boss 50 (U) 0.70
__ Weequay Thug 51 (C) 0.50
__ Young Krayt Dragon 52 (V) 30.00
__ Zuckuss 53 (R) 8.00

Miniatures Game. Champions of the Force miniatures.
__ Arcona Smuggler #55 (C) 0.50
__ Barriss Offee #20 (R) 10.00
__ Bastila Shan #1 (V) 18.00
__ Clone Commander Bacara #21 (R) 6.00
__ Clone Commander Cody #22 (R) 8.00
__ Clone Commander Gree #23 (R) 8.00
__ Corran Horn #52 (R) 8.00
__ Coruscant Guard #46 (C) 0.50
__ Crab Droid #39 (U) 4.00
__ Dark Jedi #7 (U) 1.00
__ Dark Jedi Master #8 (U) 1.00
__ Dark Side Enforcer #9 (U) 1.00
__ Dark Trooper Phase I #47 (C) 0.50
__ Dark Trooper Phase II #48 (U) 1.00
__ Darth Bane #10 (R) 23.00
__ Darth Malak #11 (V) 20.00
__ Darth Maul, Champion of the Sith #40 (R) 16.00
__ Darth Nihilus #12 (V) 24.00
__ Darth Sidious, Dark Lord of the Sith #41 (R) ..12.00
__ Darth Vader, Champion of the Sith #49 (V) 20.00
__ Depa Billaba #24 (R) 9.00
__ Even Piell #25 (R) 8.00
__ Exar Kun #13 (V) 24.00
__ General Windu #26 (R) 12.00
__ Gundark #56 (U) 0.50
__ HK-47 #57 (V) 20.00

__ Hoth Trooper with ATGAR Cannon #43 (R) 14.00
__ Jacen Solo #53 (V) 16.00
__ Jaina Solo #54 (V) 21.00
__ Jedi Consular #2 (U) 1.00
__ Jedi Guardian #3 (U) 1.00
__ Jedi Padawan #27 (U) 0.50
__ Jedi Sentinel #4 (U) 1.00
__ Jedi Weapon Master #28 (U) 2.00
__ Kashyyyk Trooper #29 (C) 0.50
__ Luke Skywalker, Young Jedi #44 (V) 18.00
__ Mas Amedda #30 (R) 8.00
__ Massassi Sith Mutant #14 (U) 0.50
__ Octuptarra Droid #42 (R) 9.00
__ Old Republic Commander #5 (U) 1.00
__ Old Republic Soldier #6 (U) 0.50
__ Queen Amidala #31 (R) 10.00
__ Qui-Gon Jinn, Jedi Master #32 (R) 9.00
__ R5 Astromech Droid #58 (C) 0.50
__ Republic Commando - Boss #33 (U) 0.50
__ Republic Commando - Fixer #34 (C) 0.50
__ Republic Commando - Scorch #35 (C) 0.50
__ Republic Commando - Sev #36 (C) 0.50
__ Saleucami Trooper #37 (C) 0.50
__ Sandtrooper 50 (C) 0.50
__ Sith Assault Droid #15 (U) 2.00
__ Sith Trooper #16 (C) 0.50
__ Sith Trooper #17 (C) 0.50
__ Sith Trooper Commander #18 (U) 1.50
__ Snowtrooper with E-Web Blaster #51 (R) 12.00
__ Ugnaught Demolitionist #59 (C) 0.50
__ Ulic Qel-Droma #19 (V) 16.00
__ Utapau Trooper #38 (C) 0.50
__ Varactyl Wrangler #60 (C) 0.50
__ Yoda of Dagobah #45 (V) 18.00

Miniatures Game. Clone Strike Game.
__ Booster Pack: Clone Trooper graphic [RPM044] 12.00
__ Booster Pack: Mace Windu graphic [RPM045] 12.00
__ Booster Pack: Super Battle Droid graphic [RPM046] 12.00
__ Starter Set [4:274] 20.00

Miniatures Game. Clone Strike miniatures.
__ Aayla Secura (VR) 20.00
__ Aerial Clone Trooper Captain (R) 17.00
__ Agen Kolar (R) 6.00
__ Anakin Skywalker (VR) 20.00
__ Aqualish Spy (C) 0.50
__ ARC Trooper (UC) 5.00
__ Asajj Ventress (R) 16.00
__ Aurra Sing (VR) 54.00

__ Battle Droid (C) 0.50
__ Battle Droid Officer (UC) 2.00
__ Battle Droid on STAP (R) 10.00
__ Captain Typho (R) 10.00
__ Clone Trooper (C) 0.50
__ Clone Trooper Commander (UC) 2.00
__ Clone Trooper Grenadier (C) 0.50
__ Clone Trooper Sergeant (C) 0.50
__ Count Dooku (VR) 26.00
__ Dark Side Acolyte (UC) 7.00
__ Darth Maul (VR) 44.00
__ Darth Sidious (VR) 26.00
__ Destroyer Droid (R) 24.00
__ Devaronian Bounty Hunter (C) 0.50
__ Durge (R) 14.00
__ Dwarf Spider Droid (R) 12.00
__ General Grievous (VR) 18.00
__ General Kenobi (R) 8.00
__ Geonosian Drone (C) 0.50
__ Geonosian Overseer (UC) 1.00
__ Geonosian Picador on Orray (R) 16.00
__ Geonosian Soldier (UC) 1.00
__ Gran Raider (C) 0.50
__ Gungan Cavalry on Kaadu (R) 7.00
__ Gungan Infantry (C) 0.50
__ Ishi Tib Scout (UC) 1.00
__ Jango Fett (R) 14.00
__ Jedi Guardian (UC) 1.00
__ Ki-Adi-Mundi (R) 15.00
__ Kit Fisto (R) 14.00
__ Klatooinian Enforcer (C) 0.50
__ Luminara Unduli (R) 12.00
__ Mace Windu (VR) 27.00
__ Naboo Soldier (UC) 1.00
__ Nikto Soldier (C) 0.50
__ Padme Amidala (VR) 22.00
__ Plo Koon (R) 12.00
__ Quarren Raider (UC) 1.00
__ Qui-Gon Jinn (VR) 24.00
__ Quinlan Vos (VR) 26.00
__ Rodian Mercenary (UC) 1.00
__ Saesee Tiin (R) 15.00
__ Security Battle Droid (C) 0.50
__ Super Battle Droid (UC) 1.00
__ Weequay Mercenary (C) 0.50
__ Wookiee Commando (UC) 1.00
__ Yoda (VR) 27.00
__ Zam Wesell (R) 15.00

Miniatures Game. Clone Wars.

__ Ahsoka Tano / Republic #02 (VR) 20.00
__ Anakin Skywalker on STAP / Republic #04 (VR) 12.00
__ Anakin Skywalker, Champion of Nelvaan / Republic #03 (R) 3.00
__ Anakin Skywalker, Jedi / Republic (R) 5.00
__ Aqualish Warrior / Fringe #34 (C) 0.25
__ ARC Trooper Sniper / Republic #05 (U) 2.00
__ Asajj Ventress, Separatist Assassin / Separatists (R) 5.00
__ Barriss Offee, Jedi Knight / Republic #06 (R) ...4.00
__ Battle Droid / Separatists #21 (C) 0.75
__ Battle Droid / Separatists #22 (C) 0.50
__ Battle Droid Sniper / Separatists #23 (U) 1.50
__ Booster Pack: Anakin and Ahsoka graphic 12.00
__ Booster Pack: Clone Trooper graphic 12.00
__ Booster Pack: Padme graphic 12.00
__ Captain Rex / Republic #07 (VR) 27.00
__ Chameleon Droid / Separatists #24 (R) 6.50
__ Clone Trooper on Gelagrub / Republic #08 (R) 3.50
__ Commander Gree / Republic #09 (R) 2.50
__ Count Dooku of Serenno / Separatists (R) 5.00
__ Darth Sidious Hologram / Sith #01 (VR) 18.00
__ Durge, Jedi Hunter / Separatists #25 (VR) 20.00
__ Elite Clone Trooper Commander / Republic #10 (U) 1.00
__ Elite Clone Trooper Grenadier / Republic #11 (C) 0.35
__ Galactic Marine / Republic #12 (U) 4.00
__ General Aayla Secura / Republic #13 (R) 5.00
__ General Grievous, Droid Army Commander / Separatists #26 (VR) 30.00
__ General Obi-Wan Kenobi / Republic (R) 5.00
__ Gha Nachkt / Fringe #35 (R) 1.25
__ Heavy Clone Trooper / Republic #14 (C) 0.50
__ Heavy Super Battle Droid / Separatists #27 (C) 0.50
__ Human Soldier of Fortune / Fringe #36 (C) 0.25
__ IG-100 MagnaGuard / Separatists #28 (U) 1.00
__ IG-86 Assassin Droid / Fringe #37 (U) 2.00
__ Luminara Unduli, Jedi Master / Republic (R) 5.00
__ Mon Calamari Knight / Republic #15 (U) 0.25
__ Neimoidian Warrior / Separatists #29 (C) 0.25
__ Nelvaanian Warrior / Fringe #38 (U) 0.75
__ Odd Ball / Republic #16 (R) 2.00
__ Padmé Amidala, Senator / Republic #17 (VR) 11.00
__ Quarren Isolationist / Separatists #30 (U) 0.25
__ Rocket Battle Droid / Separatists #31 (U) 1.50
__ Star Corps Trooper / Republic #18 (U) 4.50
__ Starter set 20.00
__ Super Battle Droid / Separatists #32 (C) 0.50
__ Techno Union Warrior / Separatists #33 (C) 1.25
__ Trandoshan Scavenger / Fringe #39 (U) 0.35
__ Utapaun Warrior / Fringe #40 (C) 0.25
__ Wookiee Scoundrel / Republic #19 (C) 0.25
__ Yoda on Kybuck / Republic #20 (VR) 15.00

Miniatures Game. Force Unleashed.

__ 2-1B / Rebels #24 (R) 4.50
__ Admiral Ozzel / Imperial #29 (R) 4.00
__ Amanin Scout / Fringe #46 (U) 0.25
__ AT-AT Driver / Imperial #30 (U) 0.75
__ Boba Fett, Mercenary / Fringe #47 (VR) 30.00
__ Caamasi Noble / Fringe #48 (C) 0.25
__ Chewbacca of Hoth / Rebels #04 (VR) 5.00
__ Cloud Car Pilot / Fringe #49 (C) 0.25
__ Dark Trooper / Imperial #31 (U) 2.50
__ Darth Revan / Sith #01 (VR) 50.00
__ Darth Vader, Unleashed / Imperial #32 (VR) ...15.00
__ Elite Hoth Trooper / Rebels #05 (C) 0.50
__ Emperor's Shadow Guard / Imperial #33 (U) 2.50
__ Evo Trooper / Imperial #34 (U) 2.00
__ Felucian Stormtrooper Officer / Imperial #35 (U) 1.25
__ Felucian Warrior on Rancor / Fringe #50 (VR) 35.00
__ Garm Bel Iblis #45 (R) 6.00
__ Golan Arms DF.9 Anti-Infantry Battery / Rebels #06 (U) 5.00
__ Gotal Imperial Assassin / Imperial #36 (C) 0.25
__ Han Solo in Carbonite / Rebels #07 (VR) 8.00
__ Han Solo of Hoth / Rebels #08 (VR) 8.00
__ Hoth Trooper Officer / Rebels #09 (U) 0.50
__ Hoth Trooper with Repeating Blaster Cannon / Rebels #10 (U) 3.00
__ Imperial Navy Trooper / Imperial #37 (C) 0.75
__ Junk Golem / Fringe #51 (U) 2.00
__ Juno Eclipse / Rebels #11 (R) 5.50
__ K-3PO / Rebels #12 (R) 6.50
__ Kazdan Paratus / Republic #02 (R) 9.00
__ Knobby White Spider / Fringe #52 (U) 1.50
__ Luke Skywalker and Yoda / Rebels #14 (VR) .20.00
__ Luke Skywalker, Hoth Pilot Unleashed / Rebels #13 (R) 11.00
__ Luke's Snowspeeder / Rebels #15 (VR) 10.00
__ Maris Brood / Fringe #53 (VR) 20.00
__ Master Kota / Rebels #16 (R) 12.00
__ Mon Calamari Medic / Rebels #17 (C) 0.25
__ Muun Tactics Broker / Fringe #54 (C) 0.25
__ Mynock / Fringe #55 (U) 1.00
__ Obi-Wan Kenobi, Unleashed / Rebels #18 (R)..8.00
__ Princess Leia of Cloud City / Rebels #19 (R) 2.50
__ PROXY / Fringe #56 (R) 6.00
__ Raxus Prime Trooper / Imperial #38 (C) 1.00
__ Rebel Marksman / Rebels #20 (U) 2.00
__ Rebel Troop Cart / Rebels #21 (U) 3.50
__ Rebel Trooper on Tauntaun / Rebels #22 (R) .10.00
__ Rebel Vanguard / Rebels #23 (U) 2.50
__ Shaak Ti, Jedi Master / Republic #03 (VR) 22.00
__ Snowtrooper / Imperial #39 (C) 0.75
__ Star Destroyer Officer / Imperial #40 (U) 0.50
__ Stormtrooper / Imperial #41 (U) 1.50
__ Telosian Tank Droid / Fringe #57 (U) 2.50
__ TIE Crawler / Imperial #42 (U) 1.50
__ Uggernaut / Fringe #58 (R) 5.00
__ Ugnaught Boss / Fringe #59 (U) 0.50
__ Ugnaught Tech / Fringe #60 (C) 0.25
__ Vader's Apprentice, Redeemed / Rebels #25 (R) 22.00
__ Vader's Apprentice, Unleashed / Imperial #43 (VR) 30.00
__ Verpine Tech / Rebels #26 (C) 0.25
__ Wedge Antilles, Red Two / Rebels #27 (R) 1.25
__ Wookiee Hunter AT-ST / Imperial #44 (R) 9.00
__ Wookiee Warrior / Rebels #28 (C) 0.50

Miniatures Game. Imperial Entanglements.

__ 181st Imperial Pilot / Imperial #16 (U) 2.00
__ Arica / Imperial #11 (R) 5.00
__ Bacta Tank / Fringe #26 (U) 2.50
__ Bespin Guard / Fringe #27 (C) 0.25
__ Bothan Commando / Rebels #01 (C) 0.25
__ C-3PO, Ewok Diety / Rebels #02 (VR) 13.00
__ Chiss Mercenary / Fringe #28 (C) 0.25
__ Darth Vader, Legacy of the Force / Imperial #12 (VR) 24.00
__ Dash Rendar, Renegade Smuggler / Fringe #29 (VR) 17.50
__ Duros Scout / Fringe #30 (C) 0.25

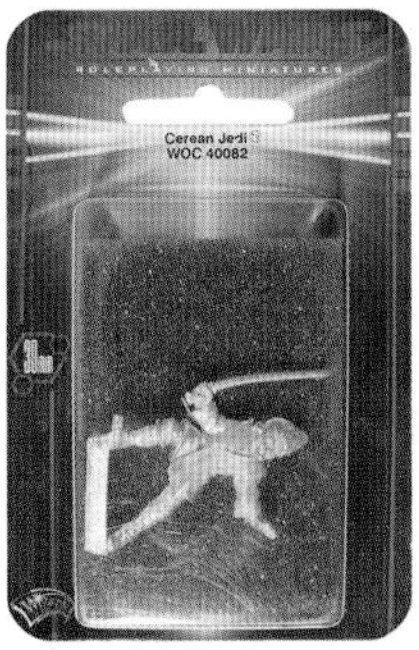

RPM035

RPM036

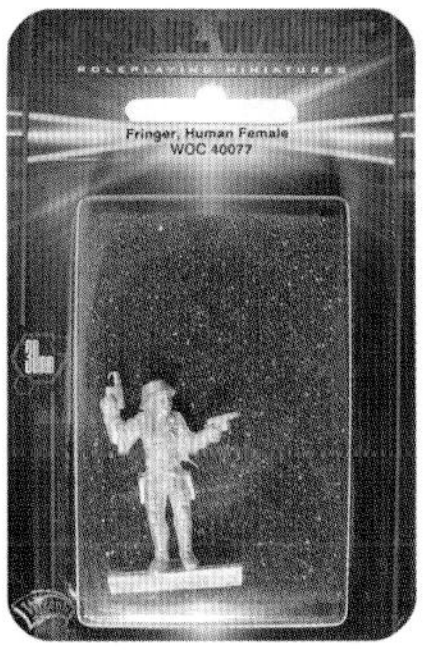

RPM037

RPM038

RPM039

RPM040

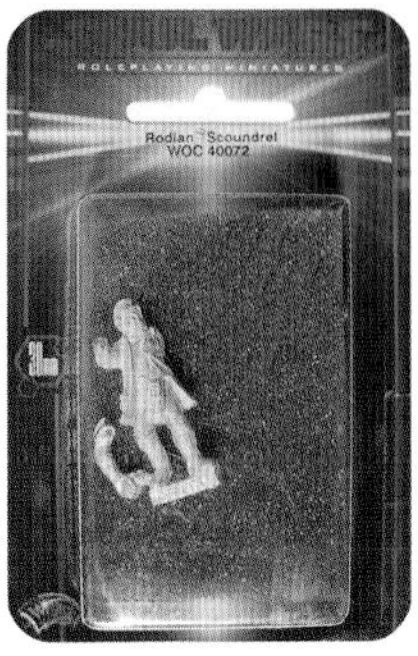

RPM041

RPM042

Role Playing Miniatures

__ Emperor Palpatine on Throne / Imperial #13 (VR) 26.00
__ Ewok Scout / Fringe #31 (C) 0.35
__ General Crix Madine / Rebels #03 (R) 4.50
__ General Rieekan / Rebels #04 (VR).................22.00
__ Imperial Dignitary / Imperial #14 (U) 1.00
__ Jawa Scavenger / Fringe #32 (C).................0.50
__ Kyp Durron / New Republic #25 (R).................5.00
__ Leia, Bounty Hunter / Rebels #05 (VR) 15.00
__ Lobot, Computer Liaison Officer / Fringe #33 (R).................3.50
__ Logray, Ewok Shaman / Fringe #34 (R) 3.50
__ Luke Skywalker, Rebel Commando / Rebels #06 (VR).................20.00
__ Mercenary Commander / Fringe #35 (U) 0.50
__ Moff Jerjerrod / Imperial #15 (R).................3.00
__ Mouse Droid / Fringe #36 (U).................3.50
__ R2-D2 with Extended Sensor / Rebels #09 (R).4.50
__ Rebel Commando Pathfinder / Rebels #07 (U) .0.75
__ Rebel Trooper / Rebels #08 (C) 0.25
__ Sandtrooper / Imperial #17 (C) 1.00
__ Sandtrooper Officer / Imperial #18 (U).............1.00
__ Scout Trooper / Imperial #19 (C) 0.50
__ Shock Trooper / Imperial #20 (U).................2.00
__ Snowtrooper / Imperial #21 (C).................0.50
__ Snowtrooper Commander / Imperial #22 (U)....1.00
__ Stormtrooper / Imperial #23 (U).................0.75
__ Thrawn (Mitth'raw'nuruodo) / Imperial #24 (R) .6.50
__ Twi'lek Black Sun Vigo / Fringe #37 (U)...........1.00
__ Ugnaught Droid Destroyer / Fringe #38 (U) 1.00
__ Veteran Rebel Commando / Rebels #10 (C).....0.50
__ Whiphid Tracker / Fringe #39 (U).................0.75
__ Xizor / Fringe #40 (VR).................20.00

Miniatures Game. Jedi Academy.
__ Anakin Solo #24 (R).................3.50
__ Antarian Ranger #12 (C).................0.75
__ Cade Skywalker, Padawan #25 (R).................2.50
__ Crimson Nova Bounty Hunter #31 (U) 1.00
__ Darth Maul Sith Apprentice #05 (VR).............26.00
__ Darth Plagueis #06 (VR).................30.00
__ Darth Sidious, Sith Master #07 (R) 13.00
__ Death Watch Raider #37 (C) 0.35
__ Disciple Of Ragnos #20 (C).................0.50
__ Exceptional Jedi Apprentice #26 (U) 1.00
__ Felucian #32 (U).................3.50
__ Grand Master Luke Skywalker #27 (R) 17.50
__ Grand Master Yoda #14 (R).................4.00
__ Heavy Clone Trooper #15 (C).................0.50
__ HK-50 Assassin Droid #33 (U).................1.25
__ Imperial Sentinel #21 (U).................1.00

RPM043

__ Jedi Battle Master #01 (U) 1.25
__ Jedi Crusader #02 (U).................1.00
__ Jensaarai Defender #34 (U) 1.00
__ Kol Skywalker #28 (VR).................25.00
__ Krath War Droid #08 (C).................0.50
__ Kyle Katarn, Combat Instructor #29 (R).................2.50
__ Leia Skywalker, Jedi Knight #30 (R) 3.50
__ Master K'Kruhk #16 (VR).................17.50
__ Naga Sadow #09 (VR).................30.00
__ Peace Brigade Thug #35 (C).................0.50
__ Praetorite Vong Priest #38 (U).................1.00
__ Praetorite Vong Warrior #39 (C).................0.50
__ Qui-Gon Jinn, Jedi Trainer #17 (R) 2.00
__ R4 Astromech Droid #36 (C).................0.35
__ Reborn #22 (C).................0.50
__ Rocket Battle Droid #19 (C).................0.50
__ Sith Apprentice #10 (U).................1.00
__ Sith Lord #11 (U).................1.00
__ Stormtrooper #23 (C).................0.75
__ The Dark Woman #13 (VR).................25.00
__ The Jedi Exile #03 (VR).................3.00
__ Vodo-Siosk Baas #04 (VR).................30.00
__ Youngling #18 (C).................0.50
__ Yuuzhan Ossus Guardian #40 (U).................1.00

Miniatures Game. Knights of the Old Republic.
__ ASN Assassin Droid #36 (U).................1.00
__ Atton Rand #01 (VR) 12.00
__ Bao-Dur #02 (R).................2.50
__ Boma #37 (U).................1.25
__ Captain Panaka #22 (R) 2.50
__ Captain Tarpals #23 (R) 4.00
__ Carth Onasi #03 (VR) 20.00
__ Czerka Scientist #38 (C) 0.25
__ Darth Malak, Dark Lord of the Sith #13 (VR)..29.00
__ Darth Sion #14 (VR) 35.00
__ Darth Vader, Scourge of the Jedi #33 (R) 6.00
__ Echani Handmaiden #39 (C) 0.50
__ Elite Sith Trooper #15 (U).................2.00
__ General Wedge Antilles #35 (R) 4.50
__ GenoHaradan Assassin #40 (C).................0.25
__ Gungan Artillerist #24 (C).................0.25
__ Gungan Shieldbearer #25 (U) 3.50
__ Gungan Soldier #26 (C) 0.50
__ Han Solo, Smuggler #30 (R) 3.50
__ Jar Jar Binks #27 (VR) 17.50
__ Jaraal #41 (R).................9.00
__ Jawa Scout #42 (U) 0.35
__ Jolee Bindo #43 (VR) 12.00
__ Juggernaut War Droid #04 (C).................0.50
__ Juhani #44 (VR).................22.00
__ Kreia #45 (VR) 28.00
__ Leia Organa, Senator #31 (VR) 13.00
__ Luke Skywalker, Jedi #32 (R).................5.00
__ Mandalore the Ultimate #55 (VR).................40.00
__ Mandalorian Captain #56 (U).................1.25
__ Mandalorian Commando #57 (U).................0.75
__ Mandalorian Marauder #58 (C).................0.50
__ Mandalorian Quartermaster #59 (U) 0.75
__ Mandalorian Scout #60 (C).................0.75
__ Massiff #46 (U).................1.00
__ Master Lucien Draay #05 (VR).................22.00
__ Mira #06 (VR).................20.00
__ Mission Vao #47 (R).................3.00
__ Obi-Wan Kenobi, Padawan #28 (VR).............18.00
__ Old Republic Captain #07 (U).................0.35
__ Old Republic Guard #08 (C).................0.50
__ RA-7 Death Star Protocol Droid #34 (U)..........1.00

__ Rakghoul #48 (U).................3.00
__ Shyrack #49 (U).................1.25
__ Sith Assassin #16 (U).................0.50
__ Sith Guard #17 (C).................0.50
__ Sith Heavy Assault Droid #18 (U).................1.50
__ Sith Marauder #19 (U).................2.00
__ Sith Scoundrel Operative #20 (C).................0.35
__ Sith Trooper Captain #21 (U).................0.75
__ Squint #09 (VR).................13.00
__ Supreme Chancellor Palpatine #29 (R).................3.00
__ T1 Series Bulk Loader Droid #50 (U).................1.25
__ T3-M4 #51 (R).................5.50
__ Tusken Raider Scout #52 (C).................0.35
__ Visas Marr #10 (R).................4.00
__ Wookiee Elite Warrior #11 (C).................0.50
__ Wookiee Trooper #12 (C).................0.35
__ Zaalbar #53 (R) 2.50
__ Zayne Carrick #54 (R).................4.50

Miniatures Game. Legacy of the Force.
__ Antares Draco / Imperial #18 (R).................3.00
__ Boba Fett, Mercenary Commander #53 (VR) ...5.00
__ Bothan Noble / Rebel #11 (U).................1.00
__ Cade Skywalker, Bounty Hunter / Fringe #40 (VR).................5.00
__ Canderous Ordo / Mandalorian #54 (R).................3.00
__ Corellian Security Officer / New Republic #30 (U) 1.00
__ Darth Cadeus / Sith #04 (R).................5.00
__ Darth Krayt / Sith #05 (VR).................5.00
__ Darth Nihl / Sith #06 (VR).................5.00
__ Darth Talon / Sith #07 (VR).................5.00
__ Darth Tyranus, Legacy of the Dark Side / Separatist #10 (R).................3.00
__ Deena Shan / Rebel #12 (R).................3.00
__ Deliah Blue / Fringe #41 (R).................3.00
__ Dug Fringer / Fringe #42 (U).................1.00
__ Duros Scoundrel / Fringe #43 (C).................0.50
__ Elite Rebel Commando / Rebel #13 (U).............1.00
__ Emperor Roan Fel / Imperial #19 (VR).................5.00
__ Galactic Alliance Scout / New Republic #31 (C).................0.50
__ Galactic Alliance Trooper / New Republic #32 (C).................0.50
__ General Dodonna / Rebel #14 (R).................3.00
__ Gotal Mercenary / Fringe #44 (C).................0.50
__ Guard Droid / Fringe #45 (C).................0.50
__ Han Solo, Galactic Hero / New Republic #33 (R).................3.00
__ Human Bodyguard / Fringe #46 (C).................0.50
__ Human Scoundrel / Fringe #47 (C).................0.50
__ Human Scout / Fringe #48 (C).................0.50
__ Imperial Knight / Imperial #20 (U).................1.00
__ Imperial Knight / Imperial #21 (U).................1.00
__ Imperial Pilot / Imperial #22 (C).................0.50
__ Imperial Security Officer / Imperial #23 (U).......1.00
__ Jagged Fel / Imperial #24 (R).................3.00
__ Jariah Syn / Fringe #49 (C).................3.00
__ Kel Dor Bounty Hunter / Fringe #50 (C).............0.50
__ Kyle Katarn, Jedi Battlemaster / New Republic #34 (VR).................5.00
__ Leia Organa Solo, Jedi Knight / New Republic #35 (VR).................5.00
__ Luke Skywalker, Force Spirit / New Republic #36 (VR).................5.00
__ Luke Skywalker, Legacy of the Light Side / Rebel #15 (R).................3.00
__ Lumiya, the Dark Lady / Sith #08 (R).................3.00
__ Mandalorian Gunslinger / Mandalorian #55 (U) .1.00

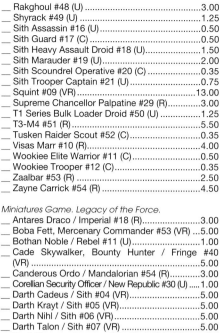

RPM044   RPM045   RPM046   RPM047   RPM048   RPM049   RPM050   RPM051

__ Mandalorian Trooper / Mandalorian #56 (U).....1.00
__ Mara Jade Skywalker / New Republic #37 (VR) 5.00
__ Marasiah Fel / Imperial #25 (R) 3.00
__ Moff Morlish Veed / Imperial #26 (VR) 5.00
__ Moff Nyna Calixte / Imperial #27 (R)....3.00
__ Noghri Commando Imperial / Imperial #28 (U).1.00
__ Nomi Sunrider / Old Republic #01 (VR) 5.00
__ Old Republic Recruit / Old Republic #02 (C)....0.50
__ Old Republic Scout / Old Republic #03 (C)......0.50
__ Rebel Honor Guard / Rebel #16 (C)....0.50
__ Republic Commando Training Sergeant / Republic #09 (U) 1.00
__ Rodian Blaster-for-Hire / Fringe #51 (U)....1.00
__ Shado Vao / New Republic #38 (R) 3.00
__ Shadow Stormtrooper / Imperial #29 (U)....1.00
__ Trandoshan Mercenary / Fringe #52 (C)....0.50
__ Twi'lek Scout / Rebel #17 (C) 0.50
__ Wolf Sazen / New Republic #39 (VR)....5.00
__ Yuuzhan Vong Elite Warrior / Yuuzhan Vong #57 (U)....1.00
__ Yuuzhan Vong Jedi Hunter / Yuuzhan Vong #58 (U) 1.00
__ Yuuzhan Vong Shaper / Yuuzhan Vong #59 (U) ...1.00
__ Yuuzhan Vong Warrior / Yuuzhan Vong #60 (C) ...0.50

Miniatures Game. Rebel Storm Game.
__ Booster Pack: Boba Fett graphic 12.00
__ Booster Pack: Han Solo graphic 12.00
__ Booster Pack: Stormtrooper graphic....12.00
__ Starter Set....20.00

Miniatures Game. Rebel Storm miniatures promotional pieces.
__ Elite Stormtrooper (P), Comic-Con 2004........15.00
__ MonCalimari Officer (P), Origins exclusive 15.00

Miniatures Game. Rebel Storm miniatures.
__ 4-LOM (R) 8.00
__ Bespin Guard (C) 0.50
__ Boba Fett (VR)....35.00
__ Bossk (R)....5.00
__ Bothan Spy (U)....1.00
__ C-3P0 (R) 6.00
__ Chewbacca (R) 6.00
__ Commando on Speeder Bike (VR)....18.00
__ Darth Vader, Dark Jedi (R) 8.00
__ Darth Vader, Sith Lord (VR)....13.00
__ Dengar (R)....6.00
__ Duros Mercenary (U)....1.00
__ Elite Hoth Trooper (U) 1.00
__ Elite Rebel Trooper (C)....0.50
__ Elite Snowtrooper (U)....1.00
__ Elite Stormtrooper (U) 1.00
__ Emperor Palpatine (VR)....20.00
__ Ewok (C)....0.50
__ Gamorrean Guard (U) 1.00
__ General Veers (R)....5.00
__ Grand Moff Tarkin (R) 5.00
__ Greedo (R)....5.00
__ Han Solo (R)....11.00
__ Heavy Stormtrooper (U)....1.00
__ Hoth Trooper (C) 0.50
__ IG-88 (R)....7.00
__ Imperial Officer (U)....1.00
__ Ithorian Scout (U)....1.00
__ Jabba the Hutt (VR) 18.00
__ Jawa (C) 0.50
__ Lando Calrissian (R)....8.00
__ Luke Skywalker, Jedi Knight (VR)....16.00
__ Luke Skywalker, Rebel (R) 18.00
__ Mara Jade, Emperor's Hand (R) 12.00
__ Mon Calamari Mercenary (C)....0.50
__ Obi-Wan Kenobi (VR)....19.00
__ Princess Leia, Captive (VR)....12.00
__ Princess Leia, Senator (R)....7.00
__ Probe Droid (VR) 18.00
__ Quarren Assassin (U) 1.00
__ R2-D2 (R) 12.00
__ Rebel Commando (U) 1.00
__ Rebel Officer (U) 1.00
__ Rebel Pilot (C) 0.50
__ Rebel Trooper (C)....0.50
__ Rebel Trooper (C)....0.50
__ Royal Guard (U) 1.00
__ Sandtrooper on Dewback (VR) 20.00
__ Scout Trooper (U) 1.00
__ Scout Trooper on Speeder Bike (VR)....20.00
__ Snowtrooper (C)....0.50
__ Stormtrooper (C)....0.50
__ Stormtrooper (C)....0.50
__ Stormtrooper (C)....0.50
__ Stormtrooper Officer (U) 1.00
__ Tusken Raider (C) 0.50
__ Tusken Raider (P)....5.00
__ Twi'lek Bodyguard (U) 1.00
__ Twi'lek Scoundrel (C)....0.50
__ Wampa (VR)....20.00
__ Wookiee Soldier (C) 0.50
__ Wookiee Soldier (P) 5.00

Miniatures Game. Revenge of the Sith Game.
__ Booster Pack: Anakin Skywalker [RPM047]...10.00
__ Booster Pack: Darth Sidious [RPM048]....10.00
__ Booster Pack: Yoda [RPM049]....10.00
__ Starter Set [RPM050]....20.00

Miniatures Game. Revenge of the Sith miniatures.
__ Agen Kolar, Jedi Master #1 (R)....8.00
__ Alderaan Trooper #2 (U)....1.00
__ Anakin Skywalker, Jedi Knight #3 (R) 12.00
__ Anakin Skywalker, Sith Apprentice #56 (VR) ..25.00
__ AT-RT #4 (VR)....22.00
__ Bail Organa #5 (VR)....9.00
__ Battle Droid #25 (C) 0.50
__ Battle Droid #26 (C) 0.50
__ Boba Fett, Young Mercenary #42 (R) 8.00
__ Bodyguard Droid #27 (U)....1.00
__ Bodyguard Droid #28 (U)....1.00
__ Captain Antilles #6 (R) 5.00
__ Chagrian Mercenary Commander #43 (U)........1.00
__ Chewbacca of Kashyyyk #7 (VR)....12.00
__ Clone Trooper #8 (C) 0.50
__ Clone Trooper #9 (C) 0.50
__ Clone Trooper Commander #10 (U) 1.00
__ Clone Trooper Gunner #11 (C)....0.50
__ Dark Side Adept #57 (U) 1.00
__ Darth Tyranus #29 (R) 12.00
__ Darth Vader #58 (VR) 20.00
__ Destroyer Droid #30 (R) 14.00
__ Devaronian Soldier #44 (C)....0.50
__ Emperor Palpatine, Sith Lord #59 (VR)....28.00
__ General Grievous, Jedi Hunter #31 (VR)....28.00
__ General Grievous, Supreme Commander (R)...6.00
__ Gotal Fringer #45 (U)....1.00
__ Grievous's Wheel Bike #33 (VR) 17.00
__ Human Mercenary #46 (U)....1.00
__ Iktotchi Tech Specialist #47 (U) 1.00
__ Jedi Knight #12 (U) 1.00
__ Mace Windu, Jedi Master #13 (VR) 22.00
__ Medical Droid #48 (R) 7.00
__ Mon Mothma #14 (VR)....9.00
__ Muun Guard #34 (U) 1.00
__ Nautolan Soldier #49 (C)....0.50
__ Neimoidian Solder #36 (U)....1.00
__ Neimoidian Soldier #35 (U) 1.00
__ Obi-Wan Kenobi #15 (R)....10.00
__ Polis Massa Medic #16 (C) 0.50
__ R2-D2, Astromech Droid #17 (VR)....18.00
__ Royal Guard #60 (U) 1.00
__ San Hill #37 (R) 4.00
__ Senate Guard #18 (U) 1.00
__ Separatist Commando #38 (C) 0.50
__ Shaak Ti #19 (R)....12.00
__ Sly Moore #50 (R) 5.00
__ Stass Allie #20 (R)....8.00
__ Super Battle Droid #39 (C)....0.50
__ Super Battle Droid #40 (C)....0.50
__ Tarfful #21 (R) 5.00
__ Tion Medon #51 (R) 7.00
__ Utapaun Soldier #52 (C) 0.50
__ Utapaun Soldier #53 (C) 0.50
__ Wat Tambor #41 (R)....5.00
__ Wookiee Berserker #22 (C)....0.50
__ Wookiee Scout #23 (U)....1.00
__ Yoda, Jedl Master #24 (R) 20.00
__ Yuzzem #54 (C)....0.50
__ Zabrak Fringer #55 (C) 0.50

Miniatures Game. Star Wars: Universe.
__ 57/60 Nom Anor #57 (R) 9.00
__ Abyssin Black Sun Thug #12 (C) 0.50
__ Acklay #13 (Huge U) 12.00
__ Admiral Ackbar #43 (VR)....12.00
__ ASP-7 #14 (U)....4.00
__ AT-ST #33 (HUGE R) 14.00
__ B'omarr Monk #15 (R)....7.00
__ Baron Fel #34 (VR)....10.00
__ Battle Droid #6 (U) 1.00
__ Bith Rebel #44 (C)....0.50
__ Chewbacca, Rebel Hero #45 (R) 10.00
__ Clone Trooper #1 (C) 0.50
__ Clone Trooper on BARC Speeder #2 (HUGE R)....14.00
__ Dark Side Marauder #35 (U) 6.00
__ Dark Trooper Phase III #36 (U) 4.00
__ Darth Maul on Sith Speeder #7 (VR)....19.00
__ Darth Vader, Jedi Hunter #37 (R)....20.00
__ Dash Rendar #16 (R)....8.00
__ Dr. Evazan #17 (VR) 8.00
__ Dresselian Commando #46 (C)....0.50
__ Elite Clone Trooper #3 (U)....1.00
__ Flash Speeder #4 (U) 8.00
__ Gonk Power Droid #18 (C)....2.00
__ Grand Admiral Thrawn #38 (VR) 24.00
__ Guri #19 (R)....1.00
__ Hailfire Droid #8 (HUGE U) 12.00
__ Han Solo, Rebel Hero #47 (R)....11.00
__ Kaminoan Ascetic #20 (C) 0.50
__ Kyle Katarn #52 (VR)....12.00
__ Lando Calrissian, Hero of Tanaab #21 (R)........6.00
__ Lobot #22 (R) 7.00
__ Luke Skywalker on Tauntaun #48 (R) 12.00
__ Luke Skywalker, Jedi Master #53 (VR) 25.00
__ New Republic Commander #54 (C)....0.50
__ New Republic Trooper #55 (C) 0.50
__ Nexu #23 (U) 4.00
__ Nien Nunb #49 (R)....6.00
__ Nightsister Sith Witch #39 (U)....5.00
__ Noghri #40 (U)....6.00
__ Nute Gunray #9 (R) 6.00
__ Obi-Wan Kenobi on Boga #5 (HUGE VR).......23.00
__ Ponda Baba #24 (R)....6.00
__ Prince Xizor #25 (VR) 16.00
__ Princess Leia, Rebel Hero #50 (R) 12.00
__ Rancor #26 (HUGE VR)....31.00
__ Reek #27 (HUGE U) 12.00
__ Rodian Black Sun Vigo #28 (U)....2.00
__ Shistavanen Pilot #29 (U)....1.00
__ Stormtrooper #41 (C)....0.50
__ Stormtrooper Commander #42 (U)....1.00
__ Super Battle Droid #10 (C)....0.50
__ Super Battle Droid Commander #11 (U)....4.00
__ Tusken Raider on Bantha #30 (HUGE U)....9.00
__ Vornskr #31 (C) 0.50
__ Warmaster Tsavong Lah #58 (VR) 14.00
__ Wedge Antilles #51 (R)....8.00
__ X-1 Viper Droid #32 (HUGE U)....8.00
__ Young Jedi Knight #56 (C)....0.50
__ Yuuzhan Vong Subaltern #59 (U)....2.00
__ Yuuzhan Vong Warrior #60 (C) 0.50

Miniatures Game. The Force Unleashed.
__ Booster Pack: 6 random figures [RPM051]....22.00

Starship Battles game.
__ Huge booster....15.00
__ Starter Set....40.00

Role Playing Miniatures: Starship Battles

Wizards of the Coast
__ Booster Pack 7 randomized, prepainted, fully assembled, durable plastic starships 22.00
__ Starter Set....40.00

Dark Side
__ Asajj Ventress's Starfighter....20.00
__ Banking Clan Frigate 15.00
__ Cloak Shape Fighter 4.00
__ Commerce Guild Destroyer 5.00
__ Darth Vader's TIE Advanced x1....20.00

Role Playing Miniatures: Starship Battles

__ Droid Trifighter 6.00
__ General Grievous's Starfighter........................20.00
__ Geonosian Starfighter...................................2.00
__ Geonosian Starfighter Ace.............................2.00
__ Imperial Interdictor Cruiser 15.00
__ Imperial Shuttle..3.00
__ Imperial Star Destroyer 5.00
__ Invisible Hand 15.00
__ Palpatine's Shuttle.......................................20.00
__ Scarab Droid Starfighter.................................2.00
__ Sith Infiltrator 3.00
__ Slave 1 (Boba Fett) 20.00
__ Slave 1 (Jango Fett) 20.00
__ Super Star Destroyer Executor........................20.00
__ Techno Union Starfighter.................................2.00
__ TIE Bomber...2.00
__ TIE Fighter..2.00
__ TIE Fighter Ace 3.00
__ TIE Interceptor...3.00
__ TIE Interceptor Ace 3.00
__ Trade Federation Battleship 10.00
__ Trade Federation Droid Control Ship...............15.00
__ Virago..15.00
__ Vulture Droid Starfighter 2.00
__ Vulture Droid Starfighter Advanced..................2.00

Light Side
__ A-wing Starfighter...2.00
__ A-wing Starfighter Ace...................................4.00
__ Anakin Skywalker's Jedi Interceptor 15.00
__ ARC-170 Starfighter 15.00
__ B-wing Starfighter Ace..................................4.00

__ Jedi Starfighter 2.00
__ Luke Skywalker's X-wing..............................15.00
__ Millenium Falcon 15.00
__ Mon Calamari Cruiser Home One...................15.00
__ Mon Calamari MC80......................................5.00
__ Mon Calamari Star Defender Viscount 15.00
__ Naboo Starfighter...2.00
__ Obi-Wan's Jedi Interceptor 15.00
__ Outrider...5.00
__ Rebel Assault Frigate....................................5.00
__ Rebel Cruiser 5.00
__ Rebel Transport 5.00
__ Republic Assault Ship....................................15.00
__ Republic Cruiser 5.00
__ Rogue Squadron X-wing................................20.00
__ SoroSuub Patrol Fighter 2.00
__ Tantive IV 15.00
__ Utapaun P-38 Starfighter................................5.00
__ V-wing Starfighter 2.00
__ Venator-class Star Destroyer...........................5.00
__ Wild Karrde 13.00
__ X-wing Starfighter 2.00
__ X-wing Starfighter Ace...................................3.00
__ Y-wing Starfighter 2.00
__ Y-wing Starfighter Ace...................................3.00

Role Playing Toys

Hasbro
__ Jedi Braid with holographic Royal Starship and holoprojector [PLS001]..................................16.00

__ Jedi Gear [PLS002].......................................35.00

Kenner
__ Boba Fett's Armor [PLS003]..........................50.00
__ Luke Skywalker's Utility Belt [PLS004]..........90.00

Kenner, Canada
Utility belts.
__ Darth Vader [PLS005]........................... 2,350.00
__ Luke Skywalker [PLS006]...................... 2,350.00
__ Princess Leia [PLS007]......................... 2,500.00

Rubies
__ Count Dooku accessory kit 15.00
__ Jedi Knight accessory kit...............................15.00

Room Alerts

Kenner
__ Boba Fett [YI001]...36.00
__ Stormtrooper [YI002] 32.00

Tiger Electronics
__ Destroyer Droid [YI003] 39.00
__ Jango Fett [YI004]...39.00

Sit-and-Spins

Kenner
__ Wicket the Ewok Sit'n Spin [YK001].............275.00

PLS001

PLS002

PLS003

PLS004

PLS005

PLS006

PLS007

YI001

YI002

YI003

YI004

YK001

__ X-Wing, inflatable [SNT001]...........................35.00

Foam snow saucers.
__ Capt. Rex, foam [SNT002]...........................25.00
__ Millennium Falcon, foam [SNT003]................40.00
__ Yoda, foam [SNT004] 40.00

Intex Recreation Corp.
__ Darth Maul Sno-Tube 39" [SNT005]...............16.00

Space Shooters

Hasbro
__ Naboo Fighter target game [TG001]...............20.00

Milton Bradley
__ Battle Belt with 32 foam disks [TG002] 11.00
__ Imperial target game [TG003] 34.00
__ Jango Fett's target game [TG004].................12.00
__ Millennium Falcon target game [TG005].........34.00

Squeaky Toys

Brazil. Unlicensed. Bagged with hang-card.
__ Darth Maul [SQU001]....................................25.00
__ Obi-Wan Kenobi [SQU002]...........................25.00
__ Queen Amidala [SQU003]..............................25.00
__ Qui-Gon Jinn [SQU004] 25.00

String / Streamer Canisters

Hasbro
Energy beam string refill canisters.
__ Clone Trooper [SCS001]..................................3.00
__ General Grievous [SCS002]...........................3.00
__ Super Battle Droid [SCS003] 3.00
__ Yoda [SCS004] 3.00

Suction Cup Toys
__ Ben Kenobi [SCU001].....................................6.00
__ Chewbacca [SCU002] 6.00
__ Darth Vader [SCU003] 6.00

SNT001

SNT002

SNT003

SNT004

SNT005

TG001

TG002

TG003

TG004

TG005

SQU001

SQU002

SQU003

SQU004

399

Suction Cup Toys

SCS001

SCS002

SCS003

SCS004

SCU001

SCU002

SCU003

SCU004

SCU005

__ Luke Skywalker as X-Wing Pilot [SCU004]...6.00
__ R5-D4 [SCU005] 6.00

Transfers

American Publishing
Presto Magix bagged sets, ESB.
__ Asteroids [CRT001]...7.00
__ Beneath Cloud City [CRT002]...........................7.00
__ Cloud City Battle [CRT003]...............................7.00
__ Dagobah Bog Planet [CRT004].........................7.00

__ Deck of the Star Destroyer [CRT005] 7.00
__ Rebel Base [CRT006]..7.00

Presto Magix bagged sets, ROTJ.
__ Death Star [CRT007]..7.00
__ Ewok Village [CRT008].....................................7.00
__ Jabba's Throne Room [CRT009] 7.00
__ Sarlacc Pit [CRT010].......................................7.00

Presto Magix boxed sets, Ewoks.
__ Ewok Hut [CRT011] 9.00
__ Ewok Village...12.00
__ Ewoks at Home [CRT012]..............................12.00

Presto Magix boxed sets, Saga.
__ Battle on Endor [CRT013]..............................15.00
__ Jabba's Throne Room [CRT014] 15.00
__ Star Wars Activity set [CRT015] 20.00

BSB
__ Death Star corridor [CRT016] 18.00

Dairylea
__ Dagobag, Bog Planet [CRT017] 9.00
__ Empire Strikes Back bumper transfer pack....65.00

Letraset
__ 1 Kidnap of Princess Leia [CRT018] 7.00

CRT001

CRT002

CRT003

CRT004

CRT005

CRT006

CRT007

CRT008

CRT009

CRT010
CRT011

CRT012

CRT013

CRT014

CRT015

CRT016

CRT017

CRT018

CRT019

CRT020

CRT021

CRT022

CRT023

CRT024

CRT025

CRT026

CRT027

CRT028

CRT029	CRT030	CRT031	CRT032	CRT033	CRT034	CRT035	CRT036	CRT037

CRT038	CRT039	CRT040	CRT041	CRT042	CRT043	CRT044	CRT045	CRT046	CRT047

__ 2 Sale on Tatooine..................................7.00
__ 3 Action at Mos Eisley [CRT019] 7.00
__ 4 Escape from Stormtroopers 7.00
__ 5 Flight to Alderaan [CRT020]..........................7.00
__ 6 Inside the Death Star [CRT021] 20.00
__ 7 Prison Break [CRT022] 7.00
__ 8 Death Star Escape [CRT023]........................7.00
__ 9 Rebel Base [CRT024].................................7.00
__ 10 Last Battle [CRT025].................................7.00
__ Part 1: Battle at Mos Eisley [CRT026].............16.00
__ Part 2: Escape from Death Star [CRT027]......16.00
__ Part 3: Rebel Air Attack [CRT028] 16.00

Nabisco Shreddies premiums.
__ C-3PO, stormtrooper, TIE, Chewbacca, R2-D2,
 Vader [CRT029]...15.00
__ Han, R2-D2, x-wing, Obo-Wan, stormtrooper,
 C-3PO [CRT030]...15.00
__ Leia, Luke, stormtrooper, TIE, Han, Chewbacca
 [CRT031]..15.00
__ Luke, C-3PO, Obi-Wan, R2-D2, TIE, Vader
 [CRT032]..15.00

Rose Art Industries
Episode III: Revenge of the Sith. Presto Magix.
__ Empire playset 7.00

Presto Magix.
__ Stick 'n Lift [CRT033] 6.00

Thomas Salter
Bagged sets, English packaging.
__ Battle on Endor...............................12.00
__ Ewok Village 10.00
__ Ewoks [CRT034] 8.00
__ Jabba the Hutt [CRT035] 8.00
__ Jabba's Throne Room 10.00

Bagged sets, multi-language packaging.
__ Battle on Endor...............................12.00
__ Ewoks [CRT036] 8.00
__ Jabba the Hutt [CRT037] 8.00
__ Jabba's Throne Room 10.00

Thomas Salter, Italy
__ N. 21 - Il Ritorno Dello JEDI [CRT038]............18.00

Walls
Vintage, mail-away premiums.
__ C-3PO [CRT039] 2.00
__ Chewbacca [CRT040] 2.00
__ Darth Vader [CRT041] 2.00
__ Jawas [CRT042] 2.00
__ Luke Skywalker [CRT043]..................................2.00
__ Obi-Wan Kenobi [CRT044] 2.00
__ Princess Leia [CRT045] 2.00
__ R2-D2 [CRT046] 2.00
__ Sandperson [CRT047] 2.00

__ Stormtrooper [CRT048] 2.00
__ TIE Fighter [CRT049]..2.00
__ X-Wing Fighter [CRT050]..................................2.00

Transformers

Hasbro
2006.
__ Anakin Skywalker/Jedi Starfighter [TST001]...20.00
__ Boba Fett / Slave I [TST002]............................20.00
__ Clone Pilot / ARC-170 Starfighter [TST003] ..20.00
__ Darth Maul / Sith Infiltrator [TST004] 20.00
__ Darth Vader/TIE Advanced Fighter [TST005]..20.00
__ Emperor Palpatine / Imperial Shuttle
 [TST006]..20.00
__ General Grievous / Wheel Bike [TST007]........20.00
__ Jango Fett / Slave I [TST008] 20.00
__ Luke Skywalker / X-Wing Fighter [TST009] 20.00
__ Obi-Wan Kenobi / Jedi Starfighter [TST010] ..20.00

2007. 30th anniversary packaging.
__ Anakin Skywalker/Jedi Starfighter [TST011]...20.00
__ AT-AT Driver / AT-AT [TST012].......................20.00
__ Clone Commander Cody / Turbo Tank
 [TST013]..20.00
__ Clone Pilot / ARC-170 Starfighter [TST014] ...20.00
__ Clone Pilot / ARC-170 Starfighter (Clone Wars
 deco) [TST015]...20.00
__ Clone Pilot / Republic Gunship [TST016] 20.00
__ Darth Vader / Sith Starfighter [TST017] 20.00
__ Emperor Palpatine / Imperial Shuttle
 [TST018]..20.00
__ Jango Fett / Slave I [TST019] 20.00
__ Luke Skywalker / Snowspeeder [TST020]......20.00
__ Luke Skywalker / X-Wing Fighter [TST021] 20.00
__ Mace Windu / Jedi Starfighter [TST022].........20.00
__ Obi-Wan / Jedi Starfighter (with hyperspace ring)
 [TST023]..20.00
__ Saesee Tiin / Jedi Starfighter [TST024] 20.00

2008. Blue and white packaging.
__ Anakin Skywalker/Jedi Starfighter [TST025]...20.00
__ Battle Droid / AAT [TST026]............................20.00
__ Boba Fett / Slave I [TST027]............................20.00
__ Captain Rex / AT-TE [TST028].........................20.00
__ Clone Commander Cody / Turbo Tank
 [TST029]..20.00
__ Clone Pilot / ARC-170 [TST030] 20.00
__ Clone Pilot / Republic Gunship [TST031] 20.00
__ Clone Pilot / V-19 Torrent Starfighter
 [TST032]..20.00
__ Darth Vader / TIE Advanced X1 Starfighter
 [TST033]..20.00
__ General Grievous / General Grievous' Starfighter
 [TST034]..20.00
__ Kit Fisto to Jedi Starfighter [TST035]..............20.00
__ Luke Skywalker / Snowspeeder [TST036]......20.00

CRT048	CRT049	CRT050

__ Luke Skywalker / X-Wing Fighter 20.00
__ Obi-Wan Kenobi / Jedi Starfighter [TST037] ..20.00
__ Plo Koon / Jedi Starfighter [TST038] 20.00
__ Shock Trooper/V-Wing Starfighter [TST039]..20.00
__ TIE Fighter Pilot / TIE Bomber [TST040].........20.00

2009. Color packaging with character graphic.
__ Ahsoka Tano / Jedi Starfighter [TST041]........20.00
__ Anakin Skywalker/Jedi Starfighter [TST042]...20.00
__ Anakin Skywalker / The Twilight [TST043]......20.00
__ Battle Droid Commander / Armored Assault Tank
 [TST044]..20.00
__ Boba Fett / Slave I [TST045]............................20.00
__ Clone Commander Cody / Clone Turbo Tank
 [TST046]..20.00
__ Clone Pilot / Republic Gunship [TST047] 20.00
__ Clone Pilot / V-Wing Starfighter [TST048] 20.00
__ Clone Trooper / AT-TE [TST049] 20.00
__ Darth Vader / TIE Advanced X1 Starfighter
 [TST050]..20.00
__ General Grievous / General Grievous' Starfighter
 [TST051]..20.00
__ Kit Fisto / Jedi Starfighter [TST052]................20.00
__ Luke Skywalker / X-Wing Fighter [TST053] ...20.00
__ Magnaguard / Magnaguard Starfighter
 [TST054]..20.00
__ Obi-Wan Kenobi / Jedi Starfighter [TST055] ..20.00
__ Y-Wing Pilot / Y-Wing [TST056] 20.00

2010. Color packaging with character graphic.
__ Anakin Skywalker to Jedi Starfighter
 [TST057]...20.00
__ Anakin Skywalker to Y-Wing Bomber
 [TST058]...20.00
__ Cad Bane / Xanadu Blood [TST059]...............20.00
__ Captain Rex / Freeco Speeer [TST060] 20.00
__ Captain Rex to AT-TE [TST061]......................20.00
__ Clone Gunner / Republic Fighter Tank
 [TST062]..20.00
__ Darth Vader to TIE Advanced x1 Starfighter
 [TST063]..20.00
__ Lieutenant Thire / Republic Attack Cruiser
 [TST064]..20.00
__ Obi-Wan Kenobi / Jedi Starfighter [TST065] ..20.00
__ Yoda to Republic Attack Shuttle [TST066] 20.00

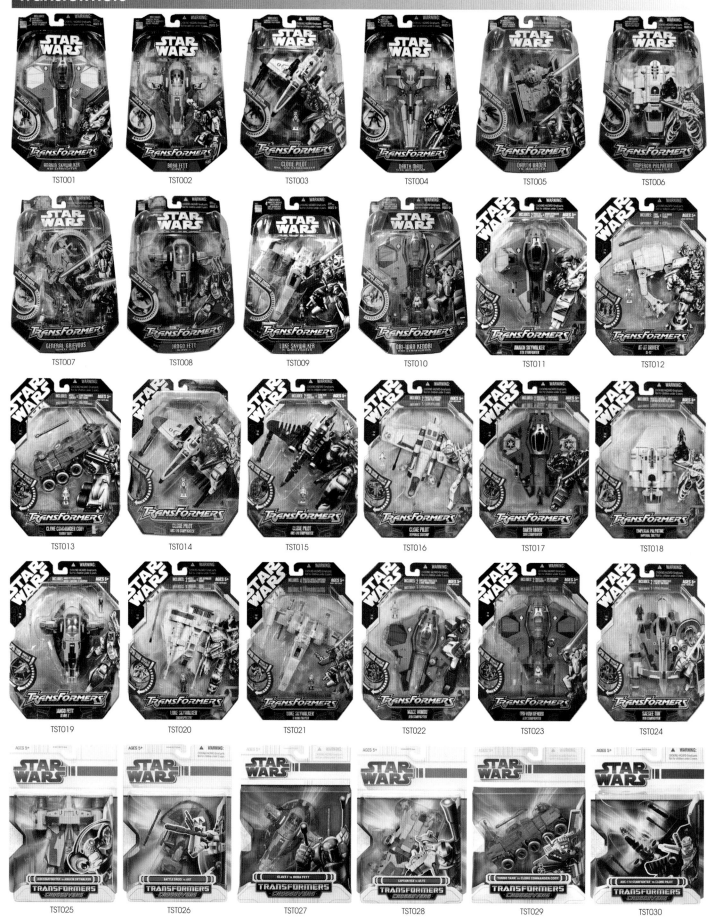

TST001 TST002 TST003 TST004 TST005 TST006

TST007 TST008 TST009 TST010 TST011 TST012

TST013 TST014 TST015 TST016 TST017 TST018

TST019 TST020 TST021 TST022 TST023 TST024

TST025 TST026 TST027 TST028 TST029 TST030

TST031

TST032

TST033

TST034

TST035

TST036

TST037

TST038

TST039

TST040

TST041

TST042

TST043

TST044

TST045

TST046

TST047

TST048

TST049

TST050

TST051

TST052

TST053

TST054

TST055

TST056

TST057

TST058

TST059

TST060

TST061

TST062

TST063

TST064

TST065

TST066

TST067

TST068

TST069

TST070

TTY001

Deluxe and multi-packs.
__ Darth Vader / Death Star [TST067] 35.00
__ Galactic Showdown Darth Vader and Obi-Wan Kenobi, exclusive to Walmart [TST068]..........45.00
__ Han Solo and Chewbacca / Millennium Falcon [TST069]..45.00
__ Han Solo and Chewbacca / Millennium Falcon with bonus Titanium vehicles [TST070].................50.00

Hasbro, UK
__ Han Solo and Chewbacca / Millennium Falcon 45.00

Transforming Toys

Takara, Japan
__ Transforming X-Wing [TTY001]....................535.00

TRK001

Trucks

__ Inter-Transmax 9968 Semi, Star Warrio [TRK001] 110.00

Vehicles, Diecast and Plastic

Clipper, Netherlands
__ Land Speeder 50.00
__ TIE Fighter..50.00
__ X-Wing Fighter 50.00

Disney / MGM
__ Parade Vehicle with R2-D2 and C-3PO..........12.00
__ Starspeeder 1000 Spaceliner Collection [TYD001]..35.00
__ Starspeeder 3000 [TYD002] 35.00

Harbert, Italy
__ Caccia Ala-X 160.00
__ Caccia T.I.E..145.00
__ Hovercraft Scooter 185.00

Kenner
Boxed.
__ Imperial Cruiser SW [TYD003] 185.00
__ Imperial Cruiser SW with background 600.00
__ Imperial Cruiser ESB...................................165.00
__ Millennium Falcon SW [TYD004] 150.00
__ Millennium Falcon SW with background 600.00
__ Millennium Falcon ESB [TYD005].................165.00
__ Tiebomber ESB [TYD006]..............................750.00
__ Y-Wing Fighter SW [TYD007] 200.00
__ Y-Wing Fighter SW with background 600.00
__ Y-Wing Fighter ESB..................................185.00

Carded.
__ Darth Vader TIE Fighter   SW large wings [TYD008]..55.00
__ Darth Vader TIE Fighter   SW small wings 2450.00
__ Darth Vader TIE Fighter ESB 55.00
__ Darth Vader TIE Fighter Catalog-order box..115.00
__ Land Speeder SW [TYD009]........................85.00
__ Land Speeder ESB 85.00
__ Land Speeder Catalog-order box.................115.00
__ Slave I ESB [TYD010] 125.00
__ Slave I ESB, 2nd cardback 170.00
__ Snowspeeder ESB [TYD011] 125.00
__ TIE Fighter SW..65.00
__ TIE Fighter SW with price box [TYD012] 215.00
__ TIE Fighter ESB..55.00
__ TIE Fighter Catalog-order box 115.00
__ Twin-Pod Cloud Car ESB [TYD013] 95.00
__ X-Wing Fighter SW [TYD014] 75.00
__ X-Wing Fighter ESB 75.00

Palitoy, UK
__ Imperial Cruiser...185.00
__ Millennium Falcon.......................................165.00

Star Force
Battery operated 'Bump and Go'.
__ Millennium Falcon [TYD015] 35.00

Diecast vehicles featuring "pull-back" action.
__ A-Wing Fighter...8.00
__ Millennium Falcon..8.00
__ MonCal Cruiser..8.00
__ X-Wing Fighter...8.00

STAR WARS
STAR TOURS

AIR ALDERAAN · TATOOINE TRANSIT · STAR TOURS · NABOO SPACELINES · DANTOOINE EXPRESS · BESPIN DIRECT
Starspeeder 1000 Spaceliner Collection

TYD001

STAR·WARS
No. 39230 Ages 4 and up.

IMPERIAL CRUISER
Authentic replica of the Empire's largest Space Craft.

Contents: Diecast and plastic ship.

Kenner

TYD003

AGES 5+

Starspeeder 3000
With Authentic Lights and Sounds!

R2-D2™ SFX · Captain Rex Voice
Shuttle Engine Sounds · Light Speed Sound Effects
Working Cabin Lights and Doors · Removable Roof
Removable Captain Rex

⚠ WARNING:
CHOKING HAZARD–Small parts.
Not for children under 3 years.

3 "AA" Batteries included.

TYD002

STAR·WARS
No. 39210 Ages 4 and up.

MILLENNIUM FALCON
Authentic replica of Han Solo's Space Cruiser.

Contents: Diecast and plastic spaceship.

Kenner

TYD004

MILLENNIUM FALCON Authentic replica of Han Solo's Space Cruiser.

No. 39210
STAR EMPIRE STRIKES BACK WARS

Contents: Diecast and plastic spaceship.

Ages 4 and up.

Kenner

TYD005

TIE BOMBER Authentic Imperial Spacecraft from STAR WARS: "The Empire Strikes Back."

No. 39260
STAR EMPIRE STRIKES BACK WARS

Contents: Diecast and plastic spaceship.

Ages 4 and up.

Kenner

TYD006

STAR·WARS
No. 39220 Ages 4 and up.

Y-WING FIGHTER
Authentic replica of the Rebel Space Craft used to attack Death Star.

Contents: Diecast and plastic spaceship.

Kenner

TYD007

No. 39160 Ages 4 and up.
STAR WARS
DARTH VADER TIE FIGHTER

Kenner

TYD008

STAR WARS
LAND SPEEDER

Kenner

TYD009

No. 39570
STAR EMPIRE STRIKES BACK WARS
SLAVE I

Kenner

TYD010

No. 39680
STAR EMPIRE STRIKES BACK WARS
REBEL ARMORED SNOWSPEEDER

Kenner

TYD011

No. 38590
STAR WARS
TIE FIGHTER

Kenner

TYD012

No. 39660
STAR EMPIRE STRIKES BACK WARS
TWIN-POD
CLOUD CAR

Kenner

TYD013

No. 39690 Ages 4 and up.
STAR WARS
X-WING FIGHTER

Kenner

TYD014

• BATTERY OPERATED

BUMP & GO

DIE CAST
STAR FORCE PLAY SET

TYD015

STAR WARS
X-WING

410025 6
16GG

TYD016

STAR WARS
No. 410201-0 (1,400)

ダイカスト
シー・スリーピーオ

ST

TYD017

STAR WARS
No. 410202-2 (1,400)

ダイカスト
ダース・ベイダー

ST

TYD018

405

TYD019

TYD020

TYD021

TYD022

MIF001

MIF002

MIF003

MIF004

MIF005

MIF006

Takara, Japan

___ X-Wing Fighter [TYD016] 195.00

Carded vehicles, similar to Kenner's line.
___ Landspeeder..95.00
___ TIE Fighter..95.00
___ X-Wing Fighter 95.00

Diecast characters, approximately 10".
___ C-3PO [TYD017]...250.00
___ Darth Vader [TYD018]....................................275.00

Space Alloy Zetca.
___ C-3PO [TYD019]..175.00
___ R2-D2 [TYD020]..175.00
___ TIE Fighter [TYD021]......................................175.00
___ X-Wing Fighter [TYD022] 175.00

Toltoys
Carded vehicles, similar to Kenner's line.
___ Land Speeder 95.00
___ TIE Fighter...100.00
___ X-Wing Fighter 114.00

Vehicles, Propeller Driven

Estes

___ Naboo Fighter electronic remote control with
display stand..18.00
___ X-Wing Sterling Model Kit Control Line Fighter
without engine 28.00
___ Y-Wing Sterling Model Kit Control Line Fighter
without engine [MIF002] 35.00

Estes / Cox

___ Darth Vader's TIE Fighter kit with engine 50.00
___ Death Star Battle Station with X-Wing control line
fighter kit, radio controller............................160.00
___ Landspeeder radio control vehicle kit with engine
[MIF001]...125.00
___ Naboo Fighter [MIF003].................................24.00
___ Snowspeeder Fighter kit with engine
[MIF004]..50.00
___ Star Wars Combat Set, X-Wing and TIE Fighter with
engines..120.00
___ Trade Federation Droid Fighter [MIF005]........24.00
___ X-Wing Fighter kit with engine [MIF006].........75.00
___ Y-Wing Fighter kit with engine.......................95.00

Voice Changers

Hasbro

___ Boba Fett [TSB001] 35.00
___ Captain Rex [TSB002] 35.00
___ Clone Commander Gear (Capt. Rex voice change
helmet with blaster gun) [TSB003].................45.00
___ Clone Trooper helmet [TSB004] 35.00
___ Clone Trooper helmet, 501st, exclusive to
Walmart...35.00
___ Clone Trooper helmet, shock trooper, exclusive to
Target [TSB005]..35.00
___ Darth Vader, 3 voice modifications, breathing,
5 pre-recorded phrases OTC packaging
[TSB006]..40.00
___ Darth Vader, 3 voice modifications, breathing, 5
pre-recorded phrases ROTS packaging
[TSB007] 35.00

___ Darth Vader, 3 voice modifications, breathing, 5
pre-recorded phrases ROTS packaging, bonus
lightsaber [TSB008] 50.00
___ Darth Vader, 30th anniversary packaging 3 voice
modifications, breathing, 5 pre-recorded phrases,
exclusive to Toys R Us [TSB009]....................35.00
___ Darth Vader, Clone Wars packaging, exclusive to
Target...35.00
___ Ultimate Darth Vader, voice changer mask, lightsaber
and cape, ROTS packaging [TSB010]............45.00

Hasbro, Canada
___ Boba Fett 35.00

Hasbro, Japan
*Authentic sounds plus speed adjustable record/
playback. U.S. releases with marketing sticker
applied.*
___ C-3PO [TSB011]..16.00

Pepsi Cola
___ C-3PO from TPM, promotional [TSB012].......15.00

Rubies
___ Belt-clipped 20.00

Tiger Electronics
*Authentic sounds plus speed adjustable record/
playback.*
___ C-3PO [TSB013]..16.00
___ Darth Vader [TSB014]....................................16.00
___ Darth Vader, alters voice to Darth Vader's
[TSB015] 25.00
___ Millennium Falcon [TSB016]..........................16.00

TSB001 TSB002 TSB003 TSB004 TSB005

TSB006 TSB007 TSB008 TSB009 TSB010

TSB011 TSB012 TSB013 TSB014 TSB015 TSB016

   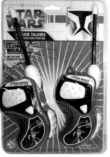 

WT001 WT002 WT003 WT004 WT005

WT006 WT007 WT008 WT009 WT010 WT011

Walkie Talkies

WG001

WG002

WG003

WG004

WG005

WG006

WG007

WG008

Walkie-Talkies

Hasbro
__ Jedi Communicators [WT001] 20.00

Jollibee
__ EPII. R2-D2 and C-3PO [WT002]....................25.00

Micro Games of America
__ Darth Vader and Stormtrooper helmets designed to
be clipped to belt [WT003]..............................24.00

TGA, Australia
__ Walkie Talkies with Morse code function
[WT004]..25.00

Tiger Electronics
__ Clone Trooper and Jango Fett [WT005] 18.00
__ Darth Vader voice changer, regular voice or altered
[WT006]..28.00
__ Imperial symbol over speaker with belt clips
[WT007]..18.00
__ Jedi Comlink [WT008]....................................10.00
__ Rebel Alliance long-range, headset with sound
effects function [WT009]................................26.00

Tiger Electronics, UK
__ View Comm walkie talkies [WT010]................30.00

Titan
__ Executive, shows R2-D2 and C-3PO on morse
code pad [WT011] 85.00

Water Guns

__ Droid rifle 6.00
__ Battle Mauser...6.00

Fun Favors
Party favors.
__ Slave I, cloud car, Millennium Falcon 24.00

Hasbro
Super soakers.
__ Wookiee Water Blaster [WG001] 25.00

Kenner
__ Water Blaster BlasTech DL-44 [WG002] 14.00

Larami
Power soakers.
__ Battle Droid Rifle [WG003]................................5.00
__ Battle Mauser [WG004]....................................5.00
__ Naboo Pistol [WG005] 5.00

Super soakers.
__ Battle Droid Rifle [WG007]..............................18.00
__ Naboo Pistol [WG006] 12.00
__ Queen Amidala Pistol [WG008] 8.00

Weapons

__ Episode I Electronic Sword [TYW001]............25.00
__ Galaxi Spacial, diecast metal cap gun 65.00
__ Star Troop Optic Saber..................................20.00

Unlicensed.
__ Professional Computer Beam Gun, Han Solo
graphics on box 55.00
__ Space sword, Star Destroyer and DS II on card
[TYW002] 5.00

Benedictine Enterprises Ltd., Hong Kong
__ Laser Sword "Glows in Dark After Use"
[TYW003] 16.00

Disney / MGM
Star Tours Power of the Jedi packaging.
__ Galactic Empire Rifle E-11 [TYW004] 25.00
__ Lightsaber..20.00
__ Rebel Alliance Blaster [TYW005] 25.00
__ Rebel Alliance Bowcaster [TYW006] 25.00

Star Tours Saga packaging.
__ Rebel Alliance Blaster [TYW007] 25.00
__ Stormtrooper Rifle 25.00

Edge Import Corp.
__ Galaxy Ray Gun, diecast metal cap gun 50.00

Harbert, Italy
__ 3-Position laser rifle 230.00
__ Laser Pistol, SW 185.00
__ Lightsaber with inflatable yellow blade.........235.00

Hasbro
__ Laser Tag Naboo Accessory Set 135.00
__ Naboo and Droid Fighter Battle [TYW008] 24.00

Lightsaber assembly kits.
__ Build Your Own Lightsaber [TYW009] 45.00
__ Build Your Own Lightsaber with bonus DVD..45.00
__ Ultimate Lightsaber, Clone Wars [TYW010] ...30.00

Lightsabers (2002). Episode II.
__ Blue [TYW011] 12.00
__ Green [TYW012]..12.00
__ Purple [TYW013]...12.00
__ Red [TYW014]...12.00

*Lightsabers (2004). Star Wars Original Trilogy Collection.
Available in blue, green, purple, red.*
__ Obi-Wan handle [TYW015] 7.00
__ Qui-Gon handle [TYW016]................................7.00

TYW001 TYW002 TYW004 TYW005

TYW006 TYW007 TYW008

Lightsabers (2005). Episode III. Available in red, blue, purple, green.
__ 2-pack [TYW017] 18.00
__ Obi-Wan handle [TYW018] 8.00
__ Qui-Gon Jinn handle [TYW019] 8.00
__ Vader handle [TYW020] 8.00

Lightsabers (2006). Saga 2. Blue, red, or green.
__ 2-packs, Jedi vs. Sith, Luke vs. Darth Vader..12.00
__ 2-packs, Jedi vs. Sith, Obi-Wan vs. Anakin ...12.00
__ 2-packs, Jedi vs. Sith, Yoda vs. Sidious 12.00
__ Darth Vader handle 7.00
__ Darth Vader handle with bonus Galactic Heroes
   figure...9.00
__ Obi-Wan handle 7.00
__ Obi-Wan handle with bonus Galactic Heroes
   figure...9.00
__ Qui-Gon Jinn handle......................................7.00
__ Qui-Gon Jinn handle with bonus Galactic Heroes
   figure...9.00

Lightsabers (2008). Clone Wars.
__ Obi-Wan handle...7.00
__ Qui-Gon handle 7.00

Lightsabers (2010). Clone Wars.
__ Blue or green blade [TYW021].......................10.00
__ Red blade [TYW022]....................................10.00

Lightsabers, electronic (1999). Episode I.
__ Darth Maul's .0000 (Design flaw could cause
   injury) 35.00
__ Darth Maul's .0200 [TYW023]........................30.00
__ Obi-Wan's (blue) [TYW024] 26.00
__ Qui-Gon's (green) [TYW025].........................20.00

Lightsabers, electronic (2002). Episode II.
__ Anakin Skywalker Interactive Jedi Training
   [TYW026] 35.00
__ Anakin's, blue [TYW027]...............................24.00
__ Count Dooku's, red [TYW028] 24.00
__ Darth Tyranus, red [TYW029] 25.00
__ Jedi lightsaber, green [TYW030].....................24.00
__ Jedi lightsaber, orange [TYW031]....................24.00
__ Mace Windu, purple [TYW032]........................24.00
__ Obi-Wan's, blue [TYW033] 26.00
__ Yoda, green [TYW034]...................................24.00

Lightsabers, electronic (2003).
__ Action packs. Random lightsaber packaged with 3
   random action figures [TYW035] 45.00

Lightsabers, electronic (2003). Star Wars Saga.
__ Anakin Skywalker [TYW036]...........................25.00
__ Count Dooku [TYW037].................................25.00
__ Darth Vader [TYW038] 25.00
__ Darth Vader, vert pkg [TYW039].....................25.00

__ Luke Skywalker [TYW040]..............................25.00
__ Luke Skywalker, vert pkg [TYW041]................25.00
__ Mace Windu, vert pkg [TYW042] 25.00
__ Obi-Wan Kenobi [TYW043].............................25.00
__ Yoda [TYW044]..25.00
__ Yoda [TYW045]..25.00
__ Yoda, vert pkg [TYW046]...............................25.00

Lightsabers, electronic (2004). Original Trilogy Collection.
__ Anakin Skywalker [TYW047] 25.00
__ Darth Vader [TYW048] 25.00
__ Luke Skywalker [TYW049] 25.00
__ Yoda [TYW050]...25.00

Lightsabers, electronic (2004). Original Trilogy Collection. Includes bonus Galactic Heroes figure(s).
__ Darth Vader, Vader and Kenobi [TYW051] 30.00
__ Luke Skywalker, Luke and R2-D2 ....30.00

Lightsabers, electronic (2005). Episode III.
__ 2-pack with 2 bonus figures and bonus poster
   [TYW052]...35.00
__ Anakin Skywalker / Darth Vader, color-change
   blade [TYW053] 20.00
__ Count Dooku [TYW054].................................20.00
__ Jedi...20.00
__ Luke Skywalker...20.00

TYW009 TYW010 TYW011 TYW012 TYW013 TYW014 TYW015 TYW016 TYW018 TYW019 TYW020

TYW021 TYW022 TYW035 TYW052 TYW074

TYW003

TYW017

TYW023

TYW024

TYW025

TYW026

TYW027

TYW028

TYW029

TYW030

TYW031

TYW032

TYW033

TYW034

TYW036

TYW037

TYW038

TYW039

TYW040

TYW041

TYW042

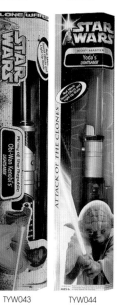

TYW043

TYW044

TYW045

TYW046

TYW047

TYW048

TYW049

TYW050

TYW051 TYW053 TYW054 TYW055 TYW056 TYW057 TYW058 TYW059 TYW060 TYW061 TYW062

TYW063 TYW064 TYW065 TYW066 TYW067 TYW068 TYW069 TYW070 TYW071

TYW072 TYW073 TYW075 TYW092 TYW093 TYW094 TYW095 TYW096 TYW097

Weapons

__ Mace Windu [TYW055] 20.00
__ Obi-Wan Kenobi, Force feedback [TYW056]..20.00
__ Yoda, training mode [TYW057].......................20.00

Lightsabers, electronic (2005). Episode III. Includes bonus Galactic Heroes figure.
__ Darth Vader (Anakin) 25.00
__ Obi-Wan figure [TYW058]......................25.00

Lightsabers, electronic (2005). Episode III. Vertical hang packaging. Walmart exclusives.
__ Jedi [TYW059]...15.00
__ Obi-Wan Kenobi [TYW060].....................15.00
__ Sith [TYW061].......................................15.00

TYW076

Lightsabers, electronic (2005). Original Trilogy Collection. Includes bonus DVD.
__ Anakin Skywalker [TYW062]..........................30.00
__ Darth Vader [TYW063] 30.00
__ Obi-Wan Kenobi [TYW064]...........................30.00

Lightsabers, electronic (2006). 30th anniversary.
__ Darth Maul 40.00
__ Darth Vader...25.00
__ Mace Windu...25.00

Lightsabers, electronic (2006). Force Action.
__ Darth Vader..30.00
__ Luke Skywalker...30.00
__ Obi-Wan Kenobi 30.00

Lightsabers, electronic (2006). Saga 2.
__ Anakin Skywalker [TYW065].......................20.00
__ Anakin Skywalker with bonus Lightsaber Action DVD..20.00
__ Darth Vader [TYW066] 20.00
__ Darth Vader with bonus Lightsaber Action DVD..20.00
__ Mace Windu [TYW067]...............................20.00
__ Obi-Wan Kenobi [TYW068]..........................20.00
__ Obi-Wan Kenobi with bonus Lightsaber Action DVD..20.00
__ Yoda [TYW069]..20.00

Lightsabers, electronic (2006). The Saga Collection.
__ 2-pack with Anakin Skywalker and Obi-Wan Kenobi figures 35.00
__ 2-pack with Darth Vader and Luke Skywalker figures 35.00
__ Darth Maul [TYW070]................................30.00

Lightsabers, electronic (2007). 30th anniversary. Force action.
__ Darth Vader...30.00
__ Luke Skywalker..30.00
__ Obi-Wan Kenobi 30.00

Lightsabers, electronic (2007). Force Unleashed.
__ Color change blade [TYW071].......................30.00

Lightsabers, electronic (2008). Clone Wars. Force action.
__ Anakin Skywalker.......................................30.00
__ Darth Vader...30.00
__ Force Unleashed...30.00

Lightsabers, electronic (2009). Duel Action.
__ Jedi / blue [TYW072]...................................40.00
__ Sith / red [TYW073].....................................40.00

Lightsabers, electronic (2009). Force Action.
__ Darth Vader...30.00

TYW077

TYW078

TYW079

TYW080

TYW081

TYW086

TYW082

TYW083

TYW087

TYW088

TYW084

TYW085

TYW089

TYW090

TYW099   TYW105   TYW106   TYW109   TYW110   TYW131   TYW146   TYW147   TYW149

TYW091   TYW098

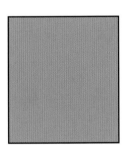

TYW100   TYW101

TYW102   TYW103   TYW104

TYW107   TYW108   TYW111   TYW112

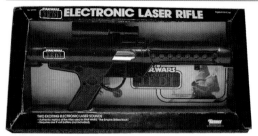

TYW113

TYW114

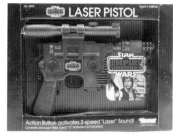

TYW115

TYW116

TYW117

TYW118

TYW119

TYW120

TYW121

TYW122

TYW123

TYW124

TYW125

TYW126

TYW127

TYW128

TYW129

TYW130

TYW132

TYW133

TYW134

TYW135

TYW136

TYW137

| TYW138 | TYW139 | TYW140 | TYW141 | TYW142 | TYW143 | TYW144 | TYW145 | TYW148 |

Lightsabers, electronic (2010).
__ Spinning electronic lightsaber [TYW074]........30.00

Lightsabers, electronic (2010). Includes bonus DVD.
__ Yoda [TYW075]..30.00

Weapons (1999). Episode I.
__ Battle Droid Blaster Rifle, electronic...............20.00
__ Naboo Foam-Firing Blaster [TYW076]............15.00
__ Tatooine Blaster Pistol, Electronic [TYW077] .22.00

Weapons (2002). Episode II.
__ Battle Droid Blaster Rifle, electronic...............20.00
__ Jango Fett's blasters 2-pack 20.00

Weapons (2005). Episode III.
__ Chewbacca's Bowcaster [TYW078] 25.00
__ Clone Trooper blaster [TYW079] 15.00
__ Energy beam blaster [TYW080] 15.00
__ General Grievous' Blaster [TYW081] 25.00

Weapons (2005). Episode III. Energy beam blaster refill canisters.
__ Clone Trooper [TYW082] 5.00
__ General Grievous [TYW083] 5.00
__ Super Battle Droid [TYW084]...........................5.00
__ Yoda [TYW085]...5.00

Weapons (2006). Saga 2.
__ Clone Trooper blaster 15.00
__ General Grievous' Blaster 25.00
__ Stormtrooper Blaster 25.00

Weapons (2007). 30th Anniversary.
__ Clone trooper with Nerf shooting mechanism 25.00
__ Rebel Trooper with Nerf shooting mechanism blue 25.00
__ Rebel Trooper with Nerf shooting mechanism green 25.00

Weapons (2008). Clone Wars.
__ Clone Trooper Blaster....................................15.00
__ General Grievous Blaster 25.00
__ Stormtrooper Blaster 25.00

Weapons (2009).
__ Clone Commander Blaster [TYW086]..............45.00
__ Clone Trooper Blaster [TYW087]....................30.00
__ General Grievous' Blaster [TYW088] 30.00
__ Stormtrooper Blaster [TYW089].....................30.00

Weapons (2010).
__ Boba Fett Blaster [TYW090] 30.00
__ Clone Trooper Blaster [TYW091] 30.00

Hasbro, Canada
Lightsabers, electronic (2002). Episode II. Tri-language packaging.
__ Anakin's, blue 30.00
__ Darth Tyranus, red 30.00
__ Obi-Wan's, blue..30.00

Lightsabers, electronic (2003). Star Wars Saga.
__ 2-pack with Anakin Skywalker and Obi-Wan Kenobi figures Multi-language packaging. 35.00
__ 2-pack with Darth Vader and Luke Skywalker figures Multi-language packaging. 35.00

Lightsabers, electronic (2004). Original Trilogy Collection. Tri-language packaging.
__ Darth Vader...20.00

__ Luke Skywalker..20.00
__ Yoda 20.00

Lightsabers, electronic (2005). Episode III. Tri-language packaging.
__ Anakin Skywalker / Darth Vader, color-change blade 20.00
__ Count Dooku..20.00
__ Mace Windu, motion activated [TYW092] 20.00
__ Obi-Wan Kenobi, Force feedback vibration [TYW093] 20.00
__ Yoda, training mode 20.00

Lightsabers, electronic (2007). 30th anniversary. Force action. Tri-language packaging.
__ Darth Vader...30.00
__ Luke Skywalker..30.00
__ Obi-Wan Kenobi 30.00

Lightsabers, electronic (2010). Clone Wars.
__ Anakin Skywalker [TYW094]...........................30.00
__ Darth Vader [TYW095]....................................30.00
__ Obi-Wan Kenobi [TYW096]..............................30.00
__ Yoda [TYW097]...30.00

Hasbro, UK
Weapons (1999). Episode I. Multi-language packaging.
__ Naboo Foam-Firing Blaster [TYW098]..............8.00

Weapons (2009).
__ Clone Commander Blaster 45.00

Kenner
POTF2 lightsabers.
__ Darth Vader's, Green packaging 55.00
__ Darth Vader's, Red packaging........................60.00
__ Luke Skywalker's [TYW099] 55.00

POTF2.
__ Chewbacca's Bowcaster [TYW100] 18.00
__ Electronic Blaster Rifle, Green package [TYW101] 45.00
__ Electronic Blaster Rifle, Orange package [TYW102] 50.00
__ Heavy blaster, Camouflage [TYW103]............26.00
__ Heavy blaster, Orange [TYW104] 22.00

Vintage lightsabers.
__ Droids with collapsible blade, green [TYW105] 275.00
__ Droids with collapsible blade, red [TYW106]275.00
__ ROTJ, red or green 45.00
__ SW with inflatable yellow blade [TYW107] ...275.00
__ SW with inflatable yellow blade, SW Kenobi / Vader pkg. [TYW108]..275.00
__ The Force, red [TYW109]................................50.00
__ The Force, yellow [TYW110]...........................50.00

Vintage.
__ Biker Scout laser pistol [TYW111] 75.00
__ Electronic laser rifle, ESB [TYW112].............275.00
__ Electronic laser rifle, ROTJ, exclusive to JC Penney [TYW113] 875.00
__ Laser Pistol, ESB [TYW114]..........................155.00
__ Laser Pistol, ESB Han Solo photo [TYW115] 490.00
__ Laser Pistol, ROTJ [TYW116] 150.00
__ Laser Pistol, SW [TYW117]...........................225.00
__ Laser rifle, 3 position [TYW118]....................240.00

Kenner, UK
__ Heavy blaster, orange [TYW119] 12.00

Larami
Electronic micro light and sound weapons. Episode I: The Phantom Menace.
__ Battle Droid Rifle [TYW120] 7.00
__ Battle Mouser [TYW121]..................................7.00
__ Naboo Pistol [TYW122].....................................7.00

Electronic micro light and sound weapons. Episode II: Attack of the Clones.
__ Anakin Skywalker, lightsaber [TYW123] 6.00
__ Jango Fett, blaster [TYW124] 6.00
__ Zam Wesell, blaster [TYW125]........................6.00

Episode II: Attack of the Clones action sets.
__ Jango Fett [TYW126] 20.00
__ Jedi Knight [TYW127] 18.00

Sound and Light Blasters.
__ Battle Droid [TYW128] 24.00
__ Jango Fett [TYW129] 16.00

Maruka, Japan
__ Lightsaber on Darth Vader header card, includes battery [TYW130] 77.00

Master Replicas
__ Force FX Lightsaber Construction Set [TYW131] 125.00

Palitoy, UK
__ 3-Position laser rifle 230.00
__ Blaster Pistol, SW 180.00
__ Lightsaber, inflatable blade, SW...................195.00

Party Express
__ Lightsaber, inflatable 8.00

Redondo
__ Galaxia laser gun 79.00

Rubies
Colored lightsabers, extend to 36 inches.
__ Blue..6.00
__ Green 6.00
__ Red 6.00
__ White...6.00

Episode I lightsabers.
__ Darth Maul, red..12.00
__ Obi-Wan, blue..12.00
__ Qui-gon, green...12.00

Episode II weapons.
__ Anakin Skywalker Lightsaber [TYW132]...........8.00
__ Anakin Skywalker Lightsaber, hang-tab package [TYW133] 8.00
__ Count Dooku Lightsaber [TYW134] 8.00
__ Jango Fett Blaster [TYW135]...........................8.00
__ Mace Windu Lightsaber [TYW136] 8.00
__ Padme Amidala Blaster [TYW137]..................20.00

Guns.
__ Clone Trooper Blaster [TYW138] 15.00
__ Han Solo's 15.00

Lightsabers.
__ Darth Vader's [TYW139] 15.00
__ Luke Skywalker's [TYW140] 15.00

TW001

TW002

TW003

TW004

TW005

TW006

ROTS. Lightsabers.
__ Anakin Skywalker [TYW141]...........................12.00
__ Count Dooku [TYW142]................................12.00
__ Darth Vader [TYW143] 12.00
__ Mace Windu [TYW144] 12.00
__ Obi-Wan Kenobi [TYW145]............................12.00

Super Live Adventure, Japan
__ Gold hilt 125.00
__ Gray hilt 145.00
__ Lightsaber...95.00

Super Sonic Toys
__ SST Laser Sword [TYW146] 45.00

Takara, Japan
__ Lightsaber [TYW147] 215.00

Tiger Electronics
Laser tag sets.
__ Naboo Assault [TYW148]...............................34.00
__ Star Wars 45.00

Toltoys
__ Laser Pistol, SW 140.00
__ Laser rifle, 3 position 360.00

Tomy, Japan
__ Lightsaber, deluxe electronic [TYW149].........45.00
__ Lightsaber, electronic 45.00
__ Lightsaber, inflatable 35.00

Weina
__ Star Wars Laser Space Pistol, released with Star Tours...100.00

Kenner, Canada
__ Wind-up walking R2-D2 [TW001] 2,250.00

Osaka
Tin Age Collection.
__ Boba Fett [TW002]......................................185.00
__ C-3PO [TW003]..185.00
__ Darth Vader [TW004] 185.00
__ R2-D2 [TW005]..225.00
__ Stormtrooper [TW006] 185.00

Takara, Japan
__ Wind-up walking R2-D2, sold in cellophane baggie..265.00

TWD001

TWD002

TWD003

TWD004

TWD005

TWD006

TWD007

TWD008

TWD009

TWD010

TWD011

TWD012

TWD013

TWD014

TWD015

TWD016

TWD017

TWD018

TWD019

TWD020

TWD021

TWD022

TWD023

TWD024

TWD025

TWD026

TWD027

TWD028

WW001

Wind-Up Toys, Deformed

__ Anakin Skywalker [TWD001]............................6.00
__ Anakin Skywalker, hands up [TWD002]............9.00
__ Anakin Skywalker, slave [TWD003] 21.00
__ Battle Droid, shot [TWD004].........................7.00
__ Battle Droid, silver [TWD005].......................8.00
__ Battle Droid, sliced [TWD006].......................7.00
__ C-3PO [TWD007]......................................15.00
__ C-3PO, TPM [TWD008]..............................9.00
__ Chewbacca [TWD009]................................15.00
__ Darth Maul empty handed [TWD010] 8.00
__ Darth Maul empty, gold [TWD011] 9.00
__ Darth Maul with hooded cloak [TWD012].........9.00
__ Darth Maul with saber [TWD013]...................11.00
__ Darth Vader [TWD014]...............................15.00
__ Emperor Palpatine [TWD015] 23.00
__ Jar Jar Binks [TWD016] 9.00

__ Mace Windu [TWD017]...................................9.00
__ Obi-Wan Kenobi [TWD018]..............................9.00
__ OOM-9 [TWD019]...9.00
__ Queen Amidala [TWD020]...............................9.00
__ Queen Amidala, hands up [TWD021]................7.00
__ Qui-Gon Jinn [TWD022].................................9.00
__ R2-D2 [TWD023]..15.00
__ Sebulba [TWD024].......................................9.00
__ Stormtrooper [TWD025]................................15.00
__ Watto [TWD026]..9.00
__ Yoda [TWD027]...15.00
__ Yoda, brown [TWD028]..................................25.00

Wonder World

Kenner
__ Wonder World [WW001] 17.00

Yo Yos

Argentina. Classic characters.
__ C-3PO [YM001]..8.00
__ Chewbacca [YM002] 8.00
__ Han Solo [YM003].......................................8.00
__ Luke Skywalker [YM004] 8.00
__ Princess Leia [YM005] 8.00
__ R2-D2 [YM006] 8.00

Argentina. Clone Wars skill game.
__ Ahsoka [YM007]...10.00
__ Anakin [YM008]...10.00
__ Asajj [YM009]...10.00
__ C-3PO [YM010]..10.00
__ Obi Wan [YM011]...10.00
__ R2-D2 [YM012]..10.00
__ Yoda [YM013]...10.00

YM001

YM002

YM003

YM004

YM005

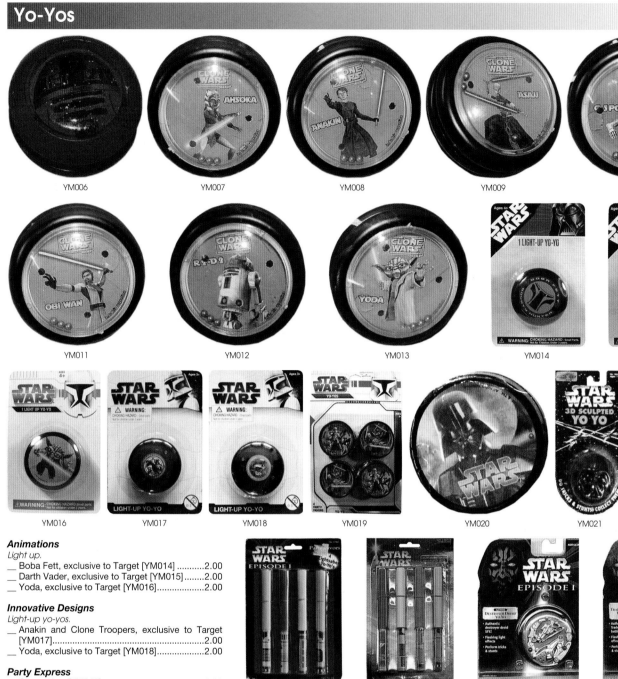

YM006   YM007   YM008   YM009   YM010

YM011   YM012   YM013   YM014   YM015

YM016   YM017   YM018   YM019   YM020   YM021   YM022

Animations
Light up.
__ Boba Fett, exclusive to Target [YM014] 2.00
__ Darth Vader, exclusive to Target [YM015].......2.00
__ Yoda, exclusive to Target [YM016]..................2.00

Innovative Designs
Light-up yo-yos.
__ Anakin and Clone Troopers, exclusive to Target
[YM017]..2.00
__ Yoda, exclusive to Target [YM018]..................2.00

Party Express
__ Clone Wars [YM019] 4.00
__ Darth Vader [YM020] 3.00

Spectra Star
3D character sculpt on sides.
__ Darth Vader [YM021] 6.00
__ Stormtrooper [YM022] 6.00

Tapper Candies
Lightsaber paper yo-yos. Packages of 4.
__ EPI:TPM [YM023]..4.00
__ EPII:AOTC [YM024] 4.00

Tiger Electronics
Electronic yo-yos with sound FX and flashing lights.
__ Destroyer Droid [YM025] 5.00
__ Trade Federation Battle Ship [YM026] 6.00

Worlds Apart, UK
__ X-Wings and TIE Fighters [YM027].................14.00

YM023   YM024   YM025   YM026

YM027 front   YM027back

Contributors

If you read Star Wars books and magazines or visit the collectibles news sites, a couple of the names below will stand out as people who have established themselves as trusted experts in the community. Also contributing are a combination of the experts who walk quietly among us and collectors who took an interest in being a part of the project. Some of them sent in photography. Some chased down and reported values from auctions and sales. A couple of them filled in checklists that had previously had a couple of holes. Several reported items exclusive to their country. It is amazing to learn how every one of them found a unique way to share their time and knowledge. What they have in common is that they all cared enough to do something to improve the documentation of Star Wars collectibles for me and for you. Please join me in honoring them for the endless facets and direction they have provided.

Chris Albright: Collector, Costumer
Jeff Allen: Costumer
John Allen: Collector
Jose Arosa: Collector (Spain)
Victor Arriaga: Collector (Mexico)
Gail Ashburn: Friend of the Book
Scott Baker: Toy Customizer
Pedro Barrios: Collector (Mexico)
Virgil Bauer: Collector
Jad Bean: Collector
Jonathon Bearrie: Collector: Vintage Action Figures
Daniel Berghelli: Collector (Argentina)
James Boryla: Collector / Dealer
Ray Bossert: Collector
Chris Brennan: Collector (Australia)
Larry Broden: Collector
Sharon Bronson: Collector
Neil Brown: Collector: Autographs
Nathan P. Butler: Timeline Archive
Bill Cable: Collector, Artist
Jose Antonio Macias Ceron: Collector (Mexico)
John Caboco: Collector
Brian Callahan: Collector: Vintage and Glass
Ardith Carlton: Sister
Kay Carlton: Daughter
Arnie Carvalho: Collector, Podcast Host
Marjorie Carvalho: Collector, Podcast Host
Gordon Chan: Collector (Hong Kong)
Mike Chockley: Collector
Robert Clark: Friend of the Book
Steve Corder: attacktix.wikia.com
Andrew Cox: Collector (New Zealand)
Mike Cramutolo: Friend of the Book
Jeff Craycraft: Disney Collector
Wayne Crews: Collector: LEGOs
Chris Da Costa: Collector (Canada)
Justin Dalby: Collector, Costumer
Anthony Damata: Collector: Vintage
Steven Davis: Collector, Costumer
Andrew Davison: Collector (United Kingdom)
Chris Dent: Collector
Thomas Derby IV: Collector: Vintage
Sophie Dessiméon: Collector (Belgium)
Ila Edger Dezarn: Collector, Costumer
Nancy Dickson: Collector (Australia)
Andy Dukes: Collector (United Kingdom)
John Eck: Collector
David Elliott: Collector: Cards (Australia)
Monty Elliott: Collector
Dan Emmons: Collector
Jeff Ensor: Collector
David Essex: Friend of the Book
Emily Facer: Fan
Erica Facer: Collector, Costumer
Chris Fawcett: Collector: Vintage and Pre-Production
Lawrence Fenton III: Son
Patricia Fenton: Daughter
Guy Fernous: Collector
Jack Flukinger: Collector, Costumer
Riley Flukinger: Friend of the Book
Dave Fox: Collector: Patches
Edgard Villasenor Franco: Collector (Mexico)

Matthew Frey: Collector: Visual Media
David Fuller: Owner: Official Star Wars Hummer
Kevin Giblin: Fan
Lori Gifford: Fan
Mike Glover: Costumer
Brian Graham: Collector
Evan Grant: Collector (Australia)
Mariyln Guyote: Collector - In Memoriam
Lindy Harisis: Collector, Costumer
Jon Harper: Collector
Jay Harris: Collector
Peter Hauerstein: Collector
Kevin Heffner: Collector (Canada)
Brian Heiar: Collector, Costumer
Jeff Hendrickson: Collector, Costumer
Mike Hessness: Collector
Paul Holstein: Collector: Trading Cards
Trevor Hopper: Friend of the Book
Scott Home: Collector
Kevin and Tanja Horn: Fans
Cole and Catherine Houston: Collectors
Shawn Houze: Collector: Beverage Bottles and Cans
Mark Huff: Gamer
David Humphries: Collector: Bootleg Action Figures
Mark Ivy: Collector
Peter Jacobsen: Fan
Warren Jacobsen: Collector, Costumer
Keith Jakubowski: Collector
Bryan Janorske: Collector
Stephen Jones: Collector (United Kingdom)
Dan Joplin: Collector: Replicas, Costumer
Cathy Kendrick: Collector: Cards / Stickers
Tim Kennedy: Collector
Deborah Kittle: Collector
"Brother Dave" Krempasky: Collector
Jason Krueger: Collector
Martin Lacy: Collector (United Kingdom)
Stacy Lehn: Friend of the Book
Richard Leigh: Collector
Tait Lifto: Collector
Ian Lindsay: Collector, Costumer
Becky Lockerby: Collector
Brian Long: Collector
Steve Loos: Fan
Joe Lynch: Collector: Micro Machines
Charles Marcus: Collector
Jim McCallum: Collector (Canada), Author
Marcella McCuiston: Collector
Karen McGoldrick: Collector (Australia)
Michael McGoldrick: Collector (Australia)
Andrew McLennan: Dealer (New Zealand)
Dennis McLeod: Collector
Jason Melton: Costumer
Jason Meixsell: Collector
Marc Miller: Collector, Costumer
Tyler Milliman: Collector
Peter Mittag: Collector (Germany)
Phil Mizzi: Collector (Australia)
Lance Moran: Collector, Costumer
Scot Alan Morrison: Collector
Glen Mullaly: Collector (Canada)
Philip Murphy: Collector (United Kingdom)

Mark Newbold: Collector
Douglas Neman: Collector
Anne Newmann: Collector, Historical Archives
Moira O'Reilly: Collector (Australia)
Barbara Ownbey: Fan
Mark Palmer: Collector (United Kingdom)
Cory Parker: Costumer, Fan
Chuck Paskovics: Collector
Camille Patterson: Costumer, Collector
Steven Peacock: Collector
Ryan Peterman: Collector
David Petty: Costumer, Collector
Kristi Pointer: Collector, Costumer
Gary Price: Celebrity Promotions
Shanon Reynolds: Collector - In Memoriam.
Mark Richert: Collector
Sandy Rivers: Collector: Martigras Coins
Dave Roberts: Collector, Dealer
Chris and Rachel Robinson: Fans
Steve Robinson: Collector
Bill Rodgers: Collector (United Kingdom)
Mark Rodnitzky: eBay ID: Playeramusement
Ross Rosemurgy: Collector
Paul Roth: Collector
Oscar Saenz: Collector
Jaclyn Tejeda Sanchez: Fan
Buddy Saunders: Owner, Lone Star Comics
Gary Saunders: Collector (United Kingdom)
Tom Schaefer: Collector
Sterling Schlangenstein: Collector
Chris Seabolt: Collector, Costumer
George Seeds IV: Collector
Joseph Setele: Collector
Helen Silver: Collector
Mark Simonetti: Collector
Duane Smith: Collector
Jeff Stagner: Collector
Jorge Stephenson: Collector
Ben Stevens: Collector, Celebrity Promotions
Tré Stratton: Collector
Amy Sullivan: Friend of the Book
Adam Sylvester: Collector
Jason Thompson: Collector (United Kingdom)
Wayne Thompson: Collector
Martin Thurn: Collector and Historical Archives
Chris Toki: Collector (New Zealand)
Corky Visminas: Sister
Curt Vigneri: Collector: Store Displays
Eric Waldmer: Collector
Charles Walker: Collector: Replicas, Costumer
Michael Walters: Friend of the Book
Pearce Weidmer: Fan, Friend of the Book
Cole Weidmer: Fan, Friend of the Book
Samantha West: Friend of the Book
Trent White: Collector: Replicas, Costumer
Scott Will: Costumer
Stuart Wilkshire: Collector (Japan)
Philip Wise: Collector, Celebrity Promoter
Matthew Wright: Collector: Media
Stone Young: Fan, Friend of the Book
Cade Young: Fan, Friend of the Book

Through a Collector's Eye

Every image used above may be found elsewhere within this book

Becoming One With The Force
BEAT THE FORCE

By Geoffrey T. Carlton

"Where did you find that old fossil?"
-Han Solo, *Star Wars: A New Hope*

In the 1990s when the Star Wars collectibles market started to regain steam there was the occasional "warehouse find" where entire cases of original unsold merchandise were discovered. To this day estate sales turn up the occasional knickknack or household item that had caught somebody's attention during the height of the original films.

Whenever treasures are brought back out into the light you can typically grab an edition of the *Star Wars Super Collector's Wish Book* and look it up to gain some insight into what it is you've scored. Occasionally really special artifacts surface that aren't documented anywhere and that's when the search for their truth begins.

Glass mirrors etched or painted with *Star Wars* and *Empire Strikes Back* images were used as midway prizes at carnivals sometime in the early 1980s. The date range was derived by absence of any authenticated *Return of the Jedi* mirrors. The game(s) used to win the mirrors have always been presumed to be of the standard carnival fare: bottle stacks, balloon boards, red star shooters, etc.

A Missouri "barn find" in late 2010 has provided an actual glimpse into the past! Amongst the remnants of discarded midway paraphernalia was part of a carnival trailer game: Beat The Force. BTF was a four stall game where players had to move a conductor from the red 'start' zone along a metal bar (without touching it!) and make contact with a "win" switch in the green "winner" zone. The metal bar is tapered with the win zone more than double the diameter of the start zone.

When the game was pulled from the trailer the power supply was not extracted with it, leaving some question about whether or not it was still functional 30 years later.

Robert Parsons and Dennis Webb, owners of American Communications, a Haltom City, Texas, electronics shop specializing in 9-1-1 consoles and severe weather warning sirens, opened up the case and built a new power system for the game to allow it to be plugged into a standard 110v outlet. As it turns out, other than some rusty contacts on the rods and replacing the keyed power switch with a simple toggle switch, the game was undamaged—ready to play!

With elbows deep in the game, Robert and Dennis did some investigation and documentation. The game itself operates using vacuum tubes. The newest component manufacturing date stamp was from December of 1979. A reasonable guess is that the game was constructed in early 1980, the year *The Empire Strikes Back* opened in theaters and when the ESB mirrors were used as midway prizes.

The back of the unit has the master power toggle, two game reset buttons per stall (win / lose), two non-resettable counters (games won / games lost), and the connection for the power supply. What is sorely lacking is any kind of volume control. Since the "lose" buzzer is designed to be heard on an open-air midway, it's an extra penalty to lose the game within the confines of an indoor room.

According to the counters at the time of acquisition, 9,206 people had beaten the force so far. When a group of 35 Star Wars fans and collectors were given 24-hour access to the game's debut event, only two were victorious: Warren Jacobsen and Amy Hestness.

Artifacts like the Beat The Force carnival game are the dinosaur bones of *Star Wars* collecting; rare, educational, insightful, and inspiring. They allow us to reconstruct the past and relive the culture that made Star Wars what it is today.

Finger Skating Star Wars

Fingerboards have progressed in design from simple trick boards to full skate parks in miniature. Standard finger skate boards come with a second set of wheels and tools to perform the transfers. The primary retail line is manufactured by Simba Toys in Germany and distributed throughout Europe. The set of twelve *Clone Wars* boards (most pictured below) were designed for precision stunts on the construct-your-own-course companion skate parks (two of four shown below).

McDonald's offered a child friendly version of *Clone Wars* finger boards in their Happy Meals in 2010. The U.S. premium toys did not offer removable wheels or miniature tools. Instead, each McDonald's finger board was packaged with a temporary character tattoo.

FGR001

FGR002

FGR003

FGR004

FGR005

FGR006

FGR007

FGR008

FGR009

FGR010

FGR011

PCT001

PCT002

PCT003

PCT004

PCT005

PCT006

PCT007

PCT008

PCT009

Fingerboards

Simba, Germany
Clone Wars fingerboard skatepark accessories.
__ Obi-Wan deck / Yoda ramp [FGR001]............30.00
__ Obi-Wan ramp / Yoda ramp 30.00
__ Yoda Ramp / Clone Trooper high rail 30.00
__ Yoda Ramp / Clone Wars rail [FGR002] 30.00

Individually packaged fingerboards with extra wheels, screws, and tools.
__ Ahsoka Tano [FGR003]................................15.00
__ Anakin Skywalker..15.00
__ Asajj Ventress [FGR004] 15.00
__ C-3PO [FGR005]..15.00
__ Clone Trooper [FGR006]...............................15.00
__ Clone Wars icons...15.00
__ General Grievous [FGR007]...........................15.00
__ General Grievous emblem [FGR008] 15.00
__ Obi-Wan Kenobi 15.00
__ R2-D2 [FGR009] 15.00
__ Yoda fighting [FGR010] 15.00
__ Yoda standing [FGR011] 15.00

Premium Toys

McDonalds
Clone Wars fingerboard skateboards from children's Happy Meals. Numbered in series. Package includes 1 fingerboard and 1 tattoo. Tattoo can come packaged in cellophane (standard) or with cardboard backer card (variation). Cardboard is less common, but does not change values. Wheels are not removable.
__ #1 Anakin Skywalker Cad Bane tattoo [PCT001] 7.00
__ #2 Captain Rex Anakin Skywalker tattoo [PCT002] 7.00
__ #3 Obi-Wan Kenobi General Grievous tattoo [PCT003] 7.00
__ #4 Yoda Asajj Ventress tattoo [PCT004]...........7.00
__ #5 General Grievous Yoda tattoo [PCT005] 7.00
__ #6 Cad Bane Commander Cody tattoo [PCT006] 7.00
__ #7 Commander Cody Obi-Wan Kenobi tattoo [PCT007] 7.00
__ #8 Mace Windu Captain Rex tattoo [PCT008]..7.00
__ #9 Asajj Ventress Mace Windu tattoo [PCT009] 7.00

Jedi Force Returns ... In a Smaller Scale

2011 saw the end of the two inch line of Hasbro's Galactic Heroes; the big-handed figures designed for a younger audience. (They also found themselves endeared to collectors of all ages, thanks to their adorable appearance.)

The name "Jedi Force" was recycled from a discontinued series of six inch figures produced in 2004-2005. The 2011 line took the form of three-inch figures and unlike the original series, the new releases feature characters from the *Clone Wars* cartoon along with classic film favorites.

Also marketed under Playskool Heroes, the semi-articulated toys are available in the popular 2-pack format, packaged as a single with a vehicle, or deluxe vehicles offer multiple figures packed in with them.

The first wave was hero-heavy, offering only Darth Vader and a Stormtrooper as intergalactic adversaries. (If Anakin and Jar Jar pursue Darth Vader for justice, will space / time become consumed by the paradox, or will that just be one more little twist in the Expanded Universe? Put a set of these into a young child's hands and watch quietly. The answer is certain to be revealed!)

Figures: Jedi Force

Hasbro

Wave 1. 2-packs.
___ Anakin Skywalker / Jar Jar Binks [P2A001]......8.00
___ C-3PO / R2-D2 [P2A002]................................8.00
___ Darth Vader / Stormtrooper [P2A003] 8.00
___ Han Solo / Chewbacca [P2A004] 8.00
___ Obi-Wan Kenobi / Clone Commander Cody
[P2A005]..8.00
___ Yoda / Luke Skywalker [P2A006] 8.00

Wave 1. Deluxe vehicles, include 2 figures.
___ Anakin's Starfighter with Anakin Skywalker and
R2-D2 [P2A007]..20.00
___ Millennium Falcon with Han Solo and
Chewbacca..35.00
___ Snowspeeder with Luke Skywalker and Han Solo
[P2A008] 20.00

Wave 1. Vehicles, includes 1 figure.
___ BARC Speeder Bike with Anakin Skywalker
[P2A009] 14.00
___ Freeco Bike with Obi-Wan Kenobi
[P2A010] 14.00
___ Landspeeder with Luke Skywalker
[P2A011] 14.00

P2A001 front

P2A001 back

P2A002

P2A003

P2A004

P2A005

P2A006

P2A007

P2A008

P2A009

P2A010

P2A011

65 Metal Slingers Medallions And The Games You Can Play With Them

A retractable / yo-yo'ish ball with a magnetic play surface, and sixty-five character points discs combine into one of the most unique and collectible *Star Wars* games available today!

Whether you're destined to become a master player or you simply enjoy the thrill of having another medium to collect, these two inch metal discs are just what you've been looking for.

The starter packs come with one slinger (the play module), three medallions, and game play instructions. The power packs have ten medallions. Booster packs are blind packed with five random discs and instructions for one of several mini-game ideas.

Discs 1-49 are Battle Medallions, 50-57 are Silver Power Medallions, and 58-65 are Gold Battle Medallions.

The colored edges of each of the slinger coins represents the level of difficulty for acquiring that particular piece in the system of blind packing the set.

Yellow is the most common, blue are uncommon, green are rare, and red are super rare. Power ups are less common than battle medallions so the red edged gold power ups are the least likely to be in any given package.

Even with the easily identifiable scarcity scale, the value of the slingers has little to no difference from medallion to medallion. They are all distributed in New Zealand, Australia, and France so to collect a set for play or display may require making new friends in a land far, far away.

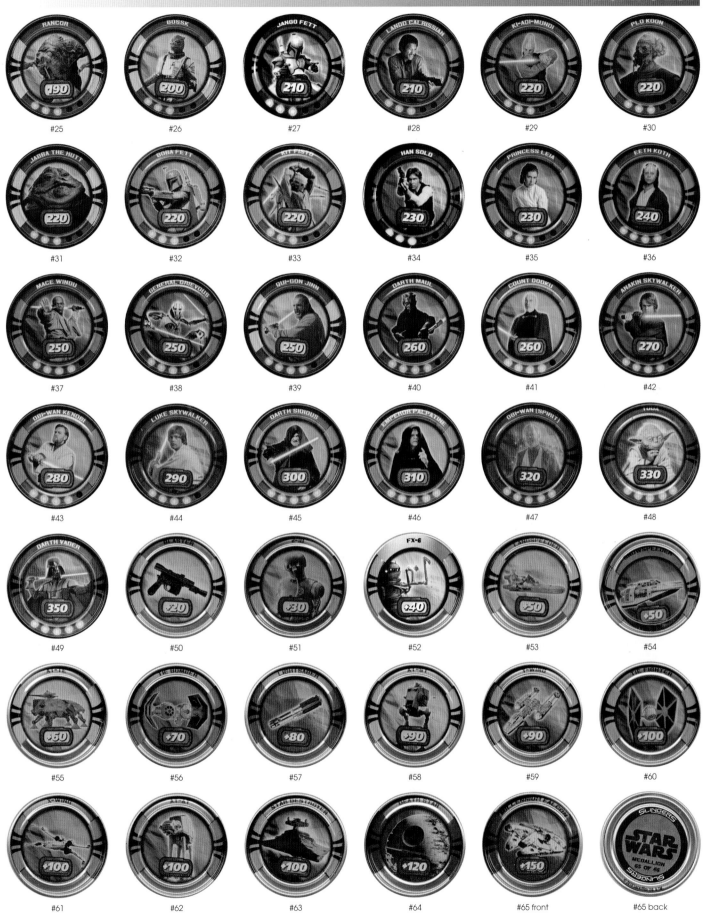

#25   #26   #27   #28   #29   #30

#31   #32   #33   #34   #35   #36

#37   #38   #39   #40   #41   #42

#43   #44   #45   #46   #47   #48

#49   #50   #51   #52   #53   #54

#55   #56   #57   #58   #59   #60

#61   #62   #63   #64   #65 front   #65 back

Topps Dog Tags, Series Two

Topps, who arguably produced the first ever of the blind-packed Star Wars collectibles with their trading card sets in 1977, have added more varieties of goods for searching, trading, and collecting.

In 2010 Topps introduced a set of 24 collectible dog tags, with images from the popular *Clone Wars* cartoon series.

2011 has seen the return of dog tags, blind packed in foil and accompanied with a matching trading card and a pictorial checklist.

The 24 tags have standardized green, red, or blue backgrounds. Every one of the characters are also available on collectible chase tags. The chase tags have an identical photo image but feature a multi-colored background. Combining trading cards with the new aspect of dog tags is helping to break Topps into new collecting communities.

#01 #02 #03 #04 #05 #06 #07 #08

#09 #10 #11 #12 #13 #14 #15 #16

#17 #17 variation #18 #19 variation #20 #21 #22 #23 #24

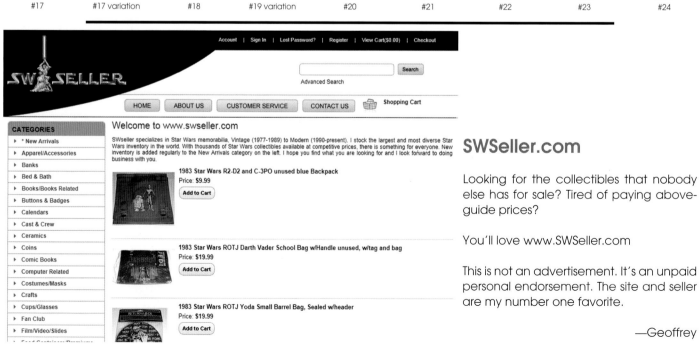

SWSeller.com

Looking for the collectibles that nobody else has for sale? Tired of paying above-guide prices?

You'll love www.SWSeller.com

This is not an advertisement. It's an unpaid personal endorsement. The site and seller are my number one favorite.

—Geoffrey

A Treasure Like No Other

By Geoffrey T. Carlton

It could be that there are thousands of these around the world. Perhaps you have one. Personally, I lost mine. And to tell you the truth, mine wasn't really that impressive. This one though, this one is my grimoire.

Back before eBay was the well prowled suburban hub that it is today, some rather exquisite items would turn up every now and again. This scrapbook was auctioned with a very humble starting bid and closed with only three of us vying for the privilege of getting to ponder its contents. Our only clue from the auction was that it had been acquired during a larger estate sale purchase in 1996 and that it had "genuine Star Wars content." (As if there could be any other?)

The inside front cover provided a hint to the style throughout. A set of Kellogg breakfast cereal stickers, some craft stickers, and a cut-out from a glossy magazine introduced materials of choice. Continuing to thumb through the pages, more memorabilia appeared as makeshift scrapbook fodder, such as the TIE Fighter paper reinforcer seen below.

Whomever created this book, for which I had become the responsible caretaker, had access to resources many kids in America only dreamed of. Photographs from press packets are sprinkled throughout, mixed in with magazine articles, newspaper advertisements, entire poster magazines (original side shown on one page and a photocopy of the back on the other page, since it was unviewable when taped down to a scrapbook page.)

As with the rest of us at the time, the young archivist was searching for answers, documenting the trail of rumors and theory behind the workings of the galaxy, and what may lie ahead for the heroes of the trilogy.

Mid-way through the tome is a mile-marker of historical significance. A ticket stub to the

Sybil Danning plays the evil witch that seduces the good Anakin to the evil side of the force.

Plitt Cagnegie Theatre for the March 28, 1985, "First Time in America" complete, uncut showing of the *Star Wars* trilogy

The event was only held at nine theaters in the USA, and this lucky fan actually got to go! Accompanying the ticket stub is a snapshot of the theater's marquis declaring, "Star Wars trilogy in 70mm"

I have great respect for and am grateful to the person who left this scrapbook behind. Through the innocence of the

moment, he/she captured magic from a time of wonder and left a reminder of the rich childhood many of us collectors have to share.

Paper Crafts with Creative Images

Scrapbooking Made Easy

Just as people no longer accept the picture quality of VHS cassettes as adequate now that blu-ray DVDs have taken over the market, those who want to create visually rich scrapbooks to chronicle their *Star Wars* memories have turned to modern materials.

Acid free archive quality pages and decor assure that the scrapbooks you put together will all remain outstanding through the progression of time.

Creative Imaginations, LLC. is officially licensed to produce *Star Wars / Clone Wars* scrapbooks and related supplies. (See their article "Star Wars Memories" by Sonia Mara Adame, "Use The Force" book craft, and "Star Wars Gift Card Holder" construction craft in the previous edition, pages 457-459.)

Their catalog of products is diverse enough to please any collector and their price point is so low you can't help but want to try your hand at scrapbooking and paper crafts.

Very few Star Wars licensees start their retail prices for as low as $1.50!

Their paper, chipboard, and epoxy sticker goods offer a combination of familiar images and framing-quality original art. You may use a traditional scrapbook, or choose one of their albums or themed mini book kits to get started.

We've classified their products into the categories: Scrap-booking Supplies, Scrapbooks, Stickers, and Transfers.

Creative Imaginations scrapbooking and paper crafting supplies can be found at local craft and hobby stores. A number of items are available for purchase directly from their website.

http://www.creativeimaginations.us

Sound like fun, but not sure where to begin? The forums at their website, under "Gallery" are filled with creative ideas to get you started quickly and provide support as you explore.

SBC001

SBC002

SBC003

SBC004

SBC005

SBC006 side 1 and side 2

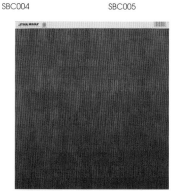
SBC007 side 1 and side 2

SBC008 side 1 and side 2

SBC009 side 1 and side 2

SBC010 side 1 and side 2   SBC011 side 1 and side 2

 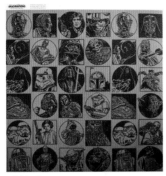  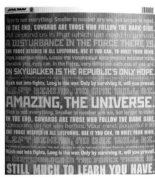

SBC012 side 1 and side 2   SBC013 side 1 and side 2

Scrapbooking Supplies

__ Scrapbook Paper Kit 4 double sided papers, 4 specialty foil papers [SBC001].......................18.00

Chipboard shapes
__ Classic Trilogy 2 sheets - 23 pieces [SBC002].6.00
__ Clone Wars 2 sheets - 23 pieces [SBC003]......6.00

Die cut shapes, 14 pieces.
__ Star Wars [SBC004].................................3.00
__ The Clone Wars [SBC005].................................3.00

__ Blueprints [SBC006] 1.50
__ C-3PO [SBC007]...1.50
__ Clone Wars icons [SBC008] 1.50
__ Clones [SBC009] 1.50
__ Darth Vader [SBC010] 1.50
__ Honor Valor [SBC011]....................................1.50
__ R2-D2 [SBC012] 1.50
__ Yoda [SBC013] 1.50

Paper, die-cut, 12"x12".
__ Black Armor [SBC014]....................................3.00
__ Stormtrooper [SBC015] 3.00
__ The Clone Wars [SBC016] 3.00

Paper, specialty foil.
__ 30th Anniversary [SBC017]..............................5.00
__ Clones [SBC018] 3.00
__ Darth Vader [SBC019] 3.00
__ ESB Crawl [SBC020] 5.00
__ Honor Valor [SBC021]....................................3.00
__ Hoth [SBC022]...5.00
__ Millennium Falcon [SBC023]...........................3.00
__ Star Wars Logo [SBC024]...............................3.00
__ Target [SBC025]...3.00
__ Use The Force [SBC026] 3.00
__ Yoda [SBC027] 5.00

SBC014   SBC015   SBC016   SBC017

SBC018   SBC019   SBC020   SBC021

Paper Crafts with Creative Images

SBC022

SBC023

SBC024

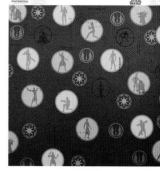

SBC025

SBC026

SBC027

SBC028

SBC029

__ Yoda Rocks! [SBC028] 3.00

Scrapbook kits. 8 double-sided papers, 12"x12" cardboard sticker, epoxy sticker.
__ Clone Wars [SBC029] 18.00
__ Star Wars [SBC030] 18.00

Scrapbooks

8x8 instant album. 20 predesigned scrapbook pages.
__ Classic [SCB001] 12.00
__ Clone Wars [SCB002] 12.00

Chipboard albums.
__ Death Star [SCB003] 9.00
__ Jedi [SCB004] 9.00

Mini book kit. 1 mini book, 8 papers, 1 chipboard sticker, 1 cardstock sticker, 1 epoxy sticker.
__ Clone Wars [SCB005] 17.00
__ Star Wars [SCB006] 17.00

Souvenir albums.
__ Darth Vader [SCB007] 10.00
__ Yoda [SCB008] 10.00

Stickers

Cardstock sticker sheets.
__ Star Wars [SV001] 4.00
__ The Clone Wars [SV002] 4.00

Chipboard sticker sheets.
__ Clone Wars [SV003] 4.00
__ Empire Strikes Back foil [SV004] 4.00
__ Star Wars [SV005] 4.00

Chipboard stickers.

SBC030

SCB001

SCB002

SCB003

SCB004

SCB005

SCB006

SCB007

SCB008

SV001

SV002

SV003

SV004

SV005

SV006

SV007

SV008

SV009

SV010

SV011

SV012

__ Clone Wars [SV006]...3.00
__ Star Wars [SV007]...3.00
__ The Empire Strikes Back [SV008].....................3.00

Epoxy sticker sheets.
__ Star Wars Icons [SV009].................................4.00
__ Star Wars Phrase [SV010] 4.00
__ The Clone Wars Icons [SV011]......................4.00
__ The Clone Wars Phrases [SV012].....................4.00

Layered sticker sheets.
__ Clone Wars [SV013]..4.00
__ Star Wars [SV014]...4.00

Scrapbook stickers, 12"x12" sheet.
__ Clone Wars [SV015]...4.00
__ Star Wars [SV016]..4.00

Sticker sheets.
__ Clone Trooper [SV017] 2.00
__ CW Logo [SV018] 2.00
__ ESB [SV019]..2.00
__ Han Solo [SV020]...2.00
__ Heroes [SV021]..2.00
__ Luke Skywalker [SV022]...................................2.00
__ Silhouettes [SV023]...2.00

__ Stormtrooper [SV024]......................................2.00
__ Stormtrooper [SV025]......................................2.00
__ SW Logo [SV026]..2.00
__ The Dark Side [SV027]......................................2.00
__ Yoda [SV028] 2.00

Transfers

4 rub down sheets.
__ Clone Wars [CRT001].......................................5.00
__ Star Wars [CRT002]..5.00

SV013

SV014

SV015

SV016

SV017 SV018 SV019

SV020

SV021

SV022

SV023

SV024

SV020 SV021 SV022 SV023 SV024 SV025 SV026 SV027 SV028 CRT001 CRT002

Momentous Discoveries
From A Micro Universe

by Jad Bean

Star Wars fans have known for years that Galoob's Micro Machines offer an affordable, diverse, and space-saving toy collection. Galoob produced hundreds upon hundreds of small yet incredibly detailed and interactive *Star Wars* toys spanning the Original Trilogy and Episode 1. Hasbro acquired Galoob in the late 1990s and has continued to release Micro Machines-scale toys under the Galoob banner, most recently in the long-running die-cast Titanium line.

While there are unfortunately no new Micro Machines toys on the horizon, collectors are currently discovering a wealth of new information about the classic Galoob toys. On my website, *StarWarsMicroMachines.wordpress.com*, you can find an ever-growing collection of photos of toy prototypes, preliminary packaging, and interviews with several people who contributed to the Star Wars Micro Machines universe.

Preliminary packaging designs provide a fascinating glimpse into the production process of the toys we love. Sometimes packaging mock-ups are carefully made to reflect the look of the final product, and sometimes they are cobbled together with whatever material is readily available. The Mini Action Transforming Playset VII packaging mockup pictured here was assembled with a spare Micro Machines Military cardback. The toys inside also have a different paint scheme than the final production versions. This set was only sold in Europe, making this an exceptionally rare find.

Packaging mockup for Mini-Action Transforming Playset VII

For all the hundreds of characters that Galoob produced, there will always be some that completist-minded collectors wish had been immortalized in plastic. A popular option for customizers is to take existing figures and repaint them to create new characters. One fan has started creating completely new Micro Machines-scale figures. Brian Webb is a talented artist and passionate Star Wars Galoob fan who contacted me after reading my website. He shared with me his desire to produce custom Micro Machines figures of the characters that should have been made but never were.

Brian's first figure, Lobot, was chosen for two reasons. First, a Lobot figure was originally planned for but not included in the Darth Vader Transforming Action Set. Second, the Star Wars Celebration V convention was eight months away, which would be the perfect avenue for a free giveaway. And since the theme of the convention was the 30th anniversary of *The Empire Strikes Back*, Lobot was the natural choice!

Using a variety of tiny sculpting tools, he meticulously refined his Lobot figure sculpt from modeler's clay. Brian then created a silicone mold of the master, from which he made multiple resin casts. Each resin figure was painstakingly hand-painted and placed in customized packaging which he designed to replicate the look of the original Galoob toys.

Brian unfortunately couldn't attend Celebration V to help me distribute his Lobot figures. Working together, we devised a system to give away the Lobot figures. Readers of my site knew that they would need to find me wearing my special Galoob t-shirt and speak the secret phrase, "Think Big, Play Small!" to receive a free Lobot figure. The giveaway was a fantastic success! Not only did several fans get to take home our "underground exclusive," but because of the contacts I made with fellow Galoob fans, I discovered and shared new pictures of unproduced Galoob toys on my site.

Brian and I remain committed to giving away his custom figures absolutely free to Galoob fans who would like one. At the time of this writing, Brian's second figure, the classic Cantina alien Hammerhead, is nearly finished. The next figure will come from *Return of the Jedi* and will be determined by readers through a poll on the site. Due to the amount of work that goes into each figure, the production runs are very small; only a few dozen of each figure are usually made. So for a chance to get yours, be sure to check the site frequently as the window of opportunity doesn't last long!

Brian Webb's custom Lobot and Hammerhead Micro Machines-scale figures are miniature works of art that in many ways surpass the work of Galoob's talented sculptors.

Resourceful Galoob fans are always discovering new treasures from the glory days of the late '90s. By reaching out to former Galoob employees, a wealth of new information has been discovered about our favorite Star Wars toy line. A special thanks goes to Jim Fong, who has generously provided several photos and information for this article. Jim was a Galoob employee who was instrumental in the design and direction of the Star Wars toy lines. Jim even managed to get himself into a few toys! His face appears in a sticker in the R2-D2 Transforming Action Set, and he recorded a line of dialogue for the X-Wing Action Fleet Flight Controller toy—though he's forgotten which one!

Galoob designer Jim Fong included his own face on a sticker in the R2-D2 Transforming Action Set.

The Micro Machines line of vehicles, playsets, and figures offered fans an entire universe of play scenarios, with two notable exceptions: the figures weren't poseable, and the accompanying vehicles were wildly out of scale and too small for the figures. Recognizing this, the Galoob team designed a completely new scale for adventure, Action Fleet. In this new assortment, the vehicles would be produced at the same six inch size, and each would include two figures with movable legs and arms. From this simple recipe, Galoob successfully expanded the Action Fleet line to include creatures, figure packs, three massive playsets, international exclusives, sets with lights and sounds, and nearly every Original Trilogy vehicle imaginable. Thanks to the generosity of Jim Fong and other former Galoob employees, new information about the fan-favorite Action Fleet line continues to be revealed.

Rare variants exist of the first seven Action Fleet toys. The first 5,000 of each ship included a limited edition, numbered sticker on the inside of the bubble. This picture is a close up of the KB Toys exclusive Landspeeder and AT-ST set.

Most fans know that Ralph McQuarrie, the original Star Wars concept artist, created new paintings for the three Action Fleet playsets and the Micro Machines Double Takes Death Star. These fantastic works were so beloved by the Galoob design team, they incorporated the artwork onto the actual playsets. High-quality art prints of these works were available as limited edition exclusives in the late '90s. At an edition run of only 1,500 each, assembling a set of all four is a challenging goal.

In addition to the four well-known paintings, Ralph also painted the artwork for the X-Wing and Darth Vader's TIE Fighter Action Fleet Flight Controller sets. These paintings were never released as art prints, however the artwork did appear on a variety of in-store display signs at Wal-Mart and other retail outlets. The Flight Controllers line continued with a TIE Interceptor and Y-Wing; the cover art for those boxes was painted by Marc Gabanna.

One of the few surviving pictures of Galoob's original Action Fleet proposal, presented to Lucas Licensing. Ships are all built from scratch. Photo provided by Jim Fong.

The Action Fleet Flight Controllers line expanded the action with lights, sounds, and firing missiles. Some of the lines of dialogue were recorded by Galoob employees.

Ralph McQuarrie's artwork for Galoob is best enjoyed in these art prints, each limited to an edition size of only 1,500.

Action Fleet Battle Pack 4, known also as "Imperial Hunters," featured a collection of familiar bounty hunters and a Sandtrooper figure sitting atop a dewback. Galoob's designers started with reference photography of the 1970s version of the dewback, which was realized as a large rubber puppet. For new scenes in the 1997 Special Edition of A New Hope, the dewback was redesigned and appeared as a computer-generated beast of burden. Battle Pack 4 was briefly delayed while Galoob updated the toy. The original catalog photography, which included the old dewback model, continued to appear on packaging and on Galoob's website long after the updated version was on store shelves.

This screencap from the original Galoob.com website shows Action Fleet Battle Pack 4 with the earlier dewback design.

A rare injection-molded plastic copy of the original Action Fleet dewback. Photo provided by Jim Fong.

It's well known that Lucasfilm artists created dozens of preliminary designs before finalizing the look of a vehicle. While the Star Wars universe is vast, there comes a point where virtually every major vehicle has been produced as a toy. Galoob expanded the Action Fleet assortment by creating the Series Alpha line. These sets paired a recognizable vehicle with a smaller version of that vehicle's earlier concept design. With Series Alpha, collectors were able to have toy versions of early concept designs for the X-Wing, AT-AT, Cloud Car, B-Wing, Snowspeeder, Y-Wing, and Imperial Shuttle.

The name Joe Johnston should be familiar to all Star Wars fans. Before directing such films as Jurassic Park III and Captain America: The First Avenger, he worked as a concept artist and art director on the Original Trilogy films. Joe's early AT-ST design was almost made as an Action Fleet vehicle. Presented here are two views of the toy prototype of his design. Certainly every Star Wars fan would have wanted to add this menacing Scout Walker to their Imperial ranks.

The Joe Johnston AT-ST would have featured an opening hatch in the front, allowing figures to fit inside. Photo provided by Jim Fong.

The Action Fleet vehicles from the mid-1990s have proven so popular and well designed that several of them were produced in die-cast metal versions for Hasbro's Titanium Ultra line, released over ten years after the originals were on shelves.

Action Fleet toys continue to be popular collectibles in today's market. Many fans would love to see Hasbro bring back Action Fleet, especially considering the variety of Prequel and Clone Wars vehicles that could be produced at an affordable and collectible price point.

Collectors and fans are gaining a new appreciation for the artistry, clever design elements, and detailed sculpting found in Micro Machines toys. Many original toy designers are sharing their fascinating pictures and stories from working at Galoob.

Talented fans are creating all-new custom collectibles as an expression of their love for the ever-expanding Micro Machines universe. There has never been a better time to enjoy Star Wars Micro Machines!

This Action-Fleet-scale prototype of Joe Johnston's early AT-ST concept, seen here from the rear, never made it to production. Photo provided by Jim Fong.

The collecting, studying, and celebrating of Galoob's Star Wars line of Micro Machines can be enjoyed at Jad Bean's website: http://starwarsmicromachines.com

Vintage Variation: Blue Snaggletooth

By Geoffrey T. Carlton

The story of Blue Snaggletooth has become a better documented phenomenon of Star Wars collecting. In 1978 Kenner produced the character Snaggletooth based upon a black-and-white production still. With no other references, the action figure they created, to be packaged with the Sears exclusive Cantina, had a blue jumpsuit, silver boots, and was of the average height of a stormtrooper.

When Kenner became aware of Snaggletooth's actual appearance, he was corrected to be short with a red jumpsuit and furry feet like a beast. At that time remaining Sears Cantinas received the corrected figure, and he was produced on his own cardback for individual sale.

For the everyday collector, that's the end of the tale. But for those in the know, that's only the first half.

A production error is what you get when a production process experiences a temporary failure. Misapplied paint schemes and incorrect packaging are common examples.

To be a true "variation," dozens to hundreds of examples of the flaw, condition, or design must exist. In the case of Blue Snaggletooth, there is a variation in the molding of the figure. At some time during production a small piece of debris found its way into the action figure's mold, giving Blue Snaggletooth's right boot a dented toe!

It's been successfully argued both ways about whether dented toe Blue Snaggletooth is more or less common, and whether he's worth more or less money to collectors. An informal study of eBay auctions shows an average of 3:2 undented boots to dented boots, with virtually no difference in their values when overall condition of the figure is considered.

Do you already own a Blue Snaggletooth? Put down the book and go and check out his right boot! Then call your collecting buddies and challenge them to a round of "Blue Snag Trivia."

Dented toe / boot Blue Snaggletooth sampled from the collection of Warren R. Jacobsen.

The Cup Collection Is Always Half Full

by Warren R. Jacobsen

I love collecting, especially Star Wars. There is nothing like the hunt for an item that you've set your sights on, and the satisfaction of finally adding a prized item to your collection.

Maybe we are all bounty hunters at heart. After 25 years of collecting, it's hard to get too excited about Hasbro's 73rd Luke figure, or the latest Star Wars toilet brush that has the same canned art that all of this year's licensees are using on their products.

What I can always count on to keep me interested is vintage collectibles. I grew up playing with Kenner action figures, carrying a metal Star Wars lunch box to school with me every day, and having cookies and milk out of Burger King Empire Strikes Back glasses. Whether it's the great artwork and packaging, the childhood memories, or just the retro feel of the items that say "1977," the entire vintage era of collectibles just screams of fun.

My latest quest has been to learn everything I can about vintage Star Wars plastic cups. Three different series of plastic cups were produced for the first Star Wars movie, and were available at convenience stores, free with the purchase of a 39 cent frozen drink. Some may have also been purchased at movie theaters. They were available from 1977-1979, with a fourth series made for Return of the Jedi in 1983. I never had any of these cups as a child. The first time I saw them in a collecting guide, I remember thinking, "I gotta collect those!" With the advent of eBay, I was finally able to buy some for myself. Each series features its own unique style of colorful artwork that you won't find on any other Star Wars collectible. My quest to collect and learn about these cups has proven quite challenging, as every time I turn around, there is a new or different variation to catalog and hunt.

The first series of Star Wars cups consists of 20 numbered cups, each featuring scenes from the movie. A paragraph on the back of the cup describes the characters and events

shown, sometimes elaborating on the qualities and motives of the characters. For example, on the Jawa cup, the little scavengers are described in great detail, going so far as to comment on their odor. "Their horrible smell attracts small insects to the dark recesses where their nostrils and mouth should be." With a description like that, you can imagine actually being on Tatooine!

The basic set of 20 cups is challenging enough to collect. The cups from all series are thin and fragile, prone to cracking. The images can wear off from excessive use or harsh storage conditions. In addition, the cups are subject to yellowing, the result of exposure to heat and sunlight. Then there are the variations. The first series has four different backs, reflecting the chain of stores where the cups were sold. All cups say "A Limited Collector's Edition From - The Coca-Cola Company." The first variation says exactly that, with no other logos. A second variation adds the name Koolee, which was a popular type of frozen drink at the time. A third version has the Koolee name, and the logo for Li'l General Stores. The fourth version has the Koolee name and the logo for Shop & Go, yet another convenience store chain. With the variations, your basic set of 20 cups has expanded to a complete set of 80.

The second series is just as challenging. It consists of 8 numbered cups, again featuring colorful artwork on the front and descriptive text on the back. The artwork of series two leans more towards character portraits, unlike the movie scenes of series one. A distinguishing feature of the series two cups is the presence of the Star Wars logo on the front of the cup, and the thin trapezoidal border framing the artwork.

Series two also has four cup variations, including two sizes of cups. The first variation is the small cup, measuring 3.25 inches across the top, and 2.25 inches across the bottom.

These small cups have only "The Coca-Cola Company" logo on the back, and the descriptive paragraph is placed higher on the cup due to its smaller size. The other three variations are all larger cups, measuring 3.5 inches across the top and 2.5 inches across the bottom. The text on these large cups is placed lower, centered between top and bottom. All three feature the Coca-Cola logo. The second cup style has no additional logos. The third variation adds the 7-Eleven Food Stores name, while the fourth variation instead says Majik Markets. If you just want a set of the different artwork, you need only find 8 cups. You'll need 16 different cups if you want all the artwork in both sizes, and for the completist, you'd better just buy all 32 variations.

But wait... there's more. Thick, straight cups featuring artwork from four of the series two cups were also available in Australia and New Zealand, from fast food chains like Kentucky Fried Chicken or Georgie Pie. The line art on these cups is thicker and less detailed, and there is no descriptive text on the back. They are also shorter than domestic cups, measuring only 12cm high, and have "Coke adds life" embossed on the bottom. Cups in this set include Darth Vader, the Droids, Han and Chewie, and the X-Wing/TIE Dogfight. In total that makes 36 variations for series two.

Series three gives collectors a much needed break. This set, released in 1979, consists of only 8 unnumbered cups, with no known variations. The cups in series three feature large black and white portraits of Star Wars characters, over a background of colorful stripes circling the cup. Secondary images are on either side of the portrait, showcasing vehicles, action poses, or background characters like the Cantina Band. The back of the cups still feature descriptive text and a small Coca-Cola company logo, but no store logos are associated with this series.

It would be four years before Star Wars convenience store cups would return, this time for Return of the Jedi. This series has 12 unnumbered cups, each featuring full color illustrations on both sides of the cup. The artwork on these cups seems to be taken straight from movie stills, and focuses on the many colorful background characters and settings. The Return of the Jedi series has proven most difficult for me to catalog and track down all the variations.

The basic domestic set consists of the 12 different cups, featuring a 7-Eleven logo on one side and "Coke is it!" on the other. Among this basic set, there is a variation to the bottom of the cup that only the most hardcore collectors will seek. The bottoms of these cups say Styroware, and have the Canada Cup name and logo. One version has a large font Styroware name, and has the Canada Cup logo centered beneath the text. The other version has a completely different, smaller font Styroware, and has the Canada Cup logo to the left of the text. This variation has been documented on cups featuring identical artwork, bringing the domestic set up to

24 cups.

To make things more complicated, the domestic set was also reportedly available in two different sizes. International cups were reportedly available in Puerto Rico at Kentucky Fried Chicken restaurants, and would likely not have a 7-Eleven logo on them. In addition, some cups (possibly the Puerto Rico cups) are known to have a Frozen Coke logo on them instead of "7-Eleven." So, a complete Return of the Jedi

set could have 48 cups or more to collect. Half the fun is discovering what else is out there.

Whether you're after a basic set of 48 cups, or a complete set of 172 or more, Star Wars cups have something to offer to every collector. If you've been bitten by the cup bug, there are other vintage plastic cups out there. For Star Wars, there are C-3PO & R2-D2 and Darth Vader cups from Grubee's stores in Canada. These cups are dated 1977, and feature watercolor style artwork on the front. On the back is descriptive text above

Grubee's and Coca-Cola logos. McDonald's in Japan offered a trio of Star Wars cups, showcasing photos of C-3PO & R2-D2, Darth Vader, and Luke & Leia.

The Empire Strikes Back had a set of three cups, found at McDonald's in Australia. These three cups featured comic style line art, with depictions of heroes, villains, or vehicles and droids.

In the United States, you could also purchase cups and pitchers at movie theaters during the 1982 re-release of Empire Strikes Back. These cups had the Star Wars name and artwork on one side, and The Empire Strikes Back name and characters on the

other. The theater cups are about the same size as the final two series of Star Wars cups. The matching pitcher measures eight inches tall.

Return of the Jedi offered more movie theater cups and pitchers in the same style. This time the cup was larger, measuring seven inches tall. The artwork wrapped around the cup, and prominently featured a light saber duel between Darth Vader

and Luke Skywalker. Other images on the cup include Jabba the Hutt and a slightly less revealing slave Leia, wearing a halter top, instead of a metal bikini. A similarly shaped and colored cup, with different artwork was available in Australia. It depicted numerous Star Wars characters around the cup, in addition to a

large Coca-Cola logo.

Last, but not least, Pepperidge Farm made a set of 5 small cups. The green Wicket, R2-D2 & C-3PO cup was available in stores, free with the purchase of one box of Pepperidge Farm Star Wars cookies. The other four cups, illustrating creatures, rebels, vehicles, and villains could be mailed away for. These are the smallest of the plastic cups, standing only four inches tall.

The lasting appeal of Star Wars cup collecting for me is the great artwork. You won't find any modern collectibles that look this cool. I'll be happy when I've tracked down a nice basic set of 48 convenience store cups. The collector in me, though, is fascinated by all the obscure variations and international offerings, and it will keep me busy for years, hunting them all.

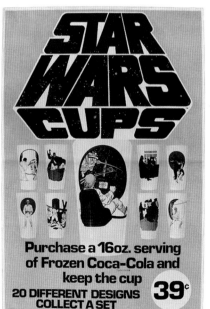

"All photography of original cups, posters, and hanging cup mobile in this article owned by Mrs. Miniver on eBay" Used with written permission and special thanks! Check out her eBay store for more incredibly rare Star Wars merchandise posters.

1977 – 1984 Australia / New Zealand Star Wars Cards

By Paul Holstein
Scans from the collection of Paul Holstein
Contact: paul@jamesbondcards.com

As a follow-up to the article in the last edition (1977 Japanese Star Wars Cards) my first thought was Latin America. I love the set from Costa Rica, and I consider the first set from Argentina to be the single hardest vintage Star Wars card set to complete. As I was gathering the cards to write about, I came across my single favorite set of all time and it changed my mind to Australia and New Zealand. But let me start from the beginning.

There were two major card manufacturers in this region, Scanlens Confectionary and Allens & Regina. Allens & Regina, in New Zealand, are part of the Scanlens confectionary group in Australia. Trading cards, both sports and non-sports, were very popular in the area and both companies produced a relatively large number of sets over the years. Other notable Star Wars sets from the period, while the movies were in theatres, were by Tip Top and Kellogg's, both producing multiple highly collectable food premium sets.

One of the earliest set is the 1977 Australia set of 72 cards. These weren't as elaborate as the U.S. and Canadian sets, or even the U.K. sets made in 1977, but they were unique. This 72 card set started with the first 66 being very near to the U.S. series one set (other than the card stock), but with cards #67-72 being added with blue borders and pictures that resembled several of the U.S. Topps stickers. I have found these (cards #67-72) to be very hard to find well centered, and in good condition. Centering is a big issue and the majority of the Chewy cards have a rub across his name that partially

wipes it out . Given the number that have this defect it must be a factory defect. A complete set of these in EX should run around $100, and a NM (pack fresh) single card #67-72 would easily fetch $20. Since the base 66 are so near the U.S. set, and almost indistinguishable from the U.K. Series One set, singles aren't traded very heavily - complete sets are more popular. I talked to vintage Star Wars collector Trevor Gaylor, who has opened Scanlens packs, and he mentioned that the "high numbers" were randomly inserted in the packs in the same way that the other cards were - they were not one to each pack like the U.S. stickers. The high numbers #67-72 and the Australian wrapper, really make this set unique and collectable.

Another very early set was the 1977 New Zealand set of 72 cards. This is another unique, and very rare set. There are 72 cards that are very similar to the Scanlens set (including the "high numbers" variation). This set differs in many ways though, including the card stock having two different variations ("Tan Backs" and "White Backs"). This set also has some completely blank backs (all of the cards that normally would have had text descriptions on the back). The "White Back" cards are on a glossy stark white stock and the "Tan Backs" are on a very thick brown cardboard non-glossy stock. As with the Scanlens, these also came in packs with a unique wrapper. Although the cards are harder to find than the Scanlens, nice condition wrappers are slightly more common.

Another difficult set to track down from New Zealand is the "Tip Top R2 D2 Space Ice" 15 sticker set from 1977. These were premiums in Tip Top Ice Cream bars and they aren't numbered. They are smaller than standard U.S. cards, about the size of a Monty card. These stickers were intended to be stuck on the game board, of the Tip Top Race-In-Space game. Condition is usually tougher when the set is a food premium, but also because food premium collectors will compete with the trading card collectors for these. An average price for a NM set of 15 has been around $100.00.

In 1980 Scanlens did a follow-up set of 132 cards for The Empire Strikes Back while Allens and Regina did not. This set contains basically the same cards as the U.S. set, with the addition of "Scanlens" in the fine print on each card and "contest" information on the backs of some cards towards the end of the series. There were also stickers to compliment the cards, but they were sold in packs by themselves. This is quite different from the U.S. packs, which included cards and stickers together in the same packs. The stickers in particular are difficult to find in good condition, as most were mis-cut, the set is big (for stickers), and very few were made.

Although New Zealand did not do the standard card set, they did produce a set of 6 stickers in 1980. These were found in boxes of Twinkies, a short promotion as Twinkies were not popular in New Zealand. These were made by the company Tip Top, that also did the Star Wars "Space Ice" set a few years earlier. The stickers are not numbered and are frequently mis-cut, but aren't extremely rare and an entire set can usually be picked up for around $20-$30.

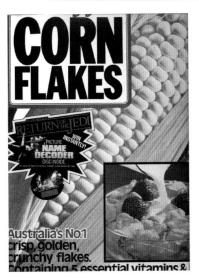

And this brings me to my all time favorite Star Wars set, the 1983 Kellogg's decoder discs from Australia. These were a set of 16 circular cards that came randomly inserted in cereal boxes (Rice Bubbles and Corn Flakes). Each card was perforated in the middle so that it had a collectable top portion and a bottom portion to be ripped off and sent in for a prize. There was a small spot to rub off to reveal a code, and the code was translated using a key on the box. I have paid upwards of $100 each to find these in mint condition, still sealed in their crimped plastic bag, untorn and unscratched. Complete cereal boxes are worth far more, due to the collectability of food premiums, and especially cereal items.

In 1983, Australia's Scanlens and New Zealand's Allens & Regina both did a Return Of The Jedi set. The Australia set had "Scanlens" prominently displayed on the front of the title and checklist cards, and also on the back of every card in the fine print. Otherwise the cards were very similar to the U.S., Canadian OPC, and New Zealand Allens & Regina sets done in the same year. One interesting fact though is that there are only three variations of the Scanlens wrappers (unlike the four variations for the U.S. set). I did not know that Allens & Regina had done a ROTJ set, until I was verifying a full Scanlens ROTJ set and found that they were mixed in. The checklists both say "Allens and Regina" on the front, and the rest of the cards say "Allens and Regina" on the back, but the title cards say "Scanlens" (you will not find a title card

with Allens/Regina on it). This has confused a lot of collectors in the past. The Allens & Regina wax box looks identical to the Scanlens wax box, except for the printing on one end, also saying "Scanlens." The wax wrapper is also very similar to the Scanlens wrapper, other than the manufacturer listed in the fine print.

A few more food premium sets can be found from New Zealand, including the 1983 Jedi Jelly set of four stickers and the 1983 Kellogg's set of 12 stickers. Jedi Jelly was an ice cream bar, making those quite hard to find (ice cream bars just didn't survive past the short time when they were available for purchase). The Kellogg's stickers came in a cereal bag, which contained Corn Flakes similar to the U.S. cereal. Each Kellogg's sticker has the Lucasfilm copyright, year (1983) and brand (Kellogg's Australia) right on the front, making this a really nice set. All of the backs of the stickers that I have say "DARTH VADER © Says Try again" indicating that there were also winner stickers, although I have never seen one.

Finally, the last set that I consider "vintage" from this region is the 1984 Australia Ewok Adventure set. This is a set of 32 total and the cards were part of the "Collect-A-Prize" game, which was for the Ewoks movie but showed scenes from Return of the Jedi. The cards are smaller than regular-sized trading cards, and came in Kellogg's cereal. There are 12 puzzle cards, 16 photo cards, and 3 instant win cards if you collect them all. These generally go for $5 to $10 each, although premiums are paid for the cards still in the original packaging and the short-printed cards.

Simple Tricks and Nonsense –
Star Wars Collecting in the eBay Era

By Cole "JediCole" Houston

If patience is a virtue then the virtuous Star Wars collector is the one who finds everything they seek at the best possible price.

Star Wars collecting, for me, began in 1977 when there was precious little to collect. More accurately my collection began in earnest in 1978, though it was kicked off by Kenner's Early Bird Set the previous year. This was of course a period when resources for collectors were limited at best. Magazines, guidebooks, and the Internet were still years to decades in the future. Back then a list of the phone numbers of every local retailer who stocked Star Wars toys was my number one tool of the trade.

At the risk of sounding like a bitter old grandpa I will say that collectors today have it so much easier. The wealth of information about and access to Star Wars collectibles is matched only by the volume of collectibles available. Collecting magazines and price guides, like this one, are readily available, as well as numerous websites. Online retailers and eBay bring a world of collectibles in front of you if there are no shops specializing in collectible in your area. Depending on where you live there may even be conventions and swap meets where you can pick up the rare finds. I am certainly appreciative of all that we, as collectors, have at our disposal today. It is how we utilize these resources that determines how much of a financial blow we take as we pursue those elusive holes in our collections.

As I pointed out at the beginning of this article, patience is your greatest ally in contemporary collecting. In this day and age with instant access to collectibles at any hour of the day or night, it is easy to pounce on the first available example of something you are seeking. Sure you pay a

premium price but that is what one must expect when making an after-market purchase, right? Well that really all depends on how willing you are to simply wait for the best opportunity to buy. If you have to have it now then you can expect to pay a higher price for that convenience. If you wait you will save money that can be funneled into even more great collectibles!

Simple Tricks

As the volume of available Star Wars collectibles increases each year it becomes harder and harder to keep up with every release. By way of example I will explore toys and statuary with anecdotes from my personal collecting experience. I am fortunate to live in an area rich with conventions and other venues for collectors throughout the course of the year. With that resource at my disposal I have been able to fill in numerous blanks in my collection in the last two years at great prices. The Concept Art Anakin Skywalker action figure was a good example of this pursuit. Repeatedly I had been outbid on eBay for this figure, which I never saw on store pegs. Loose or carded it would always exceed the price I was willing to pay, even for a rare item. I did finally stumble upon one at a convention for less than twice the original retail price, not bad for something that could not be had online for under $25.

In a similar fashion, I utilized convention finds to fill in the last blanks of my Star Wars Action Fleet collection. Darth Maul's Sith Infiltrator routinely sells for over $100, far more than I would be prepared to pay. It was just easier not to have it, no one would notice its absence but me after all. I recently purchased one of these ships, loose, at a convention for $5, along with the rare Republic Gunship, Republic Assault Ship, E-Wing Fighter, and the TIE Defender for equally low prices. Easily $200 worth of Action Fleet toys for under $25! Granted as a loose figure and toy collector, the savings I have realized are greater than they would have been if I insisted on everything being packaged. However, many items in my collection were in original packaging when I bought and later opened them. Even packaged Star Wars toys can be found at a bargain after all.

Websites like Craigslist can be excellent resources but it is rare that individuals selling through that venue are aware of what the market will bear when it comes to price. The name "Star Wars" all too often equates to multiple dollar signs in the eyes of sellers who imagine their small collection of five carded Episode 1 action figures will garner them $300. While eBay is often the bastion of high end pricing, it does still have strong potential for bargains. This is especially true if you don't mind investing in things you already have that can be resold to other collectors. I recently filled in the last blank in my collection of the Micro Machines Mini Head Playsets (4-LOM, Luke, Stormtrooper) by purchasing a lot that contained other heads I already have and playsets I did not want. Two weeks after it arrived I sold all of the unwanted Micro Machines at a garage sale for slightly more than I paid for the entire lot including shipping!

Much like purchasing in lots, buying entire collections can also serve to establish or fill in blanks of a collection quickly. The practical downside of course is the disposition of all of the extras. I would recommend against this type of purchasing on the large scale unless you have a means to recoup some of the costs and clear out the excess. Otherwise you will have quite the secondary collection on your hands. If you do not wish to become a show vendor or a long-term eBay seller, consider selling any excess from lot purchases as a single lot on eBay or Craigslist. Then put the money from that sale back into filling in even more blanks in your collection.

Nonsense

Many are the pitfalls facing collectors in the after market. The phenomenal success of Star Wars as a cultural icon has led to the name alone seeming a virtual gold mine to some. As a collector for over 30 years and a convention dealer and shop owner for over 20 I have seen the best and worst from both sides of the table.

If you shop for Star Wars collectibles of any kind at conventions, be sure to avoid the sellers who do not put pricing on their wares up front. More often than not when you inquire about pricing they whip out a guidebook as if it is a true reflection of the market. Most guides at least attempt to present an average going rate as of press time, but by publication that information is already outdated. Regardless of the accuracy of a guide's appraisal of value, these guides are not intended to be the final authority on the value or reflect a reasonable asking price. I see these types of dealers at shows with the same collectibles being offered show after show with no takers, especially since larger conventions often bring in one-time dealers looking to liquidate a collection. The important thing is to shop the room and grab what bargains you can find outright. Be sure to establish a rapport with dealers who give you a fair price. Ask if they will be at other such shows in the area.

Overpricing (or over-valuing) of the latest action figures in the Star Wars line is a practice that is not uncommon on the convention scene. Dealers will go to pains to acquire Star Wars figure waves that have not made their way into U.S. stores from suppliers in Asia. These figures they will offer at outrageous prices to the unwary buyer who "has to have it now." With few exceptions, these figures are readily available in stores nationwide within a few months. While the potential rarity is easy for a dealer to play up, time and experience have shown that it is better to hold out until retail stores receive these toys rather than pay twice as much at a show. By way of example, I was attending a convention in the Dallas area and saw the entire first wave of Episode 1 figures at one dealer's table easily six months before their release date. Later that day, I overheard someone proudly proclaiming that they had purchased the C-3PO figure from the line ... for $100! To this day, I cite this as the only time that figure would ever fetch that price. Six months later I saw no less than two dozen of them warming the pegs at a Target store.

Much to the chagrin of many Star Wars collectors, exclusivity has taken root in this genre of collectibles over the years. From Entertainment Earth's two sets of Astromech droids some years back to this year's Revenge of the Jedi Death Star Set at San Diego Comic Con, it would appear that exclusive Star Wars items will forever be a part of the collecting landscape. While this phenomenon has led many a collector to give up the chase, I advise yet again that being patient and keeping an open eye can garner even the hardest to find exclusives at a reasonable price. A good object lesson is the Jorg Sacul figure that was a Celebration II exclusive. This X-Wing Pilot figure with a George Lucas head and a Micro Machines X-Wing fighter once commanded top dollar. These days it is not uncommon to secure one for $10-15.

From One Side of This Galaxy to the Other

After thirty-three years of Star Wars collecting I have spent countless thousands of dollars purchasing everything from shampoo in a Yoda-shaped bottle to the gorgeous Attakus Oola statue. My personal collection contains vintage action figures, vehicles, and playsets that I purchased as they were released, statues and mini busts I bought during the two years that A Piece of the Action Collectibles (the business I co-owned with my wife) maintained a store, toys and collectibles from the purchase of entire collections, and even the last replica of Luke Skywalker's lightsaber an unlicensed maker was to ever produce.

With items from the collection to be found in every room of the house, I often reflect on the personal stories behind the acquisition of many pieces. Building the collection has been a long journey that took time and perseverance and continues to this day and beyond. Over the years I've made my purchases in every conceivable fashion and learned a lot about how to be an effective collector. I hope that here I have imparted some of the wisdom of my experience to my fellow collectors. While I have made the common mistakes and paid too much for things, I have also found other items in the collection at prices that offset any number of incidents of over paying. I began collecting in a time when the Internet was decades away and in that time I have constantly adapted my collecting philosophy. As collecting resources are ever-changing, we collectors should take to heart the wise words of the Jedi Master Yoda, "Patience ... patience ..."

You can read and hear even more from Cole Houston on The JediCole Universe (www.jedicole.com) and The United States of Geekdom (www.unitedstatesofgeekdom.com) websites and podcasts. A podcasting veteran and life-long collector, he has been a fixture at Texas comic, toy, and sci-fi conventions (in every capacity from attendee to vendor to emcee) for over a quarter century.

INDEX

Index

You are ready to explore Star Wars collectibles beyond the world of toys! The Star Wars Super Collector's Wish Book also has a non-toy general merchandise edition.

24,000 items with checklist-style listings, over 12,000 color photos, and accurate estimated values make the collector's guide a must-have for everybody who has ever owned merchandise produced for the Star Wars saga or who is selling or buying it now.

Items have been collected from over 50 countries and compiled together into impressive tomes from the longest running Star Wars exclusive identification guide series ever in print. Editions cover the range alphabetically from Address Books to Window Clings. From the 1976 pre-release movie paperback through the latest Clone Wars kitchenware, thirty-five years of exciting and obscure Star Wars collectibles are archived there for you to discover, marvel over, and enjoy.

Below is the list of categories covered by the non-toy edition.

Address Books
Advertising / Displays
Air Fresheners
Albums, Collecting
Answering Machines
Aprons
Arcade
__Pinball Machines
__Slot Machines
__Video Games
Armor
Art
__Animation Cels
__Crystal and Glass
__Lithography
__Metal
__Portfolios
__Prints
__Prints, ChromeArt
Autographs
Backpack Tags
Backpacks and Carry
  Bags
Badges
Bags
Bags, Gift
Bags, Nylon
Balloons
Bandages
Bank Books
Banks
Banners: Advertising
Barware
Bath Mats
Bathroom Sets
Batteries
Beachpads
Bedding
__Bed Covers
__Blankets
__Comforters
__Pillowcases
__Pillows
__Sheets
Bed Skirts
Belt Buckles
Belt Packs
Belts

Bicycle Accessories
Bicycles
Binders
Blueprints
Bobble Heads
Book Covers
Bookends
Booklists
Bookmarks
Bookplates
Books
__Activity
__Art
__Audio, Cassette
__Audio, CD
__Coloring
__Cooking
__E-Book
__Educational
__Galaxy of Fear
__Game Guides
__Graphic Novels
__Guides
__Jedi Apprentice
__Jedi Quest
__Journals, Blank
__Junior Jedi Knights
__Make Your Own
  Adventure
__Music
__Non-Fiction
__Novels
__Pop-Up / Action / Flap
__Poster
__Science Adventures
__Scripts
__Star Wars Adventures
__Story
__Technical
__Trivia
__Young Jedi Knights
__Young Reader
Bottle Cap Accessories
Bottle Caps
Bottle Openers
Bowling Ball Bags
Bowling Balls
Boxes

__Ceramic
__Plastic
__Tin
Buckets, Food
Bumper Stickers
Business Cards
Buttons
Buttons, Sewing
Cake Decorating Supplies
Cake Pans
Cakes
Calculators
Calendar Datebooks
Calendar Planners
Calendars
Calling Cards, Telephone
Cameras
Can and Bottle Holders
Candles
Candlestick Holders
Candy Covers
Candy Jars
Candy Molds
Canteens
Card Holders, Business
Cards, Trading
Cards
__24k Gold
__30th Anniversary
__501st
__Action Masters
__A New Hope
__Attack of the Clones
__Bend-Ems
__Ceramic
__Chile
__Chrome Archives
__Clone Wars
__DinaMics
__Empire Strikes Back
__Empire Strikes Back,
  Giant Photo
__Evolution
__Evolution Update
__Fanclub
__Forcecast
__French
__German

__Giant Movie Pin-Ups
__Heritage
__Italian
__Japan
__Mastervision
__Mini-Movies
__Misc.
__Movie Shots
__Parody
__Pilot Licenses
__Premiums
__Rebel Legion
__Role Playing
__Return of the Jedi
__Revenge of the Sith
__Signing
__Shadows of the Empire
__Star Wars Galaxy
  Magazine
__SW Finest
__SW Galaxy I
__SW Galaxy II
__SW Galaxy III
__SW Galaxy IV
__SW Galaxy V
__Sweden
__TCG
__TCG, Pocketmodels
__Tin
__The Phantom Menace
__TV Week
__UK
__Vehicle
__Wallet
__Widevision, 3D
__Widevision
CCG (Collectible Card
  Game)
CD Wallets
Cellular Phone
Cellular Phone
  Accessories
Cellular Phone Faceplates
Cellular Phone Straps
Cellular Phones
Centerpieces
Certificates
Chalkboards
Champagne and Wine

Checkbook Covers
Checks
Cigar Bands
Clipboards
Clippos
Clips, Snack Chip
Clocks
Clothing
__Aprons
__Bibs, Baby
__Boots
__Caps
__Earmuffs
__Gloves and Mittens
__Hats
__Jackets
__Leg Warmers
__Neckties
__Nightgowns
__Outfits, 2-Piece
__Overalls
__Pajamas
__Pants
__Ponchos
__Robes
__Scarves
__Shirts
__Shoes, Sandals, and
  Slippers
__Socks
__Suspenders
__Swimming Attire
__Undergarments
__Vests and Sweaters
__Visors
__Warm-Up Suits
__Wrist Bands
Coasters
Coin Purses
Coins
__Action Figure
__Elongated
__Geocaching
__Premiums
Collectors Box
Cologne and Perfume
Combs
Comic Books

2002

2003

2005

2007

2009

2011

__Dark Horse
__Marvel
Computers
__Cases
__Dust Covers
__Mice
__Mousepads
__Software
__USB Accessories
__USB Drives
__Wrist Rest
Condoms
Confetti
Construction Paper
Containers, Figural
Cookie Jars
Cooking Cutters
Coolers
Cork Boards
Cosmetics
Costume Accessories
Costumes
__Makeup Kits
__Masks
Coupons
Crackers
Crafts
__Art Kits
__Clip-Alongs
__Coloring Sets
__Doodle Kits
__Figure Makers
__Latchhook Kits
__Paint-By-Number
__Paintable Figures
__Poster Art Kits
__Sewing Kits
__Sun Catcher Kits
__Watercolor Paint Sets
Crayons
__"Crafts: Coloring Sets"
Credit and ATM Cards
Crowns, Paper
Cup Toppers
Cups: Disposable
Curtains
Danglers
Dartboards
Decals
Deodorant
Desktop Organizers
Diarys
Dishes
__Bowls
__Cups
__Dish Sets
__Egg Cups
__Glasses
__Glasses, Shot
__Mugs
__Pitchers
__Plates
__Steins
__Utensils
Dispensers
__Candy
__Food
__Soap / Lotion
Dog Tags
Doorknob Hangers
Drawing Instruments
Drink Holders
Drink Shakers
Earphones
Easter Egg Coloring Kits
Easter Eggs
Easter Grass
Erasers
Eyewear
__Contact Lenses

__Glasses
Fabrics
Fan Club Materials
Fans
Figures
__Ceramic
__Galactic Village
   Collection
__Metal
__Porcelain
Film
Film Frames
Fish Tanks
Fishing Accessories
Flags
Flashlights
Foam Heads
Folders
Furniture, Inflatable
Furniture
__Beds
__Bookcases
__Chairs and Sofas
__Clothes Racks
__Desks
__Nightstands
__Stools
__Tables
__Toy Chests and Storage
Game Pieces, Promotional
Gaming Controllers and
   Accessories
Gift Boxes
Gift Cards
Gift Certificates
Gift Tags
Gift Wrap
Glow In The Dark
   Decorations
Glowsticks
Glue
Gokarts
Golf Bags
Golf Ball Markers
Golf Club Covers
Goodie Bags
Greeting Cards
__Valentines, Boxed
Growth Charts
Guidemaps
Guitar Cases
Guitar Picks
Guitar Straps
Guitars
Gum Holders
Gumball Machines
Gym Sets
Hair Gel
Hairbrushes
Handbills
Handkerchiefs
Hangers
Helmets, Sports
Holiday
__Containers
__Lighting
__Ornaments
__Stockings
Holograms
Ice Skates
Inflatables
Instrument Knobs
Invitations
Ipods and Accessories
Iron-On Transfers
Jewelry
__Barrettes
__Bracelets
__Bracelets, Charm
__Cufflinks

__Earrings
__Necklaces
__Rings
Keychains
Keys, Hotel
Kites
Lamp Shades
Lamps
Lanyards
Laser Light Spinner
Laser Pointers
Laundry Bags and
   Hampers
License Plates
Lip Balm
Lotion
Lottery Scratch-Off Tickets
Lunch Boxes
Magnetic Playsets
Magnets
Matchboxes
Mats
Medallions
Media Players
__Accessories
__CD
__Digital Music
__Radio, Cassette
Media, Audio
__Cassettes
__CDs
__Records
__Tapes: 8-Track
__Tapes: Reel-to-Reel
Media, Movies
__DVDs
__Films
__Laser Discs and CEDs
__Video Cassette Storage
   Cases
__Video Cassettes
__Video Discs
Memo Boards
Memo Pads
Messengers
Milk Caps
Mirrors
Mobiles
Model Rockets
Models
__Metal
__Paper
__Plastic
__Resin
__Vinyl
__Wood / Balsa
Movie Cash Certificates
Music Boxes
Name Badges
Napkins
Nightlights
Notebooks and Tablets
Note Cards
Nut Crackers
Oil Lamps
Packaging
__Beverage
__Candy
__Cards
__Cereal
__Cheese
__Cleaners
__Cookies
__Facial Tissue
__Food Wrappers
__Fruit Snacks
__Gum
__Ice Cream
__Kids Meals
__Margarine

__Nuts
__Paper Cups
__Shoes
__Snack Chips
__Yogurt
Pads: Sports
Pails: Tin
Paint
Paper Clips
Paper Reinforcements
Paper Toweling
Paper Weights
Party
__Bags and Treat Boxes
__Banners
__Blowouts
__Decorations
__Games
__Hats
__Mazes
__Toys
Passports
Patches
Patterns
Pencil Cases / Boxes
Pencil Cups
Pencil Sharpeners
Pencil Toppers
Pencil Trays
Pencils
__"School Kits"
Pennants
Pens and Markers
Pewter
Pez Dispensers
Pez Refills
Photo Albums
Photo Frames
Piano Rolls, Player
Pinatas
Pins
Pins, Lapel
Placemats
Plate Racks
Plates
__Collector
__Paper
Play Houses
Playing Cards
Pog Slammers
Pogs
Poker Chips
Pool Toys
Pools
Popcorn Poppers
Postcards
Poster Tubes
Posters
Posters: Mini
Press Kits
Pucks
Punch-Out Activities
Purses / Carry Bags
Push Pins
Refrigerators
Remote Controls
Replicas
Rugs
Rulers
Salt Shakers
School Boxes
School Kits
Scissors
Scooters
Scrapbooking Supplies
Scrapbooks
Shades, Automobile
Sheet Music
Shoe Laces
Shoe Laces Tags

Shower Curtains
Signs
Skateboards
Skates, Roller / In-line
Slap Bands
Sleeping Bags
Snow Tubes and Sleds
Snow Globes
Soap and Body Wash
Soap Dishes
Soap
__Bubble Bath
__Shampoo
Speakers
Sponges
Sprinklers
Squeaky Toys
Stamp Collecting Kits
Stampers
Stamps, Postage
Standees
Stationary
Statues and Busts
Stencils
Stickers
__A New Hope
__Attack of the Clones
__Parody
__Premiums
__Return of the Jedi
__Revenge of the Sith
__The Phantom Menace
Straws
String Dispensers
Subway Tickets
Suitcases
Switch Plates and Covers
Table Covers
Tape Dispensers
Tattoos
Tazo
Teapots
Telephones
Tents
Thank You Cards
Thermos
Thimbles
Tickets
Tissue Covers
Toasters
Toothbrush Holders
Toothbrushes
Toothpaste
Totes, Record and Tape
Towels
__Bath
__Beach
__Hand
__Wash Cloths
Transfers
Travel Kits
Trays
Umbrellas
Vases
Vehicles, Display
Vehicles, Propeller Driven
Vehicles: Automobile
Vending Machine
   Translites
Vitamins
Walkie-Talkies
Wall Decorations
Wallets
Wallpaper
Waste Baskets
Watches
__Digital
Water Bottles
Window Clings

Epilogue

More For Next Time

by Geoffrey T. Carlton

The articles section started with "After The Bell," a listing and description of groups of items I acquired as this edition of the book was going to press. Star Wars has no "off season."

The Star Wars Super Collector's Wish Book runs in production cycles, but the buying, documenting, and photographing of collectibles is a full-time passion no matter what stage the book happens to be in. Collecting and photography work must go on.

Sometimes items get omitted for convenience. If book production is alphabetically in the T's and a new "B"oomerang arrives, it isn't always possible to go back and find room to squeeze it in. Likewise, if the book in production is the toy guide and new back-to-school supplies and lunch boxes are released, they have to wait their turn for the next general merchandise edition of the title.

Below are photos slated for the next sets of books. Your assignment is to figure out what they are, where they came from, and calculate their values. Write down your answers. When the next books come out, see if you were right!

#64617   #64513   #64155   #64222   #64618

#63793   #64152   #64217   #64099

#64520

#64545

#64139

#64146

#64465

#64614

#63713

#64127

#64224

#64620

#64461